Lecture Notes of the Institute
for Computer Sciences, Social Informatics
and Telecommunications Engineering 106

Angelos D. Keromytis   Roberto Di Pietro (Eds.)

Security and Privacy in Communication Networks

8th International ICST Conference, SecureComm 2012
Padua, Italy, September 3-5, 2012
Revised Selected Papers

 Springer

Volume Editors

Angelos D. Keromytis
Columbia University
Department of Computer Science
1214 Amsterdam Avenue, M.C. 0401
New York, NY 10027-7003, USA
E-mail: angelos@cs.columbia.edu

Roberto Di Pietro
Università degli Studi Roma Tre
Dipartimento di Matematica
Largo San Leonardo Murialdo 1
00146 Rome, Italy
E-mail: dipietro@mat.uniroma3.it

ISSN 1867-8211   e-ISSN 1867-822X
ISBN 978-3-642-36882-0   e-ISBN 978-3-642-36883-7
DOI 10.1007/978-3-642-36883-7
Springer Heidelberg Dordrecht London New York

Library of Congress Control Number: 2013931847

CR Subject Classification (1998): K.6.5, K.4.4, C.2.0-4, E.3, H.4.3

Typesetting: Camera-ready by author, data conversion by Scientific Publishing Services, Chennai, India

Printed on acid-free paper

Springer is part of Springer Science+Business Media (www.springer.com)

Preface

Secure communications continue having an impact on how society views computing and communication, as well as to which extent society can really benefit from the promises set by the ICT revolution. In particular, secure communications are a fundamental pillar for implementing the "always connected" paradigm. However, the ubiquity of digital communications has also spread the need for ubiquitous security.

As a relatively young, growing, and respected community, we are asked to continuously adapt the solutions for secure communications to cope with the related, expanding threats. To this extent, the EAI Conference on Security Communication has been a premier venue for researchers in communications privacy and security to present their latest research in the field. Moreover, it has also served as a forum for fostering international collaboration to address eminent security threats faced by our society. In particular, over the last decade we have seen an evolution in research, from traditional network security to complex security problems that cannot leverage conventional techniques. We have witnessed the emergence of new wireless systems (e.g., RFID, vehicular networks, WSNs), the widespread deployment of new communication platforms (e.g., smartphones) and of their applications (e.g., social media), the emergence of e-cash, as well as an increased interest in forensics issues (e.g., device fingerprinting). However, the most remarkable trend this year was probably the raising awareness of privacy issues associated with these emerging technologies.

The SecureComm 2012 call-for-papers attracted 73 submissions from 35 countries and four continents: Asia, Australia, Europe, and North America. Unfortunately, the acceptance rate set for this conference did not allow us to accept all the papers with relevant merits. In this respect, special thanks are due to the TPC members for their handling of the challenging, heavy, and rewarding task of selecting the papers to be included in the proceedings. We arrived at a collection of 21 papers presenting relevant, mature, and reproducible research contributions to be included in these conference proceedings.

The 21 accepted papers can be broadly classified into the following themes:

- Crypto and Electronic Money
- Wireless Security
- Web Security
- Intrusion Detection and Monitoring
- Anonymity and Privacy
- Miscellaneous

In addition to the research papers being presented at the conference, we also had two exciting keynotes, delivered by Atul Prakash, Professor in Computer Science and Engineering at the University of Michigan ("Information Confinement on Commodity Systems") and Sabrina De Capitani di Vimercati, Professor in Computer Science at Dipartimento di Informatica Università degli Studi di Milano ("Protecting Data in the Cloud: Issues and Solutions").

Last but not least, we are also grateful to the local organizers of SecureComm 2012 for providing a perfect environment for running the conference.

November 2012   Angelos D. Keromytis
                                                         Roberto Di Pietro

Organization

Program Committee

Chan Aldar C-F.	Institute for Infocomm Research, Singapore
Colantonio Alessandro	Bay31
Wespi Andreas	IBM Zurich Research Laboratory, Swizerland
Spognardi Angelo	Sapienza Università di Roma, Italy
Keromytis Angelos D	Columbia University, USA
Alomair Basel	University of Washington, USA
Christophe Bidan	Supelec
Hankin Chris	Imperial College London, UK
Soriente Claudio	University of California, Irvine, USA
Leita Corrado	Symantec Research
Yao Danfeng	Virginia Tech, USA
Nicol David	University of Illinois at Urbana-Champaign, USA
Yau David	Purdue University, USA
Cook Debra	Telcordia
Oligeri Gabriele	Università di Trento, Italy
Avoine Gildas	UCL, Belgium
Russello Giovanni	The University of Auckland, New Zealand
Chen Hao	UC Davis, USA
Yin Heng	Syracuse University, USA
Lopez Javier	University of Malaga, Spain
Seifert Jean-Pierre	Technische Universität Berlin (TUB), Germany
Lui John C.S.	The Chinese University of Hong Kong, SAR China
Rasmussen Kasper Bonne	University of California Irvine, USA
Beznosov Konstantin	UBC
Ren Kui	Illinois Institute of Technology, USA
Bai Kun	IBM T.J. Watson Research Center, USA
Manulis Mark	University of Surrey, UK
Sherr Micah	Georgetown University, USA
Cukier Michel	University of Maryland, USA
Christodorescu Mihai	IBM T.J. Watson Research Center, USA
Verde Nino Vincenzo	Università di Roma Tre, Italy
Tague Patrick	Carnegie Mellon University, USA
Gutmann Peter	University of Auckland, New Zealand
Reiher Peter	UCLA, USA
Ginzboorg Philip	Nokia
Samarati Pierangela	Università degli Studi di Milano, Italy
Poovendran Radha	University of Washington, USA

Mayrhofer Rene   Upper Austria University of Applied Sciences,
                                 Austria
Di Pietro Roberto   Università di Roma Tre, Italy
Roy Sankardas   Howard University, USA
Zhu Sencun   Penn State University, USA
Buchegger Sonja   KTH, Sweden
Ioannidis Sotiris   FORTH-ICS, Greece
Wetzel Susanne   Stevens Institute of Technology, USA
Takagi Tsuyoshi   Kyushu University, Japan
Hengartner Urs   University of Waterloo, Canada
Antonio Villani   Università di Roma Tre, Italy
Ganapathy Vinod   Rutgers University, USA
Yegneswaran Vinod   SRI International
Lou Wenjing   Virginia Polytechnic Institute and State University,
                                 USA
Robertson William   Northeastern University, USA
Zhang Xiaolan   IBM T.J. Watson Research Center, USA
Mu Yi   University of Wollongong, Australia
Andrea Zisman   City University London, UK

Additional Reviewers

Alcaraz, Cristina   Rios, Ruben
Ardagna, Claudio   Rodriguez Cano, Guillermo
Asghar, Muhammad Rizwan   Roman, Rodrigo
Backes, Werner   Stewin, Patrick
Bedi, Harkeerat   Sun, San-Tsai
Bodriagov, Oleksandr   Sun, Wenhai
Boshmaf, Yazan   Tan, Henry
Davoli, Antonio   Torabi, Sadeq
De Caro, Angelo   Wacek, Chris
Greschbach, Benjamin   Wang, Bing
Huang, Chu   Xu, Kaihe
Ion, Mihaela   Xu, Wei
Jaferian, Pooya   Xu, Yang
Jhawar, Ravi   Xu, Zhen
Kim, Hyoungshick   Yan, Lok
Kreitz, Gunnar   Yan, Qiben
Li, Fagen   Yang, Zhenyu
Martin, Benjamin   Zhang, Mingwu
Moore, Brad   Zhang, Mu
Muslukhov, Ildar   Zhang, Ning
Najera, Pablo   Zheng, Yao
Prakash, Aravind   Zhu, Youwen
Ravishankar, Borgaonkar

Table of Contents

DAFA - A Lightweight DES Augmented Finite Automaton Cryptosystem

Sarshad Abubaker and Kui Wu

Department of Computer Science
University of Victoria, Victoria BC V8P5C2, Canada
{sarshad,wkui}@uvic.ca

Abstract. Unlike most cryptosystems which rely on number theoretic problems, cryptosystems based on the invertibility of finite automata are lightweight in nature and can be implemented easily using simple logical operations, thus affording fast encryption and decryption. In this paper, we propose and implement a new variant of finite automaton cryptosystem, which we call DES-Augmented Finite Automaton (DAFA) cryptosystem. DAFA uses the key generation algorithm of the Data Encryption Standard (DES) to dynamically generate linear and non-linear finite automata on the fly using a 128-bit key. Compared to existing finite automaton cryptosystems, DAFA provides stronger security yet has similar encryption/decryption speeds. DAFA is also faster than popular single key cryptosystems such as Advanced Encryption Standard (AES). The test results on desktop and mobile phones with respect to the running speed and security properties are very promising.

Keywords: Cryptography, Finite Automata, Symmetric key, Probabilistic encryption.

1 Introduction

Smartphones and other portable devices are rapidly changing people's daily lives. More and more sensitive information such as bank accounts, birthdays and health care details are now carried over these devices, which still lag behind desktop PC's in terms of computational capability. Cryptosystems to protect the sensitive information on these devices must be computationally lightweight, or otherwise normal applications would be severely crippled when the main horsepower of the devices is spent on executing security-related primitives.

Most cryptosystems used today rely on problems based on number theory. In this paper, we explore a new type of single key cryptosystem based on the invertibility of finite automata (FA) [15,18]. These cryptosystems have relatively small key sizes and are lightweight in nature. They can be implemented easily in hardware or software using simple logical operations, thus affording fast encryption and decryption [15]. The difficulty in inverting non-linear finite automata and factoring matrix polynomials accounts for the security of these systems.

A.D. Keromytis and R. Di Pietro (Eds.): SecureComm 2012, LNICST 106, pp. 1–18, 2013.
© Institute for Computer Sciences, Social Informatics and Telecommunications Engineering 2013

An FA cryptosystem can be implemented as either a public-key system or a single-key system [15]. In the public-key cryptosystem domain, various FA cryptosystems, termed as FAPKC0, FAPKC1, FAPKC2, FAPKC93, FAPKC3 and FAPKC4 [18,15], have been proposed. Some successful attacks have been reported on certain types of FA public-key cryptosystems [2,3,5,6]. However, in the single-key cryptosystem domain, we have not seen any successful attacks on the FA cryptosystems [15].

In this paper, we focus on the single-key FA cryptosystem and further enhance its security while maintaining its fast running speed. We make the following contributions:

1. We design a DES-Augmented Finite Automaton (DAFA) cryptosystem, using DES to dynamically generate linear and non-linear finite automata on the fly. While the core encryption and decryption operations are similar to those used in FAPKC3 [11], DAFA is based on a 128-bit key and the finite automata are generated using a special modification of the key generation algorithm used in DES [12].
2. We implement DAFA over smart phones and thoroughly test its performance. Test results indicate that the statistical properties measured on the ciphertext using DAFA are satisfactory and in the same range as the properties of Advanced Encryption Standard (AES) [9]. We also demonstrate that DAFA is very competitive in terms of speed of operation.

The paper is organized as follows. We begin with a very brief introduction of the basic concepts of FA cryptosystems in Section 2. We present details of the DAFA cryptosystem in Section 3 and test its statistical features and running speed in Sections 4 and 5. We discuss some related work in Section 6 and conclude the paper in Section 7.

2 Background in FA Cryptosystems

We start with the basic definitions [15].

Definition 1. *We define an FA as a five tuple $M = \langle X, Y, S, \delta, \lambda \rangle$, where X denotes the set of all input alphabets, Y denotes the set of all output alphabets, S denotes the set of all states of the finite automaton, δ is the state transition function $\delta : S \times X \to S$, and λ is the output function $\lambda : S \times X \to Y$.*

In the context of FA cryptosystems, if we use an FA, M, to encrypt plaintext to ciphertext, we need another FA, M', to recover the plaintext. M' is called the inverse FA of M and its construction is based on the invertibility theory of FA [15].

Definition 2. *FA $M = \langle X, Y, S, \delta, \lambda \rangle$ is said to be (weakly) invertible with delay τ if for any input string $x_0, x_1, \ldots, x_\tau$ and $s \in S$, x_0 can be uniquely determined by the state s and the output string $\lambda(s, x_0 \ldots \ldots x_\tau)$.*

Definition 3. *Given two FA* $M = \langle X, Y, S, \delta, \lambda \rangle$ *and* $M' = \langle Y, X, S', \delta', \lambda' \rangle$, *states* $s \in S$ *and* $s' \in S'$ *are called a matching pair with delay* τ *if:*

$$\forall \alpha \in X_\omega, \exists \alpha_0 \in X_n : \lambda'(s', \lambda(s, \alpha)) = \alpha_0 \alpha,$$

where $|\alpha_0| = \tau$, X_ω *denotes the set of all infinite words of alphabet* X, *and* X_n *denotes the set of all finite words of alphabet* X. *In other words,* s' *matches* s *with delay* τ.

Definition 4. M' *is said to be a weak inverse with delay* τ *of* M *if for any* $s \in S$, *there exists* s' *in* S' *such that* (s', s) *is a matching pair with delay* τ.

As a special case of FA, we can define its state space $S = (Y_k \times X_h)$, where Y_k and X_h are sets of strings of length k and h, respectively. This type of FA is called (h, k)-order memory FA:

Definition 5. $M = \langle X, Y, (Y_k \times X_h), \delta, \lambda \rangle$ *is said to be an* (h, k)*-order memory FA, if there is a single-valued mapping* ϕ *from* $Y_k \times X_{h+1}$ *to* Y, *such that*

$$y(i) = \phi(y_{i-1}, \ldots y_{i-k}, x_i, \ldots x_{i-h}), i = 0, 1, \ldots$$
$$\delta(\langle y_{-1}, \ldots, y_{-k}, x_{-1}, \ldots, x_{-h} \rangle, x_0) = \langle y_0, \ldots, y_{-k+1}, x_0, \ldots, x_{-h+1} \rangle$$
$$\lambda(\langle y_{-1}, \ldots, y_{-k}, x_{-1}, \ldots, x_{-h} \rangle, x_0) = y_0$$
$$y_0 = \phi(y_{-1}, \ldots, y_{-k}, x_0, x_{-1}, \ldots, x_{-h})$$

What this means is that M needs k previous outputs and h previous inputs to generate the current output. As a special case, if the mapping ϕ is from X_{h+1} to Y, M is said to be an h-order input memory finite automaton.

Example 1. Assume that X and Y are input and output sets of 8-bit characters, respectively. An example (linear) $(1, 2)$-order FA, M, is represented as follows:

$$
y(i) = \begin{bmatrix} 0&1&1&1&0&0&0&1 \\ 0&1&1&0&0&1&1&1 \\ 0&0&0&0&1&0&1&1 \\ 1&1&0&1&1&1&1&0 \\ 0&0&0&0&1&0&1&0 \\ 0&1&0&1&0&1&0&0 \\ 1&1&1&0&1&0&0&1 \\ 0&0&1&1&0&1&0&0 \end{bmatrix} y(i-1) + \begin{bmatrix} 0&0&0&0&0&1&1&1 \\ 0&0&0&1&1&1&1&0 \\ 0&0&0&0&1&1&0&0 \\ 0&0&1&1&0&0&0&1 \\ 0&1&1&0&0&0&0&1 \\ 0&1&1&0&0&1&1&1 \\ 1&0&1&1&1&1&0&1 \\ 0&1&0&1&0&0&1&1 \end{bmatrix} y(i-2)
$$

$$
+ \begin{bmatrix} 1&0&0&0&0&0&0&0 \\ 1&0&0&0&0&0&0&0 \\ 0&0&0&0&0&0&0&0 \\ 1&0&0&0&0&0&0&0 \\ 1&0&0&0&0&0&0&0 \\ 1&0&0&0&0&0&0&0 \\ 1&0&0&0&0&0&0&0 \\ 0&0&0&0&0&0&0&0 \end{bmatrix} x(i) + \begin{bmatrix} 0&1&0&1&1&1&0&1 \\ 0&0&1&1&0&0&0&0 \\ 0&0&0&1&1&0&0&0 \\ 0&1&0&1&1&0&0&1 \\ 0&0&1&1&1&1&1&0 \\ 0&1&0&0&0&1&1&1 \\ 0&0&0&1&0&1&0&0 \\ 0&0&0&1&0&1&1&1 \end{bmatrix} x(i-1), i = 0, 1, 2, \ldots.
$$

The inverse FA of M with delay 1, M', is represented as:

$$x(i) = \begin{bmatrix} 0\,0\,1\,1\,0\,0\,0\,0 \\ 0\,0\,0\,0\,0\,0\,0\,0 \\ 0\,0\,0\,0\,0\,0\,0\,0 \\ 0\,0\,0\,0\,0\,0\,0\,0 \\ 0\,0\,0\,0\,0\,0\,0\,0 \\ 0\,0\,0\,0\,0\,0\,0\,0 \\ 0\,0\,0\,0\,0\,0\,0\,0 \\ 0\,0\,0\,0\,0\,0\,0\,0 \end{bmatrix} x(i-1) + \begin{bmatrix} 0\,0\,0\,0\,0\,0\,0\,0 \\ 1\,0\,0\,1\,0\,1\,1\,1 \\ 1\,1\,0\,1\,0\,0\,1\,0 \\ 0\,1\,0\,1\,1\,1\,0\,0 \\ 0\,1\,1\,1\,1\,1\,0\,0 \\ 1\,0\,0\,1\,0\,0\,0\,0 \\ 1\,0\,1\,0\,0\,1\,0\,0 \\ 0\,1\,1\,0\,1\,0\,0\,1 \end{bmatrix} y(i+1) + \begin{bmatrix} 0\,1\,0\,0\,0\,0\,0\,0 \\ 0\,0\,1\,0\,0\,1\,1\,0 \\ 0\,0\,1\,0\,0\,0\,0\,1 \\ 1\,1\,1\,0\,0\,1\,1\,1 \\ 1\,1\,1\,0\,1\,1\,0\,0 \\ 1\,0\,1\,0\,1\,1\,1\,1 \\ 0\,0\,1\,0\,1\,1\,1\,0 \\ 0\,1\,0\,1\,0\,0\,1\,0 \end{bmatrix} y(i)$$

$$+ \begin{bmatrix} 0\,1\,1\,0\,0\,1\,1\,1 \\ 1\,0\,1\,1\,1\,1\,1\,1 \\ 1\,0\,0\,1\,0\,1\,0\,1 \\ 0\,0\,1\,0\,1\,0\,0\,1 \\ 0\,0\,1\,0\,0\,1\,0\,1 \\ 0\,0\,1\,1\,0\,1\,1\,0 \\ 0\,1\,1\,0\,1\,1\,0\,0 \\ 0\,0\,1\,0\,0\,0\,0\,0 \end{bmatrix} y(i-1) + \begin{bmatrix} 0\,0\,0\,1\,1\,1\,1\,0 \\ 0\,0\,0\,0\,0\,0\,0\,0 \\ 0\,0\,0\,0\,0\,0\,0\,0 \\ 0\,0\,0\,0\,0\,0\,0\,0 \\ 0\,0\,0\,0\,0\,0\,0\,0 \\ 0\,0\,0\,0\,0\,0\,0\,0 \\ 0\,0\,0\,0\,0\,0\,0\,0 \\ 0\,0\,0\,0\,0\,0\,0\,0 \end{bmatrix} y(i-2), i = 0, 1, \ldots.$$

Assume that the input string is $x(0)x(1) =$ "AB", i.e., $x(0) = 0X41 = (01000001)^T$ and $x(1) = 0X42 = (01000010)^T$. Assume that the values in the initial state are set as $x(-1) = y(-2) = y(-1) = (00000000)^T$. Since M' is the inverse of M with delay 1, we append an arbitrary character, say $x(2) = 0X0 = (00000000)^T$, to the input string. We can then use M to generate output string (i.e., ciphertext) $y(0) = 0X00, y(1) = 0X01, y(2) = 0X7B$, and we can use M' to recover the input string $x(0)x(1) =$ "AB".

The above example is for illustration purpose only. Obviously, in practice, an FA is much more complex and could be linear or non-linear depending on how it is constructed. In a non-linear finite automaton, the degree of the polynomial that constitutes the FA is greater than one. Due to space limit, please refer to [15] for the details on the construction of linear/non-linear FA and the combination of several FA.

3 DES-Augmented Finite Automaton (DAFA) Cryptosystem

3.1 Basic Idea

In the section we present a new version of the single-key FA cryptosystems. Our idea is to apply the key generation algorithm of the popular and widely-used Data Encryption Standard (DES) [12] to the key generation process of FA cryptosystems. The high-level block diagram of DAFA cryptosystem is illustrated in Fig 1. In particular, DAFA operates on 64-byte plaintext blocks, and uses μ pairs of linear and nonlinear FA for encryption and decryption, where μ is a system parameter given by users. It includes three main functional components, namely (a) key processing, (b) generation of automata and starting states, and (c) encryption and decryption, which we will introduce in the sequel.

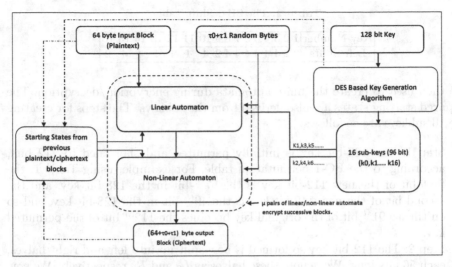

Fig. 1. High level block diagram of DAFA cryptosystem

3.2   Key Processing

We first need to describe the special treatment of the shift and permutation tables. DAFA uses various permutation tables for its operation, similar to the original DES cryptosystem. The permutation tables are randomly chosen. However, we test the tables to ensure that the permuted output is evenly spread across the entire input, and no two bits of the output are derived from the same bit of the input. Care has also been taken to ensure that there are no similar or repeating patterns among any two permutation tables. For the shift table SH-1, the sum total of all left shifts for the sixteen subkeys is 56 to ensure that at the end of the shifting process, the subkeys represent all bits of the main key and that changing even one bit of the main key will significantly affect all sixteen subkeys. An example PC-1 permutation table and an example SH-1 shift table are shown in Table 1 and Table 2, respectively.

Table 1. The PC-1 Permutation Table

57	49	41	33	25	17	9	71	105	108	72	93	78	120
1	58	50	42	34	26	18	75	86	92	104	107	83	111
10	2	59	51	43	35	27	65	102	87	99	69	95	3
19	11	127	60	52	44	36	77	116	94	118	122	74	124
63	55	47	39	31	23	15	89	98	66	112	88	81	126
7	62	54	46	38	30	22	106	113	110	119	115	79	6
14	128	61	53	45	37	29	73	90	84	97	101	114	123
21	13	5	28	20	12	4	85	67	100	80	125	70	91

DAFA is based on a 128-bit (main) key. This key is processed using a key generation algorithm similar to DES. This algorithm creates 16 subkeys, each of which are 96 bits in length and are created using the 128-bit (main) key. These subkeys

Table 2. The SH-1 Shift Table

Key Number	1	2	3	4	5	6	7	8	9	10	11	12	13	14	15	16
Left Shifts	2	2	4	4	4	4	4	4	2	4	4	4	4	4	4	2

are then used to create the finite automata during encryption/decryption. The required starting states are also derived from the subkeys. The steps for creating the 16 subkeys are as follows:

– Step 1: The 128-bit key is initially permuted and shortened to 112 bits, according to the PC-1 permutation table. For example, using Table 1, the first bit of the new 112-bit key is the 57th-bit in the 128-bit key, and the second bit of the new 112-bit key is the 49th-bit in the 128-bit key, and so on till the 91st bit of the original key becomes the 112th bit of the permuted key.
– Step 2: The 112-bit key so formed is now split up into left and right halves, each 56 bits long. We denote these halves as L_0 and R_0 respectively. We now form 16 blocks L_n and R_n for $n = 1, 2, 3, \ldots, 16$. More specifically, L_i and R_i are obtained by left shifting L_{i-1} and $R_{i-1}, i = 1, 2, 3, \ldots, 16$, respectively, according to the shift table SH-1. By left shift, we mean that we move each bit one place to the left, and the first bit is cycled to the end of the block. For instance, according to the first row of the example shift table (SH-1) shown in Table 2, L_1 and R_1 are obtained by left shifting twice of L_0 and R_0, respectively. In this way, we get 16 pairs of subkeys each 56 bits long.
– Step 3: We now concatenate the L_i and R_i pairs ($i = 1, 2, \ldots, 16$) to form 16 subkeys which are each 112 bits long. This 112-bit key is now permuted according to another permutation table PC-2 (e.g., as shown in Table 3). The example in Table 3 permutes each key to a 96-bit key. The bit numbers 9, 18, 22, 25, 35, 38, 43, 54, 64, 72, 80, 83, 96, 99, 102 and 108 are discarded in this process for each of the 112-bit keys. The choice of discarded bits is random, and given that the shift table performs a complete rotation through all 56 bits of each half of the key, this choice does not expose any vulnerability which may aid in cryptanalysis of the cipher. Thus we now have sixteen 96-bit keys generated in a fashion similar to that in the DES cipher.

Table 3. The PC-2 Permutation Table

14	17	11	24	1	5	60	87	82	105	63	70
3	28	15	6	21	10	77	73	98	86	76	57
23	19	12	4	26	8	65	94	106	111	92	81
16	7	27	20	13	2	88	85	57	109	71	66
41	52	31	37	47	55	69	93	110	104	112	78
30	40	51	45	33	48	75	79	103	67	101	91
44	49	39	56	34	53	90	100	62	107	97	68
46	42	50	36	29	32	58	95	74	84	89	61

3.3   Generation of Automata and Starting State

Once the subkeys have been derived, we need to generate the automata which will be used for encryption and decryption. The starting states for these automata will also need to be generated from the subkeys. The steps involved in this process include:

– Step 1: First we need to generate μ pairs of linear and non-linear finite automata for the cryptosystem. These finite automata will be derived using the generated subkeys described above. The linear automaton is (h_0, k_0)-order memory invertible linear FA with delay τ_0, and the non-linear automaton is h_1-order input memory FA invertible with delay τ_1, where all $h_0, k_0, \tau_0, h_1, \tau_1$ are system parameters.

– Step 2: For the linear automaton, we need to generate $h_0 + k_0$ matrices as the component matrices for generating the finite automaton. We also need to generate τ_0 full rank matrices. The specifics of how this can be generated using the subkeys is as follows. For the first $h_0 + k_0$ component matrices, we use alternate subkeys K_1, K_3, K_5 and so on in a circular manner, rolling over to the beginning when we reach K_{16}. Since we need only 64 bits in order to construct an $8X8$ bit matrix, we use three permutation tables M-1, M-2 and M-3 (e.g., as shown in Tables 4, 5, 6) to derive 64 random bits from the 96-bit keys, using the similar operations as those in the PC-1 table (refer to Step 1 in Section 3.2). These three permutation tables are used in sequence in a cyclical manner. As each 64-bit represents an $8X8$ matrix, we therefore have the $h_0 + k_0$ component matrices.

Table 4. The M-1 Permutation Table

8	34	76	13	28	2	56	7
74	20	58	40	73	31	46	79
16	59	1	47	80	91	14	22
4	32	26	55	17	77	82	83
23	65	49	68	35	61	88	95
44	29	19	62	85	5	50	37
71	11	53	38	89	52	94	92
43	64	70	86	25	67	41	10

Table 5. The M-2 Permutation Table

86	65	82	90	49	72	87	13
69	14	89	85	92	4	66	95
27	64	38	80	71	26	91	83
70	3	81	68	63	50	84	94
40	48	10	1	39	78	5	75
28	19	24	25	60	51	61	67
6	46	34	44	52	33	8	59
12	32	18	58	43	7	29	17

Table 6. The M-3 Permutation Table

```
 2 83 88 92 94 48 93 89
74 87 26 35 85 75 16 84
17 47 71  8 29 11 80 25
39 12 30 44 78 53 21 66
56 65 34 76  3 70 43 67
31 22 62 49 52  7 69 79
 4 40 15 61 24 42 13 58
38 51  6 20 57 96 33 60
```

In order to create the τ_0 full rank matrices, a slightly different approach is adopted. The τ_0 matrices are generated using the same method as for the first $h_0 + k_0$ matrices. However, to guarantee that these matrices to be full rank, we need extra processing as follows:

- First we derive the decimal representations of the 8 component bytes that make up each of the matrices so derived and raise them mod 8. If two successive values (mod 8) are the same, then the second value is incremented by 1.
- Next we make the matrices lower triangular (for linear automaton matrices) or upper triangular (for nonlinear automaton matrices) by setting all values in the diagonal to 1 and all values below or above the diagonal to 0. This ensures that our resultant matrices are full rank.
- Finally we use the decimal values derived earlier to carry out two rounds of four row swaps and additions. For example, assume that the 8 decimal values derived are 1,7,3,6,2,0,5 and 4. For round one, we first swap rows 1 and 7 and then add row 6 to row 3. Then we carry out the inverse of this operation, i.e. we now swap the rows 3 and 6 and then add row 7 to row 1 for a total of four row adds and swaps. In round two, we perform an identical operation with the last four decimal values. We first swap rows 2 and 0 and then add row 4 to row 5. Then we carry out the inverse of this operation, i.e. we now swap the rows 5 and 4 and then add row 0 to row 2. Since only basic row swaps and additions are performed, the resultant matrix will be full rank. Using this process, we can create random, full rank matrices for use in construction of the finite automata as normal (refer to [15] for the construction of finite automata using given matrices).

- Step 3: For the nonlinear automaton, we need $h_1 + 1$ component matrices. These are generated as in Step 2, except that they use the even set of subkeys K_2, K_4 and so on in a circular manner, rolling over to the beginning when we reach K_{16}. Also, as before, we use the permutation tables (e.g., M-1, M-2 and M-3) to derive the 64 random bits from the 96-bit keys. We also need τ_1 full rank matrices which are derived in a manner similar to that for the linear automaton. These component matrices, once derived, are used to create the nonlinear finite automaton as normal [15].

– Step 4: After generation of each linear/nonlinear automaton, we derive the starting state for that particular automaton before proceeding to generate the next one. The starting state is derived from alternate subkeys immediately following the last key that was used to generate a particular finite automaton. For instance, if the first linear automaton was generated, (say) using subkeys K_1, K_3 and K_5, then the three 8 bit vectors that will be required as the starting state of this automaton are generated from the sequential keys K_7, K_9 and K_{11}. For this purpose, we use random look up tables (e.g., tables SS-1, SS-2 and SS-3 shown in Table 7). These tables are used alternately in order to provide confusion as to the selection of the 8 bits from the 96-bit subkeys. That is, if SS-1 is used on K_7 to generate the first vector, then SS-2 will be used on K_9, and SS-3 on K_{11}. This cyclical process will continue for each of the starting states required for all μ pairs of linear and nonlinear automata.

Table 7. The Starting State Permutation Tables

SS-1	1	5	9	13	95	91	87	83
SS-2	40	56	9	16	11	91	34	61
SS-3	17	29	32	46	54	65	77	85

Note that the automaton and starting state creation process is designed in a manner to increase confusion and prevent cryptanalysis. This also provides for greater diffusion in the final ciphertext once encryption is performed. Based on our implementation, it has been observed that since they are based on simple bit operations, the generation of automata and starting states takes very little time even for large values of $h_0, k_0, \tau_0, h_1, \tau_1$ and μ.

3.4   Encryption and Decryption

As shown in Fig. 1, for encryption and decryption, the plaintext is split up into 64-byte blocks. Each block is encrypted with a linear and nonlinear automata pair in succession. Since there are μ different linear/nonlinear automata pairs, these are alternately cycled by the algorithm for each successive block.

As illustrated in Section 2, each FA needs to set an initial state (e.g., the values of $x(-1), y(-1), y(-2)$ in Example 1). Clearly, the number of bytes in the initial state depends on the parameters of the FA (i.e., the values of h_0, k_0, τ_0, h_1 and τ_1 in our DAFA cryptosystem). To enhance security, when we use alternative linear/nonlinear FA pairs, we create *dynamic* initial states by allowing each block (except the first one) to use the last portion of the ciphertext in the previous block as the starting state. In this way, if a single bit of the plaintext is altered, the ciphertext undergoes a drastic change.

Example 2. Assume that μ has a value of 2. Then two linear/nonlinear automata pairs are generated by the algorithm, denoted by (L_1, NL_1) and (L_2, NL_2), respectively. Assume that we split the plaintext into 64-byte blocks. For every eight blocks, denoted by $B_1, B_2, \ldots, B_8$, we can create the ciphertext c as:

$$c = B_1^{L_1, NL_1} B_2^{L_2, NL_2} \ldots B_7^{L_1, NL_1} B_8^{L_2, NL_2}$$

where $B_i^{L_1, NL_1} (i = 1, 3, 5, 7)$ returns the ciphertext of B_i encrypted using L_1 and NL_1 in sequence, and $B_j^{L_2, NL_2} (j = 2, 4, 6, 8)$ returns the ciphertext of B_j encrypted using L_2 and NL_2 in sequence (refer to Example 1 for the operation). Note that the initial states of L_1 and NL_1 when encrypting B_1 is randomly selected, but the initial states of FA when encrypting other blocks use the output of ciphertext from the previous block, i.e.,

$$B_1^{L_1, NL_1} \longrightarrow B_2^{L_2, NL_2} \longrightarrow B_3^{L_1, NL_1} \ldots \longrightarrow B_8^{L_2, NL_2},$$

where $\longrightarrow$ means setting up the initial state.

Decryption is carried out in the reverse order. Assume that the ciphertext is split up into eight 64-byte blocks $C_1, C_2, \ldots, C_8$. The plaintext p will be generated as follows:

$$p = C_1^{NL_1', L_1'} C_2^{NL_2', L_2'} \ldots C_7^{NL_1', L_1'} C_8^{NL_2', L_2'}$$

where NL_i' and L_i' are the inverse FA of NL_i and $L_i (i = 1, 2, \ldots, 8)$, respectively, $C_i^{NL_1', L_1'} (i = 1, 3, 5, 7)$ returns the plaintext of C_i decrypted using NL_1' and L_1' in sequence, and $C_j^{NL_2', L_2'} (j = 2, 4, 6, 8)$ returns the plaintext of C_j decrypted using NL_2' and L_2' in sequence (refer to Example 1 for the operation).

3.5   Features of the DAFA Cryptosystem

The DAFA cryptosystem has some nice features, including:

- It uses a 128-bit key. Unlike the traditional finite automaton cryptosystems, the key consists of a 128-bit string - not a collection of finite automata and starting states. The underlying finite automata and starting states are dynamically generated on the fly using a special modification of the key generation algorithm used in DES.
- The key space is 2^{112} bits long. Though a 128-bit key is used, 16 bits are discarded by the initial permutation, similar to DES. This security level is equivalent to that provided by triple DES, which is commonly regarded as sufficient for most applications.
- A new parameter, μ, is introduced to determine how many linear/nonlinear automaton pairs are to be generated and used for encryption/decryption purposes.
- The plaintext is split up into 64-byte blocks. Each block is encrypted by a linear and nonlinear automaton pair in succession. Further, there are μ different linear/nonlinear automaton pairs and these are alternately cycled by the algorithm for each new block. The size of each block may be user defined if required.

- Since μ can take any positive integer values, cryptanalysis on the resultant cipher is difficult since firstly, each automaton uses the encrypted values of the previous block as part of its starting state and secondly $\tau_0 + \tau_1$ random characters are added at the end of each block for encryption. This leads to probabilistic encryption results [8], as discussed in our later security analysis. The addition of two random characters to each 64-byte block of plaintext results in roughly a 3% increase in the size of the ciphertext. However, this can be reduced, if required, by increasing the size of the plaintext blocks to either 128 or 256 bytes.
- Though DAFA's key generation time is slightly larger (depending on μ) than that of the existing FA cryptosystems, the speed for encryption and decryption remains essentially the same. The security of DAFA, however, is vastly increased due to the introduction of extra randomness via the random characters appended in each block.

4   Security Analysis

The security of the FA cryptosystem has been discussed in [15]. Since DAFA consists of the same core components (i.e., the linear and nonlinear FA) used in these cryptosystems, the security of DAFA is at least as much as that afforded by these cryptosystems. Currently, there is no known attacks successful to break the single-key FA cryptosystems. In addition, the use of different automata pairs and keys along with the block-based encryption scheme introduces further randomness in the algorithm and enhances the security. We conduct extensive tests to illustrate its strong statistical properties.

4.1   Probabilistic Encryption

To be semantically secure and to avoid chosen plaintext attacks, an encryption algorithm must be probabilistic [8]. Nevertheless, most of the commonly-used single key cryptosystems such as DES and AES are deterministic in nature, i.e., given a particular plaintext and a particular key, they always encrypt to the same ciphertext. In order to achieve probabilistic encryption, DES and AES need to use other mechanisms, e.g., working with Cipher Block Chaining (CBC) [7]. In contrast, our DAFA cryptosystem integrates random padding into every block of text encrypted, resulting in a truly probabilistic symmetric encryption scheme that produces a different ciphertext each time encryption is done - even if the plaintext and the keys remain unchanged!

Two main reasons contribute to this nice feature. First, for every 64-byte block of plaintext encrypted, $\tau_0 + \tau_1$ random characters are appended at the end for encryption with the linear/nonlinear automaton pair. This is significant because it produces a *cascading* effect which alters the entire block depending on the random bytes added at the end. Second, $h_0 + k_0$ bytes need to be derived from the 128-bit key as the starting state for the first linear automaton used and $h1$ bytes need to be derived as the starting state for the first nonlinear automaton used. For the first block of data, these starting states remain constant depending on the key used. However, for all subsequent blocks, part of the encrypted values of the random characters added at the end of the current block are used as the starting state for encrypting the next block of plaintext. Thus, the starting state for the next block is random, resulting in a significant change in the ciphertext even when the same plaintext is encrypted with the same key multiple times.

In general, $\tau_0 + \tau_1$ random bytes are added to each block of plaintext processed which also affects the subsequent blocks since their encrypted values are used as the starting states for encrypting the next block of ciphertext. This results in a completely probabilistic encryption scheme, rendering our cryptosystem semantically secure and indistinguishable under a chosen plaintext attach (IND-CPA) [8]. This means that the ciphertext hides even partial information about the plaintext. This is evident from the statistical tests carried out on the cryptosystem. It adds an element of randomness to every encryption procedure and prevents partial decryption of ciphertext by ensuring that an adversary cannot recover any portion of the plaintext without knowing the decryption key.

4.2   Multiple Keys and Alternating Automaton Types

As we have seen, the 128-bit key is processed by a sophisticated key generation algorithm in order to produce sixteen 96-bit subkeys. These subkeys are used to generate the finite automata used by the algorithm. The keys are used cyclically, and the encryption algorithm uses 2μ different keys to construct different automata, among which half of the constructed automata are linear and the other half are nonlinear. Security is considerably enhanced as a result of these alternating linear/nonlinear automaton pairs. Each pair is applied alternately on successive blocks of text with the encrypted values of one block being used as the starting state of the automaton in the next block. This introduces a high degree of complexity making cryptanalysis difficult.

4.3   Statistical Analysis

We use ENT- a pseudo random number sequence test program [20] to test DAFA cryptosystem. The statistical tests are similar to those in [14]. In order to analyze if some statistical features in the plaintext carry over into the ciphertext, it is advantageous to start with plaintext which consists of highly patterned bytes and which uses a uniform key (an example of a uniform key would be PPPPPPPPPPPPPPPP). All tests have been conducted using a mix of multiple randomly generated as well as uniform 128-bit keys.

All plaintext files are 4KB in size. Four different types of plaintext have been tested. The first type, labeled as *pt1*, consists only of repetitions of the 32-byte sequence AAAABBBBCCCCDDDDEEEEFFFFGGGGHHHH. The second type, *pt2*, consists of all zeros. The third type, *pt3*, consists of all ones, and the fourth type, *pt4*, consists of random English text.

A total of 1000 test runs were conducted on the ciphertexts created with different random and uniform keys as explained earlier. The tests were conducted separately for two levels of security. In the first case, we use $h_0 = 1, k_0 = 2, \tau_0 = 1, h_1 = 2, \tau_1 = 2$ and $\mu=7$. We will refer to this security level as DAFA-121227. The second case uses a security level of $h_0 = 2, k_0 = 3, \tau_0 = 2, h_1 = 3, \tau_1 = 3$ and $\mu=7$, which we will refer to as DAFA-232337. Generally speaking, higher values result in a higher security level but a slower system, because more finite automata are used in the key generation and encryption/decryption processes. We also present the statistical results of the same tests on plaintexts encrypted using AES with a 128-bit key, under CBC mode for ready reference. We will refer to this as AES-128 in the remainder of this section. We conducted five types of test as follows.

Tests for Entropy. Entropy was first introduced by Claude Shannon [13] and is a measure of the uncertainty associated with a random variable. It refers to the expected value of the information contained in a byte of data. In other words, entropy refers to the density of the content or information contained in a file, expressed as a number of bits per character. Files which are extremely dense in information (close to 8 bits/byte) can be considered to be random. Our tests show that files encrypted with the DAFA cryptosystem, even with a lower level of security (DAFA-121227), demonstrate high average entropy (equivalent to that of AES with a 128-bit key under CBC mode) with very low levels of standard deviation. Table 8 shows the results of our entropy tests.

Table 8. Results for entropy tests using AES-128, DAFA-121227 and DAFA-232337

Plaintext Type (Size 4 KB)	Plaintext (bits/byte)	AES-128 (bits/byte)		DAFA-121227 (bits/byte)		DAFA-232337 (bits/byte)	
		Avg	S.D.	Avg	S.D.	Avg	S.D.
pt1 (AAA...HHH)	3.00200	7.95488	0.00407	7.95578	0.00915	7.95793	0.00373
pt2 (00000000...)	0	7.95479	0.00402	7.94977	0.03572	7.95770	0.00381
pt3 (11111111...)	0	7.95485	0.00414	7.94943	0.03465	7.95793	0.00358
pt4 (English Text)	4.87487	7.95477	0.00405	7.95653	0.00394	7.95818	0.00368

Chi Square (χ^2) Tests. The χ^2 test [1] with 255 degrees of freedom is a common test for measuring the randomness of data. The chi-square distribution in our tests is calculated for a stream of bytes and is expressed as an absolute number and a percentage which indicates how frequently a truly random number sequence would exceed the calculated value [1,20]. In our test, we use $\chi^2_{0.01,255}$ to test whether a given data sequence is random. We consider the test successful if the calculated χ^2 value [1] is smaller than the value of $\chi^2_{0.01,255}$.

As mentioned earlier, multiple tests were conducted with different uniform and random keys. Note that the results for the first three types of plaintext are for worst case scenarios where the plaintext is well patterned. The test result for the fourth type of plaintext is what would be the normal case scenario. As before, test results for AES-128 are also presented with DAFA-121227 and DAFA-232337 for ready reference. As is evident from Table 9, the test results for DAFA, even at the lower level of security, are comparable to AES-128.

Table 9. Results for χ^2 tests using DAFA-121227, DAFA-232337 and AES-128

Plaintext Type (Size 4 KB)	Test Runs (Unique Keys)	AES-128 % Tests Passed	DAFA-121227 % Tests Passed	DAFA-232337 % Tests Passed
pt1 (AAA...HHH)	1000	97.9	96.5	97.9
pt2 (00000000...)	1000	98.0	84.1	98.0
pt3 (11111111...)	1000	97.3	85.1	97.4
pt4 (English Text)	1000	97.2	97.2	98.6

Arithmetic Mean Tests. For the Arithmetic Mean (AM) test [20], we add the values of all the bytes in the file and divide it by the file length. If the data is random, this should be about 127.5 since there are 256 possible ASCII values that each byte of data can represent. Almost all results for our cryptosystem show values very close to 127.5. Table 10 shows the average arithmetic mean calculated from 1000 tests conducted on each type of plaintext with different keys.

Table 10. Results for AM tests using DAFA-121227, DAFA-232337 and AES-128

Plaintext Type (Size 4 KB)	Plaintext A.M	AES-128 Avg. A.M.	DAFA-121227 Avg. A.M.	DAFA-232337 Avg. A.M.
pt1 (AAA...HHH)	68.48000	127.52812	127.52098	127.51560
pt2 (00000000...)	47.99000	127.44284	127.46245	127.44099
pt3 (11111111...)	48.99000	127.49717	127.445632	127.433334
pt4 (English Text)	70.64840	127.49981	127.48059	127.57606

Tests for Monte Carlo Value for Pi (π). In the test for the Monte Carlo Value for Pi [10], successive 6-byte blocks of data are used as the source for plotting the X and Y coordinates within a square, using 24-bits for each axis. The number of points which fall within a circle inscribed in the square is used to approximate the value of Pi. As the number of points increases, the value will approach the correct value of Pi if the sequence is random [20]. Our tests in Table 11 show high accuracy in the Monte Carlo tests with a very low error percentage in the estimated value of Pi.

Table 11. Results for Monte Carlo tests for value of Pi

Plaintext Type (Size 4 KB)	Plaintext Pi	Error%	AES-128 Avg. Pi	Error%	DAFA-121227 Avg. Pi	Error%	DAFA-232337 Avg. Pi	Error%
pt1 (AAA...HHH)	4.00	27.32	3.14010	0.0474	3.14077	0.0261	3.14064	0.0302
pt2 (00000000...)	4.00	27.32	3.13981	0.0566	3.13996	0.0518	3.14270	0.0353
pt3 (11111111...)	4.00	27.32	3.13977	0.0579	3.14192	0.0105	3.14153	0.0019
pt4 (English Text)	4.00	27.32	3.14125	0.0108	3.14188	0.0092	3.13651	0.1617

The Serial Correlation Coefficient. The degree to which neighboring bytes are related to each other are measured by the Serial Correlation Coefficient (SCC). The lower the relation, the lower the value of this measure. If the bytes are totally uncorrelated, the SCC would be close to zero [20]. Table 12 shows the results of the SCC tests. We can see that in our results this value almost always converges close to zero for both levels of DAFA security tested. Note that the SCC for pt2 and pt3 is undefined since all values are equal [20].

Table 12. Results for SCC tests using DAFA-121227, DAFA-232337 and AES-128

Plaintext Type (Size 4 KB)	Plaintext S.C.C.	AES-128 Avg. S.C.C.	DAFA-121227 Avg. S.C.C.	DAFA-232337 Avg. S.C.C.
pt1 (AAA...HHH)	0.71926	-0.00031	-0.00015	-0.00019
pt2 (00000000...)	undefined	0.00023	0.00009	-0.00068
pt3 (11111111...)	undefined	-0.00020	0.00012	-0.00044
pt4 (English Text)	0.46831	-0.00026	-0.00074	-0.00005

In addition to the tests over text files, we also conducted the five types of tests of DAFA on a classic image, Lena. The test results are shown in Figure 2.

To summarize, all tests conducted with DAFA are satisfactory regarding the randomness in the ciphertext. As is evident from both the encrypted text and image files, there are no statistical patterns relating the original plaintext or image with the encrypted version.

	Before Encryption		After Encryption	
Entropy	4.488642		7.999389	
χ^2 Dist & Random %	3032081	0.01%	222.95	92.70%
Mean (Random: 127.5)	21.4564		127.6129	
Monte Carlo Pi & Error %	3.999726	27.32%	3.147025	0.17%
SCC (Random: 0)	0.219906		-0.0008	

Fig. 2. Results after encryption of a bitmap image

5   Encryption/Decryption Speed

We implemented DAFA in Java as a proof of concept in order to demonstrate its robust statistical properties and lightweight nature. We tested the performance of DAFA, as well as the AES cryptosystem with a 128-bit key using Cipher Block Chaining(CBC) for reference, on both an Intel Core 2 Duo 2.16 GHz desktop with 3GB RAM and the Nokia N900 Internet Tablet which has an ARM Cortex A8 600MHz processor with 256MB RAM. As shown in Table 13, DAFA greatly outperforms AES in terms of average encryption/decryption speed. The results shown in Table 13 are the average of 50 tests conducted on each file size with each test reflecting the average throughput for one complete encryption and decryption cycle. Note that since the DAFA encryption and decryption algorithms have similar operations on finite automata, the throughput for both are nearly identical.

Table 13. Average encryption and decryption throughput

Platform	Filesize (KB)	AES-128 (Kbit/sec)	DAFA-121227 (Kbit/sec)	DAFA-232337 (Kbit/sec)
Intel Core 2 Duo 2.16Ghz, 3GB RAM	4	516.13	2909.09	2133.33
	100	7476.64	12500.86	11940.30
	1024	47080.46	49652.76	47851.74
Nokia N900 600MHz, 256MB RAM	4	57.45	592.59	542.37
	100	1219.51	1523.81	1338.35
	1024	3955.63	4264.45	4016.32

Performance in Java is largely dependent on the JVM (Java Virtual Machine) implementation. The code is initially interpreted but parts are compiled at runtime using JIT (Just in Time) compilation [4] to boost performance for computationally intensive code. This is the main reason why generally we find that a Java program starts off slower when it is being interpreted and then rapidly picks up speed as the JIT compilatio n occurs. This can be seen in the performance results for both the AES as well as DAFA programs, where the throughput achieved is lower for the smaller files as compared to the larger ones.

The AES implementation in our test uses the Java JCE (Java Cryptographic Extension) library which is highly efficient and has been carefully optimized. Standard libraries in Java are largely programmed using native code which is much faster in terms of performance. In our profiling tests using the -Xprof option in Java, we found that roughly 25.58% of the computation time for AES encryption/decryption were handled by native method calls as compared to only 3.14% in our DAFA implementation. This is why with files of larger sizes, the relative performance of AES with respect to DAFA improves. Despite these facts, DAFA is very competitive in terms of speed even without speed and memory optimization, on both test platforms.

6   Related Work

Finite automata based public key cryptography termed FAPKC0 was introduced in [16] in 1985. Since then various public key cryptosystems based on finite automata have been proposed like FAPKC1, FAPKC2, FAPKC93, FAPKC3 and FAPKC4 [17,18,19]. In contrast to this, fewer single key cryptosystems based on finite automata have been proposed though the underlying theory behind both are similar. An excellent source for comprehensive information about both single and public key cryptosystems based on finite automata is [15]. A few attacks and suggestions on how to avoid them have been proposed in [2,3,5,6] for public key cryptosystems. However, in the single-key cryptosystem domain, we have not seen any successful attacks so far [15]. For a detailed and clear discussion about construction of finite automata required for public key cryptosystems, on which DAFA is based, readers are referred to [11]. DAFA presents an improvement on these schemes by firstly utilizing a compact key to generate finite automata on the fly and secondly by utilizing μ pairs of different linear and non-linear finite automata for encrypting successive blocks in order to increase the security afforded by the overall system.

7   Conclusion

In this paper we proposed and implemented a new variant of finite automaton cryptosystem, termed as DAFA, which uses DES to dynamically generate linear and non-linear finite automata on the fly using a 128-bit key. We conducted comprehensive statistical as well as running speed tests of DAFA on a desktop computer and on a smartphone. DAFA demonstrates strong security properties comparable to 128-bit AES, and it runs faster than AES. While our current DAFA implementation is based on Java as a proof of concept, we believe that there is large room to further improve its running speed if memory and code optimization were conducted or if implemented in assembly or C language. We expect that FA based cryptosystems, particularly the augmented variants such as DAFA, will earn credibility in the applied cryptographic world as a viable alternative to current cryptosystems and stand the tests of further cryptanalysis.

References

1. Banks, J., Carson, J.S., Nelson, B.L., Nicol, D.M.: Discrete-Event System Simulation, 5th edn. Prentice Hall (2010)
2. Bao, F., Igarashi, Y.: Break Finite Automata Public Key Cryptosystems. In: Fülöp, Z. (ed.) ICALP 1995. LNCS, vol. 944, pp. 147–158. Springer, Heidelberg (1995)
3. Bao, F., Igarashi, Y., Yu, X.: Some results on decomposition of weakly invertible finite automata. IEICE Transactions on Information and Systems E79-D, 1–7 (1996)
4. Cramer, T., Friedman, R., Miller, T., Seberger, D., Wilson, R., Wolczko, M.: Compiling java just in time. IEEE Micro 17 (1997)

5. Dai, D.W., Wu, K., Zhang, H.G.: Cryptanalysis on a finite automaton public key cryptosystem. Science in China, Ser. A 39, 27–36 (1996)
6. Dai, Z.-D., Ye, D.F., Lam, K.-Y.: Weak Invertibility of Finite Automata and Cryptanalysis on FAPKC. In: Ohta, K., Pei, D. (eds.) ASIACRYPT 1998. LNCS, vol. 1514, pp. 227–241. Springer, Heidelberg (1998)
7. Ehrsam, W.F., Meyer, C.H.W., Smith, J.L., Tuchman, W.L.: Message verification and transmission error detection by block chaining. US Patent 4074066 (1976)
8. Goldwasser, S., Micali, S.: Probabilistic encryption and how to play mental poker keeping secret all partial information. In: Annual ACM Symposium on Theory of Computing (1982)
9. Katz, J., Lindell, Y.: Introduction to Modern Cryptography. Chapman and Hall, CRC (August 2007)
10. Mathews, J.H.: Monte carlo estimate for pi. Pi Mu Epsilon Journal 5, 281–282 (1972)
11. Meskanen, T.: On finite automaton public key cryptosystems. Technical Report 408, TUCS - Turku Centre for Computer Science, Turku, Finland (2001)
12. U.S. Department of Commerce National Bureau of Standards. Data encryption standard. Federal Information Processing Standard (FIPS), Publication 46 (1977)
13. Shannon, C.E.: A mathematical theory of communication. Bell System Technical Journal 27, 379–423 (1948)
14. Hermetic Systems. Testing the me6 cryptosystem, http://www.hermetic.ch (accessed in December 2011)
15. Tao, R.J.: Finite Automata and Application to Cryptography. Tsinghua University Press (January 2008)
16. Tao, R.J., Chen, S.H.: A finite automaton public-key cryptosystem and digital signatures. Chinese Journal of Computers 8, 401–409 (1985) (in Chinese)
17. Tao, R.J., Chen, S.H.: Two varieties of finite automaton public key cryptosystem and digital signatures. Journal of Computer Science and Technology 1, 9–18 (1986)
18. Tao, R.J., Chen, S.H.: A variant of the public key cryptosystem fapkc3. Journal of Network and Computer Applications 20, 283–303 (1997)
19. Tao, R.J., Chen, S.H., Chen, X.M.: Fapkc3: A new finite automaton public key cryptosystem. Journal of Computer Science and Technology 12(4), 289–304 (1997)
20. Walker, J.: Fourmilab ent - a pseudorandom number sequence test program, http://www.fourmilab.ch/random (accessed in December 2011)

Improvement on Ahn et al.'s RSA P-Homomorphic Signature Scheme

Zhiwei Wang[1,2,3,4]

[1] College of Computer, Nanjing University of Posts and Telecommunications,
Nanjing, Jiangsu 210003, China
[2] State Key Laboratory of Information Security
(Institute of Information Engineering, Chinese Academy of Sciences),
Beijing, 100190, China
[3] Jiangsu High Technology Research Key Laboratory for Wireless Sensor Networks,
Nanjing, Jiangsu 210003, China
[4] Key Lab of Broadband Wireless Communication and Sensor Network Technology
(Nanjing University of Posts and Telecommunications),
Ministry of Education Jiangsu Province, Nanjing, Jiangsu 210003, China
zhwwang@njupt.edu.cn

Abstract. P-homomorphic signature is a general framework for computing on authenticated data, which is recently proposed by Ahn et al. With P-homomorphic signature, any third party can derive a signature on the object message m' from a signature of m, if m' and m satisfy $P(m, m') = 1$ for some predicate P which denotes the authenticatable relationship between m' and m. Ahn et al. proposed a RSA P-homomorphic signature scheme by using a RSA accumulator, which is very efficient in space. However, the computational cost of verification and derivation is very heavy. We present an improved P-homomorphic signature scheme based on factoring problem. In our construction, the time efficiency of both verification and derivation are much better than Ahn's scheme.

Keywords: P-homomorphic signature, signature derive, factoring problem, cloud computing.

1 Introduction

With the development of cloud computing, many secure problems have been proposed. One of the most important problem is that it's too much of a security risk to give a public cloud provider such as Amazon or Google access to unencrypted data. While data can be sent to and from a cloud provider's data center in encrypted form, the servers that power a cloud can't do any work on it that way. In 2009, Gentry proposed a fully homomorphic encryption scheme to make it possible to analyze data without decrypting it [1]. Up to now, some homomorphic encryption schemes have been proposed[1–3], while only a few homomorphic signature schemes have been presented.

In the past few years, there are about three research classes which have touch on this area: **quoting/redacting signature**, **arithmetic signature**, **transitive signature**. Quoting/redacting signature [4–8] is that given Alice's signature

A.D. Keromytis and R. Di Pietro (Eds.): SecureComm 2012, LNICST 106, pp. 19–28, 2013.

on some message m, any one can derive Alice's signature on a subset of m. Quoting/redacting signature is specially applied to signed text message and signed images. Arithmetic signature [9–13] is motivated by the application of secure network coding, which is that given Alice's signature on vectors $v_1, \cdots, v_k \in \mathbb{F}_p^n$, any one can derive Alice's signature on a vector in linear span of $v_1, \cdots, v_k$. In transitive signature[14–18], given Alice's signature on edges in a graph G, any one can derive Alice's signature on a pair of vertices u, v, if there exists a path from u to v in G.

Recently, Ahn et al. put forth a general framework of computing on signed data[19], which can cover all the three classes research above. Their definition is instantiated with any predicates, and allows to repeat derivation on the signatures. They call this general framework slightly homomorphic signature or P-homomorphic signature. In [19], they provide two general constructions for computing signatures on any univariate, closed predicates, namely predicates $P(M, m')$ where M only contains a single message and if $P(a, b) = P(b, c) = 1$ then $P(a, c) = 1$. The first construction is a brute force construction from any signature. Soundness of this construction follows from the underlying signature scheme. However, the signatures in this construction may become very large, which effects both the signing time and signature size. The second construction is a RSA accumulator-based construction, which can produce a short signature, but the computational cost of both verification and derivation is even worse than the first construction. The prime search component of hash function is the dominant factor. Ahn et al. [19] also proposed the third efficient construction, which is only suitable for quoting substrings and not a generic solution. Furthermore, the signature derivation procedure in this construction is very complex.

In this paper, we propose an improved generic construction of P-homomorphic signature from Ahn's RSA accumulator based construction. Our scheme is efficient in both in space and computational costs. The rest of this paper is organized as follows: In the next section, we review some preliminaries related to our construction. Then, we review Ahn et al.'s construction in Section 3. In Section 4, we propose our improved scheme. The security properties will be analyzed in Section 5. We conclude in Section 6.

2   Preliminaries

2.1   Some Concepts in Number Theory

Let $N = p \times q$ be a composite modulus, where p and q are two large prime numbers. Let $\mathbb{Q}_N$ denote the subgroup of squares in $\mathbb{Z}_N^*$. Then, it is well known that $\mathbb{Q}_N$ is a cyclic group with order $\phi(N)/4 = (p-1)(q-1)/4$ [20].

Factoring Problem. given a k-bit composite N, which is a multiple of two large primes p and q, to output p or q. Factoring problem is usually considered as a hard problem.

Theorem 2.1. *Let* $a \in \mathbb{Q}_N$, $N = p \times q$, *where* p, q *are large primes and* $p = 2p' + 1$, $q = 2q' + 1$. p' *and* q' *are also large primes. Then* $a^{2d} \equiv a \pmod{N}$, *where* $d = (N - p - q + 5)/8$.

Proof. Since $d = \frac{(N-p-q+5)}{8} = \frac{(p-1)(q-1)+4}{8} = \frac{4p'q'+4}{8}$, then $a^{2d} = a^{p'q'+1} = a$ (mod N).(We note that $\phi(N)/4 = (p-1)(q-1)/4 = p'q'$.)

Indeed, Theorem 2.1 provides a way to compute one square root of a quadratic residue $a \in \mathbb{Q}_N$.

To further understand the algorithm of computing a 2^lth root of a quadratic residue, let us introduce the following theorem.

Theorem 2.2. *Let* $N = p \times q$, *where* p, q *are large primes and* $p = 2p' + 1$, $q = 2q' + 1$. p' *and* q' *are also large primes. If* $a = x^2 \in \mathbb{Q}_N$, *then* $a^d \in \mathbb{Q}_N$.

Proof. Since p' and q' are also large primes, then $p' = 2k + 1$ and $q' = 2k' + 1$ for some integer k and k'. Then,$d = \frac{(N-p-q+5)}{8} = \frac{4p'q'+4}{8} = 2kk' + k + k' + 1$ is an integer. So we have $a^d = x^{2d} = (x^d)^2$ (mod N). Thus, $a^d \in \mathbb{Q}_N$.

From Theorem 2.1 and Theorem 2.2, we can know that a square root of $a \in \mathbb{Q}_N$ computed by a^d (mod N), still stays in $\mathbb{Q}_N$. Therefore, a 2^lth root of a can be computed as a^{d^l} (mod N),where d^l is computed over $\mathbb{Z}_{p'q'}$.

Let N be a multiple of two large primes p,q and $a \in \mathbb{Q}_N$. If s_1 and s_2 are two square roots satisfying $s_1 \neq \pm s_2$ (mod N), then N could be factored by computing $GCD(s_1 + s_2, N)$ or $GCD(s_1 - s_2, N)$ as the non-trivial divisor of N. However, if $s_1 = \pm s_2$ (mod N), it will be no useful to the factorization of N. Thus, if given two random square roots, the probability of factoring N is $1/2$.

2.2   Definition of P-Homomorphic Signature

Definition of Predicate P. Let $\mathcal{M}$ be a message space. A predicate P is defined as $P : 2^{\mathcal{M}} \times \mathcal{M} \to \{0,1\}$ which maps a set of messages and a message to a bit [19]. For the quoting application, the predicate P is defined as $P(M, m') = 1$ where $M \subset \mathcal{M}$ iff m' is a quote from the set of message M. The predicate P for arithmetic computation is defined as $P((v_1, \cdots, v_k), v) = 1$ whenever v is in the span of $v_1, \cdots, v_k$.

A P-homomorphic signature scheme Π for message space $\mathcal{M}$ and predicate P consists of four algorithms: **KeyGen, Sign, SignDerive, Verify**. Here, **Sign** is simply a special case of **SignDerive**. We describe them as follows:

KeyGen(1^λ)**:** This algorithm outputs a key pair (pk, sk). We can treat the secret key sk as a signature on the empty message ε.

Sign($sk, m \in \mathcal{M}$)**:** Given the secret key sk and a message m, the algorithm outputs a signature σ.

SignDerive($pk, (\{\sigma_m\}_{m\in\mathcal{M}}, M), m', \omega$)**:** This algorithm takes as input the public key, a set of messages M and corresponding signatures $\{\sigma_m\}_{m\in M}$, a derived message m', and possibly some auxiliary information ω. It generates a new signature σ' on m'. For complex predicate, ω can be served as a witness for $P(M, m') = 1$. For simplicity, $Sign(sk, m) = SignDerive(pk, (sk, \varepsilon), m, \cdot)$ denotes that if given sk, any messages can be derived. Here sk can be considered as a signature on the empty message ε.

Verify(pk, m, σ)**:** If this algorithm is provided with the public key, message, and the corresponding signature σ, it returns 1 when the signature is valid, otherwise, it returns 0.

We must confirm that if $P(M, m') = 1$ then

$$SignDerive(pk, (Sign(sk, M), M)m') \neq \perp,$$

and for all signature tuples $\{\sigma_m\}_{m \in M}$ satisfying

$$\sigma' \leftarrow SignDerive(pk, (Sign(sk, M), M)m') \neq \perp,$$

$Verify(pk, m', \sigma') = 1$ holds. These two rules make the signature derivation be iterative if allowed by P.

3   Review of Ahn et al.'s RSA Accumulator-Based Scheme

In Ahn et al.'s construction[19], they only focus on *univariate, closed* predicates $P(M, m')$, namely M contains a single component and if $P(a, b) = P(b, c) = 1$ then $P(a, c) = 1$. We now describe their RSA accumulator-based scheme as follows:

KeyGen(1^λ): This algorithm selects three parameters: a 20λ-bit RSA modulus N, $a \in \mathbb{Z}_N$ and a hash function H_p which maps arbitrary strings to 2λ-bit prime numbers. The public key $pk = (N, H_p, a)$, and the secret key sk is the factorization of N.

Sign($sk, m \in \mathcal{M}$): Let $U = P(\{m\}) = \{m' | m' \in \mathcal{M} and P(m, m') = 1\}$. Compute the signature as

$$\sigma = a^{1/(\prod_{u_i \in U} H_p(u_i))} \pmod{N}.$$

SignDerive(pk, σ, m, m'): In this algorithm, first check that $P(m, m') = 1$, if not then outputs $\perp$. Otherwise, let $U' = P(\{m'\})$, compute the signature as

$$\sigma' = \sigma^{\prod_{u_i \in U - U'} H_p(u_i)} \pmod{N}.$$

The signature is essentially of the form $a^{1/(\prod_{u_i \in U'} H_p(u_i))} \pmod{N}$.

Verify(pk, m, σ): Let $U = P(\{m\})$, if $a = \sigma^{\prod_{u_i \in U} H_p(u_i)} \pmod{N}$ the outputs 1, otherwise, returns 0.

This scheme can be proved secure under RSA, and the most important advantage is that signatures only require one element in $\mathbb{Z}_N^*$. However, the computational cost is very heavy. If computing an l-symbol quote from an n-symbol message requires $\mathcal{O}(n(n-l))$ evaluation of $H_p()$ and $\mathcal{O}(n(n-l))$ modular exponentiations. Verification requires $\mathcal{O}(l^2)$ evaluation of $H_p()$ and $\mathcal{O}(l^2)$ modular exponentiations. **The computational cost of prime search in $H_p()$ is the dominating factor, since the outputs of $H_p()$ must be a prime number.**

4   Our Improved Scheme

For overcoming the above shortcoming, we propose an improved scheme which can be described as follows (We also focus on *univariate, closed* predicate.):

KeyGen(1^λ): This algorithm selects a composite number N which is a multiple of two safe large prime numbers $p = 2p' + 1, q = 2q' + 1$. p and q satisfy that $(p-1)(q-1) \geq 2^l$ and $pq < 2^{l+1}$ (l is another secure parameter derived from λ). Then, computes $d = (N - p - q + 5)/8$, and chooses $h \in \mathbb{Q}_N$ and a hash function $H() : \{0,1\}^* \rightarrow \{0,1\}^l$. The public key $pk = (N, H, h)$, while the secret key $sk = d$.

Sign($sk, m \in \mathcal{M}$): Let $U = P(\{m\}) = \{m'|m' \in \mathcal{M} \quad and \quad P(m, m') = 1\}$. Compute the signature as

$$\sigma = h^{\prod_{u_i \in U} d^{H(u_i)}} \quad (\text{mod } N).$$

SignDerive(pk, σ, m, m'): In this algorithm, first check that $P(m, m') = 1$, if not then outputs $\perp$. Otherwise, let $U' = P(\{m'\})$, compute the signature as

$$\sigma' = \sigma^{\prod_{u_i \in U-U'} 2^{H(u_i)}} \quad (\text{mod } N).$$

The signature is essentially of the form $h^{\prod_{u_i \in U'} d^{H(u_i)}}$ (mod N).

Verify(pk, m, σ): Let $U = P(\{m\})$, if $h = \sigma^{\prod_{u_i \in U} 2^{H(u_i)}}$ (mod N) the outputs 1, otherwise, returns 0.

In the above scheme, signatures still requires only one element in $\mathbb{Z}_N^*$. However, the computational burden is much better than Ahn's construction. Firstly, $H()$ is a common hash function, which does not require the output must be a prime number. Thus, there exists no prime search component in $H()$, which saves a large computational cost compared with Ahn's construction. Secondly, the modular exponentiations in SignDerive and Verify algorithm can be computed very fast, since $\sigma^{\prod_{u_i \in U-U'} 2^{H(u_i)}}$ and $\sigma^{\prod_{u_i \in U} 2^{H(u_i)}}$ can be done only through *adding* and *shifting*.

5   Security Analysis

In this section, we first describe the security properties of P-homomorphic signature. Then, we prove that our improved scheme achieves the security properties.

5.1   Security Definition

The security definition of P-homomorphic signature should capture two properties: context hiding and unforgeability[19].

Context hiding means that a signature should reveal nothing more than the message being signed. If a signature on m' was derived from a signature on m, an attacker should not learn anything about m other than what can be deduced by m'. This should be true even the original signature on m is revealed. For example, in the case of quoting application, a signed quote should not reveal the length of original message, the position of the quote etc. Ahn et al. proposed a powerful statistic definition of context hiding called *Strong Context Hiding*.

Strong Context Hiding. *Let $M \subset \mathcal{M}$ and $m' \in \mathcal{M}$ such that $P(M, m') = 1$. Let (pk, sk) be the key pair. A P-homomorphic signature Π is strong context hiding if and only if the following distribution are statically close:*

$$(sk, \{\sigma_m\}_{m \in M} \leftarrow Sign(sk, M), Sign(sk, m'))_{sk, M, m'}$$

$$(sk, \{\sigma_m\}_{m \in M} \leftarrow Sign(sk, M), SignDerive(pk, (\{\sigma_m\}_{m \in M}, M), m'))_{sk, M, m'}$$

The distributions are taken over the coins of Sign and SignDerive. Here, for a set of message $M = \{m_1, m_2, \cdots, m_k\}$, it is convenient to let $Sign(sk, M)$ denote independently signing each of the k messages, which can be depicted as follows:

$$Sign(sk, M) = (Sign(sk, m_1), \cdots, Sign(sk, m_k)).$$

The above definition implies that a derived signature on m' is indistinguishable from a signature generated independently of M. Therefore, the derived signature cannot reveal any information about M other than what is revealed by m'. This definition uses statical indistinguishability meaning that even a unbounded attacker cannot distinguish the derived signatures from the fresh ones. Thus, it is called *strong context hiding*. Furthermore, Ahn et al. also proposed another definition called *context hiding* by using computational indistinguishability, which is very complex, since the attacker needs to be given a signing oracle. The relation of *context hiding* and *strong context hiding* can be proved that if a P-homomorphic signature scheme is context hiding then it is strong context hiding.

Unforgeability of P-homomorphic signature is that an attacker can adaptively choose messages and acquire the corresponding derived signatures, however, he/she cannot output a signature on a message that is not derivable from the set of signed messages at his hand. Ahn et al. presented the definition of unforgeability by extending the basic notion of adaptively chosen existential unforgeability. Ahn's definition can be defined by a game between a challenger $\mathcal{C}$ and an adversary $\mathcal{A}$ with respect to scheme Π over message space $\mathcal{M}$.

Setup: The challenger $\mathcal{C}$ runs **KeyGen**(1^λ) to obtain a key pair (pk, sk) and sends pk to $\mathcal{A}$, while keeps sk for itself. Furthermore, $\mathcal{C}$ keeps a set T that is initially empty.

Queries: $\mathcal{A}$ adaptively issues the following queries to $\mathcal{C}$

1. $Sign(m \in \mathcal{M})$: The challenger $\mathcal{C}$ runs **Sign**(sk, m) to get σ, and places (m, σ) into a table T. Then $\mathcal{C}$ returns σ to $\mathcal{A}$
2. $SignDerive(m' \in \mathcal{M})$: This challenger $\mathcal{C}$ retrieves all the tuples (σ_i, m_i) in T for $i = 1, \cdots, k$. If T is empty, then $\mathcal{C}$ returns $\perp$. Otherwise, let $M =$

$\{m_1, \cdots, m_k\}$. If $P(M, m') = 1$, then $\mathcal{C}$ runs **SignDerive**$(pk, (\{\sigma_m\}_{m \in M}, M), m')$ to obtain σ'. $\mathcal{C}$ keeps (σ', m') into T, and returns σ' to $\mathcal{A}$.

Output: Finally, $\mathcal{A}$ outputs a pair (σ', m'). If $\mathcal{A}$ wins the game, the following two conditions should be satisfied.

1. Verify$(pk, m', \sigma') = 1$;
2. Let M be the set of messages in T. $P(M, m') = 0$ must hold.

Let **ADV**$_\mathcal{A}$ denote the probability of $\mathcal{A}$ winning.

Unforgeability. *If* **ADV**$_\mathcal{A}$ *is negligible in* λ*, then A P-homomorphic signature scheme* Π *is adaptively chosen-message attacks* **unforgeable***.*

Ahn et al. also proposed a weaker notion of unforgeability[19], which is also defined by a game between challenger $\mathcal{C}$ and adversary $\mathcal{A}$. Ahn et al. call it **NHU** game, in which the adversary only makes calls to *Sign* oracle. The only difference between **NHU** game and the standard unforgeability game for a P-homomorphic signature scheme is that in this game, the adversary only wins if his forged signature on m^* such that for all $m \in T$, $P(m, m^*) = 0$, while in the standard unforgeability game, the adversary wins if his forged signature on any message that is not in T.

Ahn et al. proved that *if a P-homomorphic signature scheme is* **NHU** *unforgeable and strong context hiding, then it is standard-unforgeable.*[19] This implies that strong context hiding property can help simplify the security argument of standard unforgeability.

5.2 Security Proof

In this section, we will provide the security proof to our improved scheme.

Theorem 5.1. *If the factoring problem is hard, then our improved P-homomorphic signature scheme is unforgeable and context hiding in the random oracle.*

We proved Theorem 5.1 by showing that our scheme is strong context hiding and **NHU**-unforgeable.

Lemma 5.1. *The improved P-homomorphic signature scheme is strong context hiding.*

Proof. Let $pk = (N, H, h)$, and challenge be any m, m' where $P(m, m') = 1$. Let $U = P(m)$ and $U' = P(m')$. We can deduce that

$$Sign(sk, m) = \sigma = h^{d \prod_{u \in U} H(u)} \pmod{N}$$

$$Sign(sk, m') = \sigma' = h^{d \prod_{u \in U'} H(u)} \pmod{N}$$

$$SignDerive(pk, (\sigma, m), m') = \sigma^{2 \prod_{u \in U - U'} H(u)} \pmod{N}$$

$$= (h^{d \prod_{u \in U} H(u)})^{2 \prod_{u \in U - U'} H(u)} \pmod{N}$$

$$= h^{d \prod_{u \in U'} H(u)} \pmod{N}$$

$$= \sigma'.$$

Since $Sign(sk, m')$ equals $SignDerive(pk, (\sigma, m), m')$, the probability that an adversary can distinguish between them is exactly $1/2$. Thus, our improved P-homomorphic signature scheme is strong context hiding.

Lemma 5.1 *The improved P-homomorphic signature scheme is* **NHU**-*uforgeable if factoring problem is hard.*

Proof. We will prove this lemma through the **NHU** game discussed above. In the **NHU** game, the adversary $\mathcal{A}$ is only allowed to make *Sign* oracle queries. We suppose adversary $\mathcal{A}$ queries the random oracle on at most s unique inputs. If adversary $\mathcal{A}$ can outputs a successful forgery in **NHU** game, then we can construct a challenger $\mathcal{C}$ that solves the factoring problem with a non-negligible probability. Given a challenge N, $\mathcal{C}$'s goal is to output the factorization of N.

Setup: Challenger $\mathcal{C}$ chooses $s - 1$ $l$bits distinct integer numbers $e_1, \cdots, e_{s-1}$ at random, but all $e_i \neq 2, e_i > 0$. Let E denote $\{e_1, \cdots, e_{s-1}\}$. Then, $\mathcal{C}$ guesses a random number $i^* \in \{1, \cdots, s\}$, and keeps it. Next, $\mathcal{C}$ randomly selects $y \in \mathbb{Z}_N^*$, and computes $h = y^{\prod_{e_i \in E} 2^{e_i}}$ (mod N). Obviously, $h \in \mathbb{Q}_N$. Finally, $\mathcal{C}$ sends N, h to $\mathcal{A}$, and will ask its queries on random oracle H interactively.

Queries: $\mathcal{C}$ answers $\mathcal{A}$'s adaptively *Hash* and *Sign* queries.

- Hash queries: When $\mathcal{A}$ makes the jth query to the random oracle, if $j = i^*$, then $\mathcal{C}$ answers 2. Otherwise, if $j < i^*$, $\mathcal{C}$ answers with e_j, and e_{j-1} otherwise. Since we assume $\mathcal{A}$'s queries are different every time, let x^* as the input when $H(x^*) = 2$.
- Sign queries: When $\mathcal{A}$ makes a sign queries on message m, $\mathcal{C}$ computes $U = P(m)$, and if $x^* \in U$, then $\mathcal{C}$ aborts. Otherwise, $\mathcal{C}$ calls H on all elements of U not previously queried to H. Let $E(U)$ denote the set of integer numbers derived by calling H on every element in U. $\mathcal{C}$ computes

$$\sigma = y^{\prod_{i \in [E - E(U)]} 2^{e_i}} \quad (\text{mod } N),$$

and returns σ, m as the answer to $\mathcal{A}$.

Outputs: Eventually, $\mathcal{A}$ outputs a valid forged signature σ on message m, where m cannot be derived from any element returned by *Sign*. If m is still not queried to H, or $m \neq x^*$, then $\mathcal{C}$ aborts. Otherwise, let $U = P(\{x^*\}) - \{x^*\}$, and $E(U)$ denotes the set of integer numbers derived by calling H on every element in U. From the verification equation, the following equation holds.

$$h^{\prod_{e_i \in E(U)} d^{e_i}} = y^{\prod_{e_i \in [E - E(U)]} 2^{e_i}} = \sigma^2 \quad (\text{mod } N).$$

We computes $b = \sum_{i \in [E - E(U)]} e_i$, then $y^{2^b} = \sigma^2$ (mod N). If $\sigma \neq \pm y^{2^{b-1}}$ (mod N), $\mathcal{C}$ can factoring N by computing $GCD(\sigma + y^{2^{b-1}}, N)$ or $GCD(\sigma - y^{2^{b-1}}, N)$. Since y is randomly chosen in $\mathbb{Z}_N^*$, the probability that σ and $\pm y^{2^{b-1}}$ are distinct is $1/2$.

Probability Analysis: We assume that the attacker $\mathcal{A}$ can win the above game with the probability of ϵ. $\mathcal{A}$'s final forgery is based on the i^*th hash queries

$(1 < i^* < s)$, and i^* is randomly chosen from $\{1, \cdots, s\}$. So we can deduce that challenger $\mathcal{C}$ can solve the factoring problem through $\mathcal{A}$'s forgery with the probability of $\frac{\epsilon}{2s}$.

This completes our proof.

Note: Our improved scheme is proved secure under the hardness of the factoring problem, while Ahn et al.'s construction is proved secure under the RSA assumption. However, the hardness of RSA problem is not identical to the hardness of the factoring problem . It is generally believed that RSA assumption is stronger than factoring assumption[21].

6   Conclude

P-homomorphic signature is a general framework for computing on authenticated data, which can make any third party derive a signature on the object message m' from a signature of m, if m' and m satisfy $P(m, m') = 1$ for some predicate P. Similar with homomorphic encryption, P-homomorphic signature can also make cloud computing providers provide good services to customers. Cloud providers can directly compute on the existing signature files without secret keys. In this paper, we propose an improved P-homomorphic signature scheme, which is more efficient in computational cost than Ahn's scheme. Furthermore, our scheme can be proved under the hardness of the factoring problem.

Acknowledgments. This research is supported by the Project Funded by the Priority Academic Program Development of Jiangsu Higher Education Institutions(PAPD), the Natural science fund for colleges and universities in Jiangsu Province No. 11KJB520015, and the Program for Excellent Talents in Nanjing University of Posts and Telecommunications No. NY209014.

References

1. Gentry, C.: A fully homomorphic encryption scheme. PhD thesis, Stanford University (2009)
2. Smart, N.P., Vercauteren, F.: Fully Homomorphic Encryption with Relatively Small Key and Ciphertext Sizes. In: Nguyen, P.Q., Pointcheval, D. (eds.) PKC 2010. LNCS, vol. 6056, pp. 420–443. Springer, Heidelberg (2010)
3. van Dijk, M., Gentry, C., Halevi, S., Vaikuntanathan, V.: Fully Homomorphic Encryption over the Integers. In: Gilbert, H. (ed.) EUROCRYPT 2010. LNCS, vol. 6110, pp. 24–43. Springer, Heidelberg (2010)
4. Ateniese, G., Chou, D.H., de Medeiros, B., Tsudik, G.: Sanitizable Signatures. In: De Capitani di Vimercati, S., Syverson, P.F., Gollmann, D. (eds.) ESORICS 2005. LNCS, vol. 3679, pp. 159–177. Springer, Heidelberg (2005)
5. Miyazaki, K., Hanaoka, G., Imai, H.: Digitally signed document sanitizing scheme based on bilinear maps. In: ASIACCS 2006: Proceedings of the 2006 ACM Symposium on Information, Computer and Communications Security, pp. 343–354 (2006)
6. Haber, S., Hatano, Y., Honda, Y., Horne, W., Miyazaki, K., Sander, T., Tezoku, S., Yao, D.: Efficient signature schemes supporting redaction, pseudonymization, and data deidentification. In: ASIACCS 2008, pp. 353–362 (2008)

7. Brzuska, C., Fischlin, M., Freudenreich, T., Lehmann, A., Page, M., Schelbert, J., Schröder, D., Volk, F.: Security of Sanitizable Signatures Revisited. In: Jarecki, S., Tsudik, G. (eds.) PKC 2009. LNCS, vol. 5443, pp. 317–336. Springer, Heidelberg (2009)

8. Brzuska, C., Fischlin, M., Lehmann, A., Schröder, D.: Unlinkability of Sanitizable Signatures. In: Nguyen, P.Q., Pointcheval, D. (eds.) PKC 2010. LNCS, vol. 6056, pp. 444–461. Springer, Heidelberg (2010)

9. Boneh, D., Freeman, D., Katz, J., Waters, B.: Signing a Linear Subspace: Signature Schemes for Network Coding. In: Jarecki, S., Tsudik, G. (eds.) PKC 2009. LNCS, vol. 5443, pp. 68–87. Springer, Heidelberg (2009)

10. Gennaro, R., Katz, J., Krawczyk, H., Rabin, T.: Secure Network Coding over the Integers. In: Nguyen, P.Q., Pointcheval, D. (eds.) PKC 2010. LNCS, vol. 6056, pp. 142–160. Springer, Heidelberg (2010)

11. Boneh, D., Freeman, D.M.: Homomorphic Signatures for Polynomial Functions. In: Paterson, K.G. (ed.) EUROCRYPT 2011. LNCS, vol. 6632, pp. 149–168. Springer, Heidelberg (2011)

12. Boneh, D., Freeman, D.M.: Linearly Homomorphic Signatures over Binary Fields and New Tools for Lattice-Based Signatures. In: Catalano, D., Fazio, N., Gennaro, R., Nicolosi, A. (eds.) PKC 2011. LNCS, vol. 6571, pp. 1–16. Springer, Heidelberg (2011)

13. Wei, L., Coull, S.E., Reiter, M.K.: Bounded vector signatures and their applications. In: ASIACCS 2011, pp. 277–285 (2011)

14. Hevia, A., Micciancio, D.: The Provable Security of Graph-Based One-Time Signatures and Extensions to Algebraic Signature Schemes. In: Zheng, Y. (ed.) ASIACRYPT 2002. LNCS, vol. 2501, pp. 379–396. Springer, Heidelberg (2002)

15. Bellare, M., Neven, G.: Transitive signatures: New schemes and proofs. IEEE Transactions on Information Theory 51, 2133–2151 (2005)

16. Shahandashti, S.F., Salmasizadeh, M., Mohajeri, J.: A Provably Secure Short Transitive Signature Scheme from Bilinear Group Pairs. In: Blundo, C., Cimato, S. (eds.) SCN 2004. LNCS, vol. 3352, pp. 60–76. Springer, Heidelberg (2005)

17. Yi, X.: Directed Transitive Signature Scheme. In: Abe, M. (ed.) CT-RSA 2007. LNCS, vol. 4377, pp. 129–144. Springer, Heidelberg (2006)

18. Neven, G.: A simple transitive signature scheme for directed trees. Theoretical Computer Science 396(1-3), 277–282 (2008)

19. Ahn, J.H., Boneh, D., Camenisch, J., Hohenberger, S., Shelat, A., Waters, B.: Computing on Authenticated Data. Cryptology ePrint Archive: Report 2011/096, http://eprint.iacr.org/2011/096

20. Shoup, V.: A Computational Introduction to Number Theory and Algebra, p. 534. Cambridge University Press (2005)

21. Cao, Z., Zhu, H., Lu, R.: Provably secure robust threshold partial blind signature. Science in China Series F: Information Sciences 49(5), 604–615 (2006)

Building General-Purpose Security Services
on EMV Payment Cards*

Chunhua Chen[1,**], Shaohua Tang[1,***], and Chris J. Mitchell[2]

[1] School of Computer Science and Engineering,
South China University of Technology,
Guangzhou 510640, China
chen.chunhua@mail.scut.edu.cn, csshtang@scut.edu.cn
[2] Information Security Group,
Royal Holloway, University of London,
Egham, Surrey TW20 0EX, UK
c.mitchell@rhul.ac.uk

Abstract. The Generic Authentication Architecture (GAA) is a standardised extension to the mobile telephony security infrastructures that supports the provision of security services to network applications. We have proposed a generalised version of GAA which enables almost any pre-existing infrastructure to be used as the basis for the provision of generic security services, and have examined a GAA instantiation supported by Trusted Computing. In this paper we study another instantiation of GAA, this time building on the widely deployed EMV security infrastructure. This enables the existing EMV infrastructure to be used as the basis of a general-purpose authenticated key establishment service in a simple and uniform way, and also provides an opportunity for EMV-aware third parties to provide novel security services. We also discuss possible applications and issues of privacy and trust.

Keywords: GAA, EMV, key establishment, security service.

* This work was partially sponsored by the National Natural Science Foundation of China under Grant (No. U1135004 and 61170080), the Guangdong Province Universities and Colleges Pearl River Scholar Funded Scheme (2011), the Guangzhou Metropolitan Science and Technology Planning Project (No. 2011J4300028), the Fundamental Research Funds for the Central Universities (No. 2009ZZ0035 and 2011ZG0015), the Guangdong Provincial Natural Science Foundation (No. 9351064101000003) and the High-level Talents Project of Guangdong Institutions of Higher Education (2012).
** The author is a PhD student at the South China University of Technology. This work was partially performed during a visit to the Information Security Group at Royal Holloway, University of London, sponsored by the Chinese Scholarship Council.
*** Corresponding author.

A.D. Keromytis and R. Di Pietro (Eds.): SecureComm 2012, LNICST 106, pp. 29–44, 2013.
© Institute for Computer Sciences, Social Informatics and Telecommunications Engineering 2013

1   Introduction

Almost any large scale network security system requires the establishment of some kind of a security infrastructure. For example, if network authentication or authenticated key establishment is required, then the communicating parties typically need access to a shared secret key or certificates for each other's public keys.

Setting up a new security infrastructure for a significant number of clients is by no means a trivial task. For example, establishing a public key infrastructure (PKI) for a large number of users involves setting up a certification authority (CA), getting every user to generate a key pair, registering every user and corresponding public key, and generating and distributing public key certificates. In addition, the ongoing management overhead is non-trivial, covering issues such as revocation and key update.

At the same time, there are a number of existing security infrastructures, in some cases with almost ubiquitous coverage. When deploying a new network security protocol it is therefore tempting to try to exploit one of these existing security infrastructures to avoid the need for the potentially costly roll-out of a new infrastructure.

This is by no means a new idea (see, for example, [17,18,19,21]). However, previous proposals have been ad hoc and application-specific. The alternative approach we consider here involves building a framework on top of an existing security infrastructure, which exploits the underlying infrastructure to enable the provision of general-purpose security services. For example, 3GPP has standardised the Generic Authentication Architecture (GAA) [4], which uses the mobile telephony security infrastructures (including those for GSM[1] and UMTS[2]) to provide a set of security services. A full description of 3GPP GAA is presented in [14]. Advantages of such a general approach include the usual benefits of a layered protocol architecture, including re-usability of applications across underlying infrastructures and simplified application development.

In previous work [6,7] we proposed a generalised version of GAA, which aims to enable almost any pre-existing infrastructure to be used as a basis for the provision of generic security services. A GAA instantiation supported by the Trusted Computing (TC) infrastructure has been described [6]. In this paper we build on the widely deployed EMV [9,10,11,12] (named after Europay, MasterCard, and Visa) security infrastructure, involving the chip-based EMV credit/debit cards deployed worldwide.[3] We define a GAA instantiation building on the EMV security services, which we call EMV-GAA.

The remainder of this paper is organised as follows. In section 2 we introduce a generalised version of GAA. In section 3 we provide an overview of EMV security services. In section 4 we give details of EMV-GAA. This is followed

---

[1] The Global System for Mobile Communications.
[2] The Universal Mobile Telecommunications System.
[3] Magnetic stripe cards are even more widely deployed for credit and debit purposes than EMV cards; however, they cannot store (or process) secret keys, and hence could not be used to support GAA.

by an informal security analysis in section 5. We analyse relevant privacy and security issues, and propose a modified scheme to address possible threats in section 6. We review related work in section 7, and discuss possible applications in section 8. In section 9 we draw conclusions.

2   Generic Authentication Architecture

We start by describing the generalised version of the GAA architecture on which we build our novel scheme. We introduce the main roles in the framework, its goals and rationale, and its two main procedures. This generalised GAA architecture was first described in [7], and was elaborated in [6].

2.1   Overview of GAA

As shown in Figure 1, the following entities play a role in GAA.

- The *Bootstrapping Server Function* (BSF) *server B* acts as a Trusted Third Party (TTP), and is assumed to have the means to access credentials belonging to a pre-existing security infrastructure. B uses the pre-established credentials to provide authenticated key establishment services to *GAA-enabled user platforms* and *GAA-aware application servers*. B uses its Fully Qualified Domain Name (FQDN) as its identifier Id_B.
- A *GAA-aware application server* S is assumed to have the means to establish a mutually authenticated, confidentiality- and integrity-protected channel with B, and an arrangement to access the security services provided by B. The means by which the secure channel between B and S is established is outside the scope of the GAA framework. In practice, this could be supported by well-established techniques such as SSL/TLS channels with both server and client side certificates, IPsec tunnelling, or some other appropriate 'virtual private network'. A permanent secure channel is also potentially beneficial from an efficiency viewpoint, because it can be reused for multiple protocol executions. The functionality of a *GAA-aware application server* is also referred to as the *Network Application Function* (NAF) *server*. S uses its FQDN as its identifier Id_S.
- A *GAA-enabled user platform* P is assumed to be equipped with credentials belonging to the pre-existing security infrastructure, and accesses the security services provided by B.

The user platform and the BSF server need to interact with the pre-existing security infrastructure, whereas the application server does not (it only needs to interact with the BSF server and the user platform). Also, the user platform and the application server do not need to have a pre-existing security relationship.

GAA provides a general purpose key establishment service for user platforms and application servers. As described below, GAA uses a two-level key hierarchy consisting of a master session key and server- and application-specific

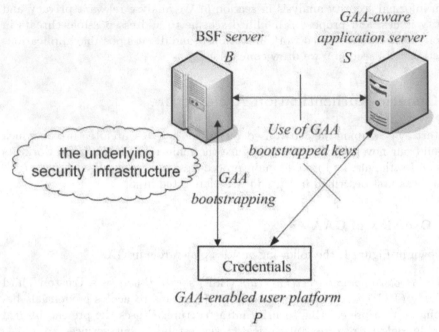

Fig. 1. GAA framework

session keys. The master session key is established using the pre-existing security infrastructure, and is not used directly to secure GAA-based applications. Instead it is used to generate the server/application-specific session keys using a *key diversification* function. By choosing a function with appropriate properties, it can be arranged that knowledge of a server/application specific session key will not reveal any information about the master session key or any other server/application-specific keys.

2.2   GAA Procedures

As we now describe, GAA incorporates two main procedures: *GAA bootstrapping* and *Use of bootstrapped keys*.

GAA bootstrapping uses the pre-existing security infrastructure to set up a shared master key MK between P and B. Also established is a Bootstrapping Transaction Identifier $B\text{-}TID$ for MK and the lifetime of this key. $B\text{-}TID$ must consist of a (statistically) unique value which identifies both an instance of *GAA bootstrapping* and Id_B.

The *Use of bootstrapped keys* procedure establishes a server/application-specific session key SK between P and S, using the master key MK shared by P and B. The procedure operates in the following way. P first derives a session key SK as:

$$SK = \mathrm{KDF}(MK, NAF\text{-}Id, \text{other values})$$

where KDF is a one-way *key diversification* function, and *NAF-Id* is an application-specific value consisting of Id_S and an identifier of the underlying application protocol. Other values may be included in the key derivation computation, depending on the nature of the underlying security infrastructure. *P* then starts the application protocol by sending a request containing *B-TID* to *S*. *S* submits the received *B-TID* and its own identifier *NAF-Id* to *B* to request the session key *SK*. Note that *B-TID* contains Id_B, so *S* knows where to send the request. As stated above, we require that *S* and *B* have the means to establish a mutually authenticated and confidential secure channel, and hence *B* can verify *S* against Id_S. If *S* is authorised, *B* derives *SK* from the *MK* identified by *B-TID*, and sends *SK*, its lifetime, and other relevant information to *S* via the secure channel. *P* and *S* now share *SK*, which they can use to secure application-specific messages.

Note that *key separation* is enforced by including *NAF-Id* as an input to the *key diversification* function. Other values used in the computation of *SK* could include identifiers for the GAA bootstrapping instance and the user platform.

3   EMV Security

In this section we provide a high-level overview of the main security features of the EMV payment system. We introduce the main roles in the system, the associated cryptographic keys and payment messages, and the processes relevant to this paper.

The EMV payment system involves five major interacting entities: a cardholder, an EMV payment card, a merchant terminal, an acquiring bank (the Acquirer) and a card issuing bank (the Issuer). The EMV specifications [9,10,11,12] define the interactions between an EMV smart card and a merchant terminal, as required to support financial transactions. Prior to engaging in such a transaction, the cardholder must complete an agreement with the Issuer, and be equipped with a chip-based EMV credit/debit card. The cardholder can then use this card to pay at merchant premises (EMV only supports transactions in which the cardholder is physically present, i.e. it does not support e-commerce or telephone transactions).

3.1   Transactions

An attempted EMV transaction can have a variety of outcomes; the transaction might be:

- approved offline;
- declined offline (by either the card or terminal); or
- sent for online approval by the card issuer.

We focus here on the case where the transaction is declined offline by the terminal, since we use the output of the card in this case as the basis of EMV-GAA bootstrapping, as described in section 4.2.

An EMV transaction that is declined offline involves the following steps. Many of the procedures involved in a typical transaction, including Data Authentication[4], Processing Restrictions, Cardholder Verification, Terminal Risk Management and Terminal Action Analysis, are omitted from this description, since they are not used in in EMV-GAA.

1. When a card is inserted into a terminal, the terminal first selects the EMV credit/debit payment application. Note that an EMV smart card could contain multiple applications, but will always contain an EMV payment application.
2. The terminal initiates Application Processing to start a new transaction session and to exchange information with the card. Note that in this mandatory step the Application Transaction Counter (ATC), a sequence number maintained by the card, is incremented.
3. The terminal reads Application Data from the card. During this mandatory step, the terminal acquires cardholder information (including the Primary Account Number (PAN) and PAN Sequence Number (PAN-SN)) from the card.
4. To decline the transaction, the terminal requests the card to generate an Application Authentication Cryptogram (AAC) (using the first GENERATE AC command [11, page 67]). The AAC is one example of an EMV-specific construct known as an Application Cryptogram (AC); an AC is a MAC computed on specific data using a key known only to a card and the card issuing bank.
5. The card performs Card Risk Management to protect the Issuer from fraud or excessive credit risk. Details of the card risk management algorithms within the card are specific to the Issuer, and are outside the scope of the EMV specifications.
6. The card performs Card Action Analysis to decide whether the transaction should be approved offline, transmitted online to be authorised by the Issuer, or declined offline. The card action analysis process is performed when the terminal issues the GENERATE AC command. Given that the card is requested to generate an AAC, the result of card action analysis is always to decline the transaction offline ([11, page 91]).
7. The card generates an AAC and returns it to the terminal. Details of this computation are described in section 3.2.
8. The terminal performs Completion, which ends processing of the current transaction.

3.2   AC Generation

In this section we provide further details of AC generation; we start by describing the secret keys involved.

---

[4] This procedure enables the terminal to verify the authenticity of the card. EMV specifies three modes of Data Authentication, namely Static Data Authentication (SDA), Dynamic Data Authentication (DDA) and Combined Data Authentication (CDA) [10, page 51]

- The Issuer possesses an AC-specific 128-bit issuer master key, IMK_{AC}, used to generate the keys required to generate and verify ACs. When personalising a card, the Issuer uses the PAN and PAN-SN for this card as diversification information to derive a card-specific 128-bit Application Cryptogram master key MK_{AC} from IMK_{AC}. This key is installed in the card during personalisation.

When the card receives a GENERATE AC command, it first derives a 128-bit Application Cryptogram session key SK_{AC} from MK_{AC}, using the current ATC as diversification information. The card then uses SK_{AC} to produce the AC, a 64-bit cryptographic MAC computed as a function of a transaction-specific byte string formed by concatenating the following data items:

- values received from the terminal, including the Amount Authorized, the Transaction Date, and the Unpredictable Number (UN);
- values from within the card, including the ATC, which identify the current transaction.

The card returns the generated AC to the terminal, together with the Cryptogram Information Data (CID), the ATC, and other relevant data.

Depending on the result of the Card Action Analysis, the card will generate one of the following three types of AC:

- a Transaction Certificate (TC), if the transaction is approved offline;
- an Authorisation Request Cryptogram (ARQC), if an online authorisation is requested;
- an AAC, if the transaction is declined offline.

The CID contains two bits indicating the type of AC generated.

The Issuer needs to recompute the AC for verification purposes. This requires that the Account Identification Data of the card (i.e. the PAN and PAN-SN), the CID, the ATC, the UN provided by the terminal, and all other data objects used to compute the AC are transmitted to the Issuer. Using the received PAN and PAN-SN, the Issuer derives MK_{AC}, and from this obtains SK_{AC} using the received ATC. The Issuer then uses SK_{AC} to compute the particular type of AC indicated by the CID.

The EMV payment system makes use of a closed PKI to support Card Authentication. We use the term EMV security infrastructure to refer to the set of EMV cards possessed by cardholders, the Issuer servers, the associated secret keys, and the supporting PKI.

4   EMV-GAA

In this section we describe a possible means of using the EMV security infrastructure to support the generic version of GAA outlined in section 2.1, which we refer to as EMV-GAA. It is important to note that the scheme we propose here works with currently deployed EMV cards, using the existing card applications. That is, card re-issue (or card update) is not required.

4.1   Architecture

As shown in Figure 2, the following EMV-specific entities play a role in EMV-GAA.

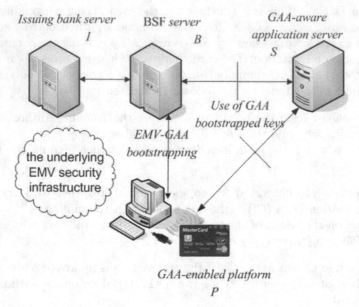

Issuing bank server   BSF server   GAA-aware
          I   B   application server
                                            S

Use of GAA
bootstrapped keys

EMV-GAA
bootstrapping

the underlying
EMV security
infrastructure

GAA-enabled platform
P

Fig. 2. EMV-GAA

- The Issuer I issues EMV-compliant cards, and possesses a master key IMK_{AC} which is used to derive the card-specific master keys MK_{AC}. I must be trusted for the purposes of supporting the EMV-GAA service by all parties using this service.
- The GAA-enabled user platform P incorporates a terminal T, an EMV-compliant card C (with an EMV debit/credit payment application), and the link between the two. To our knowledge, any EMV compliant card (SDA-, DDA-, or CDA-capable) could in principle be used to support EMV-GAA, since it does not make use of any of the Data Authentication procedures. T consists of a network access device and a card reader. A typical instantiation of T would be a Personal Computer (PC) with an attached or integrated card reader, where the card reader may or may not possess an integral keypad (as shown in Figure 2). Alternatively, T could be a mobile device (such as a Personal Digital Assistant) capable of communicating with C, e.g. using Near Field Communication. We assume that T is equipped with a supporting application that implements the EMV-GAA bootstrapping protocol described below. This supporting application could be provided by a third party trusted for the purposes of delivering the EMV-GAA service by all parties using this service.

– The BSF server B connects to I via a secure communications channel to provide the GAA services. B must be trusted by all the parties used the EMV-GAA service.

We assume that the participating entities are connected via an open network such as Internet. Note that no assumptions are made about the security properties of these communications links.

4.2 Procedures

In this section we specify the EMV-GAA bootstrapping and the EMV-GAA Use of bootstrapped keys procedures.

The EMV-GAA bootstrapping protocol involves the following sequence of steps.

1. The terminal T sends an initial request to B for the bootstrapping of a master session key MK.
2. Upon receiving the request, B generates a random number R_B, associates it with a short time interval, and caches it[5]. B then sends R_B to T.
3. T commences communications with an EMV payment card C (if necessary first prompting the cardholder to insert C into the card reader), and selects the EMV credit/debit payment application in C. T next initiates a transaction session (which automatically causes the ATC to be incremented) and reads the card information, including the PAN, PAN-SN, etc. T will always declined the transaction, and will, accordingly, request C to generate an AAC by issuing the (first) GENERATE AC command. The UN sent with the GENERATE AC command is set to R_B, as selected in step 2. The other data items sent with the GENERATE AC command can be set to fixed values (in particular the 'Amount Authorised' can be set to 0).
4. C generates the AAC and returns the generated AAC, the CID data, the ATC, and the other values necessary to verify it. We refer below to the data sent with the AAC as M.
5. T ends the current transaction session with C.
6. T generates a random number R_T, associates it with a short time interval, and caches it. T then uses the AAC as a secret key K to compute a response RES as

$$RES = f(K, R_T, R_B, \mathrm{Id}_B, M).$$

The function f can be implemented in many ways. One possibility, which complies with clause 5.1.1 of ISO/IEC 9798-4 [15], is to instantiate f using HMAC [16] based on a suitable cryptographic hash function, where the

---

[5] B will clear R_B from its cache when the bootstrapping process completes or when R_B expires.

various inputs to f are simply concatenated prior to applying HMAC. That is, RES could be computed as:

$$RES = \text{HMAC}_K(R_T \| R_B \| \text{Id}_B \| M)$$

where here and throughout $\|$ is used to denote concatenation. Note that the values $R_T \| R_B$ and Id_B play the role of the nonce and the entity identifier, respectively, in the ISO/IEC 9798-4 protocol.

7. T sends PAN, PAN-SN, R_T, R_B, M and RES to B.
8. B checks that R_B is equal to the value selected in step 2. If not, B rejects the bootstrapping request and terminates the protocol.
9. B forwards PAN, PAN-SN and M to I.
10. I uses the information received from B to recompute the AAC, and then sends PAN, PAN-SN and the AAC back to B.
11. B uses the received AAC as a secret key K to recompute RES, and compares it with the RES received in step 7. If they do not match, B rejects the bootstrapping request; otherwise, B generates the master session key MK as

$$MK = \text{KDF}(K, R_T, R_B).$$

B also sets the lifetime of MK (LT) in line with its operational policy, constructs the key identifier $B\text{-}TID$ as a combination of R_B, R_T and Id_B, and stores PAN, PAN-SN, R_T, R_B, $B\text{-}TID$, MK and LT.
12. B computes

$$XRES = f(K, R_B, R_T, \text{PAN}, \text{PAN-SN}, LT).$$

13. B sends R_B, R_T, $B\text{-}TID$, LT and $XRES$ to T.
14. T checks that R_T is the same as the value it selected in step 6. T then recomputes $XRES$, and compares it to the value received from B. If either of these checks fail, the bootstrapping fails.
15. T computes MK in the same way as B, and then stores PAN, PAN-SN, R_B, R_T, $B\text{-}TID$, MK and LT.

During bootstrapping, the card-generated AAC is used as a secret key K shared by T and B to establish the master key MK. As defined in the EMV specifications (see [11], Table 33 in Annex A), an AAC contains only 64 bits. Hence, since it is derived from K, MK has at most 64-bit security. For a stronger MK (with 128-bit security), the protocol above requires the following changes.

- T must execute two separate declined offline EMV transactions with C; that is T carries out steps 3, 4 to 5 twice to obtain two AACs, and then concatenates them to form a 128-bit key K. In this case, R_B in step 2 needs to have length double that of the UN, and is used in two parts to initiate two GENERATE AC commands belonging to two EMV transactions.
- Accordingly, I must generate the two AACs for B in step 10.

Note that the ATC is incremented for every new EMV transaction. Since the ATC is used as diversification information in the computation of AAC, the two AACs above will almost certainly be different from each other.

In the EMV-GAA Use of bootstrapped keys procedure, P and S follow the procedure defined in section 2.2 to establish a server- and application-specific session key SK. The session key SK is derived (by B and P) as follows:

$$SK = \text{KDF}(MK, R_T, R_B, \text{PAN}, \text{PAN-SN}, NAF\text{-}Id).$$

5   Informal Security Analysis

We now provide an informal security analysis of key aspects of the authentication and key establishment protocol used by the EMV-GAA bootstrapping procedure described in section 4.2. We consider a threat model in which an attacker $\mathcal{A}$ is able to observe and make arbitrary modifications to messages exchanged between B and P, including replaying and blocking messages as well as inserting completely spurious messages. This allows a trivial denial of service attack which cannot be prevented. Note that $\mathcal{A}$ is not allowed to compromise the implementations of B and P (including T and C); such attacks on system integrity cannot be prevent by the key establishment process, and are thus not addressed by the schemes we propose. We further assume that the communication channel between T and C is secure, since both devices are controlled by the user.

It is important to note that the security of EMV-GAA rests on the security of the underlying EMV security infrastructure; that is $\mathcal{A}$ is not allowed to compromise I or C.

The EMV-GAA bootstrapping protocol makes use of symmetric cryptographic techniques. The secret key K is an AAC, which can only be generated by the card C and the Issuer I (since it is a function of a key known only to them), and is securely transferred to T and B, respectively.

- *Entity authentication.* The protocol provides mutual authentication between B and T (strictly, C) using a cryptographic check function. B can verify the identity of T (strictly, C's PAN and PAN-SN); that is, the MAC generated by T on R_T, R_B and Id_B using K allows B to authenticate T (step 11). Similarly, T can authenticate B by verifying the MAC generated by B on R_B, R_T, PAN and PAN-SN (step 14). Messages exchanged in steps 2, 7 and 13 conform to the three-pass unilateral authentication protocol mechanism described in clause 5.2.2 of ISO/IEC 9798-4:1995 [15], in which the values R_B and R_T, generated by B and T respectively, serve as the nonces.
- *Confidentiality of the master session key MK.* MK is derived from K, which is shared by B and T. K is an AAC that can only be obtained by B and T. Hence, $\mathcal{A}$ cannot access MK under the assumed threat model.
- *Origin authentication.* This is achieved by B and T generating MACs on the exchanged messages using the key K. Integrity protection is also provided by the MACs. Hence, $\mathcal{A}$ cannot alter messages without being detected, since B and T will abort the bootstrapping procedure if any MAC verification fails (step 11 and 14).
- *Freshness.* R_B, generated by B, is included in the MAC sent to B in step 7; similarly R_T, generated by T, is included in the MAC sent to T in step 13.

Hence, $\mathcal{A}$ cannot replay messages to T or B, since B and T will abort the bootstrapping procedure if a received nonce is not fresh (step 8 and 14).

– *Key confirmation.* On receipt of the message in step 13, T can be sure that B has generated the MK during the current session. However, T does not confirm to B that it possesses MK. Note that $\mathcal{A}$ can block all the messages exchanged, and network errors might occur, and hence only T can be sure that it shares a fresh MK with B (until successful use of the key by T).

– *Key control.* The protocol is a key agreement process, that is B and T jointly control the inputs to the computation of MK (i.e. R_B and R_T).

6 Privacy and Security Issues

6.1 Threats

The EMV payment system is designed to be used in a closed (controlled) environment. A card terminal at a merchant typically provides a level of tamper-resistance, and is supplied by (or in conjunction with) the merchant's issuing bank. The terminal will be equipped with a pre-defined means of secure communication with the acquiring bank. By contrast, EMV-GAA operates in a more open environment. The terminal is user-controlled, and the communications with B and P are assumed to use the Internet or other public communications medium.

This change of environment gives rise to two main threats. Firstly, the scheme involves inserting the EMV card into a new type of terminal, which is itself a threat. A terminal can cause a card to perform a transaction, the precise nature of which is not apparent to the cardholder. Hence, a security threat arises whenever a card is inserted into any unauthorised terminal. Secondly, the PAN could be divulged to unauthorised entities and/or misused, including by a compromised terminal, by compromised software on a PC host, or by interception during transmission. The PAN can be regarded as Personally Identifiable Information (PII), and hence disclosure of the PAN is a privacy threat; it is also information which could be misused to conduct unauthorised transactions, and hence disclosure is also a security threat. We next consider the nature of these threats together with possible mitigations in greater detail.

Before using this service, it is likely that the cardholder will need to agree terms of use with the card issuer (and/or with the bootstrap server provider). This could include equipping the cardholder with a special card reader designed specifically for use with the EMV-GAA service—indeed, this is precisely what happens when cards are used with the CAP service, discussed below (and hence low-cost special-purpose card readers are clearly viable). This special reader could even be delivered as additional functionality in an enhanced CAP reader, further reducing deployment costs. The cardholder should in any case be advised never to insert his or her card into an unauthorised terminal. Part of the functionality of EMV-GAA could be built into the card reader (as is the case for CAP), thereby mitigating the threat of the card being forced to conduct unauthorised transactions. Finally we observe that the scheme we propose does not require use of the Personal Identification Number (PIN) of the cardholder[6], further reducing the risk of an attacker being able to use a card to create illicit PIN-authorised transactions.

The use of a special purpose card reader also mitigates the risk of PAN disclosure at the cardholder site. PAN disclosure as a result of intercepted communications can be prevented by using the modified version of the scheme outlined below; the magnitude of the threat could also be reduced through the use of SSL on the connection between B and P, a standard precaution for security-related web connections.

6.2   A Modified Scheme

We now describe a minor modification to the bootstrapping procedure, designed to remove the need to transmit the PAN. The modified scheme requires the cardholder to register the EMV card C with the BSF server prior to use. As a result of the registration procedure, the BSF stores an association between a card-specific identifier Id_C and the pair (PAN, PAN-SN) for C. The identifier Id_C must be computed as a fixed function of data stored on the card, e.g. as $h(\text{SSAD})$, where h is a cryptographic hash function and SSAD is the Signed Static Authentication Data, stored on the card and used in SDA.

The bootstrapping procedure is largely as described in section 4.2, except as follows.

- In step 3, T reads the SSAD from C, and computes Id_C for later use.
- In step 7, T sends Id_C to B instead of PAN and PAN-SN, and on receipt B uses Id_C to look up the values of PAN and PAN-SN.

7   Related Work

The Chip Authentication Program (CAP)[7] uses a EMV payment card in conjunction with a dedicated handheld device (the CAP reader) to produce one-time passwords (OTPs) for authenticating users and transactions in online banking. A dummy transaction with the card is started by requesting it to generate an ARQC, and after receipt of the ARQC the transaction is aborted. A decimal PIN is then computed as a function of the ARQC. Although the complete protocol details are not public, some information is in the public domain [8].

Urien [21] proposed the use of EMV payment cards to support the pre-shared key TLS protocol (TLS-PSK) [13]. The EMV TLS-PSK protocol provides mutual authentication, and could be used for on-line banking services. In EMV TLS-PSK, the pre-shared key identity is made of two parts: an identifier (EMV-ID) derived from parameters embedded in the card, and a set of cryptograms (i.e.

---

[6] The Cardholder Verification procedure in which the cardholder enters his or her PIN into the terminal is not used in EMV-GAA.

[7] CAP is a MasterCard brand; the corresponding Visa system is called Dynamic Passcode Authentication (DPA).

ARQCs). The pre-shared key is a fixed value, deduced from the EMV card content (EMV-PSK) and additional information. The EMV-PSK is set to $h(SSAD)$, where h is a cryptographic hash function. The EMV-ID is set to $h(h(SSAD))$.

8 Applications

GAA offers a simple and uniform interface to generic security services which operate independently of the underlying security infrastructure. Application developers are thus able to use the services provided by this interface without having to understand the detailed operation of the underlying infrastructure, substantially simplifying the development task and reducing the risk of error. Moreover, this layered approach also enables the same application to operate over a variety of different underlying infrastructures in a transparent way.

In ongoing work we are examining ways in which a range of variants of the GAA service can be used to support an OTP system [5,7] for Internet applications. Such systems could, of course, be built using the EMV-GAA service. OTP systems supported by a range of GAA services could be deployed to enable the provision of ubiquitous OTP services for a large class of users. We are also developing ways of using GAA to build more general identity management solutions, including single sign-on schemes. Work along these lines has already been standardised for 3GPP GAA, notably supporting interworking with CardSpace, OpenID and Liberty [1,3]. We are also developing a way of enhancing the 'Pwd-Hash' mechanism [20] which builds on GAA service to give a user-centric single sign-on system.

The TLS-PSK protocol using the 3GPP GAA service (as supported by the mobile telephony authentication infrastructures) has been specified by 3GPP [2].

9 Conclusions

GAA is a framework that enables pre-existing security infrastructures to be used to provide general purpose security services, such as key establishment. We have shown how GAA services can be built on the EMV security infrastructure, complementing the previously proposed GAA schemes built on the mobile telephony authentication infrastructures and Trusted Computing. Use of EMV-GAA could constitute a potentially serious security and privacy threat (including the possibility of revealing the PAN to unintended parties). To mitigate the risk, we have proposed a modified scheme to avoid the need to routinely transmit the PAN across any network links.

EMV-GAA provides a way of exploiting the now very widespread EMV infrastructure for the provision of fundamentally important general-purpose security services. Of course, application-specific security protocols building on the infrastructure can be devised independently of any generic service and, indeed, there is a large and growing literature on such schemes. However, the definition of a standard GAA-based security service enables the EMV infrastructure to be exploited in a simple and uniform way, and it also provides an opportunity for EMV-aware third parties to provide novel security services.

References

1. 3G AMERICAS: Identity Management Overview of Standards & Technologies for Mobile and Fixed Internet (2009)
2. 3rd Generation Partnership Project (3GPP): Generic Authentication Architecture (GAA); Access to network application functions using Hypertext Transfer Protocol over Transport Layer Security (HTTPS). Technical Specification TS 33.222, Version 9.1.0 (2009)
3. 3rd Generation Partnership Project (3GPP): Identity management and 3GPP security interworking; Identity management and Generic Authentication Architecture (GAA) interworking. Technical Report TS 33.924, Version 9.1.0 (2009)
4. 3rd Generation Partnership Project (3GPP): Technical Specification Group Services and Systems Aspects, Generic Authentication Architecture (GAA), Generic Bootstrapping Architecture. Technical Specification TS 33.220, Version 9.2.0 (2009)
5. Chen, C., Laitinen, P., Asokan, N., Mitchell, C.: Leveraging GAA for one-time password authentication from an untrusted computer (submitted)
6. Chen, C., Mitchell, C.J., Tang, S.: Building General Purpose Security Services on Trusted Computing. In: Chen, L., Yung, M., Zhu, L. (eds.) INTRUST 2011. LNCS, vol. 7222, pp. 16–31. Springer, Heidelberg (2012)
7. Chen, C., Mitchell, C., Tang, S.: Ubiquitous One-Time Password Service Using the Generic Authentication Architecture. Mobile Networks and Applications (to appear), http://rd.springer.com/article/10.1007/s11036-011-0329-z
8. Drimer, S., Murdoch, S.J., Anderson, R.: Optimised to Fail: Card Readers for Online Banking. In: Dingledine, R., Golle, P. (eds.) FC 2009. LNCS, vol. 5628, pp. 184–200. Springer, Heidelberg (2009)
9. EMV: EMV Integrated Circuit Card Specifications for Payment Systems Version 4.2—Book 1: Application Independent ICC to Terminal Interface Requirements (June 2008)
10. EMV: EMV Integrated Circuit Card Specifications for Payment Systems Version 4.2—Book 2: Security and Key Management (June 2008)
11. EMV: EMV Integrated Circuit Card Specifications for Payment Systems Version 4.2—Book 3: Application Specification (June 2008)
12. EMV: EMV Integrated Circuit Card Specifications for Payment Systems Version 4.2—Book 4: Cardholder, Attendant, and Acquirer Interface Requirements (June 2008)
13. Eronen, P., Tschofenig, H.: Pre-shared key ciphersuites for transport layer security (TLS). Internet Engineering Task Force, RFC 4279 (Informational) (December 2005)
14. Holtmanns, S., Niemi, V., Ginzboorg, P., Laitinen, P., Asokan, N.: Cellular Authentication for Mobile and Internet Services. John Wiley and Sons (2008)
15. International Organization for Standardization, Genève, Switzerland: ISO/IEC 9798-4:1999, Information technology—Security techniques—Entity authentication—Part 4: Mechanisms using a cryptographic check function (1999)
16. Krawczyk, H., Bellare, M., Canetti, R.: HMAC: Keyed-hashing for message authentication. Internet Engineering Task Force, RFC 2104 (Informational) (February 1997)
17. Pashalidis, A., Mitchell, C.J.: Single Sign-On Using Trusted Platforms. In: Boyd, C., Mao, W. (eds.) ISC 2003. LNCS, vol. 2851, pp. 54–68. Springer, Heidelberg (2003)

18. Pashalidis, A., Mitchell, C.J.: Using GSM/UMTS for single-sign on. In: Proceedings of SympoTIC 2003, Joint IST Workshop on Mobile Future and Symposium on Trends in Communications, pp. 146–152. IEEE Press (2003)
19. Pashalidis, A., Mitchell, C.J.: Using EMV Cards for Single Sign-On. In: Katsikas, S.K., Gritzalis, S., López, J. (eds.) EuroPKI 2004. LNCS, vol. 3093, pp. 205–217. Springer, Heidelberg (2004)
20. Ross, B., Jackson, C., Miyake, N., Boneh, D., Mitchell, J.C.: Stronger password authentication using browser extensions. In: Proceedings of the 14th USENIX Security Symposium, pp. 17–32. USENIX Association (2005)
21. Urienand, P.: Introducing TLS-PSK authentication for EMV devices. In: Proceedings of CTS 2010, International Symposium on Collaborative Technologies and Systems, pp. 371–377. IEEE Press (2010)

Anonymous Transferable Conditional E-cash

Jiangxiao Zhang[1,2], Zhoujun Li[1,2], and Hua Guo[1]

[1] State Key Laboratory of Software Development Environment,
Beihang University, Beijing 100083, China
[2] Beijing Key Laboratory of Network Technology,
Beihang University, Beijing, China
orange_0092008@163.com, zhoujun.li@263.net, hguo@buaa.edu.cn

Abstract. We present the first anonymous transferable conditional e-cash system based on two recent cryptographic primitives, i.e., the Groth-Sahai(GS) proofs system and the commuting signatures, thus the unlinkability and anonymity of the user is obtained. We solve an open problem by dividing the deposit into two parts, so that the user is unlinkable in the transferrable protocol and the deposit protocol. Comparing the existing conditional e-cash, the size of the computation and communication of our scheme is constant.

Keywords: conditional e-cash, transferability, anonymity, Groth-Sahai proofs, commuting signatures.

1 Introduction

Conditional e-cash is introduced firstly by L. Shi [11], which allows a participant to spend cash bank-issued electronic coin based on the outcome in the future. If the outcome is not favorable to the payer, he loses and the payee can cash the electronic coin from the bank; otherwise, the payer cashes back e-cash. There are many applications of conditional e-cash. For example, outsourcing computations make sure that the worker has completed the computation and can retrieve the payment simultaneously. For another example, the prediction markets obtain the outcome based the prediction in the future and the betting systems, where many people can bet in an anonymous betting systems and obtain the electronic coin depending on the result in the future.

Conditional transferable e-cash consists of the payers (the payees) $\mathcal{U}_1, \mathcal{U}_2, \cdots, \mathcal{U}_n$, the bank $\mathcal{B}$, the judge $\mathcal{J}$ and the publisher $\mathcal{P}$. Firstly, the publisher publics two commitments about two event outcomes. The user $\mathcal{U}_1$ registers one of the two outcomes at the publisher. Secondly, he withdraws a coin co from the bank $\mathcal{B}$, and then spends the coin to the user $\mathcal{U}_2$. The payee $\mathcal{U}_2$ can spend the coin to the third user $\mathcal{U}_3$, or deposit the coin to the bank $\mathcal{B}$. When the publisher publishes the outcome, only one user can win the coin, and then the user cashes from the bank $\mathcal{B}$. The bank $\mathcal{B}$ checks the coin, and decides to exchange the coin for credit to the account of the user or announce the judge to recover the identity of the double spenders. Meanwhile, traditional transferable e-cash also

A.D. Keromytis and R. Di Pietro (Eds.): SecureComm 2012, LNICST 106, pp. 45–60, 2013.

allows the user to directly spend the e-cash to other ones without depositing the e-cash into the bank.

There are some differences between transferable conditional e-cash system and traditional transferable e-cash system [7,6,13,9,5,12]. Firstly, in the transferable conditional e-cash, the user anonymously spend the conditional e-cash, while in traditional e-cash, the merchant and the user must supply the identity in order to receive money and serves respectively. Secondly, in the transferable conditional e-cash, the payee can not spend the e-cash until the outcome of the condition is published and only if the outcome is favorable to the payee, while the user can spend an e-cash without any conditional in the traditional transferable e-cash. And last, the payer can cash the e-cash in case of an unfavorable to the payee outcome of the condition, but these can not also be done in the transferable e-cash. Thus, new tools need to be developed to construct the transferable conditional e-cash.

1.1   Related Results

E-cash is the digital equivalent of regular money. It has many properties, such as divisibility, transferability, conditionality, et. al. Transferability is one of the most important properties among these basic properties. Okamoto and Ohta [16,12] proposed two transferred e-cash systems, however their systems can only provide weak anonymity. Chaum and Pedersen [7] analyzed the size of the e-cash in the transferred e-cash system, and they claimed that it is impossible to transfer a coin without increasing its size. Next, Canard et $al.$ [13] proposed an anonymous transferable e-cash system, and analyzed the anonymity [6] in transferred e-cash. To solve the problem about the size of the e-cash system, Fuchsbauer et $al.$ [9] constructed the first practical transferred constant-size fair e-cash in the standard model. However, each user has to keep in memory the data associated to all past transactions to prove her innocence in case of a fraud. Moreover, the anonymity of all subsequent owners of a double-spent coin must be revoked.

The conditional e-cash is another application in e-cash. L. Shi [11] firstly introduced the definition of the conditional e-payments, where the payer can anonymously spend the e-cash to the payee or transfer the e-cash to another. However, the conditional e-payments is on-line and depends on the expensive cut-and-choose techniques.

M. Blanton [3] improved the efficiency of the conditional e-payments and formalized it by uisng zero-knowledge proof, CL signature and verifiable encryption. However the payer can recognize a coin he has already observed previously and also decide whether he has already owned the coin he is receiving. Moreover the deposit is not anonymous.

O. Blazy et $al.$ [4] proposed an anonymously transferable e-cash, which is a traditional transferable e-cash. It achieves the optimal anonymity in the transferable e-cash, namely observe-then-receive full anonymity ($OtR - Fa$), spend-then-observe full anonymity ($StO - FA$) and spend-then-receive full anonymity ($StR - FA$).

J. Groth and A. Sahai [10] constructed the first efficient non-interactive proof systems in the standard model. It considers a large class of statements over bilinear groups. The witness indistinguishable guarantees that any adversary cannot distinguish the user uses which witness. Their randomizability allows us to improve the NIZK proofs.

G. Fuchsbauer [8] presented a system of commuting signatures and verifiable encryption. It allows one to encrypt a message and corresponding signature while preserving its public verifiability. Given a commitment, a signer can create a verifiably encrypted signature on the committed message.

1.2 Our Construction

We propose an anonymous transferable conditional e-cash based on Groth-Sahai proofs [10] and the commuting signatures [8]. In our paper, we firstly improve the commitments and the corresponding proofs by the commuting signatures, so the transferrable spending is unlinkable and the user is anonymous. Meanwhile, we divide the deposit protocol into two parts to obtain the anonymity of the user in the deposit protocol. Secondly, we introduce a publisher, who can commit two secret value for two outcomes, so the conditional e-cash is obtained. Finally, we compare the efficiency of our construction to that of [11] and [3]. our contribution is listed as follows:

- We solve an open problem, which the identity of payee is unlinkable in the conditional transfer and deposit protocol. Meanwhile, the payers cannot be linked to payees or to ongoing or past transactions.
- We present the first anonymous transferable condition e-cash.
- We compare the efficiency of our construction to that of [11] and [3], and show that the computation and communication is constant in our scheme.

1.3 Organization of the Paper

The rest of this paper is organized as follows. In Section 2, we describe the preliminaries on the various cryptographic tools and assumptions. Security model of the conditional e-cash is presented in Section 3. In Section 4, we give the general description. The main protocol is presented in Section 5. The security analysis is given in Section 6. In Section 7, we conclude the paper.

2 Preliminaries

In this section, we introduce the background knowledge that will be used for our scheme.

2.1 Bilinear Map

A pairing is a bilinear mapping from two group elements to a group element. Let $\hat{e}$ be a bilinear map such that $\hat{e} : G_1 \times G_2 \to G_3$ and the following holds.

- G_1, G_2 and G_3 are cyclic multiplicative groups of prime order p.
- Each element of G_1, G_2 has unique binary representation.
- The elements g, h generate G_1 and G_2 respectively.
- $\hat{e} : G_1 \times G_2$ is a non-degenerate bilinear map so $\hat{e}(g, h)$ generates G_3 and for all $a, b \in \mathbb{Z}_n$ we have $\hat{e}(ag, bh) = \hat{e}(g, h)^{ab}$.
- We can efficiently compute group operations, compute the bilinear map and decide membership.

2.2   Mathematical Assumptions

The security of our construction is based on the following existing mathematical assumptions, namely, the Symmetric External Diffie-Hellman(SXDH) [10] and the asymmetric double hidden strong Diffie-Hellman assumption(q-ADH-SDH) [1].

Definition 1. *Symmetric External Diffie-Hellman. Let G_1, G_2 be cyclic groups of prime order, g_1 and g_2 generate G_1 and G_2 respectively, and let $\hat{e} : G_1 \times G_2 \to G_3$ be a bilinear map. The Symmetric External Diffie-Hellman (SXDH) Assumption states that the DDH problem is hard in both G_1 and G_2 of a bilinear group pair (G_1, G_2), namely, we give $g_1, g_1^a, g_1^b \in G_1$ and $g_2, g_2^a, g_2^b \in G_2$, for random a, b, it is hard to distinguish g_1^{ab} and g_2^{ab} from G_1 and G_2 respectively. It implies that there is no efficiently computable isomorphism from G_2 to G_1 or vice versa.*

Definition 2. *q-ADH-SDH. Let $g, f, k \in G_1, h \in g_2$ and $x, c_i, v_i \in Z_n$ be random. Given $(g, f, k, g^x; h, y = h^x)$ and $(a_i = (k \cdot g^{v_i})^{\frac{1}{x+c_i}}, b_i = f^{c_i}, d_i = h^{c_i}, u_i = g_i^v, w_i = h^{v_i})$*

for $1 \leq i \leq q - 1$, it is hard to output a new tuple $(a = (k \cdot g^v)^{\frac{1}{x+c}}, b = f^c, d = h^c, u = g^v, w = h^v)$ with $(c, v) \neq (c_i, v_i)$ for all i. i.e. one that satisfies $\hat{e}(a, y \cdot d) = \hat{e}(k \cdot u, h), \hat{e}(b, h) = \hat{e}(f, d)$ and $\hat{e}(u, h) = \hat{e}(g, w)$.

2.3   Useful Tools

Groth-Sahai Proof. Groth and Sahai [10] constructed an NIZK proof system that lets us prove statements in the context of groups with bilinear maps in the standard model. In order to proof the statement, the prover firstly commits to the group elements or $\mathbb{Z}_p$ elements. Then the prover does the proof of the group elements or $\mathbb{Z}_p$ elements and sends the commitments, the proofs and corresponding parameters to the verifier. The last the verifier verifies the correct of the proof. In this paper, We use SXDH-based GS commitments and proofs to commit to elements and prove relations satisfied by the associated plaintexts. The witness indistinguishability guarantees the anonymity of the payers and the payees during the withdraw, conditional transfer and deposit.

Randomization. Belenkiy et al. [2] proposed the randomizable proofs of commitments and the NIZK proofs. For example, let $u_{1,1} = g_1, u_{1,2} = g_1^\mu, u_{2,1} =$

$g_1^v, u_{2,2} = (g_1^\mu)^v, r_1, r_2 \in \mathbb{Z}_p$, we obtain a commitment for $X \in G_1$, namely $c(X) = ((u_{1,1})_1^r \cdot (u_{2,1})_2^r, X \cdot (u_{1,2})_1^r \cdot (u_{2,2})_2^r) = (c_1, c_2)$. In order to randomize the commitment, we choose two random values $r_1', r_2' \in \mathbb{Z}_p$ and compute the randomization as $c(X)' = (c_1 \cdot (u_{1,1})^{r_1'} \cdot (u_{2,1})^{r_2'}, c_2 \cdot (u_{1,2})^{r_1'} \cdot (u_{2,2})^{r_2'})$. Meanwhile we adapt its proof (π, θ) for commitments $(c_i)_i$ to another (π, θ) for $(c_i')_i$. The property guarantees the anonymity of the payers and the payees. The bank can not link any withdrawal protocol, spending protocol and deposit protocol. Meanwhile, the randomizable proof is publicly verifiable.

Commuting Signatures. Commuting signatures and verifiable encryption [8] combines a signature scheme with GS proofs. This allows one to commit a commitment to a message, a verification or a corresponding signature and proves that the committed values are correct, as he does these to that message. We only briefly review two results of [8] relevant to our paper in the following.

SigCom allows a signer who is given a commitment c to a message, to make a commitment to c_σ to a signature on that message and a proof that c_σ contains a valid signature on the value committed in c.

AdC_κ allows anyone to commit to a key and adapt a proof, and outputs a commitment and a proof asserting that a commitment contains a valid signature on a committed message.

Following the definition of [8], we instantiate the specific signature with the Structure-Preserving signature (SP-signature) [1,15].

3   The Model

In this section, we firstly describe the algorithms for anonymous transferable conditional e-cash. The main differences between our algorithms and [4] is that we introduce a publisher and a new algorithm Publish() to give the bank the two commitments of the outcomes. We also extend the model given in [4] to include the publisher.

3.1   Algorithms

The conditional transferable e-cash system consists of withdraw protocol, spending(transferring) protocol, deposit protocol and identify procedure. We give the procedures as follows, where λ is a security parameter.

- ParamSetup(1^λ). It is a probabilistic algorithm that outputs the public parameters *params*.
- BKeyGen(),JKeyGen(),UKeyGen(),PKeyGen(). It is a probabilistic algorithm executed respectively by $\mathcal{B}, \mathcal{J}$ or $\mathcal{U}$, that output a key pairs $(pk_\mathcal{B}, sk_\mathcal{B})$, $(pk_\mathcal{J}, sk_\mathcal{J})$, $(pk_\mathcal{U}, sk_\mathcal{U})$ and $(pk_\mathcal{P}, sk_\mathcal{P})$.
- Withdraw($\mathcal{U}(sk_\mathcal{U}, pk_\mathcal{U}, pk_\mathcal{B}, pk_\mathcal{J}, C_\mathcal{B}, C_\mathcal{J}), \mathcal{B}(sk_\mathcal{B}, pk_\mathcal{B}, C_{pr}, C_{pe}, pk_\mathcal{U}))$. It is an interactive protocol where $\mathcal{U}$ withdraws one conditional transferable coin co from $\mathcal{B}$. At the end, $\mathcal{U}$ outputs a coin or $\perp$, and $\mathcal{B}$ checks the public key of the user, deducts a coin from the user and obtains a view $\mathcal{V}$ or $\perp$.

- Publish($\mathcal{B}(sk_\mathcal{B}, pk_\mathcal{B}, C_\mathcal{B}, C_\mathcal{J}).\mathcal{P}(C_{pr}, E_{pr}, C_{pe}, E_{pe})$. It is an interactive protocol between the $\mathcal{B}$ and $\mathcal{P}$. At the end, $\mathcal{B}$ obtains two commitments representing the two outcomes.
- Spend($\mathcal{U}_1(co, sk_{\mathcal{U}_1}, pk_\mathcal{B}, pk_\mathcal{J}, C_\mathcal{B}, C_\mathcal{J}), \mathcal{U}_2(sk_{\mathcal{U}_2}, pk_\mathcal{B}, pk_\mathcal{J}))$. It is an interactive protocol in which $\mathcal{U}_1$ spends/transfers the coin co to $\mathcal{U}_2$. At the end, $\mathcal{U}_2$ outputs a coin co' or $\bot$, and $\mathcal{U}_1$ outputs ok or $\bot$.
- Deposit($\mathcal{U}(co, sk_\mathcal{U}, pk_\mathcal{B}, pk_\mathcal{J}), \mathcal{B}(pk_\mathcal{B}, sk_\mathcal{B}, pk_\mathcal{U}))$. It is an interactive protocol where $\mathcal{U}$ deposits a coin co to the bank. The bank outputs a commitment and corresponding proof or $\bot$. $\mathcal{U}$ deposits corresponding coin to the bank using new commitment and corresponding proof.
- Identify($pk_\mathcal{U}, co, co', sk_\mathcal{J}$). It is a deterministic algorithm executed by the judge which outputs a public key $pk_\mathcal{U}$ of double spender.

3.2 Security Properties

In this section, we give the security definitions for the transferable conditional e-cash system. Every security property is given by a game between the adversary $\mathcal{A}$ and the challenger $\mathcal{C}$. Firstly, we describe the ability of the adversary as arbitrary and adaptive queries to oracles. The oracles are defined as follows.

- $\mathcal{O}_{Setup()}$. This oracle allows the adversary $\mathcal{A}$ to add a new user into the system, or to corrupt a honest user. When the adversary interacts with the oracle, $\mathcal{A}$ can obtain the keys of the user or the bank. If a honest user is corrupted, the secret key is $\bot$.
- $\mathcal{O}_{With()}$. This oracle can act the bank or the user in the withdrawal protocol. The adversary $\mathcal{A}$ can withdraw a conditional e-cash from the oracle acting the bank. He can also obtain some e-cash from the oracle acting the user.
- $\mathcal{O}_{Spend()}$. This oracle can allows the adversary $\mathcal{A}$ to act a payee to receive a conditional e-cash, or act a payer to spend a conditional e-cash.
- $\mathcal{O}_{Depo()}$. This oracle can act the bank or the user in the deposit protocol. The adversary $\mathcal{A}$ can obtain a conditional e-cash from the oracle acting the user, or spend some e-cash to the oracle acting the bank.
- $\mathcal{O}_{Idt()}$. This oracle can act the judge in the identity procedures. The adversary $\mathcal{A}$ can submit two e-cash to the oracle and obtain the identity of the user spending the two e-cash.
- $\mathcal{O}_{Publ()}$. This oracle can act the publisher to extract the secret value. Then the adversary $\mathcal{A}$ can obtain the secret by interacting with the oracle.

In our paper, we think the publisher, the bank and the judger are trust organizes. The judge can not remove the identity of an honest user except that the bank gives the two spending from double spenders. The publisher only publics and announces the events correctly, and can also not extract a outcome before publishing the outcome. Meanwhile, This is the request of the fair e-cash [14]. We require all the length of the conditional e-cash is the same.In the following, we will define the security properties formally.

Anonymity. We also used the definition about anonymity in [4], but our scheme only achieve the $OtR - FA(FA)$ and $StO - FA(PA_1)$. It guarantees that no coalition of users, publisher and judger can able to distinguish if the the spending protocol is executed by users or by a simulator.

Firstly, we give the security description of FA.

- (Initialization Phase.) $\mathcal{A}$ runs the $ParamSetup(1^\lambda)$ and obtains the public parameters $params$ and the key pairs $(pk_\mathcal{B}, sk_\mathcal{B})$, $(pk_\mathcal{J}, sk_\mathcal{J})$ and $(pk_\mathcal{P}, sk_\mathcal{P})$. Then $\mathcal{A}$ gives $pk_\mathcal{B}$ to $\mathcal{C}$ and keeps the $sk_\mathcal{B}$ to itself.
- (Probing Phase.) $\mathcal{A}$ can perform a polynomially bounded number of queries to the oracles in an adaptive manner. $\mathcal{A}$ can add and corrupt any user by the $\mathcal{O}_{Setup()}$. For each $\mathcal{O}_{With}()$ and $\mathcal{O}_{Spend}()$, $\mathcal{A}$ can act as bank or user in the withdrawal protocol or spending protocol. The adversary $\mathcal{A}$ can obtain the identity of the user from the $\mathcal{O}_{Idt()}$, or extract the secret value from the oracle $\mathcal{O}_{Publ()}$.
- (Challenge Phase.) $\mathcal{C}$ chooses two public keys $pk_{\mathcal{U}_0}$ and $pk_{\mathcal{U}_1}$, and presents them to $\mathcal{A}$. The two public keys must be the conditional e-cash received by the adversary $\mathcal{A}$. Then $\mathcal{A}$ acting the bank or the user interacts with the $\mathcal{C}$. $\mathcal{A}$ can specify which public $\mathcal{C}$ uses, with the restriction that he can not ask $\mathcal{C}$ to over-spend any coin, and can also not require the oracle $\mathcal{O}_{Idt()}$ and $\mathcal{O}_{Publ()}$. And last, $\mathcal{A}$ obtains a coin $co_\mathcal{M}$.
- (End Game Phase.) $\mathcal{A}$ decides which public key $\mathcal{C}$ uses.

For the security description of PA_1. The every phase is similar to the FA except that the two public keys is any keys in the Challenge Phase.

For all non-uniform polynomial time $\mathcal{A}$, the advantage breaking the anonymity is defined by

$$Adv_{TCE,\mathcal{A}}^{anon} = Pr[Exp_{TCE,\mathcal{A}}^{anon-1}(\lambda) = 1] - Pr[Exp_{TCE,\mathcal{A}}^{anon-0}(\lambda) = 1]$$

where TCE be a anonymous transferable conditional e-cash system. The $Exp_{TCE,\mathcal{A}}^{anon}(\lambda)$ is the same as that in [4] except that we give the $\mathcal{A}$ an ability to access the private key sk_{pe} and sk_{pr}.

If the $Adv_{TCE,\mathcal{A}}^{anon}$ is negligible for any polynomial-time adversary $\mathcal{A}$, we will say that our scheme is anonymous.

Unforgeability. No coalition of users and merchants can deposit more coins than they have withdrawn from the bank.

- (Initialization Phase.) $\mathcal{C}$ runs the $ParamSetup(1^\lambda)$ and obtains the public parameters $params$ and the key pairs $(pk_\mathcal{B}, sk_\mathcal{B})$, $(pk_\mathcal{J}, sk_\mathcal{J})$ and $(pk_\mathcal{P}, sk_\mathcal{P})$. Then $\mathcal{C}$ gives $pk_\mathcal{B}$ to $\mathcal{A}$ and keeps the $sk_\mathcal{B}$ to itself.
- (Probing Phase.) $\mathcal{A}$ can perform a polynomially bounded number of queries to the oracles in an adaptive manner. $\mathcal{A}$ can add and corrupt any user by the $\mathcal{O}_{Setup()}$. We define the e-cash received by the $\mathcal{A}$ is co_a and initialize it with zero. For each $\mathcal{O}_{With}()$, $\mathcal{A}$ acting as user and withdraw a conditional e-cash co_0 in the withdrawal protocol. In the transferring protocol, the $\mathcal{A}$ acting as payer transfers an e-cash co_1 to the payee, or acting as payee receives an e-cash co_2. The $\mathcal{A}$ deposit an e-cash co_de to the $\mathcal{C}$ acting as the bank in the deposit protocol. And last, the counter of the $\mathcal{A}$ is $co_a = co_0 + co_2$.

– (End Game Phase.) $\mathcal{A}$ wins the game if it can deposit $co_a + 1$ to $\mathcal{C}$, namely $co_{de} > co_a$.

For all non-uniform polynomial time $\mathcal{A}$, the advantage breaking the unforgeability is defined by

$$Adv_{TCE,\mathcal{A}}^{unfor} = Pr[Exp_{TCE,\mathcal{A}}^{unfor}(\lambda) = 1]$$

where TCE be a anonymous transferable conditional e-cash system. The $Exp_{TCE,\mathcal{A}}^{unfor}(\lambda)$ is the same as that in [4] except that we give the $\mathcal{A}$ an ability to access the private key sk_{pe} and sk_{pr}.

If the $Adv_{TCE,\mathcal{A}}^{unfor}$ is negligible for any polynomial-time adversary $\mathcal{A}$, we will say that our scheme is unforgeable.

Double-Spending. It guarantees that coalition of users and merchants can not be able to double-spend a coin with the same serial number.

This is similar to the unforgeability in the Initialization Phase.

– (Probing Phase.) $\mathcal{A}$ can perform a polynomially bounded number of queries to the oracles in an adaptive manner. $\mathcal{A}$ can add and corrupt any user by the $\mathcal{O}_{Setup()}$. In order to identify the identity of an honest user, the adversary $\mathcal{A}$ extracts the message committed in commitments and corresponding proof, and then forges a new coin. Meanwhile, the adversary can deposit the new coin to the bank, and the output of the algorithm Identify() can not output the public key. If the adversary can give a new coin as above, he must break the unforgeability of the commuting signature and the soundness and witness indistinguishability of GS proofs.
– (End Game Phase.) $\mathcal{A}$ wins the game if it can deposit a coin, the output of the Deposit() is $\bot$ and the Identify() cannot output the public key.

For all non-uniform polynomial time $\mathcal{A}$, the advantage breaking the double-spending is defined by

$$Adv_{TCE,\mathcal{A}}^{unfor} = Pr[Exp_{TCE,\mathcal{A}}^{ide}(\lambda) = 1]$$

where TCE be a anonymous transferable conditional e-cash system. The $Exp_{TCE,\mathcal{A}}^{ide}(\lambda)$ is the same as that in [4] except that we give the $\mathcal{A}$ an ability to access the private key sk_{pe} and sk_{pr}.

If the $Adv_{TCE,\mathcal{A}}^{ide}$ is negligible for any polynomial-time adversary $\mathcal{A}$, we will say that our scheme can identify the double-spending.

Exculpability. No coalition of the banks and users can accuse an honest users of have double-spending a coin.

This is shown similarly to the FA in the Initialization Phase and the Probing Phase.

– (Probing Phase.) $\mathcal{A}$ can perform a polynomially bounded number of queries to the oracles in an adaptive manner. $\mathcal{A}$ can add and corrupt any user by the $\mathcal{O}_{Setup()}$. We know the commute of the user and the bank is anonymous. If the adversary $\mathcal{A}$ wants to forge another coin and frames an honest user, he must break unforgeability of the commuting signature.

– (End Game Phase.) $\mathcal{A}$ wins the game if it can forge a corresponding e-cash and prove the spending is correct.

For all non-uniform polynomial time $\mathcal{A}$, the advantage breaking the exculpability is defined by

$$Adv_{TCE,\mathcal{A}}^{unfor} = Pr[Exp_{TCE,\mathcal{A}}^{excu}(\lambda) = 1]$$

where TCE be a anonymous transferable conditional e-cash system. The $Exp_{TCE,\mathcal{A}}^{excu}(\lambda)$ is the same as that in [4] except that we give the $\mathcal{A}$ an ability to access the private key sk_{pe} and sk_{pr}.

If the $Adv_{TCE,\mathcal{A}}^{excu}$ is negligible for any polynomial-time adversary $\mathcal{A}$, we will say that our scheme can frame an honest user making a double-spending.

Conditional Transfer. The payer can cash back his coin when an unfavorable outcome happens. The payee can anonymously transfer the coin from the payer to the payee until the time that the outcome is published. After publishing the outcome, the publisher can extract the secret value, and send it to the corresponding user and the bank. Then the user deposit the conditional e-cash to the bank. Thus, the coin can be transfer to many users.

4   General Description

In a transferable e-cash with a condition, the payer anonymously transfers e-cash before the outcome of the condition is published. The e-cash is valid to the payer and the last payee, and only one of the two users can deposit the e-cash. When the outcome is published, the publisher sends the extraction key to the winner by an authenticated and secure channel. If a user submits the e-cash to the publisher and wants to deposit the e-cash to the bank, the bank detects whether the user has happened a double-spending. If so, the bank recovers the identity of the user by the identify procedure. The transferable conditional e-cash consists of the withdrawal protocol, spending (transferring) protocol, deposit protocol and the identify procedure. We provide a new algorithm to construct the transferable e-cash system based on the outcome of a condition. The general description is given as follows.

The payer firstly withdraws an e-cash from the bank, and decides to spend the e-cash to other user based on a condition. The transferring protocol is anonymous to protect the identity of the payer $\mathcal{U}_1$ and the payee $\mathcal{U}_2$. To achieve anonymity, two tricks are adopt to our e-cash system. Firstly, commuting signature technology is used in our system. Generally, commitments and the corresponding proofs are used in the interaction between $\mathcal{U}_1$ and $\mathcal{U}_2$ to achieve anonymity. However this is not enough, i.e., if $\mathcal{U}_2$ transfers the e-cash to other payee $\mathcal{U}_3$, the bank knows that the e-cash is from the same user $\mathcal{U}_1$. Thanks to commuting signature technology, we can modify the commitments and proofs to achieve anonymity. Secondly, we divide the deposit into two parts to obtain the anonymity of the last user in the deposit protocol. More precisely, since the identity of the user is supplied in the deposit protocol, the bank can link the spending of the last user and the deposit of the user. To obtain the anonymity of the last user in the deposit protocol, we divide the deposit into two parts. The first part is exchanging in which we can exchange the spending to another spending mo provided by the bank. The other part is cashing, where the user updates the spending mo to mo' using the commuting signatures, and provides mo' and an account number to the bank. In our scheme, the most important problem is how to obtain the conditional e-cash, namely, two outcomes for the user $\mathcal{U}_1$ and another user $\mathcal{U}_i$. We achieve this goal by introducing a publisher, which gives two commitment/extraction keys. The two commitment/extraction keys commit two secret value for the two outcomes. When the outcome is favorable to a user, the corresponding secret value is sent to the corresponding user by an authenticated and secure channel. This publisher is very important, since he publishes the conditions of two events and the correct outcome to decide who can deposit the e-cash to the bank.

5   Conditional Transferable E-cash

Conditional transferable e-cash allows the user to spend a conditional e-cash to other one based on the outcome in the future. In the follow, we give the details of our scheme.

5.1   Setup

The bank $\mathcal{B}$, the judge $\mathcal{J}$, the publisher $\mathcal{P}$ and each user $\mathcal{U}$ generate key pairs $(pk_\mathcal{B}, sk_\mathcal{B})$, $(pk_\mathcal{J}, sk_\mathcal{J})$, $(pk_\mathcal{P}, sk_\mathcal{P})$ and $(pk_\mathcal{U}, sk_\mathcal{U})$ respectively. The bank also generates a pair of commitment/extraction key $(C_\mathcal{B}, E_\mathcal{B})$, which is used to committed the serial number of the e-cash. The users register their public keys to the judge as membership certificate: $cert_i = SPSign_{pk_\mathcal{J}}(pk_{\mathcal{U}_i})$, this is similar to the action that the users obtain an identity from the country and then open a bank account from the bank. The publisher gives two pairs of commitment/extraction keys, one is (C_{pr}, E_{pr}) which is used to commit the coin for the payer, and another is (C_{pe}, E_{pe}) which is used to commit the coin for the payee. If the outcome is favorable to the payer, the payer will obtain the secret key C_{pr}, otherwise the payee will obtain C_{pe}. The judge also generates two pairs of commitment/extraction keys $(C_\mathcal{J}, E_\mathcal{J})$ and (C_{sp}, E_{sp}), the first key will be used for identification of double spenders, and another key is used for the proof of our scheme. The bank maintains a database DB, which is used to save the e-cash spent. The database is initialized to empty.

5.2   The Withdrawal Protocol

The withdrawal protocol allows the user $\mathcal{U}_1$ to withdraw a coin co from the bank $\mathcal{B}$. We define the commitments of the publisher as p_n, p_m for the outcomes, which is favorable to the payer, the payee respectively, and the commitments

$\widetilde{p}_n, \widetilde{p}_{n'}$, which is used to supply some information to adversary for the security proof. The publisher publics the two commitments. And then the user registers the outcome at the publisher. The j_n and $\widetilde{j}_n$ are defined as commitments that commit a message n using $C_{\mathcal{J}}$ and C_{sp}. The b_n is defined as commitment that commits a message n using $C_{\mathcal{B}}$. The p_n and $\widetilde{p}_n$ are defined as commitments that commit a message n using C_{pr} and C_{pe}. In the following, We will give the protocol in detail.

1. $\mathcal{U}_1$ picks at random a nonce n_1 and makes commitments b_{n_1} using the commitment key of the bank, which represents the serial number of the coin, j_{n_1} to n_1 using the commitment key of the judge, which is used to verify the spending chain of users and a proof π_{n_1} that two committed values are equal [9]. Moreover, $\mathcal{U}_1$ makes commitments $j_{pk_{\mathcal{U}_1}}$, $\widetilde{j}_{pk_{\mathcal{U}_1}}$ to the public key of the user, which is used to recover the identity of users when a double-spending happens, and a proof $\pi_{pk_{\mathcal{U}_1}}$ that two committed values are equal. $\mathcal{U}_1$ also gives the commitment of the signature of the public key of user $j_{c_{\mathcal{U}_1}}$, which is made by the judge. At last, $\mathcal{U}_1$ gives the proof $\pi_{c_{\mathcal{U}_1}}$ [10,4] that the value in $j_{c_{\mathcal{U}_1}}$ is a valid signature on the value in $j_{pk_{\mathcal{U}_1}}$.
   The user $\mathcal{U}_1$ sends the following values to the bank: $\{pk_{\mathcal{U}_1}, j_{pk_{\mathcal{U}_1}}, j_{n_1}, j_{c_{\mathcal{U}_1}}, \pi_{c_{\mathcal{U}_1}}\}$.

2. In order to supply two outcomes, $\mathcal{B}$ picks at random n and m, and generates two commitments p_n and p_m using the commitment keys C_{pr} and C_{pe} respectively. $\mathcal{B}$ also gives the other two commitments $\widetilde{p}_n$ and $\widetilde{p}_m$ which is used to prove the scheme completely. Meanwhile two proofs π_n and $\pi_{n'}$ are given to prove two committed values are equal respectively. If the outcome is favorable to the payer, the publisher $\mathcal{P}$ will give the extraction key to the payer. Then the payer can open the commitment p_n and obtain the value n.

3. $\mathcal{B}$ verifies the NIZK proof $\pi_{c_{\mathcal{U}_1}}$ and the public $pk_{\mathcal{U}_1}$. If they are correct, the bank $\mathcal{B}$ chooses a random nonce n_0 for the coin and generates two commitments j_{n_0} and b_{n_0} using the commitment keys $C_{\mathcal{J}}$ and $C_{\mathcal{B}}$ respectively. The bank also gives a proof π_{n_0} that the two committed values are equal. Then the bank $\mathcal{B}$ produces a committed signature $c_{s_{c_1}}$ on the values n, m, n_0, n_1 and $pk_{\mathcal{U}_1}$ by running $SigCom$ on $p_n, p_m, j_{n_0}, j_{n_1}$ and $j_{pk_{\mathcal{U}_1}}$, and also outputs the proof π_{s_1} [10,4] that the signature $c_{s_{c_1}}$ is valid to commitments $p_n, p_m, j_{n_0}, j_{n_1}$ and $j_{pk_{\mathcal{U}_1}}$.

The bank $\mathcal{B}$ sends the following values to the user: $\{p_n, \widetilde{p}_n, \pi_n, p_m, \widetilde{p}_m, \pi_m, j_{n_0}, b_{n_0}, \pi_{n_0}, c_{s_{c_1}}, \pi_{s_1}\}$.

Finally, the user $\mathcal{U}_1$ forms the coin $co_1 = (p_n, \widetilde{p}_n, \pi_n, p_m, \widetilde{p}_m, \pi_m, j_{n_0}, b_{n_0}, \pi_{n_0}, j_{n_1}, b_{n_1}, \pi_{n_1}, j_{pk_{\mathcal{U}_1}}, \widetilde{j}_{pk_{\mathcal{U}_1}}, \pi_{pk_{\mathcal{U}_1}}, j_{c_{\mathcal{U}_1}}, \pi_{c_{\mathcal{U}_1}}, c_{s_{c_1}}, \pi_{s_1})$.

5.3 The Spending(Transferring) Protocol

This is a protocol which makes a payer $\mathcal{U}_1$ to transfer a coin to the payee $\mathcal{U}_2$. In order to obtain the anonymity of the user, $\mathcal{U}_1$ needs randomize the coin co_i before he spends the coin to the third user. $\mathcal{U}_1$ also converts the proof π_{s_i} to a new proof by running AdC_κ, which will hide the identity of the user.

1. U_2 picks at random a nonce n_2 and makes a commitments b_{n_2} using the commitment key of the bank, which represents the coin, j_{n_2} to n_2 using the commitment key of the judge, which is used to verify the spending chain of users and a proof π_{n_2} that two committed values are equal. Moreover, U_2 makes commitments $j_{pk_{U_2}}$, $\tilde{j}_{pk_{U_2}}$ and a proof $\pi_{pk_{U_2}}$ that two committed values are equal. At last, U_2 gives the proof π_{cu_2} that the value in j_{cu_2} is a valid signature on the value in $j_{pk_{U_2}}$.

   The user U_2 sends the following values to U_1: $\{j_{pk_{U_2}}, j_{n_2}, j_{cu_2}, \pi_{cu_2}\}$.

2. U_1 firstly checks the proof π_{cu_2}. If the verification is correct, U_1 randomizes co_1 to $co_1^1 = (p_n^1, \tilde{p}_n^1, \pi_n^1, p_m^1, \tilde{p}_m^1, \pi_m^1, j_{n_0}^1, d_{n_0}^1, \pi_{n_0}^1, j_{n_1}^1, d_{n_1}^1, \pi_{n_1}^1, j_{pk_{U_1}}^1, \tilde{j}_{pk_{U_1}}^1, \pi_{pk_{U_1}}^1, j_{cu_1}^1, \pi_{cu_1}^1, c_{s_{c_1}}^1, \pi_{s_1}^1)$. Then U_1 computes a committed signature $c_{s_{c_2}}$ on the values committed in $j_{n_1}^1, j_{n_2}$ and $j_{pk_{U_2}}$ using $SigCom$, and also outputs the proof π'_{s_2} that the signature $c_{s_{c_2}}$ is valid to commitments $j_{n_1}^1, j_{n_2}$ and $j_{pk_{U_2}}$. To hide the verification key of U_1, U_1 also converts π'_{s_2} to π_{s_2} by running AdC_κ.

The U_1 sends the following values to U_2: $\{co_1^1, C_{s_{c_2}}, \pi_{s_2}\}$.

Finally, the user U_2 forms the coin $co_2 = (co_1^1, j_{n_2}, b_{n_2}, \pi_{n_2}, j_{pk_{U_2}}, \tilde{j}_{pk_{U_2}}, \pi_{pk_{U_2}}, j_{cu_2}, \pi_{cu_2}, c_{s_{c_2}}, \pi_{s_2})$.

5.4 The Deposit Protocol

When the outcome is published, the winner contacts the publisher and provides the corresponding proof to the publisher by an authenticated channel. If the proof is correct, the publisher sends the secret value to the winner. Without loss of generality, the outcome is favorable to the payee, so the payee will obtain the corresponding extraction key E_{pe}. To achieve the anonymous of the user during the deposit, we divide the deposit protocol into two sections, exchanging and cashing.

Exchanging. U_i spends the coin $co_\ell = (n^\ell, p_n^\ell, m, p_m^\ell, co_1^\ell, co_2^{\ell-1}, \cdots, co_{\ell-1}^2, j_{n_\ell}^1, b_{n_\ell}^1, \pi_{n_\ell}^1, j_{pk_{U_\ell}}^1, \tilde{j}_{pk_{U_\ell}}^1, \pi_{pk_{U_\ell}}^1, c_{ju_\ell}^1, \pi_{cu_\ell}^1, c_{s_{c_\ell}}^1, \pi_{s_\ell}^1)$ to the bank, that is, U_i runs the protocol with the bank playing the role of U_2. In order to detect the double-spending, the bank firstly verifies the correctness of the secret value and commitment (m, p_m) and checks whether m equals the value committed in p_m. Then B opens the commitments $b_{n_0}^\ell, b_{n_1}^{\ell-1}, \cdots, b_{n_{\ell-1}}^2, b_{n_\ell}^1$ contained in the coin, using the extraction key of the bank. And last, the bank obtains the serial number $s = m||n_0||n_1||n_2|| \cdots ||n_\ell$, and checks whether the coin is found in the database DB. If it does not, the bank sends the value $mo = (m, c_m, c_{\sigma_m}, \pi_{c_m})$ to the user U_i, which represents a correct deposit of the user. The bank also saves the serial number to the database DB. Otherwise, the bank running the following identify procedures.

Cashing. In order to cash the coin from the bank, the user U_i converts the value $mo = (m, c_m, c_{\sigma_m}, \pi_{c_m})$ to $mo' = (m, c'_m, c'_{\sigma_m}, \pi'_{c_m})$ using AdC_κ. Then

$\mathcal{U}_i$ directly contacts the bank $\mathcal{B}$ through an authenticated channel, supplies his account number and exchanges this piece of currency for credit to his account.

If the outcome is favorable to the first payer $\mathcal{U}_1$, the user $\mathcal{U}_1$ deposits the coin to the bank as the above procedure except that the $\mathcal{U}_1$ spends the coin co_1^1 and the bank $\mathcal{B}$ will obtain the serial number $s = n||n_0||n_1|| \cdots ||n_\ell$.

5.5   The Identify Procedures

If $\mathcal{B}$ can find another serial number beginning with n in his database, i.e. $s' = n||n_0'||n_1'||n_2'|| \cdots ||n_\ell'$. He compares the two serial numbers s and s' and stops at the last t such that $n_t = n_t'$. Finally, the bank sends the two coins to the judge. In order to identify the defrauder, the judge computes the identity committed in $j_{pk_{\mathcal{U}_\ell}}$ using his extraction key $E_{\mathcal{J}}$.

5.6   Efficiency

We analysis the efficiency by comparing the computation and communication. Shi et al. [11] requires $O(m_1 m_2 k)$ computation and communication, where m_1 and m_2 are cut-and-choose parameters and k is a security parameter for RSA-based systems. We know that in cut-and-choose techniques with a parameter m a dishonest user can cheat with probability $1/m$, therefore a protocol that has the overhead of $O(m^2 k)$ is too heavy for any user. Blanton needs $O(\lambda log m_3)$, where λ is a security parameter for groups with bilinear maps and m_3 is the probability of cheating.

On a contrary, we use the commitments and corresponding proofs for representing a conditional e-cash. The proofs are given by the NIZK proof using GS proofs. Thus, the payer only needs to send some commitments and proofs to the payee in the spending protocol, transferring protocol and the deposit protocol, and the communication number only needs one time. Therefore, computation and communication in our scheme are constant, namely $O(\lambda)$, where λ is the system parameter or a security parameter for groups with bilinear maps.

6   Security Analysis

We now give the security of our scheme. The scheme fulfills the security requirements given in Section 3.

Theorem 1. *Our conditional transferable e-cash scheme provides anonymity, unforgeability, identification of double-spender and exculpability under the following assumptions: SXDH assumption, unforgeability of the commuting signature scheme, soundness of NIZK proofs and witness indistinguishability of GS proofs.*

Proof. We briefly analyze the security properties as follows.

Anonymous. The anonymous of our scheme only achieves the FA and PA_1. Our scheme commits all messages sent between the users when transferring a coin. If the adversary wants to determine which one is the user chosen by the Challenge in Challenge Phase, he needs to extract the public key committed in $j_{pk_{\mathcal{U}_i}}$. Thus, the adversary can break the soundness of NIZK proofs and witness indistinguishability of GS proofs [6].

In the following, we give the prove of the FA by a game between an adversary $\mathcal{A}$ and a challenge $\mathcal{C}$. For fair e-cash, the judge and the publisher is necessary, so they can not extract the secret key except that the bank give the proof that the user happens a double-spending.

(Initialization Phase.)Let $\mathcal{C}$ supplies a system parameter λ to the adversary $\mathcal{A}$ acting as the bank. The adversary $\mathcal{A}$ obtains the key pairs of the bank, the judge and the publisher. And then (A) sends the public keys and the commitment keys to the $\mathcal{C}$.

(Probing Phase.)In the withdrawal protocol, the $\mathcal{C}$ acting the payer withdraws conditional e-coins, then converts the coins to new coins by the algorithm $SigCom$. The $\mathcal{A}$ any payee accepts the e-coins from the $\mathcal{A}$ act the payer in the spending protocol. In the deposit protocol, the user deposits a coin to the $\mathcal{A}$ acting the bank. By the above interact, the $\mathcal{A}$ obtains some commitments and corresponding proofs. The length of the coins are the same.

(End Game Phase.)The $\mathcal{C}$ chooses two coins co_0 and co_1 from these coins in the Probing Phase, and then flips a fair coin to decide to use co_0 or co_1 for the deposit protocol. The GS proofs is soundness, so we know the commitments and the corresponding proofs are correct. If the adversary $\mathcal{A}$ can distinguish which coin the user deposits, $co_i(i=0/1)$, he must distinguish which public key the user uses, $pk_{\mathcal{U}_i}$, namely $i = 0$ or $i = 1$. We know if the $\mathcal{A}$ can solve the SXDH problem, he can distinguish which commitment the user uses. But the probability of solving the SXDH problem is ignore. For the commuting signatures, the $\mathcal{A}$ can not forge any commuting signatures, so he can not give any help to distinguish $i = 0$ or $i = 1$.

So we know the $\mathcal{A}$ can win if he can forge a commuting signature, solve the $SXDH$ problem and break the soundness of the NIZK proofs.

Unforgeability. Let $\mathcal{A}$ be an adversary. We outline the success probability of $\mathcal{A}$ is negligible by interacting with a challenger $\mathcal{C}$. The $\mathcal{C}$ gives the public key of the bank. The $\mathcal{A}$ generates the remaining parameters.

For each KeyGen(), $\mathcal{A}$ can create a new user or corrupt an honest user. So $\mathcal{A}$ obtains some key pairs. In withdrawal protocol, $\mathcal{A}$ can act as a user and withdraw some coins from the challenger, we defined the coins as co_{ui}. For each spending protocol, $\mathcal{A}$ can act as a user and spend(transfer) some coins to challenger, we defined the coins as co_{uo}. he also gets some coins from challenger, we defined the coins as co_{ui}^1. In deposit protocol, $\mathcal{A}$ deposits some coins to challenger, and other users deposit some coins which come from $\mathcal{A}$, to challenger. We defined all the deposit as co_{uo}^1. So the $\mathcal{A}$ obtains the value of the coins is $co = co_{ui} + co_{ui}^1 - co_{uo} - co_{uo}^1$. If $co > 0$, the $\mathcal{A}$ has spent a coin which is not withdrew from the bank.

We know the other users and the bank are honest, and the NIZK proof π_{s_i} is soundness. If the $\mathcal{A}$ can spend more coins which are not withdrew from the bank, he must give a forgery of a new triples $(n, n_0, pk_{\mathcal{U}_1})$ from the bank. Thus, $\mathcal{A}$ outputs a new signature on a message as a forgery, namely $\mathcal{A}$ breaks the unforgeability of commuting signature.

Double-Spending. $\mathcal{C}$ gives the public key of the judge for identifying the identity of the double-spender. $\mathcal{A}$ sets up the remaining parameters.

When $\mathcal{A}$ can spend a coin twice without revealing the identity of the $\mathcal{A}$, the output of the Identify() is not the public key of any user. Because each valid coin contains a valid certificate for the public key, by the soundness of NIZK proofs, we know the $\mathcal{A}$ must forge a new valid certificate for the public key registered in judge. Therefore, $\mathcal{A}$ breaks the soundness of NIZK proofs and the unforgeability of commuting signature.

Exculpability. The exculpability is that the $\mathcal{A}$ acting the bank can accuse an honest user of happening a double-spending. We request that the signature is issued by an honest user rather than the bank.

If a user is identified as a double spending, the $\mathcal{A}$ needs to supply two correspond spending to the user. The two spending containing two serial numbers s and s' in which $n_i = n'_i$. By the soundness of NIZK proofs, the two coins contain correct signatures. In order to accuse the honest user of happening the double-spending, the $\mathcal{A}$ forges a signature on a coin. Therefore, $\mathcal{A}$ breaks the unforgeability of commuting signature.

7   Conclusion

In this paper, we presented the first anonymous transferable conditional e-cash. One of the most features in our protocol is that the spending and deposit protocol is anonymous. In this protocol, we can modify commitments and corresponding proof using the commuting signature and the GS proofs. How to design a efficient conditional transferable e-cash will be a new think.

Acknowledgements. This work was supported by the National Natural Science Foundation of China (grant number 60973105, 90718017, 61170189), the Research Fund for the Doctoral Program of Higher Education (grant number 20111102130003) and the Fund of the State Key Laboratory of Software Development Environment (grant number SKLSDE-2011ZX-03, SKLSDE-2012ZX-11).

References

1. Abe, M., Fuchsbauer, G., Groth, J., Haralambiev, K., Ohkubo, M.: Structure-Preserving Signatures and Commitments to Group Elements. In: Rabin, T. (ed.) CRYPTO 2010. LNCS, vol. 6223, pp. 209–236. Springer, Heidelberg (2010)
2. Belenkiy, M., Camenisch, J., Chase, M., Kohlweiss, M., Lysyanskaya, A., Shacham, H.: Randomizable Proofs and Delegatable Anonymous Credentials. In: Halevi, S. (ed.) CRYPTO 2009. LNCS, vol. 5677, pp. 108–125. Springer, Heidelberg (2009)
3. Blanton, M.: Improved Conditional E-Payments. In: Bellovin, S.M., Gennaro, R., Keromytis, A.D., Yung, M. (eds.) ACNS 2008. LNCS, vol. 5037, pp. 188–206. Springer, Heidelberg (2008)

4. Blazy, O., Canard, S., Fuchsbauer, G., Gouget, A., Sibert, H., Traoré, J.: Achieving Optimal Anonymity in Transferable E-Cash with a Judge. In: Nitaj, A., Pointcheval, D. (eds.) AFRICACRYPT 2011. LNCS, vol. 6737, pp. 206–223. Springer, Heidelberg (2011)
5. Camenisch, J., Lysyanskaya, A., Meyerovich, M.: Endorsed e-cash. In: IEEE Security and Privacy 2007. Springer (2007)
6. Canard, S., Gouget, A.: Anonymity in Transferable E-cash. In: Bellovin, S.M., Gennaro, R., Keromytis, A.D., Yung, M. (eds.) ACNS 2008. LNCS, vol. 5037, pp. 207–223. Springer, Heidelberg (2008)
7. Chaum, D., Pedersen, T.: Transferred Cash Grows in Size. In: Rueppel, R.A. (ed.) EUROCRYPT 1992. LNCS, vol. 658, pp. 390–407. Springer, Heidelberg (1993)
8. Fuchsbauer, G.: Commuting Signatures and Verifiable Encryption. In: Paterson, K.G. (ed.) EUROCRYPT 2011. LNCS, vol. 6632, pp. 224–245. Springer, Heidelberg (2011)
9. Fuchsbauer, G., Pointcheval, D., Vergnaud, D.: Transferable Constant-Size Fair E-Cash. In: Garay, J.A., Miyaji, A., Otsuka, A. (eds.) CANS 2009. LNCS, vol. 5888, pp. 226–247. Springer, Heidelberg (2009)
10. Groth, J., Sahai, A.: Efficient Non-interactive Proof Systems for Bilinear Groups. In: Smart, N.P. (ed.) EUROCRYPT 2008. LNCS, vol. 4965, pp. 415–432. Springer, Heidelberg (2008)
11. Shi, L., Carbunar, B., Sion, R.: Conditional E-Cash. In: Dietrich, S., Dhamija, R. (eds.) FC 2007 and USEC 2007. LNCS, vol. 4886, pp. 15–28. Springer, Heidelberg (2007)
12. Okamoto, T., Ohta, K.: Universal Electronic Cash. In: Feigenbaum, J. (ed.) CRYPTO 1991. LNCS, vol. 576, pp. 324–337. Springer, Heidelberg (1992)
13. Canard, S., Gouget, A., Traoré, J.: Improvement of Efficiency in (Unconditional) Anonymous Transferable E-Cash. In: Tsudik, G. (ed.) FC 2008. LNCS, vol. 5143, pp. 202–214. Springer, Heidelberg (2008)
14. Canard, S., Delerablée, C., Gouget, A., Hufschmitt, E., Laguillaumie, F., Sibert, H., Traoré, J., Vergnaud, D.: Fair E-Cash: Be Compact, Spend Faster. In: Samarati, P., Yung, M., Martinelli, F., Ardagna, C.A. (eds.) ISC 2009. LNCS, vol. 5735, pp. 294–309. Springer, Heidelberg (2009)
15. Abe, M., Groth, J., Haralambiev, K., Ohkubo, M.: Optimal Structure-Preserving Signatures in Asymmetric Bilinear Groups. In: Rogaway, P. (ed.) CRYPTO 2011. LNCS, vol. 6841, pp. 649–666. Springer, Heidelberg (2011)
16. Okamoto, T., Ohta, K.: Disposable Zero-Knowledge Authentications and Their Applications to Untraceable Electronic Cash. In: Brassard, G. (ed.) CRYPTO 1989. LNCS, vol. 435, pp. 481–496. Springer, Heidelberg (1990)

Two Improvements of Random Key Predistribution for Wireless Sensor Networks

Jiří Kůr, Vashek Matyáš*, and Petr Švenda

Masaryk University, Brno, Czech Republic
{xkur,matyas,svenda}@fi.muni.cz

Abstract. Key distribution is of a critical importance to security of wireless sensor networks (WSNs). Random key predistribution is an acknowledged approach to the key distribution problem. In this paper, we propose and analyze two novel improvements that enhance security provided by the random key predistribution schemes. The first improvement exploits limited length collisions in secure hash functions to increase the probability of two nodes sharing a key. The second improvement introduces hash chains into the key pool construction to directly increase the resilience against a node capture attack. Both improvements can be further combined to bring the best performance. We evaluate the improvements both analytically and computationally on a network simulator. The concepts used are not limited to the random key predistribution.

Keywords: hash function collision, key management, random key predistribution, security, wireless sensor network.

1 Introduction

A wireless sensor network (WSN) consists of resource-constrained and wireless devices called sensor nodes. WSNs monitor some physical phenomenon (e.g., vibrations, temperature, pressure, light) and send measurements to a base station. There are several classes of sensor nodes available – ranging from high-end nodes that can easily employ public-key cryptography down to nodes that can barely make use of any cryptography at all. In our work, we consider cheap and highly constrained nodes that can use only symmetric cryptography and their storage is just a few kilobytes.

Key distribution is one of the greatest challenges in WSNs. Since network topology is usually not a priori known, every node should be able to establish a link key with a large portion of other nodes to ensure the connectivity of the network. To achieve this requirement, nodes may pre-share a single network-wide master key and use it to establish link keys. However, if a single node with the master key is captured, then the whole network gets compromised. In an alternative approach, each node pre-shares a unique link key with every node.

---

* Final work on this paper undertaken as a Fulbright-Masaryk Visiting Scholar at Harvard University.

A.D. Keromytis and R. Di Pietro (Eds.): SecureComm 2012, LNICST 106, pp. 61–75, 2013.
© Institute for Computer Sciences, Social Informatics and Telecommunications Engineering 2013

This offers much better security, yet hits the memory limits as number of nodes in the network increases.

A suitable trade-off between the two approaches comes with the random key predistribution [1]. Every node is preloaded with a fixed number of keys randomly selected from a given key pool. After the network deployment, two nodes establish a link key if they share at least one key from the key pool. The scheme can be extended to require at least q shared keys [2].

In this paper, we propose two improvements of the basic random key predistribution schemes. In the first improvement, we increase a probability that any two nodes establish a link key while maintaining memory requirements fixed. For this purpose we construct the key pool using limited length (e.g., 80-bit) collisions in a secure hash function. We also provide an evidence that such collisions can be found in a reasonably short time on today's personal computers.

The second improvement introduces hash chains into the key pool structure to directly enhance the resilience against a node capture attack. Both the improvements can be further combined together to bring the best performance. These improvements are particularly advantageous for situations in which the attacker manages to capture a significant number of nodes.

The structure of the paper is following – we review the basic random key predistribution schemes and other related work in Section 2. We present and evaluate the first improvement in Section 3 and the second improvement in Section 4. Then we evaluate their combination in the following section of this paper. We provide computational results from a network simulator and proof of concept for the collision search in Section 6, and then the last section concludes the paper. Proofs of selected equations can be found in the Appendix.

2   Background and Related Work

In this section, we provide a background knowledge on the basic random key predistribution schemes and other related work.

Our proposals modify the basic random key predistribution schemes proposed by Eschenauer and Gligor [1] and Chen et al. [2]. We refer to the schemes as to the *EG scheme* and the *q-composite scheme*, respectively, in our paper.

The *EG scheme* works as follows: in the *(i) key setup* phase, a key pool S is created by randomly taking $|S|$ keys from the possible key space. Then, for every node, m keys are randomly drawn from the key pool S without replacement and uploaded into the node. These keys form a key ring for the given node. If $|S|$ and m are chosen properly, any two nodes in the network share at least one key with a high probability. E.g., for a key pool size $|S| = 10,000$ and a ring size $m = 83$ the probability that any two nodes share a key is $p = 0.5$.

In the *(ii) shared key discovery* phase, every two neighboring nodes try to identify shared keys among their key rings. This can be done by various methods. E.g., every key can be assigned a short unique identifier that is broadcasted by the nodes that have the corresponding key in their key rings. If a shared key is found, it is used as a link key for the communication between the two nodes. If not, the link key can be established in the *path-key establishment* phase.

The *(iii) path-key establishment* phase is optional. It uses already secured links to establish link keys between two neighboring nodes that could not establish a link key directly as they had no shared key or their keys were compromised [3].

The *q-composite scheme* is a generalization of the EG scheme. In the *shared key discovery* phase, two nodes establish a link key only if they share at least q keys in their key rings. The resulting link key is derived from all the shared keys.

2.1   Node Capture Resilience

The performance of random key predistribution schemes is evaluated with respect to the node capture resilience [2]. It can be defined as the probability that a given secured link between two uncaptured nodes can be compromised by an attacker using keys extracted from already captured nodes. In other words, the node capture resilience is a fraction of secured links between uncaptured nodes that can be compromised by an attacker.

The node capture resilience is mostly influenced by the following three factors – the ring size m, the key pool size $|S|$ and the probability that any two nodes in the network can establish a link key. These values are to some extent determined by properties of the network concerned. The ring size m is limited by a storage capacity of the network sensor nodes. If we want the network to be connected by secure links, the minimum required probability of a link key establishment is given by the size of the network and by the average number of neighboring nodes (for details see [1]). Given the m and the minimum required probability, the $|S|$ is uniquely determined. Note that in the q-composite scheme also the q influences the node capture resilience and the key pool size $|S|$.

2.2   Other Related Work

The basic schemes have been modified by Ren et al. [4]. The key pool in their scheme consists of a large number of keyed hash chains where every hash chain element is considered a unique key. Every node is then assigned a number of such keys and a number of whole keyed hash chains represented by their hashing keys and chain starting points. Deterministic and hybrid approaches how to select keys for key rings based on *combinatorial design* are proposed in [5]. These approaches enhance the performance of the basic schemes and similarly to them can be also further improved with our proposals. For other key distribution schemes in WSNs see the survey [6].

Our first proposal is based on hash collisions. Rivest and Shamir took an advantage of hash collisions for a security gain in the MicroMint micro payment scheme, where an electronic coin was represented by a hash collision [7]. However, their scheme relies on the security economics rather than on computational complexity per se. An attacker with a computational power equal to the broker is able to cheat by finding a collision with given properties. In our scheme, an attacker needs to find a pre-image for a given hash.

As far as we are aware, the first usage of hash-chains for key agreement appeared in [8].

3   Collision Key Improvement

We propose a modification to the basic random key predistribution schemes. Keeping the key ring size m and the key pool size $|S|$ same as for the basic schemes, this modification additionally increases the number of keys that two nodes may share.

In our scheme, two nodes X and Y can share a key directly as in the basic schemes. Furthermore, an additional shared key C can be constructed if two nodes carry two different, but related keys K_A and K_B such that the condition $C = H(K_A) = H(K_B)$, where H is a suitable cryptographic hash function, is fulfilled. We call such related keys *colliding keys* and the resulting value C a *collision key*. Probability of two randomly chosen values for K_A and K_B being colliding keys is generally very low due to the collision resistance of the hash function. Therefore, we modify the process how keys for the key pool are selected. Instead of randomly selecting $|S|$ keys from the possible key space, $\frac{|S|}{2}$ colliding key pairs are taken to form a key pool S. Thus, the total number of keys in the key pool remains $|S|$ and the key pool gets the structure depicted in Figure 1.

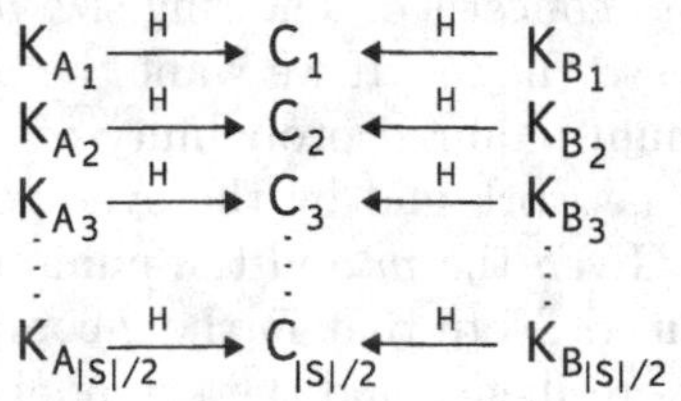

$$
\begin{array}{ccc}
K_{A_1} \xrightarrow{\ H\ } & C_1 & \xleftarrow{\ H\ } K_{B_1} \\
K_{A_2} \xrightarrow{\ H\ } & C_2 & \xleftarrow{\ H\ } K_{B_2} \\
K_{A_3} \xrightarrow{\ H\ } & C_3 & \xleftarrow{\ H\ } K_{B_3} \\
\vdots & \vdots & \vdots \\
K_{A_{|S|/2}} \xrightarrow{\ H\ } & C_{|S|/2} & \xleftarrow{\ H\ } K_{B_{|S|/2}}
\end{array}
$$

Fig. 1. Key pool structure in the collision key improvement. Colliding keys from the key pool are denoted K_A and K_B. Collision keys are depicted as C. H denotes a secure hash function.

Colliding keys long enough to withstand a brute-force attack can be efficiently generated due to the birthday paradox. In Section 6, we demonstrate that for key length of $N = 80$ bits thousands of colliding key pairs can be generated with a moderate computational power.

Beside the key pool structure, we also slightly modify the way how keys are selected to a key ring. The keys are still picked from the key pool randomly without replacement, however, we do not allow two colliding keys to be in the same key ring. Thus, if a key is picked, not only itself but also its colliding counterpart is temporarily marked off the key pool. Once the key ring is complete, all keys are put back to the key pool and the next node is processed.

In the shared key discovery phase, similarly to the q-composite scheme, two nodes X and Y can establish a link key if they share at least q keys. The shared keys can be both colliding keys drawn directly from the key rings or collision keys computed using a hash function H. Since every node has m keys in its key ring, it is also able to establish m collision keys. Thus our improvement significantly increases the effective size of the key rings as evaluated in the following subsection. Therefore, we can expand the key pool accordingly while keeping the probability of a link key establishment at the desired level. This expansion increases the node capture resilience. In the rest of the paper we refer to this improvement as to the *collision key improvement*.

3.1 Probability of Link Key Establishment

In this subsection we show how to calculate the probability that any two nodes in the network are able to directly establish a link key in the shared key discovery phase. Let us define the following notation to support readability of the subsequent analysis.

Definition 1

$$\left\{ \begin{array}{c} |S| \\ m \end{array} \right\} = \frac{|S| \cdot (|S| - 2) \cdot (|S| - 4) \cdot \ldots \cdot (|S| - 2 \cdot (m - 2)) \cdot (|S| - 2 \cdot (m - 1))}{m!}$$

The formula expresses the number of all possible key rings of size m selected from a key pool of size $|S|$ where no colliding key pair is present in the key rings. Thus it can be viewed as $|S|$ choose m, where the choice has to respect the above mentioned constraint. For justification see the Appendix.

The probability that any two nodes in the network share exactly i keys from the key pool S and exactly j collision keys that do not result from the i shared keys can be calculated as follows (see the Appendix for proof):

$$P_{SharedExactly}(i, j) = \frac{\binom{m}{i}\binom{m-i}{j}\left\{ \begin{array}{c} |S| - 2m \\ m - i - j \end{array} \right\}}{\left\{ \begin{array}{c} |S| \\ m \end{array} \right\}} \tag{1}$$

Two nodes can establish a link key if they share at least q independent keys, no matter whether these are colliding or collision keys. The collision keys are counted only if their pre-images are not. Thus the probability that any two nodes in a network are able to establish a link key is, among m and $|S|$, dependent also on the parameter q and can be calculated as:

$$P_{LinkEstablishI} = \sum_{i=0}^{m} \sum_{j=0}^{m} P_{SharedExactly}(i, j) \tag{2}$$

where $i + j \geq q$ and $i + j \leq m$.

3.2 Resulting Node Capture Resilience

In this subsection we evaluate the collision key improvement with respect to the node capture resilience. The resilience is dependent on the number of captured nodes x, the key pool size $|S|$, the key ring size m and the desired probability of a link key establishment $P_{LinkEstablishI}$. We assume that an attacker has selected the nodes to capture in a random fashion and calculate the node capture resilience as

$$P_{LinkComprI} = \sum_{i=0}^{m} \sum_{j=0}^{m} (1 - (1 - \frac{m}{|S|})^x)^i (1 - (1 - \frac{2m}{|S|})^x)^j \frac{P_{SharedExactly}(i,j)}{P_{LinkEstablishI}} \quad (3)$$

where $i + j \geq q$, $i + j \leq m$. For proof see the Appendix.

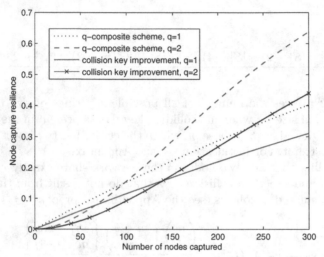

Fig. 2. Node capture resilience after x randomly selected nodes have been captured, key ring size $m = 200$, probability of link key establishment $P_{LinkEstablishI} = 0.33$

Figure 2 presents a comparison of the q-composite scheme and the collision key improvement. It is clear that our improvement provides a better node capture resilience for both values of q. E.g., if $q = 2$ and 50 nodes are captured, the resilience of the q-composite scheme is 4.7%, whereas the collision key improvement gives us the resilience of 2.7%.

4   Key-Chain Improvement

The second proposed modification of the basic random key predistribution introduces hash chains into the key pool construction. We will refer to this modification as to the *key-chain improvement*. The key-chain improvement was loosely inspired by previous work of Ren et al. [4], but our scheme utilizes hash chains in a different manner. Furthermore, we employ basic hash chains instead of the keyed ones.

In our scheme, the key pool consists of $|S|$ hash chains of a length L and every value in the chains is considered as a potential key. Thus, we refer to the hash chains as to the key-chains. The structure of the key pool is depicted in the Figure 3.

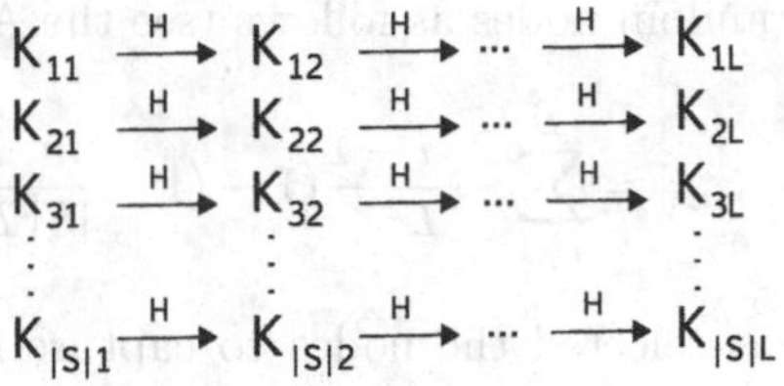

$$
\begin{array}{ccccc}
K_{11} & \xrightarrow{H} & K_{12} & \xrightarrow{H} \cdots \xrightarrow{H} & K_{1L} \\
K_{21} & \xrightarrow{H} & K_{22} & \xrightarrow{H} \cdots \xrightarrow{H} & K_{2L} \\
K_{31} & \xrightarrow{H} & K_{32} & \xrightarrow{H} \cdots \xrightarrow{H} & K_{3L} \\
\vdots & & \vdots & & \vdots \\
K_{|S|1} & \xrightarrow{H} & K_{|S|2} & \xrightarrow{H} \cdots \xrightarrow{H} & K_{|S|L}
\end{array}
$$

Fig. 3. Key pool structure in the key-chain improvement. The knowledge of a key K_{ij} enables one to compute keys K_{ik} for every $k \geq j$.

In the key-setup phase, every node is randomly assigned a key from m randomly selected key-chains. If two nodes were assigned keys from the same key-chain, they are able to calculate a shared key. A node with a value closer to the beginning of the key-chain can traverse the chain downwards to find the shared key carried by the second node.

In the shared key discovery phase, two nodes can establish a link key when sharing at least q independent keys.

The actual size of the key pool is $|S| \cdot L$, although in the subsequent analysis we shall consider the number of key-chains $|S|$ as the key pool size. The length of a key-chain L shall be taken as an independent parameter that influences the scheme security. The key-chain improvement can be further combined with the collision key improvement to get even better performance. The combination is considered in Section 5.

4.1 Probability of Link Key Establishment

The probability that any two nodes share exactly i independent keys is equal to the same probability for the basic EG and q-composite schemes. To calculate the probability we can use the formula from [2]:

$$
P_{SharedExactly}(i) = \frac{\binom{|S|}{i}\binom{|S|-i}{2(m-i)}\binom{2(m-i)}{m-i}}{\binom{|S|}{m}^2} \tag{4}
$$

Note that the probability is independent of the key-chain length L as the length influences only the node capture resilience provided by the scheme. The probability of a link key establishment for a given q is then

$$
P_{LinkEstablishII} = \sum_{i=q}^{m} P_{SharedExactly}(i) \tag{5}
$$

4.2   Resulting Node Capture Resilience

The node capture resilience is in this case dependent (among other parameters) also on the key-chain length L. To evaluate the node capture resilience, we first calculate the probability that a key from a given key-chain is compromised after an attacker captured x random nodes as follows (see the Appendix for proof):

$$P_{ChainCompr} = \sum_{i=1}^{L} \frac{2 \cdot i - 1}{L^2}(1 - (1 - \frac{m}{|S|}\frac{i}{L})^x)$$ (6)

Assuming an attacker has selected the nodes to capture in a random fashion, the node capture resilience can be calculated as

$$P_{LinkComprII} = \sum_{i=q}^{m}(P_{ChainCompr})^i \frac{P_{SharedExactly}(i)}{P_{LinkEstablishII}}$$ (7)

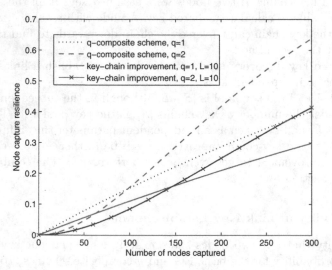

Fig. 4. Node capture resilience after x randomly selected nodes have been captured, key ring size $m = 200$, probability of link key establishment $P_{LinkEstablishII} = 0.33$, effective key-chain length $L = 10$

Figure 4 presents a comparison of the q-composite scheme and the key-chain improvement. Again, our improvement provides a better node capture resilience for both values of q. E.g., if $q = 2$ and 50 nodes are captured, the resilience of the q-composite scheme is 4.7%, whereas the key-chain improvement provides the resilience of 2.5%. Such a resilience is even better than the resilience provided by the collision key improvement proposed in Section 3.

4.3 Key-Chain Length

An important security parameter of the key-chain improvement is the length of the key-chains. It holds that the longer the key-chain, the better the node capture resilience. However, as the length of the key-chain increases, the security gain obtained for a single unit increment decreases rapidly as demonstrated in Figure 5. Also, when evaluating the node capture resilience, we have to consider the *effective length* of the key-chain, not the actual one. The effective length of a key-chain is the number of different keys from the key-chain that are actually assigned to some key ring. The effective length is dependent on the number of nodes in the network n, the size of a key ring m and the size of the key pool $|S|$. The average effective key-chain length cannot exceed $\frac{n \cdot m}{|S|}$, which is the expected number of nodes that will be assigned a key from a given key-chain. If we set the actual length to be equal to this number, the average effective key-chain length will be shorter. We can get close to the bound by setting the actual length artificially long. Yet this would increase the computational complexity of the key establishment as nodes would need to perform more hashing to establish a shared key. In practice, it is not necessary to reach the maximum length available due to the steep decrease in additional gain demonstrated in the Figure 5.

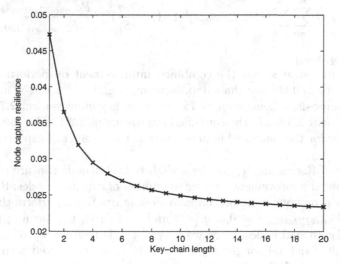

Fig. 5. Relationship between an effective length of a key-chain and node capture resilience. Key ring size $m = 200$, probability of link key establishment $P_{LinkEstablishII} = 0.33$, $q = 2$ and the number of captured nodes $x = 50$.

For most networks, a practical value of the effective key-chain length would be around $L = 10$. Such an effective length is achievable with only a slightly higher actual key-chain length for sufficiently large networks.

5 Combined Results

The key-chain improvement can be directly combined with the collision key improvement to obtain even better results with respect to the node capture resilience. To combine both improvements, the end points of the key chains should be the colliding keys. This requirement can be easily fulfilled due to the nature of the parallel collision search algorithm. If the collision is found, also the two hash chains that precede it are obtained, see Section 6.

The *probabilities of a link key establishment* between any two nodes in the network are calculated similarly as in the case of the collision key improvement using Equations 1 and 2. The size of the key pool $|S|$ is in this case defined as the number of key-chains. Thus $|S|$ has a similar meaning as in the key-chain improvement.

For given arguments, one obtains the same probability of a link key establishment for both the collision key improvement and for the combined solution. Yet there is a difference in the achieved node capture resilience, which is higher for the combined solution. The difference is dependent on the effective length L of the key-chains.

The *node capture resilience* of the combined scheme can be calculated as

$$P_{LinkComprIII} = \sum_{i=0}^{m} \sum_{j=0}^{m} (P_{ChainCompr})^i (1 - (1 - \frac{2m}{|S|})^x)^j \frac{P_{SharedExactly}(i,j)}{P_{LinkEstablishI}} \quad (8)$$

where $i + j \geq q$, $i + j \leq m$.

Figure 6 demonstrates that the combined improvement outperforms the q-composite scheme and the key-chain improvement. E.g., if $q = 2$ and 50 nodes are captured, q-composite scheme scores 4.7%, collision key improvement 2.7%, key-chain improvement 2.5% and the combined improvement 2.2%. The comparison gets even better for the combined improvement as the number of captured nodes grows.

The scheme of Ren et al. [4] provides a slightly better node capture resilience than our combined improvement for a small number of captured nodes. However, as this number grows our combined improvement starts to outperform the Ren's scheme. For $P_{LinkEstablishI} = 0.5$, $q = 2$ and $m = 161$, the turning point is around 125 of captured nodes. Since we were not able to fully reproduce Ren's analytical results (and did not get any response from the contacted authors), we did the comparison only for the parameters used in their paper.

The communication overhead of the shared-key discovery phase, when our combined improvement is used, is dependent on the discovery procedure itself. For some procedures it is similar to the overhead of the basic random key predistribution schemes. E.g., if the pseudo-random predistribution [9] is used, identifiers of keys assigned to a particular node can be calculated from the node ID. These identifiers can carry all the information necessary to discover shared keys – the key's position in a hash-chain and the hash-chain identifier. Additionally, the shared collision key can be figured out through the hash-chain identifiers when these identifiers (assigned to the colliding hash-chains) differ only in the

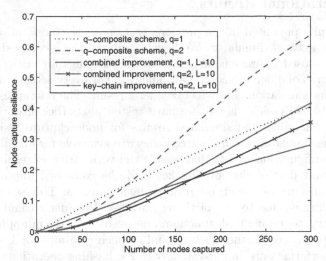

Fig. 6. Node capture resilience of the combined improvement. Key ring size $m = 200$, probability of link key establishment $P_{LinkEstablishI} = 0.33$, effective key-chain length $L = 10$.

Table 1. Probabilities that two nodes share exactly i keys from hash chains and j additional collision keys. Value i is dependent on the row and value j on the column of the table. $P_{LinkEstablishI} = 0.33$, $q = 1$, $m = 200$.

$i\backslash j$	0	1	2	3
0	0.67	0.1344	0.0134	0.0009
1	0.1344	0.0267	0.0026	0.0002
2	0.0134	0.0026	0.0003	0
3	0.0009	0.0002	0	0

least significant bit. Thus the communication overhead only covers transmission of the node IDs. Another advantage of the pseudo-random approach is that the nodes do not need to store their own key identifiers as these can be computed when actually needed.

Another interesting information concerns the composition of link keys established, e.g., what fraction of keys is based solely on the collision keys or solely on the keys from the hash chains. Such information can be calculated using Equation 1. The equation gives us the probability that two nodes share exactly i keys from hash chains and j additional collision keys. The sample probabilities for $P_{LinkEstablishI} = 0.33$, $q = 1$, $m = 200$ and different combinations of i and j are summarized in Table 1. E.g., the probability that a link key is based on exactly two keys from hash chains and a single collision key is given in the row 2, column 1. The probability that two nodes do not share any key is in the row 0, column 0. Note that the table is symmetric, i.e., both types of keys are used with an equal probability. The table is not complete, yet the probabilities of other combinations of i and j are negligible.

6   Computational Results

Analytical results presented in the previous sections were computationally verified using our network simulator. We have simulated the q-composite scheme and all the proposed improvements using various settings for critical parameters and networks of different sizes and topologies. For every setting, an average over 10 different simulation runs was taken as a result. The reference simulated network had 10,000 nodes, though we have tested also other sizes. It showed that obtained analytical and simulated results for node capture resilience are consistent. The simulator and its source codes are available for download along with sample configuration scripts that enable the verification of results[1].

The important part of the collision key and the combined improvement is a search for collisions of the cryptographic hash function. This search can be efficiently performed due to the birthday paradox. In order to find an N-bit collision in a cryptographic hash function, one needs to perform approximately $2^{\frac{N}{2}}$ hashing operations. Furthermore, to find c^2 such collisions for $1 \leq c \leq 2^{\frac{N}{2}}$, one needs to perform "only" approximately $c \cdot 2^{\frac{N}{2}}$ hashing operations [7]. Thus, once the first collision is found, additional collisions can be found increasingly efficiently. If we assume 80-bit keys are used, to create the key pool for $|S| = 2^{16}$ one needs to find 2^{15} collisions which requires approximately $2^{47.5}$ hashing operations. This can be reached with a moderate computational power. Note that 80-bit keys can be still considered as secure and appropriate for use in wireless sensor networks as attacker needs to try approximately 2^{79} values to brute force the key.

We have conducted our collision search using the parallel collision search method proposed by van Oorschot and Wiener [10]. This method is based on Hellman's time-memory trade-off approach and calculates long hash-chains. We have searched for 80-bit collisions of the SHA-256 hash function, 80-bit values were taken as an input and 80 most significant bits of the SHA-256 function as an output. We used the Gladman's implementation[2] of the hash function. The aggregate time to find over 5,000 suitable collisions was approximately 19,000 hours on a single 3GHz CPU core. The search was distributed using the BOINC infrastructure [11] to around 1,000 CPU cores so the search took less than a day. Approximately 2^{23} hash chains with an average length of 2^{24} were computed, thus about 2^{47} hashing operations were performed. The time spent and resources invested are moderate and within reasonable bounds since this procedure takes place only once in a network lifetime. The speed of the search could be significantly increased using GPUs or special purpose hardware like FPGA.

7   Conclusions

The key distribution stands among the most critical security issues for wireless sensor networks. In this paper, we proposed and analyzed two improvements

---

[1] http://www.fi.muni.cz/~xsvenda/papers/SecureComm2012/

[2] http://gladman.plushost.co.uk/oldsite/cryptography_technology/sha/index.php

(and their combination) of the random key predistribution schemes. The first improvement exploits limited length collisions in secure hash functions to increase the probability of two nodes sharing a key. The second improvement introduces hash chains into the key pool construction to directly enhance the node capture resilience. Both these improvements can be further combined to bring the best performance. Our analytical results were supported by simulations.

Our improvements are particularly advantageous for networks where the attacker manages to capture a significant number of nodes. However, the benefits of our improvements are not limited to the basic random key predistribution schemes. The improvements could be employed, e.g., in the deterministic or hybrid approach proposed in [5]. We leave the investigation of such combination for the future work. Another challenge is to analyze the improvements face to face with a clever attacker who does not capture the nodes in a random fashion. Yet the impact of such an attacker could be limited by a deterministic selection of keys to be placed into key rings.

Acknowledgements. We are grateful to the anonymous reviewers and to Luděk Smolík for their suggestions that improved the paper and to Tobiáš Smolka for his help with the BOINC infrastructure. This work was supported by the Czech research project VG20102014031, programme BV II/2 - VS. The first author is additionally supported by the project GD102/09/H042 "Mathematical and Engineering Approaches to Developing Reliable and Secure Concurrent and Distributed Computer Systems" of the Czech Science Foundation. The second and third authors are also supported by the research center Institute for Theoretical Computer Science (ITI), project No. P202/12/G061. The access to computing and storage facilities owned by parties and projects contributing to the National Grid Infrastructure MetaCentrum, provided under the programme "Projects of Large Infrastructure for Research, Development, and Innovations" (LM2010005) is highly appreciated/acknowledged.

References

1. Eschenauer, L., Gligor, V.D.: A key-management scheme for distributed sensor networks. In: 9th ACM Conference on Computer and Communications Security, CCS 2002, pp. 41–47. ACM, New York (2002)
2. Chan, H., Perrig, A., Song, D.: Random key predistribution schemes for sensor networks. In: Symposium on Security and Privacy, pp. 197–213. IEEE (2003)
3. Švenda, P., Sekanina, L., Matyáš, V.: Evolutionary design of secrecy amplification protocols for wireless sensor networks. In: 2nd ACM Conference on Wireless Network Security, pp. 225–236. ACM, New York (2009)
4. Ren, K., Zeng, K., Lou, W.: A new approach for random key pre-distribution in large-scale wireless sensor networks. Wireless Communications and Mobile Computing 6(3), 307–318 (2006)
5. Camtepe, S.A., Yener, B.: Combinatorial design of key distribution mechanisms for wireless sensor networks. IEEE/ACM Transactions on Networking 15(2), 346–358 (2007)

6. Xiao, Y., Rayi, V.K., Sun, B., Du, X., Hu, F., Galloway, M.: A survey of key management schemes in wireless sensor networks. Computer Communications 30(11-12), 2314–2341 (2007)
7. Rivest, R.L., Shamir, A.: PayWord and MicroMint: Two Simple Micropayment Schemes. In: Crispo, B. (ed.) Security Protocols 1996. LNCS, vol. 1189, pp. 69–87. Springer, Heidelberg (1997)
8. Leighton, T., Micali, S.: Secret-Key Agreement without Public-Key Cryptography. In: Stinson, D.R. (ed.) CRYPTO 1993. LNCS, vol. 773, pp. 456–479. Springer, Heidelberg (1994)
9. Di Pietro, R., Mancini, L.V., Mei, A.: Random key-assignment for secure wireless sensor networks. In: 1st ACM Workshop on Security of Ad Hoc and Sensor Networks (SANS 2003), pp. 62–71. ACM, New York (2003)
10. van Oorschot, P.C., Wiener, M.J.: Parallel collision search with cryptanalytic applications. Journal of Cryptology 12(1), 1–28 (1999)
11. Anderson, D.P.: BOINC: A system for public-resource computing and storage. In: 5th IEEE/ACM International Workshop on Grid Computing, pp. 4–10. IEEE Computer Society (2004)

Appendix: Proofs and Calculations

In this appendix we provide proofs of the selected equations and also justify the following statement that relates to the Definition 1. The formula in Definition 1 expresses the number of all possible key rings of size m selected from a key pool of size $|S|$ where no colliding key pair is present in the key rings.

Proof. We have $|S|$ possibilities how to select the first key for a key ring. After this selection, we mark the selected key and its colliding key off the key pool. Thus we have only $|S| - 2$ possibilities how to select the second key. The keys are selected in this fashion until we select the m-th key for which only $|S| - 2 \cdot (m - 1)$ possibilities remain. Since the order in which the keys were selected is not important, we divide the result by the number of permutations $m!$.   □

Proof (Equation 1). We have $\left\{ {|S| \atop m} \right\}$ possibilities how to select m keys into a key ring for any given node. Given these m keys, we have $\binom{m}{i}$ ways to select the i shared keys. Similarly, once these i shared keys have been picked, we have $\binom{m-i}{j}$ ways to select j shared collision keys that do not result from the i shared keys. Finally, we have to pick the remaining $m - i - j$ keys for the second key ring that are not the keys from the first key ring nor their colliding counterparts. Hence we pick them from the key pool without m colliding key pairs ($2m$ keys). This can be done by $\left\{ {|S| - 2m \atop m - i - j} \right\}$ ways. Thus the number of key ring assignments for two nodes such that they share exactly i keys and are able to calculate exactly j collision keys excluding the collision keys resulting from the i shared keys is $\left\{ {|S| \atop m} \right\} \binom{m}{i} \binom{m-i}{j} \left\{ {|S| - 2m \atop m - i - j} \right\}$. The total number of key ring assignments for any two nodes is $\left\{ {|S| \atop m} \right\}^2$. Thus the resulting probability is the fraction of these two values.   □

Proof (Equation 3). We follow and extend the proof from [2]. Since every node contains m keys out of $|S|$, the probability that an attacker obtains a particular key after a single node is captured is $\frac{m}{|S|}$. The probability that the attacker does not obtain the particular key after x nodes have been captured is thus $(1 - \frac{m}{|S|})^x$. Finally, the probability that the attacker compromises a link key that is based on exactly i shared keys is $(1 - (1 - \frac{m}{|S|})^x)^i$.

Similarly, the probability that the attacker obtains a particular collision key after a single node is captured is $\frac{2m}{|S|}$, because we have only $\frac{|S|}{2}$ distinct collision keys and every node is able to calculate exactly m such keys. Hence, the probability that the attacker compromises a link key based on exactly j collision keys is $(1 - (1 - \frac{2m}{|S|})^x)^j$.

Assuming a link is secured with a link key, the probability that the link key is based on exactly i shared keys and j collision keys is $\frac{P_{SharedExactly}(i,j)}{P_{LinkEstablishI}}$. $\qquad\square$

Proof (Equation 6). Assume that two nodes were assigned keys from a given key-chain, then the probability that they establish i-th key of the key-chain as a shared key is $\frac{2 \cdot i - 1}{L^2}$. Furthermore, the probability that i-th key of a given key-chain was compromised after a random node was captured is $\frac{m}{|S|} \frac{i}{L}$. The probability that an attacker has compromised i-th key of a given key-chain after he captured x nodes is $1 - (1 - \frac{m}{|S|} \frac{i}{L})^x$. $\qquad\square$

A Detection Mechanism for SMS Flooding Attacks in Cellular Networks

Eun Kyoung Kim, Patrick McDaniel, and Thomas La Porta

Dept. of Computer Science and Engineering
Pennsylvania State University, PA, USA
ekkim@cse.psu.edu

Abstract. In recent years, cellular networks have been reported to be susceptible targets for Distributed Denial of Service (DDoS) attacks due to their limited resources. One potential powerful DDoS attack in cellular networks is a SMS flooding attack. Previous research has demonstrated that SMS-capable cellular networks are vulnerable to a SMS flooding attack in which a sufficient rate of SMS messages is sent to saturate the control channels in target areas. We propose a novel detection algorithm which identifies a SMS flooding attack based on the reply rate to messages sent by a handset. We further propose a mitigation technique to reduce the blocking rate caused by the attack. Our simulation results show that the false positive and false negative rates of our detection algorithm are low even when the attack traffic is blended with flash crowd traffic and/or the attack traffic mimics flash crowd traffic, and that the blocking rate is successfully reduced through the mitigation technique.

Keywords: SMS flooding attack, DDoS attack, flash crowd, anomaly detection, modeling, cellular network.

1 Introduction

Text messages continue to grow as the most popular data service of cellular networks. The total number of text messages sent globally has tripled over the past three years to reach 6.1 trillion in 2010. In other words, people around the world are sending 200,000 text messages every second [1]. In the U.S. 66% of mobile subscribers use text messaging service and over 600 text messages on average are sent or received monthly by a subscriber [2].

With this growing popularity of text messages, the reliability of Short Message Service (SMS) is becoming increasingly important. However, previous studies have shown that the control channels in the cellular networks may be a bottleneck for both SMS and voice services due to their limited capacity and shared nature. The stand alone dedicated control channel (SDCCH) is the most vulnerable since it is used for call setup and location updates as well as SMS [3,4,5]. An abnormal increase of SMS traffic may result in high occupancy of the SDCCH and high blocking rate of text messages and voice calls threatening the reliability of cellular networks.

A.D. Keromytis and R. Di Pietro (Eds.): SecureComm 2012, LNICST 106, pp. 76–93, 2013.

There are two kinds of the events that may cause a sudden increase in the SMS traffic volume in the cellular network: flash crowds and DDoS attacks. Flash crowds are an unusual burst of legitimate traffic produced by an increased number of users; these are frequently observed during special occasions [6,7]. For example, the volume of text messages sent on the New Year's Eve increases each year [8] and the resulting congestion causes lost and delayed text messages [9].

DDoS attacks through SMS are another cause of abnormal increase of SMS traffic. Typical SMS attacks aim to degrade target networks by depleting the control channel resources with a flood of SMS messages. In previous research, the feasibility of a SMS flooding attack was proved [10], and mitigation techniques were proposed [11]. However, they do not address how to detect SMS flooding attacks.

In this paper, we propose a novel anomaly detection mechanism that identifies malicious SMS flooding traffic causing intentional congestion in cellular networks. The difficulty is that the attack traffic mimics flash crowd traffic to circumvent detection. As the traffic behavior in flash crowds and flooding attacks are very similar, we need to find some features that can be used to distinguish them to reduce the false positive rate of our detection algorithm. Due to the lack of attack traffic traces, we analyze normal SMS traffic to infer the difference between flash crowds and flooding attacks. We find through the analysis that a mobile user replies to a message from a close friend with high probability, and is unlikely to answer a message from an unknown number. Therefore, we infer that if the reply rate for a handset which sends messages into a congested network is lower than a threshold, it is likely to be a malicious handset attempting to deplete the control channels.

We also develop a mitigation technique which classifies SMS traffic as normal, suspicious, or malicious and separates the traffic into three distinct queues with decreasing priorities to reduce the blocking caused by attack traffic and allow for fast identification of malicious handsets. The blocking of the normal handsets' traffic is efficiently diminished since a higher priority for obtaining the limited control channels is given to the normal handsets rather than the suspicious and malicious handsets.

Our simulation results show that our baseline algorithm performs the detection of unmixed flooding traffic with a very low false positive rate. The detection of attacks occurring in a flash crowd event and/or mimicking flash crowds is much more challenging. The mitigation technique, however, reduces the blocking rate of the messages from normal handsets successfully.

We compare our results to those of SMS-Watchdog, the most similar algorithm to ours in the literature, and show that we are more effective at distinguishing between attack traffic and naturally occurring flash crowd traffic.

The remainder of the paper is organized as follows. In Section 2, we discuss related works. The characteristics of the SMS network architecture and the different types of SMS traffic are introduced in Section 3. Our detection algorithm follows in Section 4. We evaluate our detection algorithm and mitigation technique through simulation in Section 5 and conclude in Section 6.

2   Related Work

The increasing popularity of short messages in cellular networks has led to much research on SMS capacity. In [3], it was shown that severe congestion may occur when the SDCCH channels are exhausted as they are shared by SMS, call setup and location updates. Agarwal et al. [5] conducted capacity analysis using a queueing model to show that the SDCCHs can be a bottleneck which increases the blocking probability of SMS as well as voice calls during elevated message loads. The possibility of an attack exploiting the limited and shared property of the SDCCHs was addressed in [4].

Enck et al. [10] demonstrated that SMS-capable cellular networks are vulnerable to a SMS flooding attack where a sufficient rate of SMS messages is sent from the Internet to local cell phones in order to saturate the SDCCH capacity. Furthermore, Traynor et al. [11] evaluated the performance of this attack by modeling and simulation and proposed mitigation techniques. However, they do not address how to detect flooding attacks. We propose a detection algorithm to identify SMS flooding attacks and a mitigation technique to lower the blocking rates at the control channels.

Previous research conducted by Yan et al. [12] proposed a SMS-related attack detection scheme named SMS-Watchdog that detects abnormal activities of SMS users by checking deviations from their normal social behaviors. Their approach is applicable to SMS flooding attacks because the attacker's behavior may be changed from the behavioral profile trained before the attack starts.

However, SMS-Watchdog gives false alarms when a flash crowd event occurs because the behavioral characteristics of normal SMS users are changed during flash crowd events. On the contrary, our algorithm can distinguish flooding attacks and flash crowds reducing the false alarms.

As DoS attacks and flash crowds are the two major concerns threatening the reliability and stability of the Internet, many studies on how to discriminate them have been conducted in the IP networks [6,13,14,15]. However, the direct application of these solutions is unsuitable because the IP flow and text messages of flash crowds have different properties. For example, the flash crowd traffic in IP networks is destined to a small number of servers while the messages exchanged in flash crowd events are scattered over many users in cellular networks.

We characterize flash crowd traffic and attack traffic based on the analysis of normal SMS traffic. [7] provides us with the statistics of flash crowd traffic in cellular networks. We obtain real SMS traces of three service providers from [16] and analyze them to infer the difference between a recipient's behavior to normal messages and attack messages.

3   SMS Communication Characterization

3.1   Network Characterization

The basic network structure of SMS is depicted in Fig. 1. A mobile handset B can receive a text message from one of two sources - another mobile handset A or

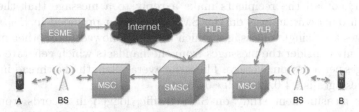

Fig. 1. SMS network structure

External Short Messaging Entity (ESME). An ESME is typically a non-mobile entity that submits messages to, or receives messages from a Short Messaging Service Center (SMSC) via the Internet. A text message from either is delivered to a recipient through a SMSC, a Mobile Switching Center (MSC), and a Base Station (BS).

A SMSC is responsible for storing and forwarding short messages to a terminating MSC. It obtains routing information from the Home Location Register (HLR) to locate the proper MSC. The MSC performs the switching functions of the system and delivers SMS messages to the specific mobile subscriber by retrieving the subscriber's location from the Visitor Location Register (VLR). A MSC can store the messages in a queue for a short time during which it retransmits the messages if acknowledgements are not received within a specific time. If a message is not successfully delivered to the mobile station after the maximum number of retransmission attempts, the MSC sends an error message to the SMSC [17,18].

Between a BS and a mobile handset, a message is delivered via the air interface using control channels. First, a BS transmits a paging request with an identifier on the Paging Channel (PCH). When a mobile handset hears its identifier, it responds to the BS on the Random Access Channel (RACH). Then, the BS assigns a SDCCH to the handset. The handset authenticates with the BS and receives the text message via the SDCCH. As a SDCCH is used for call setup and location updates in addition to SMS transfer, it may be flooded by an increase of SMS requests blocking both voice and SMS communication.

3.2   Normal Traffic Characterization

There have been prior efforts on characterizing normal SMS traffic patterns. Some researchers analyze SMS traces collected from a nationwide cellular carrier with more than 20 million subscribers over a period of three weeks [19,7]. They present thread-level characteristics in addition to the SMS message-level characteristics, where a thread is defined as messages exchanged between the same two users within a predefined timeout period. According to their analysis with 10 minutes as a timeout, the number of messages in each thread, or the thread length, is 4.9 on average and the average thread duration is 8 minutes. That implies that the average interval between receiving and responding to a message is 2 minutes.

However, not all the recipients make a reply to a message that they have received. In our own analysis on the SMS trace data provided in [16], 22% of the messages are "single" messages which are not followed by another message, where we only consider the messages from the handsets which generate at least ten messages per a day on average. Thus, the average length of a thread including "single" messages is $1 * 0.22 + 4.9 * 0.78 \approx 4$.

Another measurement study on SMS traffic, logged in records from three different companies over a one month period, examines the distribution of the intervals between messages belonging to one thread [16]. The empirical results show that the inter-arrival time and the waiting time of normal messages have power-law distribution within a thread duration and a new thread is initiated by an exponential distribution. The arrival rates of calls and SMS messages in a single sector per second and the service rates of calls and SMS messages at SDCCH are also known as shown in Table 1.

Table 1. System Variables and Parameters

λ_{call}	Arrival rate of voice calls	0.25 calls/sector/sec [11]
λ_{SMS}	Arrival rate of SMS msgs	0.7 msgs/sector/sec [11]
$\mu^{-1}_{SDCCH,call}$	Service rate of voice calls at SDCCH	1.5 sec [20]
$\mu^{-1}_{SDCCH,SMS}$	Service rate of SMS msgs at SDCCH	4 sec [4]

Flash crowd traffic shows different characteristics from regular SMS traffic. The traffic looks anomalous because cellular networks suffer a sudden increase of SMS traffic in a flash crowd event. For example, the volume of messages exchanged during the New Year's Eve in India reaches almost eightfold the normal traffic level [7]. Such an increase in traffic is affected more by an increase in the number of SMS users sending and receiving messages rather than an increment of messages per user. Therefore, the SMS communication in a flash crowd is different from a regular SMS communication in that the increased volume of traffic is caused by an increased number of users without a change in the number of messages sent by a user.

We also observe that 60% of handsets participating in a flash crowd do not send any messages in three days before the event [7]. These new participants have a higher probability to be mistakenly classified as malicious as they have weak prior relationship with legitimate recipients.

Even though flash crowd traffic may slow down the message delivery or even cause some messages to be discarded because of congestion [9], it should be serviced as legitimate because it naturally occurs from normal handsets. Therefore, we develop an anomaly detection algorithm to distinguish malicious attack traffic from flash crowd traffic even when they are intermingled and malicious attack traffic mimics flash crowd traffic to avoid the detection.

3.3   Attack Traffic Characterization

Previous studies on SMS network capacity have proven that the SDCCH can be a bottleneck in cellular networks due to its limited capacity and shared characteristics [3,5]. This makes a SMS flooding attack feasible because an attacker can paralyze cellular communications in a certain area by overloading SDCCHs in that area. Such an attack will be performed by sending enough messages to potential target lists which can be created by several efficient methods [10].

We assume that an attacker has the capability to compromise a number of handsets so that they can send attack traffic under the control of the attacker without any awareness of the owners. Even though we only consider a mobile-to-mobile attack in this paper, a SMS flooding attack using bulk messaging services can be detected if we cast each ESME of bulk messaging providers as an attacking mobile handset in the algorithm.

Furthermore, we assume that the attacker is intelligent enough to mimic the behavior of normal users in a flash crowd. The attacker can compromise a large number of handsets and make them generate bogus messages with seemingly normal rates so that the aggregated traffic saturates the SDCCHs in a target area. The attacker can even launch the attack purposely during a flash crowd event to reduce the probability of being detected.

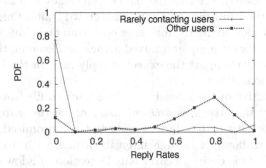

Fig. 2. Probability distribution function of reply rates

Consequently, a flooding attack and a flash crowd cannot be easily distinguished by the traffic characteristics determined by senders' behavior such as the total volume of generated messages, message generation rate per handset and contents of the messages. However, we infer that the recipients' behaviors for the messages sent by a normal user in a flash crowd event and an attacker disguised as a normal user are distinguishable.

We suppose that a user who sends out only one message to a recipient during over a one month period represents an unknown or unfamiliar sender to the recipient. Through the analysis of the SMS trace given in [16], we find that the reply rates for the unfamiliar senders and the other normal users have distinguishable distributions as seen in Fig. 2 with a 15% and 62% average value, respectively.

Since an attacker is an unknown originator from a recipient's point of view, it is expected to have a similar distribution of reply rates to that for an unfamiliar sender. Thus, we can distinguish an attack handset from a normal one based on the reply rates regardless of whether the attacker mimics a normal user's message sending characteristics.

4 Detection Algorithm

4.1 Attack Model

The purpose of a SMS flooding attack is to paralyze the cellular network in a specific area by overloading the SDCCHs. In this paper, the target of the attack is a sector served by the BS of a MSC. The handsets serviced in the target area are called local handsets and the handsets outside the targeted area are remote handsets. The incoming attack occurs from remote handsets while the outgoing attack is performed by the local handsets. Because handsets are authenticated, while they can be infected with a virus that causes them to launch an attack, their addresses cannot be spoofed.

The attack can be classified as a *mixed attack* or *unmixed attack* according to whether it occurs in concurrence with a flash crowd or not. An attacker may launch a mixed attack to accelerate the attack's efficiency and avoid detection by having the attack traffic intermingled with flash crowd traffic. Our base algorithm aims at successfully identifying the messages sent from malicious handsets among the intermingled traffic even under a mixed attack and keeping the false positive rate low by adaptively changing the expected reply rate for the benign messages during the congestion.

From the perspective of the intensity of the attack traffic from a single handset, we can classify the attack as *high-intensity* or *low-intensity*. The attacker can choose low-intensity with a large number of compromised handsets mimicking a flash crowd; however, a high intensity attack with a small number of compromised handsets is easier to carry out. Detection of a low intensity attack takes more time as the interval between attack messages sent by a handset and the number of attackers are larger. However, the blocking rate for the normal handsets decreases efficiently through our mitigation technique even when the false negative rate is not low.

Consequently, we carry out a performance evaluation for four types of attack - 1) *unmixed attack with high intensity*, 2) *unmixed attack with low intensity*, 3) *mixed attack with high intensity*, and 4) *mixed attack with low intensity*. Intuitively, the detection of the mixed attack with low intensity is the most challenging while the unmixed attack traffic with high intensity is detected with the shortest delay.

4.2 Algorithm for Identifying Attackers

We deploy a detector on each MSC to detect anomalies in air interfaces under the coverage of a MSC. Because we make use of the reply rate of mobile handsets

---

Alg. 1 : Monitor Threads

1: **for** each message M observed in W **do**
2:    **if** M is an outgoing message from L to R **then**
3:       **if** $T = (L, R)$ exists **then**
4:          Increase L_s by 1
5:       **else if** $T = (R, L)$ exists **then**
6:          Increase R_r by 1
7:       **else**
8:          Create $T = (L, R)$
9:          Increase L_s by 1
10:      **end if**
11:   **end if**
12:   **if** M is an incoming message from R to L **then**
13:       **if** $T = (R, L)$ exists **then**
14:          **if** M is delivered to L **then**
15:             Increase R_s by 1
16:          **end if**
17:       **else if** $T = (L, R)$ exists **then**
18:          Increase L_r by 1
19:       **else**
20:          **if** M is delivered to L **then**
21:             Create $T = (R, L)$
22:             Increase R_s by 1
23:          **end if**
24:       **end if**
25:   **end if**
26: **end for**

Table 2. Variables for Alg. 1

M	SMS message collected during W
T	Message thread represented by a pair of (*sender, receiver*)
L/R	Local/remote handset
L_s/R_s	The number of sent messages from L/R
L_r/R_r	The number of replies to L/R

for distinguishing benign and malicious traffic, the detector gathers (sender ID, recipient ID, timestamp) information of both outgoing and incoming messages. At the end of every time window W with duration ω, the detector looks into all the information collected during the time window and creates message threads and updates the number of sent messages and the corresponding replies for a handset as shown in Alg. 1 with the variables in Table 2.

Note that for incoming messages, only a message delivered to the destination successfully can increase R_s. Otherwise, the reply rates will be underestimated.

A detector contains an analyzer which identifies the attackers sending overloading messages. Upon the detection of congestion, the analyzer is activated and

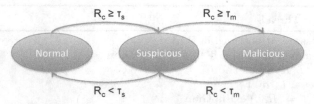

Fig. 3. SMS state transition diagram

calculates the reply rate threshold under normal network conditions, θ, considering the upper bound on the expected false positive rate for the threshold. Let X be a random variable of reply rates with finite expected value μ and non-zero variance σ^2. Given the arbitrary distribution of reply rates in the normal traffic observed before the congestion, the false positive rate is bounded to $\frac{1}{1+k^2}$ if we choose $\mu - k\sigma$ as the threshold, and consider a reply rate of less than that value as an anomaly, which is supported by the one-sided *Chebyshev's inequality*:

$$Pr(X \leq \mu - k\sigma) \leq \tfrac{1}{1+k^2}.$$

Accordingly, by setting $k = 1$ and $\theta = \mu - \sigma$, the false positive rate does not exceed 0.5. To limit the upper bound of false positive rate to 0.2, we choose $k = 2$ and $\theta = \mu - 2\sigma$. Even though a larger k and smaller θ guarantee a lower expected false positive rate, this might cause a lower detection probability and longer delay in return. The uncertainty of this effect is caused by the fact that we do not know distribution of the reply rates for malicious handsets a priori, although we expect them to be lower than that for normal handsets. In order to remove this uncertainty and resolve the trade-off, we choose $k = 1$ and $\theta = \mu - \sigma$ to increase the detection probability and reduce the detection delay, and use a scoring-based technique [21] to reduce the false positives by confirming the anomalies as attacks only when the anomaly score exceeds a threshold.

Note that θ is based on the measured distribution of reply rates during normal network conditions before the congestion occurs. The reply rate from the handsets in the area under attack will be decreased from its normal rate because the congestion in the attack area. This congestion will cause messages to be blocked and thus, send no reply. Therefore, the reply rate threshold for successfully delivered messages from a remote handset, τ_r, should be dynamically changed to reflect the blocking rate caused by congestion. As the ratio of the number of unblocked replied messages to that of replies in uncongested network is $(1 - B_{avg})$, we set τ_r to $\theta * (1 - B_{avg})$. We use B_{avg}, the moving average of blocking rate for ω_B to smooth the change of the blocking rate.

The anomaly score representing the degree to which a handset is considered an anomaly or attacker is initially set to 0. The score increases if the current reply rate is lower than θ for a normal message under current network conditions and decreases otherwise. When the anomaly score for a handset reaches a threshold designated for suspicious handsets, τ_s, the analyzer marks the handset as suspicious. If the score keeps increasing to a threshold for malicious handsets, τ_m, the handset is deemed malicious. As the analysis progresses, the score may

Alg. 2 : Identify Attackers

1: calculate θ
2: $\tau_r = \theta * (1 - B_{avg})$
3: $R_c = 0$
4: **for** each handset R in $T = (R, L)$ **do**
5:　　**if** R send or receive a message **then**
6:　　　　$R_{rr} = \frac{R_r}{R_s}$
7:　　　　**if** $R_{rr} < \tau_r$ **then**
8:　　　　　　$R_c ++$
9:　　　　**else**
10:　　　　　　$R_c = max(R_c --, 0)$
11:　　　　**end if**
12:　　　　**if** $R_c \geq \tau_m$ **then**
13:　　　　　　Mark R as malicious
14:　　　　**else if** $R_c \geq \tau_s$ **then**
15:　　　　　　Mark R as suspicious
16:　　　　**else**
17:　　　　　　Mark R as normal
18:　　　　**end if**
19:　　**end if**
20: **end for**

Table 3. Variables for Alg. 2

R_{rr}	Reply rate for R
R_c	Anomaly score representing the likelihood that R is an attacker
B_{avg}	Moving average of blocking rates for duration ω_B
θ	Reply rate threshold for normal handsets in normal network condition
τ_r	Reply rate threshold for normal local/remote handsets in congested network
τ_s	Anomaly score threshold for suspicious handsets
τ_m	Anomaly score threshold for malicious handsets

go lower and higher than the each threshold causing the change of the status of a handset as shown in Fig. 3.

The algorithm for an incoming attack is summarized in Alg. 2 and the variables used in Alg. 2 are presented in Table 3.

4.3 Mitigation Technique

We devise a 3-queue mitigation mechanism in which each kind of traffic classified by the detector - normal, suspicious, and malicious traffic - is served by one of three different queues with different weights. Weighted Fair Queueing [22] is used for scheduling messages in the queues.

Normal traffic is processed with a weight of 2 while suspicious traffic has a weight of 1. The malicious traffic is placed in the lowest priority queue and is only served when the two higher priority queues are empty. The blocking rate for the messages from normal handsets is efficiently reduced by prioritizing the process of the normal messages while reducing the number of requests for the wireless control channels by delaying or refusing service for suspicious or malicious handsets.

5   Simulation Results

In this section we evaluate our algorithm. We also compare it with the most similar related work, called SMS-Watchdog, and show that we achieve better results for the challenging circumstances.

5.1   Simulation Settings

To evaluate the performance of our algorithms, we implement a simulator based on the characteristics of SMS communication and the proposed algorithms Alg. 1 and 2. We explain the settings in our simulation.

Network Settings. Assuming a SMS network with the network components in Fig. 1, our detector modules are deployed at the MSCs because they can provide all the information - (1) the blocking rate of SDCCHs in each sector, and (2) (sender ID, recipient ID, timestamp) of messages needed to detect the attacks targeting the SDCCHs in sectors controlled by the MSCs.

The message queues for mitigation techniques are implemented in the BS. The forwarded messages from the MSC have indicators to which queue they belong. If the corresponding queue is full, the MSC retries the delivery. The maximum number of attempts is set to 2. After that, an error message returns to the SMSC and the message is deleted from the MSC.

Parameter Settings. In Alg. 1, the interval of analysis on message threads, ω, needs to be set considering the tradeoff between timely detection and computational overhead. In our simulation, we set $\omega = 10$ seconds because it is short enough to capture each message of one thread in each time window and long enough not to overload the detector. We set the value of blocking rate acceptable in cellular networks, β, to 1%. If the average blocking rate for ω is greater than β, an analyzer is activated to identify the attackers.

In Alg. 2, the duration for the calculation of the moving average of blocking rates, ω_B, is set to 120 seconds. Since the average waiting time for a reply is 120 seconds, we expect the previous message to have been transmitted 120 seconds prior to the message just received. Therefore, the average blocking rate for the last 120 seconds affects the reply rate of the message.

Traffic Settings. We simulate 24 hours of SMS communication. Local and remote handsets constantly transmit regular SMS traffic during the simulation. The regular messages are submitted by 4800 handsets at 0.7 msgs/sector/sec rate according to the normal traffic characteristics.

Attack traffic is emitted for one hour from 23 to 24 hours. The reply rates for normal handsets observed for 23 hours before the attack prevent the detector from misclassifying the normal handsets as malicious handsets due to the transient low reply rates during the congestion. The longer training period builds a stronger "send-reply" relationship among normal users making the discrimination between the normal and malicious messages easier.

The aggregated volume of the attack traffic is 8 times more than the value of regular traffic. For the mixed attack, flash crowd traffic fourfold the normal traffic is generated in addition to the attack traffic.

5.2   Performance Evaluation

We evaluate our algorithm using several fundamental metrics: false positive rate (FPR), false negative rate (FNR), and blocking rate. The false positive rate is the fraction of benign handsets that are misjudged as malicious over all benign handsets. The false negative rate is the fraction of malicious handsets that are mistakenly judged as benign over all malicious handsets. The blocking rate is the portion of messages which are blocked due to insufficient channel resources.

We show the performance of our baseline detection mechanism which identifies the malicious handsets but does not resolve the congestion, and the performance of the detector with a mitigation technique which reduces the blocking in the air interface by placing the identified attackers in a low priority queue. The algorithm performs significantly better with mitigation in places because malicious handsets are removed from the traffic flow making it easier to detect remaining malicious handsets.

Without Mitigation Techniques. We first examine the FNR and FPR of the baseline algorithm for unmixed incoming traffic with high intensity with $\tau_m = 1$, 2, and 3. The results are presented in Fig. 4a and 4b respectively for the time elapsed after the start of the attack. The FNR decreases more quickly for a smaller τ_m because the attackers' score, R_c, exceeds the threshold, τ_m, in a shorter time. When $\tau_m = 1$, however, the resulting FPR is over 5% on average whereas for $\tau_m = 2$ and 3, FPR is reliably low throughout the attack period. This is because the attack likelihood score for a normal handset which has not exchanged messages with recipients before the attack turns to 1 when the detector sees the first incoming message and exceeds the threshold in the case that $\tau_m = 1$.

Our algorithm operates even in more challenging situations. When the attacker generates a high intensity attack traffic in the middle of a flash crowd event, it is difficult to distinguish malicious traffic from benign traffic because more than a half of the benign handsets in flash crowds have not participated in conversational message threads prior to the event. However, even with the mixed traffic, our baseline algorithm identifies the attackers based on the difference between reply rates of malicious and benign messages.

Fig. 5a and 5b show more clearly that the FPR increases as τ_m decreases and the FNR increases as τ_m increases. When $\tau_m = 1$ or 2, the FPR increases to

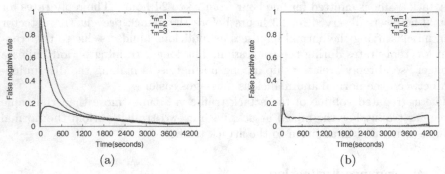

Fig. 4. (a) FNR and (b) FPR of unmixed attack traffic with high intensity without a mitigation scheme

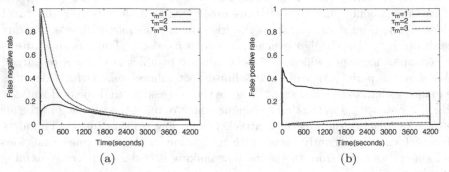

Fig. 5. (a) FNR and (b) FPR of mixed attack traffic with high intensity without a mitigation scheme

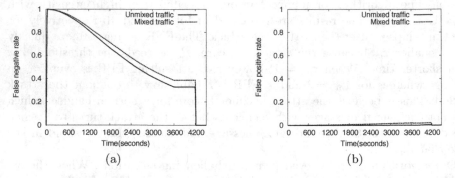

Fig. 6. (a) FNR and (b) FPR of two kinds of attack traffic with low intensity without a mitigation scheme

a high value even though the FNR decreases quickly. The dramatic increase of FPR for $\tau_m = 1$ is caused by the sudden increase of new SMS users in flash crowds. Thus, we set τ_m to 3 considering trade-off between the FPR and the FNR.

With $\tau_m = 3$, the performance of mixed and unmixed attacks with low-intensity is shown in Fig. 6. The detection of the attacks is carried out slower than the high-intensity attacks, but the false positive rates are very close to those of the corresponding high-intensity attacks. Our observation is that the intensity of attack messages initiated from a handset determines how fast the attackers can be detected and the ratio of messages from new active normal users during the attack determines the accuracy of the detection. The strength of our detection algorithm is low false positive rates even in the extreme case of the mixed traffic with low intensity even though the detection of the attacking handsets is inherently slow due to the low arrival rate of the attack messages.

With Mitigation Techniques. Our detection algorithm identifies the attacking handsets but cannot resolve the blocking caused by the attack messages. We devise a 3-queue mitigation mechanism which places the three kinds of traffic - normal, suspicious, and malicious traffic - classified by the detection algorithm into the corresponding queues and schedules each messages using Weighted Fair Queueing [22]. By providing normal messages with more wireless channel resources, the blocking rate for normal messages is efficiently reduced.

For message classification, we need to determine the proper value of τ_s for $\tau_m = 3$. The attack likelihood scores for all incoming messages after the detection starts are initially 0. A handset which has not established message threads with a recipient before the attack is likely to have 0 as a reply rate and 1 as the attack likelihood score at the first classification process. So, if we set τ_s to 1, the handset is classified as suspicious. With τ_s set to 2, the handset is still regarded as normal.

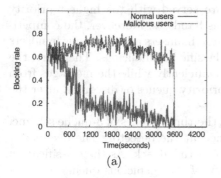 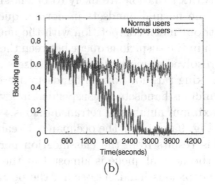

(a)   (b)

Fig. 7. Blocking rates for mixed attack traffic with low intensity when a mitigation technique is applied with (a) $\tau_s=1$ and (b) $\tau_s=2$

We determine the proper value for τ_s taking into account blocking rate as the blocking rate is the ultimate measure of the performance of the mitigation system. We show in Fig. 7 the blocking rate for the mixed attack with low intensity when the mitigation technique is applied. The blocking is mitigated most efficiently with $\tau_s = 1$, from 60% to 20% in approximately 20 minutes. Therefore, we set τ_s and τ_m to 1 and 3, respectively.

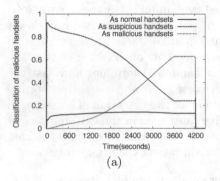 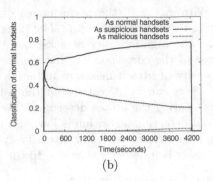

       (a)   (b)

Fig. 8. Classification of (a) malicious and (b) normal handset for mixed attack traffic with low intensity with a mitigation scheme

Fig. 8a and 8b gives us insight into how the detector with the 3-queue scheme operates to classify the message-sending handsets in case of mixed attack with low intensity. Most of the malicious handsets are considered as suspicious at first as we see in Fig. 8a. But, they are subsequently classified as malicious, and so the ratio of malicious handsets classified as suspicious starts to decrease and the ratio of malicious handsets classified correctly increases. Fig. 8b shows that the normal handsets occupy both the normal queue and the suspicious queue. This is because normal handsets from flash crowds are likely to be classified as suspicious due to the absence of previous message threads while the normal handsets which have sent messages and received replies during the prior normal network situation are likely to be classified as normal.

The normal handsets in normal queue are served with the highest priority without much competition with the malicious handsets. Moreover, the competition in the suspicious queue between the normal handsets and malicious handsets is resolved as more malicious handsets are classified as malicious. Therefore, the blocking rate for normal handsets decreases efficiently while the messages from malicious handsets are suspended in lower priority queues or discarded after the maximum number of retransmissions.

Fig. 9a presents the occupancy in each of the three queues of 3-queue scheme. This results from the classification performed at the detector. The occupancy at the normal queue is almost 1 at the start of the attack. As the classification of suspicious handsets occurs, the occupancy of the suspicious queue increases and the occupancy of the normal queue decreases. Then, the handsets in the suspicious queue are judged as normal or malicious by the detector, and the occupancy of the suspicious queue decreases. As more handsets are classified as malicious, the occupancy of the normal and suspicious queues decreases because the messages in these queues are served quickly. The blocking rate in each of the queues of the 3-queue scheme is shown in Fig. 9b. The blocking rate of a queue goes up when the occupancy of the queue is high and falls if the queue has space for new messages.

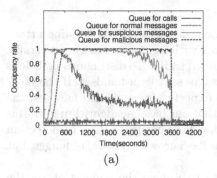 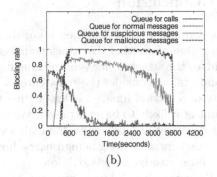

(a)   (b)

Fig. 9. (a) Occupancy and (b) blocking rate for mixed attack traffic with low intensity with a mitigation scheme

5.3   Comparison with SMS-Watchdog

The work most similar to ours is SMS-Watchdog [12]. In this work, SMS-based blending attacks are detected using each user's regular social behaviors. For example, anomalies are detected by checking if the number of recipients in a window of messages from a sender deviate significantly from the average number of unique recipients in training messages.

Because a blending attack has similar characteristics to flash crowds in terms of the increased number of recipients per sender, the SMS-Watchdog algorithms is not effective at distinguishing an attack from a flash crowd. Fig. 10a shows that the false positive rate of SMS-Watchdog's R detection scheme for a flash crowd increases to 17% and 20% for a twofold and fourfold increase in the number of recipients per sender, respectively, in a case in which the number of messages and senders increases up to 4 times more than that under regular conditions. On the contrary, our scheme has false positive rate of less than 2% as shown in Fig. 10b, which means we correctly classify flash crowd traffic.

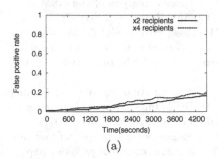 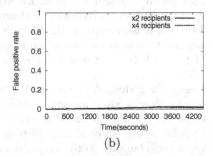

(a)   (b)

Fig. 10. False positive rates of (a) R-type detection in SMS-Watchdog scheme and (b) our scheme for a flash crowd

6   Conclusion

We propose a novel detection algorithm which identifies a SMS flooding attack regardless of whether the attack traffic is mixed with legitimate flash crowd traffic and/or the attack traffic is mimicking flash crowd traffic. To distinguish malicious handsets, we consider the reply rate to messages sent by a handset. If the reply rate of a certain handset is lower than that expected for a normal handset, the handset is likely to be an attacker. We show that our baseline algorithm performs the detection of unmixed traffic with a very low false positive rate. The detection of attackers mimicking benign users during a flash crowd event takes longer, but the false positive rate is still low.

We propose a 3-queue mitigation scheme to reduce the congestion on the wireless control channels. The mitigation scheme employs three queues with different priorities to serve normal, suspicious, and malicious traffic differentially. We show that the blocking rate of normal handsets is efficiently diminished by prioritizing normal messages.

Acknowledgment. This work was supported by the US National Science Foundation (NSF) (CNS-0905447 and CNS-0643907).

References

1. ITU, The world in 2010: Ict facts and figures, ITU. Tech. Rep. (2010),
   www.itu.int/ITU-D/ict/material/FactsFigures2010.pdf
2. Nielsen: State of the media (January 2011),
   http://blog.nielsen.com/nielsenwire/wp-content/uploads/2011/01/nielsen-media-fact-sheet-jan-11.pdf
3. Kyriazakos, S., Karetsos, G., Kechagias, C., Karabalis, C., Vlahodimitropoulos, A.: Signalling channel modelling for congestion management in cellular networks. In: IEEE VTS 54th Vehicular Technology Conference on VTC 2001 Fall, vol. 4, pp. 2712–2715. IEEE (2002)
4. Sms over ss7, National Communications System. Tech. Rep. (2003)
5. Agarwal, N., Chandran-Wadia, L., Apte, V.: Capacity analysis of the GSM short message service. In: National Conference on Communications (2004)
6. Jung, J., Krishnamurthy, B., Rabinovich, M.: Flash crowds and denial of service attacks: Characterization and implications for CDNs and web sites. In: Proceedings of the 11th International Conference on World Wide Web, pp. 293–304. ACM (2002)
7. Meng, X., Zerfos, P., Samanta, V., Wong, S., Lu, S.: Analysis of the reliability of a nationwide short message service. In: 26th IEEE International Conference on Computer Communications, INFOCOM 2007, pp. 1811–1819. IEEE (2007)
8. Cellular News. An estimated 43 billion text messages were sent globally on new years eve. (January 2008), http://www.cellular-news.com/story/28496.php
9. Cellular News. Congestion causes text message slowdown (January 2008), http://www.cellular-news.com/story/28391.php
10. Enck, W., Traynor, P., McDaniel, P., La Porta, T.: Exploiting open functionality in SMS-capable cellular networks. In: Proceedings of the 12th ACM Conference on Computer and Communications Security, pp. 393–404. ACM (2005)

11. Traynor, P., Enck, W., McDaniel, P., La Porta, T.: Mitigating attacks on open functionality in SMS-capable cellular networks. IEEE/ACM Transactions on Networking 17(1), 40–53 (2009)
12. Yan, G., Eidenbenz, S., Galli, E.: SMS-Watchdog: Profiling Social Behaviors of SMS Users for Anomaly Detection. In: Balzarotti, D. (ed.) RAID 2009. LNCS, vol. 5758, pp. 202–223. Springer, Heidelberg (2009)
13. Le, Q., Zhanikeev, M., Tanaka, Y.: Methods of Distinguishing Flash Crowds from Spoofed DoS Attacks. In: 3rd EuroNGI Conference on Next Generation Internet Networks, pp. 167–173. IEEE (2007)
14. Marnerides, A., Pezaros, D., Hutchison, D.: Flash crowd detection within the realms of an internet service provider (isp). In: The 9th Annual Postgraduate Symposium on the Convergence of Telecommunications, Networking and Broadcasting (2008)
15. Li, K., Zhou, W., Li, P., Hai, J., Liu, J.: Distinguishing DDoS attacks from flash crowds using probability metrics. In: 2009 Third International Conference on Network and System Security, pp. 9–17. IEEE (2009)
16. Wu, Y., Zhou, C., Xiao, J., Kurths, J., Schellnhuber, H.: Evidence for a bimodal distribution in human communication. Proceedings of the National Academy of Sciences (2010)
17. 3GPP, TS 23.040, Technical Realization of the Short Message Service (SMS); Release 9. v9.3.0 (2010)
18. 3GPP, TS 24.011, Point-to-Point (PP) Short Message Service (SMS) support on mobile radio interface; Release 9. v9.0.1 (2010)
19. Zerfos, P., Meng, X., Wong, S., Samanta, V., Lu, S.: A study of the short message service of a nationwide cellular network. In: Proceedings of the 6th ACM SIGCOMM Conference on Internet Measurement, pp. 263–268. ACM (2006)
20. Fonash, P., McGregor, P.: National Security/Emergency Preparedness Wireless Priority Service. In: Proc. 8th Int'l. Conf. Intelligence in Next Generation Networks
21. Chandola, V., Banerjee, A., Kumar, V.: Anomaly detection: A survey. ACM Computing Surveys (CSUR) 41(3), 15 (2009)
22. Demers, A., Keshav, S., Shenker, S.: Analysis and simulation of a fair queueing algorithm. In: Symposium Proceedings on Communications Architectures & Protocols, pp. 1–12. ACM (1989)

Set Difference Attacks in Wireless Sensor Networks

Tulio de Souza[1], Joss Wright[2], Piers O'Hanlon[2], and Ian Brown[2]

[1] Department of Computer Science, University of Oxford, UK
tulio.de.souza@cs.ox.ac.uk
[2] Oxford Internet Institute, University of Oxford, UK
{joss.wright,piers.ohanlon,ian.brown}@oii.ox.ac.uk

Abstract. We show that existing proposed mechanisms for preserving the privacy of reported data values in wireless sensor networks are vulnerable against a simple and practical form of attack: the *set difference attack*. These attacks are particularly effective where a number of separate applications are running in a given network, but are not limited to this case. We demonstrate the feasibility of these attacks and assert that they cannot, in general, be avoided whilst maintaining absolute accuracy of sensed data. As an implication of this, we suggest a mechanism based on perturbation of sensor results whereby these attacks can be partially mitigated.

Keywords: privacy, privacy-preserving, wireless sensor network, data perturbation, differential privacy, privacy-preserving data aggregation.

1 Introduction

Wireless sensor networks are increasingly being deployed to monitor a variety of real-world environments and processes. Initially designed for military applications such as battlefield monitoring or perimeter security, wireless sensor networks are now being used to monitor industrial processes, environmental pollution, marine- and land-based ecosystems, and stock control, as well as many other purposes.

The data gathered by wireless sensor networks can in many cases be sensitive, either when considered in isolation or when combined with other data. Where individuals and their actions are monitored by a wireless sensor network we desire, or may even be legally required [5], to ensure adequate protection measures for personally sensitive data. Even when data is not directly sensitive, it is good privacy and security hygiene to prevent unnecessary dissemination of readings from individual sensor nodes.

In practice, wireless sensor networks occur with varying degrees of complexity [15]. These networks can be roughly classified according to their structure, either as standalone, multi-application or federated multi-application networks.

The simplest wireless sensor networks have tended to be standalone systems running a bespoke application that defined both the constituent nodes and all

A.D. Keromytis and R. Di Pietro (Eds.): SecureComm 2012, LNICST 106, pp. 94–111, 2013.

other aspects of the network. In such a deployment, hardware requirements are tailored to fit the needs of the application in question, with the application exploiting all aspects of the network. This structure remains common today.

Increasingly, however, wireless sensor networks are being deployed in a multi-application structure comprising nodes running a common middleware that allows one or more applications to run on the same infrastructure. The use of middleware offers a flexible and standardized abstraction of the low-level characteristics of the hardware, allowing data collected by each node to serve a number of applications. This increases the range of uses for a given deployment, but also has the potential to raise privacy or security concerns.

The sharing model can be extended further by allowing *federation* of the infrastructure. A federated multi-application network allows different entities to run applications across the same set of nodes, sharing resources between multiple stakeholders. This provides an economic benefit, and can lead to longer-term deployments offering a range of sensing options, but also raises even greater privacy concerns for those individuals in the sensing environment [11].

To date, research in wireless sensor network privacy has focused largely on privacy-preserving data aggregation (PPDA) protocols that protect the data collected in sensor nodes against outside observers, or limited malicious network participants. Importantly, existing protocols have focused almost solely on standalone networks, without consideration for the more complex multi-application and federated networks.

In this work we are chiefly concerned with protecting, or conversely learning, individual readings from nodes in a wireless sensor network. Specifically, we are concerned with the potential to derive individual sensor node readings in a range of network structures, but we focus on networks that support multiple applications, even in the presence of existing privacy-preserving protocols.

The remainder of the paper is structured as follows. Firstly, we define our model and underlying assumptions, and introduce the notion of the *set difference attack*. We then explore the capabilities and goals of existing privacy-preserving data aggregation protocols, describe in detail how they fail to protect against these attacks, and analyse the potential for these attacks to function in practical deployments. Finally, we propose an initial approach towards mitigating these attacks, and explore its implications for data collection in sensor networks.

2   System and Attacker Model

We are concerned with wireless sensor networks in which multiple stakeholders deploy applications that aggregate information provided by nodes in the network.

More formally, we consider a wireless sensor network $\mathcal{W}$ as being comprised of a set of discrete sensor nodes $\mathcal{S} = \{s_1, s_2, ..., s_n\}$ along with a function mapping nodes to their reported readings modelled as simple natural numbers: $\mathcal{V} : \mathcal{S} \rightarrow \mathcal{N}$. Users query some subset of sensor nodes, corresponding to those running some application, and receive a simple addition of the individual sensor values:

$\mathcal{V}(\mathcal{A}) \mid \mathcal{A} \subseteq \mathcal{S}$; we further assume that both the set of nodes comprising a given application and the aggregate results of any queries are known[1].

Our goal is to protect or, adversarially, to learn the reading of any individual sensor: $\mathcal{V}(\{s\}) \mid s \in \mathcal{S}$.

We assume that applications aggregate a known subset of $\mathcal{S}$, reporting only an aggregate value. Intrinsically, we assume some lower limit on the size of the set $\mathcal{A} \subseteq \mathcal{S}$ in order to prevent trivially requesting the value of an individual node. We will show later how this simple defence is ineffective.

We consider two attacker models based on the standard *global passive attacker* commonly used in the field of privacy-enhancing technology research. This attacker is able to observe, but not decrypt, traffic passing between nodes but cannot alter, delay or drop communications; nor can this attacker compromise an individual node directly.[2]

We will focus on this first, truly passive, attacker restricted simply to observing the aggregate readings of applications, however the nature of our system model also naturally lends itself towards a *partially active* attacker that may deploy one or more applications subject to the limitations inherent in the system. We distinguish this from a truly active attacker in that this attacker may not drop or delay communications. These attackers correspond, respectively, to a non-stakeholder that queries the aggregate results of applications deployed by others in the network, and to a stakeholder with the ability to deploy their own applications on demand but who will not engage in openly malicious behaviour.

Further, for the current work we focus on a static moment and will not analyse in detail the potential effects of long-term analysis of sensed values. We will, however, make some mention of the effects of timing with respect to node availability in subsequent sections, but leave detailed investigation of this for future work.

The model we have described here represents recent research in federated wireless sensor network design, for example the work of Leontiadis et al. [12].

3   Set Difference Attacks

A set difference attack exploits the intersections between the sets of sensors comprising applications to discover scenarios in which individual nodes, or small clusters of nodes, are isolated.

The simplest form of this attack is demonstrated in Figure 1. The node coverage of two small applications is delineated by the light-grey regions. The first application covers the set $\{b, d, e\}$, and the second the set $\{b, c, d, e\}$. An application querying aggregate results from these two applications can trivially subtract

---

[1] While this may seem to place a great deal of information in the hands of potential attackers, it is a reasonable representation of existing wireless sensor network platforms. It should also be noted that the attacks we will describe remain feasible with greatly reduced, or more localized, information.

[2] Note that this attacker differs from the common Dolev-Yao attacker in security protocol literature in that it cannot affect messages in transit.

the aggregate of the first application from the aggregate of the second in order to learn the exact value of node c.

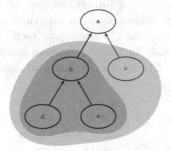

Fig. 1. Simple set differences in a WSN

This form of attack has some similarities to known attacks in statistical databases, known as *tracker attacks* [1], as well as to attacks against mix-based anonymous communications systems in the form of $(n-1)$ attacks [8]. In Section 5 we will explore more complex scenarios in which these attacks apply.

An interesting feature of these attacks is that they rely only on consideration of aggregate values reported to a sink, and thus make no attempt to read data as it passes across the network. Crucially, as we will demonstrate, this makes these attacks applicable against most well-known families of privacy-preserving protocols for wireless sensor networks proposed in the literature.

Having introduced the set difference attack, we will now describe the most common approaches towards protecting privacy of individual sensor node readings in wireless sensor networks before showing how the attack applies against these protocols.

4 Privacy-Preserving Protocols in Wireless Sensor Networks

4.1 Goals

Privacy-preserving protocols in wireless sensor networks aim to preserve the privacy of individual nodes against some combination of the *sink*, the node that aggregates values reported by other nodes, and against other nodes in the network. Different approaches have tended to focus on some combination of these, with mixed results.

The protocols shown here make various trade-offs between communication complexity, computational requirements, integrity of data, and security.

4.2 Clustering

Privacy-preserving clustering, illustrated in Figure 2, functions by forming disjoint subsets of nodes, each of which calculates an aggregate sum of their data before it is sent to the sink. A variety of approaches are possible to achieve this aggregation, but a popular approach [9] makes use of a variation on the Average Salary Problem. This algorithm, a simple instance of the more general secure function evaluation problem, allows nodes to sum their individual values without leaking any more information than the aggregate itself. The desired effect is that neither the sink, nor any node in the cluster, can learn the exact value of any individual node unless $(n-1)$ nodes in a cluster of size n collude.

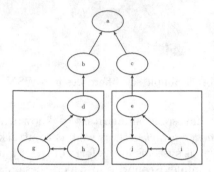

Fig. 2. Private clustering in WSNs

An advantage of the clustering approach is that it prevents both the sink and any individual nodes in the network from learning any single node's values, at the expense of the bandwidth required to form clusters and perform the secure data aggregation.

4.3   Slicing

Slicing, introduced in [9] and then expanded in [10], chiefly aims to prevent individual nodes in the network from learning the values reported by any other nodes.

To achieve this, a node divides its values into a number of randomly-sized slices and selects multiple paths through the network, as illustrated in Figure 3. Each slice is sent via a different path, and added to the total sum calculated by each intermediate node, which acts as an aggregator until the value reaches the sink. The number of paths that each node sends its data acts as a configurable parameter to the required privacy level. This simple mechanism aims at providing confidentiality against other nodes in the network as well as the sink.

4.4   Privacy Homomorphisms

Privacy homomorphism uses the well-known homomorphic properties of certain public-key encryption systems to aggregate data in transit without revealing individual values. Again, this mechanism provides protection against external attackers and malicious nodes in the network, but does not prevent the sink from learning individual values.

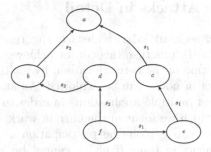

Fig. 3. Private slicing showing the path of two private data 'slices' travelling across the network from f to a

Homomorphic encryption schemes allow manipulation of message plaintexts via the corresponding encrypted ciphertexts, enabling operations such as aggregation, or summation, of messages to be performed without decryption. Many well-known encryption schemes allow restricted homomorphic operations; in the Paillier scheme, for example, the multiplication of two ciphertexts under the same public key will decrypt to the summation of corresponding plaintexts, whilst raising one ciphertext to the power of another will decrypt to the product of the plaintexts.

Gentry [7] presented a fully homomorphic encryption scheme, allowing for arbitrary operations to be performed on ciphertexts. Whilst the original scheme was extremely computationally expensive, several improved schemes have already been suggested. In practice, however, even restricted homomorphism provides powerful and practical tool for privacy-preserving protocols.

In a wireless sensor network, therefore, nodes simply encrypt their values to the public key of the sink. As the message is relayed through the network, nodes can aggregate the value of any received messages simply by aggregating the ciphertexts, as demonstrated in Figure 4. Crucially, this protects the values of any individual message from being learnt by any party except the sink.

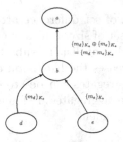

Fig. 4. Homomorphic encryption in WSNs. Values are aggregated in encrypted form at each node.

5   Set Difference Attacks in Detail

The set difference attack seeks to isolate nodes from aggregates in order to breach the privacy of their data. In practice, this can be achieved in one of two ways.

Firstly, the segmentation of the network caused by multiple applications running across disparate set of nodes can be exploited. An attacker therefore combines aggregate values of multiple applications in order to isolate single nodes. It is this approach on which we focus in the current work.

Secondly, an attacker can exploit the participation of nodes in aggregates taken at different moments in time. If nodes cannot be guaranteed always to report their values, then the aggregate value of an aggregate may include or exclude certain nodes when queried at different times. This behaviour is extremely likely to result in a set difference attack, as the set of nodes being queried is likely to remain largely the same.

These two approaches can be employed in isolation, or combined by an attacker. If the attacker can learn predictable patterns of node uptimes across the network, or can observe that certain groups of nodes are more likely to be clustered in applications, the effectiveness of the attack is increased.

While the example set difference attack shown in Figure 1 is relatively simple, the attack itself is surprisingly powerful and hard to avoid. In addition to the simple isolation of a node via finding an appropriately-sized subset, four additional cases are worthy of mention.

5.1   Isolated Cluster

Trivially, the set difference attack allows us to reveal the aggregate value of an isolated *cluster* rather than an individual node. While this is not a privacy risk equivalent to the leakage of an individual node value, the leaking of the aggregates of a small set of nodes may still be in violation of the privacy goals of the system.

5.2   Combined Subsets

Although the most basic form of set difference attack comes from observing a subset of size $n - 1$ of a given set of size n, it is of course possible for the subset to itself be the union of a number of disjoint subsets as illustrated in Figure 5.

This possibility greatly increases the likelihood of observing a successful set difference attack. Observed aggregates can be stored by an attacker and combined whenever new appropriate aggregates are found. Of course, this application of the attack is highly time-dependent.

5.3   Total Set Coverage

In general, set difference attacks are not possible where observed subsets overlap, as this includes multiple unknown values in the combined aggregates. It is possible, however, to calculate values through gathering complete collections of

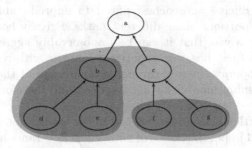

Fig. 5. A set difference attack combining multiple disjoint subsets

sets that intersect on all but one of their elements. By gathering every possible subset of size $n - 1$ from a set of size n, we can derive *all* individual values that comprise the set. The aggregate values reported for each subset form a simple system of simultaneous equations that can be solved for each individual value.

The difficulty of performing this attack relies on the size of the subsets that we observe, as we require all $\binom{n}{n-1}$ subsets of the observed subset of size n. While we will not perform a detailed analysis of the likelihood of this scenario, it relates to the well-known *coupon collector's problem* [4] in which a collector seeks to obtain a complete collection of a set of coupons, one of which is randomly included with each purchase of a given product. It is known that the number of purchases required before obtaining the entire set of coupons is of the order $n \, log(n)$, where n is the number of coupons in the set. For large networks, this scenario quickly becomes highly unlikely, however it may be practical in smaller networks or those networks where applications are likely to sample from small sets of related nodes.

5.4   Attack Recursion

The result of a successful set difference attack provides information to an attacker that can lead to further successful attacks. By learning the value of an individual node, or of a small subset of nodes, an attacker can remove that node's value from any observed aggregates in the network. This may itself reveal further isolated subsets that can themselves compromise further sets. As such, the attacker can potentially 'recurse' through several further attacks once any one attack has succeeded.

6   Attacking Existing Protocols

Existing approaches to protecting privacy in wireless sensor networks focus, to varying degrees, on manipulating data as it flows from a sensor to a sink. Clustering approaches aggregate data by combining values that are then forwarded in aggregate form. Slicing approaches split data unpredictably and randomly re-route individual portions along different paths. Privacy homomorphism encrypts data in such a way that it can be unobservably aggregated in transit. The set difference attack, however, is entirely agnostic with respect to the flow of data; instead it operates purely through examination of the final aggregate, undermining the assumptions of existing protocols and therefore rendering them vulnerable.

Clustering, in particular, may actively aid in the application of a set difference attack. As presented in [9], the choice of node clusters is random. A result of this is that multiple requests by an application are likely to result in the selection of different clusters. These, in turn, can directly cause the isolation of nodes in precisely the way envisioned in our original statement of the attack.

Slicing approaches and solutions based on homomorphic encryption share similar patterns of failure. The values of each node are protected, or at least obscured, whilst in transit, however the results are still accurately aggregated by the application. Whilst the existing protocols do provide some measure of protection against the specific threat model of an adversary that seeks to learn values in transit, they are ineffective against the attacker described in Section 2.

Ultimately, it is the requirement for accurate data reporting that results in the success of the set difference attack, and it is therefore this feature of the network that must be addressed by protocols in order to prevent the attack.

6.1   Node Availability

As we have mentioned, it is possible to perform a set difference attack through node availability rather than overlapping applications. In this case, an application that has a known, fixed set of nodes, but for which certain nodes are not always available, the absence or presence of individual nodes can clearly lead to similar attacks. Most notably, this attack will be effective even in single-application networks.

The inclusion of a time dimension in the attack clearly adds a layer of sophistication to the attack. If the availability of certain nodes is predictable, queries can be specifically targeted to take advantage of this data. Interestingly, an individual node has little power to prevent this attack in the general case, as it will be offline when the attack effectively occurs.

A slightly more nuanced version of this attack, which we leave for future work, comes from the predictability of individual nodes over time. Clearly, certain types of sensor readings will vary predictably with time, such as light levels during the day. This can lead to predictable patterns of data being reported for each node. A more sophisticated variant of the attack would be to infer variations between nodes due to the predictable variations in aggregate reports. Similar concepts have been suggested in the context of tracking of users in online anonymization services [13], however we will not consider this potential further in the current work.

7   Feasibility of Set Difference Attacks

To investigate the feasibility of the set difference attack in practice, we adopt a simulation-based approach, employing abstract networks of varying size based on the system model of Section 2.

For each experiment, randomly-sized subsets of the network were repeatedly drawn at random. Each subset was stored and compared against all previously-drawn sets, individually and in additive and subtractive operations, to determine if a set difference attack had become possible. An attack was considered to have occurred as soon as any individual node could be isolated due to the combination of any number of previously-drawn sets. Sets were drawn continually until the attack succeeded, whereupon the number of sets drawn was recorded. To prevent trivial attacks, subsets were restricted to being of cardinality three or greater, up to the size of the network. To ensure a sufficiently low error margin for the mean, experiments were repeated in the order of one thousand times for each network size.

As a practical example of a successful simulated attack, consider a network of five nodes, $\mathcal{S} = \{a, b, c, d, e\}$, in which each node is equally likely to be selected. During a particular simulation run, three subsets were drawn: $\mathcal{A}_1 = \{a, c, e\}$, $\mathcal{A}_2 = \{a, b, c, d, e\}$ and $\mathcal{A}_3 = \{a, b, d\}$. The isolation of a node occurs by subtracting the aggregate of $\mathcal{A}_2$ from that of $\mathcal{A}_1$, which is then summed with the aggregate result of $\mathcal{A}_3$. This sequence of operations will result in isolating the reported reading of node a. Note that both operations, additive and subtractive, take place over the aggregate result of a query sent towards a subset of nodes, and not as subset operations.

The results of the simulation, showing the mean number of sets drawn before a successful attack, are presented in Figure 6.

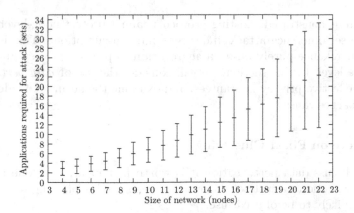

Fig. 6. Mean average and sample standard deviation of randomly-chosen sets required in networks of varying size before a successful set difference attack

As can be seen, the mean number of subsets required before isolating a single node is relatively low in the simulated networks, typically being lower than the number of nodes. The growth of the function does, however, appear to be more than linear, as might be expected due to the rate of increase of possible subsets. While this suggests that extremely large networks may not be easy targets for the set difference attack, networks of the size commonly seen in practice may well be vulnerable. Despite this it is worth noting that the lower bound for the required number of sets remains two, and simulation demonstrated such attacks occurring in practice for each network size that was tested. Due to space considerations, we leave a more detailed analysis of these results for future work.

Calculating the appropriate sets required to conduct an attack is itself extremely computationally expensive. As each new set is drawn, it must be combined with all existing sets, both in an additive and subtractive sense, to determine if an attack has been successful. The stored sets, and the number of comparisons required, grow exponentially. There are various optimizations to reduce the number of sets that must be stored and compared, and various ways to exclude sets that cannot take part in a successful attack, however the underlying complexity of the problem cannot be avoided.

For the sake of practicality, it will be possible to take a heuristic approach towards discovering set overlaps that, despite missing a proportion of successful attacks, will still result in isolating individual nodes. It is also the case that, as we have discussed, real-world networks present time constraints on the freshness and availability of sensor readings. This will present challenges to the attacker in discovering appropriate sets during a given time window, but will also greatly reduce the complexity required to perform the attack.

8 Preventing Set Difference Attacks

As has been demonstrated, existing protocols cannot protect node-level privacy against the set difference attack under reasonable assumptions. This is largely due to their reliance purely on data aggregation to provide privacy guarantees at the node level. In this section, we will consider the use of *data perturbation* to provide effective privacy guarantees, and examine the accuracy tradeoff that these approaches cause.

8.1   A Note on Fixed Clustering

Before we discuss data perturbation it is worth first mentioning one potential avenue of protection against set difference attacks, and explaining why this approach is unlikely to be of great use.

One approach that initially seems attractive for protecting against this form of attack is to enforce fixed-size clusters, or fixed size applications, and ensure the subsets of nodes resulting from these are either entirely disjoint or entirely equal. By doing so, individual nodes cannot be isolated, and thus the attack fails.

There are two major problems with this approach. Firstly, it places unreasonable constraints on applications in a multi-application or federated network. Specific deployments are likely to require specific node coverage, and the inability to choose other than a given fixed topology for applications could seriously hinder the flexibility of the network.

More seriously, this approach still cannot protect against attacks due to unavailable nodes. As is mentioned in Section 6.1, set difference attacks can arise from both predictable patterns of node availability, and potentially from predictable patterns of sensor readings. Neither of these factors will be affected by fixed-size clustering, and thus cannot provide full protection against the attack. We will therefore focus on other, fundamentally different, approaches.

8.2   Data Perturbation

To protect against a set difference attack, we propose applying random noise to sensor readings. The purpose of this is to prevent the individual value reported by a node from being meaningful even if it can be isolated by the attack. Clearly, for some applications, this *data perturbation* approach can cause an unacceptable level of inaccuracy in aggregate results. In such cases, the risks of attack must be weighed against the requirement for accurate data.

Sensor nodes can effectively obscure their data by adding random noise drawn from an appropriately-scaled symmetric probability distribution with mean 0 to their reported readings. To protect readings effectively, the standard deviation of the distribution in question should be chosen according to the possible range of values for the given reading type. Due to Chebyshev's inequality, this ensures that the value reported by a node, including noise, effectively covers a range of values that could be reported by the node with high probability. In the next section, we will discuss a well-known method for selecting privacy-preserving noise optimally according to the *differential privacy* guarantee of Dwork [2], where we will also discuss the notion of data perturbation in more detail.

Usefully, combining multiple readings and their associated random noise causes the aggregate noise to converge rapidly towards zero as the number of nodes increases, due to the weak law of large numbers. The aggregate therefore tends towards greater accuracy as the number of nodes in a given application increases, making the data perturbation approach increasingly applicable as the network scales.

For noise drawn from a Gaussian distribution the sample mean, representing the aggregate noise reported from each sensor, is a good estimator of the true mean. The mean standard error of the sample mean, therefore, describes the expected inaccuracy incurred by this method of privacy-preserving data perturbation. To summarize:

For the sample mean:

$$\bar{X} = \frac{1}{n} \sum_{i=1}^{n} X_i \tag{1}$$

The mean standard error can be described as:

$$MSE(\bar{X}) = E((\bar{X} - \mu)^2) = \frac{\sigma^2}{n} \tag{2}$$

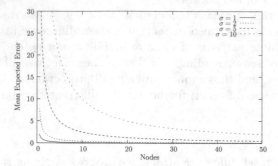

Fig. 7. Mean standard error (MSE) for various values of σ as application size increases

As can be seen from Figure 7, the expected error rapidly becomes small as the number of nodes in an application increases, even for relatively large values of σ.

Perturbation Alongside Other Mechanisms. It is important to note that the perturbation of data in the sense we have described above is largely orthogonal to the mechanisms surveyed in Section 4. As such it is entirely possible, and may indeed be advisable, for nodes to cluster, slice or encrypt their data in addition to perturbing their data. In particular, this approach has the potential to improve the node-level privacy even in situations where set difference attacks are not possible, and may add privacy properties that protect against other classes of attacker. We leave a fuller analysis of the combination of perturbation with other mechanisms for future work.

Having examined an informal approach to data perturbation, we will now discuss the more formal and optimal guarantees that can be provided by *differential privacy*.

9 Differential Privacy

The technique of gaining privacy in statistical aggregates through data perturbation is not new, and indeed represents a well-known approach that is the subject of much recent study. An important result in this area comes from Dwork [2], in which the concept of *differential privacy* is proposed. This technique aims to provide robust privacy guarantees through data perturbation, with a provably minimal addition of noise to the result of statistical queries.

The core of the differential privacy guarantee is that the existence or absence of a single record in a database should not cause a noticeable difference in the result of queries against that database. This is achieved by ensuring that databases that differ only in a single record are, in some sense, indistinguishable to any party able to make statistical queries against that database.

The purpose of this indistinguishability is to prevent an individual record from leaking useful information even in the presence of arbitrary, unknown *auxiliary information*. By ensuring that no single record is distinguishable in a statistical query, differential privacy ensures that any privacy breach involving statistical queries from a database could have occurred *without* the result of that statistical query.

More formally, differential privacy states that for any two databases D_1 and D_2 that differ only in a single data record, the result of a randomized statistical query should be almost equally probable for D_1 or D_2. Dwork's original statement of the guarantee provides that a randomised function $\mathcal{K}$ achieves ϵ-differential privacy if, for any two databases $\mathcal{D}_1$, $\mathcal{D}_2$ differing on at most one element, and all $S \subseteq Range(\mathcal{K})$:

$$\Pr[\mathcal{K}(\mathcal{D}_1) \in \mathcal{S}] \leq \exp(\epsilon) \times \Pr[\mathcal{K}(\mathcal{D}_2) \in \mathcal{S}]$$

where ϵ is a security parameter that allows security to be balanced against accuracy of results.

The probability of a given result is therefore within a small multiplicative factor regardless of whether D_1 or D_2 was queried. This ensures that the result of a statistical query cannot be used to determine with any certainty which database was queried. It thus becomes impossible for the existence or absence or a record, or its value, to be determined.

The differential privacy guarantee is extremely strong. As is clear from the definition, however, repeated queries against the same databases will reveal more information concerning the underlying probability distributions, and eventually allow the databases to be distinguished with high probability. Differential privacy therefore provides the concept of a 'privacy budget' that is partially exhausted with each query. Once that budget is exhausted, no further queries can be made against the database in question without violating the guarantee.

In practice, differential privacy is most commonly achieved by applying noise drawn from a Laplace distribution with mean 0 and standard deviation proportional to the *sensitivity* of the query and the strength of the guarantee, expressed as the probability of differentiating the two databases as a result of the query. This sensitivity, written Δf for some query function f, is the greatest value by which the result of the query can change according to the change of a single record:

$$\Delta f = max(f(D_1) - f(D_2))$$

for all D_1, D_2 that differ in at most one record. As an example, a simple count function on a database, which returns the number of records that meet a given constraint, has a sensitivity of 1, as the addition or deletion of a single record can alter the result of the count by at most 1. Clearly, for functions that have high sensitivity, such as the average height in centimetres of a small group of individuals, achieving the differential privacy guarantee may require unacceptably high costs in terms of accuracy.

Figure 8 illustrates the desirable property of the Laplace distribution for applying noise. The probability of the observed events a and b from the perspective of each probability distribution are within a small, fixed multiplicative factor, allowing each result to be convincingly drawn from either distribution.

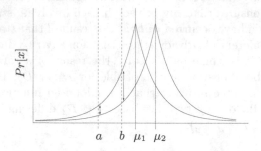

Fig. 8. Overlapping Laplace distributions, means μ_1 and μ_2, showing comparative probabilities of two values, a and b, drawn according to either distribution

A significant advantage of this differential privacy mechanism is that it is largely independent of the data itself, but provides its guarantees due to the nature of the query function.

9.1 Differential Privacy against Set Difference Attacks

Application of a differentially-private mechanism for protecting individual sensor node readings in WSNs functions similarly to the addition of random Gaussian noise as described above. The use of differential privacy, however, provides a number of attractive advantages over more *ad-hoc* methods. The guarantee provided by the mechanism gives provable privacy preservation for individual sensor nodes [2], as well as a number of attractive properties such as composability between multiple queries, at the cost of higher levels of inaccuracy. The generality of the method makes it applicable without reference to the data reported by the sensor node, relying instead on the query made by the application. Queries can be of arbitrary complexity, and are not restricted to simple functions such as counts or averages, although the noise associated with high sensitivity queries cannot be avoided. Despite this, the Laplace distribution has been shown in [3] to give a provable optimal level of noise, reducing inaccuracies in query results to the minimum required for a strong guarantee of privacy.

It is crucial to note that this framing of private data reporting is substantially different to the mechanism for differential privacy described by Dwork [2]. The original framing of differential privacy considers an accurate data store, corresponding to a sink in a wireless sensor network, that is trusted to hold and process an entire dataset. In our model, by contrast, we explicitly consider the sink as an adversary that we wish to prevent from learning individual data values, analogous to records in the database. As such, our model can best be conceived by considering each sensor node as analogous to the trusted database in Dwork [2]. Each node therefore represents a single-entry database that must, correspondingly, add a sufficient amount of noise to hide that entry. We rely on the aggregation of these single-entry databases to reduce the overall noise. The result of this is a higher level of noise than would be seen if the sink held accurate values, but with the advantage of preserving node-level privacy from all actors in the network.

10   Conclusions and Future Work

We have described the set difference attack, and shown that existing approaches to providing node-level privacy in wireless sensor networks are vulnerable to this attack under reasonable assumptions. Further, we have demonstrated that the attack is likely to be feasible in real-world networks. We propose that the weakness of existing privacy-preserving data protocols is ultimately due to their reliance on data aggregation as the sole means to achieve privacy, and thus that the ease of isolating nodes from aggregate values results in a failure to protect privacy adequately.

In response, we have proposed a countermeasure against the attack based on data perturbation and optimized with techniques from differential privacy. This approach allows for nodes to protect themselves against the set difference attack by trading accuracy of results against privacy. As we have demonstrated in Section 8.2, this tradeoff is reasonable for realistic scenarios, with the loss of accuracy decreasing quickly as the size of the network increases.

There are still a number of significant avenues to be explored in relation to this work. We have largely avoided an involved mathematical analysis of the feasibility of the set difference attacks in realistic networks, relying instead on simulation. There are many factors that can affect the feasibility of the attack in different networks, and a more rigorous mathematical analysis would be of great use in exploring these and considering approaches towards protecting networks.

The tradeoff between privacy guarantees and the accuracy of results is key to this approach. The use of the differential privacy guarantee provides a well-defined mathematical framework for this tradeoff, and allows for the security parameter to be reduced directly in favour of accuracy. Despite this, the application of the differential privacy guarantee in a wireless sensor network raises a number of issues related to distributed noise generation that we intend to explore in future work. The full implications of combining noise as we have described also remain to be investigated.

An area of great interest in data perturbation for privacy is in how strong privacy guarantees can be maintained over time series data, or highly-linked data-sets. The differential privacy guarantee is extremely strong, but is quickly violated through repeated queries of the same database. When a query can potentially cover a series of readings, the preservation of privacy without adding unacceptably high levels of noise remains open despite some initial results in this area [6, 14].

Our focus in this paper has been exclusively on data aggregation in its simplest form. In some networks, however, there may be a requirement for more complex queries to be distributed across the nodes in the network. The applications of set difference attacks, and the related perturbation defence, to more complex scenarios is worthy of attention.

Finally, the set difference attacks themselves can be extended to consider changes in the network over time. Nodes can join or leave the network, or be included in or excluded from a given aggregate. Nodes may also have predictable data patterns that can be exploited to discount their participation in a given aggregate. These last approaches, which extend the set difference attack to a far wider range of scenarios, is an avenue of great interest in extending the work presented here.

References

1. Denning, D.E., Denning, P.J., Schwartz, M.D.: The Tracker: A Threat to Statistical Database Security. ACM Transactions on Database Systems 4(1), 76–96 (1979)
2. Dwork, C.: Differential Privacy. In: Bugliesi, M., Preneel, B., Sassone, V., Wegener, I. (eds.) ICALP 2006. LNCS, vol. 4052, pp. 1–12. Springer, Heidelberg (2006)
3. Dwork, C., McSherry, F., Nissim, K., Smith, A.: Calibrating Noise to Sensitivity in Private Data Analysis. In: Halevi, S., Rabin, T. (eds.) TCC 2006. LNCS, vol. 3876, pp. 265–284. Springer, Heidelberg (2006)
4. Erdős, P., Rényi, A.: On a classical problem of probability theory. Magyar Tud. Akad. Mat. Kutató Int. Közl 6, 215–220 (1961)
5. European Commission: 95/46/EC-Data Protection Directive. Official Journal of the European Communities 281, 0031–0050 (1995)
6. Ganti, R.K., Pham, N., Tsai, Y.E., Abdelzaher, T.F.: PoolView: stream privacy for grassroots participatory sensing. In: Proceedings of the 6th ACM Conference on Embedded Network Sensor Systems, pp. 281–294. ACM (2008)
7. Gentry, C.: A fully homomorphic encryption scheme. Ph.D. thesis, Stanford University (2009)
8. Gülcü, C., Tsudik, G.: Mixing email with BABEL. In: Symposium on Network and Distributed System Security, pp. 2–16 (1996)
9. He, W., Liu, X., Nguyen, H., Nahrstedt, K., Abdelzaher, T.: PDA: Privacy-Preserving Data Aggregation in Wireless Sensor Networks. In: IEEE INFO-COM 2007 - 26th IEEE International Conference on Computer Communications, pp. 2045–2053. IEEE (May 2007)
10. He, W., Nguyen, H., Liuyi, X., Nahrstedt, K., Abdelzaher, T.: iPDA: An Integrity-Protecting Private Data Aggregation Scheme for Wireless Sensor Networks. In: IEEE Military Communications Conference on MILCOM 2008, pp. 1–7. IEEE (November 2008)
11. Huygens, C., Joosen, W.: Federated and shared use of sensor networks through security middleware. In: Sixth International Conference on Information Technology: New Generations, pp. 1005–1011 (2009)

12. Leontiadis, I., Efstratiou, C., Mascolo, C., Crowcroft, J.: Senshare: Transforming sensor networks into multi-application sensing infrastructures. In: 9th European Conference on Wireless Sensor Networks (February 2012)
13. Murdoch, S.J.: Hot or not: Revealing hidden services by their clock skew. In: 13th ACM Conference on Computer and Communications Security, pp. 27–36. ACM Press (2006)
14. Rastogi, V., Nath, S.: Differentially private aggregation of distributed time-series with transformation and encryption. In: Proceedings of the 2010 International Conference on Management of Data, pp. 735–746. ACM (2010)
15. Yick, J., Mukherjee, B., Ghosal, D.: Wireless sensor network survey. Comput. Netw. 52, 2292–2330 (2008)

JSGuard: Shellcode Detection in JavaScript

Boxuan Gu[1], Wenbin Zhang[1], Xiaole Bai[2],
Adam C. Champion[1], Feng Qin[1], and Dong Xuan[1]

[1] Department of Computer Science and Engineering,
The Ohio State University, Columbus, OH, 43202, USA
{gub,zhangwen,champion,qin,xuan}@cse.osu.edu
[2] Alliance Data System, Columbus, OH, 43202, USA
alan.bai@alliancedata.com

Abstract. JavaScript (JS) based shellcode injections are among the most dangerous attacks to computer systems. Existing approaches have various limitations in detecting such attacks. In this paper, we propose a new detection methodology that overcomes these limitations by fully using JS code execution environment information. We leverage this information and create a virtual execution environment where shellcodes' real behavior can be precisely monitored and detection redundancy can be reduced. Following this methodology, we implement *JSGuard*, a prototype malicious JS code detection system in Debian Linux with kernel version 2.6.26. Our extensive experiments show that JSGuard reports very few false positives and false negatives with acceptable overhead.

Keywords: malicious JavaScript code, shellcode detection, web security, intrusion detection, browser security.

1 Introduction

JavaScript (JS) is a scripting language that is widely used to enrich the functionality of client-side applications, e.g., Web browsers and Adobe Reader. Unfortunately, the user experience improvement brought by JS is often accompanied by security risks since JS codes can programmatically access these applications' computational objects. There are several types of JS based attacks against client-side applications [20, 40, 41], the most dangerous of which exploits target processes' memory errors using shellcodes. Shellcodes are segments of executable codes that are injected into vulnerable processes' address spaces. After the shellcodes are injected and the control flow transfers to them, attackers can execute arbitrary code in the target hosts that can steal sensitive information, furtively download and activate malware, and carry out other nefarious tasks.

A typical example of JS based shellcode injection attacks is exploiting Microsoft Internet Explorer's (IE's) *HTML object memory corruption vulnerability* [53] using an HTML document with a specially crafted JS code embedded. After IE loads the document, the JS code is parsed, compiled, and then executed, which creates large objects containing shellcodes in IE's heap via *heap*

A.D. Keromytis and R. Di Pietro (Eds.): SecureComm 2012, LNICST 106, pp. 112–130, 2013.
© Institute for Computer Sciences, Social Informatics and Telecommunications Engineering 2013

spraying [47]. The shellcodes are activated once IE's control flow is hijacked and redirected to them.

Recently, such JS based shellcode injection attacks are growing increasingly severe [14,40]. This stems from 2 facts: (1) users do not update their Web browsers in a timely manner yet spend more and more time surfing the Internet [21]; and (2) numerous browser plug-ins have been released, many of which have vulnerabilities [45]. The deteriorating situation is also witnessed by the popularity of "drive-by download" attacks [41] where users are duped into downloading JS codes that dynamically generate shellcodes and activate them via client-side vulnerabilities.

Unfortunately, existing solutions that detect JS based shellcode injection attacks are insufficient. Some approaches can miss detecting shellcodes since these approaches do not capture the accurate program execution environment, which is required for exposing the malicious features of shellcodes. Some approaches cannot effectively handle attacks in which shellcode is divided into several parts that are connected using control-flow-redirection instructions (e.g., jmp). We will present 2 representative examples in §2 that illustrate the limitations of existing detection approaches. We provide a review of existing solutions in §6.

In this paper, we focus on detecting malicious JS codes that inject shellcode into target applications. We propose a detection system that effectively overcomes the problems of existing solutions. Similar to existing work, we assume that the JS interpreter does not have exploitable memory errors and that such exploitable errors exist in the application (e.g., the Web browser) that runs the JS interpreter, plug-ins, or extension modules. We also assume that the application and its plug-ins and extensions are not malware. Therefore, we target malicious codes coming from external untrustable sources. Although we use a Web browser as an exemplary client-side target application in the rest of this paper and our prototype system is also built within a Web browser, our system can be extended to protect other client-side applications such as Adobe Reader.

To the best of our knowledge, our system is the first that creates an emulation environment *within the target application process's address space that shadows the address space information during emulation to detect malicious shellcodes in JS codes*. We perform such shadowing only when necessary. Our system accurately and comprehensively captures customized application information and real-time memory information at runtime in a lightweight manner; stand-alone machine simulators cannot easily obtain this information. From extensive experiments, we find that JSGuard yields very few false negatives and false positives. These results illustrate the promise of our detection methodology. In particular, we make the following contributions:

– We propose a new methodology that can comprehensively detect shellcodes in JS code. We propose leveraging the JS code execution environment information to instantiate a lightweight emulation environment that reveals and monitors shellcodes' real behaviors. Our emulation environment also enables examination of invoked system calls and their parameters as well as the execution flow to detect malicious shellcodes.

– We propose a technique for reducing detection redundancy at multiple levels. We fully utilize JS code execution environment information to reduce the number of times the detection system is activated and a JS string is checked. This information includes native methods, stack frames, and properties of each individual JS object.

– We implement JSGuard, a prototype system using the above methodology in Debian Linux with kernel version 2.6.26. We integrate JSGuard into the Firefox 4 Web browser. Our system is adaptive and extensible. It is designed to run in the target process's address space. JSGuard can efficiently fetch and use JS code execution environment information for shellcode detection.

– We conduct extensive experiments based on real traces and thousands of malicious shellcode samples. The experimental results show that our malicious JS code detector has high detection accuracy with acceptable overhead.

Paper Organization. The rest of this paper is organized as follows. §2 provides background information and motivating examples. §3 presents our system design and implementation. §4 presents detection examples. §5 evaluates JSGuard's performance. §6 reviews related works. §7 concludes.

2   Background and Motivating Examples

In this section, we provide a brief background on detecting shellcode in JS objects. Then we use 2 examples to illustrate the limitations of existing approaches.

2.1   Background: Detecting Shellcode in JS Objects

Malicious JS code usually places shellcode into objects generated at runtime and then activates it by exploiting vulnerable applications' memory errors. Therefore, detecting shellcode in JS objects is critical. Existing detection approaches can be classified into 2 categories: *content analysis* and *hijack prevention*.

Content Analysis. The approaches in this category are based on scanning JS objects' contents to determine if they contain malicious shellcode. It can be further divided into 2 sub-categories: *static analysis* and *dynamic analysis*. In static analysis, input data are first disassembled and then screened via code-level pattern analysis and matching. Patterns can be complicated signatures or simple heuristics that are obtained from studying known malicious codes. A representative work is Nozzle [43]. Static analysis detection is fast, but it is known that determining program behavior via static analysis is generally undecidable and, often, it can be effectively thwarted by obfuscation techniques [5].

Dynamic analysis based methods detect malicious shellcode by exploiting information generated during shellcode execution. A representative work is [18] that uses libemu [28] to detect shellcode in JS strings. The state of the art of dynamic analysis is network-level emulation, which decodes input data into instruction sequences and then emulates their execution [28, 37–39]. If any of them exhibits malicious behavior during emulation, the input data are classified as malicious.

Even though network-level emulation can achieve better detection completeness than static analysis, it is still prone to evasion. This is because it assumes that the working shellcodes either are self-contained or use specific memory access behaviors, i.e., their executions are independent of the dynamics of the JS code execution environment. Without knowledge of the execution environment, these approaches can be fooled by shellcode whose execution takes advantage of virtual memory information in the target process.

Hijack Prevention. As suggested by the name, hijack prevention approaches focus on preventing shellcode from being fully executed. This is often achieved by inserting special characters into the shellcode. A representative example is Bubble [22]. In Bubble, a JS string object is divided into multiple units, each 25 bytes long. In each unit, Bubble inserts 0xCC (i.e., int 3) into a randomly selected position. If a JS string object contains shellcode and the shellcode is executed, an interrupt handler will be activated when the control flow reaches the insertion point. However, existing hijack prevention approaches cannot effectively detect shellcodes split into parts that are "connected" at runtime via instructions that alter control flow, e.g., jmp and call.

In the following, we first introduce the heap spraying technique. Then we present 2 examples using it that can evade content analysis and hijack prevention approaches.

2.2   Heap Spraying

Heap spraying is an attack technique to thwart address space layout randomization (ASLR) [6, 36], a memory protection mechanism where objects' positions are randomly arranged in a process's address space. ASLR intents to prevent attackers from easily predicting target object addresses. However, the memory space that can be randomized is often limited, especially in 32-bit operating systems. If we allocate many large objects in the heap, then new objects will likely be placed in a contiguous memory area after a number of allocations, making their positions predictable. This technique is called heap spraying [17, 47].

2.3   Example 1: Thwarting Content Analysis Approaches

Fig. 1(a) shows a shellcode that is modified from an example illustrated in [37]. In the shellcode, eaddr is used to calculate the addresses at which the encrypted payload can be accessed. Since heap spraying can make the positions of some heap objects predictable, a skilled attacker can write JS code that first sprays target processes' heaps, and then inserts the shellcode into the objects whose addresses can be predicted and determined. In this example, we assume that the starting address of the shellcode is 0x0000 and eaddr is 0x0008.

This shellcode modifies its instructions at runtime. From address 0x0014 to address 0x0093, there is an encrypted payload, which often appears to be a meaningless or invalid instruction sequence. When the control flow reaches address 0x000a, the instruction addb $0xe2, 0xa(%esi) will be executed. This instruction modifies the contents of memory at address 0x0012. After it is executed, the

```
 1  0000  6a7f           push $0x7f                        1  0000  6a7f           push $0x7f
 2  0002  59             pop  %ecx                         2  0002  59             pop  %ecx
 3  0003  6a08           push $eaddr;eaddr=0x08            3  0003  6a08           push $eaddr
 4  0005  5e             pop  %esi                         4  0005  5e             pop  %esi
 5  0006  46             inc  %esi                         5  0006  46             inc  %esi
 6  0007  4e             dec  %esi                         6  0007  4e             dec  %esi
 7  0008  fec1           incb %cl                          7  0008  fec1           incb %cl
 8  000a  80460ae2       addb $0xe2,0xa(%esi)              8  000a  80460ae2       addb $0xe2,0xa(%esi)
 9  000e  304c0e0b       xorb %cl,0xb(%esi,%ecx)           9  000e  304c0e0b       xorb %cl,0xb(%esi,%ecx)
10  0012  00fa           addb %bh,%dl                     10  0012  e2fa           loop 0xe
11  0014                                                  11  000e  304c0e0b       xorb %cl,0xb(%esi,%ecx)
12  ........<encrypted payload>.........                  12  0012  e2fa           loop 0xe
13  0093                                                  13  ....  .........     .......................
```
                        (a)   (b)

Fig. 1. (a) Self-modifying shellcode example. The second column indicates the address of each instruction, the third column indicates the instruction binary code, and the fourth column is the IA-32 assembly code. The shellcode is mapped to address 0x0000. (b) Execution trace of the self-modifying shellcode shown in Fig. 1(a).

instruction at address 0x0012 is modified to loop 0xe, which forms a backward loop to decrypt instructions from 0x0093 to 0x0014. The loop is controlled by register ecx, which decreases by 1 upon each execution of loop 0xe. Within the loop, the instruction at address 0x000e, xorb %cl, 0xb(%esi,%ecx), is for decryption. It decrypts 1 byte per iteration. When ecx becomes 0, the loop terminates, the content stored from 0x0093 to 0x0014 is fully decrypted, and the control flow continues to the instruction at address 0x0014, the last decrypted instruction. We can see this from the shellcode execution trace shown in Fig. 1(b).

As there is no information that is dynamically generated during shellcode execution, e.g., register values at runtime, static analysis based detection approaches cannot effectively handle the decryption procedure after the shellcode is interpreted as an instruction sequence; these approaches only see the encrypted payload as a meaningless or invalid instruction sequence. Malicious behaviors that are only exhibited during execution are thus effectively concealed.

The shellcode shown in Fig. 1(a) can also be used to evade detection by current dynamic analysis based tools [18, 28, 37–39]. Given an input stream containing the shellcode shown in Fig. 1(a), network-level emulation based approaches will copy the input stream into a memory space that performs this emulation, and all read/write operations will be performed in the emulated memory space. The real contents of virtual memory units at the addresses calculated from eaddr are difficult to obtain. Then the shellcode's encrypted payload cannot be correctly decoded and emulated. In addition, these approaches do not use information in other objects to detect shellcode in the current object, which precludes shellcode detection. Since the use of heap spraying can enable prediction of objects' positions in a heap, it is not difficult for attackers to design shellcode in JS code that makes use of information stored in different objects. For example, if 2 JS objects have predictable heap positions, attackers can store shellcode in one and critical information for decryption in the other.

We also notice that some tools based on network-level emulation use heuristics based on the GetPC code [24, 37] in shellcode detection, e.g., [18] uses

```
      sub-shellcode1                        sub-shellcode2                        sub-shellcode3

1  be20010505   movl $Saddr,%esi        1  8846f7   movb %al,-0x9(%esi)      1  31db   xor %ebx,%ebx
2  8976f8       movl %esi,-0x8(%esi)    2  8946fc   movl %eax,-0x4(%esi)     2  89d8   mov %ebx,%eax
3  836ef810     subl $0x10,-0x8(%esi)   3  b00b     mov $0x0b,%al            3  40     inc %eax
4  31c0         xor %eax,%eax           4  8b5ef8   movl -0x8(%esi),%ebx     4  cd80   int $0x80
5  eb09         jmp Offset1             5  8d4ef8   leal -0x8(%esi),%ecx
                                        6  8d56fc   leal -0x4(%esi),%edx
                                        7  cd80     int $0x80
                                        8  eb04     jmp Offset2
```

Fig. 2. A shellcode can be divided into multiple parts (3 parts here). Each part, denoted by *sub-shellcode*, can be connected to another part by using a `jmp` instruction.

libemu [28]. Besides the aforementioned evasion methods, attackers can also evade detection by writing shellcode without *call group* instruction or `fstenv` instruction opcodes, e.g., using purely alphanumeric shellcode [31]. Note the shellcode shown in Fig. 1(a) has no bytes that can be decoded as the GetPC code.

2.4 Example 2: Thwarting Hijack Prevention Detection

In this subsection, we discuss how to design shellcode that evades hijack prevention detection. Fig. 2 shows a shellcode that can open a root shell. This shellcode can be divided into 3 parts as shown in Fig. 2. The first part, denoted *sub-shellcode1*, is 16 bytes long. The second part, *sub-shellcode2*, is 21 bytes long. The third part, *sub-shellcode3*, is 7 bytes long. In sub-shellcode1, Saddr is 0x05050120 pointing to some part of an object. The memory at address (Saddr-16) stores arguments of the system call used to open a root shell. These include an ASCII sequence /bin/sh. At the end of sub-shellcode1, there is an instruction `jmp Offset1`, where Offset1 is the offset between sub-shellcode1 and sub-shellcode2. This instruction diverts control flow from sub-shellcode1 to sub-shellcode2. In sub-shellcode2, Offset2 is the offset between sub-shellcode2 and sub-shellcode3. At the end of sub-shellcode2, instruction `jmp Offset2` diverts control flow from sub-shellcode2 to sub-shellcode3.

Using heap spraying, the arguments and the sub-shellcodes can be placed into 2 different objects whose positions can be predicted. Let the arguments be placed in *object1* and sub-shellcode1, sub-shellcode2, and sub-shellcode3 be placed in *object2*. Because the data structures of *object1* and *object2* are known to the attacker, it is not difficult to arrange and predict the addresses of the arguments and the above 3 sub-shellcodes in memory.

Consider a Web browser with a certain memory vulnerability that can be exploited to overwrite a function pointer and thus execute arbitrary code. The attacker can use sub-shellcode1's address to overwrite the function pointer. After the web browser's control flow is directed to sub-shellcode1 and the instruction `jmp Offset1` is executed, the control flow can be directed to sub-shellcode2, and then to sub-shellcode3 through the instruction `jmp Offset2`. In this way, the entire shellcode can be executed and a root shell is opened eventually.

Existing hijack prevention approaches may fail to detecting such shellcode with high probability. For example, if the 3 sub-shellcodes are placed at the beginning of 3 25-byte blocks in *object2*, the probability that the entire shellcode can evade detection by Bubble [22] is $(25-16)/25 \times (25-21)/25 \times (25-7)/25 = 4.1\%$. This implies, on average, more than 4 attacks can succeed per 100 trials.

Example 2 also illustrates the importance of JS code execution environment information for an attack. The arguments of the system calls used by the shellcode embedded in *object2* rely on information stored in *object1*.

These examples presented in §2 clearly demonstrate the criticality of fully leveraging JS code execution environment information in order to detect shellcode in JS objects. In addition, to guarantee detection completeness, we need to check all possible instruction sequences that can be decoded.

3   System Design and Implementation

In this section, we present the design methodology of JSGuard, its architecture and key components, and implementation. The detailed workflow will be further illustrated by examples in §4.

3.1   Design Rationale

Fundamentally, the limitations of existing approaches arise because they do not fully use the JS code execution environment information during detection. This motivates our proposal of a new detection approach that overcomes the limitations by efficiently and fully exploiting this information, including: (1) the virtual memory contents of the target application running the JS interpreter; (2) the host system's context information, e.g., system call information; and (3) the JS code semantics, which include stack frames, native method information, JS object properties, etc.

This information is used at the core of JSGuard in the following 2 ways:

– *Creating a Virtual Execution Environment for Detection.* When our detection system is activated, the real environment information at that moment is used to instantiate a virtual environment where potentially malicious JS strings are executed and monitored. Such real environment information is critical for observing the real behaviors of possible shellcodes as they exhibit real execution flow. In malicious shellcodes, process state information can be used to redirect the execution flow, e.g., for encryption or decryption (as illustrated in Example 1) or it can be leveraged to compute arguments for system calls to perform malicious actions (as illustrated in Example 2). Without precise virtual memory information, the shellcode's execution flow or characteristics can be changed and its malicious behavior may not be captured.

Using the real environment information also enables leveraging a target system's binary code to emulate system calls appearing in a decoded instruction sequence, especially those that do not change processes' states but can be used to take part in shellcode computation. This kind of emulation can help us observe more possible shellcode behaviors.

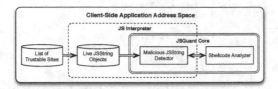

Fig. 3. The overall architecture of JSGuard

– *Facilitating Multiple-level Redundancy Reduction.* We propose reducing detection overhead at 3 levels. First, the number of JS objects to be checked should be minimal. Second, given a JS object to be checked, checking occurs only as necessary (e.g., after mutable objects have changed). Finally, the detection system should be activated as infrequently as possible.

We achieve this multiple-level redundancy reduction at JSGuard's core using the following execution environment information: stack frames, properties of JS objects, and native methods. The JS interpreter maintains a stack frame for each JS function being interpreted including its origin information. By searching the current stack frames, we can determine if JS functions are internal functions or from trustable sites. If not, objects generated in JS functions are to be checked. In addition, since external components are targets of malicious code, our detection system is activated right before control flow enters them. External components are called by JS code via external native methods. Native method information is used to distinguish built-in JS native methods that are secure (as we assume the JS interpreter is secure) from external ones that are written by users to call their external components. We only activate our detection system before external native methods are called.

3.2   JSGuard Architecture and Key Components

JSGuard aims to detect whether JS codes embedded in webpages generate malicious shellcode. If a JS code generates such shellcode at runtime, it is considered malicious. Like other work [18,22], JSGuard focuses on detecting shellcode in JS string objects, as it is difficult to insert shellcode in other types of objects.

As illustrated in Fig. 3, JSGuard resides in the address space of the target process. Besides the *JSGuard core*, the core functionality block that performs detection, JSGuard also involves the JS interpreter and a list of trustable sites. The JS interpreter determines the origins of JS functions being interpreted; only those from external untrusted sites are further checked by the JSGuard core. The list can be maintained manually or automatically. New sites can be added to it according to JSGuard's detection results for them as well as the user's knowledge. These sites can be those that are often visited by the user, e.g., the site of the company he or she is working for. They can be also those maintained by reputable companies or organizations, such as Microsoft, CNN, etc. If users are concerned about a trustable site, they can always force JSGuard to check it. The list entries can be trustable organizations' hostnames or domain names.

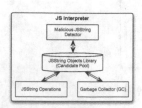

Fig. 4. Malicious JS string detector takes JS strings from a pool maintained by string-related operations and the JS interpreter's GC

```
 1  #define   BENIGN      0
 2  #define   MALICIOUS   1
 3
 4  struct JSString {
 5      size_t          length;
 6      jschar          *chars;
 7  };
 8
 9  int maliciousJSStringDetector(checkinglist) {
10      JSString *string;
11      check = checkinglist;
12      while(check != NULL) {
13          string = check->string;
14          if(ShellcodeAnalyzer(string->chars)==MALICIOUS)
15              return MALICIOUS;
16          check=check->next;
17      }
18      checkinglist = NULL;
19      return BENIGN;
20  }
```

Fig. 5. Workflow of malicious JS string detector

As shown in Fig. 3, JSGuard core has 2 key components: the malicious JS string detector and the shellcode analyzer. The malicious JS string detector runs in the JS interpreter. It prepares JS strings to be checked at runtime and then feeds them to the shellcode analyzer. The shellcode analyzer checks if an input object's content contains malicious shellcode or a part thereof and reports the results back to the malicious JS string detector. If a malicious JS string is found, interpretation stops; otherwise, it continues. In the following, we detail these components.

Malicious JavaScript String Detector. As shown in Fig. 4, the detector retrieves and checks JS strings from a checking list, which contains all JS strings that might have malicious shellcode. The checking list is maintained by instrumenting string-related operations and the JS interpreter's garbage collector (GC). In particular, when a new string JS is created, it is inserted into the checking list; when the GC reclaims a JS string, the string will be removed from the checking list after its content is zeroed.

The basic workflow of the malicious JavaScript string detector is shown in Fig. 5. The function `maliciousJSStringDetector()` has an input `checkinglist`. When called, it scans all strings in `checkinglist` and feeds them to `shellcodeAnalyzer()`, which detects malicious shellcode in JS string contents. If `shellcodeAnalyzer()` finds a JS string containing malicious shellcode, it returns `MALICIOUS` to `maliciousJSStringDetector()`. Then `maliciousJSStringDetector()` stops checking the remaining JS strings in `checkinglist` and returns `MALICIOUS` to the JS interpreter, which stops interpreting JS code. If no JS string is found to be malicious, then `maliciousJSStringDetector()` returns `BENIGN` to the interpreter, which continues interpreting JS code. In JSGuard's core, `maliciousJSStringDetector()` is called immediately before JS code calls an external component.

`checkinglist` contains the JS strings to be checked. Every time a JS string is generated, all current stack frames are checked. If there are any JS functions from external untrusted sites, then we add the JS string to `checkinglist`. We

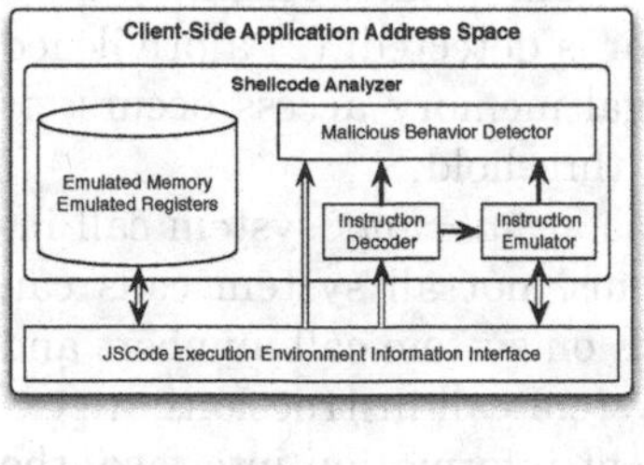

```
1  #define MALICIOUS 1
2  #define BENIGN    0
3  #define MALICIOUS_SEQUENCE 1
4  #define BENIGN_SEQUENCE    0
5
6  int ShellcodeAnalyzer(base_addr , base_size) {
7    for (i = 0; i< base_size; i++)
8      if (MaliciousInstructionSeq(base_addr + i))
9        return MALICIOUS;
10   return BENIGN;
11 }
12
13 int MaliciousInstructionSeq(addr){
14   InitializeEmulationEnvironment();
15   instruction = InstructionDecoder(addr);
16   if (End(instruction)) return BENIGN_SEQUENCE;
17   instruction.exe_depth = 1;
18   while (instruction) {
19     if (MaliciousSystemCall(instruction))
20       if (instruction.exe_depth > exe_depth_thresh)
21         return MALICIOUS_SEQUENCE;
22     InstructionEmulator(instruction);
23     UpdateEmulationEnvironment();
24     target = ComputeTarget(instruction);
25     prevInstruct = instruction;
26     instruction = InstructionDecoder(target);
27     if (End(instruction)) break;
28     SetExecutionDepth(instruction , prevInstruct);
29   }
30   return BENIGN_SEQUENCE;
31 }
```

Fig. 6. Shellcode analyzer architecture

Fig. 7. Workflow of shellcode analyzer

do so because only JS codes from external untrusted sites attempt to generate shellcode that exploits target applications' vulnerabilities. As JS strings are immutable objects, we can safely remove the strings from checkinglist after they have been checked once [22].

Shellcode Analyzer. The shellcode analyzer architecture is shown in Fig. 6. This module consists of an instruction decoder, an instruction emulator, a malicious behavior detector, an emulated memory system, and emulated registers.

Given a position in a JS string content, the instruction decoder decodes instructions starting at that position and sends each decoded instruction to the emulator. For each instruction the emulator receives, it emulates the execution thereof, for which the emulated memory system and registers provide a virtual runtime environment. The JS code execution environment information provided to the shellcode analyzer includes the target process's address space, current registers, and other context information as necessary. The emulator executes each instruction sequence and the malicious behavior detector determines whether there is any malicious behavior. If any such behavior is detected, then the instruction sequence is considered malicious. As a result, the shellcode analyzer concludes there is malicious shellcode in the content buffer. Hence the JS string object is considered malicious.

During instruction sequence emulation, if there is an instruction that reads memory, the memory values are first fetched from the real memory units in the target process's address space. Next, these values are stored in the emulated memory system. Future read operations to the same memory units will be directed to the emulated memory system. If there is a write memory operation, it will be directed to the emulated memory system. The write operation is never performed on the corresponding real memory units in the target process's address space to avoid disturbing "normal" JS code execution.

The shellcode analyzer workflow is shown in Fig. 7. From each input data position, the shellcode analyzer uses the target process's virtual memory information to emulate the execution of the decoded instruction sequence. There are 2 input parameters for `ShellcodeAnalyzer()`: (1) `base_address`, the starting address of the input data to be analyzed; and (2) `base_size`, the input data size.

The key function of the shellcode analyzer is `MaliciousInstructionSeq()`, which detects a malicious instruction sequence. The workflow of `MaliciousInstructionSeq()` is shown in lines 13–31 in Fig. 7. The `while` loop from line 18 to line 29 in Fig. 7 emulates a sequence of instructions, which continues until one of the following occurs: (1) a malicious behavior is detected; (2) a privileged or invalid instruction is encountered;[1] (3) an illegal memory access occurs; or (4) the number of executed instructions exceeds a threshold.

In our system, a *malicious behavior* is defined as a *malicious* system call invocation. In Linux and Microsoft Windows systems, not all system calls can compromise the target host's security. This depends on system call numbers and parameters, which are stored in registers before system call instructions are executed. Through the JS code execution environment information interface, the system call number and its parameters can be accurately obtained to determine if the system call invocation is intended to compromise the host's security. For example, in Linux, the system call number 11 corresponds to the system function `execve`, which executes a program. During instruction emulation, if the instruction is a system call instruction and the value of the emulated `eax` is 11, then the system call number is 11. After checking parameters stored in other emulated registers and the emulated memory system, if its first parameter is `/bin/sh`, then we can conclude that the instruction tries to open a root shell. In this case, the system call instruction will be considered malicious.

Shellcodes normally need several instructions to initialize system call parameters. Hence, we also use the `exe_depth` of an instruction that invokes a system call to decrease false positives. An instruction's `exe_depth` is defined as the number of instructions from the starting point to it during emulation of an instruction sequence. For example, suppose that a statement S in a `for` loop is executed 100 times. Then the execution depth of S is 2 (`for` statement and S).

Our system can also leverage heuristics used in current network-level emulation tools [18, 28, 37–39] to detect shellcode in JS strings during emulation. However, these heuristics are confined to detect particular types of shellcode that exhibit self-decrypting behavior [18, 28, 37, 38] or match specific memory access patterns [39]. In addition, as illustrated in §2, they are ineffective at detecting shellcode that fully exploits JS code execution environment information.

---

[1] Privileged instructions can only be executed in kernel mode; shellcodes normally run in user mode. An exception occurs if a shellcode contains a privileged instruction.

3.3   Implementation

The JSGuard prototype system is implemented in Debian Linux with kernel version 2.6.26 using C and C++ with gcc 4.3.2. The key component is the JSGuard core, which comprises 2 major parts. The first part is a modified JS interpreter integrated with the malicious JS string detector. This part is based on the Spider-Monkey JS interpreter [49], which is used in various Mozilla products including Firefox. The second part is the shellcode analyzer module. We implement it as a C library in Debian Linux system. When the malicious JS string detector calls the module, it is loaded into the address space of the application running the JS interpreter. We also implement a Firefox extension that maintains the list of trustable sites, which is loaded into Firefox's address space upon execution.

Modified JS Interpreter. In this part, we implement a malicious JS string detector, which scans JS string objects from a checkinglist and then calls the shellcode analyzer to determine if they have malicious content. The checkinglist is maintained by the code that we add into all functions related to JS string operations. First, we instrument all functions related to JS string object creation. In this way, we can track all JS string objects generated during execution of the external JS code. Populating the checkinglist with all strings fundamentally guarantees the completeness of our detection. Second, before adding a JS string to checkinglist, we also use the list of trustable sites and current stack frames to decide if the JS string should be added to checkinglist. If all JS functions being interpreted are from trustable sites or internal JS functions, the string will not be added to checkinglist; otherwise, it will.

After analyzing the source code of the SpiderMonkey JS interpreter, we find all call points that invoke native methods and insert calls to the malicious JS string detector at these points. Since the JS interpreter also uses native methods to implement some built-in JS class methods, we check if a native call is calling a JS built-in method at native call points. If this is the case, we do not activate the malicious JS string detector; otherwise, we activate it. This is due to our assumption that the JS interpreter has no exploitable memory errors. The native methods for JS built-in class methods are parts of the JS interpreter, so they do not have exploitable memory errors. However, when control flow leaves the JS interpreter to external functions, the malicious JS string detector will be activated to check all JS strings in the checkinglist.

We modify the JS interpreter's garbage collector to maintain the checkinglist and integrate the modified JS interpreter into the Firefox 4 Web browser.

Shellcode Analyzer. The shellcode analyzer prototype focuses on the IA-32 architecture and the Linux OS. We implement an instruction emulator and an instruction decoder, which is based on the Bastard project's libdisasm with version 0.23-pre [50].

When encountering a system call instruction (sysenter or int 0x80) in emulation, the shellcode analyzer will determine, with the parameters stored in the emulated memory/register system, whether it is one of 36 system calls that can be used to compromise the Linux system [32]. Besides these "malicious" system calls, we also use the exe_depth threshold to determine if the instruction truly tries to compromise the host's security; we set the threshold to 10 since most unencrypted malicious shellcodes have at least 10 instructions [38,55]. To avoid an infinite loop during instruction sequence emulation decoded from a position of a JS string's content, we set the threshold to 8000 for the number of executed instructions. According to current research, this threshold suffices to detect malicious shellcodes [37,38].

4   A Detection Example

We illustrate our detection system's effectiveness by presenting the detection procedure for Example 2 in §2.3. Example 1 in §2.2 can similarly be detected.

Assume that an attacker tries to exploit a Firefox external component in Linux using a malicious JS code. He first uses heap spraying to allocate large JS objects, then inserts the arguments and the 3 sub-shellcodes, as shown in Fig. 2, into 2 objects. We denote these objects as *object1* and *object2*. The objects are allocated in 2 contiguous memory areas and their addresses are predictable, say, 0x05250020 and 0x05350020, respectively. The JS code places the arguments in *object1* with Saddr set to 0x05250084 and places sub-shellcode1, sub-shellcode2 and sub-shellcode3 into *object2* with their addresses set to 0x05350084, 0x0535009D and 0x053500B6 respectively. Then the offset between sub-shellcode1 and sub-shellcode2 is 9 and the offset between sub-shellcode2 and sub-shellcode3 is 4. Hence, in Fig. 2, Saddr is 0x05250084, Offset1 is 9, and Offset2 is 4.

The attack starts when the 3 sub-shellcodes are ready in the heap. The JS code calls the vulnerable component. Before control flow is diverted from the JS interpreter to the external component, the JS interpreter with JSGuard invokes maliciousJSStringDetector() to check whether there are malicious JS strings arranged in the heap. maliciousJSStringDetector() will scan JS strings in checkinglist and send them iteratively to the shellcode analyzer. At a certain moment, the shellcode analyzer receives the content of *object2*.

The shellcode analyzer decodes every possible instruction sequence starting from each byte position of the content, and then executes it. Each instruction in the instruction sequence starting from the address 0x05350084 will be decoded and then executed. When the instruction jmp Offset1, i.e., jumping to 0x0535009D, is decoded and executed, the shellcode analyzer will follow the control flow and begin to decode instructions starting from 0x0535009D and execute them. Note 0x0535009D is the starting address of the sub-shellcode2 instruction sequence. In this way, the instruction sequence of sub-shellcode2 is discovered and executed. When system call instruction int $0x80 is executed, we can obtain its parameters since the contents of the emulated registers/memory system precisely reflect the runtime changes during the emulation. The shellcode analyzer discovers that this system call instruction tries to open a root shell. Meanwhile, this instruction's exe_depth exceeds the threshold. Thus this system call instruction will be considered malicious. As a result, the entire emulated instruction sequence is considered malicious. The shellcode analyzer concludes that *object2* content contains malicious shellcode and returns to `maliciousJSStringDetector()`. When the malicious JS string detector receives `MALICIOUS` from the shellcode analyzer, it in turn concludes that *object2* is a malicious JS string and the JS code being interpreted is malicious. It throws an exception and stops interpreting JS code.

5 Evaluation

We conduct extensive experiments to evaluate JSGuard, particularly its detection effectiveness and runtime overhead. We do so on a HP Pavilion a815n with an Intel Pentium 4 3.06 GHz CPU and 1 GB RAM. The computer is connected to a university campus network through 100 Mbps Ethernet; it runs Debian Linux with kernel version 2.6.26.

5.1 Effectiveness

Detection effectiveness is measured by false positives and false negatives.

– *False Positive: 0/2000.* We implement a Firefox extension that automatically fetches websites listed in a file. We set the time interval between 2 fetches to be 50 s, which is generally sufficient for JS codes embedded in a webpage to be fully executed. Every 50 s, the extension iteratively reads a URL from the file and then loads the webpage in a browser window. We construct a benign URL list containing 2000 URLs taken from the Alexa ranking of top global sites [1]. These are real websites with various content and Web applications. JSGuard classifies all of them as benign.

– *False Negative: 0/5063.* We collect 12 real world malicious webpages containing JS code that generate shellcode to launch attacks; we also collect 51 plain malicious shellcodes from the Internet. All of them target Linux systems. Based on the 51 plain shellcodes, we use the following tools to generate 5000 polymorphic or/and metamorphic malicious shellcodes: the Metasploit project's JumpCallAdditive, Pex, PexFnstenvMov, PexFnstenvSub, and ShikataGaNai [51] as well as ADMmutate [30] and TAPiON [2], which are also used in other shellcode detection tools [37, 38, 54, 55] to test their effectiveness. We then create 5051 JS codes that generate these malicious shellcodes at runtime and invoke native methods that are not built in to the JS interpreter. For example, the JS method `document.write()` eventually calls a native method. Finally we craft 5051 malicious webpages with these malicious JS codes. We put these 5051 malicious webpages and the 12 real world malicious webpages on our internal Web server and we visit them using Firefox with JSGuard on a client computer. JSGuard classifies all of them as malicious. In addition, we also write 2 heap spraying JS codes, dynamically generate the 2 shellcode examples presented in §§2.2–2.3, and feed them to JSGuard. It correctly classifies them as malicious.

Table 1. The overhead of checking trustable sites only. "Original version" is Firefox without our system. "Trustable List Only" is Firefox with our detection system enabled (JSGuard core disabled).

Firefox Version	Total Time	Time/Page	Overhead/Page
Original Version	491.953 s	1.63984 s	N/A
Trustable List Only	492.254 s	1.64085 s	0.00101 s

Table 2. The overhead purely incurred by the JSGuard core block. "JSGuard Core Only" is Firefox with our system enabled (checking trustable sites disabled).

Firefox Version	Total Time	Time/Page	Overhead/Page
Original Version	491.953 s	1.63984 s	N/A
JSGuard Core Only	1651.45 s	5.50483 s	3.86499 s

Table 3. The overhead incurred by JSGuard. The version with JSGuard is Firefox with our entire JSGuard system enabled.

Firefox Version	Total Time	Time/Page	Overhead/Page
Original Version	491.953 s	1.63984 s	N/A
With JSGuard	753.059 s	2.51019 s	0.87035 s

5.2   Overhead

To measure JSGuard's overhead, we use 2 versions of Firefox 4: one integrated with JSGuard and an "original" version without JSGuard. We use the 100 most popular websites as described by Alexa [1] as the testing dataset. In our experiments, we visit each website 3 times using each version of Firefox. The time we measured, *rendering time*, includes the times for downloading a webpage from the Internet, page parsing and rendering, and executing all JS codes therein.

We performed 3 types of experiments to measure overhead incurred: (1) by only checking trustable sites; (2) by only using the JSGuard core functionality block; and (3) by using entire JSGuard system.

In the first experiment, we disable JSGuard and measure the overhead purely incurred by checking trustable sites. We use the 10,000 most popular websites from Alexa [1] to form a list of trustable sites. The experiment results are shown in Table 1, which shows that this overhead is very low. Thus our detection system has little impact on the rendering time when all JS functions called during runtime are internal ones or from trustable sites. The second experiment measures the overhead purely incurred by running JSGuard core *without* checking trustable sites. It is an extreme case where every site the user visits is assumed to be malicious, i.e., every JS string is put into `checkinglist` so long as all interpreted JS functions are from external sites. From Table 2, the average overhead incurred by JSGuard core is 3.865 s. Note that this performance is measured in the worst-case scenario with a low-end machine. Indeed, studies show that overall user frustration increases when page load times exceed 8–10 s [8,33]. Hence, performance is acceptable even in this extreme case. The third experiment measures the overhead incurred by the entire JSGuard system. We construct a random list of 50 trustable sites from our testing dataset. The remaining 50 sites in our testing dataset are thus considered untrustable. Table 3 shows the experiment results. JSGuard's average overhead is modest: ~0.87 s.

6 Related Work

Detecting shellcode in JS objects is essential to protect vulnerable applications from JS based shellcode injection attacks. As §2.1 noted, existing shellcode detection approaches fall into 2 categories: *content analysis* and *hijack prevention*.

Content analysis is particularly popular in detecting shellcode from network messages. In [52], Toth and Kruegel proposed identifying exploit code by detecting NOP sleds. However, attacks can bypass this detection technique by either *excluding* NOP sleds or by using polymorphic techniques [11, 16, 30]. Chritodorescu and colleagues [12,13] proposed techniques to detect malicious patterns in executables using semantic heuristics. Lakhotia and Eric in [27] used content analysis techniques to detect obfuscated calls in binaries. Chinchani and van den Berg proposed a rule-based scheme in [11]. Wang et al. proposed SigFree [55] that checks if network packets contain malicious codes using "push and call" patterns and the number of useful instructions in the longest possible execution chain. These methods are based on static analysis. Although they are efficient in detecting shellcode, they still can be thwarted by using binary obfuscation [5]. To improve detection completeness, Polychronakis et al. proposed a new network-level emulation approach [37, 38] to detect polymorphic shellcode. Gene [39] used network-level emulation with specific memory access pattern heuristics to detect shellcode for MS-Windows systems. Gu et al. proposed the virtual memory snapshot based emulation approach in end systems to detect shellcode in network messages before they are processed by network server programs [23]. ShellOS provides a framework leveraging hardware visualization to detect shellcode [46]. It requires users to dump the entire target process's states and load them into ShellOS in order to construct an emulation environment. A powerful shellcode analyzer named "Shellzer" is proposed in [56]. It conducts analysis by instrumenting each instruction, which may incur undesirable overhead for online detection.

All these approaches are useful for detecting shellcode in network messages, but they are not directly applicable to detecting shellcode in JS strings, as such shellcode is not transmitted in its binary form. Instead, each byte of the shellcode is transmitted using its ASCII representation. In general, ASCII character sequences cannot be successfully decoded into the corresponding shellcode instruction sequences [18], though this is sometimes possible [35]. Nozzle is a well-known JS shellcode attack detection tool. It scans a heap object, interprets the object content to build a control flow graph (CFG), and then uses the CFG to check weather the content contains shellcode [43]. Egele et al. propose an approach that uses `libemu` [28] to check if the content of a JS string contains a sufficiently long valid instruction sequence using network-level emulation and GetPC code based heuristics. Hijack prevention based approaches can be used before or during shellcode execution. Such approaches include randomization [4, 6, 7, 26, 36], OS extension [3, 25] and flow tracking techniques [34, 42]. In general, these approaches have good detection completeness due to their extensive use of context information. However, their troubleshooting to find out the root cause is inefficient [55], which often requires heavy playback or log analysis. Recently, Gadaleta et al. proposed Bubble [22], a lightweight approach that encumbers complete execution of injected shellcode.

Recently, several machine learning based systems were proposed to detect malicious JS code. Zozzle applies Bayesian classification to hierarchical features of the JavaScript abstract syntax tree to identify syntax elements that strongly predict malware [15]. Jsand [14] emulates JS code in a virtual browser environment using machine learning methods to capture malicious features. Prophiler [9] constructs a filter that can quickly discard benign pages and forward potentially malicious pages to heavyweight analysis tools. JSGuard can complement these systems by providing malicious code training samples.

We note that some works like Cujo [44] and Blade [29] can also prevent drive-by-download attacks. However, their focus differs from ours, which is malicious shellcode detection in JS code. These works cannot prevent in-memory execution of injected shellcode. We are aware that tools like [10, 19] have been proposed to audit JS activities, but they are not malicious shellcode detection systems.

7   Conclusion

In this paper, we have proposed a new methodology to detect JS shellcode that fully uses JS code execution environment information in an efficient manner. Following the methodology, we implemented JSGuard, a prototype malicious JS code detection system on Debian Linux. Extensive experiments with real traces and thousands of malicious shellcodes illustrate our detection system's performance with acceptable overhead and very few false negatives or false positives, which validated our methodology's promise for this purpose.

References

1. Alexa Top Sites, http://www.alexa.com/topsites
2. Bania, P.: TAPiON (2005), http://pb.specialised.info/all/tapion/
3. Baratloo, A., Singh, N., Tsai, T.: Transparent Run-Time Defense Against Stack Smashing Attacks. In: USENIX Annual Technical Conf. (2000)
4. Barrantes, E.G., Ackley, D.H., Forrest, S., Palmer, T.S., Stefanović, D., Zovi, D.D.: Randomized Instruction Set Emulation to Disrupt Binary Code Injection Attacks. In: CCS (2003)
5. Bayer, U., Moser, A., Kruegel, C., Kirda, E.: Dynamic Analysis of Malicious Code. Journal of Computer Virology (2006)
6. Bhatkar, S., DuVarney, D.C., Sekar, R.: Address Obfuscation: An Efficient Approach to Combat a Broad Range of Memory Error Exploits. USENIX Security (2003)
7. Bhatkar, S., Sekar, R.: Data Space Randomization. In: Zamboni, D. (ed.) DIMVA 2008. LNCS, vol. 5137, pp. 1–22. Springer, Heidelberg (2008)

8. Bouch, A., Kuchinsky, A., Bhatti, N.: Quality is in the Eye of the Beholder: Meeting Users' Requirements for Internet Quality of Service. In: CHI (2000)
9. Canali, D., Cova, M., Kruegel, C., Vigna, G.: Prophiler: A Fast Filter for the Large-Scale Detection of Malicious Web Pages. In: WWW (March 2011)
10. Chenette, S.: Toorconx the ultimate deobfuscator (2008), http://www.toorcon.org/tcx/26_Chenette.pdf
11. Chinchani, R., van den Berg, E.: A Fast Static Analysis Approach to Detect Exploit Code Inside Network Flows. In: Valdes, A., Zamboni, D. (eds.) RAID 2005. LNCS, vol. 3858, pp. 284–308. Springer, Heidelberg (2006)
12. Christodorescu, M., Jha, S.: Static Analysis of Executables to Detect Malicious Patterns. USENIX Security (2003)
13. Christodorescu, M., Jha, S., Seshia, S., Song, D., Bryant, R.E.: Semantics-Aware Malware Detection. IEEE S&P (2005)
14. Cova, M., Kruegel, C., Vigna, G.: Detection and Analysis of Drive-by-Download Attacks and Malicious JavaScript Code. In: WWW (2010)
15. Curtsinger, C., Livshits, B., Zorn, B., Seifert, C.: Zozzle: Fast and Precise In-Browser JavaScript Malware Detection. USENIX Security (2011)
16. Detristan, T., Ulenspiegel, T., Malcom, Y., van Underduk, M.S.: Polymorphic Shellcode Engine Using Spectrum Analysis. Phrack (2003), http://www.phrack.org
17. Ding, Y., Wei, T., Wang, T., Liang, Z., Zou, W.: Heap Taichi: Exploiting Memory Allocation Granularity in Heap-Spraying Attacks. In: ACSAC (2010)
18. Egele, M., Wurzinger, P., Kruegel, C., Kirda, E.: Defending Browsers against Drive-by Downloads: Mitigating Heap-Spraying Code Injection Attacks. In: Flegel, U., Bruschi, D. (eds.) DIMVA 2009. LNCS, vol. 5587, pp. 88–106. Springer, Heidelberg (2009)
19. Feinstein, B., Peck, D.: Caffeine Monkey, http://www.secureworks.com/research/blog/wp-content/uploads/CaffeineMonkey_DEFCON15.pdf
20. Fogie, S., Grossman, J., Hansen, R., Rager, A.: XSS Attacks: Cross Site Scripting Exploits and Defense. Syngress (May 2007)
21. Frei, S., Duebendorfer, T., Ollmann, G., May, M.: Understanding the web browser threat. In: DefCon 16 (August 2008)
22. Gadaleta, F., Younan, Y., Joosen, W.: BuBBle: A Javascript Engine Level Countermeasure against Heap-Spraying Attacks. In: Massacci, F., Wallach, D., Zannone, N. (eds.) ESSoS 2010. LNCS, vol. 5965, pp. 1–17. Springer, Heidelberg (2010)
23. Gu, B., Bai, X., Yang, Z., Champion, A.C., Xuan, D.: Malicious Shellcode Detection with Virtual Memory Snapshots. In: INFOCOM, pp. 974–982 (2010)
24. Ionescu, C.: GetPC code, http://securityfocus.com/archive/82/327348/2006-01-03/1
25. Kc, G.S., Keromytis, A.D.: e-nexsh: Achieving an Effectively Non-Executable Stack and Heap via System-Call Policing. In: ACSAC (2005)
26. Kc, G.S., Keromytis, A.D., Prevelakis, V.: Countering Code-Injection Attacks with Instruction-Set Randomization. In: CCS (2003)
27. Lakhotia, A., Eric, U.: Stack Shape Analysis to Detect Obfuscated Calls in Binaries. In: IEEE Int'l. Conf. on Source Code Analysis and Manipulation (2004)
28. libemu, http://libemu.carnivore.it/
29. Lu, L., Yegneswaran, V., Porras, P., Lee, W.: BLADE: An Attack-Agnostic Approach for Preventing Drive-By Malware Infections. In: CCS (2010)
30. Macaulay, S.: ADMMutate: Polymorphic Shellcode Engine, http://www.ktwo.ca/security.html

31. Mason, J., Small, S., Monrose, F., MacManus, G.: English Shellcode. In: CCS (2009)
32. Mutz, D., Robertson, W., Vigna, G., Kemmerer, R.A.: Exploiting Execution Context for the Detection of Anomalous System Calls. In: Kruegel, C., Lippmann, R., Clark, A. (eds.) RAID 2007. LNCS, vol. 4637, pp. 1–20. Springer, Heidelberg (2007)
33. Nah, F.F.-H.: A Study on Tolerable Waiting Time: How Long are Web Users Willing to Wait? Behaviour & IT 23(3), 153–163 (2004)
34. Newsome, J., Song, D.: Dynamic Taint Analysis for Automatic Detection, Analysis, and Signature Generation of Exploits on Commodity Software. In: NDSS (2005)
35. Obscou. Building IA32 'Unicode-Proof' Shellcodes. Phrack (2003), http://www.phrack.org/
36. PaX, http://pax.grsecurity.net/docs/aslr.txt
37. Polychronakis, M., Anagnostakis, K.G., Markatos, E.P.: Network–Level Polymorphic Shellcode Detection Using Emulation. In: Büschkes, R., Laskov, P. (eds.) DIMVA 2006. LNCS, vol. 4064, pp. 54–73. Springer, Heidelberg (2006)
38. Polychronakis, M., Anagnostakis, K.G., Markatos, E.P.: Emulation-Based Detection of Non-self-contained Polymorphic Shellcode. In: Kruegel, C., Lippmann, R., Clark, A. (eds.) RAID 2007. LNCS, vol. 4637, pp. 87–106. Springer, Heidelberg (2007)
39. Polychronakis, M., Anagnostakis, K.G., Markatos, E.P.: Comprehensive shellcode detection using runtime heuristics. In: ACSAC (December 2010)
40. Provos, N., Mavrommatis, P., Rajab, M.A., Monrose, F.: All Your iFRAMEs Point to Us. USENIX Security (2008)
41. Provos, N., McNamee, D., Mavrommatis, P., Wang, K., Modadugu, N.: The Ghost In the Browser: Analysis of Web-based Malware. In: HotBots (2007)
42. Qin, F., Wang, C., Li, Z., Kim, H.-S., Zhou, Y., Wu, Y.: LIFT: A Low-Overhead Practical Information Flow Tracking System for Detecting Security Attacks. In: MICRO (2006)
43. Ratanaworabhan, P., Livshits, B., Zorn, B.: NOZZLE: A Defense Against Heap-spraying Code Injection Attacks. USENIX Security (2009)
44. Rieck, K., Krueger, T., Dewald, A.: Cujo: Efficient Detection and Prevention of Drive-by-Download Attacks. In: ACSAC (December 2010)
45. Secunia. Secunia PSI study: 28% of all detected applications are insecure (2007), http://secunia.com/blog/11
46. Snow, K.Z., Krishnan, S., Monrose, F.: Shellos: Enabling fast detection and forensic analysis of code injection attacks. USENIX Security (2011)
47. Sotirov, A.: Heap Feng Shui in JavaScript. In: BlackHat Europe (2007)
48. Sotirov, A., Dowd, M.: Bypassing Browser Memory Protections. In: BlackHat (2008)
49. SpiderMonkey JavaScript engine, http://www.mozilla.org/js/spidermonkey/
50. The Bastard Disassembly Environment, http://bastard.sourceforge.net
51. The Metasploit Project, http://www.metasploit.com
52. Tóth, T., Kruegel, C.: Accurate Buffer Overflow Detection via Abstract Payload Execution. In: Wespi, A., Vigna, G., Deri, L. (eds.) RAID 2002. LNCS, vol. 2516, pp. 274–291. Springer, Heidelberg (2002)
53. Vulnerability Note VU#492515: Microsoft Internet Explorer HTML object memory corruption vulnerability, http://www.kb.cert.org/vuls/id/492515
54. Wang, X., Jhi, Y.-C., Zhu, S., Liu, P.: STILL: Exploit Code Detection via Static Taint and Initialization Analyses. In: ACSAC (2008)
55. Wang, X., Pan, C.-C., Liu, P., Zhu, S.: SigFree: A Signature-Free Buffer Overflow Attack Blocker. USENIX Security (2006)
56. Fratantonio, Y., Kruegel, C., Vigna, G.: Shellzer: A Tool for the Dynamic Analysis of Malicious Shellcode. In: Sommer, R., Balzarotti, D., Maier, G. (eds.) RAID 2011. LNCS, vol. 6961, pp. 61–80. Springer, Heidelberg (2011)

Detection of Configuration Vulnerabilities in Distributed (Web) Environments*

Matteo Maria Casalino, Michele Mangili, Henrik Plate, and Serena Elisa Ponta

SAP Research Sophia-Antipolis, 805 Avenue Dr M. Donat, 06250 Mougins, France
{matteo.maria.casalino,henrik.plate,serena.ponta}@sap.com

Abstract. Many tools and libraries are readily available to build and operate distributed Web applications. While the setup of operational environments is comparatively easy, practice shows that their continuous secure operation is more difficult to achieve, many times resulting in vulnerable systems exposed to the Internet. Authenticated vulnerability scanners and validation tools represent a means to detect security vulnerabilities caused by missing patches or misconfiguration, but current approaches center much around the concepts of hosts and operating systems. This paper presents a language and an approach for the declarative specification and execution of machine-readable security checks for sets of more fine-granular system components depending on each other in a distributed environment. Such a language, building on existing standards, fosters the creation and sharing of security content among security stakeholders. Our approach is exemplified by vulnerabilities of and corresponding checks for Open Source Software commonly used in today's Internet applications.

Keywords: configuration validation, detection of misconfiguration, web security, distributed environments.

1 Introduction

The importance of security is nowadays well recognized and mechanisms to enforce it are being developed and adopted within enterprises. However, this is not sufficient to ensure that security requirements are met, as such mechanisms have to be correctly configured and maintained at operations time. In fact, a significant share of vulnerabilities results from security misconfiguration, as shown by data breach reports such as [1], [2] and projects such as the OWASP Top 10 [3]. The reason is that activities targeting the creation and maintenance of a secure setup, such as patch or configuration management, are labor-intense and error-prone. Software vendors, for instance, issue an increasing number of security advisories, while users, on the other hand, struggle to understand if a given vulnerability is exploitable under their particular conditions and requires immediate patching. As another example, configuration best-practice provided

---

* This work was partially supported by the FP7-ICT-2009.1.4 Project PoSecCo (no. 257129, www.posecco.eu)

A.D. Keromytis and R. Di Pietro (Eds.): SecureComm 2012, LNICST 106, pp. 131–148, 2013.
© Institute for Computer Sciences, Social Informatics and Telecommunications Engineering 2013

as prose documentation and supposingly supporting system admininistrators, is often very broad and ambiguous.

Due to such difficulties, configuration validation is needed to gain assurance about system security, but again, often requires manual intervention, and thus is time-consuming and limited to samples. New trends focus on providing standards for security automation, e.g., the Security Content Automation Protocol (SCAP, [4]), provided by the National Institute of Standard and Technology (NIST), whose specifications receive a lot of attention in the scope of the configuration baseline for IT products used in US federal agencies [4]. SCAP comprises a language that allows the specification of machine-readable security checks to facilitate the detection of vulnerabilities caused by misconfiguration. While this represents an important step towards the standardization and exchange of security knowledge, SCAP focus on the granularity of hosts and operating systems, and as such cannot be easily applied to fine-granular and distributed system components[1] independent from their environment, e.g., a Java Web Application (JWA). Furthermore, SCAP does not leverage standards and technologies in the area of system and configuration management, in order to, for instance, separate check logic and information about configuration retrieval.

To address these limitations and make the advantages of SCAP available to Web security experts, we propose a SCAP-based language and approach for the declarative specification and execution of checks for sets of fine-granular components depending on each other in a distributed environment. Moreover we separate the check logic from the retrieval of the configuration values for which we rely on existing system management procedures and technologies, e.g., Configuration Management Databases (CMDB) as defined in the IT Infrastructure Library (ITIL). Each check is essentially a set of tests over software component properties - such as the release and patch level - and configuration settings that determine a system component's behavior. Though this is not a limitation of the language, we focus on security checks, i.e., one of the most important usages is the detection of security vulnerabilities. As an example, the language allows the specification of a check to express that the deployment descriptor of any JWA deployed in a Servlet container supporting a Servlet specification version of at least 3.0 must have the `http-only` flag enabled, to prevent the access of client-side scripts to session cookies.

This paper is structured as follows. Sect. 2 introduces a sample system based on common Open Source Software (OSS), introduces a set of scenarios for configuration validation, and derives requirements for a configuration validation language. Sect. 3 presents state-of-the-art with regard to the specification of security checks for software and configuration vulnerabilities. Sect. 4 presents the configuration validation language, while Sect. 5 describes our approach. The paper concludes with an outlook on future work in Sect. 6.

---

[1] A system component hereby represents a single installation of a software component (or product) in a specific system, such as a given deployment of a Java Web Application in a Servlet container.

2 Use Case and Requirements

This section outlines an example landscape composed of a custom application on top of common OSS, and herewith prototypic for many real-life systems. An overview about network topology and installed software components is shown in Fig. 1. The service provider ACME operates this landscape for its application service "eInvoice", which allows customers to manage electronic invoices, and to make them available to their business partners through the Internet. The application front-end for managing and accessing invoices is implemented as a JWA. Instances of the application, each dedicated to one customer, are deployed in Tomcat, in customer-specific context roots. Tomcat instances run inside an internal subnet, and are proxied by the Apache HTTP Server installed on a physical machine connected to the DMZ. Requests for a customer-dedicated sub-domain of acme.com are forwarded by the reverse-proxy to the respective, customer-dedicated instance of the JWA via the Apache JServ Protocol (AJP).

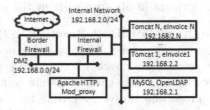

Another machine running in the internal network hosts a LDAP server for the management of user accounts, as well as a MySQL database used for persistency.

Fig. 1. ACME landscape

As the system is prototypic, so are the tasks related to configuration management and validation. In the following, we will describe different scenarios for configuration validation, different in terms of periodicity, urgency (response time), validation scope, and authorship of configuration checks.

Vulnerability Assessment (S1). This scenario focuses on the detection of known vulnerabilities. Upon disclosure of a new security vulnerability of off-the-shelf applications or software libraries, system administrators need to investigate the susceptibility of their system. First, they need to check for the presence of affected release and patch levels. This can be difficult in case of software libraries embedded into off-the-shelf applications as their presence is often unknown. Second, they need to check whether additional conditions for a successful exploitation are met. Such conditions often concern specific configuration settings of the affected software, as well as the specific usage context and system environment. The automation of both activities with help of machine-readable vulnerability checks decreases time and effort required to discover a system vulnerability, and at the same time increases the precision with which the presence of vulnerabilities can be detected. Precision is important as organizations are typically reluctant to apply patches or other measures in a productive environment unless absolutely necessary. Such checks would represent a valuable complement to textual descriptions published by security researchers or software vendors in vulnerability databases such as the NVD [4]. As an example, CVE-2011-3190[2] reports a vulnerability in the AJP connector implementation of several Tomcat releases [5], which, however, only applies under certain conditions, e.g., if certain connector classes are used, and reverse proxy and Tomcat do not use a shared secret. A machine check looking at the Tomcat release level and related configuration settings could be easily provided by the application vendor (Apache Software Foundation). An example for a critical security bug in a software library is CVE-2012-0392 which describes a vulnerability in Apache Struts, a common framework to support the Model-View-Controller paradigm in JWAs. The detection of this vulnerability is made more problematic by the fact that end-users typically do not know if applications installed in their environment make use of such library, and they cannot rely on the presence of a well-established security response process at each of their application vendors. Thus security bugs may be dormant in libraries without the service operator being aware.

Configuration Best-Practice (S2). This scenario focuses on establishing if best practices are followed. During operations time, system administrators need to periodically check whether the system configurations follow best-practices, for single and distributed system components. Today, these are often described in prose and evolve over time thus requiring continuous human intervention. Examples of best-practices are the Tomcat security guide from OWASP [6], and the SANS recommendations for securing Java deployment descriptors [7].

Example 1 (SANS recommendation on cookie-based session handling). SANS recommends to configure the cookie-based session handling for JWAs (`<cookie-config>` section of the deployment descriptor), i.e., *(i)* preventing the access to session cookies (`<http-only>` set to `true`), and *(ii)* transmitting cookies securely (`<secure>` set to `true`). In particular the `http-only` flag is an example of recommendation that only applies after the release 3.0 of the Servlet specification.

Configuration best-practices may also cover a set of distributed components, e.g., the how-to about Apache HTTP server as a reverse proxy for Apache Tomcat [8]. A language supporting the specification of such best-practice checks should support the flexible adoption to a specific environment. A recommendation related to the session timeout, for instance, may be refined by an organization to reflect its particular policy.

Compliance with Configuration Policy (S3). This scenario focuses on the periodic validation of landscape specific configuration implementing the designed policy. Such a configuration includes a set of mandated configuration settings that an organization expects to be active in its system. As an example, the configuration that enforce the ACME's access control policy embraces configuration settings of several distributed system components, e.g., the realm definition of each Tomcat instance, as well as the deployment descriptor of each Java application instance. In particular the deployment descriptor has to allow the role `admin-role` to access to the URL path `/manager/*`. Moreover the realm of

---

[2] CVE entries are maintained in vulnerability databases, e.g., NVD.

Tomcat has to refer to the LDAP server located at 192.168.2.1. This example illustrates that configuration checks aiming to assess compliance with a given configuration policy strongly reflect a particular system and environment, and are therefore authored internally to the organization rather than by externals, as in the previous scenarios.

A language for supporting the above scenarios have to fullfill the following requirements.

(RL1) The language must support the definition of configuration checks for diverse software components (e.g., network-level firewalls or application-level access control systems) and diverse technologies.

(RL2) The language must be expressive enough to cover new technologies or configuration formats without requiring extensions. This would avoid the need to update the language interpreter every time a new extension is published.

(RL3) It must be possible to specify target components by defining conditions over properties such as name, release, and supported specification, or over the existence of relationships between components. This is necessary in cases where externally provided checks must be applied to all instances of the affected software components (scenarios S1 and S2).

(RL4) Motivated by scenario S3, it must be possible to specify target components by referring to specific instances of a software component.

(RL5) It must be possible to validate the configurations of different, potentially distributed system components within one check.

(RL6) Checks must be uniquely identifiable, declarative, standardized and certifiable, to support trusted knowledge exchange among security tools and stakeholders, e.g., software vendors, experts, auditors, or operations staff.

(RL7) The language must support parametrization in order to adopt externally provided checks to a specific configuration policy.

(RL8) The specification of checks must be separated from the collection of the involved configuration settings from a given managed domain.

3   State of the Art

Prior art for the definition of the configuration validation language comprises several specifications out of the Security Content Automation Protocol (SCAP), as well as proprietary languages supported by vulnerability and patch scanners.

SCAP [11] is a suite of specifications that support automated configuration, vulnerability and patch checking, as well as security measurement. Some of the specifications are widely applied in industry, e.g., the Common Vulnerabilities and Exposures (CVE, http://cve.mitre.org), and those related to configuration validation will be discussed with regard to above-described requirements. Note that several approaches assess a system's overall security level by analyzing and reasoning about the potential combination of individual vulnerabilities (exploits) by an adversary [9], [10]. Though referring to SCAP specifications, these approaches do not look into the vulnerability specification itself, but use the language and related tools merely for the discovery of individual vulnerabilities.

Common Platform Enumeration (CPE, http://cpe.mitre.org) is a XML-based standard for the specification of structured names for information technology systems, software, platforms, and packages. It allows the definition of names representing classes of platforms which can be compared in order to establish if, e.g., two names are equal or if one of the names represents a subset of the systems represented by the other. CPE 2.3, the latest version, consists of four modular specifications which work together in layers: *(i)* CPE Naming providing a formal name format, *(ii)* CPE Language allowing the description of complex platforms, *(iii)* CPE Matching providing a method for checking names against a system, and *(iv)* CPE Dictionary binding text and tests to a name.

While the specifications CPE Naming and CPE Matching allow the definition and comparison of single software components according to properties such as vendor or product name, the CPE Language specification does not meet (RL3) with regard to component relations. It supports the specification of a complex platform through a logical condition over several CPE Names, but the semantics of their relationship is not explicitly defined. The typical interpretation used in many CVE entries is that a complex platform condition is met as soon as all software components are installed on the same machine. This interpretation, however, is in many cases not sufficient to state that a vulnerability exists. CVE-2003-0042, for instance, is only exploitable if Tomcat actually uses a given JDK version, the mere presence of both components on the same system is not sufficient. This interpretation is even more misleading if vulnerabilities are caused by combinations of client-side and server-side components, e.g., CVE-2012-0287. A special kind of relationship is the composition of software components, e.g., in the case of Java libraries. Today, each vendor of an application that embeds a vulnerable library needs to issue a dedicated CVE, as CPE insufficient to detect the use of a given library (in an application).

Open Vulnerability Assessment Language. (OVAL, [12]) defines a language for the definition of security tests detecting the presence of vulnerabilities or configuration issues on a computer system (machine). It defines several XML schemas: *(i)* OVAL System Characteristics represent system configuration information that is subject to testing, *(ii)* OVAL Definitions specify conditions for the presence of a specified machine state (vulnerability, configuration, patch state, etc.), *(iii)* OVAL Results report the assessment result, i.e., the comparison of OVAL Definitions and OVAL System Characteristics.

Since OVAL already fulfills some of the before-mentioned requirements, the language proposed in Sect. 4 is to a good extent based on OVAL concepts. According to SCAP design goals, the language supports standardized, unambiguous, and exchangeable representations of configuration checks (RL6) as well as variables for parametrization (RL7). However, a significant limitation is that OVAL checks (like CPE) work on the granularity of machines (computer systems). This impacts several other requirements. With regard to (RL1), it is difficult, sometimes impossible, to write configuration checks for fine-granular system components independently from their software computing environment (container), e.g., JWAs. The reason is that generic OVAL objects from the independent schema (e.g., textfilecontent54_object) are relative to the machine's file system, which varies from one Servlet container to the other The definition of container-specific objects (e.g., spwebapplication_object for Microsoft Sharepoint), on the other hand, restricts the use of checks to dedicated environments. Requirement (RL2) is not fulfilled as OVAL requires the extension of several schemas to address new software components. This either requires tool vendors to constantly update the language interpreter, or leads to a fragmented market where tools only support a subset of the language. We believe that the broad adoption of OVAL could be reached more easily by the use of generic types (RL2), e.g., on the basis of XML, herewith leveraging the fact that it is used for many application-level configuration formats. With regard to (RL3), (RL4) and (RL5) it is impossible in OVAL to specify a target for checks that look at distributed components, since the execution of a set of OVAL definitions and their tests are meant to be executed on a single machine. Furthermore, OVAL does not clearly separate check logic from the retrieval of the actual configuration values (RL8), herewith missing to leverage industry efforts in the area of IT Service and Application Management (ITSAM). The deployment descriptor of a JWA, for instance, can be retrieved by several means and potentially from different sources (the actual component, or a configuration store with copies). The mixture of these concerns makes the work of check authors difficult and error prone, as they cannot focus on the check logic (e.g., the session configuration of a deployment descriptor), but also care for the retrieval of values, e.g., the identification of a file path depending on installation directories and environment variables. To allow the separation of these concerns, the check language itself must be agnostic to potential configuration sources, the latter being cared for by administrators.

As representative vulnerability and patch scanner, we consider Nessus (http://www.tenable.com/products/nessus), which is a widely adopted tool and comes with a proprietary syntax for the definition of so-called audit checks. Organizations can either write custom checks according to this language, or subscribe to a commercial feed to receive compliance checks tailored for a variety of standards and regulations, e.g., PCI DSS (https://www.pcisecuritystandards.org). Having comparable expressivity, checks written in this proprietary language can be transformed into SCAP content, which is why Nessus and similar tools were SCAP-validated by the MITRE. SCAP and Nessus' proprietary language also have in common that they focus on operating systems, which makes it difficult to specify checks on a more fine-granular level, i.e., for objects which cannot be easily identified relative to the OS: *custom items* for Windows and Unix require, for instance, the specification of file paths which is not necessarily possible for JWA or Web services; *built-in* checks for Unix hide the configuration source from the check author, but instead of making the source customizable, it is hard-coded (RL9). Checks considering distributed system components are not supported at all (RL5). Nessus does also not allow to condition the applicability of the check

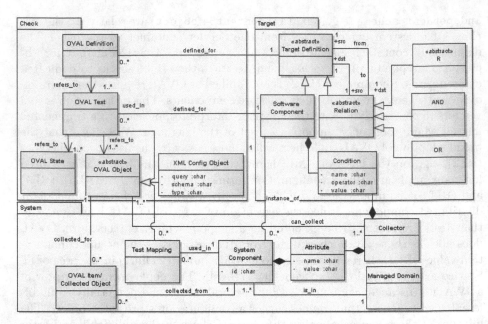

Fig. 2. Configuration validation language class diagram

on the basis of component properties (e.g., release level) or component relationships (RL3) but only on the basis of hard-coded keywords such as Unix. As a proprietary language, processed only by Nessus, it is not extensible by 3rd parties (RL3), nor standardized (RL4).

4   Configuration Validation Language

The configuration validation language allows the definition of checks for selected software components and addresses the use cases presented in Sect. 2. It includes the definition of the checks as well as of their results. This section introduces all the concepts used within the language, and defines the extensions we carried out over the OVAL standard. We formally define the semantics of the language without binding to a specific syntax. Notice that in the definitions we only consider the parts of the OVAL standard which are extended by our language. As OVAL is XML-based, a straightforward implementation of our formalism is an XML serialization.

Fig. 2 shows the main concepts of the configuration validation language. The concepts are organized into three main areas. The Check and Target areas concern the definition of the configuration checks and of the affected software components, resp., the System area contains elements corresponding to actual configurations and components of a managed domain.

The *Check* area (top left of Fig. 2) concerns the definition of checks in the form of tests comparing an expected and an actual value. This area relies on the OVAL standard [12]. The concepts we borrow and extend are shown in Fig. 2 and prefixed with "OVAL". In a nutshell, a definition is characterized by an arbitrary complex boolean combination of tests and a test defines an evaluation involving an object (possibly containing a set of other objects) and zero or more states. As described in Sect. 3, the existing OVAL objects do not fulfill requirements (RL2), and (RL8). To fulfill them, we defined a new test, object, and state, generic enough to apply to multiple configurations of multiple software components and independent from the collection mechanisms. The test and state we defined are not shown in Fig. 2 as it is the object, XML Config Object, that contains the major contributions. The XML Config Object is characterized by three attributes: the type denoting a type of configuration relevant for a software component, the schema denoting the format in which the configurations are represented, and query expressing how to identify the object within the configuration. Such object also overcomes the OVAL drawbacks about (RL1) discussed in Sect. 3.

Example 2 (Object, state, and test for http-only flag). The XML Config Object can be used to specify the recommendation described in Ex. 1. In the excerpt below, type (line 2) indicates that the configuration considered is a deployment descriptor (computing environment independent), schema (line 3) refers to the location of the schema for the deployment descriptor of J2EE web application and the Xpath query (line 4) points to the http-only configuration.

```
1   <xmlconfiguration_object id="oval:sans.security:obj:1">
2     <type>deployment descriptor</type>
3     <schema>http://java.sun.com/xml/ns/j2ee</schema>
4     <query>//*session-config/*cookie-config/*http-only/text()</query>
5   </xmlconfiguration_object>
```

By modifying only the query element, all the other recommendation of Ex. 1 can be specified. Moreover, by modifying also the type and schema, our object can be used for any other XML based configuration. The expected value for the configuration is defined through a xmlconfiguration_state defining true as expected value for the http-only tag. Finally, the OVAL test, xmlconfiguration_test, contains the object and state above which are used to evaluate the configuration.

Definition 1 (OVAL Definition). *An OVAL Definition $OD \subseteq \mathcal{T}$ is a set of OVAL Tests.*

Example 3 (OVAL Definition for SANS). The OVAL definition checking for the SANS recommendations described in Ex. 1 is a set of tests, one for each recommendation, i.e, $OD_{sans} = \{t_{http-only}, t_{secure-flag}\}$.

According to OVAL, a definition is a boolean combination of tests. As SANS requires all recommendations to be followed, all the tests involved are characterized by an OR boolean relation in order to raise an alarm whenever one of the recommendation is not followed. $t_{http-only}$ (line 3) is described in Ex. 2. All other tests can be analogously defined.

```
1   <definition id="oval:sans.security:def:1">
2     <criteria operator="OR">
3       <criterion test_ref="oval:sans.security:tst:1" comment="HttpOnly flag"/>
4       <criterion test_ref="oval:sans.security:tst:2" comment="Secure flag"/>
5     </criteria>
6   </definition>
```

Table 1. Properties description

product	Product name, e.g., Struts	unc_path	UNC path for shared location
vendor	Product vendor, e.g., Apache	ctx_root	JWA context root
release	Product release, e.g., 2.3.1.1	ip_jmx	IP address of JMX endpoint
sup_spec, req_spec	Supported/Required specification	port_jmx	Port number of JMX endpoint

Table 2. Relations description

depl_in	deployed in, models a component installed in another	comp_of	composed of, represents the internal structure of applications (e.g. linked libraries)
comm_with	communicates with, represents network communication	instr_set	instruction set, for either compiled (x86, x64) or interpreted (Java Runtime) binaries

The *Target* area (top right of Fig. 2) allows the definition of targets for the checks. A *target definition* is an abstract concept representing either a software component or a relation which can be defined over software components or relations themselves. A *software component* is characterized by a set of conditions on specific properties such as those in Tab. 1 (left side). A *relation* defines the relationship between software components. We distinguish three kinds of relations. A static relation, i.e., "composed of", which allows to represent the internal structure of a software. Run-time relations, i.e., "deployed in" and "communicates with", which allow to define relations among software components running in a landscape. Finally, boolean relations (AND, OR) combine either static or dynamic relations. Dynamic and boolean relations can be nested whereas the static relation can only be applied to software components. These types of relations, combined with the possibility to nest them, allow to define a set of software components satisfying an arbitrary complex expression.

Definition 2 (Software Component). *A software component $SC \subseteq C$ is a set of conditions. A condition $C \in C$ is a tuple $C = \langle P, \theta, V \rangle$, where*

- *$P \in \mathcal{P}$ is a property name,*
- *$\theta \in \{=, <, >, \geq, \leq\}$ is an operator,*
- *$V \in \mathrm{dom}(P)$ is a value for the property.*

We define $\mathcal{R}$ as a set of relations. Examples are listed in Tab. 2. We define $\hat{\mathcal{R}} = \mathcal{R} \times \mathbb{N}$ as the set of numbered relations where any relation can occur an arbitrary number of times and is uniquely identified by a natural number. In the examples we omit the natural number when no ambiguity arises.

Definition 3 (Target Definition). *A target definition is a tuple $TD = \langle SCS, RS, \rho \rangle$ where*

- *SCS is a set of software components (cf. Def. 2),*
- *$RS \subset \hat{\mathcal{R}}$ is a set of numbered relations,*

- $\rho : RS \rightarrow (SCS \cup RS) \times (SCS \cup RS)$ *is a total and acyclic function mapping a relation into the pair of elements, denoted as ρ_1 and ρ_2, sharing the relation (either software components or relations).*

A target definition $TD = \langle SCS, RS, \rho \rangle$ *is valid iff* $|SCS| = 1$ *when* $RS = \emptyset$.

Example 4 (Software Component and Target Definition for SANS). SANS applies to JWAs developed according to one of the releases of the Servlet specification and deployed in a web application container supporting such specification. In particular the recommendations in Ex. 1 refer to the release 3.0. According to Def. 2, a software component for the web application container can be defined as the set containing a single condition referring to the supported specification, $SC_{webappcont} = \{\langle \mathsf{sup\_spec}, \geq, \mathsf{Java\_Servlet\_3.0} \rangle\}$. As the recommendation applies to all JWAs therein deployed, the software component for the web application can be specified as an empty set $SC_{webapp} = \emptyset$. Finally, the target definition, according to Def. 3, can be expressed as $TD_{sans} = \langle SCS_{sans}, RS_{sans}, \rho_{sans} \rangle$ where $SCS_{sans} = \{SC_{webapp}, SC_{webappcont}\}$, $RS_{sans} = \{\mathsf{depl\_in}\}$, and $\rho_{1sans}(\mathsf{depl\_in}) = \{SC_{webapp}\}$, $\rho_{2sans}(\mathsf{depl\_in}) = \{SC_{webappcont}\}$.

We extend the OVAL standard by referring each OVAL definition to a target definition, i.e., to a set of related software components, and referring each OVAL test contained in the definition to a software component of the target definition. Thus we fulfill requirements (RL3) and (RL5). We name the resulting new artifact *check definition*. Note that this artifact is not represented by a single class in Fig. 2 but it involves several of the concepts therein presented and formalized above. Def. 1 and 3 provide the building blocks for the check definition.

Definition 4 (Check Definition). *A check definition is a tuple* $CD = \langle OD, TD, \tau \rangle$ *where*

- *$OD \subseteq \mathcal{T}$ is an OVAL definition,*
- *$TD = \langle SCS, RS, \rho \rangle$ is a target definition,*
- *$\tau : OD \rightarrow SCS$ is a total function that maps an OVAL test included in the definition OD into the software component to which it applies defined for the target definition TD.*

Example 5 (Check Definition for SANS). Given OD_{sans} and TD_{sans} defined in Ex. 3 and Ex. 4 resp., a check definition for SANS recommendations on cookies is $CD_{sans} = \langle OD_{sans}, TD_{sans}, \tau_{sans} \rangle$ where $\tau(t) = SC_{webapp}$ for all $t \in OD$.

The *System* area (bottom of Fig. 2) contains the concepts characterizing systems in a landscape and their configurations. A *system component* represents a single installation of a software component in a specific domain. As the purpose is to identify its configurations, the system component is defined as a set of attributes denoting how the configurations can be retrieved. The configurations required are given by the OVAL tests which are defined for software components. To evaluate the tests, the objects they contain have to be retrieved for each installation of the software component, i.e., for each system component. The tests to be performed on system components are defined through the test mapping. The set of attributes necessary to collect a configuration is given by the collector (more details about how system components are derived starting from the target definition and the collector can be found in Sect. 5). By allowing the separation of the check logic from the attributes needed for the collection, our language fulfills requirement (RL8).

Definition 5 (Collector). *A collector is a tuple $K = \langle SC_K, PS, O_K \rangle$ where SC_K is a set of conditions, $PS \subseteq \mathcal{P}$ is a set of properties, and O_K is a query over OVAL objects.*

Example 6 (Collector for Web Applications deployment descriptor). A collector for web applications deployment descriptor has to define the set of attributes for retrieving the deployment descriptor of the web application installed in the landscape. Several alternatives are viable, e.g., accessing a shared file system via the Universal Naming Convention (UNC) or relying on the JMX interface of Tomcat. These alternatives can be defined as two collectors, $K_{unc} = \langle SC_{K_{webapp}}, \{\texttt{unc\_path}\}, O_{K_{webapp}} \rangle$ $K_{jmx} = \langle SC_{K_{webapp}}, \{\texttt{ctx\_root}, \texttt{ip\_jmx}, \texttt{port\_jmx}\}, O_{K_{webapp}} \rangle$ where $SC_{K_{webapp}} = \{\langle \texttt{req\_spec}, =, \texttt{Java\_Servlet\_3.0}\rangle\}$ is the same for both as they apply to the same software component, and $O_{K_{webapp}}$ is an Xpath query over the XML serialization of the object (omitted for the sake of brevity).

Definition 6 (System Component). *A system component $SI \subseteq \mathcal{A}$ is a set of attributes. An attribute is a tuple $A = \langle P, V \rangle$, where $P \in \mathcal{P}$ and $V \in \mathrm{dom}(P)$ are properties and values, resp.*

Example 7 (System Component for SANS). The check definition for SANS in Ex. 5 includes the software component $SC_{webapp} = \emptyset$ defined in Ex. 4 which is referred to by an XML Config Test. Moreover the web application installed in the managed domain of Fig. 1 are characterized by the property of supporting the Servlet specification 3.0. Thus the collector defined in Ex. 6 can be used for establishing the set of attributes of the resulting system components. By using K_{unc}, the resulting system component for one installation of the eInvoice web application sold by ACME is $SI_{unc} = \{\langle \texttt{unc\_path}, \backslash\backslash\texttt{192.168.2.3}\backslash\texttt{path}\backslash\texttt{to}\backslash\texttt{web.xml}\rangle\}$. By using K_{jmx}, the resulting system component is $SI_{jmx} = \{\langle \texttt{ctx\_root}, \texttt{/manager/*}\rangle, \langle \texttt{ip\_jmx}, \texttt{192.168.2.2}\rangle, \langle \texttt{port\_jmx}, \texttt{8059}\rangle\}$.

Definition 7 (System Test). *A system test is $ST = \langle SIS, OD, TM \rangle$ where*

- *SIS is a set of system components,*
- *$OD \subseteq \mathcal{T}$ is an OVAL definition, i.e., a set of tests,*
- *$TM \subseteq OD \times SIS$ is a set of test mappings defining which test of the definition applies to which system component.*

Example 8 (System Test for SANS). The check definition $CD_{sans} = \langle OD_{sans}, TD_{sans}, \tau_{sans} \rangle$ defined in Ex. 5 originates several system tests, one for each set of software components installed in the managed domain fulfilling the target definition TD_{sans}. Given, $OD_{sans} = \{t_{http-only}, t_{secure-flag}\}$, $TD_{sans} = \langle SCS_{sans}, RS_{sans}, \rho_{sans}\rangle$, and $\tau(t) = SC_{webapp}$, a system test defining the tests to be performed for one possible installation of the software components is $ST_{sans} = \langle SIS_{sans}, OD_{sans}, TM_{sans}\rangle$ where $SIS_{sans} = \{SI_{jmx}\}$, and $TM_{sans} = \{(t_{http-only}, SI_{jmx}), (t_{secure-flag}, SI_{jmx})\}$. Notice that no system component for $SC_{webappcont}$ is included in SIS_{sans} as no tests apply to it.

The system test refers a test to specific system, thus (RL4) is met.

Finally, the *OVAL Item* in Fig. 2 represents the configuration collected from a system component for the OVAL object defined in the OVAL test. By evaluating such items according to the test, a boolean result for the test is produced. Based on the test results, the boolean result of the definition is also evaluated. Differently from OVAL, our OVAL Items may derive from different system, however this does not affect the evaluation algorithm defined in [12], which we rely on. A check definition originates several system tests, each one originating a check result.

Definition 8 (Check Result). *A check result is a tuple $CR = \langle ST, \omega\rangle$ where*

- *$ST = \langle SIS, OD, TM\rangle$ is a system test,*
- *$\omega : TM \to \{\top, \bot\}$ is a function that maps test mappings into its result, i.e., the boolean values true ($\top$) or false ($\bot$).*

5   Approach

The language presented in Sect. 4 separates the checks' logic from the systems to which they apply. In this section we establish the link between these two aspects, thereby describing how the checks can be instantiated and executed in a concrete landscape.

The overall approach is outlined in Fig. 3. External and internal authors (from the perspective of an organization) can define, independently from the landscape, checks CD (Def. 4) for known vulnerabilities affecting software components (cf. (S1)), and for best practices of single or multiple software components sharing relations (cf. (S2)). An additional input is the set of collector definitions $\mathcal{K}$, that has to be provided by system administrators as creates the link between the software components used in the checks and the attributes of system components which allow the collection of the configurations. The TD Evaluator module has in input the above artifacts and is responsible for producing all the system tests ST defining which test has to be executed on which system component. To produce the System Test artifact, the TD Evaluator relies on a Data Source, an authoritative source of information about the software components installed in a managed domain. We assume a single Data Source to provide information about several aspects of the managed domain, ranging from the properties of installed software (e.g. product names and vendors), or the internal structure of applications (e.g. linked libraries), up to architectural details on the deployment or the network interaction among different pieces of software. Since such information is often scattered over several repositories within an organization (e.g., CMDBs), the Data Source is a federated set of

views over these repositories, which constitute the interface to our language. Although
strong, this assumption is not unrealistic. Indeed, several theoretical formulations of this
problem are tackled in literature on data integration [13][14]. Furthermore the increasing adoption of standards such as DMTF's
CMDBf [15] demonstrates the practical feasibility of configuration data federation.

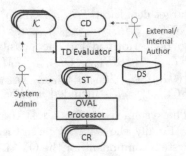

Fig. 3. Detection of vulnerabilities approach

The system test can also be manually provided by system administrators in case of
checks for selected system components (cf. scenario (S3)). System tests are then processed by
the OVAL Processor module that interprets the OVAL content and collects the
objects defined for each system component within ST. The configurations collected from distributed systems are then evaluated and check results CR are
produced, highlighting existing misconfiguration issues (if any).

A key step of the approach is the generation of the system tests based on
the data source. In the following we formally define the interpretation of target
definitions w.r.t. a data source, which provides information about the properties
of software components deployed within a managed domain. We then describe
how this leads to the generation of system tests.

Informally a data source can be seen as a particular instantiation of software
component properties (cf. Def. 2) and target definition relations (cf. Def. 3) for
a managed domain. Let $\mathcal{I}$ be the domain of instances of software components,
namely software component identifiers, containing one unique symbol for each
software component installed in a given managed domain. The data source then
maps every software component identifier to the actual values of its properties
and links it to the other software component identifiers it is related to.

Definition 9 (Data Source). *A data source is the pair of sets $DS = \langle \Pi, \Gamma \rangle$.
Π contains a partial function $\pi_P : \mathcal{I} \to \mathrm{dom}(P)$ for each property $P \in \mathcal{P}$, while
Γ includes a relation $\gamma_R \subseteq \mathcal{I} \times \mathcal{I}$ for each symbol $R \in \mathcal{R}$.*

Example 9 (Data Source). Figure 4 depicts a tabular representation of the data
source DS_1 for the example landscape of Fig. 1. Due to space limitations, only
a subset of the properties listed in Tab. 1 and relations of Tab. 2 are considered.

A software component can be seen as a simple conjunctive query ranging over
properties of software deployed within a managed domain. The data source provides the necessary views on the managed domain to answer such a query. The
answer consists of the set of software component identifiers matching to all the
conditions within the software component. If it contains no conditions, the answer is the entire domain of software component identifiers $\mathcal{I}$. This evaluation

i	$\pi_{\text{vendor}}(i)$
a	Apache
l	OpenLDAP
t_1	Apache
t_2	Apache
w_a	ACME
w_b	ACME
w_c	ACME

i	$\pi_{\text{release}}(i)$
a	2.2
l	2.4.30
t_1	7.0.18
t_2	7.0.18
w_a	1.0
w_b	1.0
w_c	1.0

i	$\pi_{\text{product}}(i)$
a	Apache HTTPd
l	OpenLDAP
t_1	Tomcat
t_2	Tomcat
w_a	Web eInvoice
w_b	Web eInvoice
w_c	Web eInvoice

i	$\pi_{\text{sup\_spec}}(i)$
t_1	Java_Servlet_2.5
t_1	Java_Servlet_3.0
t_2	Java_Servlet_2.5
t_2	Java_Servlet_3.0

i_1	i_2
w_a	t_1
w_b	t_2
w_c	t_2

(a) π_{vendor} **(b)** π_{release} **(c)** π_{product} **(d)** $\pi_{\text{sup\_spec}}$ **(e)** $\gamma_{\text{depl\_in}}$

Fig. 4. Example of data source instance

is performed by the data source interpretation of software components, given by the mapping $\lceil \cdot \rceil_{DS} : \mathcal{SC} \to 2^{\mathcal{I}}$:

$$\lceil \emptyset \rceil_{DS} = \mathcal{I} \tag{1}$$
$$\lceil \langle P, \theta, v \rangle \cup SC \rceil_{DS} = \{i \in \mathcal{I} \mid \pi_P(i)\ \theta\ v\} \cap \lceil SC \rceil_{DS}.$$

A target definition $TD = \langle SCS, RS, \tau \rangle$ is instead a more complex selection predicate (cf. Def. 3) and there can be several sets of software component identifiers which satisfy it. The interpretation of TD over a data source DS, $[\![TD]\!]_{DS}$, provides all such sets. This is done by relying on two interpretation functions, one providing the sets of software component identifiers, and one providing a function that maps each software component identifier to the corresponding software component.

The interpretation function $[\![\cdot]\!]_{DS,\rho} : (\mathcal{SC} \cup \hat{\mathcal{R}}) \to 2^{2^{\mathcal{I}}}$ associates every $SC \in \mathcal{SC}$ and $R \in \hat{\mathcal{R}}$ to a powerset of software component identifiers, as defined in (2) and (3), respectively. Notice that this function depends both on the data source DS and the function ρ that carries the structure of target definition expressions.

$$[\![SC]\!]_{DS,\rho} = \{\lceil SC \rceil_{DS}\} \tag{2}$$

$$[\![R]\!]_{DS,\rho} = \begin{cases} [\![\rho_1(R)]\!]_{DS,\rho} \times [\![\rho_2(R)]\!]_{DS,\rho} & \text{if } R = \wedge \\ [\![\rho_1(R)]\!]_{DS,\rho} \cup [\![\rho_2(x)]\!]_{DS,\rho} & \text{if } R = \vee \\ \{\{v_1, \ldots, v_n, w_1, \ldots, w_m\} \mid \{v_1, \ldots, v_n\} \in [\![\rho_1(R)]\!]_{DS,\rho}, \\ \{w_1, \ldots, w_m\} \in [\![\rho_2(R)]\!]_{DS,\rho}, \langle v_{1 \le i \le n}, w_{1 \le j \le m} \rangle \in \gamma_R\} & \text{otherwise} \end{cases} \tag{3}$$

Similarly, the interpretation function $\|\cdot\|_{DS,\rho} : (\mathcal{SC} \cup \hat{\mathcal{R}}) \to (\mathcal{I} \to \mathcal{SC})$ maps every $SC \in \mathcal{SC}$ and $R \in \hat{\mathcal{R}}$ to a function σ associating each software component identifier to the corresponding software component, according to (4) and (5).

$$\|SC\|_{DS,\rho} = \sigma, \text{ where } \sigma(i) = SC, \forall i \in \lceil SC \rceil_{DS} \tag{4}$$
$$\|R\|_{DS,\rho} = \sigma, \text{ where } \sigma(i) = \|\rho_1(R)\|_{DS,\rho}(i), \forall i \in \text{dom}(\|\rho_1(R)\|_{DS,\rho})$$
$$\text{and } \sigma(j) = \|\rho_2(R)\|_{DS,\rho}(j), \forall j \in \text{dom}(\|\rho_2(R)\|_{DS,\rho}). \tag{5}$$

Finally, the evaluation function for a valid target definition $TD = \langle SCS, RS, \rho \rangle$ over the data source DS, $[\![\cdot]\!]_{DS} : \mathcal{TD} \to \left(2^{2^{\mathcal{I}}} \times (\mathcal{I} \to \mathcal{SC}) \right)$, associates a TD to the pair $\langle I^*, \sigma \rangle$, where I^* is a powerset of software component identifiers and σ a function mapping every $i \in I \in I^*$ to a $SC \in SCS$. As expressed in (6), the definition of $[\![\cdot]\!]_{DS}$ relies on the aforementioned recursive interpretation functions of all the elements within the target definition expression, starting, in the general case, from the only relation R_0 which never appears in the ρ co-domain. In case $RS = \emptyset$, we know from Def. 3 that $\exists! \, SC_0 \in SCS$ and therefore SC_0 is the only element being interpreted.

$$[\![TD]\!]_{DS} = \begin{cases} \langle [\![R_0]\!]_{DS,\rho}, [\![R_0]\!]_{DS,\rho} \rangle, \text{with } \{R_0\} = \mathrm{dom}(\rho) \setminus \mathrm{cod}(\rho) & \text{if } RS \neq \emptyset \\ \langle [\![SC_0]\!]_{DS,\rho}, [\![SC_0]\!]_{DS,\rho} \rangle, \text{with } \{SC_0\} = SCS & \text{otherwise.} \end{cases} \tag{6}$$

Example 10. We hereby compute the interpretation of the target definition TD_{sans}, introduced in Ex. 4, w.r.t. the data source DS_1, shown in Ex. 9.

First, we recognize (Eq. (6)) that $[\![TD_{sans}]\!]_{DS_1} = \langle I^*_{sans}, \sigma_{sans} \rangle = \langle [\![\mathtt{depl\_in}]\!]_{DS_1,\rho}, [\![\mathtt{depl\_in}]\!]_{DS_1,\rho} \rangle$, since $\mathtt{depl\_in} \in \mathrm{dom}(\rho) \setminus \mathrm{cod}(\rho)$.

In order to obtain $[\![\mathtt{depl\_in}]\!]_{DS_1,\rho}$, according to (3), we now need to compute the two following terms:

(i) $[\![\rho_1(\mathtt{depl\_in})]\!]_{DS_1,\rho} = \{[\![SC_{webapp}]\!]_{DS_1,\rho}\} = \{[\![\emptyset]\!]_{DS_1}\} = \{\mathcal{I}\};$

(ii) $[\![\rho_2(\mathtt{depl\_in})]\!]_{DS_1,\rho} = \{[\![SC_{webappcont}]\!]_{DS_1,\rho}\} =$
$= [\![\{\langle \mathtt{sup\_spec}, \geq, \mathtt{Java\_Servlet\_3.0}\rangle\}]\!]_{DS_1,\rho} =$
$= \{\{i \in \mathcal{I} \mid \pi_{\mathtt{sup\_spec}}(i) \geq \mathtt{Java\_Servlet\_3.0}\}\} = \{\{t_1, t_2\}\}.$

We then have $I^*_{sans} = [\![\mathtt{depl\_in}]\!]_{DS_1,\rho} = \{\{v, w\} \mid v \in \mathcal{I}, w \in \{t_1, t_2\}, \langle v, w \rangle \in \{\langle w_a, t_1 \rangle, \langle w_b, t_2 \rangle, \langle w_c, t_2 \rangle\}\} = \{\{w_a, t_1\}, \{w_b, t_2\}, \{w_c, t_2\}\}.$

Analogously, by applying (5), we obtain $\sigma_{sans} = [\![\mathtt{depl\_in}]\!]_{DS_1,\rho} = \{w_a : SC_{webapp}, w_b : SC_{webapp}, w_c : SC_{webapp}, t_1 : SC_{webappcont}, t_2 : SC_{webappcont}\}.$

As last step, the TD Evaluator needs to identify one or more system tests, mapping each OVAL test to the system component carrying the information about how to collect the object.

A check definition $CD = \langle OD, TD, \tau \rangle$ is defined for the target definition TD, being interpreted over a data source resulting in a pair $[\![TD]\!]_{DS} = \langle I^*, \sigma \rangle$. Every $I \in I^*$ is a set of software component identifiers satisfying the TD expression. Therefore one system test has to be created for every such set I.

When the TD Evaluator processes a check definition, it must identify a *matching collector* K, among the set $\mathcal{K}$ of all the ones defined for a given managed domain. This has to be done for every software component identifier $i \in I$, and provides the set of properties PS necessary to collect the to-be-checked configurations for specific OVAL Objects from i. For this reason, every $K \in \mathcal{K}$ (cf. Def. 5) references a software component SC_K and contains a Xpath query O_K, matching to the XML serialization of the OVAL Objects it applies to. We write $t \models O_K$ whenever the XML serialization of all the OVAL Objects referenced within an OVAL Test t satisfy the Xpath query O_K.

Given a collector property set PS and a software component identifier i, Eq. (7) defines how to retrieve the corresponding system component from a data source DS, through the interpretation function $\|\cdot\|_{DS}(i) : 2^P \to \mathcal{SI}$.

$$\|PS\|_{DS}(i) = \|\{P_1, \ldots, P_n\}\|_{DS,i} = \{\langle P_1, \pi_{P_1}(i) \rangle, \ldots, \langle P_n, \pi_{P_n}(i) \rangle\}. \quad (7)$$

The conditions required to determine whether a collector matches to a software component identifier are now formalized by the following definition.

Definition 10 (Matching Collector). *For a $CD = \langle OD, TD, \tau \rangle$, where $TD = \langle SCS, RS, \rho \rangle$, let $[\![TD]\!]_{DS} = \langle I^*, \sigma \rangle$ be an interpretation of TD over DS and $\tau^{-1} : SCS \rightarrow 2^{OD}$ be the inverse of τ, mapping every SC to the set $\{t \in OD \mid \tau(t) = SC\}$. We then say that $K = \langle SC_K, PS, O_K \rangle$ matches to $i \in I \in I^*$, iff*

$$i \in \lceil SC_K \rceil_{DS} \text{ and } P \in PS \Rightarrow \exists \langle P, \cdot \rangle \in \|PS\|_{DS}(i) \text{ and } t \in \tau^{-1}(\sigma(i)) \Rightarrow t \models O_K.$$

Given the interpretation $[\![TD]\!]_{DS} = \langle I^*, \sigma \rangle$ of a target definition within a check definition $CD = \langle OD, TD, \tau \rangle$, we are now in a position to associate each $I \in I^*$ to a system test $ST_I = \langle SIS_I, OD, TM_I \rangle$, constructed as follows. (i) OD is the same OVAL Definition contained in CD. (ii) Every element $SI \in SIS_I$ is a system component, i.e. a collection of attributes associated to properties of the software component identifier which allows to collect configuration information from it. For every $i \in I$ we first need to find a matching collector K carrying such set of properties PS, and we then retrieve the system component SI, i.e. the attributes corresponding to the properties in PS, from the data source DS. (iii) TM_I maps every test $t \in OD$ to a system component $SI \in SIS_I$.

Eq. (8) finally specifies how the system test's components SIS_I and TM_I, informally described above, are built by the TD Evaluator.

$$\forall i \in I \text{ if } \exists K \in \mathcal{K} \text{ s.t. } K \text{ matches to } i, \text{ then}$$
$$\|PS\|_{DS}(i) \in SIS_I \text{ and } \langle t, \|PS\|_{DS,i} \rangle \in TM_I \; \forall t \in \tau^{-1}(\sigma(i)). \quad (8)$$

Example 11. Let us consider the check definition $CD_{sans} = \langle OD_{sans}, TD_{sans}, \tau_{sans} \rangle$, introduced in Ex. 5, and the data source interpretation of its target definition $[\![TD_{sans}]\!]_{DS_1} = \langle I^*_{sans}, \sigma_{sans} \rangle$, which has been derived in Ex. 10. Three sets of software component identifiers satisfy the target definition, namely $I^*_{sans} = \{\{w_a, t_1\}, \{w_b, t_2\}, \{w_c, t_2\}\} = \{I_a, I_b, I_c\}$, hence three system tests will be created. Among those, we shall only discuss, for brevity, the system tests ST_{I_a} and ST_{I_b}, related to I_a and I_b resp.

For the sake of this example we extend the data source $DS_1 = \langle \Pi_1, \Gamma_1 \rangle$ such that it includes the properties required by the collectors (cf. Ex. 6). Let such an extended data source be $DS'_1 = \langle \Pi_1 \cup \{\pi_{\texttt{ctx\_root}}, \pi_{\texttt{ip\_jmx}}, \pi_{\texttt{port\_jmx}}, \pi_{\texttt{unc\_path}}, \}, \Gamma \rangle$, where: $\pi_{\texttt{ctx_root}}(w_a) = $ /manager/*, $\pi_{\texttt{ip_jmx}}(w_a) = $ 192.168.2.2, $\pi_{\texttt{port_jmx}}(w_a) = $ 8059, and $\pi_{\texttt{unc_path}}(w_b) = $ \\192.168.2.3\path\to\web.xml.

According to Def. 10 the collector K_{jmx} matches to the software component identifier w_a (and not to w_b), as (i) $w_a \in \lceil SC_{K_{webapp}} \rceil_{DS}$, (ii) $\pi_{\texttt{ctx\_root}}(w_a)$, $\pi_{\texttt{port\_jmx}}(w_a)$, $\pi_{\texttt{port\_jmx}}(w_a)$ are all defined in DS (while this is not the case for w_b), and (iii) both $t_{http-only} \models O_{K_{webapp}}$ and $t_{secure-flag} \models O_{K_{webapp}}$ hold. From analogous reasoning it follows that K_{unc} matches to w_b (and not to w_a).

By applying (8) we finally derive that $ST_{I_a} = \langle \{SI_{jmx}\}, OD_{sans}, \{(t_{http-only}, SI_{jmx}), (t_{secure-flag}, SI_{jmx})\} \rangle = ST_{sans}$, as anticipated in Ex. 7 and 8. Analogously, we obtain $ST_{I_b} = \langle \{SI_{unc}\}, OD_{sans}, \{(t_{http-only}, SI_{unc}), (t_{secure-flag}, SI_{unc})\} \rangle$.

6   Conclusion and Future Work

This paper presents a formal approach to specify and execute declarative and unambiguous checks able to detect vulnerabilities caused by system misconfiguration. This paper extends the state of the art on configuration validation as security checks can be specified for fine-granular components in a distributed environment and separate the check logic from the configuration retrieval.

A proof of concept has been developed to explore the feasibility of our approach at the example of OWASP and SANS recommendations for JWA, using a CMDB as data source for resolving target definitions, and JMX for the collection of configuration settings. In future work, we will evaluate the prototype in near-world environments that comprise a greater numbers of system components. Furthermore, we plan to generate security checks and checklists in an automated fashion to facilitate scenario (S3), where checks are used for gaining assurance about compliance with system-specific configuration policies. This would allow to gain assurance without the need to manually author check on a low technical level. Lastly, we intent to investigate the usage in cloud scenarios, were cloud providers could use and offer a corresponding tool for ensuring the security of consumer-managed resources.

References

1. 7Safe, the University of Bedfordshire: Uk security breach investigations report 2010 (2010), http://www.7safe.com/breach_report/Breach_report_2010.pdf
2. Verizon: 2009 data breach investigations report. Verizon (2009), http://www.7safe.com/breach_report/Breach_report_2010.pdf
3. Williams, J., Wichers, D.: Top 10 most critical web application security risks. OWASP (2010), https://www.owasp.org/index.php/Top_10_2010-A6
4. http://{scap.usgcb.nvd}.nist.gov
5. http://tomcat.apache.org/security-6.html#Fixed_in_Apache_Tomcat_6.0.35
6. https://www.owasp.org/index.php/Securing_tomcat
7. http://software-security.sans.org/blog/2010/08/11/security-misconfigurations-java-webxml-files
8. http://tomcat.apache.org/connectors-doc/generic_howto/proxy.html
9. Chen, X., Zheng, Q., Guan, X.: An OVAL-based active vulnerability assessment system for enterprise computer networks. In: ISF, pp. 573–588 (2008)
10. Ou, X., Govindavajhala, S., Appel, A.W.: MulVal: a logic-based network security analyzer. In: USENIX Security Symposium (2005)
11. Waltermire, D., Quinn, S., Scarfone, K.: The technical specification for the Security Content Automation Protocol (SCAP): SCAP version 1.1. NIST (2011), http://csrc.nist.gov/publications/nistpubs/800-126-rev1/SP800-126r1.pdf
12. Baker, J., Hansbury, M., Haynes, D.: The OVAL language specification (version 5.10.1). MITRE Corporation (2012), http://oval.mitre.org/language/version5.10.1/OVAL_Language_Specification_01-20-2012.pdf
13. Ullman, J.D.: Information Integration Using Logical Views. In: Afrati, F.N., Kolaitis, P.G. (eds.) ICDT 1997. LNCS, vol. 1186, pp. 19–40. Springer, Heidelberg (1996)
14. Lenzerini, M.: Data integration: a theoretical perspective. In: PODS, pp. 233–246 (2002)
15. DMTF Distributed Management Task Force: Configuration Management Database (CMDB) Federation Specification. DMTF Technical Report DSP0252 (2010)

BINSPECT: Holistic Analysis and Detection of Malicious Web Pages

Birhanu Eshete, Adolfo Villafiorita, and Komminist Weldemariam

Fondazione Bruno Kessler (FBK-IRST), Trento, Italy
{eshete,adolfo,sisai}@fbk.eu

Abstract. Malicious web pages are among the major security threats on the Web. Most of the existing techniques for detecting malicious web pages focus on specific attacks. Unfortunately, attacks are getting more complex whereby attackers use blended techniques to evade existing countermeasures. In this paper, we present a holistic and at the same time lightweight approach, called BINSPECT, that leverages a combination of static analysis and minimalistic emulation to apply supervised learning techniques in detecting malicious web pages pertinent to drive-by-download, phishing, injection, and malware distribution by introducing new features that can effectively discriminate malicious and benign web pages. Large scale experimental evaluation of BINSPECT achieved above 97% accuracy with low false signals. Moreover, the performance overhead of BINSPECT is in the range 3-5 seconds to analyze a single web page, suggesting the effectiveness of our approach for real-life deployment.

Keywords: malicious web page, static analysis, lightweight emulation, machine learning.

1 Introduction

The Web has become an indispensable global platform that glues together daily communication, sharing, trading, collaboration, and service delivery. Web users often store and manage critical information that attracts cybercriminals who misuse the Web and the Internet to exploit vulnerabilities for illegitimate benefits.

Malicious web pages, that exploit vulnerabilities and launch attacks for just one time visit, take an alarmingly significant share of web-based attacks in recent years [1-4]. When an innocent victim visits a web page, an attacker might have compromised the page under visit (or crafted it purposefully) and the outcome of the visit could be stealing of critical credentials (e.g., credit card details) to impersonate the victim, installation of a malware binary on the victim's machine for future attacks, or even a complete takeover of the victim's system to remotely command and control it as a member of botnet [5-7]. In recent years, not only is the prevalence of malicious web pages on the rise but also the way in which attackers trick victims to malicious web pages is also getting sophisticated [2]. It has become a daily encounter to get contaminated search results from search

A.D. Keromytis and R. Di Pietro (Eds.): SecureComm 2012, LNICST 106, pp. 149–166, 2013.

engines on trendy terms, malicious links shared on social media, and legitimate web pages injected with malicious scripts [3].

The thus-far proposed defenses against malicious web pages fall into two major blocks, i.e., static analysis and dynamic analysis techniques. However, the use of blacklists is still a common way to facilitate and enrich these techniques by making use of heuristics and learning techniques.

Static analysis techniques, [5, 8–16], inspect web page artifacts without rendering the page in a browser. The inspection usually involves quick extraction of discriminative features from the URL string, host identity, HTML, and JavaScript code. The feature values are then encoded to train machine learning techniques to build classifiers based on which unknown web pages are classified. The major assumption in static analysis is that the statistical distribution of features in malicious URLs (e.g., spam URLs, phishing pages) tend to differ from that of benign.

In static analysis, it is difficult to detect attacks that require rendering of a page to take action. More precisely, when using page source there is a high risk of obfuscated content (e.g., JavaScript) and overlooking of malicious JavaScript that exploits vulnerabilities of browser plugins. In addition, host details of fresh (benign) URLs, registered by registrars with low reputation, are likely to be misclassified as malicious due to their low reputation scores. In effect, there is a high risk of false positives. On the other hand, false negatives may arise as well-reputed registrars may host malicious web pages which have escaped the static analysis effort. Other sources of false negatives are web pages that use free hosting services or already compromised sites with benign-looking URLs and host details. For static anlaysis relying on lexical URL features, an attentive attacker may evade these features to mislead detection techniques by carefully crafting malicious URLs which look statistically indistinguishable from the benign ones.

Dynamic analysis approaches, [11, 17–25], inspect the execution dynamics when a page is executed. Such techniques could be deployed at a proxy-level (e.g., [20]) to intercept requests (responses), visit the URL in a controlled environment (e.g., disposable virtual machine), analyze its execution dynamics for hints of malicious activity (e.g., unusual process creation, repeated redirection), and decide if it is safe to render the page in the browser. Alternatively, client-side sandboxing of critical page content (e.g., JavaScript) could be used (as in [18]) to log critical actions (e.g., invoking a plugin) and match logs with known patterns of malicious activities or apply learning-based techniques to model and classify malicious intentions.

While effective at uncovering daunting malicious web pages, dynamic analysis approaches are resource intensive as they need to load and execute the page under analysis and modern web pages are usually stuffed with rich client-side code and content which take longer analysis time. Moreover, not all web pages are likely to launch attacks when visited. There are web pages which require user interaction or wait for certain conditions to take action.

Blacklisting-based techniques maintain a list of known malicious URLs, IP addresses, and domain names collected by manual reporting, honeyclients, and custom analysis techniques. For example, Google Safe Browsing service [26] maintains a blacklist against which it checks URL requests from browsers to alert users if the requested URL happens to be in the blacklist. Another tool powered by blacklisting is McAfee Site Advisor [27] which is pluggable to Mozilla Firefox and Internet Explorer to rate safety of web pages and search engine results prior to rendering the page in the browser.

Although lightweight to deploy and easy to use, blacklisting is effective only if one can exhaustively patrol the Web to identify malicious web pages and timely update the blacklist. In practice, to do so is infeasible due to: fresh web pages are too new to be blacklisted even if they are malicious right from the outset, some web pages may escape from the blacklisting due to *'cloaking'*, and attackers may frequently change where the malicious web pages are hosted. Consequently, the URLs and IP addresses may also change accordingly [5], [17].

Heuristic-based techniques (e.g., [15]) build signatures of known attack payloads to be used by antiviral systems or intrusion detection systems to scan a web page and flag it as malicious if its heuristic pattern matches signatures in the database. Unfortunately, such signatures are easily bypassed by attackers (mainly through obfuscation) and the heuristics fail to detect novel attacks. In addition, the rate at which the signature database of heuristic-based systems is updated is way slower than the pace at which attackers overwhelm victims with novel attacks, resulting in zero-day exploits.

In addition to the afore-mentioned limitations, most approaches focus on one prominent attack while attack techniques are getting more and more complex whereby attackers use blended attack techniques by combining existing attack techniques to evade existing countermeasures. More importantly, applying static or dynamic analysis approaches in a complementary fashion is limited to capturing partial snapshot of a malicious web page.

To this end, the ideal solution is to leverage static and dynamic analysis to capture a comprehensive snapshot of a malicious web page and ensure that the overhead cost of analyzing a web page is optimal. This can be achieved by holistically characterizing and then analyzing, and detecting malicious web pages to capture a comprehensive snapshot of malicious web pages while ensuring that the analysis and detection remains lightweight in terms of its responsiveness and resource consumption.

In this paper, we present the design, implementation, and experimental evaluation of a holistic and lightweight system, called BINSPECT, that leverages a combination of static analysis and minimalistic emulation to apply supervised learning techniques in detecting malicious web pages pertinent to drive-by-download, phishing, injection, and malware distribution. BINSPECT achieved detection accuracy above 97% with low false signals and an average performance overhead of at most 5 seconds.

The contributions of this paper are the following:

- we developed a holistic approach to analyze and detect malicious web pages by leveraging static analysis and lightweight emulation of web page rendering with low performance overhead.

– we introduced novel features and enhanced existing ones so as to improve their discriminative power in the characterization of malicious and benign web pages.
– we designed, implemented, and evaluated our approach over a large dataset of malicious and benign web pages and demonstrated that our approach is effective in practice.

The paper is structured as follows. In Section 2, we present a real motivational example pertinent to malicious web pages. Section 3 covers details of holistic characterization of malicious web pages focusing on features we introduce as new and enhance from existing ones. In Section 4, a high-level description of our approach is presented. Details of the experimental setup and evaluation of our approach are discussed in Section 5. Section 6 positions our approach relative to prior work. Finally, Section 7 concludes the paper.

2   Motivational Example on Malicious Web Pages

In this section, we provide illustrations of real threats posed by malicious web pages.

A *malicious web page* is a web page that exploits one or more vulnerabilities of the browsing environment to launch one or more attacks when visited by an unsuspecting victim. Usually, malicious web pages perform attacks in four ways: *obfuscation* (e.g., obfuscated malicious JavaScript), *setting up malicious web pages* (e.g., using HTTP or JavaScript redirection), *victim luring* (e.g., social engineering tricks), and *victim takeover* (e.g., installing malware). To give context to threats of malicious web pages, in what follows we describe a real malicious website attack that compromised a high-profile website [28].

On September 26, 2011, when users visited `http://mysql.com`, the file at `http://mysql.com/common/js/s_code_remote.js?ver=20091011` was infected by a heavily obfuscated malicious JavaScript code (the de-obfuscated code is shown in Listing 1.1). The malicious code embeds an iframe to `http://falosfax.in/info/in.cgi?5&ab_iframe=1&ab_badtraffic =1&antibot_hash=1255098964&ur=1&HTTP_REFERER=http://mysql. com/` malicious domain and then throws an `HTTP 302 redirection` to load the `http://truruhfhqnviaosdpruejeslsuy.cx.cc/main.php` exploit domain. This exploit domain hosts the `BlackHole` exploit pack which, upon discovering a vulnerable browsing environment (Java plugin vulnerability in this case), leads the browser to download a malware binary to the user's machine. All this happens without the user's knowledge. In this attack, the actual payload is an exploitation of Java runtime vulnerability in the browser (`Internet Explorer 6`) to download and execute malware that steals and sends back to the attacker FTP client passwords from the user's machine. Such an attack is called *drive-by-download* [29].

```
if (document.getElementsByTagName('body')[0]){
iframer();
}else{
document.write(<iframe src='http://falosfax.in/info/in.
   cgi?5'width='10'height='10'style='visibility:hidden;
   position:absolute;left:0;top:0;'></iframe>);
}
function iframer(){
 var f=document.createElement('iframe');
 f.setAttribute('src', 'http://falosfax.in/info/in.cgi?5
   ');
 f.style.visibility='hidden';
 f.style.position='absolute';
 f.style.left='0';
 f.style.top='0';
 f.setAttribute('width', '10');
 f.setAttribute('height', '10');
 document.getElementsByTagName('body')[0].appendChild(f)
   ;
}
```

Listing 1.1. De-obfuscated JavaScript exploit code of the attack [28]

Discussion. The attack described before sounds specific to a compromised legitimate website, i.e., http://mysql.com. However, there are a couple of interesting aspects in the attack chain. First, the attacker has to target a high-profile website with solid user-base and daily traffic. Secondly, she exploited a vulnerable spot on the website (to inject malicious code) and abused HTTP redirection to lead the browser to where the actual exploit is hosted. Then after, she exploited a vulnerability of the browser extension to trick the browser into downloading a malware binary. Even if the target in this attack is the Java plugin, in principle this could have been any one of the vulnerable browser components or its extensions (e.g., PDF Renderer, Flash Player) since the malware usually runs with the privilege of the current user. The downloaded binary could be a key-stroke sniffer to steal and submit passwords and credit card details to a remote server controlled by the attacker. Or even worse, it could be a malware that compromises the victim's machine to remotely control it as a member of botnet to use it in future criminal activities (e.g., spam campaigns). Similarly, the vulnerability of the browsing environment could be of various risks depending on the client operating system, browser type and version, and browser extensions and configuration. An essential part of the attack chain is fingerprinting of the environment which provides clues to vulnerable spots based on which actual exploit is orchestrated.

3   Holistic Characterization of Malicious Web Pages

Given an unknown web page, BINSPECT analyses and classifies the web page as
malicious or benign. To do so, BINSPECT extracts features from the page under
inspection and applies a number of models that evaluate the features extracted
from the page. The models are derived from training on a known mix of benign
and malicious web pages. BINSPECT considers malicious web pages related to
drive-by-download, phishing, injection, and malware delivery.

The features on which BINSPECT bases its statistical characterization of
web pages leverages three classes of features, i.e., URL features, Page-Source
features (HTML and JavaScript), and Social-Reputation features. The underlying assumption in using these features, in prior work and in ours, is based on
the discriminative power of the statistical distribution of benign and malicious
web pages. In what follows, we describe the 39 features we extract and inspect
(focusing on the new features) which are the basis for building the models we
use to classify malicious web pages in BINSPECT.

3.1   URL Features

In BINSPECT, we rely on 11 URL features among which 8 features are reused
from prior work ([5], [10]) and we introduce 3 new features. The URL features we
reuse are: length of URL string, length of host name, number of dots ('.'), number
of hyphens ('-'), number of underscores ('_'), number of forward slashes ('/'),
number of equal signs ('='), and availability of the `client` and/or `server`
words in the URL. After evaluating the F-Score measure of candidate URL features, we found the 3 new features to be of significant relevance as a high F-score
value of a feature indicates a higher potential of the feature to split benign and
malicious web pages. These features are: `length of the path` in the URL,
`length of the query` in the URL, and `length of the file-path` in
the URL. Apart from the F-Score, manual inspection revealed that most malicious URLs have abnormally long path and query as compared to benign URLs.
In Section 5, we show the experimental verification as to the effectiveness of
these new URL features in practice.

3.2   Page-Source Features

While most prior work extract HTML and JavaScript features statically, we use
an emulated browser to parse and render the HTML and execute JavaScript
on page-load so as to capture what is manifested by JavaScript code. In this
sense, the granularity of most HTML features used in our work is high because
the JavaScript that is executed on page-load particularly enriches the HTML
features. Another reason to use an emulated browser is to capture the side-
effects of obfuscated JavaScript code that is usually executed when the page loads
because malicious JavaScript is often 'shipped' with a strong shell of obfuscation.

In total, we extract 25 Page-Source features. These are : document length,
number of words, number of lines, number of blank spaces, average length

of words, number of links, number of same-origin links, number of different-origin links, number of external JavaScript files, number of hidden elements, number of iframes, and number of suspicious JavaScript functions (including suspicious functions : `subString()`, `fromCharCode()`, `eval()`, `setTimeout()`, `document.write()`, `createElement()`, `unescape()`, `escape()`, `link()`, `exec()`, and `search()`).

Although the Page-Source features we use are mostly from prior work, we introduce new (e.g., `exec()` function) and enhance existing features for a more fine-grained characterization of web pages. For instance, apart from extracting the total number of links on the page, we split links to: `number of same-origin links`, `number of different-origin links`, and `number of external-JavaScript files`. We enhanced link features because manual analysis shows that malicious web pages link to remote origins and malicious JavaScript is often downloaded from external domains.

3.3 Social-Reputation Features

The ubiquitous effect of social network platforms, such as Facebook, Twitter, and Google Plus, is continuously changing the landscape of online social interaction and reputation building about what is shared online. Search engines are partly relying on social network reputation of URLs to enrich their ranking algorithms because of human involvement in rating URLs [30]. To evaluate if these social-reputation indicators are of use in the characterization of malicious and benign URLs, we examined the statistical distribution of URL-Sharing on Facebook and Twitter as these platforms keep track of the public share-count of URLs.

Experimental evaluation of these features suggests that for benign web pages, the share-count is usually higher as users are confident enough to share a URL that they know as harmless or they re-share after seeing that their friends have done so. On the contrary, the share-count for malicious URLs suggests that, either the URLs are not circulated across the social network or users refrain from sharing a URL they know less about.

Figure 1 shows a statistical separation in distribution of public share-counts for benign and malicious URLs on Twitter over a part of the training set we used for this work. The three new features we introduce are the `Facebook Share Count`, `Twitter Share Count`, and `Google Plus Share Count` which tell the number of times a URL is publicly shared on Facebook, Twitter, and Google Plus, respectively.

An attentive reader may argue that these features may contribute to false negatives in the case where a malicious user publicly shares a malicious URL on a social network and accumulates large share-count. However, as time passes by, the tendency that a malicious URL is circulated across the social network will reduce or the share-count of the URL does not increase because of built-in[1] URL analysis and detection techniques in the social network platform.

---

[1] Such as Link Shim of Facebook
(`http://www.facebook.com/note.php?note_id=10150492832835766`)

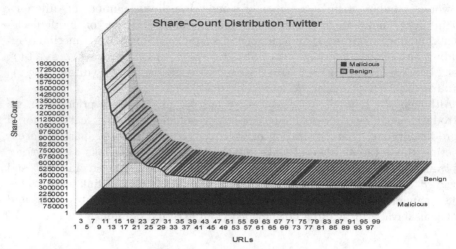

Fig. 1. Distribution of the top 100 Twitter share-counts for benign and malicious URLs on the training set

4   BINSPECT System Overview

In a nutshell, BINSPECT has three major components: feature extraction and labeling, multi-model training, and classification, as shown in Figure 2. In the following, we provide a high-level discussion of the components of BINSPECT.

Feature Extraction and Labeling. As shown in Figure 2, we use a dataset of benign and malicious samples (described in Section 5) to label the samples and extract the necessary features which characterize malicious and benign web pages. The URL feature extraction is implemented based on the URL class of Java and the features are collected by lexical scanning of the URL string. The Page-Source features are collected by visiting the page via a lightweight emulated browser so as to capture the details of what is rendered (HTML) and executed (JavaScript) using a feature extraction engine we implemented in Java. We customized the HTMLUnit [31] headless browser for the emulation and used it with two User-Agent personalities (Internet Explorer 6 and Mozilla Firefox 3). For each URL we visit for feature extraction, a fresh instance of the emulated browser is created to ensure a unique session for each URL. We used the Facebook Graph API [32], the Twitter URLs API [33], and a custom[2] script on Google Plus to automatically extract the Social-Reputation features. Features extracted from each web page are represented as a vector of the form $[v_1^{(i)}, v_2^{(i)}, ..., v_{n-1}^{(i)}, v_n^{(i)}, class^{(i)}]$ where the $v_k^{(i)}$'s are feature values ($k = 1, .., n$), n is the number of features, and $class^{(i)}$ is the class label of URL$^{(i)}$ which is either benign or malicious.

---

[2] There was not a standard API for Google Plus at the time of this experiment.

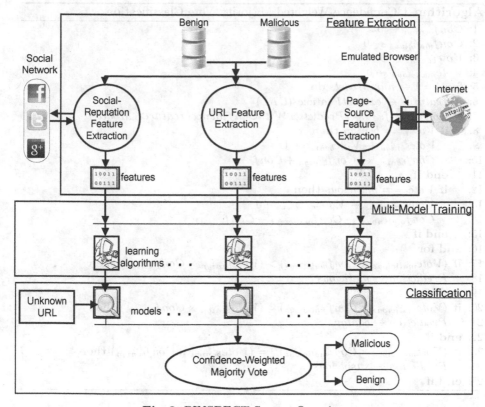

Fig. 2. BINSPECT System Overview

Multi-model Training. Using the extracted features, we train 7 supervised learning algorithms namely Decision Trees (J48, Random Tree, and Random Forest), Bayesian Classifiers (Naive Bayes and Bayes Net), Support Vector Machines, and Logistic Regression. At the end of the training, one model for each classifier is maintained as shown in the second block of Figure 2.

Confidence-Weighted Majority Vote Classification. For classification of an unknown web page using the learned models, we use the Confidence-Weighted Majority Vote algorithm that we customized (see Algorithm 1) to decide the class of the web page. To flag a page as either malicious or benign, instead of just taking the count of votes of the individual models, the vote count of the class label is multiplied with the sum of confidences with which the votes are made by each model (lines 17, 20, and 23 in Algorithm 1). The benefit of weighted-confidence majority vote is twofold. First, it minimizes the bias of relying on a single model to do classification. Secondly, it allows comparison of different models and makes the overall result more resistant to evasion attempts by attackers.

Algorithm 1 Confidence-Weighted Majority Vote Classification

1: $Conf_{benign} \leftarrow 0$
2: $Conf_{malicious} \leftarrow 0$
3: $Vote_{benign} \leftarrow 0$
4: $Vote_{malicious} \leftarrow 0$
5: **for** $i = 1 \rightarrow numModels$ **do**
6:      $features \leftarrow extractFeatures(URL)$
7:      $Vote_i, Conf_i \leftarrow getPredictionWithConfidence(features, Model_i)$
8:      **if** $Vote_i == benign$ **then**
9:          $Vote_{benign} \leftarrow Vote_{benign} + 1$
10:        $Conf_{benign} \leftarrow Conf_{benign} + Conf_i$
11:      **end if**
12:      **if** $Vote_i == malicious$ **then**
13:          $Vote_{malicious} \leftarrow Vote_{malicious} + 1$
14:          $Conf_{malicious} \leftarrow Conf_{malicious} + Conf_i$
15:      **end if**
16: **end for**
17: **if** $(Vote_{malicious} \times Conf_{malicious}) > (Vote_{benign} \times Conf_{benign})$ **then**
18:      $Prediction \leftarrow malicious$
19: **end if**
20: **if** $(Vote_{malicious} \times Conf_{malicious}) < (Vote_{benign} \times Conf_{benign})$ **then**
21:      $Prediction \leftarrow benign$
22: **end if**
23: **if** $(Vote_{malicious} \times Conf_{malicious}) == (Vote_{benign} \times Conf_{benign})$ **then**
24:      $Prediction \leftarrow suspicious$
25: **end if**

---

5   Experimental Setup and Evaluation

In this section, first we describe the data collection, dataset construction, and the experimental procedure. Then, we evaluate BINSPECT from the standpoint of its accuracy, significance of the features we introduced, its performance overhead, and its immunity to possible evasion.

5.1   Dataset and Experimental Setup

Data Source and Dataset. We collected samples from multiple sources for both malicious and benign web pages and divided the dataset into a training and a testing set. As shown in Table 1, for the malicious dataset, we collected 71,919 URLs from the malware and phishing blacklist of Google [26], the Phishtank database of collaboratively verified phishing pages [34], and the malware and injection attack URL list of MalwareURL [35]. The dataset of 414,000 benign URLs is also drawn from three popular sources. These are the Alexa Top sites [36], the Yahoo random URL generation service [37], and the DMOZ directory [38].

Table 1. Dataset for training and testing

Purpose	Benign	Malicious	Total
Training	300, 000	50, 000	350, 000
Testing	114, 465	21, 919	136, 384

Experimental Protocol. Using the training set, we extracted 39 features of which 3 are Social-Reputation features, 11 are URL features, and the remaining 25 are Page-Source features. When extracting the Page-Source features, we configured the emulated browser to manifest two different browser personalities (Internet Explorer 6 and Mozilla Firefox 3) and we used only the core components of the browser, i.e., Necko HTML Engine, Rhino JavaScript Engine, and the default CSS Parser in order to make the analysis lightweight. We used the Weka [39] machine learning toolbox to train the 7 standard classifiers with 10-fold cross validation. As a sanity check of the ground truth, we removed, from the training set, all unreachable URLs when visiting using the emulated browser.

5.2   Evaluation Results and Insights

Classification Accuracy

To decide the best combination of classifiers in BINSPECT, we evaluated the 7 classifiers in terms of accuracy, False Positive Rate (FPR), and False Negative Rate (FNR). Figures 3, 4, 5, and 6 show performance evaluation of the classifiers over the training set across the four classes of features, i.e., all features, URL features, Page-Source features, and Social-Reputation features respectively. As shown in Figure 3, training on all the features suggests that tree-based classifiers outperformed the other classifiers. In particular, the Random Tree classifier achieved 100% accuracy, 0% FPR, and 0% FNR.

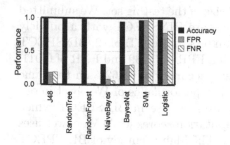

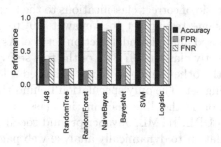

Fig. 3. With all features   **Fig. 4.** With URL features

We also evaluated how the classifiers perform on individual feature classes and the results suggest that some classifiers perform way better than the union of the features. For instance, accuracy of Naive Bayes increased by 30% (Figure 4) on URL features probably because the URL features have a statistical distribution that fits into the high degree of independence assumed in the algorithm. Another

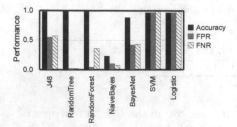   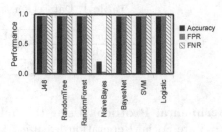

Fig. 5. With Page-Source features   **Fig. 6.** With Social-Reputation features

Table 2. Performance of BINSPECT in comparison to a public malicious web page analysis and detection service on the testing set

Measure	BINSPECT	Wepawet [40]
Classification Accuracy	97.81%	61.62%
False Positive Rate	0.189	0.983
False Negative Rate	0.011	0.073

interesting insight from Figure 6 is the high FNR of all the classifiers on social-reputation features which is attributed to the fact that malicious URLs which have higher share-count are likely to be misclassified as benign, suggesting that it is more effective to combine social-reputation features with other features to increase their predictive power. In general, the overall classification performance is better on all the features than the individual feature classes with the exception of Naive Bayes, which did not perform well in most cases (see Figures 3, 5, and 6).

For testing, we used all the classifiers except Naive Bayes due to its poor performance on the training set. Table 2 shows the overall classification accuracy of BINSPECT over the testing set. We measured the classification accuracy as the ratio of correct classifications to the total size of the testing set. We submitted the same testing set to Wepawet [40] to compare BINSPECT with a publicly deployed analysis and detection service. As can be seen from Table 2, BINSPECT correctly classified 97.81% of the test set with a FPR of 0.189 and FNR of 0.011. On the other hand, Wepawet achieved a lower accuracy of 61.62% on the same testing set. The only speculation behind the low performance of Wepawet in our opinion is the difference in the class of features we use in BINSPECT which span URL, HTML, JavaScript, and social reputation scores while Wepawet uses emulation to dynamically analyze web pages. The high accuracy of BINSPECT and its very low FNR on the testing set is an indication that our approach is effective at analyzing and detecting malicious web pages in a holistic manner with low performance overhead while covering malicious web pages leading to drive-by-download, phishing, injection, and malware delivery.

Significance of New Features
To verify whether the new features are of predictive importance in enhancing the accuracy of detecting malicious web pages, we compared the classification accuracy,

FPR, and FNR of the classifiers with and without our newly introduced (enhanced) features on the training set. As shown in Table 4, the new features, particularly the new URL features, improved the overall performance of 5 of the 7 classifiers (J48, Random Forest, Naive Bayes, Bayes Net, and Logistic Regression) shown with (↑) for accuracy and with (↓) for FPR and FNR. The new Page-Source features improved the overall performance of only 2 classifiers (Random Forest and Logistic Regression). Social-Reputation features have also improved the overall classification accuracy of Random Forest, Bayes Net, and Logistic Regression classifiers. Not surprisingly, the performance of Naive Bayes has not improved much with the new features as its overall performance is also very low.

In addition to the individual contribution of the new features, we also measured the overall improvement in accuracy of the classifiers as a result of the new features as shown in Table 3. The new features improved the accuracy of 4 of the 7 classifiers with improvements in the range 0.21% to 3.08%. Among the remaining 3 classifiers, on 2 (Random Forest and SVM), the new features seem to have no contribution on accuracy. The Random Tree classifier is an exception in this case as its accuracy was 100% even without the new features. Out of curiosity, we measured its accuracy with the new features and it remained the same, which most probably implies that this is the best classifier given the feature set and the dataset we used for training.

Table 3. Overall Contribution of new features on the accuracy of classifiers

Classifier	Without new (%)	With new(%)	Change(%)
J48 Decision Tree	98.97	99.27	↑ 0.30
Random Tree	100.0	100.0	−
Random Forest	99.94	99.94	−
Naive Bayes	28.16	30.62	↑ 2.46
Bayes Net	91.28	94.36	↑ 3.08
SVM	96.62	96.62	−
Logistic Regression	96.94	97.15	↑ 0.21

Performance Overhead

The experimental infrastructure we used is an Intel dual-core 2.66GHz CPU and 64-bit MacOSX operating system with 8GB of memory. Under this computational resource, the average time it takes to train a classifier is only 1.51 seconds. BINSPECT, took between 3 to 5 seconds (under variable system load) to analyze and detect a single page, which is an acceptable overhead given the fact that part of the analysis requires rendering the page in an emulated browser. Unfortunately, we could not compare performance overhead of BINSPECT with Wepawet due to the long delay it took to get back the results from Wepawet server which uses queueing to process batch requests for analysis.

Immunity to Evasion

Given the holistic nature of our approach, we claim that BINSPECT is not easily evadable. However, by closely inspecting the features we use, there are

Table 4. Performance of classifiers with and without new features on the training set

Classifier	Accuracy(%)	False Positive Rate	False Negative Rate
Without new features			
J48 Decision Tree	98.97	0.260	0.268
Random Tree	100.00	0.000	0.000
Random Forest	99.94	0.017	0.017
Naive Bayes	28.16	0.122	0.100
Bayes Net	91.28	0.381	0.391
Support Vector Machine	96.62	0.966	1.000
Logistic Regression	96.94	0.845	0.874
With new URL features			
J48 Decision Tree	98.98(↑)	0.254(↓)	0.262(↓)
Random Tree	100.00	0.000	0.000
Random Forest	99.95(↑)	0.014(↓)	0.014(↓)
Naive Bayes	46.45(↑)	0.184(↑)	0.171(↑)
Bayes Net	93.32(↑)	0.350(↓)	0.360(↓)
Support Vector Machine	96.62	0.966	1.000(↑)
Logistic Regression	97.05(↑)	0.798(↓)	0.825(↓)
With new Page-Source features			
J48 Decision Tree	98.93(↓)	0.260	0.268 ↑)
Random Tree	100.00	0.000	0.000
Random Forest	99.95(↑)	0.014(↓)	0.014(↓)
Naive Bayes	28.08(↓)	0.119(↑)	0.095(↓)
Bayes Net	90.85(↓)	0.381(↓)	0.391(↓)
Support Vector Machine	96.62	0.966	1.000
Logistic Regression	96.96(↑)	0.0842(↓)	0.871(↓)
With new Social-Reputation features			
J48 Decision Tree	98.99(↑)	0.265(↑)	0.274(↑)
Random Tree	100.00	0.000	0.000
Random Forest	99.95(↑)	0.014(↓)	0.014(↓)
Naive Bayes	26.69(↓)	0.075(↓)	0.051(↓)
Bayes Net	93.29(↑)	0.353(↓)	0.362(↓)
Support Vector Machine	96.62	0.966	1.000
Logistic Regression	97.06(↑)	0.806(↓)	0.834(↓)

a few things an attentive attacker has to do to try evading our analysis and detection technique. One method an attacker might use is to craft a benign-looking URL so as to imitate lexical aspects of benign URLs, which makes the URL features less useful in discriminating benign URLs from malicious ones. Another likelihood of evasion is for the attacker to use highly obfuscated client-side code (e.g., JavaScript). In such a case, BINSPECT is likely to be partly tricked because of the low consideration of obfuscated content in our approach. With regards to the Social-Reputation features, the only risk is that the attacker might lure users on social networks to publicly share a link to a malicious URL in order to collect reputation scores that could mislead BINSPECT. Even in this case, the luring would not last long because users stop sharing the link or the built-in URL scanning facility of the social network platform discovers the maliciousness of the URL. In general, it requires a great deal of effort from the attacker's side to completely bypass BINSPECT as it is quite difficult for the attacker to take control of the three complementary classes of features used in our approach and due to the nature of the classification that relies on weighted-confidence of each classifier.

6 Related Work

Canali et al. [5] proposed Prophiler, a purely static pre-filtering technique that deems web pages that launch drive-by-download attacks as likely malicious or likely benign. Prophiler achieved a very low false positive rate over a large testing set of URLs using 79 features on URL, host details, HTML, and JavaScript features. In BINSPECT, we apply static analysis and lightweight dynamic analysis to deem a web page as benign or malicious. Unlike Prophiler, where the best classifiers are used for testing, BINSPECT uses confidence-weighted majority vote for classification. Except the new features we introduced, all other features used in BINSPECT are also used by Prophiler. In BINSPECT, the number of features are half the number of features used in Prophiler.

Cova et al. [40] built Wepawet, an emulation-based dynamic analysis and detection framework for malicious content (mainly malicious JavaScript and malware). It is based on anomaly detection and the analysis and detection is available as a public service. Wepawet is reported by the authors to have a low false negative rate, particularly for drive-by-download web pages. BINSPECT, however, is a learning-based approach using mostly static features with a minimalistic emulation support.

Ma et al. [10] proposed a purely static analysis technique based on URL lexical features and host details and applied supervised learning and online learning techniques to achieve about 99% accuracy with a very low false positive rate. However, BINSPECT differs in that they use URL and host-based information only and the focus is to quickly classify URLs without further analysis of the page content and the execution dynamics in a browser. In our case, we reuse most of the URL features used by them in a statistical manner than lexical (presence/absence). More importantly, we use an emulated browser to visit and render the page and execute client-side code up on page load.

Dewald et al. [18] proposed ADSandbox, a client-side JavaScript sandboxing and signature-based, analysis technique that executes JavaScript embedded in a page within an isolated environment and logs every critical action to detect malicious web pages. ADSandbox achieved false positive close to zero but at a high performance overhead. BINSPECT, however, is a learning-based approach not only limited to web pages that host malicious JavaScript but also includes phishing pages, malware delivery pages, and pages that initiate injection attacks.

Compared to most prior work, BINSPECT characterizes malicious web pages spanning four classes of attacks (drive-by-download, phishing, malware-delivery, and injection) to build a lightweight detection system that relies on only 39 features of URL string, HTML, JavaScript, and Social-Reputation of URLs.

7   Conclusion

Existing techniques for detecting malicious web pages are effective at combating specific attack types. However, they are limited to partial snapshot of a malicious payload which limits their ability to cope up with the ever-changing and complex threats posed by malicious web pages. We presented BINSPECT, a holistic approach to defend users against malicious web pages by leveraging static analysis and lightweight emulation based on supervised learning. We have shown through large scale evaluation that BINSPECT is effective at precisely detecting malicious web pages with very low false signals. Moreover, the new features we introduced are relevant enough in improving the performance of the analysis and detection of malicious web pages. Our experiments suggest that BINSPECT incurs acceptable overhead cost to analyze web pages in a realistic scenario due to few and effective features reused from prior work and novel features.

BINSPECT lacks analysis of obfuscated JavaScript and emulation of the browser with plugins. In the future, we would like to incrementally improve BINSPECT by introducing these missing analysis steps. Another line of improvement is to further investigate additional features from social networks to characterize malicious web pages. We would also like to make BINSPECT an evolution-aware analysis and detection framework that takes into account the evolution of features and tunes its detection models accordingly.

Acknowledgments. We thank the anonymous reviewers for their insightful comments and the Authors of Wepawet for allowing us to submit and evaluate our test set.

References

1. Symantec: Symantec report on attack kits and malicious websites (July 2011), http://symantec.com/content/en/us/enterprise/other_resources/ b-symantec_report_on_attack_kits_and_malicious _websites_21169171_WP.en-us.pdf
2. Symantec: Symantec web based attack prevalence report (July 2011), http://www.symantec.com/business/threatreport/topic.jsp?id= threat_activity_trends&aid=web_based_attack_prevalence
3. WebSense: Websense 2010 threat report (July 2011), http://www.websense.com/content/ threat-report-2010-highlights.aspx/
4. Symantec: Internet security threat report 2011 trends (April 2012), http://www.symantec.com/content/en/us/enterprise/ other_resources/b-istr_main_report_2011_21239364.en-us.pdf

5. Canali, D., Cova, M., Vigna, G., Kruegel, C.: Prophiler:a fast filter for the large-scale detection of malicious web pages. In: Proceedings of WWW, pp. 197–206 (2011)
6. Stone-Gross, B., Cova, M., Cavallaro, L., Gilbert, B., Szydlowski, M., Kemmerer, R., Kruegel, C., Vigna, G.: Your botnet is my botnet: analysis of a botnet takeover. In: Proceedings of the 16th ACM CCS, pp. 635–647 (2009)
7. Eshete, B., Villafiorita, A., Weldemariam, K.: Malicious website detection: Effectiveness and efficiency issues. In: Proceedings of SysSec Workshop, pp. 123–126 (2011)
8. Ma, J.: Learning to Detect Malicious URLs. PhD thesis, University of California, San Diego (2010)
9. Ma, J., Saul, L.K., Savage, S., Voelker, G.M.: Identifying suspicious urls: an application of large-scale online learning. In: Proceedings of ICML, pp. 681–688 (2009)
10. Ma, J., Saul, L.K., Savage, S., Voelker, G.M.: Beyond blacklists: learning to detect malicious web sites from suspicious urls. In: Proceedings of KDDM (2009)
11. Thomas, K., Grier, C., Ma, J., Paxson, V., Song, D.: Design and Evaluation of a Real-Time URL Spam Filtering Service. In: Proceedings of the IEEE Symposium on Security and Privacy (2011)
12. Choi, H., Zhu, B.B., Lee, H.: Detecting malicious web links and identifying their attack types. In: Proceedings of the 2nd USENIX Conference on Web Application Development, pp. 11–11 (2011)
13. Seifert, C., Welch, I., Komisarczuk, P., Aval, C.U., Endicott-Popovsky, B.: Identification of malicious web pages through analysis of underlying dns and web server relationships. In: 33rd IEEE Conference on Local Computer Networks (2008)
14. Yung-Tsung, H., Yimeng, C., Tsuhan, C., Chi-Sung, L., Chia-Mei, C.: Malicious web content detection by machine learning. Expert Syst. Appl. 37(1), 55–60 (2010)
15. Seifert, C., Welch, I., Komisarczuk, P.: Identification of malicious web pages with static heuristics. In: Proceedings of the Australasian Telecommunication Networks and Applications Conference (2008)
16. Likarish, P., Jung, E., Jo, I.: Obfuscated malicious javascript detection using classification techniques. In: Proceedings of International Conference on Malicious and Unwanted Software (MALWARE), pp. 47–54 (October 2009)
17. Qassrawi, M., Zhang, H.: Detecting malicious web servers with honeyclients. Journal of Networks 6(1) (2011)
18. Dewald, A., Holz, T., Freiling, F.C.: Adsandbox: sandboxing javascript to fight malicious websites. In: ACM Symposium on Applied Computing, pp. 1859–1864 (2010)
19. Marco, C., Christopher, K., Giovanni, V.: Detection and analysis of drive-by-download attacks and malicious javascript code. In: Proceedings of WWW, pp. 281–290 (2010)
20. Alexander, M., Tanya, B., Damien, D., Gribble, S.D., Levy, H.M.: Spyproxy: execution-based detection of malicious web content. In: Proceedings of 16th USENIX Security Symposium, pp. 3:1–3:16 (2007)
21. Ford, S., Cova, M., Kruegel, C., Vigna, G.: Analyzing and detecting malicious flash advertisements. In: Proceedings of ACSAC (2009)
22. Ikinci, A., Holz, T., Freiling, F.: Monkey-spider: Detecting malicious websites with low-interaction honeyclients. In: Proceedings of Sicherheit, Schutz und Zuverlssigkeit, pp. 407–421 (2008)
23. Byung-Ik, K., Chae-Tae, I., Hyun-Chul, J.: Suspicious malicious web site detection with strength analysis of a javascript obfuscation. International Journal of Advanced Science and Technology, 19–32 (2011)

24. Rieck, K., Krueger, T., Dewald, A.: Cujo: efficient detection and prevention of drive-by-download attacks. In: Proceedings ACSAC, pp. 31–39 (2010)
25. Kolbitsch, C., Livshits, B., Zorn, B., Seifer, C.: Rozzle: De-cloaking internet malware. Technical report, Microsoft (2011)
26. Google: Google safe browsing api (August 2011), http://code.google.com/apis/safebrowsing/
27. McAfee: Mcafee site advisor (July 2011), http://www.siteadvisor.com
28. Armorize.: mysql.com hacked:infecting visitors with malware (September 2011), http://blog.armorize.com/2011/09/mysqlcom-hacked-infecting-visitors-with.html
29. Egele, M., Kirda, E., Kruegel, C.: Mitigating drive-by download attacks: Challenges and open problems (2009)
30. Seo, D.: Facebook and twitter's influence on google's search rankings (May 2012), http://www.seomoz.org/blog/facebook-twitters-influence-google-search-rankings
31. HtmlUnit: Htmlunit (March 2012), http://htmlunit.sourceforge.net/
32. Facebook: Facebook graph api (March 2012), https://developers.facebook.com/docs/reference/api/
33. Twitter: Twitter url api (March 2012), http://urls.api.twitter.com/1/urls/
34. PhishTank: Phishtank developer information (September 2011), http://www.phishtank.com/developer_info.php
35. MalwareURL: Malware urls (September 2011), http://www.malwareurl.com/
36. Alexa: Alexa top 500 global websites (July 2011), http://www.alexa.com/topsites
37. Yahoo: Yahoo random url generator (October 2011), http://random.yahoo.com/bin/yrl/
38. DMOZ: Open directory project (September 2011), http://www.dmoz.org/
39. Hall, M., Frank, E., Holmes, G., Pfahringer, B., Reutemann, P., Witten, I.H.: The weka data mining software: An update. SIGKDD Explorations 11 (2009)
40. UCSB: Wepawet (July 2011), http://wepawet.cs.ucsb.edu

Improving the Resilience of an IDS against Performance Throttling Attacks

Govind Sreekar Shenoy[1], Jordi Tubella[1], and Antonio González[1,2]

[1] Department of Computer Architecture,
Universitat Politècnica de Catalunya, Barcelona, Spain
[2] Intel Barcelona Research Center, Barcelona, Spain
{govind,jordit}@ac.upc.edu, antonio.gonzalez@intel.com

Abstract. Intrusion Detection Systems (IDS) have emerged as one of the most promising ways to secure systems in the network. To be effective against evasion attempts, the IDS must provide tight bounds on performance. Otherwise an adversary can bypass the IDS by carefully crafting and sending packets that throttle it. This can render the IDS ineffective, thus resulting in the network becoming vulnerable.

We present a performance throttling attack mounted against the computationally intensive string matching algorithm. This algorithm performs string matching by traversing a finite-state-machine (FSM). We observe that there are some input bytes that sequentially traverse a chain of 30 pointers. This chain of traversal drastically degrades performance, and we observe a 22X performance drop in comparison to the average case performance. We investigate hardware and software mechanisms to counter this performance degradation. The software mechanism is targeted for commodity general purpose CPUs. While the hardware-based mechanism uses a parallel traversal suitable for network processor architectures. Our results show that our proposed mechanisms significantly improves (by over 3X magnitude) string matching algorithm's worst performing cases.

1   Introduction

Intrusion Detection Systems (IDS) are emerging as one of the most promising ways of providing protection to systems on the network. By monitoring the traffic in real time, an IDS can detect and also take preventive actions against suspicious activities. To be effective, an IDS must be able to inspect packets at wire speeds. The consequences of not doing so can result either in undetected malicious packets or expensive packet drops. An adversary can also bring the IDS to this state of not being able to process packets at wire speeds. Such attempts are commonly referred to as evasion[6, 9, 18], and stem from weaknesses in some part of IDS processing.

Evasion can come in various flavors. An example of evasion is clever packet fragmentation at "malicious content" boundaries, thus tricking the IDS from inspecting malicious content. Other examples include deliberate packet header

A.D. Keromytis and R. Di Pietro (Eds.): SecureComm 2012, LNICST 106, pp. 167–184, 2013.
© Institute for Computer Sciences, Social Informatics and Telecommunications Engineering 2013

corruption and stream re-assembly. The nature and ease of evasion makes it very appealing for malicious hosts to bypass the IDS. Evasion can also occur by throttling the performance of the IDS. Since the system is unable to keep up with the wire speed, it can lead to the IDS being disabled and attack flood gates opened. For this to occur, an adversary exploits the wide performance gap between the average case and worst-case processing time[6, 15, 21]. This can also be viewed as a class of Denial-of-service (DoS) attack that targets system resource utilization[13]. Earlier works in this direction investigate attack and defense mechanisms for hash tables[6] used by an IDS. Additionally, other works explore weaknesses due to synctatics of signature specifications[21] in the Snort IDS.

In this work we present a performance throttling attack mounted against the string matching algorithm used by an IDS. An IDS like Snort[19] operates by scanning packets for malicious content using a database of >40,000 known attack strings. So Snort uses the Aho-Corasick algorithm[1] to perform a multi-string matching against the packet payload. Since the packet payload needs to be scanned and compared with a database of >40,000 strings, so it is computationally very intensive. Hence, the string matching algorithm can be susceptible to performance throttling attacks. A closer look at the processing time per payload byte of the string matching algorithm reveals a wide performance variation. We observe that there are payload bytes that need 22X processing times in comparison to the average case. Further, the cause of this variance in performance is due to the sequential traversal of a chain of pointers. Our counter-measure focuses on improving the worst-case performance by accelerating this sequential chain traversal. We propose two mechanisms - hardware-based and software-based mechanisms - to counter this performance degradation. The hardware-based mechanism is targeted for a highly parallel architecture like the network processor ([5, 11]). The software-based mechanism is for commodity general purpose CPUs. Our results indicate that our proposed mechanisms significantly improves the worst-case performance.

The rest of the paper is organized as follows. Section 2 provides a brief background on the Aho-Corasick algorithm. Section 3 presents the motivation of this work. Section 4 details our proposed counter-measure and our architecture. The simulation methodology is discussed in Section 5, and Section 6 presents the performance results. Section 7 discusses the related work in this area. Section 8 provides future directions.

2   Background

An IDS like Snort operates by inspecting packets for prior reported attacks. This database of attack strings are byte patterns that have commonly occurred and detected in attacks. The vast variety of attacks and their constant evolution bloats the attack string database. We observe that there are 42, 670 attack strings in the Snort April-2010 ruleset[1] release. So Snort commonly uses a multi-string matching algorithm like the Aho-Corasick algorithm[1] for attack detection. This algorithm works by constructing a FSM using the set of attack strings. Once the FSM is constructed, incoming bytes from packets are used to traverse this FSM. We provide a brief overview of the Aho-Corasick algorithm with an example.

Consider the set of strings: **attacker, tacked, acken, ckeh, ket**. Figure 1 shows the corresponding Aho-Corasick FSM constructed from these strings. The FSM is built in two stages. In the first stage, characters from the strings are added to the FSM. This is done in a way that strings that share a common prefix also share the same set of parents in the FSM. The edges corresponding to this stage are shown as thick lines. The nodes **9, 15, 20, 24, 27** indicate a match for **attacker, tacked, acken, ckeh, ket** respectively. These nodes also store a pointer to the list of matched strings. For example, **node 9** stores a pointer to **attacker**. The second stage in building the FSM consists of inserting failure edges. When a string match is not found, it is possible for the suffix of one string to match the prefix of another. So failure edges need to be inserted. Failure edges are shown with dotted lines. For figure clarity, only a few failure edges are shown. Once this FSM is built, the algorithm traverses it with the payload bytes. In case the payload byte does not match any of the examined edges, then the traversal is restarted from the root-node.

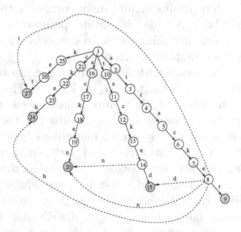

Fig. 1. Example of the Aho-Corasick Finite State Machine

An important issue with this FSM is the large storage space needed. This huge storage size requirement also impacts the performance efficiency of an IDS, due to the large working set size. Some earlier works in reducing the storage space needed for FSM have proposed removing the inherent redundancy in the FSM. A common example of redundancy is due to failure edges. Consider **node 8** and its edge **d**. This is a failure edge and is identical to the edge from **node**

---

[1] A rule in Snort typically contains multiple attack strings. We instrumented Snort to dump all the strings.

14. Thus **Node 14** is a failure pointer of **node 8**, and this traversal can also be done by jumping to **node 14**. In this way all failure edges are eliminated.

Figure 2(a) shows the FSM built with the failure pointer optimization. We observe that 93% of the edges are failure edges, and hence the failure pointer optimization provides important area benefits. As a consequence, earlier works[2, 12, 20, 22, 23, 25] have optimized the failure edges in this manner. For the rest of the paper, we consider this optimized FSM.

The FSM constructed using the Aho-Corasick algorithm is very similar to a deterministic finite automata (DFA). In fact Snort and other IDSs[16] also use regular expressions to specify attack strings. These regular expressions are again converted to DFAs or NFAs. Hence our work is equally applicable to regular expressions used in an IDS. Note that the optimized FSM thus built is very similar to a NFA. A NFA, unlike a DFA, can have multiple active states. Further these active states need to be traversed sequentially. In order to efficiently traverse the FSM, the Snort[19] IDS uses a backtracking based heuristic for traversing the NFA. This heuristic is very similar to the failure pointer optimization, and so our work can be adapted to accelerate NFA traversal in Snort.

3   Motivation

The optimization of failure chains significantly compacts the data structure. However this has a drawback. A node with failure pointers may need additional processing when there are no matching edges. In some cases we observe that this additional processing is a significant overhead.

We illustrate this more clearly with an example. Let the input bytes to the optimized FSM in Figure 2(a) be **a, t, t, a, c, k, e, t**. The first 6 bytes lead up-to **node 8**. For the final byte, **t**, the failure pointer needs to be traversed as there are no matching edges at **node 8**. Hence, **node 14** - the failure pointer of **node 8**- is accessed. Here again there are no matching edges, and so the failure pointer of **node 14** is accessed. This is repeated until a matching edge is found, or the traversal is restarted from the root-node. Note that these chain of failure pointers are accessed sequentially and sometimes wastefully as well. This can lead to significant performance degradation when large chains are visited.

Figure 2(b) shows the failure chain length distribution for various Snort database releases. We define failure chain length of a node as the maximum number of failure pointers that can be traversed starting from that node. The failure chain length of **node 8** in the above example is 4. It is very interesting to observe that there are nodes with failure chain length of up-to 31. Thus for bytes accessing failure edges of these nodes, the processing time can be high. We investigate the performance impact of traversing failure chains.

Figure 3(a) shows the CDF of processing time per byte[2]. We see that 95% of input bytes need less than **31 cc**, thus leading to an average processing time

---

[2] Processing time per byte is measured as the total number of clock cycles (cc) needed to complete the processing of a byte.

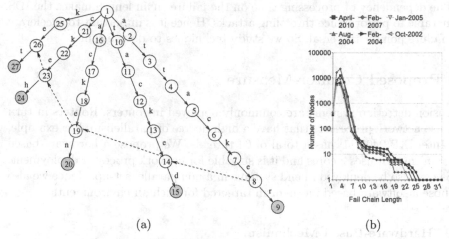

Fig. 2. Impact of Failure chain

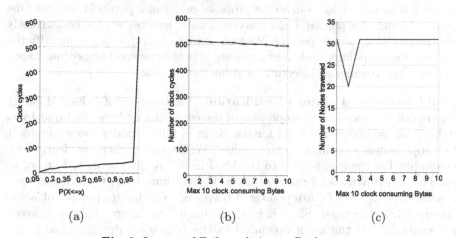

Fig. 3. Impact of Failure chains on Performance

of **23.5 cc/B**. However, there are bytes that need up-to **516 cc**. This clearly indicates that there is a wide variation in processing time. We investigate the cause of this wide variation, by examining the processing of the ten most clock consuming bytes (refer to Figure 3(b)). This is also the tail end of the CDF. As seen in Figure 3(b), we observe that these bytes need at-least **495 cc**. The cause of the enormous processing time is due to the traversal of a chain of failure pointers. In contrast, on examination of the relatively lesser clock consuming bytes (left half of 0.95 probability in the CDF plot), we observe that these bytes traverse at most 3 failure pointers. This clearly shows the significant impact of traversing a large chain of failure pointers.

The dependency of processing time on the failure chain length makes the IDS vulnerable to performance throttling attacks. Hence it is important to accelerate the failure pointer traversal. So we study techniques to do the same.

4   Proposed Counter-Measure

Intrusion detection systems are commonly deployed in routers. Routers in turn can use network processors that have a high degree of parallelism. For example, the Intel IXP 2400[11] has a total of 64 threads. We propose a hardware-based mechanism that uses 2 cores and it is suitable for network processor deployment. IDSs can also be deployed in end systems in a non parallel set-up. Hence we also propose a software-based mechanism targeted for such an environment.

4.1   Hardware-Based Mechanism

The processing of the failure chain takes a performance hit mainly due to the sequential nature of its traversal. So our proposal performs a parallel traversal. One engine performs the regular FSM traversal, while another engine concurrently finds the candidate failure pointer. We first describe a mechanism to identify the candidate failure pointer and to incorporate it in the traversal algorithm. Later, we present the parallel architecture used for the traversal.

Candidate Failure Pointer Identification. The traversal of a chain of failure pointers can be viewed as a comparison of the edges of a node to the input byte. Further, this process is repeated for the chain of failure nodes. So we break it into comparison of a chain of outgoing edges. We illustrate this more clearly with an example. Let the input bytes to the FSM in Figure 2(a) be **a, t, t, a, c, k, e, t**. The first 6 bytes lead up-to **node 8**. For the final byte, **t**, since there are no matching edges the failure pointer is traversed. The failure pointer of **node 8**, **node 14**, is traversed. Since it is a mismatch, the failure chain is followed until **node 26**. So the main operation in the failure pointer traversal is the comparison of the input byte with all outgoing edges of a node. This is checking for membership in a set of outgoing edges, and with each set corresponding to a failure pointer.

Bloom filters[3] offer a convenient and efficient way to check - without incurring any false negatives - for set memberships. We use bloom filters to do the membership check. We create a hash for each failure pointer by using its set of outgoing edges. We term it as a bloom filter signature. We illustrate this with an example. Consider **node 8** (from Figure 2(a)), we create and store bloom filter signatures for all its failure chains, namely, **nodes 14, 19, 23, and 26**. Each of these signatures are generated using outgoing edges of each node.

Figure 4 shows the signature storage of **node 8** generated in this manner. In addition to signatures, we also store offset and fan-out of the corresponding

Node 14	Node 19	Node 23	Node 26	Node 14	Node 19	Node 23	Node 26
Sig	Sig	Sig	Sig	(offset,	(offset,	(offset,	(offset,
fn(d)	fn(n)	fn(h)	fn(t)	fan–out)	fan–out)	fan–out)	fan–out)

Fig. 4. Node 6 Signature Storage

failure pointer. This is done so that when a signature matches, we can directly jump to the matching failure pointer. The traversal using bloom filter signatures is as follows. Consider traversing **node 8** with input byte as **t**. Since there are no matching edges in **node 8**, we check if there are any matching edges in the failure chain. A signature is generated using **t**, and compared against all the failure chain signatures of **node 8**. Since **node 26** has a matching signature, we directly traverse to **node 26**. Note that in case of multiple matches, the matches are traversed sequentially. This preserves traversal correctness, as the signatures are stored in the way they are originally encountered.

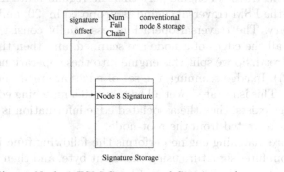

Fig. 5. Node 8 FSM Storage and Signature Access

The failure chain signature matching can be performed independently and in parallel with the conventional node processing. In the above example, the failure chain traversal is done sequentially after checking for matching edges in a node. We accelerate it by performing the failure pointer identification concurrently with the conventional node processing. If there is no need to traverse the failure pointer, then the failure pointer identification is discarded. So our proposed architecture consists of two engines: a regular FSM traversal engine and an engine to identify the candidate failure pointer. We further decouple the memory by storing the bloom filter signatures in a separate memory bank. Our memory architecture consists of two memory banks, with one containing the FSM and the other containing signatures. This helps us in decoupling the FSM traversal from the failure chain computation. Additionally, we store a pointer to the node signature in the FSM data structure. So every node also stores a pointer to the signature database and its failure chain length. Figure 5 shows the storage for **node 8**.

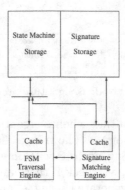

Fig. 6. Hardware Architecture

Hardware Architecture. Figure 6 shows our proposed hardware architecture. The hardware consists of a FSM traversal engine and a signature processing engine. The FSM traversal engine performs the regular state-machine traversal. We have used the FSM traversal engine as proposed in [20] and we provide here a brief summary. The traversal operations essentially consist of two steps. In the first step, all the edges of a node are scanned, and then the matching edge information is read. So we split this engine into these operations (refer to Figure 7(a), 7(b), 7(c)). In edge scanning, the set of edges are read and compared with the input byte. This is iterated over all edges until a matching edge is obtained. If a matching edge exists, then the associated edge information is read. Otherwise, the traversal is restarted from the root-node.

The signature matching engine performs the following functionalities. It generates the bloom filter signature using the input byte, and then compares it with the stored signatures. Signatures are of length 4 B and are generated using two hash functions[3]. Since the signature comparison is an AND operation, so we use 16 B AND operators for signature comparison. This allows us to compare four signatures at a time. If a signature matches, then the matched failure pointer is traversed. Figure 7(c) shows the flow-chart for the signature matching engine.

Our architecture concurrently perform signature comparison and the regular FSM traversal. Hence if the input byte matches an edge, the signature processing is flushed. However, if there are no matching edges, then the candidate failure pointer is obtained from the signature matching engine. Subsequently, this node is traversed by the FSM traversal engine.

4.2   Software-Based Mechanism

In this mechanism, the Aho-Corasick FSM is constructed so that there is an upper-bound on the failure chain length. This upper-bound can also be viewed a threshold value. In this mechanism, failure edges are inserted for nodes with failure chain lengths a multiple of this threshold value.

---

[3] A design space exploration was done to obtain these parameter values.

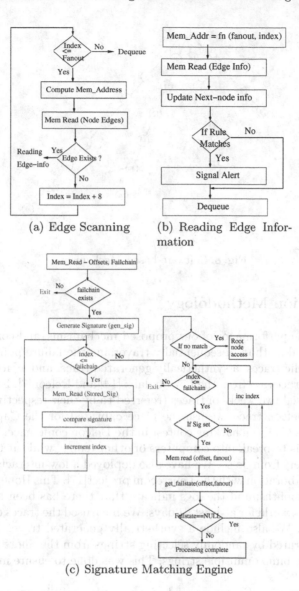

(a) Edge Scanning   (b) Reading Edge Information

(c) Signature Matching Engine

Fig. 7. Functionality of Signature Matching Engine and FSM Traversal Engine

We illustrate it more clearly with an example. Consider the FSM shown in Figure 2(a). If we use a threshold value of **3**, then failure edges are inserted for nodes with failure chain length of **3**. Hence, failure edges are inserted for **node 14**. In this way we limit the failure chain traversal to a fixed upper bound. This also enables in efficiently storing the FSM as failure edges are only inserted for selective nodes and not all the nodes in the FSM. In our simulations, we explore different values of the threshold in order to find an optimal point.

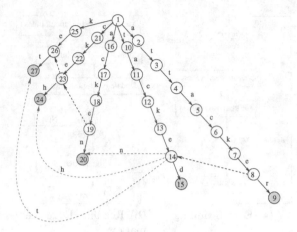

Fig. 8. Software-based Mechanism

5   Simulation Methodology

We evaluate the performance of our proposed mechanisms, and compare it with the conventional method of sequentially traversing the failure pointer. We have used three public traces, a synthetically generated trace, and a Honeypot trace.

The public traces are from the Lincoln labs [14] and Defcon[7]. For the Lincoln labs we have used two weeks of traces (referred to by their respective week) from 1999. In the Defcon trace, we use the trace captured for the Capture the flag (CTF) game[7]. CTF is a hacking contest in the Defcon conference. The objective of this contest is to break into computers of other teams, while at the same time preventing others from do so. We have also deployed a low-interaction Honeypot running in collaboration with the Leurrecom project[17]. This Honeypot has been running for 3 months, and the logs indicate that there has been an interaction with the outside world for at-least 61 days. We have used the traces collected from this Honeypot. We also include a synthetically generated trace. The synthetic trace was generated by randomly selecting strings from the Snort rule database and further combining multiple strings. This was done to ensure minimum-sized packet (64 B).

Table 1 summarizes the traces used. Note that we have inspected TCP, ICMP and UDP packets from these traces. We have used the Snort database released on April 2010 and containing 40,678 strings. We use **average number of clock cycles per incoming byte** as the metric for performance comparison. This is computed by dividing the total number of clock-cycles by the total number of bytes. Total number of clock-cycles is the sum of **total processing time** and **total memory access time**. The **total processing time** comprises of: edge-scanning, reading edge-information, signature comparison, and signature

Table 1. Summary of Traces used in the Evaluation

Data-sets	Mean Packet Size (B)	Num Packets (M)
Defcon	71.9	15.64
synthetic	73.64	0.120
Week 2	160.51	13.18
Week 3	200.01	14.91
Honeypot	205	0.46

offset computation. These processing times are obtained by assuming each of the arithmetic processing blocks need 1 cycle and branches need 2 cycles (refer to Figure 7(a), 7(b), 7(c)). With this assumption, edge scanning needs 6 cc plus the memory access latency.

The **total memory access time** is obtained from the trace-driven cache simulator [8], which was modified to model cache access times and processing times. The cache miss penalty is obtained from CACTI [24] by plugging into the SRAM model of CACTI the FSM memory sizes. We have used a 16k direct-mapped cache-configuration for the caches. Note that in case of the hardware-based mechanism, there are two caches each of 16k size. The cache hit time of 2 cc is used (also obtained from CACTI). The core frequency is assumed to be 3 GHz.

6   Results

We compare the performance of our proposed architecture with the **Baseline**. Note that the **Baseline** performs traversal using the conventional way of sequentially following failure pointers.

For the hardware-based mechanism, we have varied the minimal failure chain length. Hence signatures are kept only for those nodes with a failure chain length greater than the threshold. We have used threshold values of **1, 3, 5**. A threshold value of **1** indicates that nodes with failure chain lengths $>= 2$ have stored signatures. For the software-based mechanism, we have similarly varied the failure chain length threshold. So in this scheme, nodes with a given threshold failure chain length will have all its failure edges in place. We have used threshold values of **3, 5, 7**.

In order to evaluate the worst performance cases, we compare the processing clock cycles (cc) needed for the 10 most clock consuming bytes. Note that a byte that performs badly in one scheme may not do so in another scheme. We also compare the average-case performance. We initially report results for the synthetic trace to determine the optimal points for the hardware and software-based mechanism. Later we report results for the remaining traces.

A few terminology clarifications. **Sig-1** refers to the use of bloom-filter signatures of threshold value 1. Further, **sw-3** refers to the failure chain length of 3

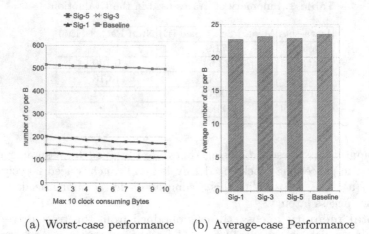

(a) Worst-case performance   (b) Average-case Performance

Fig. 9. Synthetic Trace Comparison Result for Hardware-based Mechanism

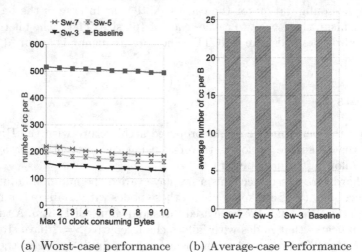

(a) Worst-case performance   (b) Average-case Performance

Fig. 10. Synthetic Trace Comparison Result for Software-based Mechanism

used in the software-based mechanism. Figure 9(a) shows the 10 most clock consuming bytes for the hardware-based mechanism for the synthetic trace. While **Baseline** needs at least **495 cc**, the use of signatures brings it down to at most **119 cc**. Additionally, on a closer examination of various threshold values, we see that **Sig-1** gives the best performance. For **Sig-1** we see a worst-case performance of **119 cc** - a 4.33X improvement over the **Baseline**. Figure 9(b) shows the average-case performance, and we see that it remains unaffected.

Figure 10 shows the comparison results for the software-based mechanism. We again observe that keeping an upper-bound of the failure chain length significantly brings down the worst-case performance. While **Baseline** needs at least **495 cc** in these bytes, the software-based mechanism reduces it to at most **219 cc**. Figure 10(b) shows the average-case performance and we see that it remains largely unaffected.

We observe that **Sig-1** is the best performing configuration for the hardware-based mechanism. Further, **sw-3** performs best for the software-based mechanism. So for the remaining traces we compare the performance of **Sig-1**, **sw-3** and **Baseline**.

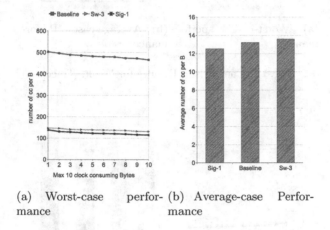

(a) Worst-case   perfor-   (b) Average-case   Performance   mance

Fig. 11. Defcon Trace Comparison Results

For Defcon trace we observe a similar performance behaviour (refer to Figure 11). Comparing the worst-case performance, the hardware-based mechanism reduces the worst-case performance to **139 cc** - over 3X improvement over the **Baseline**. On the other hand, the software-based mechanism reduces the worst-case performance to **147 cc**. On comparing the hardware-based and software-based mechanisms, we observe that the hardware-based mechanism moderately outperforms the software-based mechanism.

Figures 12, 13 and 14 show the performance results for week2, week3, and Honeypot respectively. We again observe a similar behaviour, with **Sig-1** providing the best performance for the worst-case. Note however that there is a mild average-case performance degradation for the software-based mechanism.

Our mechanisms needs additional memory in comparison to the **Baseline**. So we evaluate the additional storage space needed (measured in KBs) for our proposal. Figure 15 shows the storage space required for various schemes. The memory required has been normalized to the **Baseline** (706 KB). In case of the hardware-based mechanism, the additional storage space is between 34% and 84% to that of the **Baseline**.

In case of software-based mechanism, the additional storage space is between 1% to 140% in comparison to the **Baseline**. This exponential increase in storage

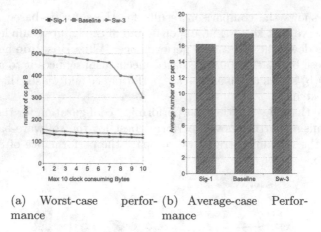

(a) Worst-case   perfor- (b) Average-case Performance   mance

Fig. 12. Comparison Results for Week2 Trace

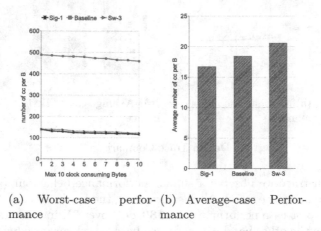

(a) Worst-case   perfor- (b) Average-case Performance   mance

Fig. 13. Comparison Results for Week3 Trace

space is due to the following. As the threshold failure chain length is reduced from **7** to **3**, the number of nodes that need to store the failure edges grows by more than 2 order of magnitude. This consequently contributes to the exponentially increased storage space.

It is interesting to note that our proposed mechanisms - hardware based and software based mechanisms - are orthogonal. These mechanisms can also be combined using an FSM constructed with an upper bound failure chain length and a parallel FSM traversal. However, we observe no significant worst-case or average-case performance improvement. Further, the combined scheme also needs additional storage space.

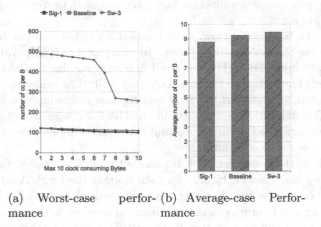

(a) Worst-case perfor-(b) Average-case Performance   mance

Fig. 14. Comparison Results for Honeypot Trace

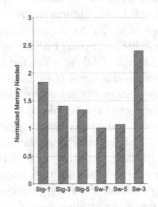

Fig. 15. Storage Space Comparison

7   Related Work

To the best of our knowledge, Crosby et al[6] were the first to introduce attacks
targeting the worst-case performance. They exploited weaknesses in the hash
tables used for port scanning in the Bro IDS[16]. A hash table needs $O(n)$ time
for insertion on an average and $O(n^2)$ in the worst-case. They carefully construct
packets that cause collision in the hash table. In this manner, the performance
of the hash table is significantly degraded. As a counter measure, they proposed
the use of universal hash functions that significantly reduces collisions.

Smith et al[21] present algorithmic complexity attacks that exploit syntactics
of rule specification. There are rules in Snort that are dependent on the relative
position of bytes in the packet. They exploited this dependency to create packets that lead to multiple repeated and often redundant processing of the same

byte. So they propose a memoization based technique to prevent such redundant processing of bytes.

Earlier works in this direction have focused on either compacting the FSM or on improving the system throughput. To compact the FSM, Kumar et al[12] used a Delayed input DFA (D^2FA). A DFA is very similar to the FSM studied in this paper. They observed that a DFA typically has numerous states with identical outgoing transitions. So they remove this redundancy using a default transition. This transition is very similar to the failure pointer studied in this paper. So our proposed architecture and traversal complements the D^2FA in improving its worst-case performance.

Tuck et al[25] study different optimizations to reduce the size of each node in the FSM. They use a 256 bit bitmap for each node in the FSM. A bit is set in the bitmap if the corresponding character is an outgoing edge. They further compact the FSM using the failure pointer optimization as discussed earlier. Hence our proposed traversal and architecture is directly applicable to this work.

Becchi et al[2] propose state merging for reducing the storage space. Two states are similar if they have multiple common output states. They combine such states to form a compact FSM. Interestingly, they use the bit mapped based implementation of Tuck et al [25] for representing states. So our proposed architecture is directly applicable to it. Song et al[23] propose using a cached DFA (CDFA) for efficient traversal. In a CDFA, a cached state is used to eliminate 1-step transitions. Among the mechanisms they investigate for compacting the FSM, they also include failure pointer optimization as discussed earlier. So again our proposed architecture is directly applicable to this work.

In addition, there have been numerous works that study a rich variety of DoS attacks. A taxonomy of DoS attacks is given in[13]. Moscibroda et al[15] study DoS attacks against DRAM scheduling in multi-cores. They observe that a malicious application can starve other benign applications, thus leading to significant performance degradation. So they propose a memory architecture that provides fairness to all executing applications. Cai et al[4] study algorithmic complexity attacks against the Unix file system. So in this attack a malicious system process tricks the OS to access system files that are not in its access privileges. They propose a defense mechanism that is provably secure. Hasan et al[10] study DoS attacks that forcefully heat up certain resources in a SMT. In this attack, a malicious thread creates a hot spot in a shared resource by repeatedly accessing it. They study several mechanisms to mitigate the hot-spot including selective throttling of threads.

8   Conclusion

In this paper, we have presented a counter-measure for a performance throttling attack against the string matching algorithm in an IDS. Our study reveals that with certain input bytes, the Aho-Corasick algorithm can end up traversing a chain of up-to 31 pointers. Our results indicate a massive performance degradation, a 22X fall in comparison to the average case performance. We investigate two mechanisms to counter this performance degradation - hardware-based mechanism and software-based mechanism. In the hardware-based mechanism we identify the candidate pointer from the chain of pointers and directly jump to it. We propose a parallel architecture for FSM traversal. The signature matching engine identifies the pointer to jump to, while the FSM engine performs the regular FSM traversal. In the software-based mechanism, we propose a modified FSM that restricts this chain of sequential pointer traversal to a fixed upper bound. Both these scheme result in over 3X improvement in the worst-case performance.

An applicability of this work is in detecting tampering of the Snort signature database. If an adversary corrupts the memory stack of the IDS using buffer overflow attempts, then the pattern matching module can be compromised. In order to detect such tampering, the hardware-based mechanism needs to be extended for detecting FSM traversal violations. Performance throttling attack is an example of an evasion attempt, there are other ways of evasion including packet re-assembly and packet fragmentation. In both of these attacks, the adversary can force the IDS to maintain an infinite number of states (TCP connections) that finally leads to memory exhaustion. Under this circumstance, even benign packets suffer massively. It will be interesting to study defense mechanisms against these attacks.

Acknowledgements. This work has been supported by the following grants: TIN2010-18368, TIN2007-61763, and SGR2009-1250. We are grateful to the Spanish Ministry and Intel Corporation for providing us the requisite monetary and logistic support.

References

[1] Aho, A.V., Corasick, M.J.: Efficient String Matching: An Aid to Bibliographic Search. Communications of the ACM 18(6), 333–340 (1975)

[2] Becchi, M., Cadambi, S.: Memory-Efficient Regular Expression Search Using State Merging. In: Proceedings of INFOCOM 2007 (2007)

[3] Bloom, B.H.: Space/time Trade-offs in Hash Coding with Allowable Errors. Communications of the ACM 13(7), 422–426 (1970)

[4] Cai, Q., Gui, Y., Johnson, R.: Exploiting Unix File-system Races via Algorithmic Complexity Attacks. In: Proceedings of IEEE Symposium on Security and Privacy (2009)

[5] Cisco Inc. The Cisco QuantumFlow Processor: Cisco's Next Generation Network Processor, http://www.cisco.com/en/US/prod/collateral/routers/ps9343/solution_overview_c22-448936.html

[6] Crosby, S.A., Wallach, D.S.: Denial of Service via Algorithmic Complexity Attacks. USENIX Security (2003)

[7] Defcon, http://www.defcon.org

[8] Edler, J., Hill, M.D.: Dinero IV Trace-Driven Uniprocessor Cache Simulator, http://www.cs.wisc.edu/markhill/DineroIV

[9] Handley, M., Paxson, V., Kreibich, C.: Network Intrusion Detection: Evasion, Traffic Normalization, and End-to-end Protocol Semantics. In: Proceedings of the 10th USENIX Security Symposium (2011)

[10] Hasan, J., Jalote, A., Vijaykumar, T.N., Brodley, C.E.: Heat Stroke: Power-Density-Based Denial of Service in SMT. In: Proceedings of HPCA (2005)

[11] Intel Corporation. Intel IXP 2400 Network Processor Hardware Reference Manual, Revision 7 (2003)

[12] Kumar, S., Dharmapurikar, S., Yu, F., Crowley, P., Turner, J.: Algorithms to Accelerate Multiple Regular Expressions Matching for Deep Packet Inspection. ACM SIGCOMM (2006)

[13] Mirkovic, J., Reiher, P.: A Taxonomy of DDos Attack and DDos Defense Mechanisms. ACM SIGCOMM Computer Communications Review 34, 39–53 (2004)

[14] MIT Lincoln Labs, DARPA Intrusion Detection Evaluation, http://www.ll.mit.edu/mission/communications/ist/corpora/ideval/

[15] Moscibroda, T., Mutlu, O.: Memory Performance Attacks: Denial of Memory Service in Multi-core Systems. In: 16th USENIX Security Symposium, pp. 1–18 (2007)

[16] Paxson, V.: Bro: a System for Detecting Network Intruders in Real Time. Computer Networks 31(23-24), 2435–2463 (1999)

[17] Pouget, F., Dacier, M., Hau, P.: Leurre.com: On the Advantages of Deploying a Large Scale Distributed Honeypot Platform. In: E-Crime and Computer Conference (2005)

[18] Ptacek, T., Newsham, T.: Insertion, Evasion and Denial of Service: Eluding Network Intrusion Detection. Secure Networks, Inc. (1998)

[19] Roesch, M.: SNORT - Lightweight Intrusion Detection for Networks. In: LISA 1999: USENIX 13th Systems Administration Conference (1999)

[20] Shenoy, G.S., Tubella, J., Gonzalez, A.: A Performance and Area Efficient Architecture for Intrusion Detection Systems. In: Proceedings of the 25th IEEE International Conference on Parallel and Distributed Processing Symposium, IPDPS (2011)

[21] Smith, R., Estan, C., Jha, S.: Backtracking Algorithmic Complexity Attacks against a NIDS. In: ACSAC (2006)

[22] Smith, R., Estan, C., Jha, S.: XFA: Faster Signature Matching with Extended Automata. In: IEEE Symposium on Security and Privacy (2008)

[23] Song, T., Zhang, W., Wang, D., Xue, Y.: A Memory Efficient Multiple Pattern Matching Architecture for Network Security. In: Proceedings of IEEE Infocom (2008)

[24] Thoziyoor, S., Muralimanohar, N., Ahn, J.H., Jouppi, N.P.: CACTI 5.1. Technical Report HP-2008-20, HP Labs (2008)

[25] Tuck, N., Sherwood, T., Calder, B., Varghese, G.: Deterministic Memory-Efficient String Matching Algorithms for Intrusion Detection. In: Proceedings of the IEEE Infocom (2004)

The Unbearable Lightness of Monitoring: Direct Monitoring in BitTorrent

Tom Chothia, Marco Cova, Chris Novakovic, and Camilo González Toro

School of Computer Science, University of Birmingham, UK

Abstract. It is known that BitTorrent file-sharing traffic is analysed to identify exchangers of copyrighted material. In general, copyright holders can perform monitoring using two approaches: *indirect monitoring*, where indirect clues of the sharing activity of a peer are considered (e.g., its presence in the peer list of a tracker), and *direct monitoring*, which establishes connections with peers to estimate their participation in sharing activity. Previous research has focused exclusively on indirect monitoring. We provide a broader characterisation of the monitoring of BitTorrent activity by considering both indirect and direct monitoring. In particular, we review previous work on indirect monitoring, provide features to detect peers engaged in such monitoring, and apply them to identify a number of monitoring organisations. Additionally, we introduce features that detect direct monitors, and provide the first ever measurements of direct monitoring, showing that it is now occurring.

Keywords: BitTorrent, P2P monitoring, copyright enforcement.

1 Introduction

BitTorrent is a decentralised peer-to-peer (P2P) protocol designed for the efficient transfer of large files. It is used by millions of users, contributing significantly to the volume of global Internet traffic [19]. BitTorrent users exchange a range of legal content: many Linux distributions rely on BitTorrent as a content delivery mechanism, and video game companies use it to provide updates and patches to their customers [2]. However, BitTorrent is also widely used (overwhelmingly so, according to one study [11]) for the illegal exchange of copyrighted material, such as music, movies and software.

Many copyright holders perceive this illegal exchange of content as a threat to their business models and have increasingly sought to prevent it. In particular, copyright holders are known to routinely monitor file-sharers, collect evidence of infringement, issue cease-and-desist letters and, in some cases, demand financial compensation from the users they deem to have infringed their copyright [8]. The task of policing BitTorrent is often outsourced to specialist *copyright enforcement agencies*.

One key aspect of BitTorrent monitoring is the precise set of techniques employed by enforcement agencies, which have never been disclosed publicly; in fact, the companies involved appear keen to avoid having their evidence being

A.D. Keromytis and R. Di Pietro (Eds.): SecureComm 2012, LNICST 106, pp. 185–202, 2013.
© Institute for Computer Sciences, Social Informatics and Telecommunications Engineering 2013

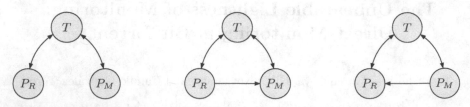

Fig. 1. Different methods by which a monitoring peer (P_M) may monitor a regular peer (P_R) via a tracker (T). From left to right: indirect monitoring; passive direct monitoring; active direct monitoring.

examined in court [8]. Nevertheless, two general approaches are possible: *indirect* and *direct* monitoring [17].

With indirect monitoring, enforcement agencies rely on indirect clues that a peer is uploading or downloading some content (i.e., by the presence of the peer's IP address in the group, or *swarm*, of peers reported by a BitTorrent *tracker* to be sharing the file — see Figure 1). A 2008 study by Piatek et al. [17] showed that indirect monitoring was extensively used by enforcement agencies. The study also demonstrated the high rate of false positives caused by this approach by implicating innocent devices such as printers and wireless access points as file-sharers, which later received cease-and-desist letters. More recent studies have confirmed that these flawed practices continue to be used [6,18].

With direct monitoring, enforcement agencies collect first-hand evidence of a peer's activity. Direct monitoring can be *active* if the monitor establishes connections with peers to confirm that they are sharing a file, or *passive* if the monitor advertises its IP address to a tracker and waits for peers to connect to it (see Figure 1). Clearly, direct monitoring techniques have the potential to gather more conclusive evidence, but are also costlier (in terms of bandwidth and computational resources) when compared with indirect techniques; methods of improving the efficiency of direct monitoring have been proposed [1]. Documents recently filed in a New York Southern District Court case imply that at least one copyright enforcement agency is using some form of direct monitoring to collect its evidence against file-sharers [15]; however, at this time it is not clear whether comprehensive direct monitoring is in widespread use.

The goal of this work is to characterise the current state of BitTorrent monitoring by investigating it from several points of view. Firstly, we review indirect monitoring and assess various features to detect peers that are engaged in this activity (*how can indirect monitoring be detected?*). Secondly, we focus on direct monitoring and study its characteristics. The occurrence of this type of monitoring has not been studied before; thus, we want to introduce features to detect peers engaging in direct monitoring (*how can direct monitoring be detected?*), as well as investigate its mechanics (*how is direct monitoring performed?*). Thirdly, we assess whether the information gathered by monitoring agencies is accurate and conclusive (*what information is really collected?*). Finally, we investigate how users can defend themselves against monitoring.

We conducted this study by measuring the activity of 1,033 swarms across 421 trackers for 36 days over 2 years, collecting over 150GB of BitTorrent traffic. We note that our aim is to design and test novel monitoring detection techniques, rather than provide a comprehensive picture of BitTorrent monitoring.

The main contributions of this study are:

- We determine that indirect monitoring is still in use against BitTorrent users and devise more effective techniques to detect peers engaging in it;
- We find indications that certain entities engage in direct monitoring of Bit-Torrent users and provide features to detect such peers;
- We also notice that direct monitoring, in its current form, falls short of providing conclusive evidence of copyright infringement.

1.1 Related Work

A number of studies have focused on measuring and characterising specific properties of BitTorrent (e.g., [5,7]); other work has introduced improvements to the measuring process itself (e.g., [24, 26, 27]). The limitations of the evidence collected through indirect monitoring for legal cases motivated Bauer et al. [1] to design BitStalker, an active probing mechanism for identifying hosts using Bit-Torrent to download files. Wolchok and Halderman [25] have shown that BitTorrent's distributed hash tables can be quickly crawled to more efficiently monitor users' activity. Similarly, Le Blond et al. [12,13] have demonstrated how protocol features can be leveraged for efficient spying on large numbers of BitTorrent users. While some of the techniques proposed in these papers are related to our work, our aims are quite different; rather than measuring the behaviour of the typical BitTorrent user, we wish to determine if and how monitoring is taking place by measuring the atypical behaviour of monitors.

The issue of detecting and understanding how the indirect monitoring of users' activity is performed on BitTorrent has received attention in the past. In a 2008 study, Piatek et al. [17] provided empirical evidence that enforcement agencies resort to indirect monitoring for identifying infringing users. They questioned the robustness of evidence collected via indirect monitoring and presented attacks that may cause arbitrary network users to be wrongly accused of infringement. Siganos et al. [20] described a set of network-level features that can be used for automatically detecting "deviant" clients, some of which are deemed to be indirect monitors. We revisit the issue of identifying indirect monitors and introduce a new and novel detection method; we show that our method is simple to compute and provides more accurate results than those of Siganos et al. [20] by ruling out false positives due to network address translation (NAT). We are the first to study whether direct monitoring is used by copyright enforcement agencies to identify file-sharers, and discuss techniques for detecting direct monitors.

A common approach to BitTorrent monitor evasion is to prevent interaction with peers that are suspected of monitoring at the transport layer (lists of suspicious peers are often referred to as *blocklists*). Potharaju et al. [18] offer a blocklist generation technique for BitTorrent based on peers' participation in multiple swarms sharing the same content, arguing that simultaneously downloading multiple copies of the same content is suspicious. The blocklist approach only prevents direct monitoring and it is only effective if reliable techniques exist for identifying monitors. We compare our results with the contents of a popular blocklist and discover a high incidence of false positives and false negatives in the blocklist we examine.

1.2 Ethical Statement

The tension between BitTorrent users and copyright enforcement agencies is often described as an arms race [17, 20, 25], in which one side attempts to share content and the other attempts to monitor and disrupt this activity. As with previous studies in this area, we do not take a side in this arms race: the results we present could benefit both users (e.g., by improving the detection and blocking of monitors) and copyright enforcement agencies (e.g., by improving monitoring techniques). Furthermore, it has been noted previously [18] that the monitoring process used by copyright enforcement agencies may wrongly implicate researchers performing experiments in BitTorrent swarms. The features we present may enable them to design more conservative research experiments or to better interpret their results.

There are significant privacy concerns when reporting on data collected from BitTorrent traffic. To protect the privacy of the peers we monitored, we do not disclose the IP addresses of individual peers, and the peer lists and peer/peer communication data that were collected during monitoring will be destroyed when they are no longer required. The web addresses of notable trackers are revealed, but since they regularly track hundreds of thousands of torrents simultaneously, this poses no risk of a privacy violation. We only disclose the identity of copyright enforcement agencies that have publicly announced that they are monitoring BitTorrent. Following previous work in this area (e.g., [18]), we indicate Autonomous Systems (ASes) that appear to host large numbers of monitors, but we do not disclose individual ranges inside an AS.

Finally, in all of our data collection processes, we were careful not to upload or download any shared files; therefore, we have not participated in any copyright-infringing activity as a result of this study. Piatek et al. [17] deliberately implicated innocent network devices (such as printers and routers) in file-sharing to draw unsubstantiated cease-and-desist letters from copyright enforcement agencies; since their study was designed to highlight the shortcomings of indirect monitoring, and ours involved communicating directly with other peers from network devices potentially capable of infringing copyright, we did not design our study in a way that would intentionally cause us to receive cease-and-desist letters.

2   Background

Firstly, we provide an overview of the BitTorrent protocol, emphasising the aspects of the protocol that are relevant to our work. We focus on the original specification of the protocol.

2.1   Protocol Overview and Terminology

The BitTorrent protocol was designed to replace the distribution of large files via other, less efficient protocols, such as HTTP and FTP.

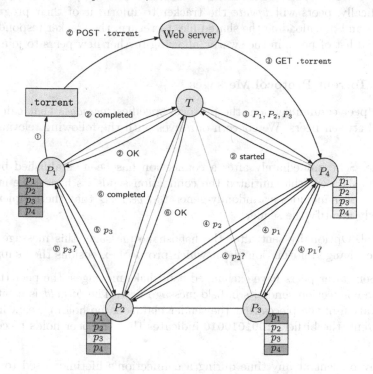

Fig. 2. A file being shared using BitTorrent

Figure 2 summarises how a file is shared using BitTorrent. The user holding the file creates a *torrent file* containing metadata about the shared file. The shared file is described in terms of smaller *pieces*, which are divided further into *blocks*. When concatenated, the pieces produce the original shared file. The torrent file also contains the URL of a *tracker*, a centralised server that tracks which peers are downloading and uploading the shared file. A SHA-1 hash — the torrent's *infohash* — is used in all subsequent peer/tracker communication to uniquely identify this torrent. The torrent file can then be published (e.g., on a web server).

Users interested in the shared file download the torrent file and report their presence to the tracker by *announcing* to it — thus they become peers, and join the collective *swarm* of peers uploading and downloading pieces of the shared file. The tracker responds with a list of up to 200 IP addresses and port numbers of other peers in the swarm. Peers that hold a complete copy of the file are *seeders*, and those that do not are *leechers*.

Peers contact other peers in the swarm using the list of IP addresses given to them by the tracker. They exchange information about which pieces of the shared file they have, and may announce their *interest* in particular pieces held by the remote peer. The remote peer may then agree to send a particular piece to the peer. When a peer holds every piece, it can reconstruct a copy of the original file. It becomes a seeder, whose role is to continue sending pieces to leechers.

Periodically, peers will *update* the tracker to inform it of their progress on uploading and downloading the shared file. In return, the tracker responds with an updated list of peers in the swarm, allowing further new peers to join.

2.2 BitTorrent Protocol Messages

For peer/peer communication, the protocol specifies *messages* that can be exchanged between peers. We concern ourselves with the following relevant messages:

handshake. Sent immediately after a connection has been established between two peers; the peer that initiated the connection sends its handshake message first. Each peer includes a randomly-generated *peer ID* that the recipient uses to uniquely identify the sender.

extprotocol. Optionally sent after the handshake message, this message allows peers to exchange information about which protocol extensions they support.

bitfield. Sent after peers have exchanged handshake messages; the peer that initiated the connection sends its bitfield message first. The *bitfield* is a bit mask representation of the pieces that the sender claims to be holding; e.g., in a 10-piece torrent, the bitfield 1001010010 indicates that the peer holds pieces 0, 3, 5 and 8.

have. May be sent at any time during a connection's lifetime. Used to inform the recipient that the sender now holds a piece that the sender was not holding when the peers exchanged their bitfields; e.g., if peer P_A has the bitfield 1000 stored for peer P_B and P_B later sends the message have(2), P_A can update its bitfield for P_B to 1010.

request. Requests that the recipient send a piece (or a block of a piece) that it has previously advertised.

piece. Contains the piece data that was requested by the recipient in an earlier request message.

keepalive. Idle peer/peer connections are usually closed after three minutes. This message is used to ask the recipient not to close the connection as a result of idleness, as the sender may send further messages later.

2.3   BitTorrent Indexing

The BitTorrent protocol does not specify how a torrent file should be circulated to other users interested in downloading the shared file. Consequently, *torrent indexing* web sites such as The Pirate Bay [21] were created to facilitate the organisation and distribution of torrent files. Many of them index copyright-infringing torrents — in the case of The Pirate Bay, this is its explicit purpose. The administrators of torrent indexing web sites are often targeted by legal action initiated by trade organisations representing copyright holders, who claim that online copyright infringement causes financial disruption to their members' businesses; these trade organisations have successfully persuaded courts in the United States, Sweden, Slovenia and other countries to order the closure of offending web sites and trackers.

3   Detecting Indirect Monitoring

A simple approach for performing indirect monitoring involves announcing to trackers and collecting the IP addresses of peers returned by the tracker. This technique offers a fast method of harvesting a large number of peers, but it has been shown by Piatek et al. [17] that IP address-based peer identification produces unreliable results. Furthermore, by announcing to trackers, monitors leave a trace of their presence: their IP addresses also appear in peer lists. We can then indirectly observe the behaviour of peers to identify differences between regular peers and monitors.

To motivate our subsequent work on direct monitoring, we first reassess techniques previously proposed to identify indirect monitors, and propose an additional novel feature for identifying them.

3.1   Methodology and Data Collection

To automatically collect information from BitTorrent trackers, we created our own indirect monitoring client that gathers newly-published torrent files from the Top 100 in each category on The Pirate Bay, and continually contacts each of the trackers and stores (IP address, port number, infohash, time) tuples from the peer lists that are returned; it then attempts to establish a TCP connection with each host and sends a handshake message to ensure that the host is in fact a BitTorrent peer. The monitor also requests from trackers the number of seeders and leechers in each swarm.

We collected data from July 21–28, 2009, routing our traffic through the Tor anonymity network [23]. This led to an excessive number of connections timing out or being dropped, so we collected data again without using Tor from August 4–6, 2009. A summary of data collected is presented in Table 1. The comparative success of the second trace when compared with the first seems to be entirely due to the poor performance of Tor.

Table 1. A summary of indirect monitoring activity

	Jul 21–28, 2009	Aug 4–6, 2009
IP addresses seen	831,039	1,351,853
(IP, port) pairs seen	894,529	1,498,015
Torrents monitored	967	690
Trackers seen	196	181

3.2   Features for Detecting Monitors

Using this data we build profiles for the behaviour of BitTorrent clients, which we can use to differentiate regular peers from monitors. The assumption is that "anomalous" profiles may be indicative of the behaviour of monitors. To build such profiles, we first consider five features that have been previously proposed in the literature:

1. The proportion of a subnet that has been seen in BitTorrent swarms. Monitoring agencies may use a large proportion of their subnet for monitoring.
2. The length of time a peer spends in a swarm. Monitors may spend more time in the swarm than regular file-sharers.
3. The number of different (IP, port, infohash) combinations per IP address. Monitoring agencies may operate many clients from a single IP address.
4. Whether a peer reported by a tracker accepts incoming connections. Monitors may block all incoming connection attempts.
5. The number of swarms in which IP addresses from a particular subnet appear. Monitoring agencies may monitor many torrents from their subnet.

Features 1–4 have been suggested by Siganos et al. [20] and Piatek et al. [17], and feature 5 by Potharaju et al. [18]. Potharaju et al. also leverage web search engines to derive a database of the content being shared by each torrent, and look for peers that download multiple copies of the same content. Another potentially useful but untested feature is whether a peer is downloading content that is likely to appeal to very different audiences (e.g., a peer that downloads both classical and pop music tracks). We do not consider either of these features, as they cannot be calculated from information provided by trackers alone.

While investigating feature 4, we found that only 16% of peers in our datasets accepted incoming connections. Given the commonness of this behaviour, we conclude that the typical behaviour of a BitTorrent client is to reject incoming connection requests. This is likely due to BitTorrent users being affected by incorrectly-configured residential routers or firewalls. We show in Section 4 that many monitors *do* accept incoming connections, therefore we do not use this feature for detecting monitors.

Our heuristic for detecting monitors relies on the remaining four features. More precisely, we consider a peer likely to be a monitor if it appears in the top first percentile for each of the features (i.e., the highest number of connections, the longest connection time, etc.); by applying this test we found 1,139 IP addresses that were in the top first percentile for all four features. To understand whether these features are effective at identifying monitors, we manually analysed these anomalies; they included IP addresses assigned to a company named Checktor [3], which offers commercial BitTorrent monitoring services, and 16 addresses assigned to a medium-sized computer security consultancy company that does not publicly acknowledge monitoring BitTorrent. Another subnet, which we saw in over 500 swarms, belongs to a company that advertises itself as providing "intellectual property advice", but does not specifically acknowledge monitoring BitTorrent. We also found two subnets assigned to hosting companies, one with IP addresses in 433 swarms and the other with IP addresses in 371 swarms. These hosting companies advertise themselves as providers of Internet services to businesses, rather than residential users, where BitTorrent traffic is more likely to be regulated. We speculate that copyright enforcement companies are using these hosting companies as a front to disguise their identities. We also identified a number of IP addresses allocated to large ISPs, such as Vodafone, Etisalat and SingNet. These ISPs have all been assigned very small subnets and therefore use NAT. Some of the 1,139 also seemed to be very active users on residential ISPs that were seeding a large number of files; while unusual, there was nothing to suggest that these peers were engaged in monitoring.

3.3   A Novel Feature

When comparing the profiles of suspicious peers that appeared to be monitoring with those that appeared to be subject to NAT, we noticed that the suspicious peers had multiple (IP, port) pairs in a number of different swarms. According to the BitTorrent protocol, a client should open a different port for each swarm that it joins; therefore, this behaviour is not expected from regular peers. While it would be possible for an (IP, port) pair to appear in more than one swarm, this should only happen when a peer has just left one swarm and joined another. The instances of peers in different swarms from ISPs that made heavy use of NAT, such as Vodafone and Etisalat, all had unique (IP, port) pairs. This observation led us to a new, sixth feature for identifying peers likely engaged in monitoring:

6. The number of times the same (IP, port) pair is observed concurrently in different swarms.

We considered any (IP, port) pair that appeared in four or more swarms to be suspicious. This feature found IP addresses assigned to Peer Media Technologies [16] (a well-known copyright enforcement agency) monitoring seven Harry Potter ebook and movie torrents, and the INRIA research institution [10], which had been overlooked by features 1–5 because so few torrents were being monitored, and because a very small proportion of INRIA's subnet was being used for monitoring. While we were collecting our data, INRIA did not publicly acknowledge monitoring BitTorrent; however, researchers there have since published work describing the detection of initial seeders of files [13].

3.4   Discussion

These results continue a line of work by Piatek et al. [17], Siganos et al. [20] and Potharaju et al. [18], who show that indirect monitoring of BitTorrent is occurring and can be detected by profiling specific characteristics of peers' behaviour.

The Stopped Message. The BitTorrent protocol allows a peer to send a stopped message in the announce to the tracker to inform it that the peer is leaving the swarm. The tracker should then remove the peer's IP address from its peer list. If a tracker correctly implements this rule of the protocol, an indirect monitor can send the message immediately after receiving a peer list and thus make itself undetectable. We tested a number of trackers' support for this message and while some trackers removed the IP address immediately, those operated by The Pirate Bay did not. By requesting from the tracker the number of completed downloads for each torrent, we found that The Pirate Bay balanced tracker load across six servers; it therefore seems probable that the two announces were being processed by different servers, which explains why peer IP addresses are not always removed from peer lists.

False Positives and Negatives. We note that, as a normal user of BitTorrent could be said to be "monitoring" the peers it connects to, it would be possible for a monitor to avoid detection by any set of features that tries to distinguish monitors from a regular peer. A monitoring client could avoid detection by our new feature by selecting a different port for each torrent, and monitoring agencies could use many different subnets and limit the amount of time that each IP address was used. This would make monitoring a much more expensive and time-consuming process, so while we cannot guarantee the detection of a monitor that deliberately tries to obscure its activities, we can detect monitors that try to maximise the number of file-sharers they find.

The suspicious behaviour we detected from the IP addresses of companies that acknowledge that they monitor BitTorrent (such as Checktor), and our detection of the INRIA monitors before they released their publication, does provide some ground truth to validate our methods. Inspecting our suspected monitors by hand, we found no results that appeared to be false positives (although we cannot absolutely rule out results that may be due to network behaviour we are unaware of). This suggests that our false positive rate is low. Inspecting a sample of the negative results, we did not find any that appeared to be monitors, although, for the reasons given above, it is harder for us to rule out false negatives.

We can make accurate comparisons between sets of features. Comparing the methods of Siganos et al., Piatek et al. and Potharaju et al. with our own, we found that they incorrectly identified IP addresses allocated to ISPs which make heavy use of NAT, such as Vodafone, Etisalat and SingNet. They also missed some of the smaller monitoring agencies such as Peer Media Technologies and INRIA. We can therefore be confident that the addition of our new feature decreases the false negative and false positive rate.

4 Detecting Direct Monitoring

Direct monitoring, in which monitors directly contact and probe other peers, was proposed by Bauer et al. as a method of improving the accuracy of file-sharing evidence collected by monitors [1]. However, it has not been shown conclusively that direct monitoring is being employed widely by copyright enforcement companies.

A direct monitor may operate *actively* (by announcing to the tracker, receiving peer lists and initiating outgoing connections to other peers), or *passively* (by placing itself into a swarm and listening for incoming connections only). Passive monitoring has the advantage of detecting peers using NAT and others that do not accept incoming connections; active monitoring can be performed more quickly and thus can monitor more peers across the same period. Initiating and listening for direct connections takes much longer than harvesting IP addresses from a tracker, so we concentrate on features that can be calculated without monitoring a large number of swarms.

4.1 Methodology and Data Collection

We created a number of customised BitTorrent clients, inserted them into swarms and observed their behaviour. Every protocol-compliant message sent to our clients was logged along with the timestamp, the message's payload, and the peer's IP address, port number and peer ID. As a side-effect of joining swarms, our clients regularly received peer lists from trackers after announcing to them, which we also stored for later use.

Table 2. A summary of direct monitoring activity

	Aug 10–23, 2010	Feb 9–18, 2011	May 3–8, 2011
IP addresses seen	311,549	112,584	98,385
(IP, port) pairs seen	2,441,555	371,572	321,949
Torrents monitored	30	20	16
Trackers seen	20	12	12

We created two classes of clients: one designed to communicate with passive direct monitors (by harvesting peer lists and attempting to connect to each peer systematically), and another designed to communicate with active direct monitors (by joining the swarm and only listening for incoming connections). Since it is possible for monitors to engage in either or both forms of direct monitoring, this allowed us to determine which (if any) form is being used most frequently.

Our clients used three different bitfield-reporting strategies to detect discrepancies between the bitfields reported by other peers, so a peer intentionally misreporting its own bitfield would be noticeable:

Mirror strategy. Designed to appear as uninteresting as possible to other peers: reports to connecting clients that it holds the same pieces as the connecting client (by "mirroring" the client's bitfield and have messages back to them), does not send request messages for pieces of the shared file, and does not respond to request or piece messages.

Empty strategy. Appears to have joined the swarm recently: per the mirror strategy, but always reports an empty bitfield and does not mirror have messages.

Full strategy. Appears to be a seeder: per the mirror strategy, but always reports a full bitfield and does not mirror have messages.

Two groups of swarms were monitored: 6 sharing public domain files, and 60 sharing copyright-infringing files. Public domain torrents were sourced from ClearBits [4] and LinuxTracker [14]. Copyright-infringing torrents were selected from a range of categories on The Pirate Bay, including music, movies, TV shows, music videos and software. Torrents were selected from both within and outside of the Top 100. Table 2 summarises the data we collected.

4.2   Features for Detecting Monitors

We identify two features for distinguishing peers likely to be performing active monitoring:

Reported Completion. Since our clients logged all bitfield messages, and most peers reconnected to our monitors, we could compare the bitfields the clients were sent and track their progression over time. Although the majority of peers reported steady progression towards completing the download, peers in 20 small subnets always reported completions of between 45% and 55%. For these IP addresses, further inspection of the bitfields showed no consistency: they appeared to be generated randomly, rather than reflecting a progressively completing download (compare Figures 3 and 4: black blocks indicate pieces of the file that a peer claims to have; white blocks are missing pieces). A peer that reports a piece as not downloaded when it had previously reported it as downloaded is lying about the parts of the shared file it is holding, and is therefore likely to be a monitor.

Connection Frequency. It is common for peers to reconnect to peers they have discovered previously to check whether they are advertising new pieces that the peer still needs to download. Most peers connected to our clients over a 40-hour period during the entire monitoring period. However, 0.05% of the peer population, scattered across a low number of small subnets, connected to our monitors over a much longer 133-hour period; all of these peers were also detected by the "reported completion" feature. This is indicative of a group of peers more interested in analysing the download progress made by other peers rather than making any download progress of their own, and is another strong feature for identifying monitors.

Peers detected using these features superficially appeared to be active, but in fact they were not downloading the shared file; their IP addresses belong to

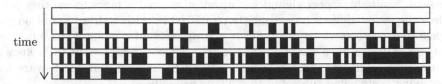

Fig. 3. The download progression of a regular peer. Its bitfield steadily progresses toward completion.

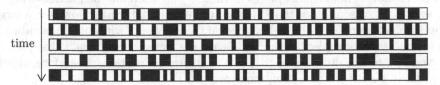

Fig. 4. The download progression of a monitoring peer. Its bitfield changes randomly over time.

subnets of three hosting companies. We can be sure that each connection was from the same BitTorrent client due to the unique peer ID in the handshake. This behaviour was not observed in any of the swarms sharing public domain content; the most likely explanation is that these were monitors. Notably, they did not request any pieces of the shared file after connecting, so it is questionable whether a copyright enforcement agency employing this technique could *prove* that other peers in the swarm were really sharing the file. We note that monitors could avoid detection by our "reported completion" feature by simulating a realistic bitfield over time, but establishing connections with other peers and then reporting a complete bitfield would be highly suspicious; additionally, as we could distribute monitors over several subnets, monitors could only avoid our "connection frequency" feature by making fewer connections, reducing their effectiveness.

We also experimented with several ineffective features; we briefly discuss them here, for the sake of completeness and to aid future research into direct monitoring:

Duration of connection. The protocol states that idle connections should be closed after 3 minutes to aid resource conservation. Peers may send keepalive messages to other peers to indicate that they wish to communicate again soon (e.g., to request a piece), and therefore want the connection to be kept alive. As there is no incentive for other peers to remain connected to our "mirror" and "empty" clients, it is expected that peers should spend little time connected to them, and conversely spend more time connected to our "full" clients; this was indeed the case, and we found no evidence that certain peers were deliberately keeping connections alive for monitoring purposes.

Protocol violations. All peers are expected to obey the protocol; e.g., if a peer advertises the availability of a piece, it should not request that piece in a future message. Similarly, a peer should not attempt to send a piece to another peer unless the receiving peer has explicitly requested it. Although we found no evidence that protocol violations indicate the presence of a monitor, instances of protocol violation were observed from 4 IP addresses assigned to ISPs known to use NAT, indicating that this may instead be another suitable feature for identifying peers being subjected to NAT or firewalling.

Number of request messages sent. Since BitTorrent is a file-sharing protocol, it follows that peers should be expected to request pieces of the shared file from others; peers that do not request pieces of the file may therefore be participating in the swarm for reasons other than file-sharing (e.g., monitoring). However, a large proportion of peers (over 99.9%) connected to our clients without ever sending a request message for a piece of the file the clients were offering, and subsequently showed progress in downloading the file in future connections; therefore, this is an unlikely feature for detecting monitors.

4.3   Discussion

ASes Involved in Monitoring. Based on the features we identify, we suspect six ASes of harbouring a total of 856 peers engaging in direct monitoring (see Table 3). Two of these ASes (AS558 and AS1213) have previously been identified in the study by Potharaju et al. [18] as potential harbourers of monitoring agencies; we suspect a further four. AS209 was considerably more active in 2010 than in 2011; it may be that this AS was once being used by monitoring agencies, but no longer is.

Incidence of Monitoring on the Pirate Bay. Our features only detected monitors in Top 100 torrents; this implies that copyright enforcement agencies are monitoring only the most popular content on public trackers. Movie and music torrents were most heavily monitored (by 65 and 26 monitors respectively), particularly by AS23504 and AS558; the other categories were less heavily monitored, although between 1 and 7 IP addresses suspected of monitoring were still present in each category.

The Use of Active vs. Passive Direct Monitoring. All of the potential monitors we have identified engaged in active direct monitoring: our clients were

Table 3. ASes suspected of engaging in direct monitoring

Number of Monitors	AS	Name
467	23504	Speakeasy, Inc.
202	174	Cogent/PSI
114	209	Qwest LLC
39	558	Net2EZ
17	27699	TELESP
17	1213	HEAnet Ltd

unable to establish outgoing connections to them. This is understandable, as monitors are able to communicate with many more peers (and therefore detect a larger number of downloaders) by harvesting peer lists and processing them systematically, as opposed to simply waiting for incoming connections for other peers.

Average Time before Monitors Connect. 40% of the monitors that communicated with our clients made their initial connection within 3 hours of the client joining the swarm; the slowest monitor took 33 hours to make its first connection. The average time decreases for torrents appearing higher in the Top 100, implying that enforcement agencies allocate resources according to the popularity of the content they monitor.

Proportion of Peers Accepting Incoming Connections. The results of our 2009 study revealed that outgoing connections could only be made to 16% of peers. This fell to 7% in 2011. Since monitors currently engage in active direct monitoring only, peers may still be able to participate in a swarm undetected by enforcement agencies, who rely solely on a peer's ability to accept incoming connections in order to communicate with them.

False Positives and Negatives. As with indirect monitoring, the rate of false negatives is difficult to quantify, because a monitor can arbitrarily behave like a regular peer. However, this comes at the cost of a far-reduced monitoring capability. The more measures a monitor takes to increase its efficiency and coverage, the more easily it can be detected. As for false positives, the suspected monitors we found showed a highly irregular download progression (as shown in Figure 4); it is impossible for a peer sharing content to behave in this way, so we can be sure that they were not regular file-sharers. While we cannot be certain that they were monitors, it seems highly likely.

Some BitTorrent clients are known to deliberately misreport their bitfields when seeding, ostensibly to evade ISPs' traffic management policies that penalise BitTorrent seeders [22]: rather than sending a complete bitfield, these clients send a partially-complete bitfield and then immediately complete it with have messages for the pieces that were omitted (a technique named *"lazy bitfield"*); we note that this behaviour is now widespread among BitTorrent clients. Our customised clients eliminate this potential source of false positives by grouping the pieces advertised in a client's bitfield message with those advertised in have messages received in the subsequent 30 seconds as if they had all been advertised in the initial bitfield message.

To corroborate the potential sources of suspicious behaviour we had detected, we compared our results with the contents of public blocklists. These are lists of peers suspected of being involved in suspicious activity, and are typically created through manual analysis by a community of concerned users. We use such lists as a baseline for comparing our results and, in particular, for gaining an understanding of potential false positives and false negatives. More precisely, we used the Anti-Infringement blocklist available from I-BlockList [9], as it is popular among BitTorrent users.

As a preliminary step, we assessed the accuracy of the Anti-Infringement list by measuring the number of false positives it contained (i.e., the number of listed peers that are unlikely to engage in monitoring activity). To do so, we leveraged the observation that enforcement agencies have no incentive to monitor public domain torrents. Therefore, we consider an entry in the blocklist to be a false positive if we find a peer in the subnet engaged in the download of public domain torrents. During 27 days of monitoring, we found 5 false positives in the blocklist (out of 2,880 total subnets), and discarded them from the rest of this analysis. We considered the remaining 2,875 to be true positives (i.e., subnets that could contain monitoring peers).

Our direct monitoring analysis produced 593 peers (out of 856) that appear in subnets listed in the Anti-Infringement list. This represents a 69% overlap between our results and the contents of the list; therefore, the majority of our results are corroborated by the results of independent blocklists. In addition, our analysis identifies 263 peers (31% of our results) that, albeit displaying the same behaviour as monitoring peers (as determined by our detection features), do not currently appear in blocklists. We consider this a strong indication that these results are true positives of our analysis that are not detected by (manual) blocklisting techniques; BitTorrent users should therefore not rely solely on such speculative blocklists to protect their privacy, and should instead combine them with blocklists based on empirical research, such as those generated by Potharaju et al. [18], to reduce the number of false negatives encountered.

Finally, we measured the number of subnets in the Anti-Infringement list that were observed during direct monitoring and were *not* detected by our techniques; we consider peers in these subnets to be potential false negatives of our analysis that warrant further examination. We found 57 such peers. There are several reasons that these peers might not have been detected by our features: 53 disconnected from our monitoring clients at unexpected times, indicating possible network connectivity problems or malfunctioning BitTorrent clients. The remaining 4 used IP addresses whose ISPs are known to use NAT, potentially limiting their ability to communicate properly with our monitoring clients; these peers showed no signs of engaging in suspicious activity, so we suspect that their subnets were mistakenly added to the blocklist.

5   Conclusion

In this paper, we examined the current state of BitTorrent monitoring. We introduced several novel techniques for identifying peers that perform monitoring and validated them on large datasets. We determined that copyright enforcement agencies use indirect monitoring (confirming the results of earlier studies) as well as direct monitoring (a novel contribution of our work) to determine users' activity. From our experiments, we derived a number of interesting properties of monitoring, as it is currently performed: e.g., that monitoring is prevalent for popular content (i.e., the most popular torrents on The Pirate Bay) but absent for less popular content, and that peers sharing popular content are likely to be monitored within three hours of joining a swarm. Finally, we found that publicly-available blocklists, used by privacy-conscious BitTorrent users to prevent contact with monitors, contain large incidences of false positives and false negatives, and recommended that blocklists based on empirical research [18] are used over speculative ones.

References

1. Bauer, K., McCoy, D., Grunwald, D., Sicker, D.: Bitstalker: Accurately and efficiently monitoring bittorrent traffic. In: Proceedings of the IEEE International Workshop on Information Forensics and Security (WIFS), London, UK (December 2009)
2. Blizzard Entertainment. Networking help for the Blizzard Downloader (2011), http://us.blizzard.com/support/article.xml?locale=en_US&articleId=21077
3. Checktor, http://www.checktor.com
4. ClearBits, http://www.clearbits.net
5. Dán, G., Carlsson, N.: Power-law Revisited: Large Scale Measurement Study of P2P Content Popularity. In: Proceedings of the International Workshop on Peer-To-Peer Systems (IPTPS), San Jose, CA, USA (2010)
6. Freedman, M.: Inaccurate Copyright Enforcement: Questionable "best" practices and BitTorrent specification flaws. Freedom to Tinker (2009), https://freedom-to-tinker.com/blog/mfreed/inaccurate-copyright -enforcement-questionable-best-practices-and-bittorrent-specificatio/
7. Guo, L., Chen, S., Xiao, Z., Tan, E., Ding, X., Zhang, X.: Measurements, Analysis, and Modeling of BitTorrent-like Systems. In: Proceedings of the USENIX Internet Measurement Conference (IMC), Berkeley, CA, USA (2005)
8. Halliday, J.: Filesharing prosecutions will face serious problems, says judge. The Guardian (2008), http://www.guardian.co.uk/technology/2011/feb/08/filesharing-prosecutions-digital-economy
9. I-BlockList, http://iblocklist.com/lists.php
10. INRIA, http://www.inria.fr/en/
11. Layton, R., Watters, P.: Investigation into the extent of infringing content on BitTorrent networks. Technical report, Internet Commerce Security Laboratory, University of Ballarat, Australia (April 2010)
12. Le Blond, S., Legout, A., Lefessant, F., Dabbous, W.: Angling for Big Fish in BitTorrent. Technical Report inria-00451282, INRIA, Sophia Antipolis, France (January 2010)
13. Le Blond, S., Legout, A., Lefessant, F., Dabbous, W., Kaafar, M.A.: Spying the World from your Laptop — Identifying and Profiling Content Providers and Big Downloaders in BitTorrent. In: Proceedings of the USENIX Workshop on Large-Scale Exploits and Emergent Threats (LEET), San Jose, CA, USA (April 2010)
14. LinuxTracker, http://linuxtracker.org
15. Malibu Media, LLC v. John Does 1–5. Exhibit A to declaration of Tobias Fieser (2012), http://beckermanlegal.com/Lawyer_Copyright_Internet_Law/malibumedia_does1-5_120706OpposDeclarationFieserExA.pdf
16. Peer Media Technologies, http://peermediatech.com
17. Piatek, M., Kohno, T., Krishnamurthy, A.: Challenges and Directions for Monitoring P2P File Sharing Networks — or — Why My Printer Received a DMCA Takedown Notice. In: Proceedings of the USENIX Workshop on Hot Topics in Security, San Jose, CA, USA (2008)

18. Potharaju, R., Seibert, J., Fahmy, S., Nita-Rotaru, C.: Omnify: Investigating the visibility and effectiveness of copyright monitors. In: Proceedings of the Passive and Active Measurement Conference (PAM), Atlanta, GA, USA (2011)
19. Sandvine. Fall 2010 Global Internet Phenomena Report (2010), http://www.sandvine.com/downloads/documents/2010GlobalInternetPhenomenaReport.pdf
20. Siganos, G., Pujol, J., Rodriguez, P.: Monitoring the Bittorrent Monitors: A Bird's Eye View. In: Proceedings of the Passive and Active Measurement Conference (PAM), Seoul, South Korea (April 2009)
21. The Pirate Bay, http://www.thepiratebay.se
22. TheoryOrg. BitTorrent Protocol Specification: bitfield (July 2012), http://wiki.theory.org/BitTorrentSpecification#bitfield:_.3Clen.3D0001.2BX.3E.3Cid.3D5.3E.3Cbitfield.3E
23. Tor Project, https://www.torproject.org
24. Wojciechowski, M., Capotă, M., Pouwelse, J.A., Iosup, A.: BTWorld: towards observing the global BitTorrent file-sharing network. In: Proceedings of the ACM Workshop on Large-Scale System and Application Performance (LSAP), Chicago, IL, USA (2010)
25. Wolchok, S., Halderman, J.A.: Crawling BitTorrent DHTs for Fun and Profit. In: Proceedings of the USENIX Workshop on Offensive Technologies (WOOT), Washington, DC, USA (2010)
26. Zhang, B., Iosup, A., Pouwelse, J., Epema, D., Sips, H.: Sampling Bias in BitTorrent Measurements. In: D'Ambra, P., Guarracino, M., Talia, D. (eds.) Euro-Par 2010, Part I. LNCS, vol. 6271, pp. 484–496. Springer, Heidelberg (2010)
27. Zhang, C., Dhungel, P., Wu, D., Ross, K.W.: Unraveling the BitTorrent Ecosystem. IEEE Transactions on Parallel and Distributed Systems 22(7), 1164–1177 (2011)

Towards Designing Packet Filter with a Trust-Based Approach Using Bayesian Inference in Network Intrusion Detection

Yuxin Meng[1], Lam-For Kwok[1], and Wenjuan Li[2]

[1] Department of Computer Science, College of Science and Engineering,
City University of Hong Kong, Hong Kong, China
ymeng8@student.cityu.edu.hk, cslfkwok@cityu.edu.hk
[2] Computer Science Division, Zhaoqing Foreign Language College,
Guangdong, China
wenjuan.anastatia@gmail.com

Abstract. Network intrusion detection systems (NIDSs) have become an essential part for current network security infrastructure. However, in a large-scale network, the overhead network packets can greatly decrease the effectiveness of such detection systems by significantly increasing the processing burden of a NIDS. To mitigate this issue, we advocate that constructing a packet filter is a promising and complementary solution to reduce the workload of a NIDS, especially to reduce the burden of signature matching. We have developed a blacklist-based packet filter to help a NIDS filter out network packets and achieved positive experimental results. But the calculation of IP confidence is still a big challenge for our previous work. In this paper, we further design a packet filter with a trust-based method using Bayesian inference to calculate the IP confidence and explore its performance with a real dataset and in a network environment. We also analyze the trust-based method by comparing it with our previous weight-based method. The experimental results show that by using the trust-based calculation of IP confidence, our designed trust-based blacklist packet filter can achieve a better outcome.

Keywords: Packet Filter, IP Confidence, Trust Calculation, Network Intrusion Detection, Bayesian Inference.

1 Introduction

Over the past ten years, network intrusion detection systems (NIDSs) [1,3] have already become an important and essential component for current network security infrastructure. These detection systems are widely deployed in various network environments (e.g., a bank) to analyze network traffic and identify different kinds of network attacks (e.g., malware, spyware). Traditionally, these detection systems can be categorized into two types: signature-based NIDS and anomaly-based NIDS. The signature-based NIDS [2,4] detects an attack in terms

A.D. Keromytis and R. Di Pietro (Eds.): SecureComm 2012, LNICST 106, pp. 203–221, 2013.

of its signatures[1] so that this kind of detection systems can only identify well-known attacks. On the other hand, the major advantage of an anomaly-based NIDS [6,7] is the ability to detect novel attacks by means of identifying significant deviations between current network traffic and its normal profile[2]. In real deployment, a NIDS usually employs both the above two detection approaches, whereas the signature-based method is more widely used [9], compared with the anomaly-based detection, as a basis for a NIDS.

However, in a large-scale network environment, it is a big bottleneck for a NIDS, especially for a signature-based NIDS, to deal with overhead network packets. The large number of network packets can heavily consume computer resources and possibly cause a NIDS to be unable to response to current network events, which can greatly decrease the effectiveness of these detection systems [12]. Take Snort [2,8] as an example, this lightweight signature-based network intrusion detection system usually spends round about 30 percent of its total computational power in conducting signature matching between its signatures and incoming packet payloads, while its computational consumption can be significantly increased when deployed in a heavy traffic network environment. Up to 80 percent or much more of its processing burden will be put into signature matching when a massive of packets arrive [13]. Overall, its computational burden is at least linear to the size of an input packet payload [14].

In this case, these detection systems are vulnerable to *denial of service* (DoS) attacks [11,10] due to their poor performance in an intensive traffic environment. The DoS (or distributed DoS) attack is an attempt to cause a computer or network resource unavailable to its users. In the context of network intrusion detection, the DoS attack can render a detection system unusable and paralyzed, which aims to lower the level of network security by sending massive network packets to exceed the maximum processing capability of the NIDSs.

To mitigate this issue, some packet filtration mechanism has been proposed in the literature. We also advocate this approach that by appropriately filtering out a number of network packets, a network intrusion detection system can achieve more reliable and desirable performance in a large-scale network environment. But how to *appropriately* filter out network packets is still a challenge in constructing such a packet filter. In our previous work [17], we have proposed and developed an adaptive blacklist-based packet filter to filter out network packets in terms of IP confidence. Our previous approach can be treated as a reputation-based method of constructing a packet filter to address the problem of overhead network packets for a NIDS, especially for a signature-based NIDS. However, for the reputation-based method, a big suffering problem is that how to *appropriately* calculate the reputation. This issue is also a big challenge for our previous

---

[1] These signatures (or rules) are predefined in a NIDS and are critical to an organization to spot and remediate unwanted events in their network.

[2] Anomaly detection refers to detecting patterns in observed events that do not conform to an established normal profile. The interesting objects of this detection are often unexpected bursts in activity.

work in which we used a method of weighted ratio-based calculation to compute the IP confidence, but the calculation lacks of theoretical basis.

In this work, we aim to construct a packet filter by using a trust-based method that refers to Bayesian inference, with the purpose of enhancing the theoretical background of computing IP confidence and further improving the performance of the packet filter in a large-scale network environment. Specifically, we design a particular component called *trust calculation engine* to calculate the trust values[3] (or IP confidence) for determining the blacklisting IP addresses. The specific calculation of trust values is referred to a Bayesian inference model. We also propose that an appropriate packet filtration mechanism should have several characteristics as follows:

- The packet filter should have a minimum impact on the network performance.
- The packet filter should indeed provide a good filtration rate.
- The packet filter should not lower the whole level of network security.

The contributions of our work can be summarized in terms of the above characteristics as below:

- We further designed a trust-based blacklist packet filter by applying Bayesian inference in calculating the trustworthiness of blacklisting IP addresses. Interfering only with abnormal traffic, the impact of our packet filter on the network performance is minimum.
- In the experiment, we evaluated our approach with Snort in real settings and the experimental results showed that our packet filter could indeed help reduce the burden of a signature-based NIDS by filtering our a number of network packets (e.g., a reduction rate between 20% and 30%).
- We further analyzed the capability of our approach in defending against the DoS attack, and discussed the impact of *impersonation attacks* [15] on the packet filter. We presented that our approach would not affect and lower the whole level of network security.

In addition to the above work, we further compared our current trust-based method with our previous weight-based method in the aspect of both false rate (false positive and false negative) and traffic sensitivity by simulating network traffic in a network environment.

The rest of this paper is organized as follows. The background of our previous work is presented in Section 2; in Section 3, we show the architecture of our designed trust-based blacklist packet filter and describe the trust calculation in details; Section 4 illustrates the experimental methodology and experimental results, and we also compare the current trust-based computation with our previous weight-based calculation; Section 5 discusses the related work and we point out the future work in Section 6. Finally, we present conclusions in Section 7.

---

[3] The term of *trust value* is used to measure the *IP confidence*, therefore, we use these two terms interchangeably throughout this paper.

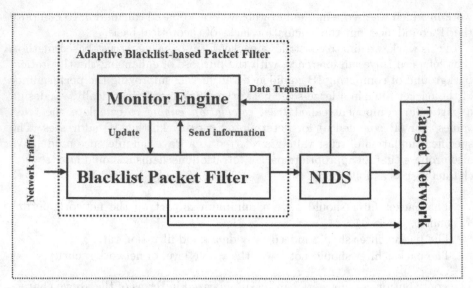

Fig. 1. The high-level architecture of the adaptive blacklist-based packet filter, which consists of a blacklist packet filter and a monitor engine

2 Background

In our previous work [17], we have proposed and developed an adaptive blacklist-based packet filter to help a NIDS filter out a number of network packets. The packet filter refines network packets depending on a blacklist, which can be generated by calculating the IP confidence. We show the high-level architecture of the adaptive blacklist-based packet filter in Fig. 1.

There are mainly two components in the *adaptive blacklist-based packet filter*: a *blacklist packet filter* and a *monitor engine*. The blacklist packet filter is responsible for filtering out network packets based on IP confidence. The monitor engine is used to collect data and update the blacklist in the *blacklist packet filter* by calculating the IP confidence.

In real deployment, this packet filter is implemented in front of the NIDS. Therefore, network traffic will firstly arrive at the *blacklist packet filter*. The filtration procedure is described as below:

- If the source IP address of a packet is not in the blacklist, then this packet will be forwarded into the NIDS for examination.
  - The NIDS examines this packet as the traditional way and decides whether to output an alarm.
  - If this packet is malicious, then the NIDS will produce an alarm and report this information to the *monitor engine*.
  - If this packet is normal, then the NIDS will send it to the target network.
- If the source IP address of a packet is in the blacklist, then this packet will be compared with the NIDS signatures stored in the *blacklist packet filter*.

- If a match is found, then the *blacklist packet filter* will generate an alarm and send a copy of this alarm to the *monitor engine*.
- If no match is identified, then the *blacklist packet filter* will directly send the packet to the target network and report the status (e.g., good or normal) of the packet (or IP address) to the *monitor engine*.

The *monitor engine* calculates the IP confidence by collecting the data from both the NIDS and the blacklist packet filter. In our previous work, we used a method of weighted ratio-based blacklist calculation. The formula of the method is shown in equation (1) (i represents the number of *good* packets, k represents the number of *bad* packets and 10 is the weighted value). In a fixed updating time, the monitor engine will update the blacklist in the *blacklist packet filter* to adapt the packet filter to the network contexts.

$$IP\ confidence = \frac{\sum_{i=1}^{n} i}{\sum_{k=1}^{m} 10 \times k}(n, m \in \mathbf{N}) \tag{1}$$

In the previous experiments, we achieved positive results that our packet filter could perform well and reduce the packets ranged from 11% to 23%. However, the IP calculation is effective and computed based on real performance. In other words, the weight-based approach of calculating the IP confidence lacks of theoretical basis. According to the work [18], the above equation is a straightforward method without the need of a distribution model, whereas it cannot accurately capture and model the uncertainty of network traffic. To improve this issue, we therefore attempt in designing our packet filter with a trust-based method of using Bayesian inference in calculating the IP confidence. Our current work aims to measure packet filtration and reduction with a theoretical model.

3   Our Proposed Method

In this section, we begin by describing the Bayesian inference and introducing its application in our designed packet filter. We then present the architecture of our further proposed trust-based blacklist packet filter and describe its components and functions in details.

3.1   Trust Value Calculation Using Bayesian Inference

In compute science, the notion of *trust* is borrowed from the social science literature aiming to evaluate and predicate the behavior of target objects. There is no clear definition for *trust* in the computer networks so that it can be interpreted as reputation, probability, trusting option, directed graphs, etc.

A lot of research work has studied and applied the notion of trust in different fields (see Section 5). In this paper, referring to some related work about IP reputation [18,19], we therefore aim to apply a trust-based method of using Bayesian inference (a theoretical model) into calculating the IP confidence for our designed trust-based blacklist packet filter, which can greatly help the packet filter deal with variants in network traffic.

As discussed in Section 2, the adaptive blacklist-based packet filter can be regarded as a reputation-based method. Thus, we can calculate the trust values (or IP confidence) by applying other trust-based approaches. In statistics, *Bayesian inference* is a method of inference in which Bayes' rule is used to update the probability estimate for a hypothesis as additional evidence. The objective of using the *Bayesian inference* in our work is to determine whether an IP address should be blacklisted. We give a major assumption as follows:

– *Assumption.* We assume that all packets are independent from each other. That is, if one packet is found to be a malicious packet, the possibility of the following packet being a malicious packet is still 1/2.

This possibility assumption indicates that the attacks may come in various forms, either in one packet or in a number of packets. To derive the calculation of trust values. We assume that N packets are sent from an IP address to the trust-based blacklist packet filter, of which k packets are proven to be *normal.* we further provide some terms as below:

$$V_i \ (means \ that \ the \ i^{th} \ packet \ is \ normal.)$$

$$n(N) \ (means \ the \ number \ of \ normal \ packets.)$$

$$P(n_i : normal) = p \ (means \ the \ possibility \ of \ the \ i^{th} \ incoming \ packet \ is \ normal.)$$

In terms of the work [18,19] and the above assumption, the distribution of observing $n(N) = k$ is governed by Binomial distribution[4] as below.

$$P(n(N) = k|p) = \binom{N}{k}p^k(1-p)^{N-k} \tag{2}$$

Then, our objective is to estimate the possibility $P(V_{N+1} = 1|n(N) = k)$. We can use the *Bayesian Inference* approach to calculate this possibility. From Bayesian equation, we can have the following probability distribution.

$$P(V_{N+1} = 1|n(N) = k) = \frac{P(V_{N+1} = 1, n(N) = k)}{P(n(N) = k)} \tag{3}$$

For the above equation, we use marginal probability distribution[5] and have:

$$P(n(N) = k) = \int_0^1 P(n(N) = k|p)f(p) \cdot dp \tag{4}$$

$$P(V_{N+1} = 1, n(N) = k) = \int_0^1 P(n(N) = k|p)f(p)p \cdot dp \tag{5}$$

---

[4] Binomial distribution is the discrete probability distribution that represents the number of successes in a sequence of n independent, which the possibility of each n is the same p.

[5] Marginal distribution of a subset of random variables is the probability distribution of the variables contained in the subset.

There is no prior information about p, so that we assume that p is determined by a uniform prior distribution $f(p) = 1$ where $p \in [0, 1]$. Therefore, using equation (2), (3), (4) and (5), we can have the following equation:

$$P(V_{N+1} = 1 | n(N) = k) = \frac{\int_0^1 P(n(N) = k|p)f(p)p \cdot dp}{\int_0^1 P(n(N) = k|p)f(p) \cdot dp} = \frac{k+1}{N+2} \quad (6)$$

Based on the equation (6), we can calculate the trust values (denoted t_{value}) for relevant IP addresses. If we set a threshold to $T \in [a, b]$ (the selection of the *threshold* will be discussed later), then we can judge a blacklisting IP address[6] to be maintained or deleted as follows:

- If $t_{value} \in T$, then the blacklisting IP address will be deleted from the black-list.
- If t_{value} is not in T, then the blacklisting IP address will be still in the blacklist.

3.2   Architecture of Trust-Based Blacklist Packet Filter

As shown in Fig. 2, we describe the architecture of our further designed *trust-based blacklist packet filter*. There are totally two major components: a *blacklist*

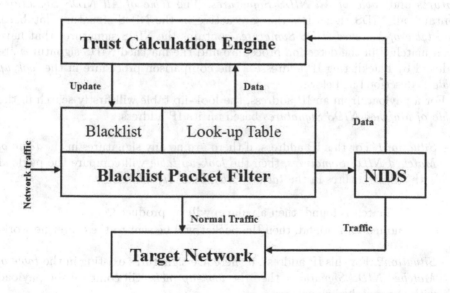

Fig. 2. The architecture of the trust-based blacklist packet filter, which consists of a blacklist packet filter and a trust calculation engine

---

[6] In the packet filter, a new IP address will be blacklisted as long as a NIDS alarm for this IP address is produced.

packet filter and a *trust calculation engine*. The blacklist packet filter is similar in our previous work and is mainly responsible for filtering out network packets based on trust values. It consists of two components: a *blacklist* and a *look-up table*. The blacklist contains all blacklisting IP addresses while the look-up table contains NIDS signatures indexed by the blacklisting IP addresses. The *trust calculation engine* is used to collect data from both the blacklist packet filter and the NIDS, and is responsible for computing trust values and updating the blacklist accordingly. When network packets arrive, the filtration procedure of the *trust-based blacklist packet filter* is described as below:

- If the IP address of a packet is in the *blacklist*, then the packet payload will be compared with the signatures stored in the *look-up table*.

  - If a match is found, then the *blacklist packet filter* will produce an alarm and send a copy of this alarm to the *trust calculation engine*.
  - If no match is found, then the packet will be sent to the target network.

- If the IP address of a packet is not in the *blacklist*, then the packet will be forwarded into the NIDS for examination

In Fig. 3, we give the construction of the *look-up table* in the blacklist packet filter. The *look-up table* contains two sub-tables: *table of Matched NIDS Signatures* and *table of All NIDS Signatures*. The *table of All NIDS Signatures* contains all NIDS signatures that are active in the NIDS signature database. The *table of Matched NIDS Signatures* contains the NIDS signatures that have been matched in the detection procedure and the matched NIDS signatures are indexed by blacklisting IP addresses. The comparison procedure in the *look-up table* is described as below:

For a payload from an IP address, the look-up table will firstly search in the *table of Matched NIDS Signatures* based on its IP address.

- *Situation1*. For this IP address, if there are no any signatures in the *table of Matched NIDS Signatures*, then the *look-up table* will compare the payload with the signatures in the *table of All NIDS Signatures*.

  - If a match is found, then an alarm will be produced.
  - If no match is found, then the packet will be sent to the target network.

- *Situation2*. For this IP address, if there are signatures existing in the *table of Matched NIDS Signatures*, then the *look-up table* will compare the payload with the matched signatures.

  - If a match is found, then an alarm will be produced.
  - If no match is found, then the *look-up table* will compare the payload with all signatures in the *table of All NIDS Signatures*. The comparison process is the same as *Situation1*.

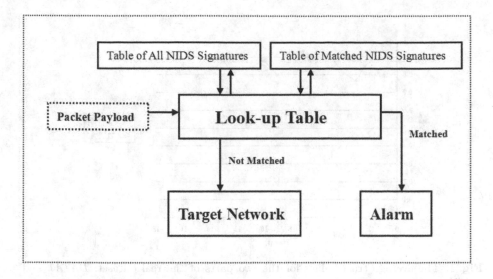

Fig. 3. The construction of the look-up table: table of Matched NIDS Signatures and table of All NIDS Signatues

4   Evaluation

To evaluate the trust-based approach, in this section, we describe the experimental methodology, illustrate how to determine the threshold in the designed packet filter, present experimental results and discuss the current approach with our previously used weight-based method.

4.1   Experimental Methodology

The first question is that how to set an appropriate threshold for distinguishing normal and abnormal IP addresses. According to the equation (6), we can calculate the trust values (t_{value}) as follows:

$$t_{value} = \frac{k+1}{N+2}$$

Therefore, if k is big enough which means that normal packets dominate the network traffic, then the t_{value} will become larger. Since k is smaller than N (the total number of packets), the value range of t_{value} is belonging to [0,1]. In this case, the best scenario for t_{value} is that its value infinitely close to 1, which means that the vast majority of current network packets are normal. On the other hand, when the t_{value} declines, it means that malicious packets are detected in the network environment. Therefore, the threshold can be initially presented as [a,1]. To determine the lower limit a of the threshold, we simulate some normal traffic to the trust-based blacklist packet filter and identify the threshold by analyzing the simulation results.

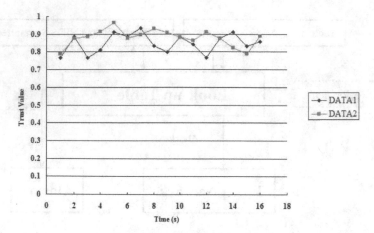

Fig. 4. The average trust values for the two parts of the real dataset: *DATA1* and *DATA2*

After obtaining the threshold, we then investigate the performance of our trust-based blacklist packet filter with a real dataset and in a network environment, comparing with the performance of Snort. At last, in the network environment, we compare the calculation of trust values with the weighted ratio-based calculation by simulating some normal and malicious packets.

4.2   Threshold Selection

In order to select an appropriate lower limit for the threshold, we conducted an experiment for the designed packet filter by using a real dataset. The real dataset was captured by a Honeypot[7] which was deployed in our CSLab. The Honeypot provided several services (e.g., FTP, HTTP) for users from outside network and recorded all incoming traffic. The incoming traffic can contain both normal and abnormal traffic.

By analyzing the captured traffic, we constructed a real dataset and divided it into two parts (called *DATA1* and *DATA2*), with about 4 to 6 million packets and the base rates are nearly $B=0.003325$ and $B=0.001723$ respectively which are regarded to be reasonable and normal in real settings. We simulated the traffic to our packet filter and the results are shown in Fig. 4.

In the experiment, the trust values will be updated in every 1 second. The average trust values are simply average values of all IP addresses in the dataset. For the *DATA1*, its average trust values are from 0.765 to 0.934, while for the *DATA2*, the average trust values are from 0.788 to 0.965. On the whole, the range of trust values is between 0.75 and 1.0. Therefore, based on the simulation results, we select the threshold to [0.75,1].

---

[7] This project is managed by HoneybirdHK (http://www.honeybird.hk/)

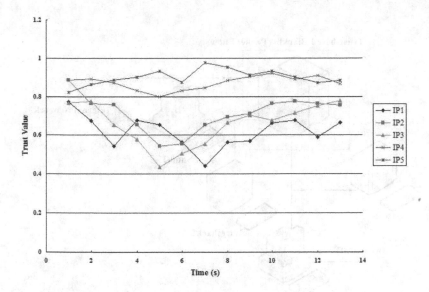

Fig. 5. The trust values for *IP1*, *IP2*, *IP3*, *IP4*, *IP5* in *DATA3*

4.3   Experiment with Real Dataset

Based on the Honeypot, we additionally constructed another dataset called *DATA3* to explore the initial performance of the trust-based blacklist packet filter. By analyzing the *DATA3* in advance, we have found some malicious packets are from the IP addresses: denoted *IP1*, *IP2* and *IP3*. We present the trust values about these possible blacklisting IP addresses in Fig. 5.

The trust values will be updated in every 1 second. It is visible that the trust values for *IP1*, *IP2* and *IP3* gradually decline below the threshold [0.75,1] when these IP addresses send some malicious packets. In comparison, we give the trust values of two normal IP addresses: *IP4*, *IP5*. As shown in Fig. 5, the trust values of these two normal IP addresses steadily fall within the threshold [0.75,1]. The results of this experiment show that the trust-based blacklist packet filter is capable of detecting the malicious IP addresses that are sending malicious packets mixing with normal packets.

In the experiment, it is hard for the trust values to reach the perfect value 1 since packet record may arrive late and the *trust calculation engine* will not count these packets in the calculation of trust values. That is, the *trust calculation engine* may not consider the late packets to be normal packets in nature. This mechanism ensures that only confirmed normal packets can be used in calculating the trust values, which can secure the trust calculation.

4.4   Experiment in a Network Environment

To further investigate the performance of the packet filter in the aspect of packet filtration, we constructed a network environment by using existing tools and

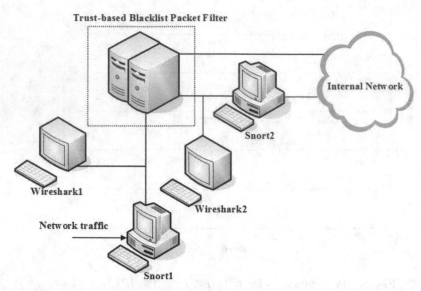

Fig. 6. The experimental deployment consists of Snort1, Wireshark1, Wireshark2, trust-based blacklist packet filter, Snort2 and Internal Network

deployed the trust-based blacklist packet filter in this network environment. The experimental deployment is shown in Fig. 6.

The network environment mainly consists of Snort, Wireshark [16] and the trust-based blacklist packet filter. In particular, we implemented two Snort in the network environment, one (named *Snort1*) is deployed in front of the *trust-based blacklist packet filter* whereas the other (named *Snort2*) is deployed behind the packet filter. Due to this deployment, we can evaluate the capability of the packet filter in reducing the burden of a NIDS by comparing the performance between *Snort1* and *Snort2*. The Wireshark is responsible for monitoring network packets and verifying the performance of our packet filter in the aspect of packet reduction by analyzing recorded packet information.

We conducted the experiment for a week and the first-day results of CPU usage between *Snort1* and *Snort2* are presented in Fig. 7. The results show that the CPU usage of *Snort1* generally larger than that of *Snort2* by implementing in the same network environment. The CPU-usage performance of other 6 days is similar to the first day, which means that our packet filter can indeed reduce the burden of a NIDS by filtering out a number of network packets. In Table 1, we show the packet reduction rate for 7 days. The information is calculated based on the recorded data from the two Wireshark tools. It is easily visible that our packet filter can achieve a packet reduction rate in the range from 21.54% to 33.87% in the experimental network environment. The results verify that our packet filter is able to filter out network packets by using the trust-based approach to calculate the IP reputation.

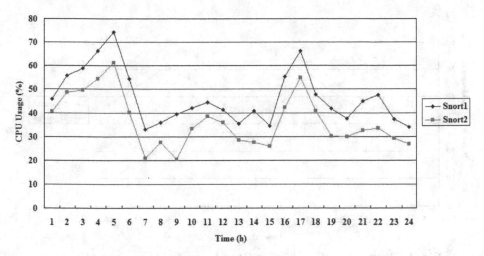

Fig. 7. The CPU usage of *Snort1* and *Snort2* for the first day

Table 1. Results of Packet Reduction Rate

Week Day	Packet Reduction Rate (%)	Week Day	Packet Reduction Rate (%)
Monday	21.54	Saturday	24.33
Tuesday	22.56	Sunday	25.80
Wednesday	31,67		
Thursday	27.84		
Friday	33.87		

The specific packet reduction rate is depending on the number of blacklisting IP addresses in the *blacklist packet filter*. In general, more IP addresses are blacklisted, bigger reduction rate can be achieved. In this case, the packet reduction rate in a real network environment may be fluctuant in terms of network contexts (i.e., when the network traffic is becoming normal, the reduction rate will be decreased, but if the network traffic contains a lot of malicious packets, then the reduction rate will be possibly increased). More future experiments can be conducted to explore this relationship.

4.5   Outcome Comparison

The above experiments show positive results of our designed trust-based blacklist packet filter in reducing the burden of a NIDS by filtering out network packets. In this section, we compare the trust-based approach with our previous weight-based method in the aspect of blacklist generation.

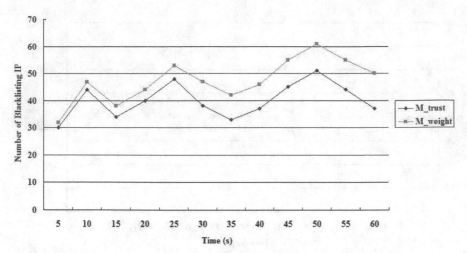

Fig. 8. The number of blacklisting IP addresses for M_{trust} and M_{weight}

Our packet filter is based on a blacklist, thus, it is very important to appropriately generate a *good* blacklist. The meaning of a *good* blacklist can be represented as follows:

– The blacklist should accurately reflect the current traffic. In other words, the false positive and the false negative of the blacklist should be low.
– The blacklist should be sensitive to the traffic change. That is, when a potential malicious IP address is detected or deleted, the blacklist should contain or remove this IP address in terms of calculated trust values or IP confidence.

To compare the two approaches (we denote our current approach as M_{trust} while our previous method as M_{weight}), we deployed these approaches in a network environment like Fig. 6 and simulated some traffic to both mechanism. During the experiment, we utilized a packet generator [5] to simulate some malicious IP addresses by sending out some malicious packets. The number of blacklisting IP addresses for both methods is shown in Fig. 8.

At the beginning, we simulated 33 malicious IP addresses. The approach of M_{trust} blacklisted 30 of them whereas the approach of M_{weight} blacklisted 32 of them. The detection rate of M_{weight} is a bit higher since we use a 10-weighted ratio based method to emphasize the impact of every malicious packet.

Then in the time interval of 5s to 10s, we additionally simulated 15 new malicious IP addresses. For the M_{trust}, it blacklisted all these new IP addresses while the number of blacklisting IP is 44 rather than 45, the reason is that 1 blacklisting IP address has become normal in terms of its trust value. For the M_{weight}, it detects all these new malicious IP with no blacklisting IP becoming normal. Subsequently, we only maintained 32 malicious IP addresses to send malicious packets between 10s and 15s. It is easily visible that M_{trust} can quickly adaptive to this change and its number of blacklisting IP addresses decreases to

34. But for M_{weight}, its number of blacklisting IP addresses only decreases from 47 to 38. During [25s,30s], [30s,35s] and [50s, 60s], we maintained the number of malicious IP addresses to 36, 30 and 34 respectively. Similarly, we find that M_{trust} is more sensitive to the traffic changes than M_{weight}.

Overall, based on the simulation results, both of the two approaches have an acceptable false positive and false negative (i.e., M_{trust} with FN 6.8% and FP 8.32%, M_{weight} with FN 2.2% and FP 15.4%). The false positive of M_{weight} is higher than M_{trust} in that we use 10 as the weighted value in calculating IP confidence which means that an IP address may be blacklisted by sending only several malicious packets. On the other hand, due to the weighted blacklist generation, M_{weight} is more powerful in detecting a malicious IP address. On the whole, the false positive and the false negative of both approaches are acceptable. Regarding to the sensitivity, the approach of M_{trust} is greatly more sensitive to the traffic changes in a network than M_{weight}. Based on the definition of a *good blacklist*, we consider M_{trust} is generally better than M_{weight} by considering both *false rate* (false positive and false negative) and *traffic sensitivity*.

4.6 Security Discussion and Potential Countermeasures

DoS Attack. As discussed before, DoS attack is a big problem for a NIDS. By implementing the packet filter, a lot of network packets can be filtered out so that the possibility of a NIDS surviving in a large-scale network environment will be increased.

For the packet filter, DoS attack is also a big challenge as for other packet filters that some countermeasures should be considered. However, the counter-measures should not affect the network security too much. We therefore consider employing a *d-threshold* into our packet filter that all packets from an IP address will be discarded if the trust value of this IP address is below the *d-threshold*. In this case, the possibility range [0,1] can be further divided into three intervals:

- *[0,d-threshold]*. When the trust values belong to this interval, all packets from these IP addresses will be discarded.
- *[d-threshold,0.75]*. When the trust values fall in this interval, all packets from these IP addresses will still be compared with NIDS signatures by the trust-based blacklist packet filter in order to keep the level of network security.
- *[0.75,1]*. When the trust values are classified into this interval, all packets will be processed into a NIDS for examination.

The DoS attack can be partly mitigated by employing a *d-threshold*. If the trust value of an IP address is smaller than this *d-threshold*, it means that this IP address is harmful to the network. Therefore, it is crucial to appropriately select this *d-threshold*. Further experiments should be conducted to collect more data to investigate this issue.

IP Spoofing. This IP spoofing attack is a kind of impersonation attacks, which refers to sending network packets by concealing the identity of the sender or impersonating another computer users. The final goal of this attack is possibly to launch a DoS attack, which affects the availability of network resources.

For our packet filter, the IP spoofing attack may succeed in bypassing the filtration of the packet filter. However, as discussed in our previous work [17], this attack will not affect the whole level of network security since the packets still need to be examined by a NIDS even if these packets bypass our packet filter. Moreover, our packet filter and the NIDS use the same NIDS signature database so that the detection capabilities of the packet filter and the NIDS are the same. To further mitigate this attack, we can develop an IP verification mechanism to verify the IP source and filter out spoofed packets. More experiments and data should be collected to evaluate this approach.

5   Related Work

Trust-based methods have been applied in many fields. Gonzalez *et al.* [19] presented a work by using Bayesian inference in defending against IP spoofing attacks at the router level. Their results showed that their application could effectively detect malicious access routers and has a low impact on the network performance. Our work is different from their work in that we apply the Bayesian inference and Bayesian model into network packet filtration to help compute IP confidence (determine blacklist) and construct a trust-based blacklist packet filter. It is visible, from our work, that the trust-based method is a promising method that can be applied into the evaluation of packet filtration. To the best of our knowledge, our work is an early work that attempts in designing a packet filter with a Bayesian model and applying this probability model into producing a blacklist. We expect to see more work to be done in this research area.

For the application of trust-based approaches, Yao *et al.* [20] proposed a Bayesian network-based trust model for a peer-to-peer file sharing application, which could present differentiated trust and combine different aspects of trust. Sun *et al.* [18] presented an information theoretical framework to quantitatively measure trust and to build a model for trust propagation in ad hoc networks. The framework was developed to secure ad hoc routing and malicious node detection. Then, Zhu *et al.* [24] extended the above idea to formalize the trusted actions by using mutual information to quantify trust and to use MaxMin mechanism to calculate trust which could be established through multiple recommendation paths in ad-hoc networks. Later, Chung *et al.* [21] presented a trust model, based on Bayesian networks, which could adapt to ad hoc networks and distributed systems. Their model evaluated the trust in a server based on two points: direct experiences with the server and recommendations concerning its service.

For filtering out packets in intrusion detection, Ioannis *et al.* [22] introduced a packet pre-filtering approach, which was a powerful hardware-based technique, as a means to resolve the burden of an intrusion detection system. They implemented the header matching portion of a NIDS system together with a small prefix match that the rules could be checked more efficiently by a full-match module. Later, Ning *et al.* [23] proposed a high-performance memory-based IDS that could be easily reconfigured for new rules by utilizing deep packet prefiltering and novel finite state encoding.

6 Future Work

A lot of studies have been conducted on constructing packet filters. But it is still a hot topic for efficiently designing such kind of filters and *appropriately* evaluating the packet filtration and reduction. Our current work aims to design a packet filter to adaptively filter out network packets by calculating IP confidence and generating a blacklist with a theoretical model. There are many possible work in future experiments. The future work could include exploring the performance of the trust-based blacklist packet filter in a distributed network environment (i.e., exploring whether the threshold is the same when deployed in a distributed network environment). Future work could also include employing more information theory (e.g., entropy theory) in calculating the IP confidence and evaluating the performance of packet filtration and reduction.

7 Conclusion

The performance of a network intrusion detection system is greatly restricted in a large-scale network environment. That is, overhead network packet can significantly reduce the effectiveness of a NIDS and heavily consume computer and network resources. To mitigate this issue, we advocate that constructing a packet filter is a promising solution.

In this work, we further design a *trust-based blacklist packet filter* to reduce the burden of a NIDS by filtering out a number of network packets. Specifically, the trust-based blacklist packet filter consists of two major components: a *blacklist packet filter* and a *trust calculation engine*. The *blacklist packet filter* is responsible for filtering out network packets in terms of IP confidence while the *trust calculation engine* is responsible for collecting data and updating the blacklist. The blacklist is generated by computing the trust values (or IP confidence) by using a trust-based approach of Bayesian inference.

In the experiment, we showed how to select an appropriate threshold for our packet filter. We then evaluated the performance of the packet filter with a real dataset and in a network environment. The experimental results show that the packet filter is effective at filtering out network packets without lowering the network security and has a minimum impact on the network performance. We further compared our current trust-based method with our previous weight-based method and the simulation results describe that the trust-based method is generally better by considering both false rate and traffic sensitivity.

Acknowledgments. We would like to thank HoneybirdHK for supporting and providing the real dataset and all anonymous reviewers for their valuable comments.

References

1. P.V.: Bro: A System for Detecting Network Intruders in Real-Time. Computer Networks 31(23-24), 2435–2463 (1999)
2. Roesch, M.: Snort: Lightweight Intrusion Detection for Networks. In: 13th Large Installation System Administration Conference (LISA), pp. 229–238. USENIX Association Berkeley, CA (1999)
3. Scarfone, K., Mell, P.: Guide to Intrusion Detection and Prevention Systems (IDPS). NIST Special Publication 800-94 (February 2007)
4. Vigna, G., Kemmerer, R.A.: NetSTAT: A Network-based Intrusion Detection Approach. In: Annual Computer Security Applications Conference (ACSAC), pp. 25–34. IEEE Press, New York (1998)
5. Colasoft Packet Builder, http://www.colasoft.com
6. Valdes, A., Anderson, D.: Statistical Methods for Computer Usage Anomaly Detection Using NIDES. Technical Report, SRI International (January 1995)
7. Ghosh, A.K., Wanken, J., Charron, F.: Detecting Anomalous and Unknown Intrusions Against Programs. In: Annual Computer Security Applications Conference (ACSAC), pp. 259–267 (1998)
8. Snort, The Open Source Network Intrusion Detection System, http://www.snort.org/
9. Sommer, R., Paxson, V.: Outside the closed world: On using Machine Learning for Network Intrusion Detection. In: IEEE Symposium on Security and Privacy, pp. 305–316. IEEE, New York (2010)
10. Carl, G., Kesidis, G., Brooks, R.R., Suresh, R.: Denial-of-Service Attack-Detection Techniques. IEEE Internet Computing 10(1), 82–89 (2006)
11. Paxson, V.: An Analysis of using Reflectors for Distributed Denial-of-Service Attacks. ACM Computer Communication Review 31(3) (July 2001)
12. Dreger, H., Feldmann, A., Paxson, V., Sommer, R.: Operational Experiences with High-volume Network Intrusion Detection. In: ACM Conference on Computer and Communications Security (CCS), pp. 2–11. ACM, USA (2004)
13. Fisk, M., Varghese, G.: An Analysis of Fast String Matching Applied to Content-based Forwarding and Intrusion Detection. Technical Report CS2001-0670, University of California, San Diego (2002)
14. Rivest, R.L.: On the Worst-case Behavior of String-Searching Algorithms. SIAM Journal on Computing 6, 669–674 (1977)
15. Michel, B., Jyanthi, H., Evangelos, K.: Detecting Impersonation Attacks in Future Wireless and Mobile Networks. In: Workshop on Secure Mobile Ad-hoc Networks and Sensors, pp. 1–16 (2005)
16. Wireshark, http://www.wireshark.org/
17. Meng, Y., Kwok, L.F.: Adaptive Context-aware Packet Filter Scheme using Statistic-based Blacklist Generation in Network Intrusion Detection. In: 7th International Conference on Information Assurance and Security (IAS 2011), pp. 74–79. IEEE Press, New York (2011)
18. Sun, Y., Yu, W., Han, Z., Liu, K.: Information Theoretic Framework of Trust Modeling and Evaluation for ad hoc Networks. IEEE Journal on Selected Areas in Communications 24(2), 305–317 (2006)
19. Gonzalez, J.M., Anwar, M., Joshi, J.B.D.: A Trust-based Approach against IP-Spoofing Attacks. In: 9th International Conference on Privacy, Security and Trust (PST 2011), pp. 63–70 (2011)

20. Yao, W., Julita, V.: Bayesian Network-Based Trust Model. In: IEEE/WIC International Conference on Web Intelligence, pp. 372–378. IEEE, New York (2003)
21. Chung, T.N., Camp, O., Loiseau, S.: A Bayesian Network based Trust Model for Improving Collaboration in Mobile ad hoc Networks. In: IEEE International Conference on Research, Innovation and Vision for the Future, pp. 144–151 (2007)
22. Ioannis, S., Vasilis, D., Dionisios, P., Stamatis, V.: Packet Pre-filtering for Network Intrusion Detection. In: ACM/IEEE Symposium on Architecture for Networking and Communications Systems (ANCS), pp. 183–192. ACM, New York (2006)
23. Ning, W., Luke, V., Benfano, S.: Deep Packet Pre-filtering and Finite State Encoding for Adaptive Intrusion Detection System. Computer Networks 55(8), 1648–1661 (2011)
24. Zhu, H., Bao, F.: Quantifying Trust Metrics of Recommendation Systems in Ad-Hoc Networks. In: 2007 IEEE Wireless Communications and Networking Conference (WCNC), pp. 2904–2908. IEEE, New York (2007)

Data Leak Detection as a Service

Xiaokui Shu and Danfeng (Daphne) Yao

Department of Computer Science
Virginia Tech
Blacksburg, VA, USA
{subx,danfeng}@cs.vt.edu

Abstract. We describe a network-based data-leak detection (DLD) technique, the main feature of which is that the detection does not reveal the content of the sensitive data. Instead, only a small amount of specialized digests are needed. Our technique – referred to as the *fuzzy fingerprint* detection – can be used to detect accidental data leaks due to human errors or application flaws. The privacy-preserving feature of our algorithms minimizes the exposure of sensitive data and enables the data owner to safely delegate the detection to others (e.g., network or cloud providers). We describe how cloud providers can offer their customers data-leak detection as an add-on service with strong privacy guarantees. We perform extensive experimental evaluation on our techniques with large datasets. Our evaluation results under various data-leak scenarios and setups show that our method can support accurate detection with very small number of false alarms, even when the presentation of the data has been transformed.

Keywords: privacy, data leak, network security, protocol.

1 Introduction

Typical approaches to preventing data leak are under two categories – host-based solutions and network-based solutions. Host-based approaches may include *i)* encrypting data when not used [4], *ii)* detecting stealthy malware with anti-virus scanning or monitoring the host [29,31,18], and *iii)* enforcing policies to restrict the transfer of sensitive data. These approaches are complementary and can be deployed simultaneously.

We present a *network-based* data-leak detection (DLD) solution that complements host-based methods. Network-based data-leak detection focuses on analyzing unencrypted outbound network traffic through *i)* deep packet inspection or *ii)* information theoretic analysis (e.g., through entropy analysis [13]). For the deep packet inspection approach, a straightforward solution requires inspecting every packet for the occurrence of any of the sensitive data defined in the sensitive database. Such solutions generate alerts if the sensitive data is found in the outgoing traffic. However, this simple solution requires storing sensitive data in *plaintext* in the detection system.

A.D. Keromytis and R. Di Pietro (Eds.): SecureComm 2012, LNICST 106, pp. 222–240, 2013.

The reason that this plaintext-based comparison mechanism is undesirable is two-fold: *i)* the machine performing the comparison may be compromised, which reveals sensitive data[1], and *ii)* it does not support the outsource of data-leak detection operations, as the provider performing the DLD service may learn or accidentally expose the sensitive data. In addition to provide the regular networking, computing, or storage services, network or cloud providers may introduce additional security protection for their customers. For their customers, these add-on security services – such as data-leak detection – are attractive, as they may have a lower cost compared to building in-house security management of their own. Thus, one may outsource the data-leak detection to a DLD provider. However, the data owner may not allow the DLD provider to access the sensitive data. *The technical challenge is that the detection algorithm needs to provide guarantees on the secrecy of customers' sensitive data while still enabling the provider to identify signs of data leak in the traffic.*

This problem of the lack of support for privacy-enhancing data-leak detection has not been systematically addressed in the security literature. In this paper we design, implement, and experimentally evaluate an efficient technique that enhances the data privacy during the data-leak detection operations. Our method is based on a fast and practical one-way computation and does not require any expensive cryptographic operations. We provide extensive experimental evidences and theoretical analysis to demonstrate the feasibility and effectiveness of our approach.

We model the DLD provider as an honest-but-curious (aka semi-honest) adversary. The DLD provider is trusted to perform inspection on network traffic, but may attempt to learn the information about the sensitive database provided by the data owner, or to discover the leaked data easily from the network traffic. Existing work on cryptography-based multi-party computation is not efficient enough for practical data leak inspection in this setting. We design, implement, and evaluate a new privacy-enhancing data-leak detection system that enables the data owner to securely delegate the traffic-inspection task to DLD providers without exposing the sensitive data. It is hard for a DLD provider to learn the *exact* value of sensitive data during the detection process.

In our model, the data owner computes a special set of digests or fingerprints from the sensitive data, and then discloses only a small amount of digest information to the DLD provider. These fingerprints have important properties, which prevent the provider from gaining knowledge of the sensitive data, while they enable accurate comparison and detection. The DLD provider performs deep packet inspection to identify whether these fingerprint patterns exist in the outbound traffic of data owner's organization or not. We perform extensive experiments with real-world datasets in various data-leak scenarios to confirm the accuracy and efficiency of our proposed solutions. Our contributions are summarized as follows.

---

[1] Sensitive data may be in encrypted storage, but is plaintext when in memory for comparison.

1. We describe a privacy-preserving data-leak detection (DLD) model for preventing inadvertent data leak in network traffic. Such a model yields a powerful and delegatable data-leak detection framework. For example, in the cloud computing environment the cloud provider can perform data-leak detection as an add-on service to its clients. We describe a quantitative privacy model needed for data-leak detection as a service.

    We design, implement, and evaluate a new and efficient technique, *fuzzy fingerprint*, for realizing privacy-preserving data-leak detection. Fuzzy fingerprints are special digests of the sensitive data that the data owner releases to the DLD provider. We describe the operations in our protocol that is run between the data owner and the DLD provider.

2. We implement our detection system and perform extensive experimental evaluation on 2.6 GB Enron dataset, Internet surfing traffic of 20 users, and also 5 simulated real-world data-leak scenarios to measure the privacy guarantee, detection rate and efficiency of our technique. Our results indicate high accuracy performed by our underlying scheme with very low false positive rate. It also shows that the detection accuracy does not degrade when only partial (sampled) sensitive-data digests are used. In addition, these partial fingerprints represent the full set of data without any bias.

The rest of the paper is organized as follows. Our models and design requirements for a privacy-preserving data-leak detection system are presented next. Details of our system including digest computation, data-inspection strategies are described in Section 3. We analyze the privacy in Section 4, and also point out the limitations of our method. Our implementation and evaluation are described in Section 5. Related work is given in Section 6. Conclusions and future work are given in Section 7.

2   Model and Overview

There is a privacy goal and threat model beside the normal security goal and threat model for any solution to outsource data-leak detection. The former is for preventing the service provider from gaining knowledge about the sensitive data during the detection, whereas the latter relates to preventing unauthorized transmission of sensitive data. There are two types of players in our model: the organization (i.e., data owner) and the data-leak detection (DLD) provider.

- *Organization* owns the sensitive data and authorizes the DLD provider to inspect the network traffic from the organizational networks for anomalies, namely inadvertent data leak. However, the organization does not want to directly reveal the sensitive data to the provider.
- *DLD provider* inspects the network traffic for potential data leaks. The inspection can be performed offline without causing any real-time delay in routing the packets. However, the DLD provider may attempt to gain knowledge about the sensitive data.

We describe the security and privacy goals in Section 2.1 and Section 2.2.

2.1   Security Goal and Threat Model

We categorize three causes for sensitive data to appear on the outbound traffic of an organization, including the legitimate data use by the employees.

– Case I *Inadvertent data leak*: The sensitive data is accidentally leaked in the outbound traffic by a legitimate user. This paper focuses on detecting this type of accidental data leaks over the network. Inadvertent data leak may be due to human errors such as forgetting to use encryption, carelessly forwarding an internal email and attachments to outsiders without encryption, or due to application flaws (such as described in [19]).
– Case II *Malicious data leak*: A rogue insider or malicious and stealthy software may steal sensitive personal or organizational data from a host. Because the malicious adversary can use strong encryption or steganography to disable content-based traffic inspection, thus this type of leaks (including covert channels) are out of the scope of our network-based solution. Host-based defenses (such as detecting the infection onset [33]) need to be deployed instead.
– Case III *Legitimate and intended data transfer*: The sensitive data is sent by a legitimate user intended for legitimate purposes. In this paper, we assume that legitimate data transfers use data encryption such as SSL, which allows one to distinguish it from the inadvertent data leak. Therefore, in what follows we assume that plaintext sensitive data appearing in network traffic is only due to inadvertent data leaks.

The security goal in this paper is to detect the inadvertent data leak in Case I. In this scenario, the traffic is usually not encrypted and thus deep packet inspection is feasible. Network-based security approaches are not effective against data leak caused by malware or rogue insiders as in Case II, because the intruder may use strong encryption when transmitting the data.

2.2   Privacy Goal and Threat Model

To prevent the DLD provider from gaining knowledge of the sensitive data during the detection process, we need to set up a privacy goal that is complementary to the security goal above. We model the DLD provider as a semi-honest adversary, who follows our protocol to carry out the operations, but may attempt to gain knowledge about the sensitive data of the data owner. Our privacy goal is defined as follows. The DLD provider is given digests of sensitive data from the data owner and the content of network traffic to be examined. The DLD provider should not find out the exact value of a piece of sensitive data with more than $\frac{1}{K}$ probability, where K is an integer representing the number of all possible sensitive-data candidates that can be inferred by the DLD provider.

We present a novel privacy-preserving DLD model with a new fuzzy fingerprint mechanism to improve the data protection against semi-honest DLD provider. We generate digests of sensitive data through a one-way function, and then hide the sensitive values among other non-sensitive values via fuzzification, The privacy guarantee is much higher than $\frac{1}{K}$ when there is no leak in traffic, because the adversary's inference can only be done through brute-force guesses.

The traffic content is accessible by the DLD provider in plaintext. Therefore, in the event of true data leak, the DLD provider may learn about the leaked information, which is inevitable for all deep-packet inspection approaches. Our unique solution confines the amount of maximally information learned during the detection and provides quantitative guarantee for the data privacy.

2.3   Overview of Privacy-Enhancing DLD

Our privacy-preserving data-leak detection method supports practical data-leak detection as a service and minimizes the knowledge that a DLD provider may gain during the process. Figure 1 illustrates the six operations between the data owner and the DLD provider in our protocol, which include PREPROCESS run by the data owner to prepare the digests of sensitive data, RELEASE for the data owner to send the digests to the DLD provider, MONITOR and DETECT for the DLD provider to collect outgoing traffic of the organization, compute digests of traffic content, and identify potential leaks, REPORT for the DLD provider to return data leak alerts to the data owner where there may be false positives (i.e., false alarms), and POSTPROCESS for the data owner to pinpoint true data leak instances. We explain the operations in details in the next section.

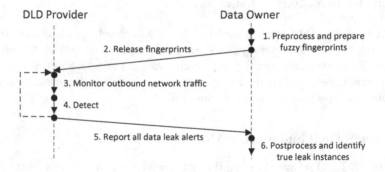

Fig. 1. Privacy-preserving DLD Model

The protocol is based on strategically computing data similarity, specifically the quantitative similarity between the sensitive information and the observed network traffic. High similarity indicates potential data leak. For data-leak detection, the ability to tolerate certain degree of data transformation in traffic is important. We refer to this property as *noise tolerance*. Our key idea for fast and noise-tolerant comparison is the design and use of a set of *local features* that are representative of local data patterns. Local features preserve data patterns even when modifications (insertion, deletion, and substitution) are made to parts of the data. To achieve the privacy requirement, the data owner generates a special type of digests, which we call fuzzy fingerprints. Intuitively, the purpose of fuzzy fingerprints is to hide the true sensitive data in the crowd so that the DLD provider is unable to learn its exact value. We describe the technical details next.

3 Fuzzy Fingerprint Method and Protocol

We describe technical details of our fuzzy fingerprint mechanism in this section.

3.1 Fingerprints

The DLD provider obtains digests of sensitive data from the data owner. The data owner uses Rabin fingerprint algorithm [24] and a sliding window to generate short and hard-to-reverse (i.e., oneway) digests through the fast polynomial modulus operation. Rabin fingerprints are computed as polynomial modulus operations, and can be implemented with fast XOR, shift, and table look-up operations. It has a unique min-wise independence property [7], which allows randomly sampling of the digests without creating any bias.

The shingle-and-fingerprint process is defined as follows. For a binary string, we first generate q-grams (shingles) using a sliding window, and then compute Rabin fingerprint of each k-bit shingle using irreducible polynomial $p(x)$:

$$f_1 = c_1 x^{k-1} + c_2 x^{k-2} + \ldots + c_{k-1} x + c_k \bmod p(x)$$

From the detection respective, a straightforward method is for the DLD provider to raise an alert if any sensitive fingerprint matches the fingerprints generated from the traffic. However, this approach has a privacy issue. In case of a data leak detected, there is a match between two fingerprints from sensitive data and network traffic. Then, the DLD provider learns the corresponding shingle, as it knows the content of the packet. Therefore, the central challenge is *to prevent the DLD provider from learning the sensitive values even in data-leak scenarios*, while allowing the provider to carry out the traffic inspection.

We propose a novel and efficient technique to address this problem. The main idea is to relax the comparison criteria by strategically introducing matching instances on the DLD provider's side *without increasing false alarms for the data owner*. Specifically, *i)* the data owner perturbs the sensitive-data fingerprints before disclosing them to the DLD provider, and *ii)* the DLD provider detects leaking by a range-based comparison instead of the exact match. The range used in the comparison is pre-defined by the data owner and correlates to the perturbation procedure. We first define the *fuzzy length* and *fuzzy set* next and then describe how they are used in our detailed protocol in Section 3.2.

Definition 1. *Given a fingerprint f, fuzzy length p_d ($p_d < p_f$) is the number of the least significant bits in f that may be perturbed by the data owner.*

Definition 2. *Given a fuzzy length p_d, and a collection of fingerprints, the fuzzy set S_{f,p_d} of a fingerprint f is the set of fingerprints in the collection whose values differ from f by at most $2^{p_d} - 1$.*

In Definition 1 for fuzzy length, p_f denotes the total length of a fingerprint. In Definition 2, the size of the fuzzy set $|S_{f,p_d}|$ is upper bounded by 2^{p_d}, but the actual size may be smaller due to the sparsity of the fingerprint space.

3.2 Operations in Our Protocol

1. PREPROCESS:
   This operation is run by the data owner on some sensitive dataset. The data owner chooses the public parameters $(k, p(x), p_d)$, where k is the length of shingles, $p(x)$ is an irreducible polynomial for computing Rabin fingerprint, and p_d is the fuzzy length. The length of a fingerprint is denoted by p_f[2].

   The data owner first computes the set S of Rabin fingerprints of the sensitive data. Then the data owner transforms each fingerprint $f \in S$ into a fuzzy fingerprint f^* as follows. Given the fingerprint f of some shingle v and a fuzzy length p_d, the data owner flips an unbiased coin p_d times to generate the new least significant p_d bits in f. The rest of the bits in f are unchanged. The transformation generates a fuzzy fingerprint f^* of f. We denote the resulting set of fuzzy fingerprints by S^*, which is the output of this operation.

2. RELEASE:
   This operation is run by the data owner. The fuzzy fingerprint set S^* obtained from the PREPROCESS operation above is released to the DLD provider for use in the detection, along with the public parameters $(k, p(x), p_d)$. The real fingerprint f and the corresponding sensitive shingle v are kept at the data owner and not released to the DLD provider.

3. MONITOR: This operation is run by the DLD provider. The DLD provider monitors the network traffic T from the data owner's organization. The header of the packet in T is removed and the payload is collected. The processed traffic $\tilde{T}$ is the output.

4. DETECT:
   This operation is run by the DLD provider on $\tilde{T}$ as follows.
   (a) The DLD provider first computes the Rabin fingerprints of traffic content $\tilde{T}$ based on the public parameters.
   (b) For each fuzzy fingerprint $f^* \in S^*$ of some sensitive data, and each fingerprint $f' \in \tilde{T}$ from the traffic, and the public parameters, the DLD provider outputs 1 (indicating possible data leak) if values of f^* and f' differ by at most $2^{p_d} - 1$, and 0 otherwise.
   (c) For all the data-leak matching instances detected during this range-based detection, the DLD provider records the set of $\{(x_1, f_1), \ldots, (x_i, f_i), \ldots)\}$ pairs, where x_i is the shingle appearing in the traffic, and f_i is its Rabin fingerprint. The DLD provider and the data owner may agree upon certain aggregation methods and a threshold for logging alerts, which we discuss more in the evaluation section 5.

Because the fuzzy set of f^* includes the original fingerprint f, thus the true data leak can be detected (i.e., true positive). Yet, due to the increased detection range, multiple values in the fuzzy set may trigger alerts. Because

---

[2] The degree of polynomial $p(x)$ is $p_f + 1$.

the fuzzy set is large for the given network flow, the DLD provider has a low probability of pinpointing the sensitive data, which can be bounded as shown in Section 4.

5. REPORT:

The DLD provider reports the set of detected candidate leak instances $\{(x_1, f_1), \ldots, (x_i, f_i), \ldots)\}$ tuples to the data owner.

6. POSTPROCESS:

This operation is run by the data owner. Given the data-leak instance candidates in the reported set of tuples $\{(x_1, f_1), (x_2, f_2), \ldots\}$, the data owner searches to see if any sensitive fingerprint $f \in \mathbb{S}$ exists in the report. If there exist $f_i = f$ and $x_i = v$, i.e., the shingle x_i and fingerprint f in the traffic match those (v, f) of the sensitive data, then there is a true data leak, otherwise the submitted candidates can be safely ignored by the data owner.

The DETECT operation can be performed between $\tilde{\mathbb{T}}$ and $\mathbb{S}^*$ via set intersection test (e.g. Formula 2 in Section 5 as one realization). The advantage of our method is that the additional matching instances introduced by fuzzy fingerprints protect the sensitive data from the DLD provider; yet they do not cause additional false alarms for the data owner, as the data owner can quickly distinguish true and false leak instances. Given the digest f of a piece of sensitive data, a large collection T of traffic fingerprints, and a positive integer $K \ll |T|$, the data owner can choose a fuzzy length p_d such that there are at least $K - 1$ other distinct digests in the fuzzy set of f, assuming that the shingles corresponding to these K digests are equally likely to be candidates for sensitive data and to appear in network traffic. A tight fuzzy length (i.e., the smallest p_d value satisfying the privacy requirement) is important for efficient POSTPROCESS operation. Due to the dynamic nature of network traffic, p_d needs to be estimated accordingly. We provide quantitative analysis on fuzzy fingerprint including empirical results on different sizes of fuzzy set.

3.3   Extensions

Fingerprint Filter. We develop this extension to use Bloom filter in the DETECT operation for efficient set intersection test. Bloom filter is a well-known space-saving data structure for performing set-membership test, and the range-based comparison in the DETECT operation can be generalized to the membership test with it. Bloom filter in combination with Rabin fingerprint is referred to by us as the *fingerprint filter*. We have implemented, evaluated, and compared this technique in our experiments in Section 5.

Bit Mask. We can generalize the PREPROCESS operation with a bit mask, which specifies any arbitrarily chosen bits or any mapped bit pattern for comparison. Details of how bit mask works are discussed in our technical report [28].

Sampling. Using the min-wise independent property of Rabin fingerprint, the data owner may *sample* the fingerprints and only reveals a subset of sensitive-data's fingerprints to the DLD provider. That is, the data owner may release a subset of $\mathbb{S}^*$

to the DLD provider in RELEASE operation. The purpose of sampling is two-fold: to increase the scalability of the comparison in the DETECT operation, and to reduce the exposure of data to the DLD provider for privacy. The subset is selected by choosing the subset of smallest fingerprints when Rabin fingerprint is equipped. More description can be found in our technical report [28].

4   Analysis and Discussion

We analyze the security and privacy guarantees provided by our data-leak detection system, as well as discuss the sources of possible false negatives – data leak cases being overlooked and false positives – legitimate traffic misclassified as data leak in the detection.

Privacy Analysis. Our privacy goal is to prevent the DLD provider from inferring the exact knowledge of all sensitive data, both the outsourced sensitive data and the matched digests in network traffic. We quantify the probability for the DLD provider to infer the sensitive shingles. Suppose there are matches between sensitive fingerprints and traffic fingerprints. Given a fuzzy length, there are multiple (e.g., K) fingerprints (including the sensitive data's fingerprint) that may trigger alerts at the DLD provider; thus, the DLD provider is unable to pinpoint which alerts are true data leaks. Therefore, even if sensitive data appeared on the traffic due to inadvertent data leak, the DLD provider has no more than $\frac{1}{K}$ probability of inferring the sensitive data, assuming that the shingles associated with the fuzzy set are equally likely to be sensitive data and appear in the network traffic. The size of fuzzy set K is upper bounded by 2^{p_d}. For a large shingle set of size $2^{p_f - p_d} \leq n \leq 2^{p_f}$, the expected value of $K = \frac{n}{2^{p_f}} \times 2^{p_d}$, assuming that the fingerprints of shingles are uniformly distributed. It is a reasonable assumption, especially when binary sensitive data is included, which expands the small distinguishable text space to the vast more well-distributed whole binary space. This privacy guarantee protects the sensitive data in the *worst-case* scenario.

If there is no match between sensitive and traffic fingerprints, then the adversarial DLD provider needs to brute force to reverse the Rabin fingerprinting computation to obtain the input shingle. The time needed depends on the size of shingle space. This brute-force attack is difficult for a polynomial-time adversary and thus the success probability is not included in Theorem 1. We summarize the above privacy analysis in the following theorem.

Theorem 1. *A polynomial-time adversary has no greater than $\frac{2^{p_f - p_d}}{n}$ probability of correctly inferring a sensitive shingle, where p_f is the length of a fingerprint in bits, p_d is the fuzzy length, and $n \in [2^{p_f - p_d}, 2^{p_f}]$ is the size of the set of traffic fingerprints, assuming that the fingerprints of shingles are uniformly distributed and are equally likely to be sensitive and appear in the traffic.*

Alert Rate. We qualify the rate of alerts expected in the traffic for a sensitive data entry (the fuzzified fingerprints set of a piece of sensitive data) given the following values: the total number of fuzzified sensitive fingerprints M, the expected traffic fingerprints set size n, fingerprint length p_f, fuzzy length p_d, sampling rate $p_s \in (0, 1]$, and the expected rate α of the leak in terms of the percentage of fingerprints in the sensitive data entry that appear in the network traffic. Based on Theorem 1, the expected alert rate R can be expressed in Equation 1. It is used to derive threshold in the detection; the detection threshold should be lower than the expected rate of alerts.

$$R = \frac{\alpha p_s KM}{n} = \frac{\alpha p_s M}{2^{p_f - p_d}} \qquad (1)$$

Collisions. Collisions may be due to where the legitimate traffic happens to contain the partial sensitive-data fingerprints by coincidence. The collision may increase with shorter shingles, or smaller numbers of partial fingerprints, and may decrease if additional features such as the order of fingerprints are used for detection. A previous large-scale information-retrieval study empirically demonstrated the low rate of this type of collisions in Rabin fingerprint [6], which is a desirable property suggesting low unwanted false alarms in our DLD setting. Collisions due to two distinct shingles generating the same fingerprint are proved to be low [5] and are negligible.

Dynamic data. For protecting dynamically changing data such as source code or documents under constant development or keystroke data, the digests need to be continuously updated for detection, which may not be efficient or practical. We raise the issue of how to efficiently detect dynamic data with a network-based approach as an open problem to investigate by the community.

Space of sensitive data. The space of all text-based sensitive data may be smaller than the space of all possible shingles. Yet, when including non-ASCII sensitive data (text in UTF-8 or binaries), the space of sensitive data can be significantly expanded. Thus, the assumption in Theorem 1 is practical.

Data modification. False negatives (i.e., failure to detect data leak) may also occur due to the data being modified by the leaking application (such as insertion, deletion, and substitution). The new shingles/fingerprints may not resemble the original ones, and cannot be detected. As a result, a packet may evade the detection. In our experiments, we evaluate the impact of several types of data transformation in real world scenarios.

5   Experimental Evaluation

We implement our fuzzy fingerprint framework in Python (version 2.7), including packet collection, shingling, Rabin fingerprinting and fingerprint filter. Our implementation of Rabin fingerprint is based on cyclic redundancy code (CRC). We use the padding scheme mentioned in [23] to handle small inputs, and map our shingle into a sparse fingerprint space. In all experiments, the shingles are in 8-byte, and the fingerprints are in 32-bit (33-bit irreducible polynomials in Rabin fingerprint). We set up a virtual network environment in Oracle VirtualBox, simulating a scenario where the sensitive data is leaked from a local network to the Internet. Valid users' hosts (Windows 7) are put into the local network, which connects to the Internet via a gateway (Linux). The gateway dumps the network traffic and sends it to a DLD server/provider (Linux). Using the sensitive-data fingerprints defined by the users in the local network, the DLD server performs off-line data leak detection. We also set up some servers (FTP, HTTP, etc.) and a hacker's host on the Internet side to which a valid user can connect to.

The DLD server detects the sensitive data within each packet on basis of a stateless filtering system. We define the sensitivity of a packet in Formula 2.

$$S_{packet} = \frac{|\underset{p_d}{\gg} \ddot{S}^* \cap \underset{p_d}{\gg} \tilde{T}|}{min(|S^*|, |\tilde{T}|)} \times \frac{|S^*|}{|\ddot{S}^*|} \tag{2}$$

$\tilde{T}$ is the set of all fingerprints extracted in a packet. S^* is the set of all sensitive fuzzy fingerprints. For each piece of sensitive data, data owner computes S^* and reveals a sample set $\ddot{S}^*$ ($\ddot{S}^* \subseteq S^*$) to the DLD server. The operator $\underset{p_d}{\gg}$ indicates right shifting every fingerprint in a set by p_d bits. The DLD server computes S_{packet} ($S_{packet} \in [0,1]$) and compares it to a threshold $S_{thres} \in (0,1)$. Packets with $S_{packet} \geq S_{thres}$ are marked sensitive.

Without the fuzzification phase, Formula 2 can be simplified to Formula 3. S is the set of all sensitive fingerprints, and $\ddot{S}$ is the revealed fingerprints set.

$$S_{packet} = \frac{|\ddot{S} \cap \tilde{T}|}{min(|S|, |\tilde{T}|)} \times \frac{|S|}{|\ddot{S}|} \tag{3}$$

Our current evaluation results reported are based on the simplified leak detection without the fuzzification phase. Additional experiments assessing the impact of fuzzification on privacy can be found in [28].

The goal of our evaluation is to answer the following questions:

1. Can our solution accurately detect sensitive data-leak in the traffic with low false positives (false alarms) and high true positives (real leaks)?
2. Does using partial sensitive-data fingerprints reduce the detection accuracy in our system?
3. What is the performance advantage of our *fingerprint filter* over traditional Bloom filter equipped with SHA-1?
4. How to choose a proper fuzzy length and make a balance between the privacy need and the number of alerts?
5. Can we experimentally validate the *min-wise independence* property of Rabin fingerprint?

The questions are experimentally addressed and answered in our following sections with the last two answered in our technical report [28].

5.1 Accuracy Evaluation

We generate 20,000 personal financial records as the sensitive data and store them in a text file. The data contains (fictitious) *person name, social security number, credit card number, credit card expiration date*, and *credit card CVV*.

To evaluate the accuracy of our strategy, we perform three separate experiments using the same sensitive dataset:

Exp.1 A user leaks the entire set of sensitive data via FTP by uploading it to a FTP server on the Internet.

Exp.2 (Base Line) The outbound HTTP traffic of Internet-surfing by 20 users are captured (30 minutes per user), and given to the DLD server to analyze, as a base line. No sensitive data (i.e., zero true positive) should be confirmed.

Exp.3 (Base Line) The Enron dataset (2.6 GB data, 150 users' 517,424 emails) as a virtual network traffic is given to the DLD server to analyze. Each virtual network packet created is based on an email in the dataset. No sensitive data (i.e., zero true positive) should be confirmed by the data onwer.

All sensitive fingerprints ($\mathbb{F}_{sens}^D = \mathbb{F}_{sens}^A$) are used in the detection, and the results are shown in Table 1. The first experiment is designed to infer the true positive rate. We manually check each packet and find out that the DLD server detects *all* 651 real sensitive packets (all of them have sensitivity values greater than 0.9). The sensitivity value is less than one, because the layered headers (IP, TCP, HTTP, etc.) in a packet are not sensitive. The next two experiments are designed to estimate the false positive rate. We found that none of the packets has a sensitivity value greater than 0.05, and the average sensitivity is very low. The results indicate that the algorithm performs as expected on plaintext.

Table 1. Mean and standard deviations of the sensitivity per packet in three separate experiments. For Exp.1, the higher sensitivity, the better; for the other two (negative control), the lower sensitivity, the better.

Dataset		Exp.1	Exp.2	Exp.3
$\mathcal{S}_{packet}$	Mean	0.952564	0.000005	0.001849
$\mathcal{S}_{packet}$	STD	0.004011	0.000133	0.002178

The data owner may reveal a subset of sensitive data's fingerprints to the DLD server for detection, as opposed to the entire set. We are particularly interested in measuring the percentage of revealed fingerprints that can be detected in the traffic, assuming that fingerprints are equally likely to be leaked (Given the *subset independence* property, sensitive-data's fingerprints are equally likely to be selected for detection). We reproduce several real-world scenarios where data leaks are caused by human users or software applications.

– In the web-leak scenarios, a user posts sensitive data on wiki (MediaWiki) and blog(WordPress) pages.

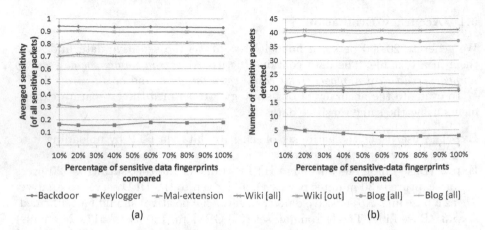

Fig. 2. Performance comparison in terms of (a) the averaged sensitivity and (b) the number of detected sensitive packets. X-axis, $\frac{|\mathbb{F}^D_{sens}|}{|\mathbb{F}^A_{sens}|}$, indicates the percentage of sensitive-data fingerprints revealed to the DLD server and used in the detection. [out] indicates outbound traffic only, while [all] means both outbound and inbound traffic captured and analyzed.

- In the backdoor scenario, a program (*Glacier*) on the user's machine (Windows 7) leaks sensitive data.
- In the email-leak scenario, a malicious Firefox extension *FFsniFF* records the information in sensitive web forms, and emails the data to the attacker.
- In the keylogging scenario, a keylogger *EZRecKb* exports intercepted keystroke values on a user's host. The keylogger records every key stroke, replacing the function keys with labels, such as "[left shift]" in its log. *EZRecKb* connects to a pre-defined SMTP server on the Internet and sends its log periodically. In this experiment, the user manually type the text, simulating typos and corrections, which bring in modifications of the original sensitive data.

In these experiments, the source file of TCP/IP page on wikipedia (24KB in text) is used as the sensitive data. Partial fingerprints are revealed for detection, the sensitivity threshold is set $S_{thres} = 0.05$, and plain set intersection test is used in DETECT operation.

Figure 2 shows the comparison of performance across various size of fingerprints used in the detection, in terms of the averaged sensitivity per packet in (a) and the number of detected sensitive packets in (b). These accuracy values reflect results computed by the data owner after running the POSTPROCESS operation. The results show that the use of partial sensitive-data fingerprints does not much degrade the detection rate compared to the use of full sets of sensitive-data fingerprints.

In Figure 2 (a), the sensitivities of experiments vary due to different levels of modification by the leaking programs, which makes it difficult to detect.

WordPress converts space into "+" when sending the HTTP POST request. Keylogger inserts function-key as labels into the original text as well as typing typos and corrections. In Figure 2 (b), [all] results contain both outbound and inbound traffic and double the real number of sensitive packets in Blog and Wiki scenarios due to HTML fetching of the submitted data.

5.2 Runtime Comparison

Our fingerprint filter implementation is based on the Bloom filter library in Python (Pybloom). We compare the runtime of Bloom filter with SHA-1 and that of fingerprint filter with Rabin fingerprint. For Bloom filters and fingerprint filters, we test their performance with 2, 6, and 10 hash functions. We inspect 100 packets with random content against 10 pieces sensitive data of various length for each point drawn in Figure 3 – there are a total of 1,625,600 fingerprints generated from the traffic and 76,160 pieces of fingerprints from the sensitive data. We show the detection time per packet in Figure 3. The time used to create the filters during the sensitive data initialization is similar to the detection phase. Therefore it is not shown in the paper due to limited space.

The result indicates that fingerprint filters run faster than Bloom filters, which is expected as Rabin fingerprint is easier to compute than SHA-1. The gap is not significant due to the fact that Python uses a virtualization architecture. We have the core hash computations implemented in Python C/C++ extension, but the remaining control flow and function call statements are in pure Python. The performance difference between Rabin fingerprint and SHA-1 is large masked by the runtime overhead spent on non-hash related operations.

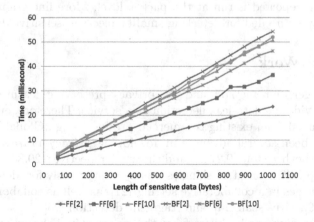

Fig. 3. The overhead of using the filters to detect data-leak, the runtime is per packet (averaged from 100 packets) against all 10 pieces of sensitive data, and the X-axis indicates the amount of sensitive information in a packet

Using fewer hash functions in Bloom filters or fewer polynomials in the fingerprint filters produces more false positives at the DLD provider. The data owner can quickly identify real data leaks from reported leaked instances. This increased collision improves the data privacy. For example, Bloom filter with 10 hashes has a collision (false positive) probability of 0.10%, 6 hashes 1.56%, and 2 hashes 25%. We expect fingerprint filter to provide similar detection accuracy to the plain set intersection realization as reported in Section 5.1. Our fuzzy fingerprint should not be confused with fuzzy Bloom filter [22].

Summary. Our detection rates in terms of the number of sensitive packets found do not decrease much with the decreasing size of fingerprint sets in Figure 2, even when only 10% of the sensitive-data fingerprints are used for detection. It is desirable for both privacy and efficiency considerations to have the data owner reveal as few fingerprints as possible. Our experiments evaluate several noisy conditions such as *data insertion* – for MediaWiki-based leak scenario, traffic contains extra HTML tags in addition to sensitive data, *data deletion* – traffic contains truncated sensitive data (not shown due to space limit), and *data substitution* – for the keylogger and WordPress-based leak scenarios, certain original data elements are replaced in the traffic. Our results indicate that the shingle-and-fingerprint method indeed can tolerate these three types of noises in the traffic to some degree. Our algorithm works well especially in the case where consecutive data blocks are preserved (i.e., *local* data features are preserved) as in the MediaWiki-based leak scenario. When the noises spread across the data and destroy the local features (e.g., replacing every space with another character), the detection rate decreases as expected. The use of shorter shingles mitigates the problem, but may increase false positives. How to improve the noise tolerance property in those conditions remains an open problem. Our fuzzy fingerprint mechanism supports the detection of data-leak at various sizes and granularities. Our evaluation reported is run at the packet level. More fine-grained segment inspection may be needed for detecting smaller pieces of sensitive data leaked.

6   Related Work

Our fuzzy fingerprint method and its privacy-preserving feature enable its adopter to provide the data-leak detection as a service. Therefore, our technique distinguishes itself from existing commercial products (e.g., Global Velocity).

There have been several advances in developing *privacy-aware* collaborative solutions from both system [9,21,27] and theory perspectives [20,34]. Specifically, Rabin fingerprint [24] based on shingles was used previously for identifying similar spam messages in a collaborative setting [21], as well as collaborative worm containment [9], virus scan [14], and fragment detection [25].

Our work fundamentally differs from the above shingle-based studies [9,14] in particular. We consider the new problem of data-leak detection in a unique outsourced setting where the DLD provider is not fully trusted. Such privacy requirement does not exist in the virus-scan paradigm [14], for the virus signatures are non-sensitive. In comparison, data-leak detection is more challenging because of the additional privacy requirement, which limits the amount of data that can be used during the detection and the amount of sensitive information gained by the DLD provider. In the meantime, the provider's detection accuracy cannot be compromised with partial digests based on the sensitive data. Our fuzzy fingerprint method is new, and our work describes the first systematic solution to privacy-preserving data-leak detection with convincing results.

Information leak through outbound web traffic was studied by Borders and Prakash [3]. Both theirs and our work detect suspicious data flow on unencrypted network traffic. Their approach is based on the key observation that network traffic has high regularities and that information (e.g., header data) may be repeated. They proposed an elegant solution that detects any substantial increase in the amount of new information in the traffic. Their anomaly-detection method detects deviations from normal data-flow scenarios, which are captured in rules. In comparison, our work inspects traffic for signatures of sensitive-data and does not require any assumption on the patterns of normal header fields or payload. Furthermore, our solution provides privacy protection of the sensitive data against semi-honest DLD providers. We also give performance evidences indicating the efficiency of our solution in practice.

A black-box approach for data leak detection was proposed in [11], which expands local data tracking to a network-wide environment. It mainly focuses on data confinement and detecting unauthorized sensitive data flow among forked processes. The specific goal makes it different from our approach to detect general data leaks over a network.

In the grid computing environment, the verification of outsourced execution was studied by Du and Goodrich in [12]. The method inserts chaff into input before outsourcing a job and verifies whether the chaff is processed or not after harvest. The threat models and security goals in our outsourced data-leak detection work and in [12] are fundamentally different.

The method of deep packet inspection is also widely used in network intrusion detection system (NIDS), such as SNORT [26] and Bro. They focus on designing and implementing efficient string matching algorithms [1] to handle short and flexible patterns in network traffic. However, NIDS is not designed for various kinds of sensitive data (e.g. long non-duplicated data), it may cause problems (e.g. large amount of states in an automaton) in data leak detection scenarios. On the contrary, our solution is not limited to very special types of sensitive data, and we provide an unique privacy-preserving feature for service outsourcing.

Encrypted traffic, which cannot be directly inspected [30], requires host-based DLD solutions to complement our network-based method. One approach is to instrument the kernel so that the inspection can be performed in the operating system of a host before data is encrypted. Existing approaches involving data flow and taint analysis [37] can be integrated.

An alternative to our approach for privacy-preserving computation is to use cryptographic mechanisms. Secure multi-party computation (SMC) is a research direction pioneered by Yao [35], where participants only learn the outcomes of computation, not the private inputs. Existing SMC solutions can support a wide range of fundamental arithmetic, set, and string operations as well as complex functions such as knapsack computation [36], automated trouble-shooting [15], network event statistics [8], private information retrieval [32], genomic computation [17], private join operations [10], and distributed data mining [16]. The provable privacy guarantees offered by SMC come at a cost in terms of computational complexity and implementation complexity as well. The advantage of our shingle/fingerprint based approach is much more efficient and simpler.

7   Conclusions and Future Work

We proposed a novel privacy-preserving data-leak detection model and its fuzzy fingerprint realization. Using special digests, the exposure of the sensitive data is kept to a minimum during the detection. We have conducted extensive experiments to validate the accuracy, privacy, and efficiency of our solutions. For future work, we plan to focus on designing a host-assisted mechanism for the complete data-leak detection for large-scale organizations.

References

1. Aho, A.V., Corasick, M.J.: Efficient string matching: an aid to bibliographic search. Commun. ACM (1975)
2. Bohman, T., Cooper, C., Frieze, A.M.: Min-wise independent linear permutations. Electr. J. Comb. 7 (2000)
3. Borders, K., Prakash, A.: Quantifying information leaks in outbound web traffic. In: Proceedings of the IEEE Symposium on Security and Privacy (May 2009)
4. Borders, K., Vander Weele, E., Lau, B., Prakash, A.: Protecting confidential data on personal computers with storage capsules. In: USENIX Security Symposium, pp. 367–382. USENIX Association (2009)
5. Broder, A.Z.: Some applications of Rabins fingerprinting method. In: Sequences II: Methods in Communications, Security, and Computer Science, pp. 143–152 (1993)
6. Broder, A.Z.: Identifying and Filtering Near-Duplicate Documents. In: Giancarlo, R., Sankoff, D. (eds.) CPM 2000. LNCS, vol. 1848, pp. 1–10. Springer, Heidelberg (2000)
7. Broder, A.Z., Charikar, M., Frieze, A.M., Mitzenmacher, M.: Min-wise independent permutations. Journal of Computer and System Sciences 60, 630–659 (2000)
8. Burkhart, M., Strasser, M., Many, D., Dimitropoulos, X.: SEPIA: Privacy-preserving aggregation of multi-domain network events and statistics. In: Proceedings of USENIX Security (2010)
9. Cai, M., Hwang, K., Kwok, Y.-K., Song, S., Chen, Y.: Collaborative Internet worm containment. IEEE Security and Privacy 3(3), 25–33 (2005)
10. Carbunar, B., Sion, R.: Joining Privately on Outsourced Data. In: Jonker, W., Petković, M. (eds.) SDM 2010. LNCS, vol. 6358, pp. 70–86. Springer, Heidelberg (2010)
11. Croft, J., Caesar, M.: Towards practical avoidance of information leakage in enterprise networks. In: USENIX HotSec (August 2011)
12. Du, W., Goodrich, M.T.: Searching for High-Value Rare Events with Uncheatable Grid Computing. In: Ioannidis, J., Keromytis, A.D., Yung, M. (eds.) ACNS 2005. LNCS, vol. 3531, pp. 122–137. Springer, Heidelberg (2005)

13. Fawcett, T.W.: ExFILD: A tool for the detection of data exfiltration using entropy and encryption characteristics of network traffic. Thesis submitted to Delaware University
14. Hao, F., Kodialam, M., Lakshman, T.V., Zhang, H.: Fast payload-based flow estimation for traffic monitoring and network security. In: ANCS 2005: Proceedings of the 2005 ACM Symposium on Architecture for Networking and Communications Systems, pp. 211–220. ACM, New York (2005)
15. Huang, Q., Jao, D., Wang, H.J.: Applications of secure electronic voting to automated privacy-preserving troubleshooting. In: Proceedings of the 12th ACM Conference on Computer and Communications Security, CCS (2005)
16. Jagannathan, G., Wright, R.N.: Privacy-preserving distributed k-means clustering over arbitrarily partitioned data. In: Proceedings of the Eleventh ACM SIGKDD International Conference on Knowledge Discovery in Data Mining (2005)
17. Jha, S., Kruger, L., Shmatikov, V.: Towards practical privacy for genomic computation. In: IEEE Symposium on Security and Privacy, pp. 216–230. IEEE Computer Society (2008)
18. Jiang, X., Wang, X., Xu, D.: Stealthy malware detection and monitoring through VMM-based "out-of-the-box" semantic view reconstruction. ACM Trans. Inf. Syst. Secur. 13(2) (2010)
19. Jung, J., Sheth, A., Greenstein, B., Wetherall, D., Maganis, G., Kohno, T.: Privacy Oracle: a system for finding application leaks with black box differential testing. In: Proceedings of Computer and Communications Security, CCS (2008)
20. Kleinberg, J., Papadimitriou, C.H., Raghavan, P.: On the value of private information. In: TARK 2001: Proceedings of the 8th Conference on Theoretical Aspects of Rationality and Knowledge, pp. 249–257. Morgan Kaufmann Publishers Inc., San Francisco (2001)
21. Li, K., Zhong, Z., Ramaswamy, L.: Privacy-aware collaborative spam filtering. IEEE Transactions on Parallel and Distributed systems 20(5) (May 2009)
22. Mayer, C.P.: Bloom filters and overlays for routing in pocket switched networks. In: Proceedings of ACM International Conference on emerging Networking EXperiments and Technologies (CoNEXT) Student Workshop (2009)
23. Rabin, M.O.: Digitalized signatures as intractable as factorization. Tech. Rep. MIT/LCS/TR-212. MIT Laboratory for Computer Science (January 1979)
24. Rabin, M.O.: Fingerprinting by random polynomials. Tech. rep., Center for Research in Computing Technology, Harvard University, TR-15-81 (1981)
25. Ramaswamy, L., Iyengar, A., Liu, L., Douglis, F.: Automatic detection of fragments in dynamically generated web pages. In: Proceedings of the 13th International World Wide Web Conference (WWW) (May 2004)
26. Roesch, M.: Snort-lightweight intrusion detection for networks. In: Proceedings of the 13th Conference on Systems Administration, LISA 1999 (1999)
27. Sarwar, B., Karypis, G., Konstan, J., Riedl, J.: Item-based collaborative filtering recommendation algorithms. In: Proceedings of the 10th International Conference on World Wide Web (2001)
28. Shu, X., Yao, D.: Data leak detection as a service: challenges and solutions. Technical Report TR-12-10, Computer Science, Virginia Tech. (2012)
29. Stefan, D., Wu, C., Yao, D., and Xu, G.: Cryptographic provenance verification for the integrity of keystrokes and outbound network traffic. In Proceedings of the 8th International Conference on Applied Cryptography and Network Security (ACNS) (2010).
30. Varadharajan, V.: Internet filtering issues and challenges. Journal of IEEE Security & Privacy, 62–65 (2010)

31. Wang, Y.-M., Beck, D., Jiang, X., Roussev, R., Verbowski, C., Chen, S., King, S.: Automated web patrol with Strider HoneyMonkeys: Finding web sites that exploit browser vulnerabilities. In: Proceedings of the Annual Symposium on Network and Distributed System Security, NDSS (2006)
32. Yoshida, R., Cui, Y., Sekino, T., Shigetomi, R., Otsuka, A., Imai, H.: Practical searching over encrypted data by private information retrieval. In: Proceedings of the Global Communications Conference, GLOBECOM (2010)
33. Xu, K., Yao, D., Ma, Q., Crowell, A.: Detecting infection onset with behavior-based policies. In: Proceedings of the Fifth International Conference on Network and System Security (NSS) (September 2011)
34. Xu, S.: Collaborative Attack vs. Collaborative Defense. In: Bertino, E., Joshi, J.B.D. (eds.) CollaborateCom 2008. LNICST, vol. 10, pp. 217–228. Springer, Heidelberg (2009)
35. Yao, A.C.: How to generate and exchange secrets. In: Proceedings of the 27th IEEE Symposium on Foundations of Computer Science, pp. 162–167. IEEE Computer Society Press (1986)
36. Yao, D., Frikken, K.B., Atallah, M.J., Tamassia, R.: Private information: to reveal or not to reveal. ACM Trans. Inf. Syst. Secur. 12(1) (2008)
37. Yin, H., Song, D., Egele, M., Kruegel, C., Kirda, E.: Panorama: Capturing system-wide information flow for malware detection and analysis. In: Proceedings of the 14th ACM Conferences on Computer and Communication Security, CCS (2007)

Revealing Cooperating Hosts by Connection Graph Analysis

Jan Jusko[1,2] and Martin Rehak[1,2]

[1] Faculty of Electrical Engineering, Czech Technical University in Prague
{jan.jusko,martin.rehak}@fel.cvut.cz
[2] Cognitive-Security s.r.o., Prague, Czech Republic

Abstract. In this paper we present an algorithm that is able to progressively discover nodes cooperating in a P2P network. Starting from a single known node, we can easily identify other nodes in the peer-to-peer network, through the analysis of widely available and standardized IPFIX (NetFlow) data. Instead of relying on the analysis of content characteristics or packet properties, we monitor connections of known nodes in the network and then progressively discover other nodes through the analysis of their mutual contacts. We show that our method is able to discover all cooperating nodes in many P2P networks. The use of standardized input data allows for easy deployment onto real networks. Moreover, because this approach requires only short processing times, it scales very well in larger and higher speed networks.

1 Introduction

Peer-to-peer networks generate a significant amount of traffic in today's Internet. Peer-to-peer protocols are popular with file sharing applications, are implemented for a VoIP application (Skype) and have also been adopted by malware as a Command & Control (C&C) channel. The ability to observe peer-to-peer networks is useful — it can be used to manage networks more effectively thus providing better quality of service, to detect and mitigate botnets employing P2P for their C&C architecture, etc. Furthermore, peer-to-peer traffic can degrade the performance of anomaly detection techniques. The detection rate can decrease by up to 30% and false positive rate can increase by up to 45% [9].

In this paper we propose a method that tries to exploit the inherent properties of the peer-to-peer networks to find *cooperating* hosts in the network. We consider two hosts to be cooperating if they are part of the same *overlay* network. We find cooperating hosts by observing their mutual peers. It shows that if two hosts are in the same overlay network their sets of peers overlap. Some theoretical ground for this observation in connection with random graphs can be found in [4].

While graphs and graph algorithms are used to detect peer-to-peer networks in [4,10] our approach differs in both the graph representation and the employed graph algorithm. In [4] the graph is created based on all network traffic and only afterwards the likely members of a peer-to-peer botnet are identified by a graph algorithm. In [10] the graph is created based on flows grouped together by

A.D. Keromytis and R. Di Pietro (Eds.): SecureComm 2012, LNICST 106, pp. 241–255, 2013.
© Institute for Computer Sciences, Social Informatics and Telecommunications Engineering 2013

clustering and afterwards its properties are evaluated. Based on the properties the algorithm decides whether the flows were induced by peer-to-peer network or not. Unlike the two, we employ a graph *construction* algorithm and the graph constructed by this algorithm represents a single peer-to-peer network.

In our evaluation we show that the algorithm is able to link hosts cooperating in the usual peer-to-peer networks, such as KAD, Gnutella, BitTorrent and Skype P2P network; and also to link hosts infected by the same malware using peer-to-peer as its C&C channel. Knowing which hosts are engaged in the same overlay with the infected host might help to mitigate the botnet in the network. We believe that this method can be used as a pre-processing layer for packet inspection based detection, where we would first find clusters of hosts in the network and then perform the detection only for few of them and extend the results on the remaining hosts in the cluster.

2   Related Work

There is a plethora of research in the field of peer-to-peer networks. One can find studies of BitTorrent in [17,12,18], BitTorrent's DHT [5], KAD (which is based on Kademlia) in [19,14] and Gnutella in [13,1,15]. There are also many works proposing various improvements to peer-to-peer protocols, but those are not of primary interest here.

Peer-to-peer architecture is now often used by botnets for their C&C. An overview of peer-to-peer botnets and an analysis of one of them can be found in [7]. A peer-to-peer based C&C is, on an example of Kademlia, analyzed theoretically in [8], where the authors show that P2P based C&C is harder to monitor compared to the centralized C&C architecture. Besides that, they also propose several mitigation techniques.

Detection of peer-to-peer networks is another topic often dealt with. There are three main groups of detection methods — packet payload based, flow based methods and graph methods. Within all three groups the detection can be based on the observation of either the specific peer-to-peer network behavior or inherent peer-to-peer networks properties. We do not dive into packet payload based methods in this overview and also skip the methods based on specific peer-to-peer protocol features.

A flow-based method to detect peers using inherent properties of peer-to-peer networks is introduced in [2]. The method itself does not use any protocol-specific features and thus, in theory, might be used for any peer-to-peer network. The authors validate the method on BitTorrent and Gnutella networks.

As an example of graph methods, we can mention one introduced in [3]. The method is agnostic of any specific peer-to-peer protocol features. It creates a connection graph of the peers communicating on a given port and based on the network diameter and number of hosts that function as both client and server determines whether they constitute a peer-to-peer network.

Graphs were used to even greater extent in [10], where they are used to determine whether certain group of flows was generated by the peers in a peer-to-peer

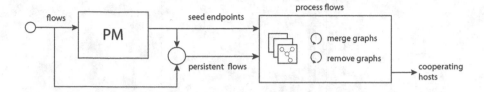

Fig. 1. Schema of the detector. As an input it takes flows from the network which are processed by the Persistence Module (denoted by the PM). The set of seed endpoints is then transferred to the Graph module which processes the flows induced by persistent endpoints and merges and deletes graphs as needed. The output of the detector are sets of endpoints that appear to be cooperating in peer-to-peer networks.

network. The groups of flows are identified based on packet payload inspection, which might limit the potential use of this method. Traffic Dispersion Graphs are also used in [11] to analyze the network traffic and identify unwanted applications.

Peer-to-peer architecture of the botnet C&C is used against the botnet itself to detect its members knowing one starting bot [4]. Their proposed method is similar to ours; it also starts with one known node of a given P2P network and is based on monitoring of mutual contacts. However, they use a rather different graph representation and determine the detected node's confidence after the graph is constructed.

In this work we also use ideas from paper aimed at detecting botnet C&C [6]. The authors focus on observing long term connections that are possible used for botnet C&C. They use whitelists and any long-lasting connection not whitelisted is considered a C&C channel.

3   Detection Method

We propose a detector that takes network traffic as input and finds hosts cooperating in peer-to-peer networks. The detector is composed of two separate modules. At the core of the detector there is the *Graph Module* which constructs graphs around starter nodes, further called *seed nodes*. Nodes are a representation of hosts participating in peer-to-peer networks and each graph represents a single peer-to-peer network. Seed nodes are selected by the *Persistence Module*. The schema of the two is depicted in Fig. 1 and both are further explained in detail in Sections 3.1 and 3.2.

The network traffic processed by the detector is represented by set of *flows*, where flow is a tuple

$$\text{(src ip, src port, dst ip, dst port, protocol)}.$$

Flows can be constructed either from NetFlow data or packet capture.

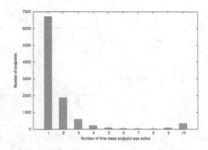

Fig. 2. The histogram shows that majority of endpoints are active only one or two time intervals. Then we can see only a marginal number of endpoints being active between three and nine time steps. All services that run steadily and are regularly used are active all 10 time windows.

The goal of the detection method is to find cooperating hosts in the network. We consider two hosts in the network to be cooperating if they are participating in the same peer-to-peer network. Any host that is participating in an arbitrary peer-to-peer network needs to listen for incoming connections from other peers within the same network — thus it has to keep an open port. Therefore, each peer in a peer-to-peer network can be represented as a tuple *(ip address, port)* which we call *endpoint*.

In reality, the host can participate in more peer-to-peer networks. For each peer-to-peer network it uses, the host needs to keep a listening port open. For each such host, different peer-to-peer networks are represented by independent endpoints, enabling us to separate peer-to-peer networks effectively.

Note that the aforementioned nodes used in the Graph Module and selected by the Persistence Module are in fact endpoints.

Our choice of node representation is different to the one used in [4] because we argue that one host may be taking part in several peer-to-peer networks, e.g. downloading music on BitTorrent, using Skype and at the same time be infected by a P2P botnet. If the authors in [4] chose such a host as a starter node in their graph algorithm, we believe they would suffer a hight false positive rate. We show in the evaluation that using endpoint as the node representation can overcome this issue. In our approach, such a host would simply appear as three distinct endpoints that belong to different graphs.

We would like to note that, while the algorithm could process flows continuously, we process flows in 5-minute batches, i.e. we collect flows for five minutes, which are then processed at once. It follows that observation window size, tryout and ignore periods and memory limit can only be a multiple of 5 minutes.

3.1   Persistence Module

The graph algorithm used in the Graph Module needs a *seed* node around which it constructs the connection graph. The sole purpose of this module is to find such nodes. We already established that nodes representing peers have the form of *endpoints*. There are two criteria for choosing the seed endpoints — the persistence criterion and peers count criterion.

The persistence criterion means that we choose endpoints that are *persistent*, i.e. are sending or receiving data for longer periods of time. During normal network operation, a single host uses many ports to communicate with other hosts. Most of these ports are used only for a short period of time. However, there are some ports that are kept open — these are usually used for listening for incoming connections. We performed a small experiment on the University network, in which we monitored network traffic in ten 5-minute intervals. In the first time interval we recorded all observed endpoints in our network. In the following 9 time intervals we recorded whether the given endpoints were reused. This way, we were able to create a histogram showing the number of endpoints used in either one, two or up to ten time intervals. The histogram can be found in Fig. 2. We can see that most endpoints were used only in one time interval during the experiment. Then the trend is declining with exception of endpoints that were used during all time intervals. We believe that these are the endpoints that represent services (such as web servers or IMAP servers) or active peers of peer-to-peer networks.

To define persistence of endpoints formally, we use simplified method of measuring persistence introduced in [6]. The original method was focused on revealing hidden C&C channels. We, on the other hand, are interested only in persistence of endpoints, no matter where they connect to. We are not trying to detect exact periodicity of connections but an ongoing character of a connection. For this purpose, the regularity of an endpoint activity is observed by a sliding window W, which is split into n bins. This window is called *observation window* and bins are called *measurement windows*. We can write $W = [b_1, b_2, b_3, ..., b_n]$. We then formally define persistence of an endpoint as:

$$p(e, W) = \frac{1}{n} \sum_{i=1}^{n} \mathbf{1}_{e, b_i}$$

where e is the endpoint for which the persistence is calculated, W is the observation window and function $\mathbf{1}_{e, b_i}$ is equal to 1 if at least one connection to or from the endpoint e occurred during the measurement window b_i, otherwise it is equal to 0.

The persistence calculation itself is based on three parameters — *measurement window size*, which states how long the connections are recorded into one bin before proceeding to another, *observation window size*, which determines how many bins there are in the observation window and the *threshold persistence p^**. This parameter determines how many seed endpoints are passed to the Graph Module.

When moving to the next observation window, we calculate persistence for all endpoints. We select those with the persistence exceeding the threshold p^* and apply the second criterion, which is the number of contacted peers during the last observation window. We assume that any peer communicates with more than one other peer in the peer-to-peer network. Therefore, from the persistent endpoints

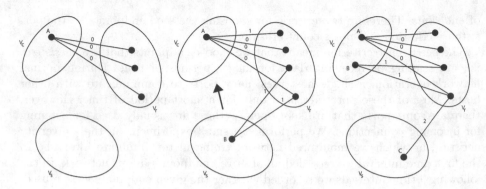

Fig. 3. Algorithm illustration. First we have a seed node A with 3 recorded contacts. In the second time interval, another node, B, is observed, sharing two mutual contacts with A. If we consider $K = 2$, then in the third step, node B is already moved to the V_c. Moreover, the algorithm detected yet another node, which has only one mutual contact with a node from V_c. Note that the weights of the edges in the graph are determined by the time step in which they occurred most recently.

we select those that had at least two peers in the last observation window. This effectively removes long lasting connection between only two peers. These could be clients downloading large files from the Internet or users connecting to other computers via Remote Desktop or SSH.

In the end, only endpoints that exceed the persistence threshold and have at least two peers in the last observation window are passed to the Graph Module as the seed endpoints.

3.2   The Graph Module

The graph module is responsible for

- constructing graphs around the seed endpoints received from the persistence module,
- merging similar graphs,
- removing graphs that failed to find any cooperating host for the given seed endpoint.

Before describing the Graph Module in detail, where we work with the term *graph* extensively, we first introduce its formal definition. Graphs can be used to represent a P2P network, where vertices represent nodes participating in the P2P network and edges represent connections between two nodes participating in the P2P network. To detect the nodes of a P2P overlay network within our network we use a 3-partite weighted graph

$$G = (V, E, w)$$

where

$$V = V_c \cup V_s \cup V_r.$$

V_c is a set of nodes from our network we *believe* are participating in the P2P network, V_s is a set of nodes from our network that we *suspect* are participating in the P2P network and V_r is a set of nodes from outside of our network communicating with nodes from $V_c \cup V_s$. E is a set of edges. Function w assigns each edge a weight — a value equal to the time when the edge was added to the graph. We ignore all intra-network communication and cannot see communication between the nodes that are outside of our network. Therefore the graph we define is indeed a 3-partite weighted graph. This also implies that $G = ((V_c \cup V_s) \cup V_r, E)$ can be considered a bipartite graph.

The algorithm for constructing graph around a seed node is explained later in this section. Graph Module, just like the Persistence Module processes flows collected in the network. Here, however, we process only flows that originate from or are directed towards a persistent endpoint. We do that because we assume, just like in the Persistence Module, that all endpoints representing peers in an arbitrary peer-to-peer network are persistent. Then removing flows assigned to non-persistent endpoints does not compromise the ability of the module to find cooperating peers.

However, before the module can construct any graph, it first needs to receive seed endpoints from the Persistence module. The persistence module feeds seed endpoints to the graph module periodically. When the module receives the first set of seed endpoints it creates a graph for each of them. For every subsequent set of received seed endpoints it checks whether given seed endpoints are already recorded in any of the graphs. For those that are not, it creates new graphs. This way we prevent the creation of duplicate unnecessary graphs.

Since we expect this method to find cooperating endpoints (which are believed to be persistent) we should, after some time, construct graphs that are very similar and describe the same peer-to-peer network despite starting from different seed endpoint. There is no point in keeping such graphs separate so the module joins them together. It rises a question though, how to define "similarity" of two graphs. Two graphs that represent the same P2P network should have similar sets V_c by some measure. However, since both graphs were iteratively constructed from different seed nodes, they do not necessarily contain similar sets of edges or set V_r. Therefore we define *similarity* of two graphs G_1 and G_2 as

$$s(G_1, G_2) = \frac{\mid V_c^{G_1} \cap V_c^{G_2} \mid}{min(\mid V_c^{G_1} \mid, \mid V_c^{G_2} \mid)}$$

where $V_c^{G_1}$ resp. $V_c^{G_2}$ represents V_c of graph G_1 resp. G_2. This definition ensures that similarity of two graphs G_1, G_2 is high (in fact equal to 1) even in the case when $V_c^{G_1} \subset V_c^{G_2}$ and $\mid V_c^{G_1} \mid \ll \mid V_c^{G_2} \mid$. This is a case of two graphs that represent the same P2P network but one of them is much smaller (either because it was created later or because the seed was not as "active" as the seed of the other graph). We merge two graphs if their similarity is greater than the *merge overlap threshold*, which is another algorithm parameter.

There is, of course, a possibility that the graph algorithm will not be able to find any cooperating hosts for certain seed. This might happen when the seed is the only peer of the respective peer-to-peer overlay in the network, or when the seed node around which we tried to construct a graph was a service, e.g. an email server. If any graph fails to find at least one cooperating endpoint in the network for certain period of time called the *tryout period* it is removed from the module. Even thought we remove the graph, it might be recreated next time the seed nodes are received from the persistence module, because the endpoint might be active despite the fact it has no cooperating nodes. Therefore we define another time parameter, the *ignore period*, that determines how long after removing a graph with a specific seed node, this seed node may not be used to construct another graph. We do not want to ignore the given seed endpoint forever, because service using the port may change or a cooperating peer might appear later.

The Graph Algorithm. As we already mentioned, P2P networks can be represented by a graph. We try to exploit this graph structure to find other participating P2P nodes using one starter node. To achieve this, we traverse the edges of the graph which is constructed on the basis of observed network communication. Since P2P overlay networks are dynamically changing, so should the graph that represents a P2P overlay network.

The detection algorithm monitors network traffic and constructs (modifies) the graph defined in the beginning of the section based on the observed network activity in the following way:

- the graph starts with only the seed node $n \in V_c$,
- when a network connection occurs between any node $n \in V_c$ and some node m outside of our network then there are two options:
    - $m \in V_r$ already; in this case we just update $w(\{m, n\}) = current\_time()$,
    - $m \notin V_r$ yet; in this case we add m to V_r and $\{m, n\}$ to E and set $w(\{m, n\}) = current\_time()$.
- when a network connection occurs between any local node not yet in the graph and some node $m \in V_r$, we add n to V_s, add $\{m, n\}$ to E and set $w(\{m, n\}) = current\_time()$,
- any edge $e \in E$ for which $t_{now} - w(e) > t_L$ is removed from the graph,
- any node $n \in V$ is removed from the graph when it does not have any incident edge (it has a zero degree),
- if $(\exists m \in V_s)(\exists n \in V_c)(| Adj(m) \cap Adj(n) | > K)$ then we move m from V_s to V_c, where $Adj(n)$ is a set of vertices adjacent to n.

The output of the algorithm is the set V_c which at any given moment contains a list of active P2P nodes in the local network. There are two parameters used in this algorithm:

- a *memory limit*, t_L, which specifies how long a recorded connection (an edge in the graph) is kept in memory,
- a *mutual contacts overlap threshold*, K, which specifies how many mutual adjacent vertices a node from V_s needs to have with any node from V_c to be moved to V_c, i.e. to consider it a P2P node.

First three steps of such an algorithm can be found in Fig. 3.

Table 1. List of peer-to-peer networks with their respective clients installed on the client hosts in the control set. Last column specifies how many hosts is running given client application.

network	client application	hosts
Skype	official client	18
BitTorrent	μTorrent	26
KAD	eMule	15
Gnutella	Phex	18

4   Evaluation

4.1   Experiment Setup

To evaluate the detector we deployed it in the University network consisting of approximately 1000 hosts. Since we did not have access to all the computers and could not establish the ground truth concerning the network activity, i.e. what service did every endpoint in the local network belong to, we chose 155 hosts from two subnets for a small control set.

The first subnet contains 36 hosts of which 18 are running Windows XP, 15 are running Windows 7 and 3 are running Linux. We refer to these hosts as *client hosts*. The client hosts were engaged in casual Internet activity, such as browsing the web, working with email, listening to music, watching videos, sharing files, etc. On these we also installed client applications for several P2P networks, where one host can participate in several peer-to-peer networks. The list of installed client applications can be found in Table 1.

To examine whether the algorithm is capable of linking hosts participating in a botnet, we infected three computers with *Trojan.Sirefef-6* malware, which uses peer-to-peer for its C&C [16]. To ease up the determination of the ground truth for the client hosts we set all client applications belonging to the same peer-to-peer network to use the same port. This has no effect on detection capabilities of our algorithm.

The second subnet contains servers - we refer to this hosts as *server hosts*. None of the them is running any of the aforementioned applications. They run many services, such as web servers, IMAP/POP services and other.

We were collecting network traffic for 20 hours during a working day. The traffic was collected in form of NetFlow data by a network probe. Flows were always collected for five minutes and then sent in a batch to our algorithm. Number of flows within one 5 minute interval ranges from 37000 at night to 240000 during peak hours. To establish the ground truth for the client hosts in the control set, we collected `netstat` information on each client host every five minutes. This was necessary since many applications tend to open more ports than the main port. This way we were able to determine what application did every endpoint of the client hosts belong to. Ground truth for the server hosts was determined in cooperation with their administrators.

Table 2. Parameters and their values used in the experiment

parameter	values
persistence threshold	$0.5, 0.8$
mutual contacts overlap threshold	$3, 4, 5, 6$
memory limit	$60, 90, 120$ minutes
merge overlap threshold	$0.3, 0.5, 0.7$

Some of the parameters mentioned in the previous sections do not have any impact on detection performance. They are used to tune the memory and processing power requirements of the detector. These are tryout period, ignore period, and measurement and observation window sizes. In our experiments we fixed value of tryout period to 1 hour. Ignore period was set to 1 hour as well, however, every consecutive time the graph around a certain seed node is removed because it failed to find cooperating peers, the ignore period for the given seed increases by 1 hour. Observation window size is 5 minutes, which is also the smallest value we can set (because we process flows in 5-minute batches). Resorting to higher values would extend the time an endpoint needs to become persistent. Measurement window size was chosen in accordance with [4].

The remaining parameters and their values used in the experiment are summed up in Table 2.

4.2   Evaluation Methodology

Since the algorithm runs continually and modifies the graphs according to the changes in the network (hosts joining/leaving peer-to-peer networks) we need to choose a point in time when we evaluate the detection performance. In our control set we started the client application and let them run for several hours. Therefore we decided to choose the point when the numbers of detected nodes of the peer-to-peer networks in their respective main graphs stabilize, i.e. the numbers are same for at least three consecutive time intervals.

It is possible that endpoints participating in the same peer-to-peer network will be spread in several graphs. Therefore we need to choose the *main* graph - the graph that managed to link most of the cooperating hosts from the given peer-to-peer network. We use this graph for the performance evaluation.

Please note that the algorithm does not detect any endpoint until it receives first data from the Persistence Module.

Once we choose the point in time and graphs representing the peer-to-peer networks, we determine the *detection rate* and number of *false positives*.

Client applications used for various peer-to-peer networks differ in usage of ports. Some applications use more than 1 listening port, a typical example being Skype. Another difference is in the number of used ephemeral ports. While clients for peer-to-peer networks based on UDP use only one or small number of ports, clients for TCP based peer-to-peer networks are very eager in using ephemeral ports, e.g. Bit-Torrent. For each peer-to-peer network and its client application we are interested

Table 3. Detection rate for various *memory limit* and *mutual contacts threshold* values. Memory limit values are intentionally chosen very lower so that the relationship between the two is obvious. Higher mutual contacts threshold may require longer memory limit in order to attain "comparable" detection rate. Memory limit is in first row in minutes, mutual contacts threshold in the first column.

(a) Skype

	5	10	15	25	45
2	94.4	94.4	94.4	94.4	94.4
3	94.4	94.4	94.4	94.4	94.4
4	94.4	94.4	94.4	94.4	94.4
5	94.4	94.4	94.4	94.4	94.4
6	72.2	83.3	94.4	94.4	94.4
7	16.7	22.2	22.2	27.8	83.3
8	16.7	16.7	22.2	22.2	38.9

(b) BitTorrent's DHT

	5	10	15	25	45
2	96.2	100	100	100	100
3	53.8	76.9	92.3	100	100
4	34.6	57.7	69.2	88.5	100
5	34.6	42.3	61.5	73.1	92.3
6	34.6	42.3	57.7	65.4	84.6
7	34.6	42.3	42.3	65.4	76.9
8	34.6	42.3	42.3	61.5	65.4

in the main listening port. In some graphs we may observe several endpoints associated with a single host, especially if they represent a peer-to-peer network using TCP as transport protocol. In a rigorous understanding, these endpoints are *true positives* because they are used for the communication in the peer-to-peer overlay. To keep the things simple, we ignore all endpoints that are in fact true positives but are not associated with the main listening port. If we did not ignore such endpoints we would have issues with the detection rate calculation as we do not know the exact number of ephemeral ports used by a client.

Identification of false positives differs among the peer-to-peer networks. For KAD, Gnutella, BitTorrent and Trojan.Sirefef-6 we consider every detected endpoint not associated with the host from the control set and the respective listening port of the client application to be a false positive. We can do so since these peer-to-peer networks are used only rarely at the University. Using this approach we determine the upper bound of the false positives detected by our algorithm. We cannot do the same with Skype as it is very popular at the University. Therefore we evaluate false and true positives only on the control set.

4.3   Evaluation Results

We evaluated the algorithm performance for all combination of parameters, summed up in Table 2. Before we move on to the actual results of the detection we describe the effect of the particular parameters on the detection performance of the algorithm.

Increasing the persistence threshold in general lowers the number of graphs in the Graph Module. This is important for the performance consideration, especially on huge networks. Having too many graphs in the model can result in exhaustion of the system resources. To focus on detection performance, rising the persistence threshold lowers the number of endpoints induced by the client application but not associated with the main port. It does not seem to have any significant impact on false positives rate.

Table 4. Parameters used for the evaluation of the algorithm. These provide the best results, however they are not the only choice of parameters that attains the same detection performance.

parameter	value
persistence threshold	0.8
mutual contacts overlap threshold	5
memory limit	90 minutes
merge overlap threshold	0.3

Choice of memory limit has a minor impact on false positives rate — the rise of the memory limit is accompanied by the rise of the false positive rate. On the other hand, it can have severe impact on the detection rate (explanation of the connection to mutual contacts overlap threshold, will be introduced shortly). This parameter also impacts memory requirements, high memory limit result in increased memory requirements of the algorithm.

Mutual contacts overlap threshold is the parameter that we believe has the greatest impact on the false positive rate. Increase in its value is accompanied by the drop of the detection rate. There is some boundary (determined by the peer-to-peer protocol) exceeding which the detection rate would drop considerably. This can be easily seen in Table 3a. When using memory limit of 5 minutes, the change from mutual contacts overlap threshold from 6 to 7 causes a significant drop in the detection rate. However, under this limit value, we can attain the same detection rate for various values of mutual contacts overlap threshold just by adjusting the memory limit.

There is a connection between the memory limit and mutual contacts overlap threshold parameters. Rising the mutual contacts threshold while fixing the memory limit lowers the detection rate. On the other hand, raising the memory limit while keeping the mutual contacts threshold fixed improves the detection rate. This is best seen in Table 3.

We did not notice any impact of the merge overlap threshold value on the detection results.

We do not present results for all combinations of parameters, since there are too many of them and many bring the same results. We rather present only the results for one combination of parameters that brings the best results. For the parameters please refer to Table 4.

Detection Rate. The algorithm was able to find all cooperating hosts in Skype, BitTorrent, Kademlia and Trojan.Sirefef-6 peer-to-peer networks. On the other hand, detection rate for Gnutella was considerably lower — 44%.

While Gnutella uses TCP protocol for its communication, Skype, Kademlia and Trojan.Sirefef-6 all use UDP for their peer-to-peer overlay. Finally, newest BitTorrent protocol implementations use both UDP and TCP. In BitTorrent, TCP is used for communication in *swarms*, i.e. the communities created to share files listed in a single torrent file and UDP is used in BitTorrent's DHT implementation, which is utilized for distributed tracker functionality.

As was mentioned before, the algorithm attained 100% detection rate for Bit-Torrent clients. However, these were detected based on BitTorrent's DHT implementation which is used for distributed tracker functionality and not based on the BitTorrent protocol. The question is whether the algorithm would be able to detect BitTorrent clients that do not use DHT. To verify the detection performance on clients using only BitTorrent protocol without any DHT we ran the algorithm again with the same parameters, while ignoring all UDP connections from or to the μTorrent listening port (effectively removing the DHT traffic).

Here we need to realize the difference between the BitTorrent protocol and the other peer-to-peer protocols in this evaluation. While other peer-to-peer networks maintain an overlay network at all times, the BitTorrent client is not part of any overlay (if it is not using DHT) unless it wants to download a file and joins a swarm. Therefore, when we talk about detecting cooperating hosts for BitTorrent using only the BitTorrent protocol, we mean hosts that are members of the same swarm.

With such setting, we were able to detect all peers cooperating in the same BitTorrent swarm. This shows that even without DHT we were able to find cooperating hosts and that the algorithm is not restricted only to the UDP-based peer-to-peer networks and can be effective for TCP-based peer-to-peer networks as well.

Detecting Gnutella peers seems to be much harder. The algorithm found only 8 peers which constitutes around 44% of all peers. Gnutella uses TCP for communication. Unlike protocols that use UDP and the listening port is used for both incoming and outgoing connections, Gnutella uses the listening port only for incoming connections. Outgoing connections are sent through an ephemeral ports that are assigned and changed at the discretion of the operating system. That makes the detection much harder. Gnutella has two types of peers, *leaf nodes* and *ultrapeers*. Leaf nodes only connect to the ultrapeers and ultrapeers connect to both ultrapeers and leaf nodes. Ultrapeers have higher frequency of connections with other peers and are thus more likely to be linked together. Most of the cooperating hosts found for the Gnutella network were in fact ultrapeers.

The important thing to note here is that linking cooperating hosts (with the exception of BitTorrent peers detection without DHT) did not require any user activity besides connecting (and logging in) to the network.

False Positive Rate. For four of the peer-to-peer networks we experimented on we encountered no false positives. These were Skype, KAD, Gnutella and Trojan.Sirefef-6. Only one false positive was found when linking cooperating hosts in the BitTorrent's DHT network. Due to the low number of false positives we refrain from calculating the false positive rate, since it would only have a negligible value.

5   Conclusion

In this paper we presented a novel method that links cooperating hosts in the same peer-to-peer network by exploiting the inherent properties of peer-to-peer networks. It tries to reconstruct the peer-to-peer overlay based on the observed connection in the network.

The method managed to detect all cooperating peers in most of the networks and attained almost zero false positive rate.

Since the method does not use neither packet payloads nor flow statistics, it is a viable option for deployment on the backbone network where computationally expensive models are not an option.

We believe that this method presents a viable approach to detecting peers in overlay networks, both well known file sharing networks and specialized peer-to-peer networks used by botnets as a C&C channel.

Acknowledgement. This material is based upon work supported by the ITC-A of the US Army under Contract W911NF-12-1-0028 and by ONR Global under the Department of the Navy Grant N62909-11-1-7036. Also supported by Czech Ministry of Interior grant number VG2VS/189.

References

1. Acosta, W., Chandra, S.: Trace Driven Analysis of the Long Term Evolution of Gnutella Peer-to-Peer Traffic. In: Uhlig, S., Papagiannaki, K., Bonaventure, O. (eds.) PAM 2007. LNCS, vol. 4427, pp. 42–51. Springer, Heidelberg (2007)
2. Bartlett, G., Heidemann, J., Papadopoulos, C.: Inherent behaviors for on-line detection of peer-to-peer file sharing. In: IEEE Global Internet Symposium, pp. 55–60 (May 2007)
3. Constantinou, F., Mavrommatis, P.: Identifying known and unknown peer-to-peer traffic. In: Fifth IEEE International Symposium on Network Computing and Applications, NCA 2006, pp. 93–102 (July 2006)
4. Coskun, B., Dietrich, S., Memon, N.: Friends of an enemy: identifying local members of peer-to-peer botnets using mutual contacts. In: Proceedings of the 26th Annual Computer Security Applications Conference on ACSAC 2010, pp. 131–140. ACM, New York (2010)
5. Falkner, J., Piatek, M., John, J.P., Krishnamurthy, A., Anderson, T.: Profiling a million user dht. In: Proceedings of the 7th ACM SIGCOMM Conference on Internet Measurement, IMC 2007, pp. 129–134. ACM, New York (2007)
6. Giroire, F., Chandrashekar, J., Taft, N., Schooler, E., Papagiannaki, D.: Exploiting Temporal Persistence to Detect Covert Botnet Channels. In: Balzarotti, D. (ed.) RAID 2009. LNCS, vol. 5758, pp. 326–345. Springer, Heidelberg (2009)
7. Grizzard, J.B., Sharma, V., Nunnery, C., Kang, B.B., Dagon, D.: Peer-to-peer botnets: overview and case study. In: Proceedings of the First Conference on First Workshop on Hot Topics in Understanding Botnets, HotBots 2007, p. 1. USENIX Association, Berkeley (2007)
8. Ha, D.T., Yan, G., Eidenbenz, S., Ngo, H.Q.: On the effectiveness of structural detection and defense against p2p-based botnets. In: DSN, pp. 297–306. IEEE (2009)
9. Haq, I.U., Ali, S., Khan, H., Khayam, S.A.: What Is the Impact of P2P Traffic on Anomaly Detection? In: Jha, S., Sommer, R., Kreibich, C. (eds.) RAID 2010. LNCS, vol. 6307, pp. 1–17. Springer, Heidelberg (2010)

10. Iliofotou, M., Kim, H.-C., Faloutsos, M., Mitzenmacher, M., Pappu, P., Varghese, G.: Graption: A graph-based p2p traffic classification framework for the internet backbone. Comput. Netw. 55(8), 1909–1920 (2011)
11. Iliofotou, M., Pappu, P., Faloutsos, M., Mitzenmacher, M., Singh, S., Varghese, G.: Network monitoring using traffic dispersion graphs (tdgs). In: Proceedings of the 7th ACM SIGCOMM Conference on Internet Measurement, IMC 2007, pp. 315–320. ACM, New York (2007)
12. Kryczka, M., Cuevas, R., Guerrero, C., Azcorra, A.: Unrevealing the structure of live bittorrent swarms: Methodology and analysis. In: 2011 IEEE International Conference on Peer-to-Peer Computing (P2P), August 31-September 2, pp. 230–239 (2011)
13. Li, C., Chen, C.: Topology analysis of gnutella by large scale mining. In: International Conference on Communication Technology, ICCT 2006, pp. 1–4 (November 2006)
14. Liu, X., Li, Y., Li, Z., Cheng, X.: Social Network Analysis on KAD and Its Application. In: Du, X., Fan, W., Wang, J., Peng, Z., Sharaf, M.A. (eds.) APWeb 2011. LNCS, vol. 6612, pp. 327–332. Springer, Heidelberg (2011)
15. Evangelos, P.: Markatos, Tracing a large-scale peer to peer system: An hour in the life of gnutella. In: Proceedings of the 2nd IEEE/ACM International Symposium on Cluster Computing and the Grid, CCGRID 2002, p. 65. IEEE Computer Society, Washington, DC (2002)
16. McNamee, K.: Malware analysis report - botnet: Zeroaccess/sirefef (February 2012), http://www.kindsight.net/sites/default/files/ Kindsight_Malware_Analysis-ZeroAcess-Botnet-final.pdf
17. Móczár, Z., Molnár, S.: Characterization of BitTorrent Traffic in a Broadband Access Network. In: Szabó, R., Zhu, H., Imre, S., Chaparadza, R. (eds.) AccessNets/Selfmagicnets 2010. LNICST, vol. 63, pp. 176–183. Springer, Heidelberg (2011)
18. Qi, J., Zhang, H., Ji, Z., Yun, L.: Analyzing bittorrent traffic across large network. In: 2008 International Conference on Cyberworlds, pp. 759–764 (September 2008)
19. Steiner, M., En-Najjary, T., Biersack, E.W.: A global view of kad. In: Proceedings of the 7th ACM SIGCOMM Conference on Internet Measurement, IMC 2007, pp. 117–122. ACM, New York (2007)

New Multi-dimensional Sorting Based K-Anonymity Microaggregation for Statistical Disclosure Control

Abdun Naser Mahmood[1], Md. Enamul Kabir[1], and Abdul K. Mustafa[2]

[1] School of Engineering and Information Technology,
University of New South Wales Australian Defence Force Academy
Canberra, ACT 2600, Australia
[2] University of Canberra, ACT, Australia
{Abdun.Mahmood,m.kabir}@unsw.edu.au, abdul.mustafa@jcu.edu.au

Abstract. In recent years, there has been an alarming increase of online identity theft and attacks using personally identifiable information. The goal of privacy preservation is to de-associate individuals from sensitive or *microdata* information. Microaggregation techniques seeks to protect microdata in such a way that can be published and mined without providing any private information that can be linked to specific individuals. Microaggregation works by partitioning the microdata into groups of at least k records and then replacing the records in each group with the centroid of the group. An optimal microaggregation method must minimize the information loss resulting from this replacement process. The challenge is how to minimize the information loss during the microaggregation process. This paper presents a new microaggregation technique for Statistical Disclosure Control (SDC). It consists of two stages. In the first stage, the algorithm sorts all the records in the data set in a particular way to ensure that during microaggregation very dissimilar observations are never entered into the same cluster. In the second stage an optimal microaggregation method is used to create k-anonymous clusters while minimizing the information loss. It works by taking the sorted data and simultaneously creating two distant clusters using the two extreme sorted values as seeds for the clusters. The performance of the proposed technique is compared against the most recent microaggregation methods. Experimental results using benchmark datasets show that the proposed algorithm has the lowest information loss compared with a basket of techniques in the literature.

Keywords: Privacy, Microaggregation, Microdata protection, k-anonymity, Disclosure control.

1 Introduction

In recent years, the phenomenal advance of technological developments in information technology enable government agencies and corporations to accumulate

A.D. Keromytis and R. Di Pietro (Eds.): SecureComm 2012, LNICST 106, pp. 256–272, 2013.
© Institute for Computer Sciences, Social Informatics and Telecommunications Engineering 2013

an enormous amount of personal data for analytical purposes. These agencies and organizations often need to release individual records (microdata) for research and other public benefit purposes. This propagation has to be in accordance with laws and regulations to avoid the propagation of confidential information. In other words, microdata should be published in such a way that preserve the privacy of the individuals. Microdata protection in statistical databases has recently become a major societal concern and has been intensively studied in recent years. Microaggregation for Statistical Disclosure Control (SDC) is a family of methods to protect microdata from individual identification. SDC seeks to protect microdata in such a way that can be published and mined without providing any private information that can be linked to specific individuals. SDC is often applied to statistical databases before they are released for public use.

To protect personal data from individual identification, SDC is often applied before the data are released for analysis [2,26]. The purpose of microdata SDC is to alter the original microdata in such a way that the statistical analysis from the original data and the modified data are similar and the disclosure risk of identification is low. As SDC requires suppressing or altering the original data, the quality of data and the analysis results can be damaged. Hence, SDC methods must find a balance between data utility and personal confidentiality.

Various methods for Microaggregation has been proposed in the literature for protecting microdata [3,4,7,8,11,12,20,23]. The basic idea of microaggregation is to partition a dataset into mutually exclusive groups of at least k records prior to publication, and then publish the centroid over each group instead of individual records. The resulting anonymized dataset satisfies k-anonymity [18], requiring each record in a dataset to be identical to at least $(k-1)$ other records in the same dataset. As releasing microdata about individuals poses privacy threat due to the privacy-related attributes, called quasi-identifiers, both k-anonymity and microaggregation only consider the quasi-identifiers. Microaggregation is traditionally restricted to numeric attributes in order to calculate the centroid of records, but also has been extended to handle categorical and ordinal attributes [4,8,19]. In this paper we propose a microaggregated method that is also applicable to numeric attributes.

The effectiveness of a microaggregation method is measured by calculating its information loss. A lower information loss implies that the anonymized dataset is less distorted from the original dataset, and thus provides better data quality for analysis. k- anonymity [17,18,21] provides sufficient protection of personal confidentiality of microdata, while ensuring the quality of the anonymized dataset, an effective microaggregation method should incur as little information loss as possible. In order to be useful in practice, the dataset should keep as much informative as possible. Hence, it is necessary to seriously consider the tradeoff between privacy and information loss. To minimize the information loss due to microaggregation, all records are partitioned into several groups such that each group contains at least k similar records, and then the records in each group are replaced by their corresponding mean such that the values of each variable are the same. Such similar groups are known as clusters. In the context of data mining, clustering is a useful technique that partitions records into groups such that records within a group are similar to each other, while records in different groups are most distinct from one another. Thus, microaggregation can be seen as a clustering problem with constraints on the size of the clusters.

Many microaggregation methods derive from traditional clustering algorithms. For example, Domingo-Ferrer and Mateo-Sanz [3] proposed univariate and multivariate k-Ward algorithms that extend the agglomerative hierarchical clustering method of Ward et al. [24]. Domingo-Ferrer and Torra [6,7] proposed a microaggregation method based on the fuzzy c-means algorithm [1], and Laszlo and Mukherjee [13] extended the standard minimum spanning tree partitioning algorithm for microaggregation [27]. All of these microaggregation methods build all clusters gradually but simultaneously. There are some other methods for microaggregation that have been proposed in the literature that build one/two cluster(s) at a time. Notable examples include Maximum Distance [15], Diameter-based Fixed-Size microaggregation and centroid-based Fixed-size microaggregation [13], Maximum Distance to Average Vector (MDAV) [8], MHM [9] and the Two Fixed Reference Points method [28]. Most recently, Lin et al. [29] proposed a density-based microaggregation method that forms clusters by the descending order of their densities, and then fine-tunes these clusters in reverse order.

The reminder of this paper is organized as follows. We introduce the problem of microaggregation in Section 2. Section 3 introduces the basic concept of microaggregation. Section 4 reviews previous microaggregation methods. We present a brief description of our proposed microaggregation method in Section 5. Section 6 shows experimental results of the proposed method. Finally, concluding remarks are included in Section 7.

2 Problem Statement

The algorithms for microaggregation works by partitioning the microdata into groups, where within groups the records are homogeneous but between groups the records are heterogeneous so that information loss is low. The similar groups are also called clusters. The level of privacy required is controlled by a security parameter k, the minimum number of records in a cluster. In essence, the parameter k specifies the maximum acceptable disclosure risk. Once a value for k has been selected by the data protector, the only job left is to maximize data utility. Maximizing utility can be achieved by microaggregating optimally, i.e. with minimum within-groups variability loss. So the main challenge in microaggregation is how to minimize the information loss during the clustering process. Although plenty of work has been done, to maximize the data utility by forming the clusters, this is not yet sufficient in terms of information loss. So more research needs to be done to form the clusters such that the information loss is as low as possible. This paper analyses the problem with a new multi-dimensional sorting algorithm such that the information loss is minimal.

Observing this challenge, this work presents a new clustering-based method for microaggregation, where a new multi-dimensional sorting algorithm is used in the first stage. In the second stage two distant clusters are made simultaneously in a systematic way. According to the second stage, sort all records in ascending order by using a sorting algorithm in the first stage explained in Section 5) so that the first record and the last record are most distant to each other. Form a cluster with the first record and its $(k-1)$ nearest records and another cluster with the last record and its $(k-1)$ nearest records. Sort the remaining records $((n-2k)$, if dataset contains n records) by using the same sorting algorithm and continue to build pair clusters at the same time by using the first and the last record as seeds until some specified records remain. Finally form one/two cluster(s) depending on the remaining records. Thus all clusters produced in this way contain k records except the last cluster that may contain at the most $(2k-1)$ records. Performance of the proposed method is compared against the most recent widely used microaggregation methods. The experimental results show that the proposed microaggregation method outperforms the recent methods in the literature.

3 Background

Microdata protection through microaggregation has been intensively studied in recent years. Many techniques and methods have been proposed to deal with this problem. In this section we describe some fundamental concepts of microaggregation.

When we microaggregate data we should keep in mind two goals: data utility and preserving privacy of individuals. For preserving the data utility we should introduce as little noise as possible into the data and preserving privacy data should be sufficiently modified in such a way that it is difficult for an adversary to reidentify the corresponding individuals. Figure 1 shows an example of microaggregated data where the individuals in each cluster are replaced by the corresponding cluster mean. The figure shows that after aggregating the chosen elements, it is impossible to distinguish them, so that the probability of linking any respondent is inversely proportional to the number of aggregated elements.

Consider a microdata set T with p numeric attributes and n records, where each record is represented as a vector in a p-dimensional space. For a given positive integer $k \leq n$, a microaggregation method partitions T into g clusters, where each cluster contains at least k records (to satisfy k-anonymity), and then replaces the records in each cluster with the centroid of the cluster. Let n_i denote the number of records in the ith cluster, and $x_{ij}, 1 \leq j \leq n_i$, denote the jth record in the ith cluster. Then, $n_i \geq k$ for $i = 1$ to g, and $\sum_{i=1}^{g} n_i = n$. The centroid of the ith cluster, denoted by $\bar{x}_i$ is calculated as the average vector of all the records in the ith cluster.

In the same way, the centroid of T, denoted by $\bar{x}$, is the average vector of all the records in T. Information loss is used to quantify the amount of information of a dataset that is lost after applying a microaggregation method. In this paper we use the most common definition of information loss by Domingo-Ferrer and Mateo-Sanz [3] as follows:

$$IL = \frac{SSE}{SST} \tag{1}$$

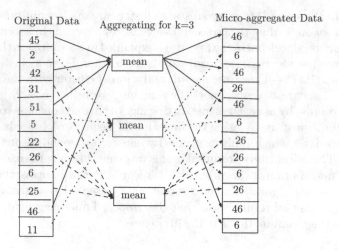

Fig. 1. Example of Microaggregation using mean

where SSE is the within-cluster squared error, calculated by summing the Euclidean distance of each record x_{ij} to the average value $\bar{x}_i$ as follows:

$$SSE = \sum_{i=1}^{g} \sum_{j=1}^{n_i} (x_{ij} - \bar{x}_i)' (x_{ij} - \bar{x}_i) \qquad (2)$$

and SST is the sum of squared error within the entire dataset T, calculated by summing the Euclidean distance of each record x_{ij} to the average value $\bar{x}$ as follows:

$$SST = \sum_{i=1}^{g} \sum_{j=1}^{n_i} (x_{ij} - \bar{x})' (x_{ij} - \bar{x}) \qquad (3)$$

For a given dataset T, SST is fixed regardless of how T is partitioned. On the other hand, SSE varies of a dataset depending on the partition of the dataset. In essence, SSE measures the similarity of the records in a cluster. The lower the SSE, the higher the within-cluster homogeneity and the higher the SSE, the lower the within cluster homogeneity. If all the records in a cluster are the same, then the SSE is zero indicating no information is lost. On the other hand, if all the records in a cluster are more diverse, SSE is large indicating more information is lost. In this paper, we used SSE as a measure of similarity indicating a record will be included in a particular cluster if it causes least SSE among all other records in the dataset. Therefore, the microaggregation problem can be enumerated as a constraint optimization problem as follows:

Definition 1 (Microaggregation Problem). Given a dataset T of n elements and a positive integer k, find a partitioning $G = \{G_1, G_2, ..., G_g\}$ of T such that

1. $G_i \cap G_j = \Phi$, for all $i \neq j = 1, 2, ..., p$,
2. $\cup_{i=1}^{p} G_i = T$,
3. SSE is minimized,
4. for all $G_i \in T$, $\mid G_i \mid \geq k$ for any $G_i \in \mathbf{G}$.

The microaggregation problem stated above can be solved in polynomial time for a univariate dataset [12] but has been shown to be NP hard for multivariate dataset [14]. It is a natural expectation that SSE is low if the number of clusters is large. Thus the number of records in each cluster should be kept close to k. Domingo-Ferrer and Mateo-Sanz [3] showed that no cluster should contain more than $(2k - 1)$ records since such clusters can always be partitioned to further reduce information loss.

4   Previous Microaggregation Methods

Previous microaggregation methods have been roughly divided into two categories, namely fixed-size and data-oriented microaggregation [3,9]. For fixed-size microaggregation, the partition is done by dividing a dataset into clusters that have size k, except perhaps one cluster which has a size between k and $(2k-1)$, depending on the total number of records n and the anonymity parameter k. For the data-oriented microaggregation, the partition is done by allowing all clusters with sizes between k and $(2k - 1)$. Intuitively, fixed-size methods reduce the search space, and thus are more computationally efficient than data-oriented methods [29]. However, data-oriented methods can adapt to different values of k and various data distributions and thus may achieve lower information loss than fixed-size methods.

Domingo-Ferrer and Mateo-Sanz [3] proposed a multivariate fixed-size microaggregation method, later called the Maximum Distance (MD) method [15]. The MD method repeatedly locates the two records that are most distant to each other, and forms two clusters with their respective $(k - 1)$ nearest records until fewer than $2k$ records remain. If at least k records remain, it then forms a new cluster with all remaining records. Finally when there are fewer than k records not assigned to any cluster yet, this algorithm then individually assigns these records to their closest clusters. This method has a time complexity of $O(n^3)$ and works well for most datasets. Laszlo and Mukherjee [13] modified the last step of the MD method such that each remaining record is added to its own nearest cluster and proposed Diameter-based Fixed-size microaggregation. This method is however not a fixed size method because it allows more than one cluster to have more than k records.

The MDAV method is the most widely used microaggregation method [15]. MDAV is the same as MD except in the first step. MDAV finds the record r that is furthest from the current centroid of the dataset and the record s that is furthest from r instead of finding the two records that are most distant to each other, as is done in MD. Then form a cluster with r and its $(k-1)$ nearest records and form another cluster with s and its $(k - 1)$ nearest records. For the remaining records, repeat this process until fewer than $2k$ records remain. If between k and $(2k - 1)$ records remain, MDAV simply forms a new group with all of the remaining records. On the other hand, if the number of the remaining records is below k, it adds all of the remaining records to their nearest clusters. So MDAV is a fixed size method. Lin et $al.$ [29] proposed a modified MDAV, called MDAV-1. The MDAV-1 is similar to MDAV except when the number of the remaining records is between k and $(2k - 1)$, a new cluster is formed with the record that is the furthest from the centroid of the remaining records, and its $(k - 1)$ nearest records. Any remaining records are then added to their respective nearest clusters. Experimental results indicate that MDAV-1 incurs slightly less information loss than MDAV [29]. Another variant of the MDAV method, called MDAV-generic, is proposed by Domingo-Ferrer and Torra [8], where by the threshold $2k$ is altered to $3k$. If between $2k$ and $(3k - 1)$ records remain, then find the record r that is furthest from the centroid of the remaining records and form a cluster with r and its $(k - 1)$ nearest records and another cluster with the remaining records. Finally when fewer than $2k$ records remain, this algorithm then forms a new cluster with all the remaining records. Laszlo and Mukherjee [13] proposed another method, called Centroid-based Fixed-size microaggregation that is also based on a centroid but builds only one cluster during each iteration. This algorithm first find a record r that is furthest from the current centroid of the dataset and then find a cluster with r and its $(k - 1)$ nearest records. For the remaining records repeat the same process until fewer than k records remain. Finally add each remaining record to its nearest clusters. This method is not a fixed-size method as more than one cluster has more than k records. Solanas et $al.$ [16] proposed a variable-size variant of MDAV, called V-MDAV. V-MDAV first builds a new cluster of k records and then tries to extend this to up to $(2k - 1)$records based on some criteria. V-MDAV adopts a user-defined parameter to control the threshold of adding more records to a cluster. Chang et $al.$ [28] proposed the Two Fixed Reference Points (TFRP) method to accelerate the clustering process of k-anonymization. During the first phase, TFRP selects two extreme points calculated from the dataset. Let N_{min} and N_{max} be the minimum and maximum values over all attributes in the datasets, respectively, then one reference point G_1 has N_{min} as its value for all attributes, and another reference point G_2 has N_{max} as its value for all attributes. A cluster of k records is then formed with the record r that is the furthest from G_1 and the $(k - 1)$ nearest records to r. Similarly another cluster of k records is formed with the record s that is the furthest from G_2 and $(k - 1)$ nearest records to s. These two steps are repeated until fewer than k records remain. Finally, these remaining records are assigned to their respective nearest clusters. This method is quite efficient as G_1 and G_2 are fixed throughout the iterations. When all clusters are generated, TFRP applies a enhancement step to determine whether a cluster should be retained or decomposed and added to other clusters.

Lin et $al.$ [29] proposed a density-based algorithm (DBA) for microaggregation. The DBA has two different scenarios. The first state of DBA (DBA-1) repeatedly builds a new cluster using the k-neighborhood of the record with the highest k-density among all records that are not yet assigned to any cluster until fewer than k unassigned records remain. These remaining records are then assigned to their respective nearest clusters. The DBA-1 partitions the dataset into some clusters, where each cluster contains no fewer than k records. The second state of DBA (DBA-2) attempts to fine-tune all clusters by checking whether to decompose a cluster and merge its content with other clusters. Notably, all clusters are checked during the DBA-2 by the reverse of the order that they were added to clusters in the DBA-1. After several clusters are removed and their records are added to their nearest clusters in the DBA-2, some clusters may contain more than $(2k-1)$ records. At the end of the DBA-2, the MDAV-1 algorithm is applied to each cluster with size above $(2k-1)$ to reduce the information loss. This state is finally called MDAV-2. Experimental results show that the DBA attains a reasonable dominance over the latest microaggregation methods.

All of the microaggregation methods described above repeatedly choose one/two records according to various heuristics and form one/two cluster(s) with the chosen records and their respective $(k-1)$ other records. However there are other microaggregation methods that build all clusters simultaneously and work by initially forming multiple clusters of records in the form of trees, where each tree represent a cluster. The multivariate k-Ward algorithm [3] first finds the two records that are furthest from each other in the dataset and build two clusters from these two records and their respective $(k-1)$ nearest records. Each of the remaining record then forms its own cluster. These clusters are repeatedly merged until all clusters have at least k records. Finally the algorithm is recursively applied to each cluster containing $2k$ or more records. Domingo-Ferrer et $al.$ [10] proposed a multivariate microaggregation method called μ-Approx. This method first builds a forest and then decomposes the trees in the forest such that all trees have sizes between k and $\max(2k-1,3k-5)$. Finally, for any tree with size greater than $(2k-1)$, find the node in the tree that is furthest from the centroid of the tree. Form a cluster with this node and its $(k-1)$ nearest records in the tree and form another cluster with the remaining records in the tree.

Hansen an Mukherjee [12] proposed a microaggregation method for univariate datasets called HM. After that Domingo-Ferrer et $al.$ [9] proposed a multivariate version of the HM method, called MHM. This method first uses various heuristics, such as nearest point next (NPN), maximum distance (MD) or MDAV to order the multivariate records. Steps similar to the HM method are then applied to generate clusters based on this ordering. Domingo-Ferrer et $al.$ [7] proposed a microaggregation method based on fuzzy c-means algorithm (FCM) [1]. This method repeatedly runs FCM to adjust the two parameters of FCM (one is the number of clusters c and another is the exponent for the partition matrix m) until each cluster contains at least k records. The value of c is initially large (and m is small) and is gradually reduced (increased) during the repeated FCM runs to reduce the size of each cluster. The same process is then recursively applied to those clusters with $2k$ or more records.

5   The Proposed Approach

This section presents the proposed sorting algorithm and pairwise systematic algorithm for microaggregation that minimizes the information loss and satisfies the k-anonymity requirement.

It has been observed that the reason many of the existing techniques has high information loss is due to some clusters containing very *different* observations which increases the information of a cluster. Therefore, the initial choice of cluster(s) is often difficult since these observations are not known in advance. The proposed technique solves this problem by applying a multi-dimensional sorting on the dataset in a particular way so that the different observations are at opposite ends of the sorted dataset. This process is explained in Section 5.1. Next, a pairwise systematic method takes this sorted dataset to create two clusters repeatedly by minimizing information loss and observing k-anonymity. The algorithm is described in Section 5.2.

5.1   Sorting Technique

Before describing the sorting technique, first we consider a simple example. Consider Table 1 which consists of two variables V_1 and V_2. Rank/Index each of the variables in ascending order individually and create a table where the columns indicates the **position** of the value in the original data (Table 1). For example, the first rank (3) of column 1 in Table 2A indicates the position of smallest value of the first variable (1) in Table 1. Similarly, the second (4) and third (2) ranks indicate the positions of second smallest (2) and third lowest (3) values respectively. The second column is also created in the same way. Now sum the positions of each rank. For example, in Table 2B rank 1 comes from the positions of 5th row of first column and 4th row of second column, rank 2 comes from the positions of third row of first column and fifth row of second column and so on, i.e., $1(9), 2(8), 3(4), 4(3), 5(6)$, where first number is the rank and the number in bracket is the sum of the respective positions. The last column is the rank of the sum-values in bracket of the previous column. For example, $4(3)$ is ranked 1, since 3 is the smallest sum in $9, 8, 4, 3, 6$. Thus according to this sorting algorithm, the first record in the sorted table (see Table 3) should be the 4th row, the second record should be third row of original table in Table 1 and so on. The sorted table is presented in Table 3. The algorithm of this sorting technique is presented in Table 4.

Using the algorithm in Table 5, it is expected that the first record and the last record are more distant and there is zero probability that the first record and the last recorded will be included in the same cluster.

5.2   Pairwise-Systematic Microaggregation Algorithm

The Pairwise-Systematic (P-S) microaggregation proposed by Kabir *et al.* [22] is a practical microaggregation algorithm that creates two distant clusters in a systematic way. Based on the information loss measure in equation (1), the

Table 1. Original variable

V_1	V_2
5	6
3	10
1	3
2	1
4	2

Table 2. A.Rank of sorted values B.Sum of Ranks and final positions

R_1	R_2
3	4
4	5
2	3
5	1
1	2

Rank Sum	R
1(5+4)=1(9)	5
2(3+5)=2(8)	4
3(1+3)=3(4)	2
4(2+1)=4(3)	1
5(4+2)=5(6)	3

Table 3. Sorted variables

V_1	V_2
2	1
1	3
4	2
3	10
5	6

sorting algorithm in Table 5 and the definition of the microaggregation problem, the Pairwise-Systematic (P-S) microaggregation algorithm is as follows. Please refer to Kabir *et al.* [22] for detailed of the algorithm.

According to this method, first sort all records of n in the dataset T in ascending order by using the algorithm in Table 5. Thus in the sorting dataset, the first record and the last record are the most distant to each other among all other pair records in the dataset T. The algorithm (see Table 5) repeatedly builds pair clusters using the first record and the last record in the sorting dataset and their corresponding $(k-1)$ nearest records until fewer than $3k$ records remain (see steps 2-6 of Table 5). The nearest records in a cluster are chosen in such a way that the inclusion of these records causes less SSE than the other records in the dataset. If between $2k$ and $(3k-1)$ records remain, then sort these records in ascending order by using the same sorting algorithm in Table 5 and find the first record f. Form a cluster with f and its $(k-1)$ nearest records, and another cluster with the remaining records (see step 7 of Table 5). Moreover, if fewer than $2k$ records remain, then form a new cluster with all remaining records (see step 9 of Table 5).

The proposed algorithms stated above endeavours to repeatedly build two clusters simultaneously in a systematic way. As the records in the dataset T are

Table 4. Multi-dimensional Sorting Algorithm

---

function $[C, IX]$= MultiDSort(X)

Input: X is a d-dimensional matrix with m rows or instances
Output: C is a d-dimensional matrix, IX is index of the sorted matrix

For $n = 1$ to d
$Y = \text{Sort}_n(X)$ along dimension n
Create an index array IA such that the value at $IA(i) = j$ represents $X(i)'$s
position/index in the sorted array Y(j)(n)
End For

For $p = 1$ to m
    For $n = 1$ to d
        Let z be an m dimensional array containing indeces of the
multidimensional sorted matrix, then
           $Z(p) = Z(p) + Y(p)(n)$
    End For
End For

End function

---

arranged in ascending order and the first record and the last record are most distant to each other, building clusters in this systematic way, the algorithm easily captures if there are any extreme values in the dataset.

Definition 2 (Systematic clustering-based microaggregation decision problem). In a given dataset T of n records, there is a clustering scheme $G = \{G_1, G_2, ..., G_g\}$ such that

1. $\mid G_i \mid \geq k, 1 < k \leq n$: the size of each cluster is greater than or equal to a positive integer k, and
2. $\sum_{i=1}^{g} IL(G_i) < c, c > 0$: the total information loss of the clustering scheme is less than a positive integer c.

where each cluster $G_i(i = 1, 2, ..., p)$ contains the records that are more similar to each other such that the cluster means are close to the values of the clusters and thus cause the least information loss.

6   Experimental Results

This section presents the experimental results and compares the results with several existing techniques. The objective of this experiment is to investigate the

Table 5. P-S microaggregation algorithm

Input: a dataset T of n records and a positive integer k
Output: a partitioning $\boldsymbol{G} = \{G_1, G_2, ..., G_g\}$ of T, where $g = |\boldsymbol{G}|$ and $G_i \geq k$ for $i = 1$ to g.

1. Let $\boldsymbol{G} = \Phi$, and $T' = T$;
 2. Sort all records in T' in ascending order by using the algorithm in Table 5;
 3. Find the first $f \in T'$ and the last record $l \in T'$;
 4. Form a cluster G_1 containing first record f and its $(k-1)$ nearest records in T';
     and another cluster G_2 containing last record l and its $(k-1)$ nearest records in T';
 5. Set $\boldsymbol{G} = \boldsymbol{G} \cup G_1 \cup G_2$ and $T' = T' - G_1 - G_2$;
 6. Repeat steps 2-4 until $|T'| < 3k$;
 7. If $2k \leq |T'| \leq (3k - 1)$;
     (i) Go to step 2;
     (ii) Form a cluster containing the first record $f \in T'$;
        and its (k-1) nearest records in T';
     (iii) Form another cluster with remaining records in T';
 8. else;
 9. If $T' < 2k$;
     (i) Form a new cluster with all the remaining records in T'.

effectiveness of the proposed algorithm in terms of measured information loss of represented cluster data. The following three datasets [9], which have been used as benchmarks in previous studies to evaluate various microaggregation methods, were adopted in the experiments.

1. The "Tarragona" dataset contains 834 records with 13 numerical attributes.
2. The "Census" dataset contains 1,080 records with 13 numerical attributes.
3. The "EIA" dataset contains 4,092 records with 11 numeric attributes (plus two additional categorical attributes not used here).

To accurately evaluate our approach, the performance of the proposed algorithm is compared in this section with various microaggregation methods. Tables 6-8 show the information losses of these microaggregation methods. The lowest information loss for each dataset and each k value is shown in bold face. The information losses of methods DBA-1, DBA-2, MDAV-1 and MDAV-2 are quoted from [29]; the information losses of methods MDAV-MHM, MD-MHM, CBFS-MHM, NPN-MHM and M-d (for $k = 3, 5, 10$) are quoted from [9]; the information losses of methods μ-Approx and M-d (for $k = 4$) are quoted from [10], and the information losses of methods TFRP-1 and TFRP-2 are quoted from [28]. TFRP is a two-stage method and its two stages are denoted as TRFP-1

Table 6. Information loss comparison using Tarragona dataset

Method	$k = 3$	$k = 4$	$k = 5$	$k = 10$
MDAV-MHM	16.9326		22.4617	33.1923
MD-MHM	16.9829		22.5269	33.1834
CBFS-MHM	16.9714		22.8227	33.2188
NPN-MHM	17.3949		27.0213	40.1831
M-d	16.6300	19.66	24.5000	38.5800
μ-Approx	17.10	20.51	26.04	38.80
TFRP-1	17.228	19.396	22.110	33.186
TFRP-2	16.881	19.181	21.847	33.088
MDAV-1	16.93258762	19.54578612	22.46128236	33.19235838
MDAV-2	16.38261429	19.01314997	22.07965363	33.17932950
DBA-1	20.69948803	23.82761456	26.00129826	35.39295837
DBA-2	16.15265063	22.67107728	25.45039236	34.80675148
Multi-DSort	**9.8572**	**11.9989**	**18.17**	**32.1338**

Table 7. Information loss comparison using Census dataset

Method	$k = 3$	$k = 4$	$k = 5$	$k = 10$
MDAV-MHM	5.6523		9.0870	14.2239
MD-MHM	5.69724		8.98594	14.3965
CBFS-MHM	5.6734		8.8942	13.8925
NPN-MHM	6.3498		11.3443	18.7335
M-d	6.1100	8.24	10.3000	17.1700
μ-Approx	6.25	8.47	10.78	17.01
TFRP-1	5.931	7.880	9.357	14.442
TFRP-2	5.803	7.638	8.980	13.959
MDAV-1	5.692186279	7.494699833	9.088435498	14.15593043
MDAV-2	5.656049371	7.409645342	9.012389597	13.94411775
DBA-1	6.144855154	9.127883805	10.84218735	15.78549732
DBA-2	5.581605762	7.591307664	9.046162117	13.52140518
Multi-DSort	**2.0954**	**3.6254**	**3.4595**	**6.8497**

Table 8. Information loss comparison using EIA dataset

Method	$k = 3$	$k = 4$	$k = 5$	$k = 10$
MDAV-MHM	0.4081		1.2563	3.7725
MD-MHM	0.4422		1.2627	3.6374
NPN-MHM	0.5525		0.9602	2.3188
μ-Approx	0.43	0.59	0.83	2.26
TFRP-1	0.530	0.661	1.651	3.242
TFRP-2	0.428	0.599	0.910	2.590
MDAV-1	0.482938725	0.671345141	1.666657361	3.83966422
MDAV-2	0.411101515	0.587381756	0.946263963	3.16085577
DBA-1	1.090194828	0.84346907	1.895536919	4.265801303
DBA-2	0.421048322	0.559755523	0.81849828	2.080980825
Multi-DSort	**0.4048**	**0.5299**	**0.7956**	**1.7709**

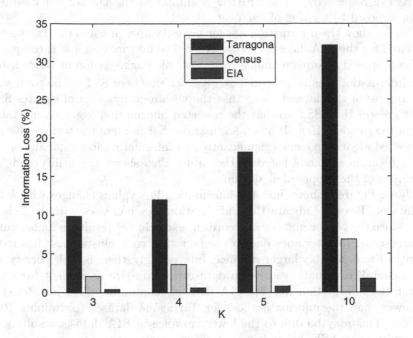

Fig. 2. Information Loss vs k for Tarragona, Census, and EIA datasets

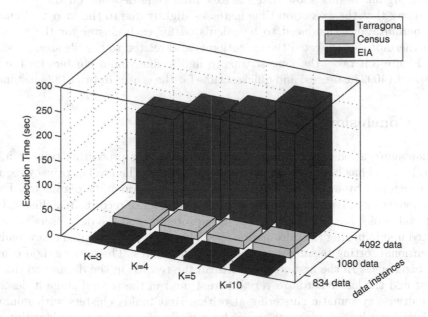

Fig. 3. Execution time vs k

and TRFP-2 respectively. The TFRP-2 is similar to the DBA-2 but disallows merging a record to a group of size over $(4k - 1)$.

Tables 6-8 show the information loss for several values of k and the Tarragona, Census and for the EIA datasets respectively. The information loss is compared with the proposed algorithm among the latest microaggregation methods listed above. Information loss is measured as $\frac{SSE}{SST} \times 100$, where SST is the total sum of the squares of the dataset. Note that the within-groups sum of squares SSE is never greater than SST so that the reported information loss measure takes values in the range [0,100]. Tables 6-8 illustrate that in all of the test situations, the proposed algorithm causes significantly less information loss than any of the microaggregation methods listed in the table. This shows the utility and the effectiveness of the proposed algorithm.

Analysis: Figure 2 shows how the information loss values changes with k for each dataset. Results indicate that information loss increases with k. This is obvious since the higher number of records in each cluster results in higher sum-of-squared-error (SSE) values due to the fact that each cluster now has more observations and possibly larger variance. Interestingly, there is little correlation between overall information loss of a dataset and its size as evident from the fact that the information loss for CIA dataset (containing 4092 instances) is much lower than the information loss for Tarragona dataset (containing 1082 instances). This may be due to the lower variance in EIA dataset resulting in clusters with lower SSE, hence lower information loss.

Figure 3 shows the how the execution time varies with k and different file sizes. Again, results show that the execution time depends on the value of k. It shows that the execution time increases slightly due to the increased number of permutations that need to be calculated for each cluster for the higher k. Furthermore, as expected the execution is also related to the file size. As shown in Figure 3 it takes the longest time to find k-anonymous clusters for the EIA dataset (4092 instances) and quickest time for the census dataset (834 instances).

7   Conclusion

Microaggregation is an effective method in SDC for protecting privacy in microdata and has been extensively used world-wide. The level of privacy required is controlled by a parameter k, often called the anonymity parameter. For k-anonymization, k is basically the minimum number of records in a cluster. Once the value of k has been chosen, the data protector and the data users are interested in minimizing the information loss. This work has presented a new multidimensional sorting technique for numerical attributes. The new method consists of two stages. In the first stage it sorts all the records in the dataset so that the first and the last record are very different, and in the second stage it describes a pairwise systematic clustering algorithm that builds clusters with minimum information loss. A comparison has been made of the proposed algorithm with the most widely used microaggregation methods using the three most popular benchmark datasets (Tarragona, Census and the EIA). The experimental results show that the proposed algorithm outperforms all the tested microaggregation methods with respect to information loss. Thus the proposed method is very effective in preserving the privacy microdata sets and can be used as an effective privacy preserving k-anonymization method for Statistical Disclosure Control.

References

1. Bezdek, J.C.: Pattern recognition with fuzzy objective function algorithms. Academic Publishers, Norwell (1981)
2. Domingo-Ferrer, J., Torra, V.: Privacy in data mining. Data Mining and Knowledge Discovery 11(2), 117–119 (2005)
3. Domingo-Ferrer, J., Mateo-Sanz, J.: Practical data-oriented microaggregation for statistical disclosure control. IEEE Transactions on Knowledge and Data Engineering 14(1), 189–201 (2002)
4. Domingo-Ferrer, J., Torra, V.: Extending microaggregation procedures using defuzzification methods for categorical variables. In: 1st international IEEE Symposium on intelligent Systems, Verna, pp. 44–49 (2002)
5. May, P., Ehrlich, H.-C., Steinke, T.: ZIB Structure Prediction Pipeline: Composing a Complex Biological Workflow Through Web Services. In: Nagel, W.E., Walter, W.V., Lehner, W. (eds.) Euro-Par 2006. LNCS, vol. 4128, pp. 1148–1158. Springer, Heidelberg (2006)
6. Domingo-Ferrer, J., Torra, V.: Towards fuzzy c-means based microaggregation. In: Grzegorzewski, P., Hryniewicz, O., Gil, A. (eds.) Soft Methods in Probability, Statistics and Data Analysis. Advances in Soft Computing, vol. 16, pp. 289–294. Physica-Verlag, Heidelberg (2002)
7. Domingo-Ferrer, J., Torra, V.: Fuzzy microaggregation for microdata protection. Journal of Advanced Computational Intelligence and Intelligent Informatics 7(2), 153–159 (2003)
8. Domingo-Ferrer, J., Torra, V.: Ordinal, continuous and heterogeneous kanonymity through microaggregation. Data Mining and Knowledge Discovery 11(2), 195–212 (2005)
9. Domingo-Ferrer, J., Martinez-Balleste, A., Mateo-Sanz, J.M., Sebe, F.: Efficient multivariate data-oriented microaggregation. The VLDB Journal 15(4), 355–369 (2006)
10. Domingo-Ferrer, J., Sebe, F., Solanas, A.: A polynomial-time approximation to optimal multivariate microaggregation. Computer and Mathematics with Applications 55(4), 714–732 (2008)
11. Han, J.-M., Cen, T.-T., Yu, H.-Q., Yu, J.: A multivariate immune clonal selection microaggregation algorithm. In: IEEE International Conference on Granular Computing, Hangzhou, pp. 252–256 (2008)
12. Hansen, S., Mukherjee, S.: A polynomial algorithm for optimal univariate microaggregation. IEEE Transactions on Knowledge and Data Engineering 15(4), 1043–1044 (2003)
13. Laszlo, M., Mukherjee, S.: Minimum spanning tree partitioning algorithm for microaggregation. IEEE Transactions on Knowledge and Data Engineering 17(7), 902–911 (2005)
14. Oganian, A., Domingo-Ferrer, J.: On the complexity of optimal microaggregation for statistical disclosure control. Statistical Journal of the United Nations Economic Commission for Europe 18, 345–354 (2001)

15. Solanas, A.: Privacy protection with genetic algorithms. In: Yang, A., Shan, Y., Bui, L.T. (eds.) Success in Evolutionary Computation. SCI, vol. 92, pp. 215–237. Springer, Heidelberg (2008)
16. Solanas, A., Martinez-Balleste, A., Domingo-Ferrer, J.: $V-MDAV$: A multivariate microaggregation with variable group size. In: 17th COMPSTAT Symposium of the IASC, Rome (2006)
17. Samarati, P.: Protecting respondent's privacy in microdata release. IEEE Transactions on Knowledge and Data Engineering 13(6), 1010–1027 (2001)
18. Sweeney, L.: k-Anonymity: A model for protecting privacy. International Journal on Uncertainty, Fuzziness and Knowledge-based Systems 10(5), 557–570 (2002)
19. Torra, V.: Microaggregation for Categorical Variables: A Median Based Approach. In: Domingo-Ferrer, J., Torra, V. (eds.) PSD 2004. LNCS, vol. 3050, pp. 162–174. Springer, Heidelberg (2004)
20. Kabir, M.E., Wang, H.: Systematic Clustering-based Microaggregation for Statistical Disclosure Control. In: IEEE International Conference on Network and System Security, Melbourne, pp. 435–441 (2010)
21. Kabir, M.E., Wang, H., Bertino, E., Chi, Y.: Systematic Clustering Method for l-diversity Model. In: Australasian Database Conference, Brisbane, pp. 93–102 (2010)
22. Kabir, M.E., Wang, H., Zhang, Y.: A Pairwise-Systematic Microaggregation for Statistical Disclosure Control. In: IEEE International Conference on Data Mining, Sydney, pp. 266–273 (2010)
23. Kabir, M.E., Wang, H.: Microdata Protection Method Through Microaggregation: A Median Based Approach. Information Security Journal: A Global Perspective 20(1), 1–8 (2011)
24. Ward, J.H.J.: Hierarchical grouping to optimize an objective function. Journal of the American Statistical Association 58(301), 236–244 (1963)
25. Wang, H., Zhang, Y., Cao, J.: Effective collaboration with information sharing in virtual universities. IEEE Transactions on Knowledge and Data Engineering 21(6), 840–853 (2009)
26. Willenborg, L., Waal, T.D.: Elements of statistical disclosure control. Lecture Notes in Statistics, vol. 155 (2001)
27. Zahn, C.T.: Graph-theoretical methods for detecting and describing gestalt clusters. IEEE Transactions on Computers C-20(1), 68–86 (1971)
28. Chang, C.-C., Li, Y.-C., Huang, W.-H.: TFRP: An efficient microaggregation algorithm for statistical disclosure control. Journal of Systems and Software 80(11), 1866–1878 (2007)
29. Lin, J.-L., Wen, T.-H., Hsieh, J.-C., Chang, P.-C.: Density-based microaggregation for statistical disclosure control. Expert Systems with Applications 37(4), 3256–3263 (2010)

More Anonymity through Trust Degree
in Trust-Based Onion Routing

Peng Zhou, Xiapu Luo, and Rocky K.C. Chang

Department of Computing, The Hong Kong Polytechnic University, Hunghom, Hong Kong
{cspzhouroc,csxluo,csrchang}@comp.polyu.edu.hk

Abstract. Trust-based onion routing employs users' own trust to circumvent compromised onion routers. However, it runs a high risk of being deanonymized by the inference attack based on a priori trust relationship. In this paper, we first observe that the onion routers with higher trust degree (e.g., those that are trusted by more users) are more effective in defending against the inference attack. We therefore incorporate trust degree into trust-based onion routing. With a rigorous theoretical analysis, we devise an optimal strategy for router selection and an optimal routing algorithm for path selection. Both minimize the risk of deanonymization by the inference attack without sacrificing the capability of evading compromised routers. Moreover, simulation-based experiments on top of real-world social networks confirm the effectiveness of the optimal router selection.

Keywords: trust degree, anonymity, trust-based onion routing.

1 Introduction

Recently, trust-based models have attracted growing research interests in the anonymous communication area [1–4], especially for onion routing [5–7]. Onion routing networks protect anonymity with the help of onion routers. However, since onion routers are usually deployed by volunteers whose identities and technical competence are not verified [7], users cannot easily detect compromised routers. And even worse, various attacks employ compromised routers to deanonymize users [8–20]. The most recent research proposes trust-based onion routing algorithms to address this problem [2,4]. By considering the trust that an user assigns to routers' owners, he can select routers from trusted individuals, hence circumventing the compromised routers.

In existing trust-based onion routing networks, a user only considers its own trust and believes that routers with equal trust can protect its anonymity equivalently. However, confronting the adversary who can observe the routers in users' connections and perform inference attack based on a priori trust relationship, users are more likely to be deanonymized if they select the routers that are rarely trusted by other users. As studied in [4,21], this inference attack is a major threat to trust-based onion routing. Therefore, besides the user's own trust for router selection, the trust from other users also plays a very important role in protecting anonymity. In this paper, we find that the routers are more effective for a user in defending against the inference attack, if these routers are

A.D. Keromytis and R. Di Pietro (Eds.): SecureComm 2012, LNICST 106, pp. 273–291, 2013.
© Institute for Computer Sciences, Social Informatics and Telecommunications Engineering 2013

trusted by more other users. We thus define a router's trust degree with respect to a user as the sum of trust from other users in this router.

Figure 1 illustrates the effectiveness of trust degree in protecting anonymity. In this example, users can only select their trusted onion routers to make their connections. Alice trusts Bob and Ken equally, both of them operate onion routers. Pete is an adversary who knows the trust relationship among users and routers. If Pete observes Bob's router in Alice's connection, he can deanonymize Alice directly as Bob is only trusted by Alice. However, Pete cannot deanonymize Alice by observing Ken's router, because Ken is also trusted by many other users.

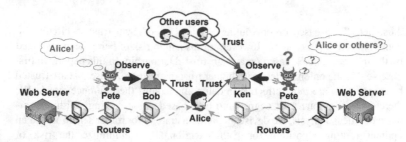

Fig. 1. Trust degree in protecting anonymity

Moreover, since we observe in real world that each person's friends are always trusted by different numbers of other people, an average person can potentially gain more anonymity by considering trust degree in trust-based onion routing networks. To support this assertion, we analyze a public data set from the Facebook reported in [22]. This data set regards other people in a person's friend list as friends with equal trust. The authors of this data set crawl the New Orleans regional network in Facebook from December 29th, 2008 to January 3rd, 2009 and collect more than 1.5 millions social links from about $60,000$ people to their friends. And $53,609$ of them have more than one friend.

Figure 2 illustrates the distribution of trust degrees of these $53,609$ people's friends in [22]. We calculate a friend's trust degree with respect to a person as the number of other people who have this friend in their friend lists. The horizontal axis represents the person index while the vertical axis shows the trust degree of people's friends. To ease the explanation, we sort these people in an ascending order according to their trust degree distance, which can be computed by subtracting the smallest trust degree from the largest one of each person's friends. As can be seen, more than 99.6% of the people have friends with different trust degree. In particular, for more than 80% of them, their friends' trust degree varies larger than 50.

Trust degree is an intuitive, and effective, feature in defending against the inference attack, but past work neglects it. By selecting routers with a large trust degree, users can intelligently hide their identities with the help of many other users, hence obtaining more protection for their anonymity. In this paper, we incorporate trust degree into the trust-based onion routing. In particular, we make three major contributions:

1. To the best of our knowledge, we are the first to incorporate trust from other users into the trust-based onion routing.

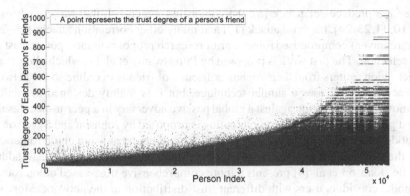

Fig. 2. The distribution of trust degrees of 53, 609 people's friends

2. More importantly, we prove an optimal router selection strategy based on the trust from other users. This minimizes the chance of deanonymization through inference, but does not sacrifice the capability of evading compromised routers. We evaluate this strategy in both simulation and real-world social networks. Experimental results show the user anonymity can be effectively improved.
3. We also prove an optimal trust degree aware routing algorithm for path selection.

The remainder of this paper is organized as follows. We review related works in Section 2. Section 3 introduces necessary preliminaries, including the trust model, the adversary model, the definition of trust degree, and the definition of anonymity. In Section 4, we present an optimal strategy for router selection that incorporates trust degree. We also analyze the anonymity improvement in both simulation and real-world social networks. In Section 5, we prove an optimal trust degree aware routing algorithm for path selection. We finally conclude this paper in Section 6.

2 Related Work

Trust-based onion routing appears recently and attracts growing interests from both industrial and academic communities [1–4]. Trust is effective in identifying compromised routers [2, 4], thus defending against correlation-like attacks [8–20]. However, users who select routers according to trust run a high risk to be deanonymized by the adversary who knows a priori trust relationships [4, 21].

In this section, we review three kinds of past work in the literature. We first present a brief description of the attacks that rely on compromised routers. We then review existing trust-based anonymous communications. Moreover, we discuss the side effect if the trust models are used to protect anonymity.

In onion routing networks, users anonymously access the Internet through layered encrypted circuits. These circuits are established by dynamically selected onion routers [5–7]. However, without an effective mechanism to verify routers' identities, onion routing networks are vulnerable to compromised routers. A number of attacks exploit compromised routers to compromise anonymity in onion routing networks. This includes the predecessor attack [8], the congestion attack [9], the traffic analysis attacks [10, 11, 23, 24], the sybil attack [12] and many other correlation attacks [13–20].

To circumvent compromised routers, prior research proposes to incorporate trust into router selection. The first work is proposed by Puttaswamy et al. [1] which allows users to select onion routers from their friends or friends of friends in online social networks [8]. Drac system [3] uses a similar technique, but it is mainly designed to facilitate anonymous communication against a global passive adversary in a peer-to-peer fashion. The first general trust model for onion routing is proposed by Johnson and Syverson [2]. This model reasons about the trust as the difficulty of compromising onion routers, but ignore the fact that different users may trust different parts of the network. To address this issue, Johnson et al. [4] presents a more comprehensive trust-based onion routing. This model considers users with different trust distribution in the network. Moreover, Marques et al. [25] report a preliminary survey for trust models used in anonymous communication.

Although trust models help evade compromised routers, the adversary who has the knowledge of a-priori trust relationships is more likely to deanonymize users by making inference. Diaz et al. [21] present a pioneer research to discuss this attack. It assumes the source and destination of a communication in a mix-based network [26, 27] are also members of a social network. The adversary who obtains the social network graph in advance can reduce the anonymity protected by the mix-based network. Johnson et al. [4] also discuss a similar attack against trust-based onion routing. They propose a downhill algorithm to mitigate the adversary's inferences. Since the compromised routers in a user's connection close to this user are more effective in attacking anonymity than the routers far away from this user, the downhill algorithm allows users to select routers from sets with a decreasing minimum trust threshold. This algorithm does not leverage trust degree information in the design space, thus losing the chance to further improve anonymity by selecting onion routers that are trusted by more other users.

The trust we consider in this paper is very different from another two notions of trust. One is the behavioral trust that represents the performance reputation [28–32], and the other is the environmental trust that defines the security of software and hardware platforms where the anonymity toolkits run [33].

3   Preliminaries

In this section, we first present a general trust model for trust-based onion routing. We then elaborate on the adversary model. After that, we formalize the trust degree, and give a brief description of the anonymity protected by onion routing networks.

3.1   The Trust Model

We consider the general trust model proposed by Johnson et al. [4]. It provides a foundation for trust-based onion routing in several aspects. First, this model reasons about trust for the onion routing protocol and describes the notion of trust as the difficulty of compromising the onion routers. This difficulty represents the probability that the adversary is failed to compromise the routers. Second, this model considers a very coarse level of trust in onion routers. It is a reasonable consideration because users need outside knowledge to estimate the trust. This includes the knowledge of the technical competence of individuals who operate the routers, the computer platform where the routers are running in, and the likelihood that the router is deployed by the adversary, etc. Therefore, it is unrealistic to expect an accurate trust assigned to the routers. Third, since different users have different adversaries, this model investigates different users with different distributions of trust in routers. For example, organizations may deploy onion routers to serve their own members but attack the users from their rival.

In this model, V is the set of nodes in a trust-based onion routing network. $V = U \bigcup R \bigcup \Delta$, where U is the set of users (e.g., the human beings or their computers), R is the set of onion routers, and Δ is the set of the destinations (e.g., the web servers). c_{ij} is the probability that the onion router $r_j \in R$ is successfully compromised by u_i's adversaries. $C = [c_{ij}]^{|U| \times |R|}$ is the matrix of the probabilities for each user's adversaries compromising each router in the network. $|U|$ and $|R|$ are the number of users and onion routers in the network, respectively. $T = [t_{ij}]^{|U| \times |R|} = [1 - c_{ij}]^{|U| \times |R|} = I - C$ is the matrix of users' trust distributions over routers. $t_{ij} = 1 - c_{ij}$ is the trust u_i assigns to r_j. Since this model only takes coarse level of trust into account, there are a very limited number ν of distinct values of trust in T. Such as in [2,4], only $\nu = 2$ and $\nu = 3$ have been studied.

We use the terms "path" and "connection" interchangeably in the rest of the paper to represent an onion route consisting of several onion routers. We regard a position of a connection as a hop of this connection. To establish a connection, a user should select onion routers to fill in all the hops of its connection. In trust-based onion routing, a user makes a connection with several hops and actively selects onion routers according to T for these hops. $P = [p_{ij}]^{|U| \times |R|}$ is the matrix of probabilities that users use to select routers based on T.[1]

3.2 The Adversary

We consider two kinds of adversary in this paper. The first kind attempts to compromise onion routers in the network. If some routers in an user's connection are compromised, especially if the routers in both the first and last hops are compromised, various attacks [8–20] can be launched to deanonymize the user. The adversary could manipulate onion routers by two means. One is to compromise legal routers that already exist in the network, and the other is to deploy its own malicious routers in the network. In some worse conditions, the adversary could compromise a significant fraction of the network, such as launching the Sybil attack [12]. The trust-based onion routing algorithms are originally proposed to defend this kind of adversary. With the help of users' own trust in onion routers, they identify and exclude compromised routers in their connections.

Although the trust model can defend against the adversary who compromises onion routers, a new kind of adversary appears and poses a significant threat to trust-based onion routing [4]. This adversary deanonymizes users by making inference based on a priori trust relationships. In particular, this adversary could exploit compromised routers

---

[1] $P = [p_{ij}]^{|U| \times |R|}$ may be different when users select routers for different positions of their connections. This will be elaborated on in Section 5.

or malicious destinations (e.g., malicious web servers) to observe routers in connections, and then infer the original user of the connection according to the fact that users prefer to choosing their trusted routers in trust-based onion routing. In this paper, we follow prior work [4] and assume that, the adversary can only employ compromised routers to observe the routers in adjacent positions of the connections (i.e., adjacent hops), or use the malicious destinations to observe the router in the last hop. To face this adversary, the user runs a high risk to be deanonymized if she selects a router barely trusted by other users.

Prior research [4, 21] shows it is feasible for an adversary to make inference in practice, although this adversary is required to know users' trust distributions over onion routers in advance. In realistic environment, the adversary could estimate these trust distributions through outside knowledge [2, 4]. For example, the users belonging to an organization may be more likely to trust the routers deployed by this organization. In particular, if both users and routers' owners are members of social networks, the adversary can profile the trust relationships by crawling and deanonymizing online social networks [34, 35]. Moreover, since the trust-based onion routing algorithm may be set up by default in softwares and shared in the public, the adversary who knows the trust distributions can also infer users' router selection probabilities [2].

In this paper, we focus on defending against the adversary who makes inference to deanonymize the user without sacrificing the capability of defending against the adversary who attempts to compromise onion routers.

3.3 The Trust Degree

Existing trust-based onion routing networks employ users' own trust to improve anonymity by thwarting the adversary who attempts to compromise routers [4], but do not consider the trust from other users. However, if the adversary deanonymizes the user by making inference based on the knowledge of a priori trust distributions, the trust from other users plays a very important role in protecting anonymity.

We define a router's trust degree with respect to a user as the sum of other users' trust in this router. Let d_{ij} be the trust degree of the router $r_j \in R$ with respect to the user u_i as:

$$d_{ij} = \sum_{u_x \in U} t_{xj} - t_{ij} = \sum_{u_x \in U/u_i} t_{xj} \tag{1}$$

where t_{ij} is the trust u_i assigns to r_j, t_{xj} is the trust $u_x \in U/u_i$ assigns to r_j and U/u_i is the set of users excluding u_i.

As elaborated on in Section 3.2, the adversary can estimate the trust-based router selection distributions if they have the knowledge of a priori trust relationships and the corresponding trust-based router selection strategies. However, a user's router selection distribution may not be the same as this user's trust distribution over routers. For example, according to the trust-based algorithms proposed by Johnson and Syverson [2], if the adversary compromises a significant fraction of the network, u_i should choose the most trusted routers with the probability 1 rather than $\frac{\max_{r_j \in R} t_{ij}}{\sum_{r_j \in R} t_{ij}}$ to maximize the capability of keeping from compromised routers. The adversary could infer the user with higher accuracy by using the router selection distributions rather than the trust distributions. Therefore, a more accurate definition of a router's trust degree with respect to a user could be the sum of other users' selection probabilities for this router:

$$d_{ij} = \sum_{u_x \in U} p_{xj} - p_{ij} = \sum_{u_x \in U/u_i} p_{xj} \tag{2}$$

where p_{ij} is the probability that u_i uses to select r_j and p_{xj} is the probability that $u_x \in U/u_i$ uses to select r_j. In the rest of the paper, we use Eqn.(2) to calculate d_{ij}.

3.4 The Anonymity

The onion routing protocol keeps the adversary from linking the source and destination of a connection that a user [2] makes, hence protecting the information of who is talking to whom in a communication [6]. As a result, the path anonymity of a connection can be protected if the user or the destination of this connection can be concealed. When the source link (i.e., the user) of a connection can be observed by the adversary, the path anonymity depends on the destination's anonymity. In this case, Johnson et al. [4] conclude that the path anonymity can be best protected if users select one of their most trusted routers to make a single hop connection.

But if the destination link of a connection can be observed, the protection of path anonymity relies on the protection of the user anonymity. This is a common scenario in real world. For example, an organization imposes censorship on some sensitive web sites and attempts to record who access these sites. In this paper, we focus on the problem of protecting the user anonymity when the destination link can be observed.

4 Trust Degree in Router Selection

In existing trust-based onion routing networks, users select routers only according to their own trust, thus being vulnerable to the adversary who makes inference based on a priori trust relationship [4]. However, we find that the routers trusted by more other users are more effective in defending against this inference. Therefore, we incorporate the trust from other users into trust-based onion routing.

In this section, we elaborate on selecting routers for a single hop based on trust degree information. Section 4.1 defines the metric of anonymity for router selection. In particular, we use the chance of a user to be inferred by the adversary to measure anonymity. Section 4.2 presents the optimal router selection strategy by considering routers' trust degree to maximize anonymity. We also analyze the anonymity improvement with the help of the optimal strategy in both simulation and real-world social networks in Section 4.3. This is compared with existing trust-based strategy. Table 1 summarizes important notations used in this section.

---

[2] In this paper, a user actively selects routers to initiate a connection and access a destination through this connection.

Table 1. Important notations in Section 4

Symbol	Definition		Symbol	Definition
$|A|$	the size of set A		$[a_{ij}]^{I \times J}$	an $I \times J$ matrix of elements a_{ij}
t_{ij}	u_i's trust in router r_j		d_{ij}	r_j's trust degree with respect to u_i, $d_{ij} = \sum\limits_{u_i \in U \setminus u_i} p_{ij}$
p_{ij}	u_i's probability to select router r_j		R_e	a set of routers that u_i equally trusts, $\forall r_j \in R_e, t_{ij} = t_e$
$U \setminus u_i$	the set of users excluding u_i		$p_i\{R_e\}$	u_i's strategy to select routers from R_e, $p_i\{R_e\} = [p_{ij}]^{1 \times |R_e|}$
			$\Gamma(p_i\{R_e\})$	the expectation of the chance to infer u_i for strategy $p_i\{R_e\}$
D_e	$D_e = \sum\limits_{r_j \in R_e} d_{ij}$		θ_e	$\theta_e = \sum\limits_{r_j \in R_e} p_{ij}$

4.1 Minimizing the Chance of Being Inferred in Router Selection

We investigate a user u_i who is aware of routers' trust degree with respect to a population of other users whose trust distributions and router selection strategies are known. To preserve the capability of defending against compromised routers, we only consider the trust degree information for the routers equally trusted by u_i. The number of routers equally trusted by u_i could be large due to the small number of distinct trust levels considered in existing trust-based onion routing [2, 4]. Moreover, as a person's friends always receive different amount of trust from other persons [22], the routers equally trusted by u_i are more likely to have different trust degrees.

We consider the scenario that the adversary makes inference according to the observation on a single hop of u_i's connection. It may be the case that the adversary manipulates the destination and observes the last hop (i.e., the Hop-X in Figure 3).

Fig. 3. An example of the single hop that can be observed

Since the adversary has the knowledge of a priori trust relationships and users' router selection strategies in the network, she gets the probability $\frac{p_{ij}}{p_{ij}+d_{ij}}$ to infer u_i if the router r_j is observed, where d_{ij} can be calculated by Eqn.(2). Moreover, if u_i has the probability p_{ij} to choose r_j for the exposed hop, the adversary has the probability p_{ij} to observe r_j in this hop of u_i's connection. Therefore, u_i has the probability $p_{ij} \cdot \frac{p_{ij}}{p_{ij}+d_{ij}}$ to be inferred through r_j in the exposed hop.

We consider the problem of minimizing u_i's chance of being inferred when a single hop of u_i's path is observed by the adversary. The objective function is defined as:

$$\Gamma(p_i\{R_e\}) = \sum_{r_j \in R_e} p_{ij} \cdot \frac{p_{ij}}{p_{ij}+d_{ij}} \tag{3}$$

where, $R_e \subseteq R$ is a set of routers to which the user u_i assigns the equal trust t_e, i.e., $\forall r_j \in R_e, t_{ij} = t_e$. R is the set of onion routers in the entire network. $p_i\{R_e\} = [p_{ij}]^{1 \times |R_e|}$ is a selection strategy that u_i uses to select a router from R_e for the exposed hop. Herein, p_{ij} is a probability for u_i to select router r_j, the matrix $[p_{ij}]^{1 \times |R_e|}$ consists all the p_{ij}s for $r_j \in R_e$ and $|R_e|$ is the size of set R_e.

The objective function $\Gamma(p_i\{R_e\})$ calculates the expectation of the chance to be inferred when u_i uses strategy $p_i\{R_e\}$ to select routers from R_e. A lower chance of being inferred means more anonymity for u_i. To maximize u_i's anonymity, we should find the optimal strategy $p_i^*\{R_e\}$ to minimize $\Gamma(p_i\{R_e\})$. We formalize this as:

$$p_i^*\{R_e\} = \arg \min_{p_i\{R_e\}} \Gamma(p_i\{R_e\}), \quad subject\ to \sum_{r_j \in R_e} p_{ij} = \theta_e \qquad (4)$$

where, $\theta_e = \sum_{r_j \in R_e} p_{ij}$ is the sum of u_i's probabilities of choosing routers from R_e. Existing trust-based algorithms decide θ_e. For example, If u_i is only allowed to select the most trusted routers, $\theta_e = 1$ for R_e with $t_e = \max_{r_j \in R} t_{ij}$ and $\theta_e = 0$ for other R_e. Since a user's trust in a router is modeled as the difficulty of this user's adversary in compromising this router [2,4], the routers with equal trust from a user should have the same probability of being not compromised by this user's adversary. Therefore, to preserve the capability of defending against compromised routers, we should not change the value of θ_e when we minimize $\Gamma(p_i\{R_e\})$.

4.2   The Optimal Router Selection Strategy

As existing trust-based algorithms do not consider routers' trust degree, u_i can only use an equal probability to select routers with equal trust (i.e., $p_{ij}^= = \frac{\theta_e}{|R_e|}$ for $r_j \in R_e$) [2,4]. However, by considering the trust from other users, u_i can intuitively gain more anonymity by using a higher probability to select routers trusted by more other users.

Let $[d_{ij}]^{1 \times |R_e|}$ be the matrix of d_{ij} for $r_j \in R_e$. Let $D_e = \sum_{r_j \in R_e} d_{ij}$ be the sum of trust degree d_{ij} for $r_j \in R_e$.

Considering $[d_{ij}]^{1 \times |R_e|}$, we prove an optimal router selection strategy for u_i to minimize the chance of being inferred. Lemma 1 gives this optimal solution $p_i^*\{R_e\}$ and shows the minimal chance of being inferred $\Gamma(p_i^*\{R_e\})$ in theory. In $p_i^*\{R_e\}$, u_i's probability of choosing a router $r_j \in R_e$ is proportional to d_{ij}. The minimal chance $\Gamma(p_i^*\{R_e\})$ is inversely proportional to D_e.

Lemma 1. *Subject to* $\sum_{r_j \in R_e} p_{ij} = \theta_e$, *the optimal strategy* $p_i^*\{R_e\}$ *for minimizing* $\Gamma(p_i\{R_e\})$ *is* $p_i^*\{R_e\} = [p_{ij}^*]^{1 \times |R_e|} = \frac{\theta_e}{D_e} \cdot [d_{ij}]^{1 \times |R_e|}$. *The minimum chance is* $\Gamma(p_i^*\{R_e\}) = \sum_{r_j \in R_e} p_{ij}^* \cdot \frac{p_{ij}^*}{d_j} = \frac{(\theta_e)^2}{\theta_e + D_e}$.

Proof. In R_e, we have $|R_e|$ routers denoted as $r_1, r_2, \cdots, r_{|R_e|}$. We assume the sum of probability that u_i uses to choose r_1 and r_2 is $\beta \le \theta_e$. We first consider the problem of finding the optimal strategy for u_i to select r_1 and r_2 and minimize $p_{i1} \cdot \frac{p_{i1}}{p_{i1}+d_{i1}} + p_{i2} \cdot \frac{p_{i2}}{p_{i2}+d_{i2}}$. This problem can be formalized as below:

$$p_i^*\{r_1, r_2\} = \arg \min_{p_i\{r_1, r_2\}} (p_{i1} \cdot \frac{p_{i1}}{d_{i1}+p_{i1}} + p_{i2} \cdot \frac{p_{i2}}{d_{i2}+p_{i2}}), \quad s.t.,\ p_{i1} + p_{i2} = \beta \le \theta_e$$

As $p_{i2} = \beta - p_{i1}$, $\min\limits_{p_i(r_1,r_2)} (p_{i1} \cdot \frac{p_{i1}}{d_{i1}+p_{i1}} + p_{i2} \cdot \frac{p_{i2}}{d_{i2}+p_{i2}})$ can be written as $\min\limits_{p_{i1} \in [0,\beta]} f(p_{i1})$,

where, $f(p_{i1}) = p_{i1} \cdot \frac{p_{i1}}{d_{i1}+p_{i1}} + (\beta - p_{i1}) \cdot \frac{(\beta-p_{i1})}{d_{i2}+\beta-p_{i1}}$. We know that, if $f(p_{i1})$'s second

derivative is larger than 0, $f(p_{i1})$ has a minimum value. And this minimum value can be

obtained when $f(p_{i1})$'s first derivative equals to 0. Such that, if $f''(p_{i1}) = \frac{d^2 f(p_{i1})}{d^2 p_{i1}} > 0$,

$f(p_{i1})$ reach its minimum when $f'(p_{i1}) = \frac{df(p_{i1})}{dp_{i1}} = 0$. As $\beta \geq p_{i1} \geq 0$ and $d_{i1} > 0, d_{i2} > 0$, then we have:

$$f''(p_{i1}) = 2d_{i2}^2 \cdot p_{i1} + 2d_{i1}^2 (\beta - p_{i1}) + 2d_{i1}(d_{i1}d_{i2} + d_{i2}^2) > 0.$$

Therefore, $f(p_{i1})$ has a minimum value when $f'(p_{i1}) = 0$, such as:

$$f'(p_{i1}) = (d_{i2}^2 - d_{i1}^2) \cdot p_{i1}^2 + 2d_{i1}(d_{i1}d_{i2} + d_{i1}\beta + d_{i2}^2) \cdot p_{i1} - d_{i1}^2 \beta (2d_{i2} + \beta) = 0$$

By solving this quadratic equation, we can get two roots. But considering $p_{i1} \geq 0$, we only use the positive result $p_{i1} = \frac{d_{i1}}{d_{i1}+d_{i2}} \cdot \beta$. We thus have:

$$p_{i1}^* = \frac{d_{i1}}{d_{i1}+d_{i2}} \cdot \beta, \quad p_{i2}^* = \beta - p_{i1} = \frac{d_{i2}}{d_{i1}+d_{i2}} \cdot \beta$$

and the minimum value of $(p_{i1} \cdot \frac{p_{i1}}{d_{i1}+p_{i1}} + p_{i2} \cdot \frac{p_{i2}}{d_{i2}+p_{i2}})$ is:

$$\min\limits_{p_i(r_1,r_2)} (p_{i1} \cdot \frac{p_{i1}}{d_{i1}+p_{i1}} + p_{i2} \cdot \frac{p_{i2}}{d_{i2}+p_{i2}}) = p_{i1}^* \cdot \frac{p_{i1}^*}{d_{i1}+p_{i1}^*} + p_{i2}^* \cdot \frac{p_{i2}^*}{d_{i2}+p_{i2}^*} = \frac{\beta^2}{d_{i1}+d_{i2}+\beta}$$

Based on that, we have:

$$(\frac{p_{i1}^2}{d_{i1}+p_{i1}} + \frac{p_{i2}^2}{d_{i2}+p_{i2}}) \geqslant \frac{\beta^2}{d_{i1}+d_{i2}+\beta} = \frac{(p_{i1}+p_{i2})^2}{d_{i1}+d_{i2}+(p_{i1}+p_{i2})}$$

and when $p_{i1} = \frac{d_{i1}}{d_{i1}+d_{i2}} \cdot \beta$, $p_{i2} = \frac{d_{i2}}{d_{i1}+d_{i2}} \cdot \beta$, the equality satisfies.

Subject to $\sum\limits_{r_j \in R_e} p_{ij} = \theta_e$, we minimize $\Gamma(p_i\{R_e\})$ using above inequation as:

$$\Gamma(p_i\{R_e\}) = \sum_{j=1}^{|R_e|} p_{ij} \cdot \frac{p_{ij}}{d_{ij}+p_{ij}} = (\frac{p_{i1}^2}{d_{i1}+p_{i1}} + \frac{p_{i2}^2}{d_{i2}+p_{i2}}) + \sum_{j=3}^{|R_e|} p_{ij} \cdot \frac{p_{ij}}{d_{ij}+p_{ij}}$$

$$\geq \frac{(p_{i1}+p_{i2})^2}{d_{i1}+d_{i2}+(p_{i1}+p_{i2})} + \frac{p_{i3}^2}{d_{i3}+p_{i3}} + \sum_{j=4}^{|R_e|} p_{ij} \cdot \frac{p_{ij}}{d_{ij}+p_{ij}}$$

$$\geq \frac{(p_{i1}+p_{i2}+p_{i3})^2}{d_{i1}+d_{i2}+d_{i3}+(p_{i1}+p_{i2}+p_{i3})} + \frac{p_{i4}^2}{d_{i4}+p_{i4}} + \sum_{j=5}^{|R_e|} p_{ij} \cdot \frac{p_{ij}}{d_{ij}+p_{ij}}$$

$$\geq \cdots \geq \frac{(\sum\limits_{r_j \in R_e} p_{ij})^2}{\sum\limits_{r_j \in R_e} p_{ij} + \sum\limits_{r_j \in R_e} d_{ij}} = \frac{(\theta_e)^2}{\theta_e + \sum\limits_{r_j \in R_e} d_{ij}} = \frac{(\theta_e)^2}{\theta_e + D_e}$$

When $p_{ij} = \frac{d_{ij}}{D_e} \cdot \theta_e$, all the equalities satisfy.

Therefore, we have the optimal strategy $p_i^*\{R_e\} = [p_{ij}^*]^{1 \times |R_e|} = \frac{\theta_e}{D_e} \cdot [d_{ij}]^{1 \times |R_e|}$ to

minimize $\Gamma(p_i\{R_e\})$, i.e., $\min\limits_{p_i\{R_e\}} \Gamma(p_i\{R_e\}) = \Gamma(p_i^*\{R_e\}) = \sum\limits_{r_j \in R_e} p_{ij}^* \cdot \frac{p_{ij}^*}{p_{ij}^*+d_{ij}} =$

$\frac{(\theta_e)^2}{\theta_e + D_e}$. Lemma 1 is proved.   □

4.3 More Anonymity through Trust Degree

We demonstrate that u_i can gain more anonymity by considering routers' trust degree in both simulation and real-world social networks. This is compared with the strategy used by existing trust-based algorithms, where the equal probability is used to select routers with equal trust [4]. We denote this existing trust-based strategy as $p_i^=\{R_e\} = [p_{ij}^=]^{1 \times |R_e|}$, where $p_{ij}^= = \frac{\theta_e}{|R_e|}$ for $\forall r_j \in R_e$. Although the optimal strategy $p_i^*\{R_e\}$ is proved to be able to maximize u_i's anonymity, we show that u_i can gain different anonymity improvement in the context of different $[d_{ij}]^{1 \times |R_e|}$. We use $\Gamma(p_i\{R_e\})$ as the metric for u_i's anonymity. A smaller $\Gamma(p_i\{R_e\})$ represents more anonymity. As θ_e will not affect our analysis, we simply consider $\theta_e = 1$.

Simulation. We consider the case that u_i has 10 equally trusted routers (i.e., $|R_e| = 10$) and the sum of d_{ij} for $r_j \in R_e$ is 100 (i.e., $D_e = 100$). Figure 4(a) shows the heat map for 1000 different samples of $[d_{ij}]^{1 \times |R_e|}$ that we randomly generate. The dark color indicates a large d_{ij} while the light color means a small value. Figure 4(b) illustrates the comparison of u_i's anonymity for these 1000 samples of $[d_{ij}]^{1 \times |R_e|}$ between existing trust-based strategy (i.e., $p_i^=\{R_e\}$) and the optimal strategy (i.e., $p_i^*\{R_e\}$). In Figure 4(a), we sort the indexes of the 1000 samples of $[d_{ij}]^{1 \times |R_e|}$ in an ascending order according to $\Gamma(p_i^=\{R_e\})$ of these samples and arrange d_{ij}s in each $[d_{ij}]^{1 \times |R_e|}$ in a descending order according to r_j.

Figure 4(b) shows that the $\Gamma(p_i^*\{R_e\})$ stays at 0.0099 for any $[d_{ij}]^{1 \times |R_e|}$. The value 0.0099 is the minimal chance of inferring u_i when $D_e = 100$ and $\theta_e = 1$ because $\frac{(\theta_e)^2}{\theta_e + D_e} = \frac{1}{101} = 0.0099$. Refer to Figure 4(a), we find that, a larger anonymity improvement (i.e., a larger $\frac{\Gamma(p_i^=\{R_e\})}{\Gamma(p_i^*\{R_e\})}$) could be achieved in the context of $[d_{ij}]^{1 \times |R_e|}$ whose d_{ij}s vary more significantly. In particular, when $[d_{ij}]^{1 \times |R_e|}$ satisfies $\exists d_{ij} = 100$ and other d_{ij}s are all equal to 0, the $\Gamma(p_i\{R_e\})$ is reduced from 0.9001 in $p_i^=\{R_e\}$ to 0.0099 in $p_i^*\{R_e\}$. The value 0.9001 indicates u_i suffers more than 90% probability to be inferred while 0.0099 represents this probability is less than 1%. Even when $[d_{ij}]^{1 \times |R_e|}$ are uniformly distributed, i.e., d_{ij}s for $\forall r_j \in R_e$ are all the same and equal to $\frac{D_e}{|R_e|} = 10$, the optimal strategy can at least keep anonymity the same as in existing strategy (i.e., $\frac{\Gamma(p_i^=\{R_e\})}{\Gamma(p_i^*\{R_e\})} = 1$).

Real-World Social Networks. We also investigate the optimal strategy $p_i^*\{R_e\}$'s effectiveness by using the public data set from the Facebook [22]. This set includes more than 1.5 millions social links from 53,609 persons to their friends. Each person has more than one friend and all these 53,609 persons have 63,406 friends in total. We thus regard the 53,609 persons as the users in onion routing networks and assume the 63,406 friends deploy onion routers. We consider all these 53,609 persons as to be u_i one by one, and compare u_i's anonymity between the optimal strategy $p_i^*\{R_e\}$ and existing trust-based strategy $p_i^=\{R_e\}$. Each person equally trusts the routers set up by their friends, but distrusts other routers (i.e., two levels of trust are considered). Persons only select routers from their friends (i.e., $\theta_e = 1$ for R_e where $t_e = \max_{r_j \in R} t_{ij}$). We measure u_i's anonymity using $\Gamma(p_i\{R_e\})$ and a smaller $\Gamma(p_i\{R_e\})$ indicates more

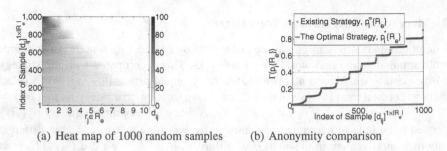

(a) Heat map of 1000 random samples   (b) Anonymity comparison

Fig. 4. Anonymity comparison between existing trust-based strategy and the optimal strategy for 1000 random samples of $[d_{ij}]^{1 \times |R_e|}$ when $|R_e| = 10$ and $D_e = 100$

anonymity. Note that, when a person is considered as u_i, we calculate d_{ij} for this person in the case that other persons use existing trust-based strategy to choose routers.

Figure 5 shows the results for these 53, 609 users. The D_es of these users are from 0.01 to 2491. In accordance with Lemma 1, although $\Gamma\left(p_i^*\{R_e\}\right)$ decreases when D_e increases, $\Gamma\left(p_i^*\{R_e\}\right)$ is consistently smaller than $\Gamma\left(p_i^=\{R_e\}\right)$ for any D_e. By analyzing the results in depth, we find more than 99.6% users can improve their anonymity with the help of the optimal strategy $p_i^*\{R_e\}$ (i.e., $\frac{\Gamma\left(p_i^=\{R_e\}\right)}{\Gamma\left(p_i^*\{R_e\}\right)} > 1$). In particular, more than 65.6% users obtain at least 1.5 times improvement for their anonymity (i.e., $\frac{\Gamma\left(p_i^=\{R_e\}\right)}{\Gamma\left(p_i^*\{R_e\}\right)} > 1.5$). The largest improvement is $\frac{\Gamma\left(p_i^=\{R_e\}\right)}{\Gamma\left(p_i^*\{R_e\}\right)} = 31.1$. It can be seen that the user anonymity can be improved by considering routers' trust degree in practice.

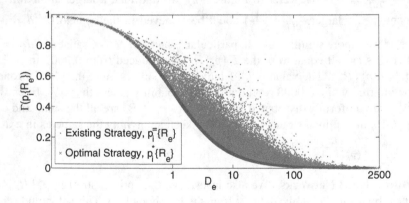

Fig. 5. Anonymity comparison between existing trust-based strategy and the optimal strategy in real-world social networks [22]

5   Trust Degree Aware Routing Algorithm for Path Selection

The scenario discussed in Section 4 assumes the adversary only observes a single hop of a connection. However, a more common scenario is that the adversary can observe more than one hop in a connection. By taking this general case into account, we design trust degree aware routing algorithms for path selection. We still only consider trust degree information among the routers equally trusted by a user. This helps preserve the capability of circumventing compromised routers.

Section 5.1 first formalizes the metric of anonymity for path selection. In particular, we measure anonymity by using the chance of a user to be inferred by the adversary who observes multiple hops of this user's connection. Section 5.2 then gives a general version of the optimal trust degree aware routing algorithm for path selection in theory.

Table 2 summarizes important notations used in this section.

Table 2. Important notations in Section 5

Symbol	Definition
$A \setminus B$	the set A excluding a sub set $B \subseteq A$ or an element $B \in A$
h_k	the k-th hop in u_i's path
O	the set of hops exposed to the adversary
o_n	the n-th element of set O
t_k	a trust threshold for u_i to select routers in hop h_k
p_{ij}^k	u_i's probability to select router r_j for hop h_k
R_+^n	a set of routers where $r_j \in R_+^n, t_{ij} \geq t_n$
R_e^n	a set of routers with equal trust from u_i, $r_j \in R_e^n, t_{ij} = t_e \geq t_k$
$p_i\{R_+^k\}\|_O$	a routing algorithm $p_i\{R_+^k\}\|_O = \{p_i\{R_+^k\}, h_k \in O\}$
$p_i\{R_e^k\}\|_O$	a sub routing algorithm $p_i\{R_e^k\}\|_O = \{p_i\{R_e^k\}, h_k \in O\}$
N	$N = \|O\|$ be the number of exposed hops
$\Gamma\left(p_i\{R_+^k\}\|_O\right)$	the expectation of the chance to infer u_i if $p_i\{R_+^k\}\|_O$ is used
θ_e^k	$\theta_e^k = \sum_{r_j \in R_e^k} p_{ij}^k$
$D_e^{(n)} \cdot d_{ij}^{(n+1,N)}$	$\sum_{r_j \in R_e^k, h_k = o_n} \cdots \sum_{r_j \in R_e^k, h_k = o_1} \sum_{u_x \in U \setminus u_i} \prod_{h_k \in O} p_{xj}^k$

5.1   Minimizing the Chance of Being Inferred when Multiple Hops Exposed

Similar to Section 4.1, we focus on a user u_i who is aware of routers' trust degree with respect to a population of other users whose trust distributions and routing algorithms are known. Given a path of u_i, the adversary attempts to compromise routers in this path and employs the compromised routers to observe routers in adjacent hops. In particular, if the destination (e.g., a web server) is compromised, the last hop can be observed by the adversary. Based on the knowledge of a priori trust relationships, the adversary infers u_i by observing routers in exposed hops.[3]

Given a L-hop path of u_i. Let h_k be the k-th hop in the path. Let O be the set of hops exposed to the adversary. Therefore, u_i has the probability $\prod_{h_k \in O} p_{ij}^k \cdot$

$\prod_{h_k \in O} p_{ij}^k / \sum_{u_x \in U} \prod_{h_k \in O} p_{xj}^k$ to be inferred through r_j in each of these exposed hops, where p_{ij}^k is the u_i's probability to select r_j for the k-th hop (i.e., hop h_k) in u_i's path.

Let $o_n \in O$ be the n-th element of the set O. Let $N = |O| \leq L$ be the number of exposed hops.

---

[3] Prior research [4] assumes the length of users' paths is fixed and known. The adversary thus can know the number of unexposed hops in the path and make some inference based on these unexposed hops. In this paper, we do not consider the inference based on unexposed hops because the user can simply establish path with random length to evade such inference.

We consider the problem as minimizing the chance of being inferred when a set O of hops in u_i's path are observed by the adversary. The objective function is:

$$\Gamma\left(p_i\{R_+^k\}|_O\right) = \sum_{r_j \in R_+^k, h_k = o_N} \cdots \sum_{r_j \in R_+^k, h_k = o_1} \frac{\prod\limits_{h_k \in O} p_{ij}^k \cdot \prod\limits_{h_k \in O} p_{ij}^k}{\sum\limits_{u_x \in U} \prod\limits_{h_k \in O} p_{xj}^k} \tag{5}$$

where, $p_i\{R_+^k\}|_O = \{p_i\{R_+^k\}, h_k \in O\}$ is a routing algorithm consisting of $N = |O|$ router selection strategies for these exposed hops belonging to O in the path. Each $p_i\{R_+^k\} = [p_{ij}^k]^{1 \times |R_+^k|}$ is a router selection strategy for the k-th hop (i.e., h_k). $R_+^k \subseteq R$ is the set of candidate routers that u_i can select for hop h_k, i.e., $\sum_{r_j \in R_+^k} p_{ij}^k = 1$. Existing trust-based routing algorithms will use a trust threshold t_k to restrict u_i's router selection for its hop h_k, such as $\forall r_j \in R_+^k, t_{ij} \geq t_k$. In particular, the downhill algorithm [4] uses a decreasing trust threshold in the hops from the user to the destination, i.e., $t_k \leq t_{k-1}$. But if u_i is only allowed to select the most trusted routers for its connection, $t_k = \max\limits_{r_j \in R} t_{ij}$ for $\forall k \in [1, L]$.

Let R_e^k be a set of routers with equal trust $t_e \geq t_k$ (i.e., $r_j \in R_e^k, t_{ij} = t_e \geq t_k$). We can express R_+^k as $R_+^k = \bigcup_{t_e \geq t_k} R_e^k$.

The object function $\Gamma\left(p_i\{R_+^k\}|_O\right)$ calculates the expectation of the chance that u_i can be inferred when the routing algorithm $p_i\{R_+^k\}|_O$ is used. As a lower chance of being inferred indicates more anonymity, we maximize u_i's anonymity by finding the optimal routing algorithm $p_i\{R_+^k\}|_O^*$ to minimize $\Gamma\left(p_i\{R_+^k\}|_O\right)$ as:

$$p_i\{R_+^k\}|_O^* = \arg \min_{p_i\{R_+^k\}|_O} \Gamma\left(p_i\{R_+^k\}|_O\right), \text{ where, } R_+^k = \bigcup_{t_e \geq t_k} R_e^k$$
$$\text{subject to } \sum_{r_j \in R_e^k} p_{ij}^k = \theta_e^k \text{ for } t_e \geq t_k \text{ and } h_k \in O \tag{6}$$

where, θ_e^k is the sum of u_i's probabilities of choosing routers with equal trust $t_e \geq t_k$ for hop h_k in u_i's connection. We should keep any θ_e^k the same as in existing trust-based algorithms when we explore the optimal $p_i\{R_+^k\}|_O^*$, because the same θ_e^k means the same capability of defending against compromised routers.

Let $p_i\{R_e^k\}|_O = \{p_i\{R_e^k\}, h_k \in O\}$. As $R_+^k = \bigcup_{t_e \geq t_k} R_e^k$, the object function in Eqn.(5) thus can be re-expressed as:

$$\Gamma\left(p_i\{R_+^k\}|_O\right) = \sum_{t_e \geq t_k, h_k = o_N} \cdots \sum_{t_e \geq t_k, h_k = o_1} \Gamma\left(p_i\{R_e^k\}|_O\right),$$
$$\text{where, } \Gamma\left(p_i\{R_e^k\}|_O\right) = \sum_{r_j \in R_e^k, h_k = o_N} \cdots \sum_{r_j \in R_e^k, h_k = o_1} \frac{\prod\limits_{h_k \in O} p_{ij}^k \cdot \prod\limits_{h_k \in O} p_{ij}^k}{\sum\limits_{u_x \in U} \prod\limits_{h_k \in O} p_{xj}^k} \tag{7}$$

Therefore, to facilitate the exploration of the minimal $\Gamma\left(p_i\{R_+^k\}|_O\right)$ without changing the value of any θ_e^k for $t_e \geq t_k, h_k \in O$, we can find the minimal $\Gamma\left(p_i\{R_e^k\}|_O\right)$ subject to each θ_e^k instead. When all the minimal $\Gamma\left(p_i\{R_e^k\}|_O\right)$s for $t_e \geq t_k, h_k \in O$ are found, the minimal $\Gamma\left(p_i\{R_+^k\}|_O\right)$ is also reached. The optimal routing algorithm $p_i\{R_+^k\}|_O^*$ consists a set of sub optimal routing algorithms $p_i\{R_e^k\}|_O^*$ for $t_e \geq t_k, h_k \in O$.

5.2   The Optimal Trust Degree Aware Routing Algorithm in Theory

Intuitively, we expect the sub optimal routing algorithm $p_i\{R_e^k\}|_O^*$ can be implemented by applying the single hop's optimal router selection strategy $p_i^*\{R_e\}$ proposed in Section 4 to each of the $N = |O|$ exposed hops independently, i.e., $p_i^*\{R_e^k\} = p_i^*\{R_e\}$ for $h_k \in O$. However, it is not the case because the router selection strategies $p_i^*\{R_e^k\}$ for these N exposed hops are correlated. To illustrate it, we give an example in Figure 6. We assume u_i equally trusts routers r_1, r_2 and r_3. If only hop h_2 is exposed to the adversary, according to the single hop's optimal router selection strategy $p_i^*\{R_e\}$, we should have a larger probability to choose r_1 than r_2 for hop h_2, because r_1 is trusted by two other users (i.e., u_1 and u_2) but r_2 is just trusted by one (i.e., u_3). However, if hop h_3 is also exposed and r_3 is already selected for hop h_3, the adversary can deanonymize u_i directly if u_i selects r_1 for hop h_2. The reason is that, except u_i, no other users trust both r_1 and r_3 in Figure 6. In this situation, we cannot minimize the adversary's chance of inferring u_i by applying the single hops's optimal strategy to hop h_2 independently.

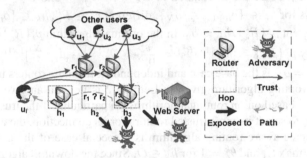

Fig. 6. An example to show the router selection strategies in different exposed hops are correlated

Based on the analysis of Figure 6, we find that the joint probabilities of selecting routers for multiple exposed hops are correlated. We consider u_i selects routers for its connection in a descending order (i.e., given $h_k, h_{k'}$ and $k' > k$, u_i first selects routers for $h_{k'}$). In this case, to minimize the chance of being inferred, u_i's probability of selecting a router for a hop $h_k \in O$ should depend on the routers already selected in hops $h_{k'} \in O, k' > k$.

Lemma 2 gives the optimal routing algorithm $p_i\{R_e^k\}|_O^*$ and the minimal $\Gamma\left(p_i\{R_e^k\}|_O\right)$ using this algorithm. Due to the page limit, we omit the proof of Lemma 2 in this paper.

We sort O in an ascending order, i.e., for $h_k = o_n$ and $h_{k'} = o_{n+1}$, we have $k < k'$.

Let $D_e^{(n)} \cdot d_{ij}^{(n+1,N)} = \sum\limits_{r_j \in R_e^k, h_k = o_n} \cdots \sum\limits_{r_j \in R_e^k, h_k = o_1} \sum\limits_{u_x \in U \setminus u_i} \prod\limits_{h_k \in O} p_{xj}^k$, where $U \setminus u_i$

is the set of users excluding u_i. In particular, $D_e^{(0)} \cdot d_{ij}^{(1,N)} = d_{ij}^{(1,N)} = \sum\limits_{u_x \in U \setminus u_i} \prod\limits_{h_k \in O} p_{xj}^k$

and $D_e^{(N)} \cdot d_{ij}^{(N+1,N)} = D_e^{(N)} = \sum\limits_{r_j \in R_e^k, h_k = o_N} \cdots \sum\limits_{r_j \in R_e^k, h_k = o_1} \sum\limits_{u_x \in U \setminus u_i} \prod\limits_{h_k \in O} p_{xj}^k$.

Lemma 2. *Subject to* $\sum_{r_j \in R_e^k} p_{ij}^k = \theta_e^k$ *for* $t_e \geq t_k, h_k \in O$, *the optimal routing algorithm* $p_i\{R_+^k\}|_O^*$ *for minimizing* $\Gamma\left(p_i\{R_+^k\}|o\right)$ *consists of a set of sub optimal algorithms* $p_i\{R_e^k\}|_O^*$ *for* $t_e \geq t_k, h_k \in O$. *In each* $p_i\{R_e^k\}|_O^*$, *for* $h_k = o_n$, *we have:*

$$p_i^*\{R_e^k\} = [p_{ij}^{k*}]^{1 \times |R_e^k|} = \frac{\theta_e^k}{D_e^{(n)} \cdot d_{ij}^{(n+1,N)}} \cdot D_e^{(n-1)} \cdot [d_{ij}^{(n,N)}]^{1 \times |R_e^k|}$$

where, the hop h_k *is the* n-*th element in* O (*i.e.,* $h_k = o_n$). *Using this optimal routing algorithm, the chance can be minimized to be:*

$$\min_{p_i\{R_+^k\}|o} \Gamma\left(p_i\{R_+^k\}|o\right) = \sum_{t_e \geq t_k, h_k = o_N} \cdots \sum_{t_e \geq t_k, h_k = o_1} \frac{(\prod_{h_k \in O} \theta_e^k)^2}{\prod_{h_k \in O} \theta_e^k + D_e^{(N)}}$$

Where, $D_e^{(n-1)} \cdot [d_{ij}^{(n,N)}]^{1 \times |R_e^k|}$ is a matrix of $D_e^{(n-1)} \cdot d_{ij}^{(n,N)}$s for $r_j \in R_e^k, h_k = o_n$. Moreover, $D_e^{(n)} \cdot d_{ij}^{(n+1,N)}$ can be considered as the sum of $D_e^{(n-1)} \cdot d_{ij}^{(n,N)}$s over $r_j \in R_e^k, h_k = o_n$. Since the calculation of $D_e^{(n-1)} \cdot d_{ij}^{(n,N)}$ and $D_e^{(n)} \cdot d_{ij}^{(n+1,N)}$ are based on the p_{ij}^ks for $h_k \in \{o_{n+1}, \ldots, o_N\}$, different $r_j \in R_e^k, h_k \in \{o_{n+1}, \ldots, o_N\}$ will lead to different $p_i^*\{R_e^k\}, h_k = o_n$. In the optimal algorithm $p_i\{R_e^k\}|_O^*$, the router selection strategy $p_i^*\{R_e^k\} = [p_{ij}^{k*}]^{1 \times |R_e^k|} = \frac{\theta_e^k}{D_e^{(N)}} \cdot D_e^{(N-1)} \cdot [d_{ij}^{(N,N)}]^{1 \times |R_e^k|}$ for the last exposed hop $h_k = o_N$ is the base case and independent from the routers in other hops.

The optimal routing algorithm given in Lemma 2 is general and we can use it to improve any trust-based onion routing algorithms. In particular, if the trust-based algorithm restricts u_i to select its most trusted routers for its connection, the corresponding optimal trust degree aware routing algorithm is a special case of the general version when $t_k = t_e = \max_{r_j \in R} t_{ij}$ and $\theta_e^k = 1$ for $h_k \in O$. Since the downhill algorithm uses the same probability to select routers from R_+^n [4], the optimal trust degree aware downhill algorithm can be the special case of the general version when $t_k \leq t_{k-1}$ and $\theta_e^k = \frac{|R_e^k|}{|R_+^n|}$ for $t_e \geq t_k, h_k \in O$.

An Example. We give an example to help understand Lemma 2 in depth. In this example, we design an optimal trust degree aware routing algorithm for u_i given the last two hops exposed (i.e., $O = \{o_1 = h_2, o_2 = h_3\}$) in Figure 6. We assume the network only includes four users (i.e., u_i, u_1, u_2 and u_3) and three onion routers (i.e., r_1, r_2 and r_3). We investigate u_i who considers trust degree information with respect to other users (i.e., u_1, u_2 and u_3) who use the equal probabilities to select routers with equal trust. We consider two levels of trust (i.e., trust and distrust) and users are restricted to select their trusted routers. u_1 and u_2 trust r_1 but distrust r_2 and r_3. u_3 equally trusts r_2 and r_3 but distrusts r_1. Therefore, we have $p_{11}^k = p_{21}^k = 1$ and $p_{32}^k = p_{33}^k = 0.5$ for $h_k \in O = \{h_2, h_3\}$. Moreover, u_i equally trusts r_1, r_2 and r_3, we have $R_+^2 = R_e^2 = R_+^3 = R_e^3 = \{r_1, r_2, r_3\}$ and $\theta_e^2 = \theta_e^3 = 1$.

If u_i uses the same probability to choose routers with equal trust for its connection (i.e., u_i's routing algorithm is $p_i\{R_+^k\}|_{\{h_2, h_3\}}^=$ where $p_{ij}^{k=} = \frac{1}{3}$ for $r_j \in R_+^k, h_k \in \{h_2, h_3\}$), the adversary has the chance $\Gamma\left(p_i\{R_+^k\}|_{\{h_2, h_3\}}^=\right) = 0.587$ to infer u_i. But if u_i uses the optimal trust degree aware routing algorithm $p_i\{R_+^k\}|_{\{h_2,h_3\}}^*$ for the 2 exposed hops according to Lemma 2, the adversary's chance of inferring u_i is minimized to $\Gamma\left(p_i\{R_+^k\}|_{\{h_2,h_3\}}^*\right) = 0.25$. It can be seen, u_i obtains more than 2 times improvement for its anonymity (i.e., $\dfrac{\Gamma\left(p_i\{R_+^k\}|_{\{h_2,h_3\}}^=\right)}{\Gamma\left(p_i\{R_+^k\}|_{\{h_2,h_3\}}^*\right)} > 2$). Table 3 gives this optimal algorithm. The probabilities of selecting routers for hop h_2 depend on the routers that are already selected in hop h_3.

Table 3. The optimal trust degree aware routing algorithm $p_i\{R_+^k\}|_{\{h_2,h_3\}}^*$ of u_i in Figure 6

$r_j \in R_+^3$	r_1	r_2	r_3
p_{ij}^{3*}	0.6667	0.1667	0.1667

$r_j \in R_+^2$	r_1	r_2	r_3	r_1	r_2	r_3	r_1	r_2	r_3
p_{ij}^{2*}	1	0	0	0	0.5	0.5	0	0.5	0.5

6 Conclusions

In this paper, we show that the user can gain more anonymity by considering routers' trust degree in trust-based onion routing networks. With solid theoretical analysis, we propose the optimal trust degree aware solutions to maximize anonymity for both router selection and path selection. This is a theoretical foundation for trust degree aware onion routing. Our results benefit future research for practical applications.

Acknowledgements. We thank the anonymous reviewers for their very helpful comments. This work is partially supported by grants G-U386 from The Hong Kong Polytechnic University, 60903185 from NSFC, 2012M511058 from CPSF and 12R21412500 from STCSM.

References

1. Puttaswamy, K.P.N., Sala, A., Zhao, B.Y.: Improving anonymity using social links. In: Proc. Workshop on Secure Network Protocols (2008)
2. Johnson, A., Syverson, P.: More anonymous onion routing through trust. In: Proc. IEEE CSF (2009)
3. Danezis, G., Diaz, C., Troncoso, C., Laurie, B.: Drac: An Architecture for Anonymous Low-Volume Communications. In: Atallah, M.J., Hopper, N.J. (eds.) PETS 2010. LNCS, vol. 6205, pp. 202–219. Springer, Heidelberg (2010)
4. Johnson, A., Syverson, P., Dingledine, R., Mathewson, N.: Trust-based anonymous communication: Adversary models and routing algorithms. In: Proc. ACM CCS (2011)
5. Goldschlag, D.M., Reed, M.G., Syverson, P.F.: Hiding routing information. In: Proc. Workshop on Information Hiding (1996)
6. Syverson, P.F., Goldschlag, D.M., Reed, M.G.: Anonymous connections and onion routing. In: Proc. IEEE Symposium on Security and Privacy (1997)
7. Dingledine, R., Mathewson, N., Syverson, P.: Tor: The second-generation onion router. In: Proc. USENIX Security Symposium (2004)

8. Wright, M., Adler, M., Levine, B.N., Shields, C.: The predecessor attack: An analysis of a threat to anonymous communications systems. ACM Transactions on Information and System Security (2004)

9. Evans, N.S., Dingledine, R., Grothoff, C.: A practical congestion attack on Tor using long paths. In: Proc. USENIX Security Symposium (2009)

10. Troncoso, C., Danezis, G.: The Bayesian traffic analysis of mix networks. In: Proc. ACM CCS (2009)

11. Agrawal, D., Kesdogan, D.: Measuring anonymity: the disclosure attack. IEEE Security & Privacy (2003)

12. Douceur, J.R.: The Sybil Attack. In: Druschel, P., Kaashoek, M.F., Rowstron, A. (eds.) IPTPS 2002. LNCS, vol. 2429, pp. 251–260. Springer, Heidelberg (2002)

13. Syverson, P., Tsudik, G., Reed, M., Landwehr, C.: Towards an analysis of onion routing security. In: Proc. Designing Privacy Enhancing Technologies: Workshop on Design Issues in Anonymity and Unobservability (2000)

14. Murdoch, S., Danezis, G.: Low-cost traffic analysis of Tor. In: Proc. IEEE Symposium on Security and Privacy (2005)

15. Øverlier, L., Syverson, P.: Locating hidden servers. In: Proc. IEEE Symposium on Security and Privacy (2006)

16. Bauer, K., McCoy, D., Grunwald, D., Kohno, T., Sicker, D.: Low-resource routing attacks against Tor. In: Proc. ACM Workshop on Privacy in the Electronic Society (2007)

17. Fu, X., Ling, Z.: One cell is enough to break Tor's anonymity. In: Proc. Black Hat DC (2009)

18. Ling, Z., Luo, J., Yu, W., Fu, X., Xuan, D., Jia, W.: A new cell counter based attack against Tor. In: Proc. ACM CCS (2009)

19. Zhu, Y., Fu, X., Graham, B., Bettati, R., Zhao, W.: Correlation-based traffic analysis attacks on anonymity networks. IEEE Transactions on Parallel and Distributed Systems (2009)

20. Hopper, N., Vasserman, E.Y., Chan-Tin, E.: How much anonymity does network latency leak? ACM Transactions on Information and System Security (2010)

21. Diaz, C., Troncoso, C., Serjantov, A.: On the impact of social network profiling on anonymity. In: Proc. Workshop on Privacy Enhancing Technologies (2008)

22. Mislove, A.: Wosn 2009 data sets (2009), http://socialnetworks.mpi-sws.org/data-wosn2009.html

23. Luo, X., Zhou, P., Zhang, J., Perdisci, R., Lee, W., Chang, R.K.C.: Exposing invisible timing-based traffic watermarks with backlit. In: Proc. ACSAC (2011)

24. Luo, X., Zhang, J., Perdisci, R., Lee, W.: On the Secrecy of Spread-Spectrum Flow Watermarks. In: Gritzalis, D., Preneel, B., Theoharidou, M. (eds.) ESORICS 2010. LNCS, vol. 6345, pp. 232–248. Springer, Heidelberg (2010)

25. Marques, R., Zúquete, A.: Social networking for anonymous communication systems: A survey. In: Proc. International Conference on Computational Aspects of Social Networks (2011)

26. Chaum, D.: Untraceable electronic mail, return addresses, and digital pseudonyms. Communications of the ACM (1981)

27. Danezis, G., Dingledine, R., Mathewson, N.: Mixminion: Design of a type iii anonymous remailer protocol. In: Proc. IEEE Symposium on Security and Privacy (2003)

28. The Tor Project. Tor path selection specification (2009), http://tor.hermetix.org/svn/trunk/doc/spec/path-spec.txt

29. Snader, R., Borisov, N.: A tune-up for Tor: Improving security and performance in the Tor network. In: Proc. ISOC Network and Distributed System Security Symposium (2008)

30. Snader, R., Borisov, N.: Improving security and performance in the Tor network through tunable path selection. IEEE Transactions on Dependable and Secure Computing (2010)

31. Dingledine, R., Freedman, M.J., Hopwood, D., Molnar, D.: A Reputation System to Increase MIX-Net Reliability. In: Moskowitz, I.S. (ed.) IH 2001. LNCS, vol. 2137, pp. 126–141. Springer, Heidelberg (2001)
32. Dingledine, R., Syverson, P.: Reliable MIX cascade networks through reputation. In: Proc. International Conference on Financial Cryptography (2003)
33. Böttcher, A., Kauer, B., Härtig, H.: Trusted computing serving an anonymity service. In: Proc. International Conference on Trust & Trustworthy Computing (2008)
34. Gross, R., Acquisti, A.: Information revelation and privacy in online social networks. In: Proc. ACM Workshop on Privacy in the Electronic Society (2005)
35. Narayanan, A., Shmatikov, V.: De-anonymizing social networks. In: Proc. IEEE Symposium on Security and Privacy (2009)

Privacy Preserving Back-Propagation Learning Made Practical with Cloud Computing

Jiawei Yuan and Shucheng Yu

University of Arkansas at Little Rock, USA
{jxyuan, sxyu1}@ualr.edu

Abstract. Back-propagation is an effective method for neural network learning. To improve the accuracy of the learning result, in practice multiple parties may want to collaborate by jointly executing the back-propagation algorithm on the union of their respective data sets. During this process no party wants to disclose her/his private data to others for privacy concerns. Existing schemes supporting this kind of collaborative learning just partially solve the problem by limiting the way of data partition or considering only two parties. There still lacks a solution for more general and practical settings wherein two or more parties, each with an arbitrarily partitioned data set, collaboratively conduct learning.

In this paper, by utilizing the power of cloud computing, we solve this open problem with our proposed privacy preserving back-propagation algorithm, which is tailored for the setting of multiparty and arbitrarily partitioned data. In our proposed scheme, each party encrypts his/her private data locally and uploads the ciphertexts into the cloud. The cloud then executes most of the operations pertaining to the learning algorithms with ciphertexts but learns nothing about the original private data. By securely offloading the expensive operations to the cloud, we keep the local computation and communication costs on each party minimal and independent to the number of participants. To support flexible operations over ciphertexts, we adopt and tailor the BGN 'doubly homomorphic' encryption algorithm for the multiparty setting. Thorough analysis shows that our proposed scheme is secure, efficient and scalable.

Keywords: privacy reserving, learning, neural network, back-propagation, cloud computing, computation outsource.

1 Introduction

Back-propagation[17] is an effective method for learning neural networks and has been widely used in various applications. The accuracy of the learning result, despite other facts, is highly affected by the volume of high quality data used for learning. As compared to learning with only local data set, collaborative learning improves the learning accuracy by incorporating more data sets into the learning process[19,11]: the participating parties carry out learning not only on their own data sets, but also on others' data sets. With the recent remarkable growth of new computing infrastructures such as Cloud Computing, it has been more convenient

A.D. Keromytis and R. Di Pietro (Eds.): SecureComm 2012, LNICST 106, pp. 292–309, 2013.

than ever for users across the Internet, who may not even know each other, to conduct joint/collaborative learning through the shared infrastructure[12,13].

Despite the potential benefits, one crucial issue pertaining to the Internet-wide collaborative learning is the protection of data privacy for each participant. In particular, the participants from different trust domains may not want to disclose their private data sets, which may contain privacy or proprietary information, to anybody else. In applications such as healthcare, disclosure of sensitive data, e.g., protected health information (PHI)[2], is not only a privacy issue but of legal concerns according to the privacy rules such as Health Insurance Probability and Accountability Act(HIPAA)[1]. In order to embrace the Internet-wide collaborative learning, it is imperative to provide a solution that allows the participants, who lack mutual trust, to conduct learning on neural networks jointly without disclosing their respective private data sets. Preferably, the solution shall be efficient and scalable enough to support an arbitrary number of participants, each possessing arbitrarily partitioned data sets.

Related Work. Theoretically, secure multiparty computation (SMC)[20] can be used to solve problems of this kind. But the extremely high computation and communication complexity of SMC, due to the circuit size, usually makes it far from practical even in the two-party case. In order to provide practical solutions for privacy preserving back-propagation network (BPN) learning, several schemes have been proposed recently. Schlitter[18] introduces a privacy preserving BPN learning scheme that enables two or more parties to jointly perform BPN learning without disclosing their respective private data sets. But the solution is proposed only for horizontal partitioned data. Moreover, this scheme cannot protect the intermediate results, which may also contain sensitive data, during the learning process. Chen et. al.[6] proposes a privacy preserving BPN learning algorithm for two-party scenarios. This scheme provides strong protection for data sets including intermediate results. However, it just supports vertically partitioned data. To overcome this limitation, Bansal et. al.[4] enhanced this scheme and proposed a solution for arbitrarily partitioned data. Nevertheless, this enhanced scheme, just like [6], was proposed for the two-party scenario. Directly extending them to the multi-party setting will introduce a computation/communication complexity quadratic in n, the number of participants. In practical implementation, such a complexity represents a tremendous cost on each party considering the already expensive operations on the underlying groups such as Elliptic Curves. To our best knowledge, there is no efficient and scalable solution that supports collaborative BPN learning with privacy preservation in the multiparty setting over arbitrarily partitioned data.

Our Scheme. In this work, we address this open problem by incorporating the computing power of the cloud. The main idea of our scheme can be summarized as follows: each participant first encrypts her/his private data with the system public key and then uploads the ciphertexts to the cloud; cloud servers then execute most of the operations pertaining to the learning process over the ciphertexts and return the encrypted results to the participants; the participants jointly decrypt the results with which they update their respective weights for the BPN. During this process, cloud servers learn no privacy data of a participant even if they collude with all the rest participants. Through off-loading the computation tasks to the resource-abundant cloud, our scheme makes the computation and communication complexity on each participant *independent* to the number of participants and is thus highly scalable. For privacy preservation, we decompose most of the sub-algorithms of BPN into simple operations such as addition, multiplication, and scalar product. To support these operations over ciphertexts, we adopt the BGN 'doubly homomorphic' encryption algorithm [5] and tailor it to split the decryption capability among multiple participants for collusion-resistance decryption. As decryption of [5] is limited to small numbers, we introduce a novel design in our scheme such that arbitrarily large numbers can be efficiently decrypted. To protect the intermediate data during the learning process, we introduce a novel random sharing algorithm to randomly split the data without decrypting the actual value. Thorough security analysis shows that our proposed scheme is secure. Performance evaluation shows that our scheme is efficient and highly scalable.

Contribution. Our contribution can be summarized as follows:

- To our best knowledge, this paper is the first that provides privacy preservation for multiparty (more than two parties) collaborative back-propagation network learning over arbitrarily partitioned data;
- Thorough analysis shows that our proposed scheme is secure and efficient;
- We tailor [5] to support multiparty secure scalar product and introduc designs that allows decryption of arbitrary large messages. These improvements can be used as independent general solutions for other related applications.

The rest of this paper is organized as follows. Section 2 presents the models and assumptions. In section 3 we introduce technique preliminaries which is followed by detailed description of our proposed scheme in section 4. Section 5 evaluates our proposed scheme. We conclude our work in section 6.

2 Models and Assumptions

2.1 System Model

We consider a system composed of three major parties: a *trusted authority* (TA), the *participating parties* and the *cloud servers* (or *cloud*). TA is the party only responsible for generating and issuing encryption/decryption keys for all the other parties. It will not participate in any computation other than key generation and issuing. Each participating party s, denoted as P_s, owns a private data set and wants to perform collaborative BPN learning with all other participating parties. That is, they will collaboratively conduct learning over the arbitrarily partitioned data set, which is private and cannot be disclosed during the whole learning process. We assume that each participating party stays online with broadband access to the cloud and is equipped with one or several contemporary computers, which can work in parallel if there are more than one.

2.2   Security Model

Our scheme assumes the existence of a trusted authority who is trusted by all the parties, TA has the knowledge of system secret key and will not participate in any computation besides the key generation and issuing. TA is allowed to learn about each party's private data whenever necessary. We claim that the existence of TA is useful when investigation is needed in case some malicious party intentionally interrupts the system, say using bogus data sets. In real life, parties such as the government agents or organization alliances can be the TA. Although the existence of TA is helpful, we leave the completely distributed solution as a future work.

The participating parties do not fully trust each other. Therefore, they do not want to disclose their respective private data(except for the final weights learned by the network) to any other parties than TA. The cloud is not fully trusted by the participating parties either, i.e., the cloud is not allowed to learn about the sensitive information, such as original data sets and intermediate data. In this paper, we follows the curious-but-honest model[8]. That is, all the parties (i.e., all the participating parties and the cloud) will honestly follow our protocol but try to discover others' private data as much as possible. A number malicious of participating parties may collude among themselves and/or with the cloud.

2.3   Design Goals

- The multiple (two or more) participating parties can jointly perform a BPN learning over arbitrarily partitioned data. Specifically, the parties shall be able to jointly execute all the learning steps as defined by the BPN algorithm [17], which mainly includes a feed forward stage and a back-propagation stage.
- Confidentiality of private data shall be protected during the joint learning process. Specifically, we want to protect confidentiality of each party's private data set as well as all the intermediate results during the learning process, which means each party learns nothing but the final learned neural network.
- The system shall be efficient and scalable. In particular, the cost introduced on each party shall not grow with the number of participating parties. The computation tasks can be securely offloaded to the cloud without compromising data privacy. But the processing time on the cloud shall be less than or comparable to that on each participant. The overall execution time of the learning algorithm shall be practically acceptable.

3   Technique Preliminaries

3.1   Arbitrarily Partitioned Data

In this paper, we consider arbitrarily partitioned data as Bansal et al. did in[4] among multi-parties, say Z parties($Z > 2$). For arbitrarily partitioned data, each party $P_s, 1 \leq s \leq Z$, holds parts of the data set without any specific order. Specifically, consider a data set D with N rows $\{DB^1, DB^2, \cdots, DB^N\}$, and each row $DB^v, 1 \leq v \leq N$ has m attributes $\{x_1^v, x_2^v \cdots, x_m^v\}$. DB_s^v is the subset of data set owned by P_s, we have $DB^v = DB_1^v \bigcup DB_2^v \cdots \bigcup DB_Z^v$ and $DB_1^v \bigcap DB_2^v \cdots \bigcap DB_Z^v = \emptyset$. For each DB^v, P_s has t_s^v attributes(i.e. $|DB_s^v| = t_s^v$), where $\sum_{s=1}^{Z} t_s^v = m$, and each $t_s^v, 1 \leq v \leq N$ does not have to be equal. When $t_s^1 = t_s^2 = \cdots = t_s^N$ and the attributes owned by a party in each row are at the same position, the arbitrary partitioning becomes vertical partitioning. Similarly, it is horizontal partitioning if each P_s completely holds some DB^v.

3.2   Back-Propagation Network Learning

Back-Propagation Network[17] is one of the most widely used model in neural network learning. The multi-layer BPN can approximate any nonlinear function.

BPN learning algorithm is mainly composed of two stages: $feed\ forward$ and $error\ signal\ back - propagation$. As shown in Figure.1, there is a configuration for a three layer(a-b-c) BP network: vector $\{x_1, x_2, \cdots, x_a\}$ contains the values of input nodes, vector $\{h_1, h_2, \cdots, h_b\}$ represents values of hidden nodes and the values of output nodes are $\{o_1, o_2, \cdots, o_c\}$. w_{jk}^h denotes the weight connecting the input layer node k and the hidden layer node j. w_{ij}^o denotes the weight connecting j and the output layer node i, where $1 \leq k \leq a, 1 \leq j \leq b, 1 \leq i \leq c$.

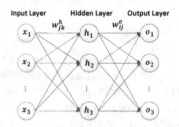

Fig. 1. Configuration of BP Network

During the BPN learning process, the goal is to model a given function by modifying internal weights of input signals to generate an expected output signal. As described in Algorithm 1, all the weights are initialized as small random numbers[10,7,14]. In the $FeedForwardStage$, values at each layer are calculated using the weights, the sigmoid function, and the values at the previous layer. In the $signalBack - Propagationstage$, the algorithm checks whether the error between output values and target values is within the threshold. If not, all the weights will be modified according to Eq.(1),(2) and the learning procedure is repeated. The learning will not be terminated until the error is within the threshold or the max number of iterations is exceeded. After the learning, the final weights on each link are the used to generate the learned network. Ref.[17] describes details of the BPN algorithm.

$$\Delta w_{ij}^o = -(t_i - o_i)h_j \tag{1}$$

$$\Delta w_{jk}^h = -h_j(1 - h_j)x_k \sum_{i=1}^{c}[(t_i - o_i) * w_{ij}^o)] \tag{2}$$

Algorithm 1. Back-Propagation Learning Algorithm

Input: N input sample vectors $V_i, 1 \leq i \leq N$, with a dimensions, $iteration_{max}$,learning rate η,target value t_i,sigmoid function $f(x) = \frac{1}{1+e^{-x}}$

Output: Network with final weights: $w_{jk}^h, w_{ij}^o, 1 \leq k \leq a, 1 \leq j \leq b, 1 \leq i \leq c$

begin

 Randomly Initialize all w_{jk}^h, w_{ij}^o.

 for $iteration = 1, 2 \cdots, iteration_{max}$ **do**

  for $sample = 1, 2 \cdots, N$ **do**

   //**Feed Forward Stage:**

   for $j = 1, 2 \cdots, b$ **do**

    $h_j = f(\sum_{k=1}^{a} x_k * w_{jk}^h)$

   for $i = 1, 2 \cdots, c$ **do**

    $o_i = f(\sum_{j=1}^{a} h_j * w_{ij}^o)$

   //**Back-Propagation Stage:**

   if $Error = \frac{1}{2}\sum_{i=1}^{c}(ti - oi)^2 > threshold$ **then**

    $\Delta w_{ij}^o = -(t_i - o_i) * h_j$

    $\Delta w_{jk}^h = -h_j 1 - h_j x_k \sum_{i=1}^{c}[(t_i - o_i) * w_{ij}^o)]$

    $w_{ij} = w_{ij} - \eta \Delta w_{ij}$

    $w_{jk}^h = w_{jk}^h - \eta \Delta w_{jk}^h$

   else

    //**Learning Finish**

    break

3.3 BGN Homomorphic Encryption

Homomorphic encryption is a form of encryption that enables operations on plaintexts to be performed on correspondingly ciphertexts without disclosing the plaintexts. Most existing homomorphic encryption schemes only support single operation - either addition or multiplication. In [5], Boneh et al. introduced a public-key 'doubly homomorphic' encryption scheme which simultaneously supports one multiplication and unlimited number of addition operations. Therefore, given ciphertexts $C(m_1), C(m_2), \cdots, C(m_i)$ and $C(\hat{m}_1), C(\hat{m}_2), \cdots, C(\hat{m}_i)$, one can compute $C(m_1\hat{m}_1 + m_2\hat{m}_2 + \cdots + m_i\hat{m}_i)$ without knowing the plaintext, where $C()$ is the ciphertext encrypted by the system's public key. Specifically, this scheme can be described as follows.

- **KeyGen:** Generate two cyclic groups G and G_1 of order $n = q_1 q_2$ as well as a bilinear map $e : G \times G \to G_1$, where q_1 and q_2 are large primes. Randomly pick two generators $g, u \leftarrow G$ and set $h = u^{q_2}$. The public key is published as $PK = (n, G, G_1, e, g, h)$ and the private key is $SK = q_1$.
- **Encrypt:** Pick a random number $r \leftarrow Z_n$ and encrypt the message M as: $C = g^M h^r$, where C is the ciphertext.
- **Decrypt:** Obtain q_1. Compute $C^{q_1} = g^{Mq_1} h^{rq_1}$. As $h^{rq_1} = 1$ and g^{q_1} can be easily computed, the message M can be decrypted using Pollard's lambda method[15] as long as the message is not large.

Apparently, this scheme is homomorphic under the addition operation. It is easy to verify that one multiplication operation over the message can still be applied using bilinear map, after which unlimited number of addition operations can be applied. Details of this scheme is described in [5].

We shall point out that this scheme is designed for two parties. Moreover, due to message decryption involves solving discrete logarithm of the ciphertext using Pollard's lambda method, this algorithm just works with small numbers. While it is easy to extend the work to decrypt long messages (in which the message is treated as a bit string) using a mode of operation, it remains open to efficiently decrypt large numbers (wherein the final message is interpreted by its value and unknown to the encryptor after homomorphic operations).

4   Our Proposed Scheme

4.1   Problem Statement

In this paper, we aim at enabling multiple parties to jointly conduct back-propagation network learning without revealing their private data. The input data sets owned by the parties can be arbitrarily partitioned. The computational and communicational costs on each party shall be practically efficient and the system shall be scalable.

Specifically, we consider a 3-layer(a-b-c configuration) neural network for simplicity but it can be easily extended to multi-layer neural networks. The learning data set for the neural network, which has N samples(denoted as vector$\{x_1^m, x_2^m, \ldots, x_a^m\}$, $1 \leq m \leq N$), is arbitrary partitioned into $Z(Z \geq 2)$ subsets. Each party P_s holds $x_{1s}^m, x_{2s}^m, \cdots, x_{as}^m$ and have:

$$x_{11}^m + x_{12}^m + \cdots + x_{1Z}^m = x_1^m \tag{3}$$
$$\cdots\cdots$$
$$x_{a1}^m + x_{a2}^m + \cdots + x_{aZ}^m = x_a^m \tag{4}$$

Each attribute in sample $\{x_1^m, x_2^m, \ldots, x_a^m\}$, $1 \leq m \leq N$, is possessed by only one party - if P_s possesses $x_k^m, 1 \leq k \leq a$, then $x_{ks}^m = x_k^m$; otherwise $x_{ks}^m = 0$. In this paper, we use w_{jk}^h to denote the weight used to connect the input layer node k and the hidden layer node j; w_{ij}^o to denote the weight used to connect the hidden layer node j and the output layer node i, where $1 \leq k \leq a, 1 \leq j \leq b, 1 \leq i \leq c$ and a, b, c are the number of nodes of each layer as we describe in Figure.1. For collaborative learning, the main task for all the parties is to jointly execute the operations defined in the Feed Forward stage and the signal back-propagation stage as shown in Algorithm 1. During each learning stage, except for the final learned network, neither the input data of each party nor the intermediate results(weights, value of hidden layer node, value of output layer node, etc) generated can be revealed to anybody else other than TA.

4.2   Privacy Preserving Multi-party Neural Network Learning

In this section, we introduce our cloud based privacy preserving multi-party BPN learning algorithm over arbitrarily partitioned data. As we described in Algorithm 2, all the parties generate and assign random weights w_{jks}^h and w_{ijs}^o to each

---

Algorithm 2. Privacy Preserving Multi-Party BPN Learning Algorithm

---

begin

    Input: each P_s's data set for N data samples,$x_{1s}^v, x_{2s}^v, \cdots, x_{as}^v, 1 \leq v \leq N$, w_{jks}^{hv} and w_{ijs}^{ov}
        for N samples, $iteration_{max}$, η, target value t_i

    Output: Network with final weights: $w_{jk}^h, w_{ij}^o, 1 \leq k \leq a, 1 \leq j \leq b, 1 \leq i \leq c$

    for $iteration = 1, 2, \cdots, iteration_{max}$ **do**

        for $v = 1, 2, \cdots, N$ **do**

            //**Feed Forward Stage**: **for** $j = 1, 2, \cdots, b$ **do**

                Using Algorithm 3 and Algorithm 4, each P_s obtain random shares φ_{vs} for
                $\sum_{k=1}^a (x_{k1}^v + x_{k2}^v + \cdots + x_{kZ}^v) * (w_{jk1}^{hv} + w_{jk2}^{hv} + \cdots + w_{jkZ}^{hv})$
                Using Algorithm 5, all the parties compute the sigmoid function and obtain the
                random shares h_{vjs}, $\sum_{s=1}^Z h_{vjs} = h_{vj}$ and $h_{vj} = f(\sum_{s=1}^Z \varphi_{vs})$, where $f()$ is
                the approximation for the sigmoid function as described in section4.6.

            for $i = 1, 2, \cdots, c$ **do**

                Using Algorithm 3,Algorithm 4 and Algorithm 5, each P_s obtain random shares
                o_{vis} for $f(\sum_{j=1}^b (h_{vj1} + h_{vj2} + \cdots + h_{vjZ}) * (w_{ij1}^{ov} + w_{ij2}^{ov} + \cdots + w_{ijZ}^{ov}))$

        //**Back-Propagation Stage**: Using Algorithm 3, all the parties and cloud calculate
        $Error = \frac{1}{2} \sum_{i=1}^c (t_i - o_i)^2$

        if $Error > threshold$ **then**

            for $i = 1, 2, \cdots, c$ **do**

                //(step 1)
                Using Algorithm 4 and Algorithm 3, each P_s obtains random share Δw_{ijs}^{ov} for
                $\Delta w_{ij}^{ov} = (-(t_{vi} - \sum_{s=1}^Z o_{vis}) * (\sum_{s=1}^Z h_{vjs})$

            for $j = 1, 2, \cdots, b$ **do**

                //(step 2)
                Using Algorithm 4 and Algorithm 3, each P_s obtains random share μ_s^v for
                $\sum_{i=1}^c [(\sum_{s=1}^Z o_{vis} - t_{vi}) * (\sum_{s=1}^Z w_{ijs}^{ov})]$
                //(step 3)
                Using Algorithm 4 and Algorithm 3, each p_s obtains random share κ_s^v for
                $\sum_{s=1}^Z x_{ks}^v * \sum_{s=1}^Z \mu_s^v$
                //(step 4)
                Using Algorithm 4 and Algorithm 3, each P_s obtains random share ϑ_s^v for
                $\sum_{s=1}^Z h_{vjs} * (1 - \sum_{s=1}^Z h_{vjs})$
                //(step 5)
                Using Algorithm 4 and Algorithm 3, each P_s obtains random share Δw_{jks}^{hv} for
                $\Delta w_{jk}^{hv} = \sum_{s=1}^Z \kappa_s^v * \sum_{s=1}^Z \vartheta_s^v$

            Each P_s updates $w_{ijs}^{ov} = w_{ijs}^{ov} - \eta * \Delta w_{ijs}^{ov}$ and $w_{jks}^{hv} = w_{jks}^{hv} - \eta * \Delta w_{jks}^{hv}$

        else

            Learning Finished;

P_s and make agreement on the max number of learning iteration $iteration_{max}$, the learning rate η, error threshold and target value t_i of each output layer node at the beginning of learning. In the Feed Forward Stage, all the parties agree on the terms of approximation for the sigmoid function according to their accuracy requirement(details given in section 4.5) and obtain random shares h_{js} for value of hidden layer node and o_{is} for value of output layer node. After the Feed Forward Stage, all the parties work together to check whether the network has reached the error threshold. If not, they go into the Back-Propagation Stage, which aims at modifying the weights so as to achieve correct weights in the neural network. For the weights of each output layer node w_{ij}^o, each P_s obtains random shares of the changes in weights, denoted as Δw_{ijs}^o, for Δw_{ij}^o from Eq. (1) by using the cloud based Algorithm 3 and Algorithm 4. For the weights of each hidden layer node w_{jk}^h, instead of directly computing the changes in weights according to Eq. (2), our proposed scheme divided it into four step computation: $\sum_{i=1}^{c}[(t_i - o_i) * w_{ij}^o)]$, $x_k \sum_{i=1}^{c}[(t_i - o_i) * w_{ij}^o)], -h_j(1 - h_j)$ and Δw_{jk}^h, and let each P_s obtains the random shares$(\mu_s, \kappa_s, \vartheta_s, \Delta w_{jks}^h)$ for each computation step respectively by using Algorithm 3 and Algorithm 4. Finally, each P_s updates its own weights with their shares and learning rate η.

4.3 Secure Scalar Product and Addition with Cloud

In this subsection, we tailor Ref.[5] and propose an algorithm that allows multiple parties to perform secure scalar product and homomorphic addition operations on ciphertexts using cloud computing. Specifically, each party encrypts his data with the system public key and uploads the ciphertexts to the cloud. The cloud servers compute the sum of original messages based on their ciphertexts. If the original messages are vectors, the cloud computes the scalar product of the vectors. During this process, the cloud does not need to decrypt nor learn about the original messages. The final result of the sum or scalar product is returned to all the parties in ciphertext. Decrypting the results needs the participation of all the parties. Due to efficiency limitation of the Pollard's lambda method, the algorithm in [5] can only work well with relative small numbers. We overcome such a limitation and make it suitable for large numbers. Our algorithm is presented in Algorithm 3.

Decryption of Large Numbers: Message decryption in the BGN algorithm involves solving the discrete log using Pollard's lambda method[15]. On a single contemporary computer, for example, the Pollard's lambda method is able to decrypt numbers of up to 30-40 bits within a reasonable time slot (e.g., in minutes or hours). Decryption of larger numbers is usually believed less practical in terms of the time complexity. In practice, however, it is hard to guarantee that the final results (numbers) are always small enough for the Pollard's lambda method to efficiently decrypt. This is either because the numbers contained in the vectors are too large, or the vectors are too long (of high dimension). To overcome this limitation, we propose to let the data holders divide the numbers, if they are large, into several numbers, and the cloud then decrypt the smaller "chunks" with which the final result can be recovered. The decryption process can be parallelized for efficiency. Assuming that the cloud is able to efficiently decrypt the result if each input number is less than d bits, our solution for supporting large numbers can be described as follows. W.l.o.g., we just consider the scalar product operation over input numbers of $3d$ bits.

Let $V_A = (A_1, A_2, \cdots, A_k)$ and $V_B = (B_1, B_2, \cdots, B_k)$ be two vectors, where A_i and B_i are $3d$-bit numbers for $1 \leq i \leq k$. Each vector can be represented as:

$$A_i = A_{i2} * 2^{2d} + A_{i1} * 2^d + A_{i0}$$
$$B_i = B_{i2} * 2^{2d} + B_{i1} * 2^d + B_{i0}$$

We can compute the product of $A_i * B_i$ as follows:

$$A_i * B_i = 2^{4d}(A_{i2} * B_{i2}) + 2^{3d}(A_{i2} * B_{i1} + A_{i1} * B_{i2}) + 2^{2d}(A_{i2} * B_{i0} + A_{i0} * B_{i2} + A_{i1} * B_{i1}) + 2^d(A_{i1} * B_{i0} + A_{i0} * B_{i1}) + A_{i0} * B_{i0}$$

Algorithm 3. Secure Scalar Product and Addition

- **Key Generation:**
  TA generates two cyclic groups G and G_1 of order $n = q_1 q_2$, where q_1 and q_2 are large primes, and a bilinear map $e : G \times G \to G_1$. Then it picks two random generators $g, u \in G$ and computes $h = u^{q_2}$. TA splits q_1 as $q_1 = (q_{11} + q_{12} + \cdots + q_{1Z}) \mod n$, where q_{1s} is randomly chosen from Z_n for $1 \le s \le Z$. For $1 \le s \le Z$, TA sends q_{1s} to party P_s as her/his secret key. The public key is published as $PK = (n, G, G_1, e, g, h)$, and the system master key is $SK = q_1$ which is only known to TA.

- **Encryption:** Given a message M, encrypt it as: $C = g^M h^r \in G$, $r \xleftarrow{R} Z_n$.

- **Secure Scalar Product:** Given the ciphertexts of vector $(M_{11}, M_{12}, \cdots, M_{1v})$ and $(M_{21}, M_{22}, \cdots, M_{2v})$, the cloud computes their scalar product as:

$$C(prod) = h_1^r * \prod_{i=1}^{v} e(C_{1i}, C_{2i}),$$

where $h_1 = e(g, h)$, C_{1i} and C_{2i} are the ciphertexts of message M_{1i} and M_{2i} respectively.

- **Secure Addition:** Given the ciphertexts of message $M_1, M_2, \cdots, M_v$, the cloud computes their sum as:

$$C(sum) = \prod_{i=1}^{v} C_i$$

- **Decryption:** W.l.o.g., we just demonstrate the decryption of $C(sum)$ as follows. The cloud broadcasts $C(sum)$ to each party. On receiving the ciphertext, each party P_s computes $C(sum)^{q_{1s}}$ and returns the result to the cloud.

  With the results from all the parties, the cloud computes:

$$\prod_{j=1}^{Z} C(sum)^{q_{1s}} = C(sum)^{q_1}.$$

Since $C(sum) = \prod_{i=1}^{v} C_i = \prod_{i=1}^{v} g^{M_i} h^{r_i}$, we have:

$$C(sum)^{q_1} = (g^{\sum_{i=1}^{v} M_i} \prod_{i=1}^{v} h^{r_i})^{q_1} = (g^{q_1})^{\sum_{i=1}^{t} M_i}$$

Note that $h^{q_1} = 1$. $\sum_{i=1}^{v} M_i$ can be efficiently solved using Pollard's lambda method[15] given g^{q_1}. The encrypted scalar product can be decrypted jointly in the similar way.

The scalar product of V_A and V_B can be calculated as follows:

$$\sum_{i=1}^{k} (A_i * B_i) \tag{5}$$

$$= 2^{4d} \sum_{i=1}^{k} (A_{i2} * B_{i2}) + 2^{3d} \left(\sum_{i=1}^{k} (A_{i2} * B_{i1}) + \sum_{i=1}^{k} (A_{i1} * B_{i2}) \right)$$

$$+ 2^{2d} \left(\sum_{i=1}^{k} (A_{i2} * B_{i0}) + \sum_{i=1}^{k} (A_{i0} * B_{i2}) + \sum_{i=1}^{k} (A_{i1} * B_{i1}) \right)$$

$$+ 2^{d} \left(\sum_{i=1}^{k} (A_{i1} * B_{i0}) + \sum_{i=1}^{k} (A_{i0} * B_{i1}) \right) + \sum_{i=1}^{k} (A_{i0} * B_{i0})$$

Therefore, instead of directly calculating $\sum_{i=1}^{k} (A_i * B_i)$, the participants can first compute $\sum_{i=1}^{k} (A_{i0} * B_{i0}), \cdots, \sum_{i=1}^{k} (A_{i2} * B_{i2})$ separately and finally recover $\sum_{i=1}^{k} (A_i * B_i)$ using Eq. (5). For this purpose, the data holders need to split A_i and B_i and encrypt A_{i0}, A_{i1}, A_{i2} and B_{i0}, B_{i1}, B_{i2}, which are d-bit numbers. By doing this, the encryption cost on each data holder increases by x times, where x is the number of smaller numbers that each large number is broken into. In the above example $x = 3$. The cloud needs to perform x^2 more time operations on ciphertexts than for a single scalar product. x^2 more decryptions will be performed by participants and the cloud. If x is fixed, the expansion of computation/communication cost is of constant time. Usually, x will not be large. For example, if 30-bit numbers can be efficiently decrypted, our technique can efficiently decrypt 90-bit numbers with $x = 3$.

4.4 Secure Sharing of Scalar Product and Sum

As the intermediate results generated during the BPN learning process may be used to derive some privacy information, the actual intermediate results cannot be known to each party as well as the cloud server. However, the 'BGN' algorithm[5] only supports one step multiplication over ciphertext and need to decrypt the intermediate results first, which will disclose some privacy data, for further privacy-preserving learning operations. To protect these intermediate results(scalar products or sum), we introduce a secure sharing algorithm in Algorithm 4, which enables each participating party to get a random share of the intermediate result without knowing its actual value. As described in Algorithm 3, Z parties can efficiently perform secure scalar product and addition computation with the help of cloud. To securely share the result, say ϵ, each party first generates a random number $L_s \leftarrow (0, u)$, where u is the upper bound of ϵ, and encrypts it as: $C(L_s) = g_1^{L_s} h_1^{r_s q_2}$, where $g_1 = e(g, g), h_1 = e(g, h), r_s \overset{R}{\leftarrow} Z_p$. Then all the parties uploads the ciphertexts of L_s to the cloud and the cloud securely calculates the ciphertext of $sumL = \sum_{s=1}^{Z} L_s$ as:

$$C(sumL) = \prod_{s=1}^{Z} C(L_s) = g_1^{L_1 + L_2 + \cdots + L_Z} h_1^{q_2 \hat{r_s}}$$

where $\hat{r_s} \overset{R}{\leftarrow} Z_p$. All the parties work together to decrypt the difference between ϵ and $sumL$ as $\hat{L} = |\epsilon - sumL|$ and send it to P_1. Note that $0 < \sum_{s=1}^{Z} L_s < Z * u, 0 < \epsilon < u$, we have $-u < \sum_{s=1}^{Z} L_s - \epsilon < Z * u$. As the cloud is able to efficiently decrypt numbers as large as u, it can decrypt $\sum_{s=1}^{Z} L_s - \epsilon$ efficiently as long as Z is not very large. Finally, all each P_s get its secure share ϵ_s of ϵ. For P_1, $\epsilon_1 = L_1 + \hat{L}$ and for other parties, $\epsilon_s = L_s$.

To ensure the efficiency for computing $\hat{L}$, we consider about the following two possible cases: $Case1$: $\epsilon > \sum_{s=1}^{Z} L_s$ and $Case2$: $\epsilon < \sum_{s=1}^{Z} L_s$. In multi-party scenarios($Z \geq 2$), as $L_s \overset{R}{\leftarrow} (0, U)$, there is a high possibility that $\epsilon < \sum_{s=1}^{Z} L_s$. At the same time, $\sum_{s=1}^{Z} L_s$ will not be much larger than ϵ(in 10 party scenarios, $\sum_{s=1}^{Z} L_s$ is at most 4bits larger than ϵ). Therefore, the cloud and all the parties can start decryption from $Case2$. If the successfully decryption of $\hat{L}$ cannot be achieved in empirical time using Pollard's lambda method, we can change to decrypt $\hat{L}$ process in $Case1$.

4.5 Approximation of Activation Function

In this subsection, we introduce the approximation of activation function using Maclaurin series expansion[3] and its secure sharing based on Algorithm

Algorithm 4. Secure Share of Scalar Product and Sum

Input: Ciphertext of ϵ
Output: Shares of ϵ: ϵ_s for $P_s, 1 \leq s \leq Z$
begin

    for $s = 1, 2 \cdots, Z$ **do**

        Choose $L_s \xleftarrow{R} (0, u)$
        $C(L_s) = g_1^{L_s} h_1^{r_s q_2}$
        //where u is the upper bound of ϵ

    //Cloud Calculates:
    $C(sumL) = \prod_{s=1}^{Z} C(L_s)$
    case 1.$\epsilon > \sum_{s=1}^{Z} L_s$
        $C(\hat{L}) = C(\epsilon) * C(sumL)^{-1}$

    case 2.$\epsilon < \sum_{s=1}^{Z} L_s$
        $C(\hat{L}) = C(sumL) * C(\epsilon)^{-1}$

    Decrypt $C(\hat{L})$ with Algorithm 3 and send $\hat{L}$ to P_1
    //Output Shares:
    $\epsilon_1 = L_1 + \hat{L}$
    for $i = 2, 3 \cdots, Z$ **do**
        $\epsilon_s = L_s$

    end

3 and Algorithm 4. Since the 'BGN' encryption does not support exponentiation operations over ciphertext(i.e. calculating $C(e^x)$ given $C(x)$) and cannot directly support the secure computation of sigmoid function $\frac{1}{1+e^{-x}}$, we utilize Maclaurin series expansion to approximate the sigmoid function and make it suitable for our proposed Algorithm 3 and Algorithm 4. Since the sigmoid function $\frac{1}{1+e^{-x}} \in (0,1)$, we can guarantee the converge of its Maclaurin series and approximate it as:

$$\frac{1}{1+e^{-x}} = \frac{1}{2} + \frac{x}{4} - \frac{x^3}{48} + \frac{x^5}{480} + O(x^6) \tag{6}$$

Due to the property of Maclaurin series, the terms in the expansion can be decided depends on the accuracy requirement. As shown in the approximation of sigmoid function in Eq. (6), the major challenge of secure computation for the equation becomes how to compute $x^k, 2 \leq k \leq n$ and share it without disclosing any privacy data. Based on the aforementioned Algorithm 3 and 4, Z parties are allowed to securely calculate and share x. With these properties, we proposed Algorithm 5 to securely share x^k. Using x^2 for instance, Z parties first work together to get the secure shares of x using Algorithm 3 and 4, denoted as x_s for each P_s. With the ciphertext of x and x_s, each P_s then calculates $\hat{C}_s(x) = C(x)^{x_s}$ and uploads it to the cloud. Cloud computes $C(x^2)$ using secure addition in Algorithm 3 and finally all the parties securely get the shares of x^2 with Algorithm 4. The scenarios of $x^k, k > 2$ can be easily extended as x^2. Due to spcae limitation, we provide the correctness of this algorithm in Appendix.

4.6   Security Analysis

In this section, we sketch the prove that our scheme is semantically secure under the subgroup decision assumption. As stated in section 4.1, our scheme is

---

Algorithm 5. Secure Share of Activation Function

Input: x_s, ciphertext of x: $C(x)$
Output: Shares of x^k, x_s^k for P_s, $1 \leq s \leq Z$
begin
    for $j = 2, 3 \cdots, k$ **do**
        //each P_s calculate:
        $\hat{C}_s(x^{j-1}) = C(x^{j-1})^{x_s}$
        Cloud Calculate $C(x^j)$ using Algorithm 3.
        $C(x^j) = \prod_{s=1}^{Z} \hat{C}_s(x^{j-1})$
        Call Algorithm 4, generate secure shares of x_s^j

---

composed of four sub-algorithm and we first analyze the security of Algorithm 4, since the other three algorithm are based on it:

Theorem 1. *Algorithm 3 is semantically secure assuming the group G satisfies the subgroup decision assumption.*

Proof. First, in our scheme, the secret key q_1 is randomly split into Z parts, and each part is distributed to a data holder. Therefore, unless all the data holders work together, they cannot recover the secret key q_1 with their own parts. Suppose a polynomial time adversary B, which is also a involved data holder in the collaborative computation and can collude with less than other $Z - 2$ data holders and the cloud server, is able to break the semantic security of the scheme with non-negligible advantage. We can construct an algorithm A that breaks the subgroup decision assumption with the same advantage. The construction of the algorithm A is the same as that in [5].

Security of Algorithm 4: To share one number, each party P_s independently chooses a random number L_s and encrypts it locally before he uploads to the cloud. Since Algorithm 3 is secure according to the above theorem, the random number chosen by each party is well protected. The decrypted data, i.e., the difference between ϵ and the sum of all the local random numbers, is indistinguishable from a random number as long as at least one of the local random numbers is not disclosed. This means that the data confidentiality of ϵ, which can be an intermediate value, can be well protected under the random oracle model as long as there is at least one non-malicious party.

Security of Algorithm 5: To share the result of approximation of activation function, we utilize the Algorithm 3 and Algorithm 4. Since we do not introduce any other steps to Algorithm 5 beside Algorithm 3 and Algorithm 4, we can achieve the same data confidentiality in Algorithm 5 as Algorithm 3 and Algorithm 4 did.

Security of Algorithm 2: In Algorithm 2, all the data exchange for parties are during the the secure computation of $step 1, 2, 3, 4, 5$. All these steps are based on Algorithm 3, Algorithm 4 and Algorithm 5, which has been proved secure in terms of data confidentiality. Thus, we can prove that the same security for Algorithm 5 as Algorithm 3, Algorithm 4 and Algorithm 5 according to the composable security model.

5   Performance Analysis

5.1   Complexity Analysis

In this section, we numerically evaluate the performance of our proposed scheme in terms of computation cost and communication cost and compare it with the existing techniques. Since our scheme is composed of four sub-algorithms, we first give the analysis of each sub-algorithm and then provide the complexity of whole scheme. For expression simplicity, in the following part of this section, we denote time complexity of one multiplication operation on Group G as MUL[1] and that of one exponentiations operation on Group G as EXP.

Complexity of Algorithm 3: In multi-party scenarios, when all the parties need to jointly perform a secure scalar product or addition computation, each party P_s first needs to encrypt all his data attributes once, which costs $2n_s$ EXP and n_s MUL, where n_s is the number of data attributes owned by P_s. Then cloud would calculate the ciphertext of scalar product or sum based on encrypted data uploaded by each party and send back the ciphertext of result to each party. After receiving the ciphertext of result, each P_s just needs to perform one EXP and upload it into cloud for generate the final result. Therefore, the total computation cost for each party P_s for the secure computation for scalar product or sum is $2n_s$ EXP and $(n_s + 1)$ MUL. Note, $2n_s$ EXP and n_s MUL in our scheme is one time cost, it does not need to be performed in each secure computation round. For communication cost, each P_s needs to exchange $(n_s + 2)$ messages with cloud, where $|G|$ bits for each of n_s messages and $|G_1|$ bits for the other two. Note, n_s messages are also one time cost.

Complexity of Algorithm 4: To securely get the random share of the result of scalar product or addition, each P_s first needs to perform 2 EXP and one MUL to encrypt its chosen random number. After the cloud calculates the ciphertext of difference between the result the sum of all the local random number based on the uploaded ciphertexts, another EXP is needed for each P_s to decrypt the difference. Therefore, the total cost for each P_s during the secure sharing process is 3 EXP and one MUL. For communication cost, only 3 messages exchange are needed for each party P_s and cause $3|G_1|$ bits cost.

Complexity of Algorithm 5: To jointly perform the approximation of activation function(here we choose 5 terms for our approximation to achieve acceptable accuracy as in [21]), each party P_s needs to perform 8 EXP and 2 MUL besides the cost in Algorithm 3 and 4. For communication cost, 9 more messages, which have $9|G_1|$ bits are needed for each party besides cost in Algorithm 3 and 4.

Complexity of the Whole Scheme: In this part, we analyze the computation cost and communication cost of our whole privacy preserving multi-party neural network learning scheme. Considering the neural network configuration(a-b-c) as described in section 3.2, each party P_s first needs to encrypt all its privacy data once using Algorithm 3 with $2(n_s + b + c)$ EXP and $(n_s + b + c)$ MUL, where n_s is the number of data attributes holed by P_s, a, b and c represent the number

---

[1] When the operation is on the elliptic curve, EXP means scalar multiplication operation and MUL means one point addition operation.

Table 1. Computation/Communication Cost of Privacy-Preserving BPN Learning Schemes. n_s: number of data attributes owned by party P_s; Z: number of participating party; G and G_1: size of messages

	Our Scheme	Bansal's scheme	Chen's Scheme
Comp.	$(31b + 18c + 2n_s)$EXP $+(8b + 6c + n_s)$MUL	$Z^2 * (4n_s(a + 4b + c + bc))$ $*$(EXP+MUL) $+Z^2 * (12b$EXP$+8b$MUL$)$	$Z^2 * (5ab + 2bc$ $+abc)$(EXP+MUL) $+Z^2 * (4n_s(2bc + 4ab$ $+b))$(EXP+MUL)
Comm.(bit)	$n_s * a * |G| + (24b + 5c) * |G_1|$	$Z^2 * (ab + 3bc + 4b + 2)|G|$ $+2n_s|G|$	$Z^2 * (b + 2bc + 4ab + 2)|G|$ $+2n_s|G|$

of input layer nodes, hidden layer nodes and output layer nodes respectively. Note: this is the one time cost and do not need to be performed again during the whole learning process. In the Feed Forward Stage, by using Algorithm 4 and Algorithm 5, each P_s performs $11(b + c)$ EXP and $3(b + c)$ MUL to get the random shares of every hidden layer node value and output layer node value. In the Back-Propagation Stage, to get the random share of changes for each output layer nodes, $step1, 3$ cost each P_s $5c$ EXP+$2c$ MUL and $5b$ EXP+$2b$ MUL respectively; $step1, 3$ both need $3b$ EXP and b MUL and $step5$ needs $7b$ EXP and $3b$ MUL. Thus P_s needs to perform $(18b + 5c)$ EXP+$(4b + 2c)$ MUL using Algorithm 3 and Algorithm 4.

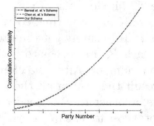

Fig. 2. Cost Influence of Party Number

Combining the cost for the two stages, the computation complexity for each party P_s of one round privacy preserving back-propagation neural network learning in multi-party scenarios is $31b + 18c + 2n_s$ EXP and $8b + 6c + n_s$ MUL. For cloud side, it needs to perform $4 + a + b + c$ pairing operations on Group G, $Z * (8b + 14c)$ MUL and 11 decryption, where the complexity of each decryption is $O(\sqrt{K})$ and K is the size of message for decryption. Although the computation cost on cloud side will linearly increase with the party number, cloud can handle it in parallel efficiently. For communication cost, each party P_s needs to exchange $n_s * a + 24b + 5c$ messages with $(n_s * a * |G| + (24b + 5c) * |G_1|)$ bits during the one round privacy preserving BPN learning process. By securely outsource most computation tasks to the cloud server, our scheme makes the cost of each party independent to the number of participating parties, which is a significant difference with the excising scheme[4,6] as we shown in Figure.2. To compare our scheme with existing ones[4,6], we summarize the cost of our scheme and Ref.[4,6] in Table.1. Considering the same neural network configuration(a-b-c), when extending scheme in Ref.[4] to Z parties scenarios, which utilized ElGamal[9] for secure computation, $Z^2 * (4n_s(a + 4b + c + bc))*(\text{EXP}+\text{MUL})+Z^2 * (12b\text{EXP}+8b\text{MUL})$ are needed for each party P_s for computation. When compared with scheme in Ref.[6], which can support two party privacy preserving back-propagation neural network learning over vertical partitioned data, Z parties scenario will introduce $Z^2 * (5ab + 2bc + abc + 4n_s(2bc + 4ab + b))(\text{EXP}+\text{MUL})$ computation cost to the each party. For communication cost, schemes in Ref.[4,6] will cause $Z^2 * (ab + 3bc + 4b + 2) * |G_1| + 2n_s * |G_1|$ bits and $Z^2 * (b + 2bc + 4ab + 2) * |G_1| + 2n_s * |G_1|$ bits respectively for Z parties scenarios. Different form our scheme, both [4] and [6] will introduce a computation/communication complexity quadratic in Z for Z parties scenario and make their scheme unpractical. As a result, by offloading most computation cost to the cloud, our proposed scheme significantly outperforms the existing works in multi-party scenarios without any limitation on the type of data partition.

5.2 Accuracy Analysis

In our proposed scheme, the only place that introduces accuracy loss is the approximation for the activation function. As described in section 4.5, we achieve the approximation by using Maclaurin series expansion, whose accuracy can be adjusted by modifying the number of series terms according to the system requirement. Due to the property of Maclaurin series, our scheme can achieve any higher accuracy by adding more series terms in approximation. Similar method of approximation with Maclaurin series expansion is used in [21], but it just supports two party setting. Moreover, the cost brought by the increasing accuracy requirement in our scheme is lightweight. Taking the a-b-c configuration BPN for an example, it will cause $8(b + c)$ EXP $2(b + c)$ MUL for each party if we extend 5 series terms to 9 series terms for more accuracy. Compared with the existing schemes in [4,6], which use the piecewise linear approximation[16] for the activation function and introduce about only $3\% - 6\%$ more error rate than none privacy-preserving scheme, our approximation can achieve at least the same accuracy as these works. Furthermore, due to limitation of finite fields for secure computation, both schemes in [4] and [6] need to map the real numbers in sigmod function to fixed-point representations in every step of Feed Forward Stage and Back-Propagation Stage, which will lead to further loss in accuracy. However, our proposed scheme can omit this limitation and be efficiency performed on the sigmod function without any accuracy loss during the secure computation process by utilizing the cloud server.

6 Conclusion

In this work, we proposed the first secure and practical multi-party BPN learning scheme over arbitrary partitioned data. In our proposed approach, the parties encrypt their arbitrarily partitioned data and upload the ciphertexts to the cloud. The cloud can execute most operations pertaining to the BPN learning algorithm without knowing any private information. The cost of each party in our scheme is independent to the number of parties. This work tailors the BGN homomorphic encryption algorithm to support the multi-party scenario, which can be used as an independent solution for other related applications. Complexity and security analysis shows that our proposed scheme is scalable, efficient and secure. As a future work, we will study the feasibility of performing secure multiparty learning without the help of any trusted authority.

References

1. The health insurance portability and accountability act of privacy and security rules, http://www.hhs.gov/ocr/privacy
2. National standards to protect the privacy of personal health information, http://www.hhs.gov/ocr/hipaa/finalreg.html
3. Abramowitz, M., Stegun, I.A.: Handbook of Mathematical Functions: with Formulas, Graphs, and Mathematical Tables. Dover Books on Mathematics. Dover, New York (1964)
4. Bansal, A., Chen, T., Zhong, S.: Privacy preserving back-propagation neural network learning over arbitrarily partitioned data. Neural Comput. Appl. 20(1), 143–150 (2011)
5. Boneh, D., Goh, E.-J., Nissim, K.: Evaluating 2-DNF Formulas on Ciphertexts. In: Kilian, J. (ed.) TCC 2005. LNCS, vol. 3378, pp. 325–341. Springer, Heidelberg (2005)
6. Chen, T., Zhong, S.: Privacy-preserving backpropagation neural network learning. Trans. Neur. Netw. 20(10), 1554–1564 (2009)
7. Cun, L., Boser, B., Denker, J.S., Henderson, D., Howard, R.E., Hubbard, W., Jackel, L.D.: Handwritten digit recognition with a back-propagation network. In: Advances in Neural Information Processing Systems, pp. 396–404. Morgan Kaufmann (1990)
8. di Vimercati, S.D.C., Foresti, S., Jajodia, S., Paraboschi, S., Samarati, P.: Over-encryption: management of access control evolution on outsourced data. In: Proceedings of the 33rd International Conference on Very Large Data Bases, VLDB 2007, pp. 123–134. VLDB Endowment (2007)
9. El Gamal, T.: A Public Key Cryptosystem and a Signature Scheme Based on Discrete Logarithms. In: Blakely, G.R., Chaum, D. (eds.) CRYPTO 1984. LNCS, vol. 196, pp. 10–18. Springer, Heidelberg (1985)
10. Fahlman, S.E.: Faster-learning variations on Back-propagation: An empirical study, pp. 38–51. Morgan Kaufmann (1988)
11. Flouri, K., Beferull-lozano, B., Tsakalides, P.: Training a svm-based classifier in distributed sensor networks. In: Proceedings of 14nd European Signal Processing Conference, pp. 1–5 (2006)
12. Grossman, R., Gu, Y.: Data mining using high performance data clouds: experimental studies using sector and sphere. In: Proceedings of the 14th ACM SIGKDD International Conference on Knowledge Discovery and Data Mining, KDD 2008, New York, USA, pp. 920–927 (2008)
13. Grossman, R.L.: The case for cloud computing. IT Professional 11(2), 23–27 (2009)

14. Law, R.: Back-propagation learning in improving the accuracy of neural network-based tourism demand forecasting. Tourism Management 21(4), 331–340 (2000)
15. Menezes, A.J., Oorschot, P.C.V., Vanstone, S.A., Rivest, R.L.: Handbook of applied cryptography (1997)
16. Myers, D., Hutchinson, R.: Efficient implementation of piecewise linear activation function for digital vlsi neural networks. Electronics Letters 25(24), 1662–1663 (1989)
17. Rumelhart, D.E., Hinton, G.E., Williams, R.J.: Learning internal representations by error propagation. In: Parallel Distributed Processing: Explorations in the Microstructure of Cognition, vol. 1, pp. 318–362. MIT Press, Cambridge (1986)
18. Schlitter, N.: A protocol for privacy preserving neural network learning on horizontal partitioned data. In: Proceedings of the Privacy Statistics in Databases (PSD) (September 2008)
19. Yang, B., Wang, Y.-D., Su, X.-H.: Research and Design of Distributed Neural Networks with Chip Training Algorithm. In: Wang, L., Chen, K., S. Ong, Y. (eds.) ICNC 2005, Part I. LNCS, vol. 3610, pp. 213–216. Springer, Heidelberg (2005)
20. Yao, A.C.: Protocols for secure computations. In: Proceedings of the 23rd Annual Symposium on Foundations of Computer Science, SFCS 1982, Washington, DC, USA, pp. 160–164 (1982)
21. Zang, S., Zhong, S.: A privacy-preserving algorithm for distributed training of neural network ensembles. To appear in Neural Computing and Applications

Appendix

Correctness of Algorithm 5

This section proves the correctness of Algorithm 5 and shows how to compute any $x^k, k \in Z_R$ for the approximation of activation function.

Proof. 1. When $k = 1$, $x^k = x$, as aforementioned in *Section* 4.3, it can be securely calculated without disclosing any privacy information.

2. If when $k = n$, multi-party can securely compute x^n without revealing any privacy information. For $k = n+1$, we have: $C(x^n) = g_1^{x^n} h_1^{r_n}$, $\hat{C}(x^n)_s = C(x^n)^{x_s} = g_1^{x^n * x_s} h_1^{r_n * x_s}$, where $C(x^n)$ is the ciphertext of x^n based on Algorithm 3 and x_s is the random share of $x(\sum_{s=1}^{Z} = x)$ for party P_s by using Algorithm 4. After each P_s uploading his $\hat{C}(x^n)_s$ to cloud, cloud can calculates as:

$$\prod_{s=1}^{Z} \hat{C}(x^n)_s \tag{7}$$

$$= g_1^{\sum_{s=1}^{Z} x^n * x_s} h_1^{\sum_{s=1}^{Z} r_n * x_s} = g_1^{x^n * \sum_{s=1}^{Z} x_s} h_1^{\sum_{s=1}^{Z} r_n * x_s}$$

$$= g_1^{x^n * x} h_1^{x * \sum_{s=1}^{Z} r_n} = g_1^{x^{n+1}} h_1^{x * r_{n+1}} = C(x^{n+1})$$

With the ciphertext of x^{n+1}, all the parties can utilize Algorithm 3 and Algorithm 4 to securely get the random share of $x^n + 1$.

Random Host Mutation for Moving Target Defense

Ehab Al-Shaer, Qi Duan, and Jafar Haadi Jafarian

Department of Software and Information Systems
University of North Carolina at Charlotte
Charlotte, NC, USA
{ealshaer,qduan,jjafaria}@uncc.edu

Abstract. Exploiting static configuration of networks and hosts has always been a great advantage for design and launching of decisive attacks. Network reconnaissance of IP addresses and ports is prerequisite to many host and network attacks. At the same time, knowing IP addresses is required for service reachability in IP networks, which makes complete concealment of IP address for servers infeasible. In addition, changing IP addresses too frequently may cause serious ramifications including service interruptions, routing inflation, delays and security violations. In this paper, we present a novel approach that turns end-hosts into untraceable moving targets by transparently mutating their IP addresses in an intelligent and unpredictable fashion and without sacrificing network integrity, manageability or performance. The presented technique is called Random Host Mutation (RHM). In RHM, moving target hosts are assigned virtual IP addresses that change randomly and synchronously in a distributed fashion over time. In order to prevent disruption of active connections, the IP address mutation is managed by network appliances and totally transparent to end-host. RHM employs multi-level optimized mutation techniques that maximize uncertainty in adversary scanning by effectively using the whole available address range, while at the same time minimizing the size of routing tables, and reconfiguration updates. RHM can be transparently deployed on existing networks on end-hosts or network elements. Our analysis, implementation and evaluation show that RHM can effectively defend against stealthy scanning, many types of worm propagation and attacks that require reconnaissance for successful launching. We also show the performance bounds for moving target defense in a practical network setup.

1 Introduction

In the current Internet architecture, network configuration parameters such as IP addresses are mostly static and easily discoverable. Although this simplifies reachability and manageability, it gives adversaries significant advantage to remotely scan networks and identify their targets accurately and quickly using off-the-shelf scanning tools [1,2]. Despite firewall deployment, most enterprise networks have many public and private hosts accessible from outside. Using the

A.D. Keromytis and R. Di Pietro (Eds.): SecureComm 2012, LNICST 106, pp. 310–327, 2013.
© Institute for Computer Sciences, Social Informatics and Telecommunications Engineering 2013

existing dynamic IP assignment techniques like *DHCP* does not protect from scanning, and using *NAT* makes it difficult to reach legitimate hosts remotely. In addition, these techniques are insufficient to provide proactive countermeasure because the IP mutation is infrequent and traceable.

In this paper we propose a novel proactive moving target defense, called *Random Host Mutation (RHM)*, that challenges the principal assumptions of scanning adversaries in cyber warfare: "if you can scan it (*i.e.*, a response received), you can find it. Otherwise, it is an unused address". We propose a mutable network architecture that mutates IP addresses of designated moving target (MT) hosts randomly and frequently so that the attackers' premises about the network fail. The goal of these mutations is to make the hosts untraceable via network reconnaissance attacks. However, developing an efficient and practical scheme that can be deployed on general networks requires careful consideration of tough challenges: (1) IP mutation must be transparent to the end-host to prevent disruption of active connections, (2) the integrity of end-to-end Internet reachability should be maintained, (3) IP mutations should be fast and unpredictable to deceive scanners by optimally using the whole available address range, (4) IP mutations should avoid service interruptions, routing inflation, delays and security violations, (5) RHM should be seamlessly deployed in any existing networks without requiring any changes in the end-host or network infrastructure.

RHM addresses each of these challenges and develops an optimized moving target defense architecture that maximizes the uncertainty on the adversary discovery, while satisfying the configuration management constraints. To keep the IP addresses of end-hosts unchanged, RHM creates routable short-lived virtual IP addresses (vIP) that will be changed randomly, consistently and synchronously in the network to allow unpredictable, yet safe mutation. The vIP addresses will be used for routing and are automatically translated into the real IPs (rIP) and vice versa at the network edges (subnet) close to the destination. Using rIP and vIP addresses allows for separating network administration and mutation management, making mutation transparent to administrators and end-host configuration. Under RHM architecture, a MT host is reachable by a name that is then resolved to a vIP address. However, scanners do not often query DNS for scanning networks because (1) it increases detection probability [3], and (2) not all hosts names are necessarily known by scanners or DNS. Although users commonly use named servers to reach their destinations, RHM allows only authorized users (e.g., administrators) to reach MT hosts based on policy-based access control predefined by RHM managers for each MT host.

To optimize IP mutation, the mutant vIPs are selected randomly from the entire unused address space in the network in order to increase unpredictability while satisfying various mutation speed requirements of different MT hosts, routing table size bound, routing convergence, and network operation integrity. We formulate this problem as a constraint satisfaction problem and solve it using Satisfiability Modulo Theories [4] (SMT) solvers. To allow for the maximum use of unused address space for mutation while considering routing convergence, RHM employs two-phase mutation: (1) *low frequency mutation (LFM)* that solves the constraint satisfaction problem to select an optimal assignment of MT hosts to random mutation range of vIPs, and (2) *high frequency mutation (HFM)* that uses a cryptographic random function to select from a designated range a specific mutant vIP randomly, yet synchronously across RHM components in the network. In both mutations, active sessions are maintained.

The RHM architecture was implemented and tested in our university campus, and comprehensive evaluation were conducted to study the effectiveness and limitations of RHM. Our theoretical analysis, simulation and experimentation results show that RHM can protect up to $40 - 90\%$ of the network host from reconnaissance attacks lunched by scanning tools or vicious random scanning worms.

Previous works [5,6,7,8] propose techniques to allow for changing or hiding IP address using consecutive DHCP updates [5], encrypting headers [6], translation [7], or rerouting to another server [8]. These solutions are very limited as they do not support wide range of IP mutation. Also, they are not readily deployable solutions as they do not address the challenges discussed before.

The rest of the paper is organized as follows. Section 2 describes the related works. Section 3 presents the formulation and algorithms for RHM. In Section 4 the RHM architecture and protocol are described; Section 5 describes the required re-configurations. Section 6 presents implementation, analysis and evaluation, and Section 7 concludes the paper.

2   Related Works

A few research proposals on dynamically changing IP addresses for proactive cyber defense have been presented in the literature. The APOD (Applications That Participate in Their Own Defense) scheme [8] uses *hopping tunnels* based on address and port randomization to disguise the identity of end parties from sniffers. However, this approach is not transparent as it requires cooperation of both client and server hosts during the IP mutation process.

The DyNAT provides a transparent approach [9] for IP hopping by translating the IP addresses before packets enter the core or public network in order to hide the IP address from man-in-the-middle sniffing attacks. Although this technique will make network discovery infeasible for sniffers, it does not work for scanners who rely on probe responses for discovering the end-hosts.

A network address space randomization scheme called NASR [5] was proposed to offer an IP hopping approach that can defend against hitlist worms. NASR is a LAN-level network address randomization scheme based on DHCP update. NASR is not transparent to the end-hosts because DHCP changes are applied to the end-host itself which results in disruption of active connections during address transition. Moreover, it requires changes to the end-host operating system which makes its deployment very costly. Also, NASR provides very limited unpredictability and mutation speed because its IP mutation is limited on the LAN address space and will require DHCP and host to be reconfigured for this purpose (the maximum IP mutation speed is once every 15 minutes).

A technique called OF-RHM (OpenFlow Random Host Mutation) was proposed in [10]. OF-RHM offers an IP mutation technique for software-defined networks. Although the technique is transparent to end-hosts and provides high mutation rate, it is not deployable on traditional networks.

Yegneswaran et al. [11] and Cai et al. [12] present techniques for defending honeynets from systematic mappings that aim at differentiating live IPs from monitored ones and blacklisting monitored IPs for efficient target selection. RHM completely wipes out systematic mapping attacks, because generated blacklists are only valid for a relatively short interval.

In summary, none of the previous techniques provides a deployable transparent mechanism for IP mutation that can defend against external and internal scanning attacks without changing the configuration of the end-hosts. RHM implement an efficient IP mutation in term of unpredictability, mutation speed and configuration management. Unlike the previous techniques, RHM uses the entire address space to increase unpredictability and updates configurations at real-time while preserving network operation integrity.

3   Host Mutation Optimization

Maximizing mutation unpredictability and mutation speed are primary objectives of RHM. To achieve the first goal, RHM uses the maximum portion of unused address space for mutation. However, achieving the second goal is limited by the routing convergence time and table size bounds. Thus increasing the mutation speed implies bounding the mutation space to local ranges. To satisfy these conflicting objectives, RHM uses two levels of random mutation granularity: *Low Frequency mutation (LFM)* and *High Frequency mutation (HFM)*. LFM is used for selecting a random network address, denoted as *virtual address range (VAR)* for the MT hosts, and HFM is used to select a random vIP within VAR assigned during LFM. Combining the two levels of mutation, enhance not only the mutation unpredictability and speed but also the network manageability.

The duration of an LFM or HFM is called an LFM or HFM interval, respectively. An LFM interval contains multiple HFM intervals, and in every HFM interval the MT host will be associated with a unique vIP from the designated VAR of that particular host. Since LFM is more expensive than HFM, LFM interval is fixed, while the HFM interval is customized based on the required mutation speed of each MT host. To maintain connectivity with MT hosts, MT hosts engaged with active sessions will retain their vIPs in addition to new ones during mutation. Therefore, a MT host might be associated with more than one vIP simultaneously.

In the following, we describe the main phases of RHM algorithm: (1) generation of unused *VARs*, (2) LFM for optimal assignment of VARs to MT hosts, (3) VAR segmentation, and (4) HFM for random and synchronized vIP selection within the allocated VARs for each MT host. The configuration management and session tracking for active connections will be discussed in subsequent sections.

Table 1. Description of parameters

b_{ij}	denotes whether range r_j is assigned to host h_i ($b_{ij} \in \{0,1\}$)
$\{h_1, \ldots, h_n\}$	set of MT hosts
$\{r_1, \ldots, r_m\}$	set of VARs
B_{kj}	denotes whether range r_j is assigned to at least one of the host in subnet S_k ($B_{kj} \in \{0,1\}$)
E_i	The expected value of vIP repeat probability in LFM interval for host h_i
F_i^p	set of address ranges used by those hosts similar to host h_i in the last p LFM intervals
N_i	The number of vIP mutations in an LFM interval for host h_i
S^l	set of address ranges uses by any host in the previous l LFM intervals
$\{S_1, \ldots, S_z\}$	set of subnets
T_d	maximum routing update propagation delay
$R_i = 1/T_{HFM_i}$	mutation speed of host h_i
T_{LFM}	length of an LFM interval
U	upper bound for routing table size
V_i	minimum required address space for h_i

3.1   VAR Generation

The first step of each LFM interval is to generate unused address blocks (VARs) in the network address space. The unused address space is defined as the address space that includes rIPs and vIPs that are currently in-use for active sessions. Given used address ranges $A_1, \ldots, A_u$ of the network and vIPs, $q_1, \ldots, q_k$ vIP addresses used in currently active sessions, we can generate contiguous blocks of unused address space by simply masking the full network address space A as follows:

$$\{r_1, r_2, .., r_m\} \leftarrow A \wedge \neg(A_1 \vee \ldots \vee A_u \vee q_1 \vee \ldots \vee q_k) \tag{1}$$

We implemented this by encoding A, $A_1, \ldots, A_u$, and $q_1, \ldots, q_k$ as Boolean expressions using Binary Decision Diagram (BDD) [13] operations.

In addition, LFM will require sufficient unused address space to allow for swapping VARs during mutation. This means that the unused address space should be at least twice the total mutation space required by all MT hosts (formally, $2 \sum_{1 \leq i \leq n} V_i \leq \sum_{1 \leq j \leq m} |r_j|$, where V_i is the minimum required address space for MT h_i).

3.2   LFM Formulation

The core problem of LFM is to assign VARs to MT hosts at each interval such that (1) mutation unpredictability can be maximized, (2) mutation speed, and (3) routing table size constraints are satisfied. Suppose we currently have a set of MT hosts $\{h_1, \ldots, h_n\}$, VARs $\{r_1, \ldots, r_m\}$, mutation rate (R_i) for each host h_i, the expected value of vIP repeating probability (E_i) for each h_i, maximum routing convergence time T_d, and the upper bound for the routing table size

(U). Each host belongs to a subnet in the set $\{S_1, ..., S_k\}$, where subnet is a group of hosts that are physically connected through a switch. We can then formulate LFM constraint optimization problem using the following SMT-based (Satisfiability Modulo Theories [4]) formulas:

The following is the description of these constraints. Table 1 describes the important parameters of our formalization.

VAR Allocation Constraint: Eq. 2 is to guarantee that at least one VAR must be assigned to each MT host.

Unpredictability Constraint: Eq. 3, 4, and Eq. 6 are used to maximize unpredictability during LFM and HFM, respectively. Eq. 3 is to guarantee that VARs used in the past l intervals (S^l) will not be repeated for *any* host during the coming LFM interval. Similarly, Eq. 4 is to avoid using the same VAR that has been used by another host with similar characteristics in last p intervals (F_i^p represents the list of VARs used by hosts similar to h_i). This is important to countermeasure fingerprinting attacks by preventing scanners from utilizing vulnerability information discovered for another host. A longer interval assures that, similar hosts share vIPs less frequently. Users can increase l and p (usually $p > l$) to achieve the desired level of unpredictability.

$$\sum_{1 \leq j \leq m} b_{ij} \geq 1 \tag{2}$$

$$b_{ij} = 0, \text{if } r_j \in S^l \tag{3}$$

$$b_{ij} = 0, \text{if } r_j \in F_i^p \tag{4}$$

$$\sum_{1 \leq i \leq n} b_{ij} \, V_i \leq |r_j| \tag{5}$$

$$V_i \geq \frac{(N_i - 1)}{2E_i} \tag{6}$$

$$b_{ij} \leq B_{kj}, \forall h_i \in S_k \tag{7}$$

$$\sum_{1 \leq k \leq z} \sum_{1 \leq j \leq m} B_{kj} \leq U \tag{8}$$

$$b_{ij}, B_{kj} \in \{0, 1\}, 1 \leq i \leq n, 1 \leq j \leq m, 1 \leq k \leq z$$

Mutation Speed Constraint: RHM allows each MT host to specify the target mutation rate (mutation per second) it requires based on its security requirements. During each LFM interval the size of allocated VARs should be sufficient for the mutation rate of each and all moving hosts. Each MT host h_i has a mutation rate R_i, based on which the HFM interval of the host, T_{HFM_i}, is calculated: $T_{HFM_i} = 1/R_i$. Also, during an LFM interval all the vIPs of a host are selected from the same VAR. T_{LFM} is greater than the maximum routing convergence time: $T_{LFM} > T_d + \delta$, where T_d is the routing convergence time and δ is the LFM planning time.

Thus total number of vIPs selected by RHM during an LFM interval will be $N_i = \lceil T_{LFM}/T_{HFM_i} \rceil$. We can then calculate the probability of repeating a vIP for a MT host after selecting j^{th} vIP as $P_i = (j-1)/V_i$, where V_i is the minimum required size of the VAR associated with a host. Therefore, we can then calculate the *expected value* of the repeating probability in HFM interval as follows:

$$E(P_i) = \frac{1}{N_i} \sum_{j=1}^{N_i} \frac{j-1}{V_i}$$

$$= \frac{N_i - 1}{2V_i}$$

where $1 \leq i \leq n$. Therefore:

$$E_i \geq \frac{N_i - 1}{2V_i}$$

The constraint in Eq. 6 is to guarantee that V_i has minimum addresses required to ensure that the expected value of P_i will not exceed the expected threshold (E_i) associated with this host. Since a VAR can be assigned to more than one MT host, Eq. 5 is used to ensure that VAR size ($|r_j|$) is large enough to accommodate MT hosts sharing the same VAR, r_j.

Routing Table Size Constraint: We should minimize the routing table size incurred by the VAR assignments. To this aim, one should assign those hosts that are in the same subnet with VARs that have the same prefixes. We define B_{kj} as a Boolean parameter (that is, $B_{kj} \in \{0,1\}$) to indicate if range r_j is assigned to at least one host in subnet S_k. Eq. 7 denotes that if a range r_j is assigned to a host h_i ($b_{ij} = 1$) in subnet S_k, then the routing entry for r_j must be added to the total routing entries of the subnet.

Eq. 8 constraint is used to bound the number of distinct VARs assigned to different subnets, S_k. This consequently implies assigning minimum number of VARs to moving hosts that are in the same physical subnet to minimize the routing table size (supernetting or route aggregation).

3.3   VAR Segmentation

RHM allows more than one MT host to share the same VAR in order to optimize the use of VAR spaces and allow for maximizing the possibility of supernetting for MT hosts in the same subnet. To avoid address collision within a VAR, participating MT hosts will be eventually allocated non-overlapping ranges within the shared VAR. Since a VAR r_j may be assigned to multiple MT hosts,

$\sum_{1 \le i \le n} b_{ij} = p$ means that r_j is allocated to p MT hosts. So r_j must be divided into p separate sub-VARs proportional to the V_i requirement for each MT host. The assignment of sub-VARs is randomized to minimize the possibility that the same host uses the same sub-VAR in two consecutive LFM intervals.

3.4   HFM Formulation

Each host h_i has a specific HFM interval T_{HFM_i}, which is determined based on the security requirements of the MT host. To achieve synchronization in HFM, every MTG of the network will use a pre-established hash function H and a shared key K to compute virtual addresses for all moving hosts in its subnet. The shared key is distributed by the MTC. Suppose there are p available vIPs $\{a_1, a_2, \ldots, a_p\}$ for host h_i in the current LFM interval, then the MTG can compute the vIP of HFM interval I_j of MT host h_i as:

$$A(I_j, h_i) = a_{(H(K,j) \bmod p)+1} \tag{9}$$

Here j is the index of the current HFM interval which can be calculated from the mutation speed of the MT host. The *mod* operation guarantees that the computed address index fall into the valid range between 1 and p. The randomness (or unpredictability) of the vIP mutations in VAR is guaranteed by the randomness of the hash function. However, Eq. 6 guarantees that for a host h_j, even in case of uniform vIP selection, the repeat probability never surpasses E_i.

This synchronization of MTGs is not precise time synchronization. Instead it is a loose synchronization that is realized via sharing of K, mutation index j and the designated VARs of MT hosts. The sharing allows each MTG to compute the active vIP addresses of every MT host in the network. In the case when a MTG crashes, it can still get the shared key and mutation index from the MTC to resume the IP mutations of the MT hosts within its subnet.

4   RHM Architecture and Protocol

4.1   Architecture

The main architecture of RHM network is depicted in Figure 1. The tasks of assigning a VARs to MT hosts (Sections 3.1, 3.3 and 3.2) are performed by a MTC. At each LFM interval, MTC selects new VARs for each MT hosts such that it satisfies constraints in Section 3. Then, the new designated VARs are announced to MTGs, which are boxes deployed at the boundary of subnets (between subnet switch and the core).

Each MTG is responsible for management of MT hosts in one subnet. MTG has various functions. Firstly, it selects a vIP from the current VAR of a MT host using a cryptographic function and a secret random key to guarantee unpredictability and intractability (Section 3.4). Secondly, it translates source rIP to vIP for outbound, and destination vIP to rIP for inbound packets. MTG stores the mapping between rIP and vIP in a translation table and performs address

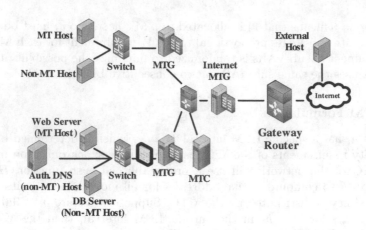

Fig. 1. The Architecture of moving target network

translation for incoming and outgoing packets. Active connections using old vIP will be maintained by storing the information of forwarding flows in the connection table. MTG will forward packets from old connections until the session is terminated (*e.g.*, FIN for TCP) or expired (*i.e.*, long inactive time for both TCP and UDP). Thirdly, it advertises routing updates of assigned VARs (for MT hosts in its subnet) by using the appropriate Interior Gateway Protocol (Section 5). Finally, it is responsible for changing DNS responses of local authoritative DNS servers (Section 4).

In addition to VAR selection, MTC is responsible for management of MTGs, key distribution for HFM vIP selection, and authorization of rIP-based flows (Section 4).

4.2   Protocol

There are two ways to communicate with MT hosts: using host name or host rIP. These two scenarios are depicted in Figures 2 and 3, respectively. These figures show a scenario where a MT host communicates with another MT host. Other scenarios (*e.g.*, non-MT host communicating with a MT host) are special cases of this scenario.

Figure 2 shows that when a DNS query is sent to resolve the name of an MT host, the DNS response is intercepted by the MTG and the rIP of the MT server is replaced with its current vIP (steps 1-3). Moreover, the MTG also sets the TTL value in the DNS response according to the HFM interval. As a result, clients will receive the vIP mapping to MT host name and initiate their connections accordingly (steps 3-4).

Figure 3 shows how authorized users (*e.g.*, administrators) can reach MT hosts using rIPs. In this case, MTG will request and authorize access for this source from MTC (steps 1-4). If access is granted, the MTG of the source will translate the rIP of the destination to the corresponding vIP and update its translation table

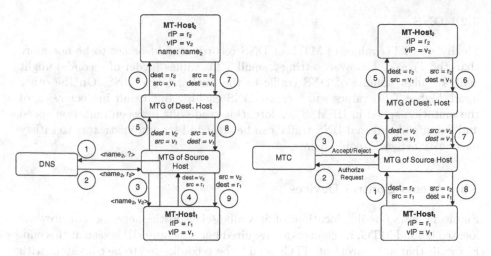

Fig. 2. hosts communicating with moving hosts through name

Fig. 3. hosts communicating with moving hosts through IP address

accordingly. It is important to note that this authorization is performed once per every session that includes rIP as destination. MTC access control policy can be managed by administrators based on the criticality of the MT host. In both scenarios (access by name or rIP) the source rIP is always translated to vIP.

As a result, RHM protocol restricts routing to vIP destinations in order to (1) ensure MT host mutation in the network, and (2) filter out traffic destined to rIPs and inactive vIPs that can be generated randomly by internal scanners at source MTG.

5   Reconfiguration Planning

RHM deployment does not require any change to current Internet infrastructure. In this section, we describe required reconfigurations that must be considered for deployment of RHM in current setting of Internet infrastructure.

5.1   Session Tracking

In order to prevent the disruption of active sessions, the MTG stores the rIP-vIP mapping of each flow in its translation table, and does not delete them until the termination of the flow. Active sessions continue using their vIPs without any disruption, and MTG handles their packets based on the translation table. The vIP is evicted from the available unused address space, and thus will not be assigned to any other MT host. However, the MT host will be assigned a new VAR that will be used for the next HFM. Therefore, an MTG might keep multiple vIP entries for the same MT host in its translation table in order to handle old and new active sessions.

5.2 DNS

Ideally, the TTL values of MT host DNS records should be set to be not more than the T_{HFM_i}. However, setting a small TTL values (order of seconds) might generate high volume of DNS traffic to the authoritative DNS. On the other hand, higher TTL values will increase DNS cashing but result in decreasing of the mutation speed in HFM. Therefore, this trade-offs between mutation speed and volume of external DNS traffic can be adjusted by administrators to satisfy particular network requirements.

5.3   Access Control Devices

Figure 1 shows possible locations of firewall devices in the network. For firewalls located behind MTG, no changes are required because only rIP is seen at this end. Firewalls that are in front of MTGs need to be reconfigured to be consistent with recent vIP changes. However, from a practical perspective, firewall polices that are in front of MTGs usually use domain/subnet ranges instead of specific IP addresses.

Thus a simple approach is to use default-accept in these firewalls for only the unused address space leaving the responsibility of filtering out the actually unused address space to MTGs. Since allocated VARs are strictly from the unused address space, this will not overlap with any of the existing rules in the firewall. This simply implies delegating the filtering out of the traffic destined to the unused addresses to MTGs, which eliminates spurious traffic by discarding any traffic not destined to an active vIP [14].

We assume that IDS/IPS devices are deployed behind the MTGs which is practically sound for most networks. Moreover, MTG bypasses hosts that use IPSec traffic because they are inherently protected from scanning attacks by IPSec gateways.

5.4   Routing

For implementation of RHM, no change is required on gateway and other external routers, because they simply route the traffic to/from our network. Routing updates must be advertised for internal routers. To address the routing convergence time, which is relatively small, MTC pre-computes VAR assignments one LFM interval before using them for mutation. Therefore, routing updates can be propagated in a timely and conflict-free manner.

For non-MT hosts using real IP address no routing update is required. MTC delegates routing update responsibility to MTGs, because they act as the gateway between routers and subnets. MTC informs MTGs of the next set of designated VARs for their MT hosts. MTGs generate initiates and broadcast advertisement messages as new VARs being assigned. If authentication is required, MTG will be given the credentials to authenticate itself to routers in the network. MTG triggers updates both periodically (required for most interior gateway protocols), and upon receiving new VAR assignments from MTC.

5.5   Implementation and Deployment

To study and demonstrate the feasibility of RHM, we implemented a proof-of-concept for RHM in a designated class C subnet in our university campus network. The network is further divided into 3 subnets each containing up to 3 MT hosts. The MTG and MTC components are implemented on Linux-based (Ubuntu) boxes and given privilege to interact with RIP-2 based routers and local firewalls. One RHM subnet includes an *Apache* Web Server, an *Apache* FTP server, and an OpenSSH server that reside on different MT hosts. To update routing information, MTC pre-computes and distributes VAR assignments to all MTGs for every LFM interval. MTG boxes implement RIP-2 protocols to communicate and advertise VARs to routing devices.

Our implementation proved that the RHM approach is feasible. We run several network activities during mutation: downloading files from FTP server and SSH server, video streaming from the HTTP server, and web browsing. Availability of these surfaces was not affected and long-lived connections functioned soundly and accurately, even after numerous LFM intervals. The routing propagation convergence was fast and the delay was negligible (less than 60 seconds). This shows that RHM is deployable and manageable on real networks. However, the implementation may not measure the scalability of the approach, since scalability evaluations require thousands of network elements. For this purpose, to show the effectiveness and scalability of RHM approach we performed analytical studies and simulation experiments, and we provide this result in Section 6.

6   Analysis and Evaluation

In this section, we evaluate RHM effectiveness against attacks and the overhead it incurs on the network. We use analytical modeling, experimentation and simulation to evaluate RHM.

6.1   Effectiveness

We evaluate the RHM effectiveness against scanning external and internal scanners.

External Scanners. The prolonged interval between target discovery and attack allows RHM to mutate the vIP of the scanned host before the actual launching of the attack. RHM can prevent information gathering by external scanners, which may be used for various purposes including hitlist attacks effectively, since the IP addresses in the hitlist will be soon out-of-date. Due to high mutation speed, and unpredictability of vIP assignments, our solution will be the *optimal* solution for defense against hitlist worms. To show the effectiveness of RHM against hitlist attacks, we run 100 different *Nmap* scanning over 90 minutes for a class B RHM network of up to $10 - 20\%$ MT hosts. Then, after comparing all the hundred scanning reports with the ground truth we found not more than 3% of actual IP addresses has been discovered, as shown in Figure 4.

Internal Scanners. Internal network scanning is performed via sequence of probes sent to random IPs, usually by random scanning worms. We can further classify random scanning worms into two categories: the first category is non-repeat random scanning worms, which never repeat addresses that have been scanned before. This can be achieved by some periodic pseudo-random generators or more sophisticated cooperative scanning approaches such as divide-and-conquer, or sequential scanning [15]. The second category is repeatable random scanning worms, which may choose a repeated address during random scan. In this section, we study the effectiveness of RHM on random scanning worms using the following two metrics: (1) *The mutation success probability*: the probability that a host is not hit by a scanner; and (2) slow-down rate of worm propagation: the total infection time with and without RHM.

Mutation Success Probability: Suppose there are N addresses in the available address space of the MT host and the MT host will use a random address from the address space in any HFM interval. Assume a non-repeat uniform scanner that is scanning an RHM network. We define speed ratio k as scanning rate of scanners on mutation speed of MT host. It can be shown that for N scans and $k = 1$, the scanner will miss the target with probability

$$P_{miss} = \left(1 - \frac{1}{N}\right)^N \approx e^{-1} = 0.37 \qquad (10)$$

Given k and N, for a non-repeat random scanner, the scanner will miss the target with the following *mutation success* probability:

$$M = \prod_{j=0}^{\lfloor \frac{N-k}{k} \rfloor} \left(\frac{j \cdot k}{N} + \frac{N - j \cdot k}{N} \prod_{i=0}^{k-1} \left(1 - \frac{1}{N - j \cdot k - i}\right) \right)$$

Figure 5 shows the theoretical and simulated mutation success probability of the moving hosts with $N = 30000$, 60000 and 120000 and different k values for the non-repeatable scanners. The scanner makes a total of 30000 scans, which means the scan ratios are 1, 0.5, 0.25 respectively in the three cases. In the simulation, every data point is the average of 10 runs, and there are 10% MTs in the network. The mutation success probability is the percentage of the MTs that are not infected at the end of the simulation. We can see that the simulated result is roughly consistent with the theoretical analysis. We can also see that the mutation success probability is stable when k is less than some threshold. If the scanner can scan the whole mutation address space, the mutation success probability can reach a maximum value about 0.4. If the scanner cannot scan the whole space, the mutation success probability can be much higher than 0.4. When the scanner can only scan one quarter of the address space, the mutation success probability can reach about 0.8.

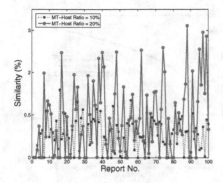

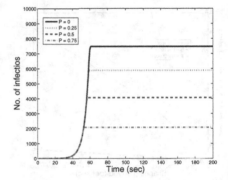

Fig. 4. Ratio of common IP addresses between Nmap reports

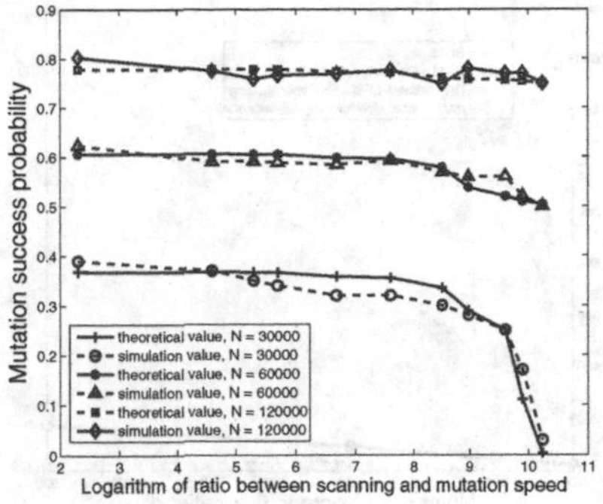

Fig. 5. Mutation success probability of a MT host for non-repeatable scanners

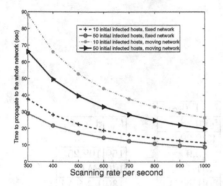

Fig. 6. Worm propagation speed comparison for fixed and moving networks

Fig. 7. Worm propagation in RHM network with various safe-area migration probabilities

For a repeatable uniform scanner, if a host uses a fixed or moving address and the scanner uses a random address from a set that has N possible addresses for every scan, then the scanner may hit the host with probability $1/N$ for every scan. In other words RHM has no effect on the repeatable scanners. For routing worms [16], the worm scanning space is determined based solely on BGP routing data, and the RHM effect is similar to uniform scanners.

Slow-Down Rate of Worm Propagation: The ideal case of non-repeatable scanning can be achieved via cooperative scanning, such as divide-and-conquer scanning [15]. Based on our analysis of non-repeat scanner in equation 10, a cooperative will miss about e^{-1} (more than one third) portion of the vulnerable hosts (this can be considered to be equivalent to that the whole network only contains $e^{-1}V$ vulnerable hosts). Also, the propagation speed will also decrease because the total number of hittable vulnerable hosts decreases.

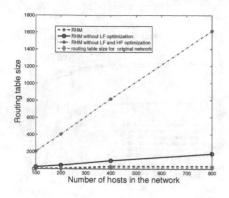

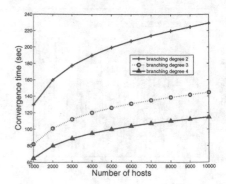

Fig. 8. Routing table size for different RHM settings

Fig. 9. Routing convergence for different network sizes

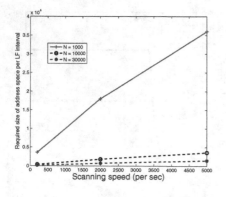

U	T (sec)
50	0.28
45	0.29
40	0.9
35	1.52
30	UNSAT

U	T (sec)
160	87.94
150	109.25
140	FAIL
130	UNSAT

Fig. 10. Address space requirement   **Fig. 11.** Case 1   **Fig. 12.** Case 2

Based on [15], in a moving target network, the propagation model for an ideal non-repeat cooperative scan worm is

$$\frac{dI(t)}{dt} = \begin{cases} \frac{(1-e^{-1})\eta}{N}VI(t) & I(t) < V \\ 0 & I(t) = V \end{cases} \tag{11}$$

The solution of the equation is:

$$I(t) = I(0)e^{a(1-e^{-1})t} \quad \text{for } I(t) < (1-e^{-1})V \tag{12}$$

Here $a = \frac{\eta V}{N}$ and $I(0)$ is the number of infected hosts in the beginning. We calculated the worm propagation speed based on the above analysis. Fig. 6 shows the time (in seconds) for the worm to propagate a class A network (2^{24} total addresses) with 10000 vulnerable hosts.

We can see that with RHM, worm propagation takes about two times more than usual time. This means that RHM can slow down the worm propagation significantly. We also integrated IDS feedback in mutation decision, in order to move MT hosts to scanned safe area with a probability P. Figure 7 shows that the mutation success probability will be improved to 40 to 80% with IDS feedback.

6.2   Overhead Evaluation

In this section, we evaluate (1) the required address space overhead with varying scanning rate, (2) the computational complexity of the constraint satisfaction solution, and (3) the routing and firewall overheads.

Address Space Overhead. The required address space necessarily depends on mutation speed. Similarly, the HF and LF mutation speed is dependent on targeted attack model.

To maximize the defense benefit of RHM, enough addresses for an LFM interval should be provisioned. For example, based on our analysis for non-repeat uniform scan worm in Section 6.1, if we want to keep the mutation success probability to be over 0.3, then the size of the address space assigned to a single MT host for an LFM interval should be at least

$$(\text{scanning speed}/P_{0.3}) \cdot T_{LFM} \tag{13}$$

Here $P_{0.3}$ is the mutation speed that can achieve mutation success probability 0.3 for this scanning speed. Figure 10 shows the required size of address space with network size $N = 1000, 10000$ and 30000.

SMT Formalization. We also tested the feasibility of the constraint satisfaction algorithm for LFM VAR assignment. We use the Z3 SMT solver [4] for our evaluation. The running time of the SMT instance is very sensitive to the selection of the upper bound U of the routing table size in Eq. 8. Figure 11 shows the running time of the SMT formalization for a network with 100 moving hosts, 40 empty address ranges, while the demand of every host is a random number between 1 and 5, the size of the empty ranges is a random number between 10 and 20. In the table, "UNSAT" means the SMT solver reported that the instance is unsatisfiable. In this case one must relax some of the parameters (such as decreasing the routing table size upper bound or increasing the size of empty address ranges) to get a feasible solution.

Figure 12 shows the running time of the SMT formalization for a network with 300 moving hosts, 120 empty address ranges. In the table, "FAIL" means the SMT solver failed to solve the instance. This means that the upper bound used in the constraint is beyond the solving ability of the SMT solver. In this case one also needs to relax some of the parameters to get a feasible solution.

Routing and Firewall Updates Overhead. The overhead of routing update is proportional to the routing table size after every LF mutation. Suppose the total number of hosts in a subnet is H_t, and the number of moving hosts in the subnet is H_m. We also assume that in the LFM optimization algorithm we can arrange N_h moving hosts with the address ranges that have the same prefix (route summarization). Then we can see that the total number of routing entries needed for the subnet in one LFM interval is $1 + (H_m/N_h)$. Here (H_m/N_h) are the routing entries required for the moving hosts, and we need to add 1 entry for all fixed hosts in the same subnet. If no LFM optimization is adopted, then the total number of routing entries needed for the subnet in one LFM interval will be close to $1 + H_m$, because RHM will assign different address blocks for different moving hosts, which requires a different entry in the routing table. If there is no LFM and HFM optimization and the motion is completely random, and there are on average N_{HFM} HFM intervals in a LFM interval, then the total number of routing entries needed for the subnet in one LFM interval will be close to $1 + H_m \cdot N_{HFM}$, because we need to use a different entry in the routing table for every host in every HFM interval.

We simulated RHM in networks with various sizes, ranging from 100 to 800 hosts. The networks contain up to 16 subnets and every subnet contains up to 50 hosts respectively. Fig. 8 shows the routing table size for every LFM interval for different kinds of RHM setting. We can see from the figure that LFM and HFM optimization can greatly reduce routing table size.

We also simulated the routing convergence time for different network sizes. We assumed each subnet includes 50 hosts, and the network uses *RIP* for routing advertisements. In RIP, each router broadcasts its routing table every 30 seconds. We assumed the routers form a full tree and simulated routing convergence time for branching degrees 2, 3, and 4. As represented in Figure 9, the convergence time for branching degree 2 and a network including 10000 hosts is less than 4 minutes.

For firewall updates, the analysis and results are similar. The firewall updates occurs for new VARs in each LFM interval, and the firewall updates are basically equal to routing updates. The only difference is that for firewalls we have to evict old entries, while in routers unadvertised destinations will be excluded after a certain timeout interval.

7   Conclusion and Future Work

Moving target is a game changing technique that puts the defender in a stronger position with proactive rather than reactive defense. In this paper we present a novel framework called Random Host Mutation (RHM). We formulated intelligent host randomization with constraint satisfaction problem to achieve high unpredictability and speed while satisfying routing and configuration constraints. We implemented RHM in existing network without requiring changes in endhosts or network infrastructure. We performed rigorous theoretical analysis and experimentation to evaluate the effectiveness and overhead of RHM.

We evaluated RHM through implementation, experimentation and simulation. Our experimentation shows that RHM can defeat scanning tools by invalidating at least 97% of its discovery. We also show that RHM can defeat random scanning worms by decreasing the number of infected hosts by 40 to 80% and by slowing down the propagation speed by 50%.

Our implementation and simulation also shows that the routing update overhead is tens of times smaller than random mutation without optimization and the average packet translation and lookup overhead is less than one tenth of a millisecond.

In the future, we plan to study reliability and security issues with RHM operation. For example, we would like to study impact of failures and attacks on RHM devices. We also plan to investigate other related moving target techniques such as random route mutation and deceptive fingerprinting.

References

1. Lyon, G.F.: Nmap Network Scanning: The Official Nmap Project Guide to Network Discovery and Security Scanning. Insecure, USA (2009)
2. Laudicina, A.P.: Nessus - a powerful, free remote security scanner. Sys. Admin. 11(5) (2002)
3. Whyte, D., Kranakis, E., van Oorschot, P.C.: DNS-based Detection of Scanning Worms in an Enterprise Network. In: Proceedings of The 12th Annual Network and Distributed System Security Symposium (February 2005)
4. Bjørner, N., de Moura, L.: $z3^{10}$: Applications, enablers, challenges and directions. In: CFV 2009 (2009)
5. Antonatos, S., Akritidis, P., Markatos, E.P., Anagnostakis, K.G.: Defending against hitlist worms using network address space randomization. Comput. Netw. 51(12), 3471–3490 (2007)
6. Kewley, D., Fink, R., Lowry, J., Dean, M.: Dynamic approaches to thwart adversary intelligence gathering. In: DARPA Information Survivability Conference and Exposition, vol. 1, p. 0176 (2001)
7. Michalski, J.T.: Network security mechanisms utilising network address translation. International Journal of Critical Infrastructures 2(1), 10–49 (2006)
8. Atighetchi, M., Pal, P., Webber, F., Jones, C.: Adaptive use of network-centric mechanisms in cyber-defense. In: ISORC 2003, p. 183. IEEE Computer Society (2003)
9. Kewley, D., Fink, R., Lowry, J., Dean, M.: Dynamic approaches to thwart adversary intelligence gathering. In: Proceedings of DARPA Information Survivability Conference Exposition II, DISCEX 2001, vol. 1, pp. 176–185 (2001)
10. Jafarian, J.H., Al-Shaer, E., Duan, Q.: Openflow random host mutation: Transparent moving target defense using software defined networking. In: Proceedings of HotSDN workshop at SIGCOMM 2012, Helsinki, Finland (2012)
11. Yegneswaran, V., Alfeld, C.: Camouflaging honeynets. In: Proceedings of IEEE Global Internet Symposium (2007)
12. Cai, J.-Y., Yegneswaran, V., Alfeld, C., Barford, P.: An Attacker-Defender Game for Honeynets. In: Ngo, H.Q. (ed.) COCOON 2009. LNCS, vol. 5609, pp. 7–16. Springer, Heidelberg (2009)
13. Chakravarty, S.: A characterization of binary decision diagrams. IEEE Trans. Comput. 42(2), 129–137 (1993)
14. Al-Shaer, E.S., Hamed, H.H.: Discovery of policy anomalies in distributed firewalls. In: Twenty-Third Annual Joint Conference of the IEEE Computer and Communications Societies, INFOCOM 2004, vol. 4, pp. 2605–2616 (March 2004)
15. Zou, C.C., Towsley, D., Gong, W.: On the performance of internet worm scanning strategies. Elsevier Journal of Performance Evaluation 63, 700–723 (2003)
16. Zou, C.C., Towsley, D.: Routing Worm: A Fast, Selective attack worm based on IP address information. In: Workshop on Principles of Advanced and Distributed Simulation (PADS 2005), pp. 199–206 (2005)

Towards a Framework for Evaluating the Security of Physical-Layer Identification Systems

Ryan M. Gerdes[1], Mani Mina[2], and Thomas E. Daniels[2]

[1] Utah State University, Logan, UT 84322, USA
ryan.gerdes@usu.edu
[2] Iowa State University, Ames, IA 50011, USA
{mmina,daniels}@iastate.edu

Summary. In recent years researchers have shown that the analogue signalling behaviour of digital devices can be used for identification and monitoring purposes. The basic postulate of these so-called physical-layer identification (PLI) approaches is that devices are sufficiently variable in their behaviour to be distinguishable and that an attacker would be unable to adequately emulate this behaviour. Recent work, however, has shown that at least some PLI implementations can be defeated using electronic equipment capable of generating arbitrarily shaped signals known as arbitrary waveform generators (AWGs).

In this work we first present a framework to determine whether an AWG, specified in terms of resolution, sampling rate, distortion, and noise parameters, could be used to defeat a given PLI system. We then utilise this framework in the formulation of a cost-minimisation problem to find the most cost-effective values of these parameters; i.e. we characterise the least expensive, and hence lowest performing, AWG an attacker would require to defeat a PLI system. The use of the framework is illustrated by applying it to a previously proposed PLI approach. Results indicate that the PLI system could be defeated using an AWG with a substantially lower sampling rate and resolution than the PLI system sampler.

1 Introduction

Identifying digital devices based on signalling differences manifested at the physical layer (known as physical-layer identification or PLI) has been shown to be effective for a wide range of technologies. From wired [1] and wireless [2–6] networking devices to sensor [7, 8] and RFID devices [9–11], PLI approaches are able to reliably distinguish between highly similar devices with accuracies of over 90% [12, 13].

The methodology of PLI is similar to that of biometrics [14]: (1) identify and acquire a recurring and ubiquitous signal, S, to serve as a 'fingerprint', (2) extract a set of features from the signal, $L = f(S)$, and (3) employ a classification technique to compare a test feature set with a database of existing feature sets in order to verify the purported identity of the test subject. When a threshold technique is used in (3) to compare feature sets, a reference feature set, L_R, is

A.D. Keromytis and R. Di Pietro (Eds.): SecureComm 2012, LNICST 106, pp. 328–348, 2013.

used with a distance measure, $d(\cdot)$, to check whether the differences between L and L_R are within a certain threshold, $d(L_R, L) \leq th$.

While PLI could be used to corroborate higher layer mechanisms used for authentication, intrusion detection, and forensics, its use in these areas is predicated on the belief that the slight variations in the signalling behaviour of devices are difficult, if not impossible, to control and duplicate. In light of recent work by Danev et al. [15] and Edman and Yener [16], which showed that wireless signals can be successfully forged using arbitrary waveform generators (AWGs), it is no longer possible to merely assert the inherent unreproducibility of signals. Instead, we now require a framework to not only judge the security of PLI systems, in absolute terms and in relation to each other, with respect to existing AWGs but one that also specifies the performance an AWG of the future would need to defeat a given PLI system.

1.1 Paper Contributions and Structure

While existing work has shown that certain PLI systems can be defeated using AWGs, ours is the first work to consider the problem of whether a specific AWG can defeat an arbitrary PLI system. In what follows we propose, and provide implementation details of, a general framework for determining whether an AWG, characterised by sampling rate, resolution, signal-to-noise ration, and total harmonic distortion, could produce a forged signal that would be accepted by a given PLI system. By estimating the cost associated with an increase or decrease in each parameter, we can also find the least expensive—i.e. lowest performing—AWG necessary to defeat the PLI system.

As a result of this work, researchers and designers of PLI systems will be able to 1) determine if a PLI system is secure from an attacker using a given AWG; 2) compare and evaluate the relative security of systems; 3) investigate the strengths and weaknesses of different PLI methodologies to decide which features and comparison techniques are most effective in securely identifying devices; and 4) evaluate the trade-offs associated with selecting higher or lower performing equipment for acquiring device signals.

In the next subsection we provide an overview of the two works that motivated our research: we discuss which PLI systems were attacked, the equipment used, and the authors' results. In Section 2 we describe two ways in which PLI systems can be subverted, define our threat model, and note the most relevant parameters used to characterise AWGs. The modelling of the attacker's AWG is detailed in Section 3, where we also discuss how a cost minimisation problem can be defined that utilises the model to determine the most cost-effective values for the AWG performance parameters. In Section 4 we demonstrate the use of the framework by analysing the matched filter PLI system outlined by Gerdes et al. in [1, 12].

1.2 Related Work

In both [15] and [16] two types of attacks were carried out against the PLI approach (which utilised the demodulation characteristics of 802.11b signals) proposed by Brick et al. [5]; in addition, a transient-based PLI approach for sensor nodes proposed by Danev and Capkun [8] was also examined in [15]. The PLI system of [5] was compromised in both works by creating signals with the features of known devices and through the replay of observed frames. For the former attack, false-accept rates (FAR) of 98% and 75% were reported for [15,16], respectively; in the latter attack, the FAR for [16] was 55% while the replay attack met with similar success as the generation attack for [15]. The difference in attack success rates can probably be attributed to not only the threat models but the vastly different hardware used to implement the PLI system and carry out the attacks.

In [15] universal software radio peripherals (USRP) operating at 128 Megasamples/s and controlled with the GNU Radio library were used for both the genuine and attacker devices, with the attacker device being programmed to produce the features of the genuine devices as measured by, and at, the PLI system (which consisted of an Agilent Digital Signal Analyser operating at 40Gigasamples/s with 8000MHz of bandwidth). The replay attack was carried out using a Tektronix AWG 7000 (20 Gigasamples/s); the frames used for the replay were captured at the attacker's location using the PLI system. In [16] both the PLI system and the attacking device were built using the same USRP (14-bit analogue-to-digital converter operating at 100 Megasamples/s and dual 16-bit digital-to-analogue converter operating at 400MHz). The attacker sought to reproduce or generate signals, which it captured, from one of three laptops used to represent legitimate users.

In their analysis of the PLI system of [8], Danev $et~al.$ were able to successfully replay frames captured by the PLI system over a wired channel; however, when a wireless channel was used the system could only be defeated if the attacker assumed the genuine device's physical location.

2   Preliminaries

The following notation and nomenclature will be used when discussing the analogue signalling behaviour of digital devices and the PLI system used to identify those devices. We will also assume that devices transmit data using frames, as in IEEE 802.3 and 802.11b.

A record, r, is defined as a discrete time/voltage sampled version (obtained using an analogue-to-digital converter) of the analogue signal that makes-up the data frame. For the PLI system, L_i^j is used to represent the feature vector derived from the jth frame of the ith device; $L_i^j(k)$ denotes access to the kth element of the feature vector. In addition, a collection of feature vectors from the ith device are denoted as $\mathbf{L}_i$, where $\mathbf{L}_i(j)$ is used to refer to the individual vector L_i^j. The feature vectors of frames that are to be tested by the system are always accompanied by the subscript T; the reference feature vector(s) used to establish a device's baseline behaviour by the subscript R. A generic analogue signal is denoted by $\tilde{s}$ and a sampled version of it s.

2.1   Attack Types

We define and discuss the two classes of attacks that can be used against PLI systems.

Type I Attack. We define a type one attack as an attack in which an attacker is attempting to accurately reproduce those portions of a device's signal used for identification. In the terminology of [15], this type of attack can be carried out through *feature replay* or *signal replay*. In the former case, the attacker attempts to replicate only the specific features used by the PLI system for identification; those portions of the signal not used for identification needn't be considered. For a signal replay attack, the attacker acquires a sampled version of a device's signal and attempts to produce near-perfect copies of those portions of the signal used for identification using an AWG.

We provide a demonstration of how our framework can be used to measure the resiliency of PLI systems to signal replay attacks in Section 4. Because the PLI system analysed in that section uses each sample point of the device's signal as features, the feature replay attack is not examined in this work. We note that the framework can be used to evaluate feature replay, though.

Type II Attack. In a type two attack the attacker does not seek to produce a high-fidelity copy of a device's signal but rather exploits the limitations of the identification technique used by the PLI system. For example, consider a PLI system using a threshold-based approach where the distance measure is simply the sum of the differences between the test and reference feature vectors $(d(L_R, L_T) = L_R(1) - L_T(1) + \ldots + L_R(n) - L_T(n)$, with $d(L_R, L_T) \leq th$ for L_T to be accepted). To defeat the PLI system the individual differences between all the elements of the feature vectors needn't be sufficiently small, only the sum of the differences; thus an attacker could simply engineer a signal such that $L_T(n) \geq th - L_R(1) + L_T(1) - \ldots - L_R(n)$ to satisfy the threshold.

A type two attack could be effected through manipulation of a signal generated by a device under the attacker's control or the attacker could craft a signal using an AWG. The only limitation faced by the attacker is that their signal must behave according to the standard governing data transmission for the device (for example, in the case of 10Mb Ethernet the voltage levels, signal transitions, etc must be in accordance with those specified in the 802.3 standard [17]).

To carry out such an attack, however, requires more knowledge of the PLI system and associated target device than a type one attack. Whereas a type one attack can be carried out simply by observing frames from the targeted device, in a type two attack, assuming a threshold scheme is used by the PLI system, the attacker must possess both the device's reference feature set and thresholds for future outputs to be able to construct their signal. By knowing these along with the distance measure, an attacker might be able manipulate their signal, in whole or in part, to produce a signal falling within the threshold for the device. We are aware of no attacks of this type having been demonstrated against PLI systems.

While this type of attack is not amenable to a general analysis, due to the complicated and PLI-specific relationship between the signal, feature vectors, and distance function, so long as an AWG is used to actually generate a specially crafted signal our framework can be used to determine if the attack would succeed for a given AWG. A type two attack is proposed and evaluated in Section 4.

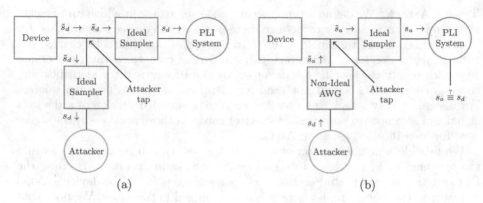

Fig. 1. (Threat model) Assuming lossless channel (a) attacker and PLI system, using the same samplers, are able to measure device's signal $\tilde{s}_d$ and obtain same sampled version s_d, and (b) attacker uses a non-ideal AWG to synthesise the analogue signal $\tilde{s}_a$ from s_d, and the PLI system, using the same sampler as in (a), measures $\tilde{s}_a$ to determine whether the attacker's signal is distinguishable from s_d

2.2   Threat Model

To simplify our analysis we chose to ignore channel effects and equip both the attacker and PLI system with ideal samplers of the same resolution and sampling rate (these parameters are explained below). In consequence of these assumptions, an attacker would be able to 1) capture the same device signal, $\tilde{s}_d$, as the PLI system (Figure 1a), and 2) generate a forged version of $\tilde{s}_d$, denoted by $\tilde{s}_a$, using an AWG and know it be identical to what will be measured at the PLI system, taking into account differences in the sample rates and resolutions of the AWG and PLI system sampler, to produce the sampled signal s_a (Figure 1b).

To justify ignoring channel effects at this time, despite the very real obstacle they present to an attacker, as demonstrated in [13], we note that a non-ideal channel is not only a problem for an attacker. Simply changing a device's position with respect to the PLI system significantly degrades our ability to re-identify it (unless training data has been previously acquired for the new position) [8]. Our analysis thus presents a best-case scenario for the attacker. In actuality an attacker would be required to model the channel and integrate its effect into the signal to be produced by the AWG.

The decision to provide the attacker and PLI system with identical samplers was mostly a practical matter: doing otherwise would have required multiple oscilloscopes to carry out our experiments. It is also difficult to see the benefit of an attacker using a sampler with a higher resolution and sampling rate than the PLI system as, irrespective of the sampling rate and resolution of the attacker's AWG, the forged signal would be downsampled at the PLI system. In addition, we would argue, and indeed it is assumed in our AWG framework, that an attacker captures $\tilde{s}_d$ at a resolution and sampling rate greater than or equal to that of their AWG for the simple reason that upsampling the captured signal could add no new information. Both of these cases could be tested at a future

Fig. 2. (Arbitrary waveform generator) the code specifies the levels of discrete signal $\hat{x}$, which the low-pass filter smooths to create $\tilde{x}$ (NOTE: $\hat{x}$ has discrete levels but is continuous in time)

time, and the framework is, in any case, flexible enough as-is to accommodate different samplers for the attacker and PLI system.

We also note that while both the channel and tap of Figure 1 are depicted using lines, this is not meant to imply that the framework is limited to analysing wired PLI systems. In the case of a wireless channel, an antenna would serve as the tap and if down-mixing were used by the PLI system (as in [8]) appropriate mixers could be placed in front of the ideal samplers and after the non-ideal AWG. If down-mixing were not used by the wireless PLI system, we could either stipulate that the sampling rate of the non-ideal AWG be no less than twice the carrier frequency used by the devices or place a mixer after the AWG to up-mix the generated signal.

2.3 AWG Characteristics

An arbitrary waveform generator creates an analogue version of a digitized waveform. The three core components of an AWG are the waveform source memory, digital-to-analogue converter (DAC), and low-pass filter (Figure 2); optional components include scaling circuits, DC offset circuits, and differential outputs [18]. An analogue signal is created by feeding the binary values of the digitized waveform (known as codes) to the DAC, where a stepped, analogue output is generated; the stepped output is smoothed by the low-pass filter.

Because of the central role of the DAC in recreating the digital signal, we will concentrate our performance analysis exclusively on it and assume the other components of the AWG to be ideal. In any case, the parameters related to the DAC we will be discussing are always given with respect to the output of the AWG, so we are merely overestimating the minimum performance of the AWG.

According to [19], the most important specifications used to evaluate the dynamic performance of a DAC are settling time, glitch impulse area, distortion, spurious free dynamic range (SFDR), and signal-to-noise ratio (SNR). In addition to these parameters, we will also discuss DAC resolution. Definitions for each of these parameters may be found in the appendix. Static performance measures (gain, offset, differential non-linearity [DNL], and integral non-linearity [INL], see [20]) are not discussed due to the fact that dynamic non-linearities dominate at high frequencies [21]. Our distortion model does, however, allow us incorporate errors due to static non-linearities.

3 Framework Overview

A system diagram of our framework is given in Figure 3. The attacker begins with s_d, a sampled version of some authenticated device's signal, $\tilde{s}_d$, that is acquired at the PLI systems sampling rate, f_p, and resolution, R_p. Because of

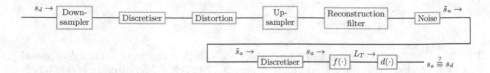

Fig. 3. (Framework overview) Operations used to simulate (red) attacker producing analogue signal $\tilde{s}_a$ from authentic device's sampled signal s_d, and (blue) PLI system sampling and comparing attacker's forged signal to baseline behaviour of device to determine whether authentic and forged signal are distinguishable

the lossless channel assumed in our threat model, s_d is the same for the attacker and the PLI system. The first step the attacker takes is to downsample s_d to the sampling rate of their AWG. Allowing $f_a = P/Q \times f_p$ ($P/Q \leq 1$) to be the sampling rate of the AWG, s_d is downsampled by P/Q. The downsampled signal is then discretised according to the resolution of the AWG, R_a. To simulate the distortion and noise present in all real-world AWGs, the downsampled signal must be passed through a distortion function and have noise (in our case, additive white gaussian noise) added to the resulting signal to produce the attacker's output, $\tilde{s}_a$. However, before noise is added to the distorted signal, it is upsampled to the PLI system rate—i.e. it is upsampled by Q/P—and a reconstruction filter is applied. Upsampling at this point is done for two reasons.

In the first place, distortion and noise measurements of actual AWGs are made after the generated signal has passed through a reconstruction (low pass) filter. Applying our distortion model to an upsampled signal would introduce high frequency distortion components that would otherwise be filtered by the AWG's reconstruction filter. Secondly, since we are synthesising signals for the PLI system to compare with actual sampled data to determine the similarity between the two, the synthesised data must be at the same sample rate as the original. In actuality the attacker's AWG would produce a continuous-time signal that would then be sampled by the PLI system at the rate f_p; upsampling the discrete representation of the attacker's signal simulates this sampling.

At the PLI system, $\tilde{s}_a$ is discretised according to the sampler resolution R_p (the sampling of the signal having been accomplished by the AWG model).

The preceding involves only the first step of the PLI methodology; steps two and three, wherein the attacker's signal is subjected to feature extraction and comparison, are specific to the PLI system under examination.

The methodology used to model the attacker's AWG and the PLI system is detailed in the next subsection, while a cost-based method for determining the most economical values for the parameters outlined in Section 2.3 for the AWG are covered in Section 3.2.

3.1   AWG and Sampler Models

The functionality of the AWG and sampler models of the framework are explained within the context of the performance parameters given in Section 2.3. Note: the text in parenthesis immediately following each parameter indicates which aspect of the framework (with reference to Figure 3) the parameter bears upon.

Settling Time. (*Down-sampler, Up-sampler, Reconstruction filter*) It is the settling time of the DAC used in the AWG that sets the ultimate limit on the maximum sampling rate of the AWG. Allowing τ to denote the settling time of the DAC, the sampling rate of the AWG, f, must be less than or equal to the inverse of the settling time ($f \leq 1/\tau$). If we stipulate that the settling time of the attacker's AWG, τ_a is much less than the inverse of the sampling rate, f_p, of the PLI system sampler ($\tau_a << 1/f_p$) the settling time may be ignored as it unlikely that the attacker's signal would be sampled during the transition period (modern AWGs are capable of meeting this requirement, see [22]). By this assumption, the glitch area may be similarly ignored.

Based on the above, we need focus only on the sampling rate of the AWG and PLI system sampler. To simulate the attacker downsampling the signal s_d by integer amounts—i.e. the new sample rate is given by $1/n \times f_p$, where n is an integer—we can simply discard every n^{th} data point; however, to downsample by a non-integer factor, of say P/Q requires upsampling (insertion of P zeros between data points), application of an anti-alias filter, and downsampling (discarding every Q datapoints) [23]. An FIR least-squared filter with a cutoff frequency of $P/Q * f_p/2$ (the Nyquist frequency) is used as the anti-aliasing filter in our implementation. The Nyquist frequency of the attacker's AWG was chosen as most commercially available DACs are able to generate signals up to their own Nyquist frequency [24].

The same procedure is used to restore the attacker's signal to the PLI system sample rate (the signal is upsampled by Q/P).

Resolution. (*Discretisers*) Because of the filtering used to downsample and upsample signals, the sample points of the resampled signals will not be exact multiples of the increment voltage of either the attacker's AWG or the PLI system's sampler. In order to incorporate the effects of the finite resolution of the AWG and sampler, it is therefore necessary to discretise these signals by rounding each sample to the nearest multiple of the increment voltage. (Algorithm 1 details how the sampled signal s is discretised for an n-bit AWG/sampler with full-scale voltage V_{FS}.)

Algorithm 1. Set resolution

Input : s, n, and V_{FS}
Output: $\mathbf{s}^*$ (n-bit representation of $\mathbf{s_d}$)
foreach $s_i \in \mathbf{s}$ **do**

$\quad i \leftarrow \arg\min_m \left(\left| s_i - m\frac{V_{FS}}{2^n - 1} \right| \right)$; $\qquad\qquad$ //m is an integer

$\quad \mathbf{s}^* \leftarrow \mathbf{s}^* \cup \left(i \times \frac{V_{FS}}{(2^n - 1)} \right)$;

end

Distortion. (*Distortion*) A full and proper accounting of how the output of a DAC deviates from its ideal output depends not only on the behaviour of the non-ideal components used to construct the DAC [25] but also on its architecture [26,27]. As such, it is not possible to utilise a single distortion model in our framework. Rather, an attacker would need to select (based upon market availability or the manufacturing resources at their disposal) a distortion model for the DAC used in their AWG. While several so-called behavioural models have been proposed for many different DAC architectures and deployments [28–32], to simply illustrate how distortion models can be used in our framework we have selected a model that, while not tied to any particular architecture, nonetheless produces adjustable amounts of static and dynamic distortion.

Allowing $s[i]$ to denote the ith sample point of the sampled signal s and s^* the distorted version of s, distortion of both types can be introduced using the polynomial [33]

$$s^*[i] = D(s[i]) = \beta + \alpha s[i] + \gamma \times (\beta + \alpha s[i])^2 + \delta \times (\beta + \alpha s[i])^3$$
$$+ \eta \times (\beta + \alpha \times (s[i] - s[i-1]))^2 + \kappa \times (\beta + \alpha \times (s[i] - s[i-1]))^3 \quad (1)$$

In (1), static distortion is generated through the scaling of individual sample points, while dynamic distortion is introduced by taking the difference between two sample points.

To achieve a certain amount of distortion using this model one would create a test signal (see the [34]), apply (1) to it, and vary the coefficients until the desired THD was reached. Unfortunately, we are aware of no set procedure for how the coefficients should be modified. In the absence of formal guidelines, we follow [33] and set the initial values of the coefficients to $\alpha = 1, \beta = 0$ (no gain or offset error, as these can be compensated for), $\gamma = 0.003, \delta = 0.0001, \eta = 0.0001, \kappa = 0.002$ and vary each coefficient (excepting α and β) by a constant multiple, m, to achieve a specified distortion. Our distortion model is then

$$s^*[i] = D(s[i], m) = \beta + \alpha s[i] + m \times \gamma \times (\beta + \alpha s[i])^2$$
$$+ m \times \delta \times (\beta + \alpha s[i])^3 + m \times \eta \times (\beta + \alpha \times (s[i] - s[i-1]))^2$$
$$+ m \times \kappa \times (\beta + \alpha \times (s[i] - s[i-1]))^3 \quad (2)$$

In our framework the THD of the AWG is established using a procedure similar to that of real AWGs: Equation 2 is applied to a test signal[1], consisting of a single period of a 10 MHz sine wave, sampled at the sample rate of the AWG, and m varied until the THD equals the value specified. Common test signals used in real world measurements for several DACs we examined were 1,2,4,5, and 10 MHz (see [35], e.g.). A 10 MHz test signal was selected due to the fact that the PLI system used to illustrate our framework extracts features from a 5 MHz square wave and 10 MHz sits between the fundamental frequency and the first harmonic of 15 MHz (see Section 4.3). As noted at the beginning of Section 3, the test signal is upsampled before the distortion measurements are made.

Having found an m that produces the specified THD, (2), is applied to the attacker's signal and the resulting distorted signal upsampled by Q/P to the PLI system sample rate (Algorithm 2).

---

[1] The attacker's signal is not used with the model to establish the THD of the AWG because it is composed of multiple frequencies, and while the THD can be calculated for any particular frequency over the bandwidth of the signal, we cannot say which particular THD represents the THD of the AWG.

Algorithm 2. Set distortion

Input : s, P, Q, and *thd*
Output: s^* (distorted version of s)
$s_t \leftarrow$ create test signal;
$s_D \leftarrow s_t$;   //distorted test signal
$m \leftarrow 1$;
//$THD(\cdot)$ calculates THD using Equation 2 of [34]
while $THD(s_t, s_D) \neq thd$ do
   if $THD(s_t, s_D) > thd$ then decrease m;
   else increase m;
   foreach $s_i \in s_t$ do
     | $s_D \leftarrow s_D \cup D(s_i, m)$;
   end
   $s_D \leftarrow upsample(s_D, Q, P)$;
end
foreach $s_i \in s$ do
  | $s^* \leftarrow s^* \cup D(s_i, m)$;
end
$s^* \leftarrow upsample(s^*, Q, P)$;

Spurious Free Dynamic Range (SFDR). The distortion model described above only allows one or the other of THD/SFDR to be specified (the other may be calculated). We chose to specify THD as it more informative, in the sense that the SFDR may remain constant while harmonic distortion continues to increase.

Noise. (*Noise*) Just as is the case for distortion, there are several ways to model the noise performance of DACs [36,37]. Again, for the purposes of illustration, we have selected a simple, non-behavioural model that uses additive white Gaussian noise (AWGN) for the attacker's AWG.

As noted in [34], the signal-to-noise ratio of an AWG is calculated in such a way as to exclude the effects of distortion. Therefore, we use the signal produced by the distortion model in the numerator of the SNR ratio (see Equation 1 of [34]); i.e. a distorted signal, s, produced using (2), is defined as being free of noise. Having calculated the power of this signal, $p_s = P(s)$, to achieve a specified signal-to-noise ratio, *snr*, we need merely generate a noise signal, s_n of equal length with power $P(s_n) = p_s/snr$ and add the two to produce a signal with both distortion and noise, $s^* = s + s_n$ (Algorithm 3).

Algorithm 3. Set SNR

Input : s and *snr*
Output: s^* (noisy version of s, with SNR of *snr*)
$p_s \leftarrow P(s)$;   //$P(\cdot)$ calculates power
$p_n \leftarrow p_s/snr$;
$s_n \leftarrow$ create signal of white Gaussian noise, having power p_n;
$s^* \leftarrow s + s_n$;

3.2   Finding Minimum AWG Performance

By following the procedure outlined above, it is possible to simulate an attacker generating a forgery of an authenticated device's signal using an AWG of a specified sample rate, resolution, THD, and SNR. This forged signal can then be used in steps two and three of the PLI methodology (feature extraction and comparison) to determine whether the attacker's AWG is sufficient to defeat a given PLI system.

To judge the security of any particular PLI system, one could of course gather performance information on all the AWGs currently available, construct AWG models for each, and simulate attacker signals. To evaluate the relative security of different systems a similar process would be followed for each, with the system that required the most expensive AWG necessary to defeat it adjudged the most secure. Consider, however, a PLI system for which no existing AWG is capable of defeating. While, through trial and error, the framework could be used to find a number of AWGs that would defeat the system, if we wished to actually manufacture such an AWG, how would we decide which combination of performance parameters would be cost-effective?

This is to say, given two theoretical AWGs capable of defeating a particular PLI, the same in every respect except that one has five bits of resolution and a THD of -90 dBc while the other has a resolution of six bits and a THD of -70 dBc, the attacker would want to select the cheaper of the two to manufacture. Finding the most cost-effective AWG may be accomplished by utilising the above framework in the constraint function of a cost-minimisation (constrained optimisation) problem that accounts for the marginal cost for improvements in each performance parameter. Such a formulation would also be useful in the case where a wide enough gap exists between the cost of manufacturing an AWG capable of defeating the system and simply purchasing an existing AWG that is known to be able to defeat it. Similarly, we would need to know the lowest performing theoretical AWG necessary to defeat a system to be able to say that the system is secure against attacks using AWGs with sample rates, resolutions, THDs, and SNRs below a certain level.

Cost Minimisation Formulation. The cost, or objective, function in our formulation, $f_c(f, n, snr, thd)$, returns the cost necessary to obtain an AWG with a sampling rate of f, resolution of n, SNR of snr, and THD of thd. Allow $s_a = AWG(s_d, f, n, snr, thd)$ to be the attacker's forgery of an authenticated device's signal, s_d, produced using the AWG with the aforementioned parameters. Furthermore, let $th = d(L_R, f(s_T))$ be the maximum distance allowed between a signal, s_T, claiming to originate from the device and the device's feature set, L_R, where the function $f(\cdot)$ extracts features specific to the PLI approach from the sampled signal s_T and $d(\cdot)$ is the distance measure the approach employs. Our minimisation problem is then

$$\min_{f,n,snr,thd} f_c(f, n, snr, thd) \text{ subject to } d(L_R, f(s_a)) \leq th \qquad (3)$$

The derivation of a sample cost function is covered in Section 4.4.

Equation 3 describes a mixed-integer non-linear programming problem, with black box constraints. To ease the process of solving of it, we can impose upper and lower boundaries on each parameter, in addition to stipulating integer values for each.

Given the assumptions of our threat model, the upper bounds for the sampling rate and resolution must be those of the PLI system sampler. Modern DACs are capable of achieving THDs < -80 dBc [35] and SNRs > 75 dB [38], so our theoretical DAC must be capable of exceeding at least these numbers. Lower bounds are calculated using the framework by setting all parameters to their upper values and then choosing one parameter to decrease until the signal generated by the AWG model violates the constraint of (3); the value at which the constraint is violated is then the lower bound for that parameter. This process is repeated for each parameter. Lower bounds are thus specific to the PLI system under consideration.

To convert (3) to an integer non-linear problem, we mandate that thd and snr be integers (n is already an integer), while for the sampling rate we define f_a to be some fraction P/Q of the PLI system sampling rate (where P and Q are integers, passed separately to the optimiser). As the signal the attacker is attempting to forge is sampled at the PLI system sampler rate, and our upsampling/downsampling routine will first upsample by P and then downsample by Q, the attacker's effective sample rate would be $P/Q \times f_p$.

4   Framework Application

We demonstrate the use of the framework on the PLI approach of Gerdes *et al.*, which was proposed to identify wired Ethernet devices. In what follows we provide a brief overview of their PLI approach, describe our implementation of it, and detail how the framework was used to analyse the security of it.

4.1   Overview of PLI Approach

Using the nomenclature of Section 2 and the generic PLI methodology of Section 1, the PLI approach of Gerdes *et al.* is to [12]: (1) capture the beginning of a 10Mb Ethernet frame, known as the synchronisation signal, where a slope-based trigger is used by the sampler to detect the beginning of the frame, (2) extract a specified number of contiguous sample points, using the triggering sample point as a reference for which sample point to start with, and (3) check if the inner product of the extracted features and reference features lies between the two thresholds established for the device.

More explicitly, as laid out in Sections 4.2–3 of [12], for device k to be accepted as device i the inner product between the reference features, L_{Ri}, of the ith device and the features, L_{Tk}^j, extracted from the jth record, r_k^j, of the kth device must fall between the thresholds th_{+i} and th_{-i}.

The reference feature vector, derived from an arbitrary record, r_i^l, of the ith device is $L_{Ri} = r_i^l[trg_i^l + m : trg_i^l + n]$, where trg_i^l is the sample point in the record r_i^l at which the scope triggered and m and n are the first and last sample points, relative to the trigger, of the span of sample points used as the feature set for the device. To account for triggering error and slight deviations in signal levels, the test feature set is actually taken to be $L_{Tk}^j = f(r_{Tk}^j, trg_k^j) = r_{Tk}^j[trg_k^j + m - \delta : trg_k^j + n + \delta]$, where δ is the number of extra sample points to include in the feature vector.

Stating the preceding in terms of a constraint equation, we have that for a record from device k to be identified by the PLI system as having originated from device i, it must satisfy

$$th_{-i} \le \max \left(\sum_{h=1}^{n-m} L_{Ri}[h] \times L_{Tk}^j[h + \Delta] \right) \le th_{+i} \qquad (4)$$

where Δ may vary from $0 \ldots 2 \times \delta$ and $th_{+/-i}$ are established using the last 25 accepted records but only updated after 20 records are accepted (see Sections 4.2.2.3 and 4.3.3 of [12]).

4.2   Attacks Against PLI Approach

Type I Attack. For the type one attack the attacker attempts to replay the synchronisation portion of the original waveform, but with a different payload, using the lowest performing AWG possible.

Type II Attack. As an example of a type two attack, let us assume that the attacker is still attempting to produce a high fidelity copy of the targeted device's signal but wishes to compensate for the inherent error of their DAC so that a lower performing AWG can be used. If the error distribution of the DAC is such that it is just as likely to overshoot the desired output value as undershoot it, for the attacker to maximise the amount of allowable error between the forged signals and the authentic signals they should construct a single frame based upon the average of multiple observed waveforms and transmit it with a custom payload. The proof follows.

Following the procedure set out in Section 4.3.3 of [12], the thresholds for the next m records from device i are determined by taking the mean of distance measures for the previous n records and adding, for the upper threshold, or subtracting, for the lower threshold, the standard deviation of those same measures times some constant, K. Allowing the output of the distance measure for the jth record to be represented by $d^j = d(L_{Ri}, f(s_i^j, trg_i^j))$ the thresholds are then

$$th_{+/-i}(d^j \cdots d^{j+m-1}) = \mu(d^{j-n} \cdots d^{j-1}) \pm K \times \sigma(d^{j-n} \cdots d^{j-1}) \qquad (5)$$

where $\mu(\cdot)$ and $\sigma(\cdot)$ are the mean and standard deviation, respectively.

As $d(\cdot)$ is the sum of products, forging a signal that produces $(th_+ + th_-)/2$ allows for the maximum, equal amount of deviation for each sample point in either direction. The average of the signals used to calculate the thresholds is just such a signal.

We note that $d(\cdot)$ for this PLI approach is effectively using correlation to find the maximum alignment between L_R and L_T, and by extension the records, s_R and s_T, used to create the feature vectors. Allow L_{T*} to equal those elements of

L_T found to produce the maximum output of the distance measure with L_R and l to be number of elements of L_R (i.e. we extract the $m - n$ contiguous sample points from s_T that produce the maximum correlation with the $m - n$ sample points of s_R that constitute L_R). The distance measure for the jth record may then be simplified to

$$d^j = \sum_{k=1}^{l} L_R[k] \times L_{T*}^j[k] \qquad (6a)$$

$$= L_R \cdot L_{T*}^j \qquad (6b)$$

The mean of the distance measure for n training records can be expressed by

$$\mu(d^1 \cdots d^n) = \frac{d^1 + d^2 +, \ldots, + d^n}{n} \qquad (7a)$$

$$= \frac{L_R \cdot L_{T*}^1 + L_R \cdot L_{T*}^2 +, \ldots, + L_R \cdot L_{T*}^n}{n} \qquad (7b)$$

$$= \frac{L_R \cdot (L_{T*}^1 + L_{T*}^2 +, \ldots, + L_{T*}^n)}{n} \qquad (7c)$$

$$= L_R \cdot \mu \left(L_{T*}^1 \cdots L_{T*}^n \right) \qquad (7d)$$

It is worth noting that although an infinite number of arbitrary signals (though not an infinite number of signals falling within the guidelines set by the 802.3 standard [17]) could be generated to produce a distance measure equal to the mean of the previous n records, finding the average signal only requires that an attacker observe n waveforms, align, and then average them. Of course an attacker could not know the which frames would exactly constitute the n training records, and while the attacker can align and average observed waveforms, there is no guarantee that the resulting signal, even if reproduced perfectly, would be aligned with L_R in such a way as to produce a distance measure of $(th_+ + th_-)/2$.

4.3   Experimental Validation of PLI Approach

To ensure that the devices we intended to forge were identifiable using the matched filter PLI system we collected data from 27 different Ethernet cards; using the matched filter PLI approach outlined above, we were able to identify the cards with $\approx 94\%$ accuracy (false-reject rate of 0.2%).

Our experimental setup consisted of two PCs: one to act as the Test PC (TPC), which housed the Ethernet card to be fingerprinted, while the other, the Data Acquisition PC (DAQPC), made use of a passively tapped internal Ethernet card to capture Ethernet frames sent to it over a crossover cable by the TPC. A Tektronix 4032 digital phosphor oscilloscope (DPO), interfaced via USB and controlled by MATLAB, was used as the PLI system sampler. As per our threat model, both the attacker and the PLI system used the data collected by the DAQPC.

In order to generate traffic for the DAQPC to capture, the TPC was instructed to ping the DAQPC. During a typical data acquisition period the TPC would ping the DAQPC 10,000 times over the course of approximately three hours. To ensure that only traffic from the TPC was captured and that the measurement equipment did not affect the load characteristics of the DAQPC, as seen by the TPC, only the receiving pins of the DAQPC's Ethernet card on the secondary side of the transformer were connected to the oscilloscope. In this way the DAQPC could respond to the TPC's pings and ensure that the data acquisition process didn't cause packet loss or affect the transmitting circuitry of the TPC. Upon detection of an Ethernet frame (a simple slope-based threshold was used) the oscilloscope began to sample the signal at a rate of 2.5 Gigasamples/s; the signal was sampled 1,000,000 times, for a total of 400 micro-seconds. The oscilloscope had 8-bits of resolution.

Finally, the data collected during sampling was sent to the DAQPC via USB interface, where a MATLAB routine monitoring the interface accepted the data and stored the values in a vector called a record, which was subsequently written to disc. Each captured frame was stored in its own record; all of the records collected for a device during a session are said to encompass its dataset.

We note that a 10Mb Ethernet frame is transmitted using a differential signal to lessen the effects of environmental noise. The frame is reconstructed at the receiver by taking the difference of the received signals. In what follows, we apply the framework to the reconstructed 10Mb Ethernet waveform, which we found by taking the difference of the signals captured at the receive pins on secondary side of the DAQPC's transformer. This results in a loosening of the constraints placed on an attacker, as in actuality an attacker would be required to forge two signals when attempting to defeat the system. We make this simplification as the PLI approach of Gerdes *et al.* uses the reconstructed signal for identification.

In addition, as each channel of the oscilloscope used to acquire device signals had 8 bits of resolution, and we take the difference between the channels to reconstruct the Ethernet Frame, the device signals should actually be considered 9-bit: the maximum of the absolute value of any of the binary sample points that make up the waveforms was greater than 127 but less than 255; 8 bits, plus another bit for the sign, are required to represent this data then. The y-scale, or voltage, increment used in the capturing routine was 0.02 volts, which leads to an effective full-scale voltage of -5.12 to +5.10 V (binary values for the sample points range from -256 to 255).

4.4   Cost Function Estimate

To estimate the cost of acquiring an arbitrarily specified AWG, we assumed a linear relationship between cost and each performance parameter; i.e. we assumed that DAC performance scales linearly with cost, so that, for example, all other parameters being equal, a DAC with an SNR of 65 dB would cost more than one with an SNR of 50 dB.

Pricing information for 37 different DACs from Analog Devices was obtained using their online tool *ADIsimDAC*, which suggests DACs that meet certain user specifications, along with their cost [39]. Since we wished to obtain pricing data on as many DACs as possible, we only specified the dynamic range (-4 to 4 V) and minimum sampling resolution of 100 MS/s. We note that even though the PLI system sampler has a dynamic range of $\approx\pm5.12$ V, only $\approx\pm4$

V is necessary to forge the reconstructed Ethernet frame, as the signal does not exceed ± 3.5 V. Furthermore, while an attacker could utilise a DAC with a different dynamic range, by scaling and applying an offset to the DAC output using an amplifier, this would introduce additional distortion and noise that would need to be included in the AWG model [40].

Having found DACs meeting these two specifications, we then extracted sample rate, resolution, noise, and distortion parameters from their datasheets. Of the 37 DACs meeting our requirements, 17 reported inter-modulation distortion (IMD) and noise-spectral density (NSD) instead of THD/SNR. While these measures could be used with our framework, by using different test signals with the distortion model and performing different noise measurements, they are nonetheless incompatible with—i.e. cannot be converted to—THD/SNR measures; as such, they were discarded. Seven DACs reported THD/SINAD instead of THD/SNR; because of the relationship between THD, SINAD, and SNR noted in Section 2.3 we were able to convert the SINAD measure to SNR. If multiple test signals or bandwidths were used to give a range of values for a particular parameter, we selected the signal with the highest frequency, at the highest output current, with measurements made over the largest bandwidth.

Using these data we performed a multiple linear regression (R^2 of 0.8185) to obtain the following cost function

$$f_c(P, Q, n, snr, thd) = 0.0693 \times P/Q \times 2500 + 1.6201 \times n - 0.1518 \times thd$$
$$+ 0.0164 \times snr - 26.4959 \quad (8)$$

Where the sampling rate is defined, in units of Megasamples/s, as a fraction of the PLI system sampling rate $f_p = 2500$, resolution (n) in bits, THD (thd) in dBc, and SNR (snr) in dB.

When examining the datasheets, we noticed that in general DACs with higher resolution and sample rate tended to have higher THD. This implies that is very costly to achieve small amounts of distortion at higher resolutions and sampling rates. However, when linear regression was performed using THD values from the datasheets, a positive coefficient was reported. As THD is negative, increasing the absolute value of the THD (i.e. decreasing the distortion) within the framework would actually lead to a lowering of the cost. Thus, a solver employing a cost function with a positive coefficient for THD would tend to drive it to $-\infty$ (zero distortion). To counter this we transformed the THD values by adding a positive scalar greater than any of the THD values and taking the negative of the result.

4.5   PLI System Evaluation Setup and Results

To evaluate the security of the PLI system, we first incorporated (4) into the cost-minimisation formulation given in (3), which lead to

$$\min_{f,n,snr,thd} f_c(f, n, snr, thd) \text{ subject to } d(L_R, f(s_a, trg_a)) \leq th_+$$
$$th_- \leq d(L_R, f(s_a, trg_a)) \quad (9)$$

where $d(\cdot) = \max\left(\sum_{i=1}^{n} L_R[i] \times L_T[i + \Delta]\right)$, n is number of elements in L_R, $s_a = AWG(s_d, f, n, snr, thd)$, and trg_a is the sample point in the attacker's record, s_a, at which the PLI system sampler triggered.

Equation 9 is then used, along with the cost function defined by (8), to find the lowest-cost AWG necessary to successfully carry out a type one replay attack and a type two attack against each of the devices used for the experimental validation of the PLI. A randomly selected record was used in the type one attack, while the type two attack used a synthesised record based on the average of 25 records.

A lower bound for each of the AWG parameters was established by decreasing or increasing their value (the former in the case of sampling rate and resolution and the latter for SNR and THD), while the other parameters were set to their ideal values, until either of the constraints of (9) were violated by the resulting record. The lower bounds were found to be $f_a = 2/100 \times 2500 = 50$, $n = 5$, $thd = -25$, and $snr = 20$; should any one of the parameters fall below these values, the resulting record would be automatically rejected. Upper bounds were $f_a = 2500$, $n = 9$, $thd = -90$, and $snr = 100$.

Record Selection. To select the record(s) to be forged, we first chose 44 sequential records (the first record was chosen randomly, though it had to number 1000 or greater to ensure that the device was operating outside the warming-up period); the first 25 records were used to establish thresholds for the remaining 19. For the type one attack, one of the 19 records was chosen, at random, to be reproduced using the AWG model; for the type two attack a combination of 25 records were chosen from the training records and the remaining 19, with at most 24 records selected from the training set (again, these were selected sequentially). To create the averaged record, each of the 25 selected records was aligned with the first and the average computed. The reference features were extracted from the first record of each device's dataset.

In [12], 25 records are used to establish thresholds for the next 20 records. We limited our selection of records usable for forgery to only the next 19 (and stipulated that the attacker could only use at most 24 of 25 training records for averaging) because if record 20 should be selected randomly (or the attacker begins averaging with the first record), the attacker would be forging a record used as training data to determine the thresholds for the forgery. This case should be examined separately to see how much, if any, advantage is gained by the attacker. We also checked to be sure that the single record used in the type one attack would have been accepted by the PLI system—an attacker would not be able to guarantee this, which is another reason for them to use an average of several records.

Results. A summary of the AWG characteristics for each of the attacks, found using the genetic algorithm solver included in the Global Optimisation toolbox for MATLAB, are given in Tables 1a and 1b. As can be seen from examining the best-case scenario (when the attacker is required to utilise the most expensive AWG), the sampling rate and resolution of an AWG necessary to defeat a matched-filter based PLI system would need to be substantially less than those

Table 1. Characteristics of highest, mean (rounded), and lowest cost AWGs required to carry out the (a) type one attack using randomly selected signal and (b) type two attack

Parameter	Highest	Mean	Lowest	Parameter	Highest	Mean	Lowest
Resolution (bits)	5	5	5	Resolution (bits)	5	5	5
Sample rate (MS/s)	53	50	50	Sample rate (MS/s)	53	51	50
THD (dBc)	-35	-30	-26	THD (dBc)	-37	-32	-25
SNR (dB)	21	22	20	SNR (dB)	22	22	20
	(a)				(b)		

of the sampler used in our implementation (for the PLI system sampler, $n = 9$ and $f_p = 2500$ MS/s). In the worst-case scenario (lowest cost to attacker), the sampling rate, resolution, SNR, and THD are at the lower bounds (or nearly so), while for the mean case only the SNR and THD are appreciably distant from the lower bounds. In any case, the sampling rate, resolutions SNR, and THD of each of the DACs used for the cost function estimation of Section 4.4 are in excess of those reported in the tables.

Both the average and maximum costs for the type two attack are (slightly) higher than those of the type one, contrary to the results of Section 4.2. This is in spite of the fact that when the AWG attacker's averaged record was tested directly (i.e. it did not pass through the AWG model) with the reference feature set the resulting distance measure was almost exactly $(th_+ + th_-)/2$. It seems possible that the averaged sample point values, when they are discretised, are biased slightly towards one of the higher or lower level, instead of being equally distributed among the two (as assumed in our proof).

It should also be mentioned that because of the randomness of the noise an attacker record will sometimes be rejected at the reported minimum SNRs. Having repeatedly checked for constraint violations using the same SNR, it appears that the more the noise changes the trigger point of the attacker record relative to the record used for the reference feature set (i.e. as $|trg_p - trg_a|$ grows larger) the more likely it is that the record will be identified as a forgery. To ensure acceptance, the attacker should employ an AWG with a slightly higher SNR (≈ 2 dB).

5   Conclusion

We have proposed, and illustrated the use of, a framework to determine whether an attacker could defeat a given PLI system by replaying a record using an AWG of a specified sample rate, resolution, THD, and SNR. The framework is flexible enough to be used in evaluating arbitrary PLI system implementations, using different threat models and AWG models. We also showed how the framework can be used with a cost-minimisation problem to find the lowest performing AWG necessary to defeat a PLI system. Given a particular pricing model for the sample rate, resolution, THD, and SNR, the cost-minimisation formulation can also be used to determine the most cost-effective AWG.

For the reasons given in Section 2.2, this version of the framework did not incorporate channel effects and assumed ideal/identical samplers for the attacker and PLI system. In order to better evaluate the security of PLI systems, we will extend our work by integrating both channel models and models for non-ideal/differing samplers into the framework. To widen the application of the framework, we will use it to evaluate and compare PLI approaches for the wireless domain and investigate the feature replay attack mentioned in Section 2.1. Finally, the immediate focus of our future work will be to experimentally confirm the predictions of the framework for the PLI system of Gerdes *et al.*

References

1. Gerdes, R.M., Daniels, T.E., Mina, M., Russell, S.F.: Device identification via analog signal fingerprinting: A matched filter approach. In: Proceedings of the 2006 Network and Distributed System Security Symposium (NDSS 2006). The Internet Society (2006)
2. Hall, J., Barbeau, M., Kranakis, E.: Detection of transient in radio frequency fingerprinting using signal phase. In: Proceedings of the 3rd IASTED International Conference on Wireless and Optical Communications (WOC 2003), pp. 13–18. ACTA Press (2003)
3. Hall, J., Barbeau, M., Kranakis, E.: Enhancing intrusion detection in wireless networks using radio frequency fingerprinting. In: Proceedings of Communications, Internet and Information Technology (CIIT 2004). ACTA Press (2004)
4. Ureten, O., Serinken, N.: Wireless security through rf fingerprinting. Canadian Journal of Electrical and Computer Engineering 32, 27–33 (2007)
5. Brik, V., Banerjee, S., Gruteser, M., Oh, S.: Wireless device identification with radiometric signatures. In: Proceedings of the 14th ACM International Conference on Mobile Computing and Networking (MobiCom 2008), pp. 116–127. ACM (2008)
6. Shi, Y., Jensen, M.: Improved radiometric identification of wireless devices using mimo transmission. IEEE Transactions on Information Forensics and Security 6(4), 1346–1354 (2011)
7. Rasmussen, K.B., Capkun, S.: Implications of radio fingerprinting on the security of sensor networks. In: Proceedings of the Third International Conference on Security and Privacy in Communications Networks and the Workshops (SecureComm 2007), pp. 331–340. IEEE Computer Society (2007)
8. Danev, B., Capkun, S.: Transient-based identification of wireless sensor nodes. In: Proceedings of the 2009 International Conference on Information Processing in Sensor Networks (IPSN 2009), pp. 25–36. IEEE Computer Society (2009)
9. Saparkhojayev, N., Thompson, D.R.: Matching electronic fingerprints of rfid tags using the hotelling's algorithm. In: Proceedings of the IEEE Sensors Applications Symposium (SAS), pp. 19–24. IEEE Computer Society (2009)
10. Danev, B., Heydt-Benjamin, T.S., Capkun, S.: Physical-layer identification of rfid devices. In: Proceedings of the USENIX Security Symposium (USENIX-SS 2009), pp. 199–214. USENIX Association (2009)
11. Zanetti, D., Danev, B., Capkun, S.: Physical-layer identification of uhf rfid tags. In: Proceedings of the 16th ACM Annual International Conference on Mobile Computing and Networking (MOBICOM 2010), pp. 353–364. ACM (2010)
12. Gerdes, R.M.: Physical layer identification: methodology, security, and origin of variation. PhD thesis, Iowa State University, Ames, IA (2011)
13. Danev, B.: Physical-layer Identification of Wireless Devices. PhD thesis, ETH Zurich, Zurich, Switzerland (2011)
14. Bolle, R.M., Connell, J.H., Pankanti, S., Ratha, N.K., Senior, A.W.: Guide to Biometrics. Springer (2004)

15. Danev, B., Luecken, H., Capkun, S., Defrawy, K.E.: Attacks on physical-layer identification. In: Proceedings of the Third ACM Conference on Wireless Network Security (WiSec 2010), pp. 89–98. ACM, New York (2010)
16. Edman, M., Yener, B.: Active attacks against modulation-based radiometric identification. Technical report, Rensselaer Polytechnic Institute, Department of Computer Science (2009)
17. IEEE: IEEE 802.3-2008 ieee standard for information technology-specific requirements–part 3: Carrier sense multiple access with collision detection (cmsa/cd) access method and physical layer specifications. Technical report, IEEE, IEEE Std 802.3–2008 (2008)
18. Burns, M., Roberts, G.W.: An introduction to mixed-signal IC test and measurement. Oxford University Press (2001)
19. Kester, W.: Evaluating high speed dac performance. Technical report, Analog Devices, MT-013 Tutorial (2008)
20. Balestrieri, E., Moisa, S., Rapuano, S.: Dac static parameter specifications some critical notes. In: Proceedings of the 10th IMEKO TC-4 Workshop on ADC Modelling and Testing, vol. 1, pp. 81–86 (2005)
21. Hendriks, P.: Specifying communications dacs. IEEE Spectrum 34, 58–69 (1997)
22. Tektronix USA: AWG7000B Series AWG Data Sheet
23. Oppenheim, A.V., Schafer, R.W. (eds.): Discrete-Time Signal Processing. Prentice Hall (1989)
24. Analog Devices USA: (AD9734/AD9735/AD9736 Series DAC Data Sheet)
25. Wambacq, P., Sansen, W.M. (eds.): Distortion Analysis of Analog Integrated Circuits. Springer (1998)
26. Andersson, K.O.: Studies on Performance Limitations in CMOS DACs. PhD thesis, Linkopings universitet, Linkoping, Sweden (2002)
27. Wikner, J.J.: Studies on CMOS Digital-to-Analog Converters. PhD thesis, Linkopings universitet, Linkoping, Sweden (2001)
28. Chan, K.L., Zhu, J., Galton, I.: Dynamic element matching to prevent nonlinear distortion from pulse-shape mismatches in high-resolution dacs. IEEE Journal of Solid-State Circuits 43(9), 2067–2078 (2008)
29. Naoues, M., Morche, D., Dehos, C., Barrak, R., Ghazes, A.: Novel behavioral dac modeling technique for wirelesshd system specification. In: Proceedings of the IEEE Electronics, Circuits and Systems (ICECS 2009), pp. 543–546 (2009)
30. Wit, P.D., Gielen, G.: Efficient simulation model for dac dynamic properties. In: Proceedings of the IEEE Circuits and Systems (ISCAS 2010), pp. 2896–2899 (2010)
31. Andersson, N.U., Andersson, K.O., Vesterbacka, M., Wikner, J.J.: Models and implementation of a dynamic element matching dac. Analog Integrated Circuits and Signal Processing 34, 7–16 (2003)
32. Vandenbussche, J., der Plas, G.V., Gielen, G., Sansen, W.: Behavioral model of reusable d/a converters. IEEE Transactions on Circuits and Systems II: Analog and Digital Signal Processing 46, 1323–1326 (1999)
33. Riley, K., Hummels, D., Irons, F., Rundell, A.: Dynamic compensation of digital to analog converters. In: Proceedings of the IEEE Instrumentation and Measurement Technology Conference (IMTC 1999), vol. 2, pp. 1310–1315 (1999)
34. Gerdes, R.M., Mina, M., Daniels, T.E.: Awg characterisation definitions. Technical report (2012), http://www.eng.usu.edu/ece/faculty/rgerdes/papers/tech/awgCharDef.pdf
35. Analog Devices USA: AD9763/AD9765/AD9767 Series DACData Sheet
36. Maloberti, F., Estrada, P., Valero, A., Malcovati, P.: Behavioral modeling and simulation of data converters. In: Proceedings of IMEKO 2000, vol. 10, pp. 229–236 (2000)

37. Liu, E.W.Y.: Analog Behavioral Simulation and Modeling. PhD thesis, University of California, Berkeley, CA (1993)
38. Analog Devices USA: AD9777 Series Data DAC Sheet
39. Analog Devices: Design Tools ADIsimDAC (2011),
    http://designtools.analog.com/dtSimDACWeb/dtSimDACMain.aspx
40. Aksin, D.Y., Maloberti, F.: Non-linear behavioral model of a bipolar track and hold amplifier for high-speed and high-resolution adcs. In: Proceedings of the IEEE Electronics, Circuits and Systems (ICECS 2005), pp. 1–4 (2005)

A Voice Spam Filter to Clean Subscribers' Mailbox

Seyed Amir Iranmanesh[1], Hemant Sengar[2], and Haining Wang[1]

[1] Department of Computer Science, College of William and Mary,
Williamsburg, VA 23187, USA
{sairan,hnw}@cs.wm.edu
[2] Technology Development Department, VoDaSec Solutions,
Fairfax, VA 22030, USA
hsengar09@gmail.com

Abstract. With the growing popularity of VoIP and its large customer base, the incentives of telemarketers for voice spam has been increasing in the recent years. If the threat of voice spam remains unchecked, it could become a problem as serious as email spam today. Compared to email spam, voice spam will be much more obnoxious and time consuming nuisance for telephone subscribers to filter out. In this paper, we propose a content-based approach to protect telephone subscribers voice mailboxes from voice spam. In particular, based on Dynamic Time Warping (DTW), we develop a speaker independent speech recognition system to make content comparison of speech messages. Using our system, the voice messages left on the media server by callers are matched against a set of spam filtering rules involving the study of *call behavioral* pattern and the analysis of *message content*. The uniqueness of our spam filtering approach lies in its independence on the generation of voice spam, regardless whether spammers play same spam content recorded in many different ways, such as human or machine generated voice, male or female voice, and different accents. We validate the efficacy of the proposed scheme through real experiments, and our experimental results show that it can effectively filter out spam from the subscribers' voice mailbox with 0.67% false positive rate and 8.33% false negative rate.

Keywords: VoIP, voice spam, content filtering, Dynamic Time Warping.

1 Introduction

IP telephone service providers are moving fast from low-scale toll bypass deployments to large-scale competitive carrier deployments; thus giving an opportunity to enterprise networks for supporting less expensive single network solution rather than multiple separate networks. The broadband-based residential customers also switch to IP telephony due to its convenience and cost effectiveness. On the contrary to traditional telephone system in which the end devices are dumb, the VoIP architecture pushes intelligence towards the end devices like PCs and IP phones, creating many new services. This flexibility coupled with

A.D. Keromytis and R. Di Pietro (Eds.): SecureComm 2012, LNICST 106, pp. 349–367, 2013.

the growing number of subscribers has attracted attackers for malicious resource abuse. As the number of VoIP subscribers hits a critical mass, it is expected that voice spam will emerge as a serious threat. In fact in Japan where VoIP market is much more mature than USA, has witnessed some recent voice spam attacks. The SoftbankBB, a VoIP service provider with 4.6 million users has reported three incidents of spam attacks within its own network [20]. These incidents include unsolicited messages advertising an adult website, scanning of active VoIP phone numbers and requesting personal information of users. Similarly, Columbia University experienced a voice spam attack, with someone accessing the SIP proxy server and "war dialing" a large number of IP phone extensions [21]. There are many reported incidents of spam messages on Google voice too [7]. Evidently, the effectiveness of telephone calls presents strong incentives for spammers to establish voice channels with many subscribers at the same time. Such machine generated unsolicited bulk calls known as SPIT (Spam over Internet Telephony) may hinder the deployment of IP telephony, and if the problem remains unchecked then it may become as potent as email spam today. In many aspects, the voice spam is similar to an email spam. Moreover, voice spam will be much more obnoxious and harmful than email spam. The ringing of telephone at odd time, answering of spam calls, phishing attacks and inability to filter spam messages from the voicemail box without listening each one are real nuisance and waste of time.

In the past, a number of anti-spam solutions have been proposed. Both academic and industry research groups have made some efforts to address the voice spam problem. Most of the ideas are borrowed from the data security field, using the techniques such as intrusion detection systems, black and white lists, Turing tests, computational puzzles, reputation systems, and rate throttling at the gatekeeper. These solutions generally distinguish a legitimate subscriber from a spammer using only SIP signaling messages. However, in this paper we take a radically different approach. Instead of analyzing the SIP signaling messages and identifying the spam originating source(s) or ascertaining the real identity of spammers, we try to avoid spam message deposition on the subscribers' voice mailboxes. The goal of the proposed approach is two-pronged. First, we allow only legitimate messages to be deposited on the subscribers' mailbox account, unsolicited spam messages are blocked at the media server itself. Secondly, the proposed approach also provides a way to identify spamming sources based on spam messages. To the best of our knowledge, this is a first attempt to clean subscribers' voice mailboxes from voice spam messages.

Beyond the basic observation that SIP signaling messages needs to be analyzed for its source and caller identification, we make three additional observations that are central to our approach. First, the spammers would prefer to see high hit ratio for their spamming attacks. Thus, most of the spamming attacks are expected to occur in bulk (i.e., as much spam as possible within a short duration of time) and most of the spam messages will be delivered to voice mailboxes. Second, during the spam attack instance, a spammer will play pre-recorded messages to many of the spam victims at the same time. Third, the originating spam source is expected to be some sort of interactive voice response (IVR) system, which can interact with the users if the calls are answered and it should also be able to leave a voice mail if the calls are not answered. However, it should be noted that in most of the spam attacks the voice stream originating from the spam source is machine generated. Based on these observations, we design and develop a voice mailbox filtering approach.

In our approach, we first segment voice messages in their voiced segments using a silence removal technique. Our silence removal technique is based on two audio features; the *signal energy* and the *spectral centroid*. After calculating the partial similarity between each pair of voiced segments coming from two different voice messages, we can determine how similar are the two voice messages content-wise. To measure the similarity between two voiced segments as a metric for content comparison, we use the technique of Dynamic Time Warping (DTW) to compute the cosine similarity between two sequences of speech feature matrices. A popular speech feature representation known as RASTA-PLP (Relative Spectral Transform - Perceptual Linear Prediction) is used to extract speech feature matrices from voice messages. After a message is left on the server by a caller, it is divided into voiced segments using our segmentation method and RASTA-PLP spectra for its voiced segments being calculated. Using our DTW based system, the RASTA-PLP matrix is then matched against a set of spam signatures. If a match is not found, our system is further coupled with Bayesian filtering to reveal the hidden spam words/phrases within a voice message to show how closely (probabilistically) it matches with the known spam messages seen in the past. Normally during a spam attack, many of the deposited voice messages share the same content, we finally use our speaker independent speech recognition technique to find how many similar messages (in content) are deposited within a predefined time interval of ΔT.

We conduct two sets of experiments to evaluate the effectiveness of our proposed solution against realistic spam attack scenarios. In the first experiment, we investigate the most generic spam attack scenario, where a spammer repeatedly sends the same spam message to many of the subscribers at the same time. Three hundred voice messages in various size are deposited from thirty speakers with different accents (such as American, British, or Indian English), different sex and ages to form the scenario. In the second set of experiment, we investigate the power of our method to classify voice messages as spam and non-spam, in which the deposited voice messages include spam words/phrases. Our experimental results show that our approach is computationally efficient, and speaker independent to identify a common segment of voice message out of a database of known spam signatures and classify the voice message correctly.

The remainder of the paper is structured as follows. The basic VoIP architecture, SIP-based IP telephony, voice message deposition process, and a brief overview of the proposed approach are presented in Section 2. In Section 3, we describe the technical details on voice message signature construction. In Section 4, we detail spam detection methodology. Section 5 analyzes the performance of the proposed solution. Section 6 surveys related work. Finally, Section 7 concludes the paper.

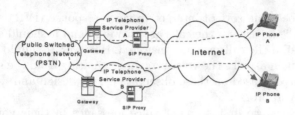

Fig. 1. Island-based SIP VoIP Deployment

2   Background

Voice spam is an extension of email spam in the VoIP domain. The technical know-how and execution style of email spam can easily be adapted to launch voice spam attacks. For example, a voice spammer first harvests user's SIP URIs or telephone numbers from the telephone directories or by using spam bots crawling over the Internet. Then, a compromised host is used as a SIP user agent (UA) that sends out call setup request messages. Finally, the established sessions are played with a pre-recorded .wav file. However, voice spam is much more obnoxious and harmful than email spam. The ringing of telephone at odd time, answering of spam calls, phishing attacks and inability to filter spam messages from the voicemail box without listening each one are real nuisance and waste of time.

Before we delve into voice spam problem, we briefly describe the basic VoIP architecture as it serves two purposes: first, it explains as why we do not hear much of voice spam attacks today as compared to email spam; second, it also describes as why it could be a serious problem for VoIP subscribers in the near future.

2.1   VoIP Architecture

As shown in Fig. 1, in today's IP telephony world most of the VoIP service providers (such as Vonage, AT&T Callvantage, and ViaTalk) operate in partially closed environments and are connected to each other through the public telephone network. VoIP service providers allow only their own authenticated subscribers to access SIP proxy server resources. The authentication of call requests is feasible because user accounts are stored locally on the VoIP service provider's SIP servers. However, in general the threat of spam calls is associated with the open architecture of VoIP service, where VoIP service providers interact with each other through the IP-based peering points. It provides an ability for individual subscribers to connect with each other without traversing the PSTN cloud. Therefore, it is quite possible that an INVITE message received by a VoIP service provider from another service provider (through IP network) for one of its subscriber may not have any type of authentication credentials for the calling party.

Recently, we are witnessing a large demand for SIP trunks. A SIP trunk is a service offered by a VoIP service provider permitting business subscribers to reach beyond the enterprise network and connect to the PSTN through IP-based connections. Generally most of the SIP trunks are set up without authentication. Only few of the service providers use TLS or IPSec to secure SIP signaling. In

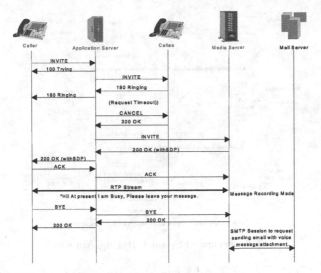

Fig. 2. Voice Message Deposition

this scenario, a spam attack can be launched from within the enterprise network (e.g., a corporate network is infected with malicious worm) or by a man-in-the-middle where SIP signaling is transported over the Internet in plaintext without any encryption.

2.2 SIP-Based IP Telephony

The Session Initiation Protocol (SIP) [15], belonging to the application layer of the TCP/IP protocol stack, is used to set up, modify, and tear down multimedia sessions including telephone calls between two or more participants.

SIP-based telecommunication architectures have two types of elements: end devices referred to as user agents (UAs) and SIP servers. Irrespective of being a software or hardware phone, UAs combine two sub-entities: the connection requester referred as the user agent client (UAC) and the connection request receiver referred to as the user agent server (UAS). Consequently, during a SIP session, both UAs switches back and forth between UAC and UAS functionalities.

SIP messages consisting of request-response pairs are exchanged for call set up, from six kinds including INVITE, ACK, BYE, CANCEL, REGISTER, and OPTIONS - each identified by a numeric code according to RFC 3261 [15].

2.3 Voice Mail Deposition

A simple voice message deposition scenario is shown in Fig. 2. A caller calls a callee who is busy and unable to take phone call, in this particular case, the call is answered by a voice messaging system. The call is set up between caller and callee's voice messaging system that plays a "busy" greeting message and asks the caller to leave a voice message. The caller records the voice message and then hangs up. With the *SendMail* command, the application (i.e., call control)

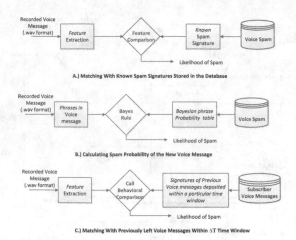

Fig. 3. Overview of Spam Filtering Approach

server requests the media server to deliver the recorded voice message to the callee's inbox. The media server sends email with the recorded message as an attachment (in .wav file format) to the user account on SMTP mail server.

2.4   Overview of Spam Filtering Approach

As shown in Fig. 3, our spam filtering approach can be briefly described as a three-step process. Given a recorded voice message, we first verify if it matches with any of the known spam signatures stored in the database. For example, when a caller leaves a voice message for a callee, media server records the RTP stream and converts it into a .wav file. The *feature extraction* process takes this .wav file as an input and extracts few features from the corresponding spectrogram. This set of features is searched in the database to find a match with known spam signatures. In the second step, even if a match is not found with known spam signatures, we observe the words and phrases and their spamicity. The overall spam score of the message determines its likelihood of being a spam message. In the third step, we observe how many similar messages (in content) are deposited within a predefined time interval of ΔT.

3   Voice Message Signature Construction

This section provides technical details as how we can extract some specific features from a recorded message on the media server, which later on can be used to construct a signature of the deposited message.

3.1   Visual Representation of a Voice Message

Now assume that a telemarketer has left a voice message in one of the callees voice mailbox saying:

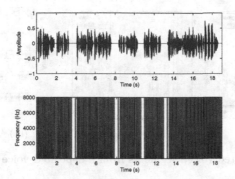

Fig. 4. Speech Waveform and Spectrogram (US Female Speaker)

Take off those unwanted pounds - without strict diets. Just because you live a busy life doesn't mean you can't lose weight. Look and feel 20 years younger. You will Love how it makes you feel. Please give us a call now at 777 666 5555

When we analyze the recorded .wav file, Fig. 4 shows the visual representation of human speech vibrations in the form of *waveform* and *spectrogram*. At the top, the waveform tracks variation in pressure as a function of time for a given point in space. Although we can learn quite a lot by a visual inspection of a speech waveform, it is impossible to detect individual speech sounds from waveforms because a speech consists of vibrations produced in the vocal tract. The vibrations themselves can be represented by speech waveforms. To read the *phonemes* in a waveform, we need to analyze the waveform into its frequency components, i.e., a spectrogram which can be deciphered (the bottom of Fig. 4). In the spectrogram, the darkness or lightness of a band indicates the relative amplitude or energy present at a given frequency.

3.2 Silence Removal From Deposited Voice Message

In our spam content analysis, we are interested in only voiced portions of the deposited message. Therefore, we need a method to remove all silence periods and segment the deposited message in voided segments. We use a method based on two simple audio features, namely the *signal energy* and the *spectral centroid*. In order to extract the feature sequences, the signal is first broken into non-overlapping short-term-windows (frames) of 50 msec. length. For each frame, the two features, described below, are calculated, leading to two feature sequences for the whole deposited voice message.

Signal Energy: Let us assume that the deposited voice message's i^{th} frame has N audio samples $x_i(n), n = 1, 2, ..., N$. The ith frame energy is calculated as:

$$E(i) = \frac{1}{N} \sum_{n=1}^{N} |x_i(n)|^2 \tag{1}$$

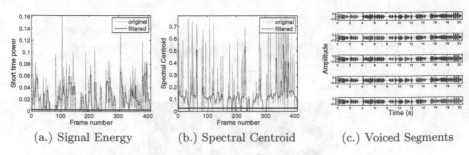

(a.) Signal Energy   (b.) Spectral Centroid   (c.) Voiced Segments

Fig. 5. Detected voiced segments from a deposited voice message

Spectral centroid: The spectral centroid, C_i , of the ith frame is defined as the center of gravity of its spectrum

$$C_i = \frac{\sum_{k=1}^{N}(k+1)X_i(k)}{\sum_{k=1}^{N}|X_i(k)|^2} \tag{2}$$

where $X_i(k)$, k=1,2,...,N, is the Discrete Fourier Transform (DFT) coefficients of the ith short-term frame, where N is the frame length.

Estimating two thresholds – $T1$ and $T2$, the two feature sequences are compared with their respective thresholds. The voiced segments are formed by successive frames for which respective feature values are larger than their thresholds. The detailed description of the method can be found in [6]. We use the same example spam message recorded by Crystal, a US native English speaker and apply silence removal method. Fig. 5 (a) and (b) show energy and spectral centroid sequences and their threshold values, respectively. The detected voice segments are shown in Fig. 5 (c). These individual voiced segments serve as fundamental units to build our spam detection methodology.

3.3   RASTA-PLP Spectrogram Characterization

As the first step towards comparing two voiced segments, Short-time Fourier transform (STFT) can be adopted. Using STFT features, the sinusoidal frequency and phase content of local sections of a signal as it changes over time, can be determined. Since STFT, similar to most of speech parameter estimation techniques, is easily influenced by the frequency response of the speech channel, e.g. from a telephone line, we use another popular speech feature representation known as RASTA-PLP, an acronym for Relative Spectral Transform - Perceptual Linear Prediction. PLP is a speech analysis technique for warping spectra to minimize the differences between speakers while preserving the important speech information [9]. RASTA was proposed to make PLP more robust to linear spectral distortions. RASTA applies a band-pass filter to the energy in each frequency subband to remove any constant offset resulting from steady-state spectral factors of the speech channel and to tolerate short-term noise variations [10]. After a deposited message is segmented to voiced segments, RASTA-PLP spectra for

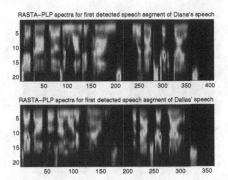

RASTA–PLP spectra for first detected speech segment of Diane's speech

RASTA–PLP spectra for first detected speech segment of Dallas' speech

Fig. 6. RASTA-PLP spectral features for the first voiced segment of Diane (Female) and Dallas (Male) Native Speakers

all voiced segments of the voice message is calculated. For each spam voice message, its RASTA-PLP spectral matrices, corresponding to its voiced segments, are stored in the spam signature database. Fig. 6 shows the RASTA-PLP spectrograms for the first voiced segment ("Take off those unwanted pounds without strict diets.") of two deposited messages from different speakers, Diane (Female English speaker) and Dallas (Male English speaker), with the same content.

3.4   Matching Process

The spam filtering architecture can work in a standalone or distributed collaborative manner. In the standalone mode, the voice messages left by the callers are undergoing through the behavioral analysis and signature matching based on the locally stored signatures. However, in the collaborative distributed mode, a group of disparate VoIP service providers work together. A centralized spam database can be queried as per need basis by individual service providers for signature matching, and at the same time newly found spam message is made available to the database so that it can be signaturised and used by the other service providers.

For signature matching and call behavior analysis, the newly arrived voice message is divided to voiced segments and corresponding RASTA-PLP matrices are calculated. The database of known spam signatures is queried to find the voice spam message that has similar content to the newly arrived voice message. If the computed cosine distance between the newly arrived and an already known spam message is less than a threshold, we confidently declare that a match has been found. However, in case there is no match found, then we perform call behavior analysis. Within a predefined time interval of ΔT (say 5 minutes), we segment all of the voice messages left on the media server to their voiced segments and calculate their corresponding RASTA-PLP matrices to observe how many messages are of similar content. Beyond a threshold value (say 3 messages per 5 minutes), the matched messages are considered to be a part of an impending spam attack and demand further analysis. The unmatched messages are deposited to their respective user accounts (i.e., mailboxes).

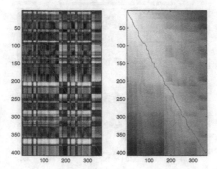

Fig. 7. Using DTW to find similarity between constructed scores matrices for the first voiced segment of Diane's speech and Dallas's speech

4   Detection Methodology

To either find if the newly arrived voice message has similar content to a spam signature or observe as how many similar messages (content-wise) are recorded on the media server within a predefined time interval, we propose a speaker independent speech recognition method. The newly deposited message is first divided into small voiced segments using the silence removal technique described in Section 3.2. For each of the voiced segments, we create RASTA-PLP matrices. As a similarity measure, we use Dynamic Time Warping (DTW) method and calculate the cosine distance for each pair of voiced segments coming from two different voice messages. Based on these partial scores for the corresponding speech segments, we finally determine if the two voice messages are similar enough and a match is found. The details of these phases are presented as follows.

4.1   Scoring Similarity between Two Speech Segments

Constructing Scores Matrix. Cosine Similarity is considered here as the similarity measure between two speech segments. We calculate the cosine distance between every pair of frames from RASTA-PLP spectral matrices for two segments, and then we construct the *local match* scores matrix. The left side of Fig. 7 shows spectrogram-like scores matrix for the first voiced segment ("Take off those unwanted pounds without strict diets.") of two speech snippets of Diane (female) and Dallas (male) native speakers. High similarity values can be seen as a dark stripe approximately down the leading diagonal in the figure.

Dynamic Time Warping (DTW). Although two different voice segments (speaker's utterances) with same content have more or less the same sounds in the same order, the durations of each sub-segment (words and letters) may not match. As a consequence, matching between two voice segments without temporal alignment may fail. To cope with different speaking speeds and differences in timing between two segments, we use a dynamic programming method named

Dynamic Time Warping (DTW) [5]. Considering a 2D space with the X-axis of time frames from one segment and the Y-axis of time frames from another segment, DTW tries to find the path through this 2D space that maximizes the local match between the aligned time frames. The total *similarity cost* found by DTW can be considered as a proper indication of how well these two segments match. The right side of Fig. 7 illustrates how DTW finds the lowest-cost path between the opposite corners of the scores matrix. As we can see in the right side of Fig. 7, the path on the scores matrix follows the dark stripe depicted in the left side of Fig. 7.

Similar to other dynamic programing, the bottom right corner of the *minimum-cost-to-this point* matrix returns the cost of minimum-cost alignment of the two speech segments. This value as a partial score, can be used as our similarity measure. The smaller is a partial score, the closer are the two corresponding segments of different voice messages. Since the value of the partial score has a relationship with the size of spectral matrices (duration of voiced segments), we divided the partial score by the minimum duration of two segments to define a more comparable weighted partial score. To specify a threshold to find if two segments are similar enough, the method against many different voice messages is tested. Hence, we empirically found 10 as the proper threshold for acceptance or rejection of similarity between two segments.

4.2 Voice Message Content Matching

To find if two speech messages are similar enough, weighted partial scores for all pair of corresponding segments of both messages are calculated. After comparing the weighted partial scores to the threshold value of 10 for each pair of corresponding segments, we can determine if the two segments have same content. If a certain number of corresponding segments for both messages have same content, the two whole speech messages are also similar enough and a match has been found.

4.3 Bayesian Content Filter

Based on the idea of Bayesian filtering for email spam, we propose a similar method for voice spam filtering. In this method, we have a database of known spam words named spam speech database. In the training phase, the spam words are converted to speech using text-to-speech (TTS) system and stored in the spam speech database. Speech words here can be a single word, a combination of words (i.e., phrase), phone number or URL address with high spamicity. In other words, we transform the known email spam database and its probabilities to voice spam world. Since there is no speaker independent speech segmentation method (without language-specific knowledge) to perfectly segment speech messages at the word level, we take an alternative approach. In our approach, entries of the spam speech database are tested against the voice message to find if the voice message includes an entry of the database. As an example, suppose Mike left a voice message, "Free mortgage consultations available now", for his friend. To check if the deposited message is spam, entries of the database are tested against this voice message. Assuming that "mortgage" is an entry in the spam speech database, that was previously detected from another speaker (Crystal) and stored in the database, we try to find if the voice message includes this speech word "mortgage". Starting from the beginning of the voice message, a frame in size of the entry of the database (speech word "mortgage") traverses the waveform of the speech message. While the frame traversing the message, the dissimilarity of the current frame of the speech message and the speech word from database ("mortgage") is calculated using DTW. Reaching the end of the speech message, the frame of speech message with maximum similarity is the determiner if the message includes the spam word ("mortgage"). This similarity score is compared to a threshold to find if the speech message includes that spam word. Using Bayes' Formula and based on the number and spamicity of spam words from the database that the spam message contains, we can decide if the the speech message is spam or not. To justify the threshold, as the most important part of this method, we have tested the method for different words and phrases in different sizes. Hence, it is empirically found that the similarity score using DTW is tightly related to the size of speech words. For example, DTW similarity score for word in size of "mortgage" is about 4.5-5, and for word in size of "777 5555 666" (as a phone number) is about 50. Therefore, the threshold is set in a dynamic way based on the size of the speech word to be tested.

4.4   Searching

As explained in Section 3, we construct two separate databases to store RASTA-PLP matrices; Spam Signature Database for spam signatures, and Spam Speech Database for spam words and phrases with high spamicity. After voice messages are left on the media server by callers, the Spam Signature Database is first queried to find a match. Entries in the Spam Signature Database can be organized in categories based on VoIP service providers where they have been locally stored from to speed up the search process. In case a match is not found (i.e., signature does not exist in the Spam Signature Database), entries of the Spam Speech Database are searched against the voice message to find if the voice message includes that entry of the database. After performing this search, Bayesian spam filtering is used to determine the final probability of the voice message being spam. To reduce the search time, we propose a cluster-like structure for the Spam Speech Database, where cluster heads are speech words with the highest probabilities in each cluster. For example, two clusters of the database are described here:

- Cluster 1:
  - cluster head: Viagra
  - cluster members: sex, cheap, night, www.buyviagraonline.com

- Cluster 2:
  - cluster head: Mortgage
  - cluster members: 100% free, lower interest, "555 666 7777" (phone number)

To perform a search, we start with cluster heads. If none of the cluster heads matches, the voice message is classified as non-spam. If one of the cluster heads matches, we narrow our search to the corresponding cluster to consider all other relevant words in relevance order. The Baye's Formula will take care of calculating the probability of being spam based on the number of spam segments it contains and their spamicities.

5   Performance Evaluation

We conduct a series of experiments to evaluate the performance of our solution. In our experiments, we left voice messages on Google voice [7] and then later on analyzed for their legitimacy and spam detection rate. In addition to these manually deposited voice messages, three popular TTS systems are used to generate various voice messages with different speakers in different sizes. Eight speakers were selected from AT&T Natural Voices® TTS system [1]. Twelve speakers were selected from Cepstral engine [3], as a TTS system that makes realistic synthetic voices. Moreover, ten speakers were selected from PlainTalk [22], the advanced built-in TTS technology of Mac OS. These thirty selected speakers have different accents (such as American, British or Indian English), different sex (male and female) with ages ranging from 10 to 60 years old.

5.1   Arrival of Same Content Voice Messages

This is a most generic spam attack scenario where a spammer repeatedly sends the same spam message to many of the subscribers at the same time. If a newly arrived voice message matches with any of the signatures stored in the database, the message is categorized as a spam message.

Ten totally different text messages with different size and content were converted to voice messages spoken by the thirty above mentioned different speakers to form 10 different sets of 30 voice spam messages with same content. All of these 300 different voice messages were first segmented into small voiced speech segments. Then the RASTA-PLP spectral matrices for all segments were calculated as well. After randomly selecting 3 voice messages of different speakers out of total 30 messages from each set of speech messages (with same content), a database with 30 entries were generated. For each sub-experiment, this process was repeated 10 times and each time one voice message from one of 10 sets is selected to check if it is spam. Iterating the sub-experiment 10 times forms a complete experiment. To take average, the complete experiment was conducted three times and the results are summarized in Table 1:

In our experiments, we found that our speaker independent spam detection algorithm can detect similar content message with 91% accuracy while generating 0.67% false positive rate and 8.33% false negative rate. However, if the newly arrived message does not match with any of the spam signatures stored in the database, we recorded its signature and observed if this signature matches with any of the future deposited messages within a predefined time interval of ΔT

Table 1. False Positive and False Negative rates of Voice Message Content Filtering

Case	Correct	False Positive	False Negative
#1	91	0	9
#2	87	1	12
#3	95	1	4

($\simeq$ 5 minutes). The similar message count beyond a threshold value within a time period can be categorized as an impending spam attack and needs further analysis.

We are aware that there are some legitimate applications that can generate calls in bulk. For example, it is possible that an emergency response system within a company, city or college may call many of the telephone numbers at the same time alarming about some untoward incidents. It is also possible for a credit card company to send a prerecorded generic message at a particular time to many of its customers regarding fraudulent activity in their accounts. In all such cases, there will be a number of matches (beyond a defined threshold value) within a predefined time interval ΔT and therefore possibly be labeled as spam messages without delivering to their respective mailboxes.

These legitimate call scenarios may cause false positives. To avoid such false positives, before labeling these legitimate voice messages as spam, our Bayesian content filtering method is used to calculate the probability of being spam for one of the newly deposited voice messages. Moreover, if we are provided with the calling numbers and the originating source IP addresses used by these bulk call applications in advance, then combining the SIP signaling information and content filtering approach can also avoid such false positives.

5.2   Hiding Spam Words/Phrases within a Voice Message

In this set of experiments, the Spam Speech Database was built with 137 entries in five clusters: Employment, Financial (Business and Personal), Marketing, Medical, and Calls-to-Action. In addition to having one or more cluster heads, each cluster has several cluster members converted from email spam trigger words/phrases, and some special elements, such as URL address, email address and phone number, which have been extracted from our Spam Signature Database. Table 2 summarizes the details of the clusters in our Spam Speech Database.

To evaluate the efficiency of the proposed Bayesian based content filtering method, we recorded 30 various voice messages in different size from mentioned speakers with different accents, genders, and ages. This set of voice messages includes three types of voice messages as follows:

(1) *Spam voice message*: a voice message that includes at least one cluster head and either at least one special element or significant number of relevant cluster members. This type of voice messages should be classified as spam.

Table 2. Cluster details of the Spam Speech Database

Cluster	# of cluster members	# of special elements
Employment	24	4
Financial (Business)	15	2
Financial (Personal)	18	2
Marketing	35	5
Medical	18	3
Calls-to-Action	9	2

(2) *Doubtful voice message*: a voice message that includes at least one cluster head but neither special element nor significant number of relevant cluster members. Although this type of voice messages could be classified as either spam or non-spam, our system classifies it as non-spam to reduce the false positives. In other words, a few relevant words/phrases from a cluster of the Spam Speech Database do not classify a deposited message as spam. There have to be enough words/phrases with a high spamicity to outweigh the rest of the voice message that includes words/phrases with a low spamicity. For example, a voice message from your spouse taking out a second mortgage on the house should not be misclassified as spam.

(3) *Non-spam voice message*: a voice message that does not include even one cluster head. This type of voice messages should be classified as non-spam.

Our Bayesian based spam detection method is used to classify the test set of voice messages. The results show that the method can correctly classify 83.33% of voice messages while 13.33% of either non-spam or doubtful voice messages are misclassified as spam and 20% of spam voice messages are not detected. We further looked into the results and details of the method to find the causes of these false positives and false negatives. It is discovered that the problem arises when voice messages are deposited by speakers with accents rather than US English, such as British or Indian English. Since the entries of our Spam Speech Database are converted by Crystal, a US native English speaker from spam email world, the dissimilarity score computed by our DTW based algorithm is not dependable enough to compare the small-size speech words of those speakers with different accents.

6   Related Work

The SIP IETF working group has published a couple of informational drafts proposing (1) *computational puzzles* to reduce spam in SIP environments and (2) an extension of SIP protocol to send user's feedback information to the SPIT identification system [12,14]. To some extent, the combination of user's whitelist with the Turing tests or computational puzzles can prevent spam calls. However, the capability of a SIP UA to solve the computational puzzle relies on its computing resources. Therefore, it cannot be ignored that a spammer can potentially have significantly more resources than a normal user. The solving of audio Turing tests requires caller's time and manual intervention. Still, the Turing tests cannot be a solution for deaf (or blind) users and can be thwarted by employing cheap labor. Recently, a number of products such as Sipera's IPCS [19] and NEC's VoIP SEAL [11] incorporate audio Turing test to solve the voice spam problem. However, an attacker may abuse these security devices as reflectors and amplifiers to launch a stealthy DDoS attack [16]. Now we review some other related work on SPIT prevention.

Inferring Spoken Words. The closest work to our approach is a method in which the spam detection module detects spoken words within an established voice stream. The most intuitive way to detect a spam message is to use *"speech-to-text"* engine, where deposited voice messages can be converted to text format and then the well-known email filtering approaches can be used for detection. However, the performance of speech-to-text engine is largely depends on speaker, speaking style, ambient environment, and language. Because of the high error rate, this approach is still far away to become a commercially viable solution to filter voice spam messages.

Collaborative Approach. Google Voice [7] has a feature to report calls as spam and block future calls from that number. This is a reactive approach requiring spam call be received by a user and then block that number. It has a few drawbacks to be applicable in telecommunication networks: (1) what will happen if the spam message is generated from a spoofed number, e.g., every time a new telephone number is used to send a spam message; (2) the current generation of hardphones do not provide any button to send feedback about received spam calls; (3) it is based on inferring spoken words and thus suffers from the same drawback as discussed above; and (4) there is no previous study on what will happen if the message content itself mutates (i.e., spam messages use different accents or male/female speakers), making it difficult to infer spoken words.

Content Analysis. The *V-Priorities* [8] system developed by Microsoft is explored to filter spam calls. V-Priorities works on three levels: first, analysis examines the prosody – rhythm, syllabic rate, pitch, and length of pauses – of a caller's voice; secondly, rudimentary word and phrase recognition is done to spot target words that could indicate the nature of a call; and finally, at the third level analysis involves metadata, such as the time and length of a message. The voice content analysis does not require maintenance of caller's call history and remains independent of signaling. However, this approach suffers from scalability issue since it is difficult to monitor hundreds of voice streams simultaneously. The real-time content analysis is an exceedingly difficult task. By the time, calls are analyzed to be spam calls, it has already affected the receiver (human recipient or voice mailbox). The prosody analysis of machine generated voice may give different results compared to human generated voice. As mentioned earlier, inferring spoken words makes it error-prone and its success largely depends upon users, ambient environment, and language.

Black/Whitelists, Trust and Reputation System. The unwanted callers and domains are blacklisted so that their future calls can be filtered as spam calls. By contrast, the known callers are put in a whitelist and the calls from such callers are given preference by allowing them to go through. The trust and reputation system is used in conjunction with black/whitelists. The *social network* mechanism is used to derive a reputation value for a caller. Dantu et al. [4] used the Bayesian algorithm to compute the reputation value of a caller based on its past behavior and callee's feedback. Rebahi et al. [13] derived caller's reputation value by consulting SIP repositories along the call path from call's source to its destination. As an anti-spam solution, Sipera's IPCS [19] also relies on caller's reputation value. These solutions can block the spam call during the call setup phase. However, the derivation of caller's reputation value requires building a social network. The notion of user's feedback requires the modification of SIP clients and an extension of SIP protocol [12]. The construction of a whitelist suffers from the *introduction problem* and the calculation of a reputation value is vulnerable to "bad-mouthing attacks", where malicious users may collude and provide unfair ratings for a particular caller. Furthermore, these schemes rely on caller's identity which can be spoofed.

Call Duration-Based Approach. Sengar et al. [17] observed the significance of call duration in spam detection and raised a fundamental question about how small it could be for normal conversations. Their proposed statistical approach lacks the consideration of those calls that are hidden behind a firewall, SBC or B2BUA agents. Balasubramaniyan et al. [2] used the call duration to develop call credentials. A caller provides a call credential to the callee when he makes a call. However, a spammer could set up at least two accounts to build call credentials by calling each other and then later on use these trusted accounts to launch spam attacks.

Recently, Wu et al. [23] proposed a spam detection approach involving user-feedback and semi-supervised clustering technique to differentiate between spam and legitimate calls. However, the current generation of telephone sets do not provide an option to give feedback of a call to service provider's system. Sengar et al. [18] used callers calling behavior (day and time of calling, call duration etc.) to detect an onslaught of spam attack. However, it is difficult to capture calling pattern for each of the subscribers and, being an after-the-fact method, by the time we detect a spam attack many of the subscribers must have already been affected by the spam.

7 Conclusion

Although there are very few reported incidents of voice spam today, with the growth of VoIP and its openness, the voice spam could become a serious threat in the near future. The heart of the problem lies in the fact that a spammer can send unsolicited advertisements and messages with low or no cost while being anonymous. Unfortunately, many of the mechanisms which work for email spam fail completely in the context of VoIP. Most of the previous solutions against voice spam are proposed to distinguish a legitimate subscriber from a spammer using SIP signaling messages. Instead of analyzing the SIP signaling messages to identify the spammer, this paper proposes a speaker independent speech recognition scheme for content filtering to avoid spam message deposition on the subscribers' voice mailboxes. Being a speaker independent, computationally efficient, and scalable solution, our proposed approach can effectively protect subscribers' voice mailboxes from spam messages. Our work is evaluated in real-world experiments. The experimental results show that our spam filtering approach can successfully classify a voice message into spam with 91% accuracy, while having 0.67% false positive rate and 8.33% false negative rate.

References

1. AT&T Labs Research. At&t natural voices® text-to-speech system, http://www2.research.att.com/ttsweb/tts/
2. Balasubramaniyan, V., Ahamad, M., Park, H.: CallRank: Combating SPIT Using Call Duration, Social Networks and Global Reputation. In: The Fourth Conference on Email and Anti-Spam (2007)
3. Cepstral®. Cepstral text-to-speech engine, http://www.cepstral.com/
4. Dantu, R., Kolan, P.: Detecting spam in voip networks. In: Proceedings of the Steps to Reducing Unwanted Traffic on the Internet on Steps to Reducing Unwanted Traffic on the Internet Workshop (2005)
5. Ellis, D.: Dynamic time warp (dtw) in matlab. Web resource (2003), http://www.ee.columbia.edu/~dpwe/resources/matlab/dtw/
6. Giannakopoulos, T.: A method for silence removal and segmentation of speech signals, implemented in matlab. Web resource (2010), http://www.mathworks.com/matlabcentral/fileexchange/authors/30223
7. Google. Google Voice (2011), http://www.google.com/voice
8. Graham-Rowe, D.: A Sentinel to Screen Phone Calls (2006), http://www.technologyreview.com/communications/17300/?a=f
9. Hermansky, H.: Perceptual linear predictive (PLP) analysis of speech. The Journal of the Acoustical Society of America 87(4), 1738–1752 (1990)
10. Hermansky, H., Morgan, N.: RASTA processing of speech. IEEE Transactions on Speech and Audio Processing 2(4), 578–589 (1994)
11. NEC Corporation. NEC Develops World-Leading Technology to Prevent IP Phone SPAM. Product News (2007), http://www.nec.co.jp/press/en/0701/2602.html
12. Niccolini, S., Tartarelli, S., Stiemerling, M., Srivastava, S.: SIP Extensions for SPIT identification. draft-niccolini-sipping-feedback-spit-03, IETF Network Working Group, Work in Progress (2007)
13. Rebahi, Y., Al-Hezmi, A.: Spam Prevention for Voice over IP. Technical report (2007), http://colleges.ksu.edu.sa/ComputerSciences/Documents/NITS/ID143.pdf
14. Rosenberg, J., Jennings, C.: The Session Initiation Protocol (SIP) and Spam. RFC 5039, IETF Network Working Group (2008)

15. Rosenberg, J., Schulzrinne, H., Camarillo, G., Johnston, A., Peterson, J., Sparks, R., Handley, M., Schooler, E.: SIP: Session Initiation Protocol. RFC 3261, IETF Network Working Group (2002)
16. Sengar, H.: Beware of New and Readymade Army of Legal Bots. USENIX; login (October 2007)
17. Sengar, H.: Voice Spam (SPIT) Problem (March 2007), http://www.vodasec.com/
18. Sengar, H., Wang, X., Nichols, A.: Call Behavioral Analysis to Thwart SPIT Attacks on VoIP Networks. In: Rajarajan, M., Piper, F., Wang, H., Kesidis, G. (eds.) SecureComm 2011. LNICST, vol. 96, pp. 501–510. Springer, Heidelberg (2012)
19. SIPERA: Sipera IPCS: Products to Address VoIP Vulnerabilities (April 2007), http://www.sipera.com/index.php?action=products,default
20. VOIPSA. Confirmed cases of SPIT. Mailing list (2006), http://www.voipsa.org/pipermail/voipsec_voipsa.org/2006-March/001326.html
21. VOIPSA. VoIP Attacks in the News (2007), http://voipsa.org/blog/category/voip-attacks-in-the-news/
22. Wikipedia. Plaintalk, Website, http://en.wikipedia.org/wiki/PlainTalk
23. Wu, Y.-S., Bagchi, S., Singh, N., Wita, R.: Spam Detection in Voice-Over-IP Calls through Semi-Supervised Clustering. In: IEEE Dependable Systems and Networks Conference (DSN 2009) (June-July 2009)

Author Index